NetWare Supervisor's Guide

NetWare Supervisor's Guide

Covers version 4.0

The definitive technical reference for NetWare supervisors

John T. McCann

with Steven L. Guengerich and Adam T. Ruef

M&T Books
A Division of MIS:Press
A Subsidiary of Henry Holt and Company, Inc.
115 West 18th Street
New York, New York 10011

Printed in the United States of America

Library of Congress Cataloging-in-Publication Data (to be assigned)

McCann, John T.
BSG's NetWare supervisor's guide : the definitive technical reference for NetWare supervisors / John T. McCann ; with Steven L. Guengerich and Adam T. Ruef.
p. cm.
Rev. ed. of: Business System Group's NetWare supervisor's guide.
1st ed. 1989.
Includes index.
ISBN 1-55851-284-5 : $29.95
1. Local area networks (Computer networks) — Management.
2. NetWare (Computer file) I. Guengerich, Steven L. II. Ruef, Adam T. III. McCann, John T., 1966- Business Systems Group's NetWare supervisor's guide. IV. Business Systems Group. V. Title. VI. Title: NetWare supervisor's guide.
TK5105.7.M4 1993
004.6'8dc20

93-8635
CIP

96 95 94 93 4 3 2 1

Project Editor: Carol King
Technical Editor: Charles Rose
Copy Editor: Kristen Little
Production: Charlene M. Carpentier
Cover Design: Lauren Smith Design

Dedicated to my mother and father,
who have helped me become everything I can be.
Thanks.

Table of Contents

Preface to Fifth Edition

In 1989, BSG and M&T Books, Inc. collaborated to produce the first edition of the *NetWare Supervisor's Guide*. Since that time, this book has become one of the best selling books written on NetWare of all time. This fifth edition, we believe, will be even more useful to network administrators as LANs become more prevalent, and Novell continues to improve upon its existing operating systems.

Now, as then, we believe this book is unique because of the practical perspective it lends to the complicated, everyday challenges of supervising NetWare LANs. At BSG we've built our reputation as a national systems integration firm by addressing just such challenges through effectively utilizing talented teams of consultants, instructors, and communicators to provide information solutions.

It is this belief in teaming up the best people with the right perspective for approaching a job that is behind the features that set this NetWare book apart from others. First, it makes no attempt to replace the NetWare manuals, except to augment the Novell documentation. In the more recent versions of NetWare, the NetWare manuals offer adequate explanation of the use of NetWare, so it did not seem necessary to reproduce that information in this book.

The second unique feature of this book is its emphasis on technical information. Any experienced LAN administrator knows to make backups on a regular basis, and to enforce good security practices. However, questions such as, "how does the server store information on the hard disk" and "what does an IEEE 802.3 packet frame look like compared to Ethernet" have previously gone unanswered. You will find answers to these and many other questions in the pages that follow.

Since its initial release in 1982, NetWare has grown to support hundreds of thousands of LANs and millions of users. Many of the people administering the LANs have outgrown the technical depth of the information currently available. This book will fill in the missing pieces for the experienced NetWare LAN administrator who has technical questions and concerns. Many of the sections in this book are designed to address some commonly asked questions about NetWare. This book could save calls to one of the "pay-as-you-go" support services offered for NetWare users.

An additional feature that many readers of this book have found refreshing is the inclusion of historical information concerning NetWare and the growth of the LAN industry. We have tried to include anecdotes and interesting information that may provide you with insights into the development of network computing.

Another obvious audience for this information is the software developer. As with the experienced user perspective, the author of this book has first-hand experience in the development of NetWare applications. Much of the detailed technical information contained herein is the result of research performed during software development. Anyone involved in applications development for the NetWare environment will find this a valuable reference for undocumented technical aspects of NetWare.

Even if you don't use NetWare, you'll find much detailed information about non-NetWare specific topics, such as topologies and protocols. This book caters to anyone using Ethernet, token ring or ARCNET, and covers such topics as CSMA/CD and TCP/IP.

The material for this book was written by John T. McCann. He is currently developing new NLM technologies and previously developed SiteLock and QueueIT! SiteLock was first released under John's company banner, Integerity Software, and was later marketed by Brightwork, Inc. John has installed more than 600 NetWare networks and has written several utility programs. His background includes graduate studies and teaching in Computer Science at Texas A&M University as well as several published technical works on telecommunications and networking.

Much of John's in-depth knowledge of NetWare is freely shared via CompuServe's NetWire forum. His invaluable contribution to NetWire as a SYSOP earned John the title of "Wizard" on that bulletin board. He has helped thousands of NetWare users solve some of their most difficult problems. Many of these users came to him after other consultants had failed to provide the correct answer. It is safe to say that, if there is a problem with NetWare John doesn't know about, it won't be long before he has an answer.

The project to get this book in print was managed by Steve Guengerich of BSG in Houston, Texas. Steve is BSG's Chief Infrastructure Officer and Editor-in-Chief of its publications. Adam Ruef contributed additional material and edited the manuscript. Others at BSG involved in the original editing, production, and review of the work included David Menendez, Keith Nickerson, Susan Leighton Wilson, Hendrik Stokvis, Stephen Wilson, and Mike Culp. Subsequent editions have received additional technical editing and review by Joel Brandon, Robert Stephenson, and Boyd Brown, all Certified NetWare Instructors for BSG Educational Services, a Novell Authorized Education Center, and Bob Janusaitis, Dave Cornell, Craig Janssen, and Stephanie Deming of BSG Consulting.

What's New in the Fifth Edition

With the recent changes in Novell policies and strategy, and the rapid changes in network computing overall, this newest edition has much new material. Though Novell has further segregated its product line into NetWare 2.2, NetWare 3.11, and now NetWare 4.0, we have retained material pertaining to older versions of NetWare as well. In this book, we define NetWare/286 as all of the NetWare 2.x family; likewise NetWare/386 includes all versions of the NetWare 3.x and 4.x families. When there is information specific to a certain version within the general /286 or /386 categories, we have indicated it specifically.

How to Read This Book

While it is possible to read it sequentially, this book is organized as a handbook—to take its rightful place alongside many of the other dog-eared, coffee-stained, buried-someplace-on-the-desk, and invaluable information sources that LAN supervisors live by. Therefore, extra effort has been invested in producing a detailed index, organized to highlight several logical groupings.

Chapter 1

This chapter provides background, history, and general introductory information about NetWare LANs. NetWare and networking are explained in this chapter and will provide a useful tool to anyone wondering what networking is all about.

Chapter 2

This chapter offers general NetWare installation pointers. Taken as a whole, the chapter serves as a good overall checklist for installation.

Chapters 3 Through 10

These chapters discuss each of the components of a NetWare LAN in a detailed fashion—from file servers to routers; from workstations to printers.

Chapters 11 and 12

These chapters shift to the big picture, providing tips, tricks, and techniques for managing and troubleshooting NetWare LANs.

The Appendixes

Although they relate to the book's main content, the appendixes stand alone as rich sources of information for LAN supervisors.

As stated at the beginning of many sections throughout the book, the examples and products presented are only a sampling of what is available. It would be impossible to show all variations on a usage technique or to list all products in a particular category, so an attempt has been made to offer representative samplings.

Thank you for your interest in BSG's *NetWare Supervisor's Guide*. The authors, editors, producers, and publishers hope you will find the information it presents useful.

Steven G. Papermaster, Chairman
BSG Capital Corp.
April, 1993

Acknowledgments

Thanks to:

Doug Woodward, Grant Echols, Warren Harding, Van Harris, Jamie P. Sanders, Doug Baird, Corey Krebs, John Crook, Keith Fenstermaker, Graig Taylor, Scott Raban, Skip Addison, and Jason Lamb of Novell.
Kyle Powell, Drew Major, and Dale Neibaur, of Superset
Brian Meek of Excelan
Glenn Fund of the Boston Area NetWare User's Group
Jeff Chumbley
Walt Thirion of Thomas-Conrad
Scott Hutchinson
Christopher C. Cleveland of IBM
Les Lovesee
Mickey Applebaum
Bart Mellink of Cyco Automation
Paul D. Griendling of Micro One Dallas
Rick Segal of Microsoft
Randy Doss of Microtest
Jeff Plummer of Compaq
Rich Adams
Clarke Williams
Art Rothstein
Dave Kearns
Jeff Grammer
Don Crawford
Doug Lindhout

Trademarks:

Why This Book Is for You

If you are a network supervisor, consultant, installer, or power user of NetWare, this book is for you. *NetWare Supervisor's Guide* is a complete resource for managing a NetWare LAN. Comprehensive discussions and valuable tips familiarize you with the features and requirements of your network, teaching you how to effectively approach and resolve the problems you face on a day-to-day basis. You'll learn how to install a NetWare LAN, choose a file server, manage the workstation environment, troubleshoot your network, and much more.

Whether you're involved in planning a NetWare installation, actually installing a network, or managing an installed network, you'll find this book an invaluable reference to have on hand.

CHAPTER 1

Introduction to Local Area Networks

In the beginning, there was the personal computer (PC). It processed words, figures, and information. Life for the PC user was simple, and soon every user had his own little world. Self-containment was the rule, from word processing to spreadsheets to databases. The trouble was, many of these worlds had to function together.

These isolated PCs could no longer be islands unto themselves. Not only did the product of each user increasingly need to interact with the products of other users, but an increasing need to share resources emerged—resources that would aid in bringing their work together. More and more users needed to access the same printers, plotters, backup units, modems, hard disk drives, compact disc-read-only memory drives (CD-ROMs), and write once read many drives (WORMs).

The solution? Local Area Networks, or LANs.

Traditionally, a network is thought of as any one of many different types of complex communications systems. Just as a telephone company is made up of a network of telephone lines, the data communications resources of a mainframe computer constitute a network. A LAN, like most complex constructions, is the sum of its parts. A LAN involves methods of connections between those providing services and those receiving services. In the following section, LANs will be discussed in this context. A LAN is limited in physical size, and is usually confined to a single campus or building. It usually consists of personal computers and related devices linked together via high-speed media for the purpose of sharing computing resources. A unique feature of LANs is that they are privately owned. LANs, like most types of networks, including multiuser systems, may be linked together through public or private data lines.

A LAN also differs from a traditional multiuser system in that, while the devices attached to a multiuser system are usually non-programmable displays and printers, the devices attached to a LAN, such as PCs, are "intelligent." Once a device is connected to the LAN, it is capable of exchanging data with other devices.

Files can always be shared using the "sneakernet" approach (a.k.a. "doing the floppy shuffle"), but in installations with more than a few workstations, physically carrying disks from place to place wastes time and energy. By sharing program files using a LAN, updating to a new version of a program can be done once per file server rather than separately at each workstation.

Without a LAN, sharing output devices such as printers is a relatively crude process. It is workable, but only for small groups of PCs that are physically close to one another. There are several printer sharing devices on the market, but they do have drawbacks. In a typical non-LAN environment, a printer is connected to a serial device concentrator that channels communications from each connected PC to the printer. If the communicating PC ceases transmission for a period greater than the concentrator's "time-out" period, another PC could start communicating with the device. This type of conflict could cause the output from both PCs to be interspersed, resulting in garbage. Ultimately, both sending PCs would have to begin again. Caching programs, also known as print spoolers, can minimize the effect of printer contention on parallel printer sharing devices, but they are not available for all types of serial output.

The benefits of sharing hard disks are best illustrated with an example. Consider the case of 100 similar stand-alone PCs, each with a 40 megabyte (MB) hard disk. On each disk is the same 20MB of applications and utilities and 10MB of common templates and/or database files. The remaining 10MB contain workstation/user-specific data. In a LAN environment, just four or five 250MB hard disk drives satisfy the same needs.

Now consider what happens when users outgrow their current 40MB drives and they need 60MB drives "just to survive." The stand-alone workstations will require 100 new 60MB drives (or 100 new 20MB drives). The LAN requires only the purchase of another set of four 250MB drives, all of which could be added to the LAN server(s). If the new disk space is needed for programs, then much less additional disk space (if any at all) would be required at the file server(s).

There are also benefits to sharing backup units with a LAN. There are two methods of doing backups without a LAN; one is simple but tedious and unreliable; the other is complex, expensive, and unreliable. A simple backup scheme entails users performing their own backups on floppy disks or tape drives. The more complex option, that allows sharing of a backup device, entails installing the adapter for a tape drive, Bernoulli Box, or WORM drive in each PC. With the adapter installed, the backup unit can be moved, with some effort, from PC to PC.

With both of these schemes, there is still the problem of reliability. Even if every PC were to have a tape drive, Bernoulli Box, or even a floppy disk drive, users typically don't have the discipline to perform regular backups. There is the added problem of collection and off-site storage of these backups.

The sharing of backup devices with a LAN means purchasing fewer devices overall. Instead of supplying every PC user with a large hard disk and a tape unit for backup, a shared tape drive is used to back up one shared hard disk.

This logic holds true for CD-ROM and WORM devices as well. CD-ROM devices are sometimes used in a manner that is specific to a particular user, lessening the need to share CD-ROM devices. WORM drives are typically used for archiving purposes and are best implemented in a shared manner.

In addition to eliminating the cost of adding a new modem for each new workstation, connecting a pool of modems at a LAN modem server eliminates the need to wire an extra phone line to and support a modem at each workstation.

Networks offer the additional advantage of support for electronic mail (E-mail) systems. E-mail is an application that functions only if some sort of network is in place. (E-mail is discussed in greater depth later in this chapter.)

Finally, the sharing of connections to minicomputers or mainframes can be facilitated by a LAN. Modem sharing can be used to connect to a minicomputer that has asynchronous ports. In addition, many mainframe gateways facilitate communication between microcomputers and mainframes via a LAN.

Indeed, LAN technology offers a wide variety of options. Today, few computing applications remain that are unable, in some way, to reap the benefits of a LAN.

Types of LANs

LANs vary widely in the degree of functionality they offer. At the most primitive level, a LAN supports "disk serving." LANs such as Corvus's Constellation which linked Apple II computers had a central disk server available to all users on the LAN, but the disk was partitioned into many pieces so that each user received a separate piece. One user could not utilize information on another's partitioned section(s). Thus, only the physical disk was shared, not the files.

More sophisticated LANs are capable of "file serving." This technology requires a more complex server that actively manages access to the disk. All users can share the same file space and use each other's files. To protect sensitive information, file servers use one or more layers of file and directory security.

Some LANs employ the concept of peer-to-peer resource sharing. This approach offers even more flexibility, as each user determines when and if a central server is needed at all. Peer-to-peer in this case, however, typically involves communication between two devices on a LAN, which usually bypass the file server.

The term peer-to-peer is expanded to refer to sharing different hard disks in PC workstations. There is no requirement in this environment for a central file server or disk server. Rather, all PCs participate in the sharing of file and disk space. An example is the Sitka networking products. Because of this distributed style of file sharing, peer-to-peer LANs require careful planning to ensure an adequate file system. LANs that support peer-to-peer communication technology enable all intelligent networked devices to communicate with each other via a higher layer of the OSI model, e.g., using a predefined session or transport layer protocol. (See Appendix F for a discussion of the seven-layer OSI reference model.)

The most sophisticated LANs use a mixture of centralized file serving and peer-to-peer resource sharing techniques. One example is a Systems Network Architecture (SNA) gateway to a mainframe. The gateway node communicates with other nodes via peer-to-peer protocols. At the same time, the LAN also uses centralized file serving for applications such as word processing. LANs can be linked, or "bridged," to form Wide Area Networks (WANs) via public or private data lines, although this is not yet a widespread practice.

Physical LAN topologies are divided into three main types: bus, star, and ring. In the case of bus and ring topologies, the difference is sometimes only discernible to those who examine the lower levels of the OSI model, e.g., the data-link layer. Figures 1-1, 1-2, and 1-3 show layouts of the bus, ring, and star topologies. (Topologies are discussed in great detail in Chapter 7.)

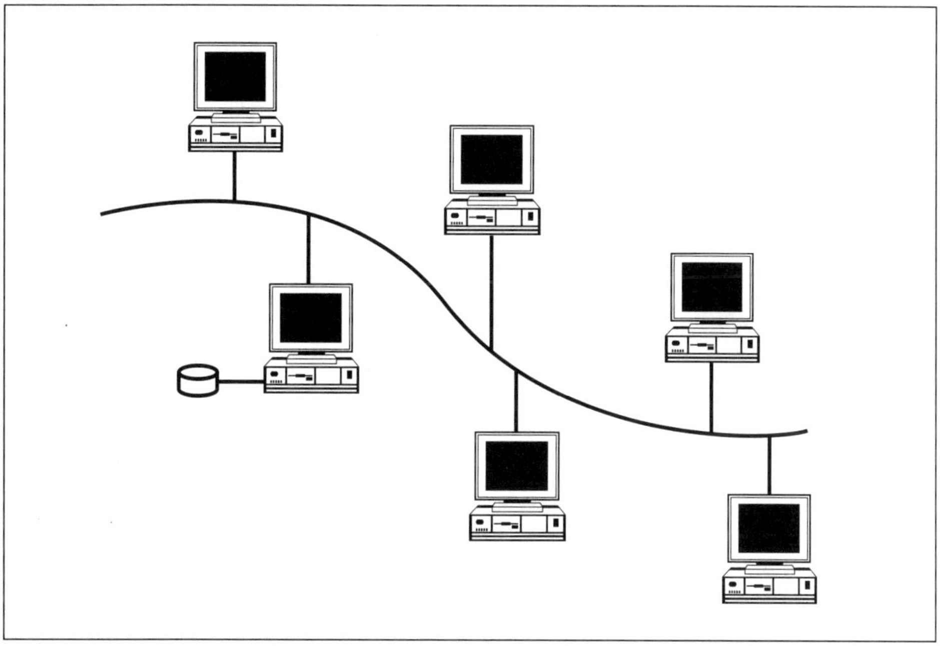

Figure 1-1. Bus topology

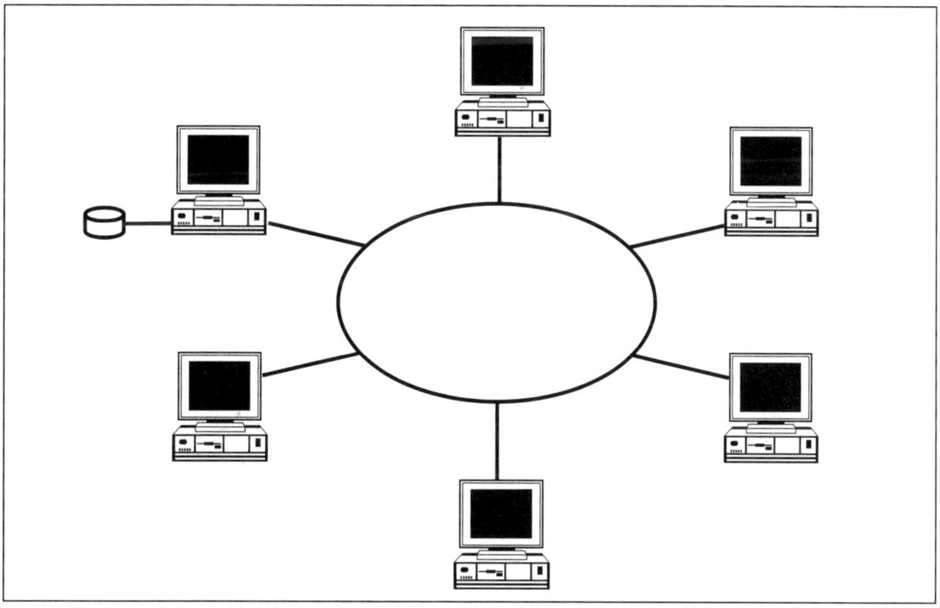

Figure 1-2. Ring topology

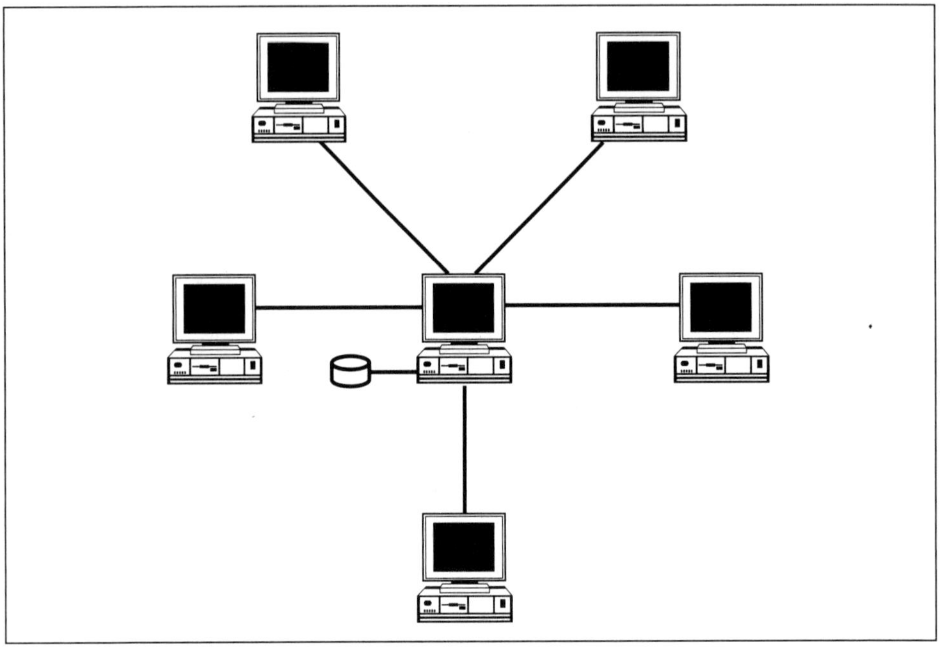

Figure 1-3. Star topology

Selecting a LAN

Selection of the appropriate LAN is dependent upon the specific needs of the users. It's best to begin by drawing up a list of the resources and applications to be shared. The next step is to determine the manner in which these resources and applications will best be shared, i.e. through a peer-to-peer network or one that combines peer-to-peer connections and file serving. The latter is most often the preferred choice because when a LAN incorporates both peer-to-peer and fileserving, it allows for more functionality. The LAN can be adapted to suit the needs of its applications. Hence this type of LAN is preferred to a LAN that only provides one of the services. Figure 1-4 lists some of the mainstream LAN operating systems in use in 1993.

Manufacturer	Product
Apple	AppleTalk
Artisoft, Inc	LANtastic
AT & T	StarGROUP
Banyan, Inc.	VINES
Datapoint	DataLAN
DEC	Pathworks
IBM	LAN Server
Microsoft	LAN Manager, Windows for Workgroups
Novell	NetWare, NetWare Lite
Sun Microsystems	Sitka
Ungermann-Bass, Inc.	NET/ONE

Figure 1-4. LAN operating systems

When choosing a LAN operating system, there are several questions to consider: How mature is the product? Is the vendor still actively updating the operating system? (If updates are not actively pursued, such as with IBM's PC Network, then the product may fall short in supporting new technology.) Finally, how important is the product to the vendor? (In the case of CBIS Inc., Banyan Systems, Inc., and Novell Inc., the LAN operating systems they sell are their primary products. This means there is a greater chance that the product will continually be refined to take advantage of technology advancements.)

With the above considerations in mind, select an initial list of LAN systems that will suit the users' requirements. Next, based on existing applications and hardware, determine which system will be compatible with each of the LAN products chosen. Also take into consideration the applications to be implemented as part of the overall LAN installation, such as links to other microcomputers, minicomputers, and mainframes, and sharing of printers and modems.

Selecting a LAN Dealer

Once the applications software choices are made, the success of a LAN installation depends on the source chosen for service and support of the LAN operating system, in this case, NetWare, and on the LAN hardware selected. An authorized dealer can be a computer retailer, a consultant, a Value-Added Reseller (VAR), or a systems integrator.

Each type of dealer has a different level of technical and analytical expertise. The selection should be based on how well expectations of what the LAN will accomplish are understood. There are a few tests to determine a dealer's ability. These tests can be applied to all dealers, regardless of type.

First and foremost, ask for references from other customers. Call these references to find out what went right and what went wrong. Take time to visit potential dealers to see their offices. Do they have LANs of their own? What type of LANs are they and do they actually use them in operating their businesses? Do the dealers offer training? Do they offer you the option of receiving training at their offices or on-site?

Next, determine the quality of the dealer's technical support staff and their level of training. With the advent of Novell's Certified NetWare Engineer (CNE) program, it is preferable to find a dealer with CNEs or Enterprise CNEs on staff. However, know that the title CNE/ECNE does not convey relevant, hands-on LAN experience for all aspects of LANs. These titles signify only that an individual has passed written tests by Novell, and not necessarily that he or she has gone through Novell's authorized training. Just as important as the titles is that your chosen LAN dealer have experienced support personnel or technicians with a track record of successful LAN installs. Also, find out if the dealers maintain a stock of replacement parts. Many times a good maintenance contract will call for a dealer to maintain a spare parts inventory for the sole purpose of client support.

These are only a few of the considerations when selecting a dealer, offered as a basic set of parameters to which other criteria can be added. Unless your organization chooses to be self-sufficient for LAN technical support, dealer selection can be an important aspect of a successful LAN implementation.

Once a dealer has been selected, the only pre-installation step left is to determine the desired LAN design. The network operating system, LAN topology, file server hardware, workstation configurations, and disk drives are all complex and necessary considerations.

History of NetWare

In the late 1970s, Novell Data Systems, Inc. (NDS) of Orem, Utah, was founded as a vendor of general purpose computer equipment. NDS built a line of Z-80-based microcomputers and sold them with private-labeled printers, software, and other items. (NDS-labeled printers can still be found in use in a few dark dusty corners of Novell's headquarters in Provo, Utah.) NDS looked like one of the many "pre-IBM PC," CP/M microcomputer vendors that would be soon doomed to extinction unless they drastically changed their business plans.

In the early 1980s NDS began to set themselves apart from the typical CP/M PC vendor by developing a series of networking products. The heart of this new network system was a server designed and built by NDS. Based on Motorola's 68000 processor, the NDS server supported a star topology and maintained direct attachments to each workstation over a modified RS-422 connection running at 232 Kilobits (Kb) per second. The server had 256 Kilobytes (K or KB) of Random Access Memory (RAM) and could support one to four "MUX boards." Each MUX board served as an integrated, six-channel RS-422 multiplexor supporting the direct attachment of up to six workstation connections for a system maximum of 24 users.

The software to run the server was developed by a group of new Brigham Young University graduates working as independent consultants calling themselves "Superset." Superset started work on this project under a six week contract to write a disk serving operating system to support CP/M and, at a later time, UNIX workstations. (That's why early versions of the NetWare file system supported file naming with eight character names and eight character extensions.)

The original contract was extended several times as the scope of the project grew. Superset borrowed from UNIX and VMS in developing the directory and security structures, to form the basis of what would eventually become NetWare. The authors also began incorporating elements of file serving, as opposed to disk serving.

The effort toward networking was nearly for naught as NDS went bankrupt in the early 1980s. Safeguard Scientifics, which had provided much of the start-up capital for NDS, came in to oversee the reorganization.

Amid the reorganization of Novell Data Systems, Inc. into Novell, Inc., the authors of the new operating systems purchased one of the first IBM PCs available and almost immediately began developing "shells" that would allow this machine, running either CP/M-86 or MS/PC-DOS to interact with the NDS file server operating system on the 68000-based server.

After reorganization, Novell, Inc. emerged in 1983 with Ray Noorda as its new president and CEO. The only products that survived the reorganization were the 68000-based file server and a revamped file serving operating system called ShareNet.

ShareNet was also the name of Novell's PC network package for IBM PCs. It included the 68000-based file server with 256K, a processor board, and a MUX board. Some early models incorporated a 5MB removable Winchester drive as the primary shared storage. PCs were supported by installing a Network Interface Card (NIC). NDS's original design had integrated the equivalent of the ShareNet NIC into the NDS CP/M workstations.

With IBM's release of the PC/XT, ShareNet was renamed NetWare/S-net as Novell repositioned its product for the introduction of a system that would allow this new, hard disk-based PC to be used as a file server in small networks. S-Net referred to the star topology used by the file server. The "all-PC" network was to be based on a new board developed by a start-up networking company, Gateway Communications. NetWare/X (later renamed NetWare/G) was the first of literally hundreds of network adapters that would eventually be supported by NetWare.

NetWare was introduced back in 1983 when no one was sure which operating system would become dominant on the IBM PC. Many early PC-clone vendors bundled both operating systems with their respective machines. A large base of applications were being ported from CP/M-80 to CP/M-86. MS/PC-DOS actually appeared to be the early underdog. Novell supported both and even went as far as building special versions of the S-Net NIC for the TI Professional and the Victor 9000. This is particularly impressive when considering how many networking companies are just now addressing the issue of supporting multiple workstation operating systems and types. Support for CP/M-86 lingered on until 1986, long after it was clear that Microsoft had beaten Digital Research in the battle for dominance in the fledgling PC industry.

Novell extended NetWare to the IBM PC/XT architecture with the introduction of NetWare/86. NetWare/86 continued ShareNet's file serving concept, called a remote file system. The remote file system concept is key to NetWare today. Rather than simply responding to workstation requests for data, NetWare acts as an overseer and protector of files; all requestors who want access to files must have permission from NetWare to do so. This feature allows true multiuser applications to exist on a LAN, because access to the data is truly arbitrated by the NetWare operating system.

This remote file system scheme has become the cornerstone of NetWare's versatility. Since it is not tied to any one operating system (such as DOS, Unix, etc.),

NetWare can be linked to many operating system platforms. This is accomplished by offering users a variety of different "shells" that can be accessed when communicating with a NetWare file server. Examples that demonstrate the flexibility of NetWare's design include the 1988 releases of NetWare products for DEC's VMS operating system and Apple's AppleTalk Filing Protocol (AFP), and the 1989 release of NetWare for Unix, a version which runs on a variety of computer platforms.

Another concept introduced with NetWare was the idea of network hardware independence. No longer were users tied to a specific network hardware topology. Rather, users could use the network hardware of their choice (although only one type of hardware could be used at any one time). The 1986 release of Advanced NetWare version 2.0 added the flexibility of linking dissimilar network topologies either at the file server or via an external bridge server.

To support applications, Novell initiated a two-fold program in 1984 to encourage Independent Software Vendors (ISVs) to make their applications NetWare-specific. The first part of the program offered a COBOL compiler that allowed existing multiuser systems running on minicomputers to be ported to NetWare. By 1986, this program had resulted in more than 2,000 multiuser applications for use specifically with NetWare. Note that Novell also offered a run-time system for Ryan-McFarland's RM/COBOL, and one for applications written in Control-C Software's Multi-user BASIC.

The second part of the program offered Application Program Interfaces (APIs) to ISVs. These APIs resolved many programming issues for which the ISVs had previously been responsible, greatly simplifying the development of NetWare-specific applications.

The momentum established with these breakthroughs enabled Novell to move further forward with the release of Advanced NetWare (ANW) 1.0 in 1985, and ANW 2.0 in 1986 in both 808x and 80286 versions. One of the "firsts" offered by version 2.0 was full DOS 3.1 compatibility. The 80286 version of NetWare, Advanced NetWare/286 2.0, offered support for the Intel Corp. 80286 microprocessor's protected mode. This support allowed NetWare to perform true multitasking at its kernel, resulting in higher levels of throughput. Indeed, this use of the Intel 80286 in its protected mode was two years ahead of Microsoft Corp's use of this mode in its OS/2 product.

Novell also initiated LAN fault tolerance with its release of the first System Fault Tolerance (SFT) version of NetWare in 1986. This first version, called SFT NetWare Level I, incorporated the use of HOTFIX, a utility that effects compensation for defective areas on the hard disks of the file server. Two other forms of SFT were included in a second version, called SFT NetWare Level II, which was released in December 1986. An additional safety measure included in this version was disk mirroring. To protect data from disk drive or drive controller failure, this feature ensures that each bit of data is written on two disk drives instead of one. The Transaction Tracking System (TTS) was then added to ensure database integrity. The real beauty of TTS is that applications do not need to be modified to take advantage of the TTS feature. (For more information about HOTFIX, disk mirroring, and TTS, see Chapter 5.) The features of SFT NetWare Level I were incorporated in the NetWare/68 and /286 versions of the operating system, while Level II features were incorporated only into the /286 version of NetWare. Advanced NetWare/86 did not benefit from any SFT features until the release of ELS II 2.12.

In late 1987, NetWare ELS I (Entry Level Solution) was introduced. This version of NetWare was based upon NetWare/286 2.0a, but allowed only four concurrent users. In mid-1988, ELS II 2.12 was released. As the name implies, ELS II 2.12 was based upon ANW 2.12. In mid-1989, ELS II 2.15 was introduced. In March 1990, NetWare ELS I 2.12 was released.

Also in late 1987, SFT 2.1 of NetWare was released. Every version of NetWare now included the SFT Level I utility HOTFIX. All versions of NetWare that included disk mirroring and TTS were now called SFT NetWare. Advanced NetWare referred to versions that did not have disk mirroring and TTS options. Advanced NetWare also enabled the file server to run in nondedicated mode. This meant the server could be used as a DOS workstation while performing its NetWare file serving duties. This capability has been available since the release of NetWare/86 in 1983.

The last release for the venerable NetWare/68 of file servers (S-Net) was 2.1. The last release for NetWare/86 was 2.0a, which ran on IBM PC/XT compatibles. It should be noted that ELS II 2.12 does allow NetWare to run on IBM PC/XT compatibles in dedicated mode only. Therefore, it can be considered the last /86-style version of NetWare.

In 1988, Novell introduced versions of NetWare for two completely different hardware platforms. The first was NetWare for VMS, providing support for DEC's

VAX series of minicomputers. Based on NetWare 2.0a, NetWare for VMS allows a VAX minicomputer to run as a NetWare server. In late 1989, Novell released NetWare for VMS 2.1. The second new version, 2.15, added the ability to connect Apple Computer's Macintoshes to a NetWare file server.

In the spring of 1989, Portable NetWare was introduced. Not meant for retail sale, this product is meant to be modified by computer and operating system manufacturers to run in their specific environments. As with NetWare for VMS, which Novell created just for the DEC VAX minicomputer world, Portable NetWare allows NetWare to exist on a variety of other hosts and host-specific operating systems.

In September 1989, Novell began shipping NetWare/386, version 3.0. This new breed of NetWare uses 386- and 486-based machines for file servers, providing a new foundation for large LANs. And, in the summer of 1990, NetWare/386 3.1 was shipped. It offered advanced debugging features for server application developers and fixes for many little inconsistencies found in NW386 3.0. For instance, NetWare/386 3.1 rearranges the file tables on its volumes to expedite mounting of volumes. Instead of five minutes to mount a 300MB volume, it now takes less than a minute to mount a volume of this size. In March, 1991 Novell began shipping NetWare 2.2 and 3.11.

At Networld Dallas, 1992, Novell showed and began the release of NetWare SFT III—the result of years of effort. This first release of NetWare SFT III was part of the NetWare 3.11 operating system. SFT III allows for the full mirroring and duplexing of file servers.

In March 1993 Novell released NetWare 4.0. This version of NetWare brings many new enhancements including directory services, security auditing, the ability to run NLMs in protected memory (ring 3), file compression, direct support for data migration, and small block allocations. The small block allocation enhancement keeps smaller files from using up an inordinate amount of disk space.

Data Migration—A Short Story

Until NetWare 4.0, Novell did not support data migration. The DM concept provides for storage of old, infrequently used data in media other than primary file server(s), while retaining important information about the data in the main file server(s), so that it can be easily located and retrieved.

For example, say there is a file on the file server that is currently unneeded. Without DM, recovering the disk space occupied by this file requires that the file be backed up (assuming the file is worth keeping) and then deleted from the disk. Then, the next user needing the file has to track the file down via various manual or automated backup systems. Finally, once the file is located, it must be recovered to the main file server's disk.

With DM, the processes of backing up and deleting the file and subsequently recovering it are all automated. A system process detects that a file is ready to be "migrated" to a slower, less expensive medium based on the amount of time since it was last used. (This is supervisor-configurable.) The process then continues with the migration and, once it is complete, the file is removed from the file server hard disk. However, instead of disappearing from the directory listing, as it would have in the previous scenario, the file remains listed. All of its attributes, even its size, are displayed as if the file were still resident on the file server hard disk. This file alias (the file name and all of its attribute information) allows users to query and find the file, and, with the appropriate utilities, "see" that the file has been migrated. When a user tries to open a migrated file, it must be remigrated or recovered to the file server hard disk. During this time the user will be alerted that the file is being recovered and that it may take some time, depending on the file's current location, which could be on an alternate medium, like tape, WORM, or another file server. All in all, the DM process allows for more efficient use of server hard disk space.

NetWare 4.0 supports DM directly by including file attributes that indicate if a file is migrated and retain the migrated file's size, even though, technically, it no longer occupies any space. Also, NetWare 4.0 has system APIs, which are "hooks" that can signal to other processes (system or user programs) that a user is attempting to use a migrated file. At that point, if a process responds that it is able to recover the file, it is given the opportunity to do so. When done, it notifies the server process that the file has been recovered, then allows the user access to the file. Until the recovered file is either deleted or migrated off the server again, full access is allowed.

Unfortunately, direct support for DM is not recognized by desktop operating systems such as MS-DOS Windows. Currently, special utilities need to be used to identify migrated files. While there is a file attribute (NetWare allows up to 32 different file attributes, not all of which are defined yet) that indicates that a file has been migrated, at this time no desktop operating system recognizes that attribute.

An example of what results from the lack of direct, innate support for DM at the desktop follows:

A user requests the use of a migrated file. The file recovery process begins, but there is nothing that identifies this to the user (because of the lack of desktop support), so he or she begins to think the workstation is "hung" and thus resets his or her PC by pressing CTRL-ALT-DEL. Once the PC is reset, the user then reattempts to access that file. If its recovery is incomplete, he or she will subsequently assume that the workstation is once again hung. The cycle continues until file access can be gained.

Until there is direct support for data migration in the desktop operating system, general DM facilities will be slower to develop than specialized DM facilities. For instance, Kodak has an imaging system that uses NetWare 4.0's DM; however, their image files are accessed via specialized ones. These facilities allow migrated file-sensitive operations, such as the identification of migrated files and user prompts that explain that it will take a certain amount of time to recover the files, thus giving users the choice of migrating the files or not. This approach differs from a more generalized desktop approach because a user will have more control over when a migration occurs. Until generalized facilities are available on the desktop, giving knowledge of which files are migrated (remember, they appear to be there in directory listings), users will unknowingly start the recovery process of one or more migrated files, resulting in wasteful activities, especially if the user was just browsing and really did not require access to the migrated file.

In summary, NetWare 4.0's introduction of direct support for data migration is a set of powerful new features, but it is a first step with more needed, especially at the desktop, in order for users to fully benefit from it.

History of Other Novell Products

In addition to this full line of network operating systems, the NetWare banner includes other products from Novell, most of which are the results of corporate mergers and acquisitions.

In the mid-1980s, Novell acquired CXI, Inc., a minicomputer and mainframe communications company. Renamed the Novell Communications Products division, the products from the CXI acquisition are largely mainframe connectivity products such as Systems Network Architecture (SNA) gateways, LU/6.2 programming tools, and workstation emulation tools. CXI also has various T1, X.25, Transmission Control Protocol/Internet Protocol (TCP/IP) connectivity products.

In March 1987, Novell acquired SoftCraft, Inc., a database management software manufacturer. Renamed the Novell Development Products division, SoftCraft's line of Btrieve and Xtrieve products were integrated into the NetWare product line. Since the acquisition, a line of SQL-based products have emerged, based on existing SoftCraft products. As a result, each copy of NetWare now includes the Btrieve Value-Added Process (VAP) or NetWare Loadable Module (NLM). (VAPs and NLMs are discussed in Chapter 4.)

In June of 1989, Novell merged with Excelan, Inc. This merger brought a line of Ethernet hardware and TCP/IP software to Novell's portfolio of products. Excelan brought long-missing TCP/IP expertise to Novell and gave Novell a foothold in the OSI marketplace.

In October 1991, Novell announced its desire to acquire Digital Research, makers of DR-DOS. When the acquisition was completed a few months later, the company had gained its first desktop operating system.

In February 1993, Novell acquired UNIX Systems Labs (USL). USL was formerly a subsidiary of AT&T and chiefly known for bearing the standard for the most widely used version of UNIX: System V, Release 4 (also known as SVR4). Through these acquisitions, Novell joined desktop operating systems to complement its NetWare server operating system—providing a complete computing platform solution. More important for Novell, though, these acquisitions provide users with alternatives to Microsoft's Windows and Windows NT operating systems.

In addition to these acquisitions and mergers, Novell has depended on strategic Original Equipment Manufacturers (OEMs) to provide NetWare-certified products to the marketplace. Some of these sources include Eicon Technology Corporation for the Novell X.25 Gateway, Samsung Information Systems, Inc., and Hyundai Electronics America for file servers and terminals, and Action Technologies, Inc. for E-mail services.

NetWare Operating Fundamentals

The following information provides an outline of how NetWare works. It is provided primarily for those readers with a limited technical understanding of NetWare. Additional documents devoted to the NetWare Theory of Operations for the various platforms—NetWare/286, NetWare/386, NetWare 4.0, NetWare for UNIX—can be obtained directly from Novell by calling (800) RED-WORD, or (512) 346-8380 outside the United States.

At each workstation, two components form what NetWare users refer to as the "shell." The first component is the Internetwork Packet Exchange/Sequenced Packet Exchange (IPX/SPX) interface. This interface provides the hardware-specific communications routines that enable the workstation to communicate with its installed network card, which in turn communicates with other devices (primarily file servers) on the network. Note that communications between the shell and the file servers is via IPX, not SPX. Further, these communications are also referred to as NCP communications or NCP (NetWare Core Protocol).

The other component of the shell is the interpreter interface (NETX.COM). This module monitors all user commands and determines if they are bound for NetWare or DOS. If a command is intended for NetWare, then the IPX component is used to establish a communication session with the file server. The entire setup is simple and straightforward. With NetWare 4.0 the architecture of the shell has been changed. Instead of running "ahead" of DOS and intercepting every interrupt call, the NetWare shell (now the NetWare requester), with version 4.0, sits "behind" DOS and only processes those interrupt calls passed from DOS.

The shell or the requestor requires 20K to 80K of a workstation's base 640K RAM to operate. The exact amount of memory necessary depends largely on the underlying network hardware and user-selected installation options, such as the number of concurrent file handles or the number of cache buffers selected. (These options are detailed further in Chapter 6.)

The file server runs a program called NET$OS (SERVER for NetWare/386). NET$OS has primary responsibility for the fulfillment of user requests. When the /286 version of NET$OS is loaded, it demands and uses all of the available extended memory in the file server machine. In its dedicated form, NET$OS can be loaded from a floppy disk, from a hard disk that boots DOS, or from the NetWare disk itself.

All nondedicated versions of NET$OS must be loaded after DOS. NET$OS still uses all of the extended memory (NetWare/286), and up to 25K of RAM in the file server/workstation's 640K base of memory. This is approximately equal to the RAM required for IPX/SPX, which does not need to be loaded at a nondedicated file server. Roughly the same amount of RAM is available after the network shell has been loaded as in a regular workstation.

Today, by far, the most serious users of networks and networking technology consider only dedicated file servers, and hence dedicated versions of NetWare. While the nondedicated mode is appealing in that it offers the opportunity to use the file server as a workstation, it is rarely the choice today with the lower costs of hardware and the higher costs of having LAN performance or integrity jeopardized by a user on a nondedicated file server.

Differences in NetWare Operating Systems

On the following pages are listed the major features of the various versions of NetWare and their differences. There are at least three distinct NetWare categories: NetWare/68, NetWare/286, and NetWare/386. In 1993, Novell's operating system offerings were NetWare 2.2 (NetWare/286), NetWare 3.11 (NetWare/386), NetWare 4.0 (NetWare/386) and SFT III NetWare 3.11 (NetWare/386). Before the release of 2.2, there were three major product offerings in the NetWare/286 category: Entry Level Solution (ELS), Advanced NetWare (ANW), and System Fault Tolerance (SFT).

Although as of March, 1988 Novell had discontinued the NetWare/68 operating system, Federal Technologies Corporation still maintains the aftermarket to support and maintain the Star 68A and 68B file servers. The NetWare operating system 2.1 heralded the end of the line for the Novell Star operating systems. Now, all current versions require at least a PC/AT-type file server, while the most recent versions of NetWare released, NetWare 3.11, NetWare 4.0 and SFT III NetWare 3.11, require a server with a 386 or 486 microprocessor.

Features/Limitations of the NetWare/68 operating system:

- Hot Fix
- Connections to other servers
- Support for the RXnet (ARCNET) LAN board
- Up to 254 concurrent users
- All of the NetWare security innate to the 2.1x product line
- Up to 4,000 concurrently open files
- 2 gigabytes (GB) storage

- 1-8MB RAM
- 16 drives

Features/Limitations of all NetWare/286 versions:

- Hot Fix
- Connections to other servers
- Support for VAPs (except for ELS II 2.12 dedicated mode)
- Ability to use Novell's Disk Coprocessor Board (DCB)
- Ability to use any LAN driver available
- Runs on AT-compatibles and PS/2s using Intel 80286/386/486 microprocessors
- No keycard (except for 2.1 and 2.11)
- Files up to 255MB in size
- Up to 1,000 concurrently open files
- Up to 200 concurrent TTS transactions
- Ability to use disk drives that are larger than 255MB
- All of the NetWare security innate to the 2.1x product line
- UPS monitoring
- 1.5-16MB of RAM

Features/Limitations of ELS NetWare Level I 2.12:

- Up to 4 concurrent users
- Ability to run in nondedicated mode
- Password encryption on the wire
- Unable to use Value Added Disk Drivers (VADDs)
- Unable to support Value Added Processes (VAPs)
- Unable to participate in a network with other servers
- No Async remote bridge support
- No Macintosh support
- Does not support Novell's DCB

Features/Limitations of ELS NetWare Level II 2.15:

- Up to 8 concurrent users
- Unable to use Value Added Disk Drivers (VADDs)

- Does not support Novell's DCB
- Only one LAN adapter allowed; an asynchronous (COM) adapter option is allowed in addition to the LAN adapter, and the NL1000 is allowed for Macintosh connections without compromising the choice of a single LAN adapter

Features/Limitations of ANW 2.15:

- Limited to 100 concurrent users
- Ability to run in nondedicated mode
- Support for VADDs
- Unable to use a PC/XT-compatible as file server
- Up to 4 LAN adapters per server
- Ability to run in nondedicated mode
- Ability to connect to AppleTalk networks

Features/Limitations of SFT NetWare 2.15:

- Limited to 100 concurrent users
- Support for VADDs
- Unable to use a PC/XT-compatible as file server
- Up to 4 LAN adapters per server
- Unable to run in nondedicated mode
- Ability to connect to AppleTalk networks
- Ability to do disk mirroring, disk mirroring across disk channels (disk duplexing), and to use TTS

Features/Limitations of SFT NetWare 2.2:

- Offered with maximum concurrent users of 5, 10, 50, and 100
- Support for VADDs
- Unable to use PC/XT-compatible as file server
- Up to 4 LAN adapters per server
- Ability to run in nondedicated mode
- Ability to do disk mirroring, disk duplexing
- Requires the use of TTS in dedicated operation
- The ELS and Advanced versions of NetWare are discontinued

- Ability to set WATCHDOG interval (default: 15 minutes)
- Ability to add printers to server dynamically (for information on these last two features, see Chapter 2)

Features/Limitations of NetWare/386:

- Hot Fix
- Connections to other servers, including servers down to the release of 2.0a
- Support for NLMs, but not for VAPs or VADDs
- Ability to use Novell's DCB
- Runs on 386 compatibles and PS/2s using Intel 80386/486 microprocessors
- No keycard
- File sizes up to 4GB
- Up to 100,000 concurrently open files
- Up to 25,000 concurrent TTS transactions
- Support for disk drives that are larger than 255MB, and allowing volumes up to 32 terabytes (32 million million bytes!)
- Ability to link up to 32 physical drives to form one virtual volume
- Up to 250 concurrent users
- Dynamic allocation of resources as needed, such as memory for loadable applications, i.e., NLMs, disk caching, file service processes, etc.
- Ability to connect to AppleTalk networks
- Ability to do disk mirroring, disk mirroring across disk channels (disk duplexing), and to use TTS
- 2.5MB-4GB of RAM
- UPS monitoring
- Password encryption on the wire
- 18 LAN Adapters per server
- All of the NetWare security innate to the 2.1x product line and more

Features/Limitations of NetWare 3.11

- Offered with maximum concurrent users of 5, 10, 20, 50, 100, and 250
- Ability to support AppleTalk Phase I networks
- Ability to support AppleTalk Phase II networks
- Ability to dynamically configure AppleTalk network data
- Support for TCP/IP and OSI
- Support for IPX tunneling over TCP/IP
- Support for 64 LAN Adapters per server
- Support for native filenames for OS/2 (HPFS), FTAM, and NFS, in addition to support for DOS and Macintosh

Features/Limitations of SFT III NetWare 3.11

- No support for Macintoshes
- No support for NFS

Features/Limitations of NetWare 4.0

- Ability to run NLMs in Ring 3
- File compression on "unused" files
- Sub-allocation (disk sizes <4K)
- Support for Data Migration
- Directory Services
- Support for up to 1000 users

NetWare 2.2 and 3.11 present a new product stratification from Novell. Figure 1-5 compares the two side-by-side.

	2.2	3.11
Maximum number of users	5	5
	10	10
		20
	50	50
	100	100
		250
Run Dedicated	yes	yes
Run Nondedicated	yes	no
Dynamic resource allocation	no	yes
MEMORY:		
Novell's recommended minimum server RAM (with 50 active users)	2.5MB	6.0MB
Maximum RAM	12MB	256MB (4GB)
Maximum cache RAM	12MB	256MB (4GB)
Disk space needed by operating system and utilities	5MB	9MB
VOLUMES:		
Total disk storage	2GB	32TB (2048GB)
Maximum partition size	255MB	unlimited
Maximum volume size	255MB	32TB (2048GB)
Maximum volumes per server	32	64
Maximum physical drives per server	32	4096
Volumes and Files able to span multiple drives	no	yes
FILE SYSTEM:		
Support for DOS, OS/2 (HPFS) and Macintosh	yes	yes
Support for NFS	no	yes

Figure 1-5. Comparison of NetWare 2.2 and NetWare 3.11

	2.2	3.11
PERFORMANCE:		
Dynamic cache buffer pool	no	yes
Split Seeks	yes	yes
Data Scattering		
(same file scattered on many drives)	no	yes
Dynamic volume sizing	no	yes
Dynamic directory entry sizing	no	yes
COMMUNICATION PROTOCOLS:		
IPX/SPX	yes	yes
NetBIOS	yes	yes
AFP	yes	yes
TCP/IP	no	yes
OSI	no	yes
IPX tunneling via TCP/IP	no	yes
LAN ADAPTER SUPPORT:		
Multiple NICs (maximum per server)	4	18 (64)
Support for 32bit data paths	no	yes

Figure 1-5. Comparison of NetWare 2.2 and NetWare 3.11

Advantages of NetWare

A hallmark of NetWare has been its constant refinement. NetWare incorporates innovative technology into each major release, solidifying its market position. Novell's obvious commitment to its product leads one to the conclusion that implementing NetWare is a choice with a future.

One NetWare innovation is the ability to network dissimilar LAN topologies through the use of routers, formerly called bridges by Novell. Disparate topologies can be routed (bridged) "internally," using the file server, or they can be routed (bridged) "externally," using a device outside the file server. Up to four topologies can be routed with various versions of NetWare released prior to NetWare/386. With NetWare/386 3.1x, up to 64 topologies can be routed, subject to the limitations of the hardware being used. The routed topologies can be the same, with each routed portion representing a different network segment. By having more than one network segment, the bandwidth of the network is expanded and performance is potentially improved.

In order to route different LAN topologies, some overhead is required, causing a reduction in performance. This overhead only affects performance when network traffic crosses a router, such as when communicating with file servers externally across a router to the intervening file server or routing server. Each time a bridge is "crossed" some performance is lost due to the overhead of "moving" the packet between the different LAN topologies. Also, performance will be further impaired if the bridging is done between topologies of high throughput and those of lower throughput. Remember, throughput is not solely calculated by a topology's "megabit per second (Mb/s)" speed rating. For instance, 4Mb/s IBM Token-Ring can have lower throughput than 2.5Mb/s ARCNET. In addition, when bridging dissimilar topologies, performance is limited to the speed of the slowest topology involved. Also, the speed and loading of the intervening servers and routers can noticeably affect performance.

NetWare can also provide connectivity to non-PC computers without changing their native environments. Novell started with connections to DEC's VMS system, has continued with NetWare for Macintosh, and also supports Sun Microsystems Inc.'s Network File System (NFS). Portable NetWare for UNIX, which is based on NetWare/386 with all non-portable code removed, is Novell's Original Equipment Manufacturer (OEM) version of NetWare. It is intended to allow NetWare to exist on 32-bit systems, regardless of platform. For instance, installations with Data General Corp., Prime Computer, Inc., or NCR Corp. minicomputers could incorporate their own versions of Portable NetWare. Also, Sun and NeXT are expected to have versions of Portable NetWare made available for their workstations. This would allow the heterogeneous minicomputers and PCs to share resources on a homogeneous network.

The OEM versions of NetWare for UNIX are all derivatives of a base-line "generic" implementation based on UNIX. All current OEMs are based on UNIX or its derivatives. Novell is considering other base-line implementations for the

AS/400 and IBM 370-compatible mainframes. Most mainframes and minis could be considered potential targets for NetWare.

Because it is dedicated to the long-term success of NetWare and the development of products based on the NetWare System, Novell has opened its internal protocols and functions to allow for third-party support. Thousands of NetWare-aware applications exist, from databases to system-level utilities. This openness has had far-reaching effects. For instance, a competing LAN manufacturer, Banyan Systems, Inc., actually emulates some NetWare calls in an attempt to allow some NetWare-aware applications to run under its operating system, VINES. One of the more important results of this extensive third-party support is the assurance that NetWare will remain a viable product for a long time to come.

The long list of NetWare advantages continues to grow with the improved design of NetWare. Among the leading LAN operating systems, such as Microsoft Corp.'s LAN Manager, and Banyan's VINES, NetWare is the only one designed from the ground up to be a total network operating system. The other leading vendors have products that are based on other operating systems. These other operating systems, OS/2 for 3+Open and UNIX for VINES, are not designed for network performance. This is especially true of OS/2. The main drawback of basing a LAN operating system on another non-network operating system is that the LAN inherits that system's pitfalls. Also, these non-network-specific operating systems include general OS features that serve to slow network-specific operations. Designed from the ground up as a network operating system, NetWare avoids any such encumbrances.

Planning a NetWare LAN

The planning process is extremely important in the overall implementation of a LAN. This process immediately raises questions that might otherwise be put off. For example, what will be the tangible costs and benefits of the LAN? How much will the LAN need to grow? How will changes in business affect the LAN? Answering these questions by using current information and by making projections will provide a much better basis for specific choices when planning the LAN's components.

One important design consideration is to always plan on the high side. For instance, if you are unsure your LAN will eventually service 100 or 200 users, use 200 as your margin for planning. Always allow for more capacity than you think you will ever need. By doing so, you better ensure that your LAN will perform well and it will continue to work smoothly as it grows. Also, be sure to allow for growth when choosing servers, workstations, cabling, etc.

In many cases, the process of planning the LAN is actually a small part of an overall strategic systems plan. The LAN selection is often preceded by the selection of business applications and design. In these instances, it is only after an organization has chosen the software that best fits its needs that it turns to planning the most appropriate LAN to support the applications.

When planning a NetWare LAN, the most essential step is selecting the NetWare version. The choice of topology is not as pertinent as the version of NetWare chosen because almost all versions allow use of any LAN topology. Disk space requirements, number of users, and applications to be used are also factors in choosing a version of NetWare. Thus, the essential first decision is what NetWare version will be used. This issue can affect several other decisions, including the file server hardware needed. Once the choice has been made, proceed with the steps that follow. Note that the /286 version of NetWare has been succeeded by NetWare /386.

Cable Considerations

One of the most common cable types used for LANs is unshielded twisted pair (UTP) cabling. There is also the much lesser used shielded twisted pair. For instance, the telephone wire in your company's building is most likely UTP. Another common, though increasingly less frequently used, cable type is coaxial cable, or coax. This cable type is similar to that used to connect a television to a cable TV subscription service.

Regardless of which type of cable is used, some precautions should be taken to avoid unnecessary performance and reliability problems. Foremost, as with all metal-based cabling, avoid electromagnetic fields. This may seem easy to do, but it is important to note that many sources of magnetic fields are easily overlooked. For example, running a cable near the ballast of a fluorescent light is commonly a cause of LAN difficulties. Another trouble spot occurs when cable is run along elevator shafts. It's important to stay clear of any power transmission equipment for the elevator.

Another less common phenomenon involves grounding loops. These loops occur when workstations and file servers on the same physical LAN connection are plugged into different power sources. If there is more than one power transformer, there may be more than one power source. This arrangement is common in older buildings, such as those often used by departments of the government. Grounding loops tend to unbalance the signal in the LAN cable. One solution is to ground the LAN cable at one end, preferably to a true earth ground rather than to a conduit or building ground.

Fire codes must also be considered when installing LAN cable. Most cities have adopted some form of the National Electrical Code. As a result, many LANs installation sites require Teflon-jacketed cable rather than PVC (Polyvinyl Chloride). Teflon-jacketed cable is also referred to as plenum-rated, meaning it is safe to use in the air handling spaces of a building. PVC breaks down and gives off chlorine gas in a fire, making it unsuitable for use in any air plenums (such as the suspended ceiling in most offices).

A third commonly used cable type is fiber-optic cable. Handling and installation of fiber-optic cable should be performed only by a professional cable installer. The complexities of splicing and installing fiber-optic cable are beyond the scope of this book. If the LAN is small, and prefabricated lengths of fiber-optic cable can be used without splicing, its installation could be performed by a novice.

Workstation Considerations

Many different types of personal computers can be connected to a NetWare LAN. Virtually any Compaq or other IBM-compatible PCs, Apple Macintoshes, and other types of workstations can participate in a NetWare LAN.

It is important to note that the workstation is the user's view into your network's "world." If it is slow or underequipped, your user will see a slow network. This only serves to frustrate the users and will hamper their work. With the price of 386/486 based workstations dropping everyday, it would seem foolish to not equip a user with such a machine. Also, if using a Graphical User Interface (GUI), be sure to include enough RAM to avoid the memory-to-disk swapping penalty, a real problem when there is too little RAM.

Network Interface Card Adapters

The Network Interface Card (NIC) adapter selected for the workstation is of primary concern. It is important to verify that the NICs chosen for workstations will operate properly. Remember, as with the choice of workstation, the choice of NIC will also define the user's perception of the network's speed. Thus, incorporate the best performance, as defined in the following paragraphs, in a NIC that you can afford. The combination of a high performance workstation with a high performance NIC will offer the user the best "view" when accessing the network. In other words, the user's workstation will not be "the" bottleneck.

The bus speed of the PCs to be connected to the network is also of critical concern. Most PCs adhere to the IBM AT standard (i.e., non-MCA) 8MHz bus speed setting, but many compatibles do not. It may be necessary to actually set up a workstation to determine if a particular NIC adapter will work. The following guidelines should be considered when trying a particular workstation/NIC combination for the first time.

- Test more than one card; you never know when a defective card will show up.
- Use the latest driver for the chosen NIC.
- Remember that most electronic component failures occur during the first 10 days of use.
- If it won't work in one slot, try moving the NIC to another slot in the workstation.

When selecting the network cards, it is important to determine if 16-bit boards exist for your selected topology. 16-bit implies that a card has two edge connectors, thus using both the long and short connectors available to many of the card slots in 80x86 (x=2,3,4, etc.) (AT class) machines.

A card with a 16-bit connection is able to move data through the machine faster. Instead of data moving one byte (8 bits) at a time, it can be moved two bytes (or a word) at a time. This alone can account for the increased speed as compared to 8-bit cards. Using the same software (perhaps with different drivers), the 16-bit card will be able to transport the data quicker, thus allowing for higher performance. If it is not possible to place 16-bit cards in all of the workstations, either due to a lack of 16-bit slots or funding, be sure to include them in the file servers. The result will be a file server that has increased ability to handle network traffic. However, other bottlenecks in the system, such as the disk drive channel, access to RAM, and file server processes, may result in no net performance benefit.

An added benefit of many 16-bit NICs is their ability to use hardware interrupts 9 and above, often called cascaded interrupts. This allows the otherwise impossible use of network cards.

For newer systems, 32-bit NICs are or will be available. As with 16-bit cards, 32-bit cards offer increased performance. Look for 32-bit cards in 386 and 486 systems using IBM's Micro Channel, or in other systems using EISA.

When installing NICs in a PC, a conflict may arise with other cards already installed in the same PC. Such conflicts can be resolved by determining the options used by each card. (Many common options are discussed in Chapter 6.)

Occasionally a video card or internal modem located next to a NIC adapter may prevent the NIC adapter from working properly. As a test, try rearranging the cards so that they are separated by at least one slot.

Diskless Workstations

Often called "LAN workstations," diskless workstations are specialized PCs that do not have any form of disk drive. This makes it impossible to copy data from the network onto a diskette. Having fewer parts, diskless workstations tend to be less expensive than regular, disk-drive equipped PCs. Diskless workstations are typically used in environments where security and cost are of major concern.

Diskless workstations do have some drawbacks. Since the PC does not have a disk drive, it must boot from the network file server. This is accomplished via firmware, i.e., software encoded on memory chips, installed on the NIC adapter (also known as boot ROMs), with a boot image copied onto the file server. With the exception of IBM Token-Ring and its RPL (Remote Procedure Load) ROMs, upgrade of boot ROMs is very costly. The chips are expensive and installing them requires disassembling the PC and possibly removing the NIC adapter.

One drawback associated with NetWare run on diskless workstations is that new boot ROMs are often needed when there is a change in the major and/or minor revision of the operating system. Novell uses a system to identify different versions of NetWare. Usually NetWare versions are named with three numbers, two numbers and one letter, or rarely, three numbers and one letter. Major revisions, which require new boot ROMs, are indicated by a change in the character to the left of the decimal (the "ones" position) and minor revisions are indicated by a change in the character to the right of the decimal (the "tenths" position). For example:

- An upgrade of NetWare version 1.0 to 2.0 requires a new boot ROM.
- Upgrading version 2.0 to 2.1 also requires a new boot ROM.
- Upgrading version 2.11 to 2.15 does not require a new boot ROM.

Another drawback of using diskless workstations concerns upgradeability. Often the NIC adapter is integrated into the system board, or "motherboard," of the workstation. If an improved NIC adapter becomes available, it is impossible to install the NIC without replacing the machine or, at the least, its motherboard. Sometimes it is possible to disable the native NIC and insert another one to be used in its place. This close integration of components also means that other areas are often not upgradeable, such as video type and amount of RAM.

File Server Considerations

When selecting a file server, the most important consideration is the manufacturer. Keep in mind that the file server is one of the most critical parts of the entire network. A savings of a few thousand dollars may be more than offset by service costs and lost business due to LAN downtime if the file server proves unreliable. In addition, a lower quality file server may have upgrade limitations, such as requiring expensive optional parts from a sole supplier as opposed to more commodity-oriented alternatives. It is recommended that any machine chosen be a file server of high quality, manufactured by a widely recognized and well regarded company.

While it is true that even a machine from a superior manufacturer can have problems, the risk is much higher with a lesser known manufacturer's machine. The following scenarios are actual examples of problems caused by the use of inferior equipment.

A clone machine offered up to 8MB of RAM on the motherboard with the promise of an additional 8MB module in the future (to bring the total RAM to 16MB). The manufacturer later reneged and owners of the machine had to go elsewhere to expand their RAM base.

On another occasion, a machine of lesser quality failed to even boot up NetWare. Instead it spewed out errors, including GPI and Invalid op code interrupts. The same thing happened in another off-brand machine, but in that case the solution was to replace the "no-name" disk controller with one from a manufacturer who maintained high standards for disk controllers.

Yet another machine ran the bus at the same speed used by the CPU. Better-designed clones (using an ISA-based bus) operate the bus at 8MHz regardless of the processor speed being used. In this case, the processor was running at 16MHz, twice the speed of a "standard" AT bus. As a result, most of the expansion cards refused to operate. The solution was to operate the machine at 8MHz, yielding a somewhat crippled but usable machine.

File server quality is largely influenced by the degree of the machine's compatibility with NetWare. At least two different classes of NetWare compatibility exist. The first class includes machines that can function as file servers. The second class consists of PCs rated as NetWare Compatible workstations. Some manufacturers advertise their product as NetWare Compatible, implying compatible "as a file server" (i.e., the first class) when they are actually only certified for use as workstations.

The issue of NetWare compatibility is further complicated by the existence of an official compatibility program from Novell. In order to receive Novell's stamp of approval, a PC manufacturer must make a substantial investment and submit a machine to Novell for compatibility testing. For a fee (roughly $10,000), Novell applies a series of compatibility tests to the manufacturer's PC. If the machine passes all the tests, it is said to be NetWare Compatible. Not every PC manufactured, however, is submitted for testing. Consequently, a machine that is 100 percent NetWare compatible may never have been tested by Novell simply because the manufacturer did not submit it to Novell for testing. Just the same, most 386/486 machines produced now are capable of successfully running NetWare 3.1x and NetWare 4.0. Given this fact, it is likely that the next generation Intel microprocessor-based PCs (known as Pentiums, not 586s) will also run NetWare.

If you will be running SFT III NetWare, it is important to use file servers verified by Novell to run SFT III.

Another important file server consideration is specifying RAM, which is treated in detail in Chapter 3. The memory you specify for the file server needs to be extended memory. The other type of RAM, expanded memory, is not used by the NetWare operating system.

Also important is site planning, specifically, selecting a physical location for the file server. Sufficient ventilation and cooling, along with adequate power protection, are prerequisites for a suitable file server location. In addition, if an uninterruptable power supply (UPS) or other specialized power system is used with the file server, printers cannot be connected to the same UPS. Due largely to the electromagnetic (or electrostatic) motors used in most printers, they should be placed on separate power filtering devices.

Printer Considerations

Each file server is capable of supporting up to five file-server-attached network printers. Connecting these printers can be accomplished via either a serial or parallel connection. Note that NetWare does not use hardware interrupts when communicating with attached printers. This frees the interrupts normally used by serial and parallel ports for use by NIC adapters. (More on the file server's use of interrupts is offered in Chapter 3.)

When printing in a LAN environment, print data from the workstation is captured in a file on the file server. All of the jobs for a given network printer are stored in a queue. The file server takes completed jobs out of the queue and sends them to the print server (which may be a VAP or NLM running with the operating system). The more printers that are used in the network, the more administrative tasks are required to effectively route data and to group users.

In general, it is not preferred to connect printers to the server. Rather, use of Novell's or third party print products and nonserver based printers is recommended.

An increasingly popular option is direct connection to the network. Many high performance printer manufacturers are providing Ethernet and token ring connection options for their printers (e.g., HPLaserJet IIIsi). This allows the printer itself to be connected to the LAN as if it were a workstation. Printing speed can be greatly increased as the data is delivered directly to the printer's memory at network speed, bypassing the much slower parallel port.

Disk Drive Considerations

Whether adding disks to an existing file server or selecting disks for a new installation, choosing the proper disk drive can be difficult. Often the selection process becomes confused with terms such as Small Computer Systems Interface (SCSI), Enhanced Small Driver Interface (ESDI), Run Length Limited (RLL), Integrated Drive Electronics (IDE), and Redundant Array of Inexpensive Disks (RAID). A number of factors need to be considered when choosing a disk drive.

The first and most obvious consideration is the amount of disk space needed. Less obvious is the need to calculate the disk space needed. NetWare usually requires about 5MB for system files which reside on the first volume, SYS:. And, storage of dynamic printer (spooler) files defaults to the SYS: volume, although this may be changed with NetWare version 2.1 and higher (see Chapter 10, Changing Queue Directory's Location). If additional capacity is needed in anticipation of more users, start by calculating the average amount of disk space required by each user. Estimate requirements based on the nature of the application. Add 33 percent for contingency, and multiply the result by the number of additional users expected. Be sure to include room for occasional fluctuations in the amount of data on the file server, such as those that occur during a closing period in an accounting environment. In any event, it is always a good idea to arrive at an estimate that keeps disk space usage below 75 percent of the total available space. This approach allows for system overhead and can prevent unanticipated or sooner-than-expected "disk full" messages.

When the amount of disk space has been determined, look for likely disk drive candidates. Ignore specifications such as SCSI, ESDI, Run Length Limited (RLL), etc., unless there is a specific environment required for a drive of a certain type. The terms ESDI, SCSI, RLL, and ST-506 relate to disk operations. For instance, ESDI and ST-506 are interfaces between the disk drive and the PC. RLL and Modular Frequency Modulation (MFM) refer to different ways of controlling the manner in which data is encoded onto the disk's magnetic platters. Generally speaking, the interface used is more important than the data encoding technology. (These terms are discussed in-depth in Chapter 5.)

Once the disk drive is selected, the next consideration is deciding on the system interface, which is provided by the disk drive controller. Some combinations of disk drives/controllers are not feasible. Figure 1-6 contains a list of drive sizes, disk drives, and controllers that work together, ranging from 70MB to 1080MB. This list is by no means intended to be complete. Instead, it offers a few "plug-and-play" options requiring no special, non-Novell utilities and lists those that can be used in any 286 or 386-based NetWare file server.

Size(MB)	Drive Model	Controller
76	Fujitsu M2243	Adaptec 4070 (A4070) + Novell's DCB*
90	Priam/Vertex V170	Adaptec 4070 + DCB
109	Priam/Vertex V185	Adaptec 4070 + DCB
117	Maxtor XT1140	type 9 drive/normal AT controller
126	Maxtor XT1140	Adaptec 4000 (not A4070, the A4000) + DCB
155	CDC Wren III	DCB + (embedded-onboard SCSI)
183	Maxtor XT1240	Adaptec 4070 + DCB (the 1140 could be used)
245	Priam ID130	Adaptec 4070 + DCB (used with v2.0a)
280	CDC Wren IV	DCB (v2.1x + Generic SCSI [embedded SCSI] driver)
480	Fujitsu FJ2623A/S	IDE or SCSI (DCB)
660	Micropolis MC1624	SCSI (DCB)
1080	Fujitsu FJ2266S	SCSI (DBC)

* **DCB** stands for Disk Coprocessor Board, Novell's disk drive controller's controller

Figure 1-6. Sample drive/controller combinations

Note that many third-party utilities for NetWare/286, such as OnTrack Computer Systems, Inc.'s Disk Manager-N, allow different drive and controller combinations. In addition, many manufacturers are making PCs with drive types that allow different drives to use the internal disk controller. The LAN dealer you select should be able to specify drives that will work in these environments.

Finally, several manufacturers make drive systems that incorporate the use of a NetWare feature called Value Added Disk Driver (VADD) in NetWare/286 and NetWare Loadable Module (NLM) in NetWare/386. (VADDs and NLMs are covered in more detail in Chapter 4.)

Electronic Mail Considerations

In some respects, electronic mail (E-mail) is the one true network application in that it would not exist without some sort of network in place—there is no such thing as single-user E-mail. This makes E-mail a fundamental consideration in LAN planning.

With NetWare versions up to and including 2.1, Novell included a simple, single server-based, E-mail facility. Beginning with version 2.11, Novell stopped bundling the E-mail program with NetWare. To purchase Novell Mail for NetWare 2.1x and newer versions, order part number 883-000606-001. However, Novell Mail is NOT recommended, because of its lack of minimally acceptable features for an enterprise E-mail system. Instead, an E-mail system based on Novell's MHS (Message Handling Service) is recommended as it is sure to interface with many other E-mail products because of the widespread use of MHS. You can even use MHS E-mail to communicate with others via CompuServe.

All NetWare versions 2.1 and above include the MHS facility (or a coupon for it). MHS is the message "agent" for any E-mail applications that use MHS's functions. For instance, E-mail packages like DaVinci Mail, The Coordinator, and cc:Mail all support MHS. MHS is a kind of "background" application and is not itself an actual electronic mail application. Some of the products that use MHS have their own message agents built in, but the option to support MHS can make it possible to connect to other types of electronic mail systems. Novell makes MHS available at no charge to NetWare users who request it.

CHAPTER 2

Installing NetWare

Once plans for a LAN have been completed, all of the components selected, and the hardware and communications components purchased and assembled, NetWare can be installed. This chapter covers installation of NetWare on the file server, as well as user and applications installations. The emphasis in this chapter is placed on installation of NetWare on the file server, as this is where most of the NetWare operating system files are stored.

File Server Installation

Although the great majority of NetWare dealers provide some installation assistance as a part of their service, installing NetWare on a file server is typically a routine operation. In fact, most of the information needed to complete the process can be obtained from the NetWare manuals.

Figure 2-1 contains a high-level listing of the major steps (or utilities) required to install the operating system and workstation shells.

	2.0x	2.1x	2.2	3.x	4.0
To generate and install the operating system	GENOS INSTALL (/68 2.02x) COMPSURF PREPARE SYSGEN (/68 prior to version 2.02)	NETGEN INSTALL (/68 version) ELSGEN	INSTALL	INSTALL	INSTALL
To generate workstation shells	GENSH	SHGEN	WSGEN	WSGEN	INSTALL

Figure 2-1. Utilities to install the operating system and workstation shells

The information in this section should be used to supplement, rather than to replace the step-by-step instructions provided by the Novell documentation. In addition, there are three miscellaneous points to consider that are not covered well in the Novell manuals. These are:

- Disk drive installation
- Disk drive preparation, especially using COMPSURF
- Disk drive partitioning

Disk Drive Installation

A NetWare file server sold in a "factory" configuration does not always fit the needs of a particular LAN. Because not all manufacturers offer standard machines with disk drive capacities exceeding 300MB, additional disk drives or large capacity third-party drives are sometimes required.

While third-party disk drives typically come with installation instructions, it is easy to miss a key step which can create a problem that only becomes visible later. Most of the problems that result from improper disk drive installation are related to placement of terminating resistors, cabling, and device addressing. Following are ten steps that provide some guidelines for installing disk drives in a NetWare file server.

1. Have the necessary terminating resistors for each hard disk.
2. Know how to set up the drive as drive 0 or 1, and where the terminating resistor(s) are to be placed.
3. Make sure both drives are terminated when using the type of 34-pin ribbon cable that has a "twist" in it. Otherwise, only drive 0 should be terminated.
4. Usually, one edge of the disk drive ribbon cable is color coded. This indicates pin 0 or 1 of the connector at each end. Sometimes the connector at either end of the cable is stamped with a 0 or a 1. In either case, be sure to line up the connectors on the ribbon cable with the correct pins on the drive and controller.

5. Make sure there are enough connections from the power supply to handle all of the internal disk drives. If not, 'Y' adapters or power splitters are available to increase the number of power connections available from the power supply.
6. Verify that you have the correct internal bus cable for the number of controllers and/or drives you are installing.
7. Make sure you know how to set the controller's address. This is most important when dealing with SCSI controllers.
8. Drive 0 is always terminated and is the last drive in the physical chain. Likewise, controller 0 is always terminated and the last controller in the physical chain. This is most essential when dealing with SCSI controllers. (Point #3 above is the exception.)
9. When installing a controller for a Novell Star system (68A, 68B), the tape drive, if installed, is controller 7 (where the range of addresses is 0-7).
10. If installing an embedded SCSI drive and you are using Novell's DCB, be sure to disable parity checking on the disk drive controller.

WARNING: Some older IDE/ATA drives will be rendered useless if low level formatted. Check with the manufacturer to determine the safe method to COMPSURF the drive.

Disk Drive Preparation and COMPSURF

For NetWare 3.x and 4.x installations the following section does NOT apply. COMPSURF stands for COMPrehensive SURFace analysis, a standard utility delivered with NetWare. (NetWare/386 incorporates COMPSURF's operation within the INSTALL utility.) COMPSURF formats and tests file server disk drives. The benefits of COMPSURF are twofold. First, it prepares a low-level format on the disk. Second, by thoroughly testing the surface of a hard disk at the time of installation, COMPSURF alerts installers to many problems that may occur with hard disk media.

When COMPSURF is executed, it uses information contained in the file server to identify all of the hard disks in the system. The origin of this information depends on the PC and the components used as the file server. COMPSURF seeks these sources in a predetermined order.

For NetWare /286:

- Value Added Disk Driver (VADD), whose routines, in turn, search for drives
- Disk controller ROM of XT (808x CPU)
- CMOS setup information of AT (80x86 CPU)
- DCB EEPROM of Novell's Disk Coprocessor Board

For NetWare /386:

- DSK drivers which have been loaded

Once it has gathered all of the information it has sought for the disk drives in the file server, COMPSURF is ready to prepare and test them. Since it has a very specialized function, it is necessary to understand some of the nuances of COMPSURF's operation.

For all drive types other than drives defined in the AT's setup information CMOS, COMPSURF issues a single format directive and the disk drive's controller formats the disk drive. When it is finished, the controller reports back to COMPSURF that it is done.

In the case of AT drives defined in the CMOS, COMPSURF must issue thousands of format commands, formatting one track at a time. This is because the unusual design of the AT's disk controller allows it to format only one track at a time. Besides taking an unnecessarily long period of time, the result is confusing to the AT's disk drive and its controller and does not always produce an ideal format. Therefore, if the disk drive being installed is defined in the CMOS of an AT-class file server, more commonly known as the DRIVE TYPE entered at SETUP time, COMPSURF should not be used to low-level format the disk drive. Instead, the manufacturer's low-level format routine should be used. In low-level format, a sequence of address and control information is written by the disk controller at the beginning of each sector of the hard disk. This enables the disk controller to locate each sector on the disk, and is either performed at the factory or delivered with the disk drive.

COMPSURF also performs extensive testing of the hard disk drives. Properly preparing a large hard disk (300MB) can require as many as 72 hours of COMPSURFing. The need for such extensive testing was minimized when Novell added the feature, Hot Fix, to all 2.1x versions of NetWare. Hot Fix monitors disk writes while the file server is operating. When a write error is detected, Hot Fix automatically marks the bad area of the disk as unusable and moves the data to another part of the disk. Since Hot Fix can adjust for media errors "on the fly," the testing performed by COMPSURF isn't needed beyond a couple of passes (requiring approximately one to three hours). This initial testing is still necessary since the Hot Fix option is not in operation during the installation process. On versions of NetWare that do not use Hot Fix (most versions older than 2.1x), COMPSURF should be run longer in order to obtain a complete testing of the disk.

As a final note, Disk Manager/N, from Ontrack Computer Systems, Inc., provides COMPSURF-equivalent utilities that can be used instead of COMPSURF. Besides operating quicker than COMPSURF, these utilities also allow for more types of disk drives to be used.

Included with NetWare 2.2 is a new utility called ZTEST. ZTEST is a scaled down version of COMPSURF which only runs the Track 0 test. Usually ZTEST takes less than five minutes to complete.

Disk Drive Partitioning

The space on a hard disk can be divided into one or more partitions. This allows more than one type of operating system to access the disk, although only the appropriate operating system can be used to access its corresponding partition. For example, a disk drive may have both a DOS and a NetWare partition. However, only DOS can be used to access the DOS partition, and only NetWare can access the NetWare partition. With NetWare/386, access to the server's DOS partition(s) can be achieved via NLMs designed to do so. Within a NetWare partition there can be one or more volumes. Each volume can be treated as a separate and distinct drive, often referred to as a virtual drive.

All NetWare versions support only ONE NetWare partition per physical disk. NetWare version 2.0x supports a maximum partition size of 255MB. Version 2.1x and 2.2x have no such limit. All versions of 2x allow up to 255MB per volume. Thus, with version 2.1x/2.2x it is possible to use a 300MB disk and divide it into two or more volumes; with version 2.0x, only the first 255MB of the disk can be used. (Note that Racet Computers offered the ability to break the 255MB partition boundary in NetWare 2.0x.) It is important to note that the NetWare partition must be the first partition, i.e., the partition starting with cylinder 0, on a disk drive for any NetWare version 2.x or older. NetWare/386 removes many limitations, including the location where the NetWare partition begins, the maximum size of the NetWare partition and the maximum size of a NetWare volume within a NetWare partition.

Further, NetWare/386 allows up to 8 volumes per NetWare partition and each volume may use a different block size (described in the following section).

At one time, a primary rationale for partitioning the disk drive on a file server was to allow it to be used as a workstation, i.e., as a nondedicated server. The idea was to load the network operating system (NetWare) in one partition and the workstation operating system (DOS) in another. However, there are several reasons why nondedicated use is ill-advised.

First, NetWare 2.2x and older must occupy the beginning (i.e., track 0) of a hard disk, making it the first partition on the disk. Therefore, DOS or other non-NetWare partitions must come after the NetWare partition. Since the DOS, or non-NetWare, partition must be at the end of the disk, the potential exists for that partition to be overwritten with file server data by the Hot Fix feature. This is because Hot Fix reserves space at the end of the disk drive to store data from "bad spots" on the disk. Any data written to the DOS partition may overwrite Hot Fix data. Note that NetWare 2.15c corrects Hot Fix so it does not overwrite the DOS partition at the end of the disk.

Second, most versions of DOS limit the size and placement of partitions. These limitations may make having a DOS partition unworkable. For example, with some versions of DOS, the disk drive can be no larger than 32MB if the intention is to boot the disk with DOS.

Third, performance is greatly reduced on a nondedicated file server when there is I/O activity for a DOS partition. This is a result of the difference in performance between NetWare's elevator-seeking logic during disk access and DOS's slower disk-access technique.

Finally, some versions of NetWare/286 may interpret that the whole disk belongs to the network operating system even though there is a DOS partition on the disk. The dual results of this are that: (1) NetWare starts to consume space in the DOS partition; and (2) when DOS accesses its own partition, it ends up overwriting the data written by NetWare. Given all of the shortcomings of writing multiple partitions, the best approach is to use a separate disk drive for each operating system on the file server. NetWare/386 does not have any of these difficulties in handling multiple disk partitions.

Volumes and Block Sizes

With NetWare/386 3.x you may have up to 8 volumes per NetWare partition. Volume names must be at least 2 characters long and may be up to 15 characters long. Each volume may be of a different block size. The block size controls how much disk space is minimally occupied. The default block size is 4K; you may alternately use 8K, 16K, 32K, or 64K. Finally, a NetWare volume must be at least 1MB in size.

Larger block sizes are preferable in a transaction-based environment. For instance, the performance of a system that experiences a lot of database activity would improve with the use of a larger block size because the typical high-use database setup has, as its basis, large data files. As portions of these files are accessed, they are read into memory. A larger block size reads in more data and makes it immediately available, whereas using a smaller block size requires multiple, separate reads to access the same data contained within the previously mentioned, larger block. However, this block size affects ALL files on that volume. Thus, if you have a few batch files, perhaps each being a couple hundred bytes long, each would be located in a separate disk block resulting in a larger amount of wasted disk space. (NetWare 4.0 cures this dilemma with its small-block allocation feature. For instance, if a 64K block size was used, each batch file would occupy a 64K block of the disk.)

The volume block size is defined when creating the volume with the INSTALL utility. Once set, it is not possible to change it without first removing the volume. Removing a volume results in the loss of all data for that volume, so be careful when choosing your block size. When in doubt, use the default 4K.

With NetWare/386 3.x and beyond, a single volume may consist of up to 32 separate physical disk drives, without the aid of any specific hardware, such as RAID, to "link" the drives. By defining a volume with multiple segments you realize a volume size much greater than any single disk could offer. However, if any drive in the "link" goes offline, the whole volume will become inaccessible. To help prevent this real possibility from disabling your volume, use disk mirroring (Chapter 5). In fact, disk mirroring is always recommended in any environment in which the cost of a day of downtime is more than the cost of disk mirroring.

Operating System Reconfiguration

Part of the process of installing the operating system involves specifying the types of network adapters installed in the file server and their settings. This is done using GENOS (version 2.0x), NETGEN, ELSGEN (version 2.1x.), or INSTALL (version 2.2x). Should the need arise to alter the settings of any of the network adapters after the operating system is generated and installed, there is a way to make such a change without rerunning the entire installation procedure.

If you are using version 2.1x/2.2x, use the DCONFIG utility that can be found on many disks delivered with NetWare, including the disks labeled SHGEN-2 and AUXGEN. For version 2.0x, use the SCONFIG utility found on the GENOS-3 disk (or possibly on GENOS-4). In both cases, when either utility is executed from the command line, a list of the operating options that can be changed will be listed. Figures 2-2, 2-3, and 2-4 provide examples of how to use DCONFIG and SCONFIG to reconfigure the operating system.

Figure 2-2 lists options available by typing DCONFIG without any parameters.

```
J:\V2.15\NETWARE\AUXGEN> dconfig
Usage: dconfig [volume:]file [parameter list] or
 or
dconfig -i[volume:]file (Take input from specified file.)

Where [parameter list] is zero or more of:
A-E: [net address], [node address], [configuration #];
C0-7: [driver  type], [configuration #];
OTHER: [signature], [Configuration #];
SHELL: [node address], [configuration #];
BUFFERS: [number of buffers];

     J:\V2.15\NETWARE\AUXGEN>
```

Figure 2-2. Options used with DCONFIG

Note that DCONFIG can also be used to reconfigure workstation shells. It can also be used to reconfigure the BACKUP and RESTORE utilities for Novell's high-speed internal tape backup unit.

The SCONFIG utility, like DCONFIG, can be used not only to reconfigure NET$OS, but also to reconfigure 286-based BACKUP and RESTORE Novell utilities.

Figure 2-3 lists the options available by typing SCONFIG without any parameters.

```
F:\V2.0A\NETWARE\GENOS-3> sconfig
Usage: SCONFIG <filename> [<lan>: [<net #>][,[<node #>][,<config #>]]] ...
  [<net #> and <node #> fields are hexadecimal. <config #> is decimal]
```

Figure 2-3. Options used with SCONFIG

```
F:\V2.0A\NETWARE\SYSTEM> sconfig

Novell 68000 OS Configuration Program v2.01
(C) Novell Inc. 1986
USAGE: SCONFIG filename parameters
```

Figure 2-4. Options used with SCONFIG for S-net file servers

There is also a version of SCONFIG for Novell S-net file servers. The version of SCONFIG designed for S-net servers is only useful on NetWare versions 2.01 or later. Figure 2-4 lists the options available by typing SCONFIG without any parameters.

The parameters in this version of SCONFIG include:

```
B: [Buffers]
S: [Star LAN address]
R1: [RXNET board 1 LAN address]
```

Note that SCONFIG can be used to view the NetWare operating system file NET$OS.SYS directly by typing the file name as an explicit argument, as shown in Figure 2-5.

```
F:\V2.0A\NETWARE> sconfig net$os.sys

OS FILE: net$os.sys

Buffers [200]
S-Net Boards [004A414E]
RX-Net Board 1 [1234FADE]
```

Figure 2-5. Using SCONFIG to reconfigure NET$OS.SYS

To complete this reconfiguration example, if it is determined that the number of buffers used by the operating system needs to be increased, the buffer parameter (B:) is used to submit the new number, as shown in Figure 2-6.

```
F:\V2.0A\NETWARE> sconfig net$os.sys b:232
OS FILE: net$os.sys

Buffers [232]
S-Net Boards [004A414E]
RX-Net Board 1 [1234FADE]

Checksuming file

1f573978
Checksum has been updated
```

Figure 2-6. Using the SCONFIG buffer parameter

It is often useful to know the configuration data for NetWare 2.1x when preparing to use DCONFIG. The data is stored in the file CONFIG.DAT found on the disk labeled SUPPORT. If NETGEN or ELSGEN is run from a hard disk, it will be in the SUPPORT subdirectory.

Booting the File Server

Booting the file server can be accomplished in a variety of ways. If a nondedicated version of NetWare is used, the file server must boot DOS first before NetWare is loaded. The NetWare operating system may be composed of one or three files. If it is one file, it will be a NET$OS or a SERVER executable file that is several hundred kilobytes in size. If the operating system has three files, they will be the files NET$OS.EXE, NET$OS.EX1, and NET$OS.EX2. All three files must exist in the same directory, unless they are on different floppy disks. If they are on different floppy disks, NetWare will prompt the user for them. In the case of either one or three files, executing NET$OS (pre-NetWare/386) or SERVER (NetWare/386) from the command line will load NetWare.

If a dedicated version of NetWare is used, the file server can be booted in one of two ways. It can boot DOS first, then load NET$OS, just as with nondedicated NetWare, or the file server can boot directly from the NetWare SYS: volume, which is the first volume in the system. To boot from the SYS: volume, NET$OS.EXE (or NET$OS.SYS if /68) must be in the SYS:SYSTEM directory. The NetWare cold boot loader will search for NET$OS in this directory, load, and run it.

If the file server contains one of Novell's Disk Coprocessor Boards (DCBs), booting directly from the NetWare disk may not be possible, unless the file server is a specialized Novell 286B or 386AE model. If this is the case, DOS must be booted first, then NetWare. There are some third-party DCBs that can boot NetWare directly without the need for the intervening DOS boot step, such as the DCBs available from ProComp USA, Inc.

With NetWare/386, reconfiguration of the operating system is a far more trivial task than it is under NetWare/286. Loading and unloading of drivers allows for quick updating of driver (disk, LAN card, UPS, and so on) in a matter of seconds, without bringing the server down.

If, under NetWare/386, you have volumes with many files (>2000) and those volumes seem to mount slowly, try increasing the minimum directory cache buffers count. For instance:

```
Set Minimum Directory Cache Buffers = 100
```

Cold Boot Loader Problems

The cold boot loader program bootstraps NetWare into memory. Beginning with NetWare version 2.12, this program began causing problems when booting the file server, thus requiring the remedial step of booting DOS first.

If a problem with the cold boot loader is suspected, a correcting file (called LOAD21.ARC) can be obtained from Novell via the CompuServe bulletin board,

NetWire. This file contains a cold boot loader that can be used with all versions of NetWare 2.1x. NETGEN is used to install the new cold boot loader on the network.

If you are having problems when directly booting your NetWare/286, that is, not from DOS, you may find the easiest and quickest solution to be simply booting from DOS (preferably a floppy so as not to waste any disk space). These boot time problems such as "error hole in file" are usually related to incompatibilities or problems with the cold-boot loader. As such, they do not directly impact NetWare once it is running, thus, bypassing it altogether and booting from DOS will not incur any problems. Do NOT, however, use MS DOS 5.0. The file server will not come up, but will simply leave a blank screen with a blinking cursor in the top left corner. Use a DOS version prior to 5.0, such as 3.3 or 3.31.

Setting PROMPT on Nondedicated File Servers

The DOS command, PROMPT, is useful when custom-tailoring the command line prompt, particularly to display the current volume and subdirectory being used. It is normally set in the AUTOEXEC.BAT file of a PC, e.g., PROMPT = PG. However, when it is used in the AUTOEXEC.BAT file of a nondedicated NetWare file server, the PROMPT command can cause the workstation side of the file server to fail. The usual result is the message "invalid COMMAND.COM," which is received upon the termination of an application and followed by the PC/file server "locking up."

If PROMPT is set in a batch file other than AUTOEXEC.BAT, this problem doesn't occur. The same is true if PROMPT is set from the command line. The best solution is to move PROMPT to another batch file which is called by the nondedicated file server's AUTOEXEC.BAT. Regular workstations on the LAN do not have a problem when PROMPT is set in AUTOEXEC.BAT.

Note that the definition of PROMPT is not the only cause of "invalid COMMAND.COM" messages. For example, the COMMAND.COM file could actually be bad or the COMSPEC command might be improperly set.

Errors Linking NET$OS [NETGEN]

While designed to provide a user-friendly approach to generating the NetWare network operating system, NETGEN is far from foolproof. One of the errors that can be encountered, error 9, produces the following system message:

```
AN ERROR OCCURRED WHILE LINKING NET$OS ERROR = 9
```

This error usually occurs during the first stage of NETGEN, the linking process. The essence of the problem is that NLINK (NetWare Linker) cannot find a specific .OBJ file in a specific directory, or on a specific disk if NETGEN is being run from diskettes. Typically, this error occurs when adding a new driver to the operating system, especially if it is a driver that was not included in the original NetWare packages.

All drivers for NETGEN are defined in two places. The first is typically in the AUXGEN directory (or disk) where the .LAN files are found. These files define the options that the actual driver (.OBJ) files contain. They also include the location of the driver (.OBJ) files. The second place is the subdirectory (or disk) in which the driver files themselves are located.

It is this separation of driver files into two distinct directories that is the source of linking error 9. What usually precipitates this error is that the .LAN file is found and is included in the NETGEN driver selection, but the directory and/or file with the .OBJ file is not found during the actual link process. This happens because the .OBJ file has unknowingly been placed in the wrong subdirectory.

To solve this error, you must determine the correct name of the subdirectory in which the driver files are located. The DEBUG utility can be used to read the LAN file to determine the directory in which its associated .OBJ files are located, as shown in Figure 2-7.

```
L:\V2.15\NETWARE\AUXGEN> debug tccmdrv.lan
-d100 10F <enter>
61E7:0100  0B 4C 41 4E 5F 44 52 56-5F 31 38 30 39 54 68 6F   .LAN_DRV_1809Tho
```

Figure 2-7. Using DEBUG to determine location of .OBJ files

In Figure 2-7, the first byte after the address is 0B. This is the length of the directory/drive in which the .OBJ files should be located. In HEX, B is 11, so the next 11 characters represent that directory/disk name, in this case, “LAN_DRV_180.” Because DOS does not allow directory names to be formed in an 11-character stream, the actual name would be “LAN_DRV_.180.” Thus, all of the driver .OBJ files associated with this .LAN file would be located in a directory/disk named

"LAN_DRV_.180." This approach will eliminate most errors in linking driver files during NETGEN.

Another error that NETGEN can produce is an error 10. This error indicates that there is no free disk space available. Here you would exit NETGEN and ensure there is at least 2MB of free disk space. To further prevent error 10 from recurring, have at least 5MB free.

While errors 9 and 10 are more common, there are actually 14 different error codes that can result from NLINK errors. Figure 2-8 lists a summary of these NLINK error codes. While we have focused on NLINK errors encountered when using NETGEN, remember that these errors can occur when NLINK is used by SHGEN as well, to create the shells and operating system.

NLINK Error Codes

CODE	MEANING
1.	Unable to open the argument input file
2.	Memory allocation error
3.	Error reading the file
4.	Unknown object record type
5.	Bad segment alignment
6.	Bad combine type in segment
7.	Public multiply defined
8.	Public specified to wrong group
9.	Unable to open a file
10.	Unable to write to a file, out of disk space
11.	Bad frame method in fixup
12.	Bad relative fixup mode
13.	Fixup target not reachable from frame
14.	Unable to open a mapfile

Figure 2-8. Summary of NLINK error codes

Configuration Files for Version 2.1x

Once the file server has been booted and you have logged in for the first time, there are a few more file server options to consider. These involve the initialization of the file server at boot time. Most of this additional initializing is activated by using the AUTOEXEC and CONFIG files allowed by NetWare.

NetWare 2.2 Issues

The latest version of NetWare/286 is 2.2. NetWare 2.2 contains fixes for many previous problems with NetWare/286. You should be aware of some of the new items in 2.2, including the following:

- FSPs
- Dynamic Memory Pool 4 (DMP4)
- Mandatory TTS with dedicated operation
- New Rights Mask and File Attributes
- Revised Printing Services

2.2 FSPs

One of the most vexing limitations of old versions of NetWare/286 was insufficient FSPs on NetWare/286 file servers. This problem is not completely solved with NetWare 2.2, however, you should find that there is some improvement. For a more complete discussion of FSPs, see Chapter 3.

2.2 DMP4

NetWare 2.2 adds an additional dynamic memory pool not previously included in NetWare/286. It is used for mapping directories and its size cannot be configured.

2.2 Mandatory TTS

With NetWare 2.2, Transaction Tracking System (TTS) is required when the operating system is set up for dedicated operation. If it is set up for nondedicated operation, you will be unable to use TTS or disk mirroring. This means if you upgrade to version 2.2 and you do not have a TTS volume, you will have to create one for a dedicated server to run. To create a TTS volume you must reinitialize the disk volume where it is created. This area is required whether you have applications that use TTS or not.

2.2 New Trustee Assignments

Trustee Assignments for NetWare 2.2 have changed. The new Trustee Assignments or Rights for NetWare 2.2 more closely resemble the Trustee Assignments for NetWare/386 than for NetWare versions prior to 2.2. For more information see the section titled "NetWare/286 and /386 Trustee Rights Compared" later in this chapter.

2.2 INSTALL Options

The following are command line installation options available using NetWare 2.2's INSTALL utility:

-c Create Utilities
-e Advanced Install
-l Link and Install
-m Maintenance
-n No configuration or linking
-u Upgrade

These are well covered in the NetWare 2.2 documentation, but the above is offered as a little crib sheet.

If you are doing an operating system upgrade from earlier versions of NetWare to 2.2, keep in mind the following cautions about using the INSTALL options. Several INSTALL options will destroy all information on the hard disk. In particular, the option -L, which runs the ZTEST module, should never be used during an upgrade. ZTEST checks track 0 of the hard disk, destroying all data on the disk. If track 0 of the hard disk was inoperative, the server would not boot. The ZTEST needs to be run for new hard drives.

The -U, -M, and -F options also should be used with caution, since they display the File Server Definition screen. Any changes you make to the size, volumes, or partitions on the hard drive in the Definition screen will destroy your ability to access the data on the drive.

Server-Attached Printers

A NetWare file server uses AUTOEXEC.SYS (NetWare/286)/AUTOEXEC. NCF (NetWare/386) in the same way that DOS uses AUTOEXEC.BAT. While this file is optional, it is often used to store instructions that the file server executes at boot time. It is created by using the SYSCON utility's SUPERVISOR options and is kept in the SYS:SYSTEM directory. If the AUTOEXEC.SYS/AUTOEXEC.NCF file does not exist (this is the default), then the file server automatically establishes connections, or "mappings," between default printer queues and server-attached printers. These default printer mappings follow a simple pattern, beginning with PRINTQ_0 being mapped to PRINTER 0, and so on. However, if AUTOEXEC.SYS/AUTOEXEC.NCF is found, no such default action will occur and all print queue-to-printer mappings must be explicitly defined in the AUTOEXEC.SYS/AUTOEXEC.NCF file.

With regard to AUTOEXEC.SYS/AUTOEXEC.NCF, the key printing consideration is that all print queues must be assigned to each server-attached printer in this file. Otherwise, the printer will not be active when the file server boots. This is often the source of problems when a file server is rebooted after already having been in use; someone has created or modified the AUTOEXEC.SYS/AUTOEXEC. NCF file in SYS:SYSTEM.

2.2 and Dynamic Printer Configuration

With versions of NetWare/286 prior to 2.2, all printer definitions occur within NETGEN (or other appropriate utility). With 2.2, printer definitions can occur in AUTOEXEC.SYS/AUTOEXEC.NCF or as a result of typing them at the server console. These new commands are listed in Figure 2-9.

The PSERVER.VAP is a major improvement over core printing services. Not only does the VAP print faster than core services, it also allows you to dynamically reconfigure all print service parameters. The VAP itself must be loaded at boot time. It then remains loaded until the server is downed.

The VAP supports a Print Server which services the network print queues. You can stop and start this print server from the file server console using PSERVER STOP and PSERVER START. You can use PCONSOLE to reconfigure the print server, which file servers it will service, which queues, which printers, etc., and then stop and restart the print server using these commands so that the changes you made can take effect. The file server does not have to be brought down.

P n CREATE device	Used to create a printer definition
P n CONFIG baud, wordsize, Stopbits, Parity, XonXoff	Used to configure the printer
P n REMOVE	Used to remove a printer definition
P n POLL x	Used to change the polling interval for how often the specific printer port's print queue is checked for new print jobs, 1 to 60 seconds NOTE: This polling time is 15 seconds with previous versions!

The "n" in the above is the printer port number, 0, 1, 2, etc.

Figure 2-9. COMMANDS to perform printer definitions with NetWare 2.2

The VAP also supports the PSERVER.EXE program. With PSERVER.EXE, you can set up a dedicated workstation to do the work of the print server. This frees up the file server CPU for other duties. If you use PSERVER.EXE, you can stop or down it by using PCONSOLE. To start it, you run the program from the workstation.

2.2 Watchdog Setup

With NetWare 2.2 it is now possible to set the watchdog timeout. In previous versions the time was set at 15 minutes. This resulted in an "are you there?" message being sent to all current workstations every five minutes. If a workstation did not respond to the query, another "are you there?" message would be sent every minute for 10 more minutes. After this 15 minute period the workstation would have its connection cleared and its user automatically logged out. This might happen if users shut off their machines without logging off or if the machine locked up and the user did not reboot before the fifteen minutes expired.

Use the following server console command to set the watchdog interval:

```
WATCHDOG start=N interval=M count=0
```

N and M are in seconds, and O is the number of times to repeat the interval (M). For instance, the default 15 minutes would be declared:

```
WATCHDOG start=600 interval=60 count=10
```

i.e.,

600 seconds = 5 minutes
60 seconds = 1 minute
10 repetitions of 1 minute = 10 minutes

Shortening the Watchdog timeout will help in freeing up a connection more quickly when someone disconnects from the network. This can be very useful when ALL available connections are being used for a particular file server. Otherwise, by default it will take 15 minutes after someone disconnects before another can use that connection.

If you want to have this new timeout always in effect, put the appropriate Watchdog timeout commands in the AUTOEXEC.NCF so they will execute each time the file server is booted.

UPS Monitoring

For NetWare version 2.1x, except for version 2.15, the file CONFIG.UPS is used to define uninterruptible power source (UPS) monitoring hardware. Beginning with NetWare version 2.15, several boot-time options, including those previously specified using CONFIG.UPS, are handled using SERVER.CFG. This special file specifies how certain operations that boot and run the file server will take place. (Details of both CONFIG.UPS and SERVER.CFG are in Appendix B of the respective NetWare Installation manuals.)

With the newer approach, SERVER.CFG is a text file that is placed in the SYS:SYSTEM directory. When the file server boots, it searches for this file. When this file is found, the operating system (NET$OS) reads and interprets the commands within it. These commands include provisions to generate error messages when file server data cannot be deciphered.

VAP WAIT and TTS WAIT

NetWare 2.15 and later has the "VAP WAIT xxx" option. This command, specified in SERVER.CFG, instructs the file server to wait a specified number of seconds before automatically loading any VAPs in the SYS:SYSTEM directory. The "xxx" parameter in the VAP WAIT command indicates the number of seconds that the file server will wait. The range is 10 to 360 seconds but, if no number is specified, a minimum wait time of 10 seconds is used. For some VAP applications the VAP WAIT time specified should be 45 seconds, i.e., VAP WAIT 45. This 45 second "wait" period allows for some internal processes of NetWare to complete their initialization so that incoming VAPs will not cause a system crash due to incomplete server init routines

When the file server is booted, it will wait the specified number of seconds before loading the VAPs found in SYS:SYSTEM. If any key on the file server keyboard is pressed while it is counting down, NetWare will abort the loading of all VAPs. Otherwise, VAPs will be loaded and the file server will continue booting. This option can be useful in determining whether or not a VAP is causing a file server problem.

Without the VAP WAIT command, the file server will wait for a manual "Y" or "N" response to be typed to indicate whether to load a VAP. If the question remains unanswered, the file server will not finish booting.

In addition, there is the "TTS WAIT xxx" command for SFT NetWare. It is used in the same manner as VAP WAIT. Pressing a key while the server is counting down the TTS WAIT time causes the transaction backout feature of SFT NetWare to be aborted.

Connecting Multiple File Servers

As a network grows, new file servers are sometimes needed. Adding file servers to a Novell network is relatively simple, but there are a few configuration issues to consider. The following discussion assumes that the new server has been prepared and is ready to begin service.

First, there is the consideration of how the file servers are actually interconnected. Figure 2-10 demonstrates a network in which the file servers share a "file server only" backbone.

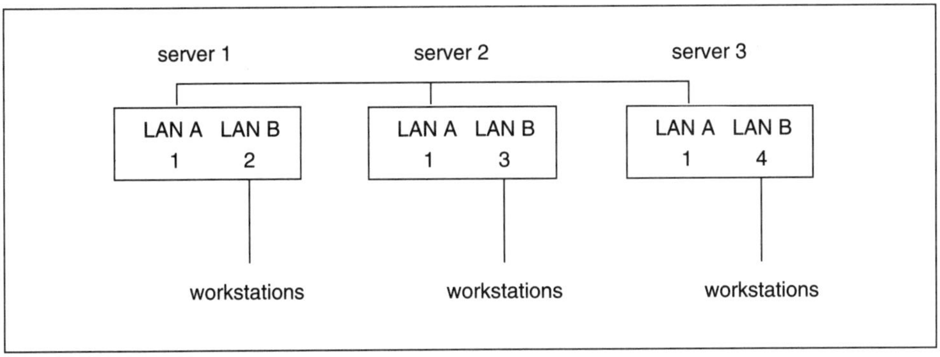

Figure 2-10. Shared file server network

Once workstations are connected to a file server, they can connect to other file servers on the backbone. In this configuration, the Network Interface Cards (NICs) that connect the file servers together must be configured to share the same internetwork address. (In NETGEN, the internetwork address is referred to as the "Network Address.") On the other hand, all file server LAN interfaces not connected to the backbone must use unique internetwork addresses. For instance, if address 2 is used on one file server where the LAN interface only connects to workstations, no other file server can use address 2 for any of its LAN interfaces. Note that the internetwork or network address is not the same as a NIC's node address.

In either case, proper addressing is important. If internetwork addresses do not match properly, communication between file servers is impossible. On the other hand, if there are duplicate non-backbone internetwork addresses, an error message similar to the following will appear:

```
!!!ROUTER CONFIGURATION ERROR!!! Router 10005A389B10 claims LAN A is
  00000123!
```

Figure 2-11 demonstrates a network in which the file servers and workstations share a common backbone.

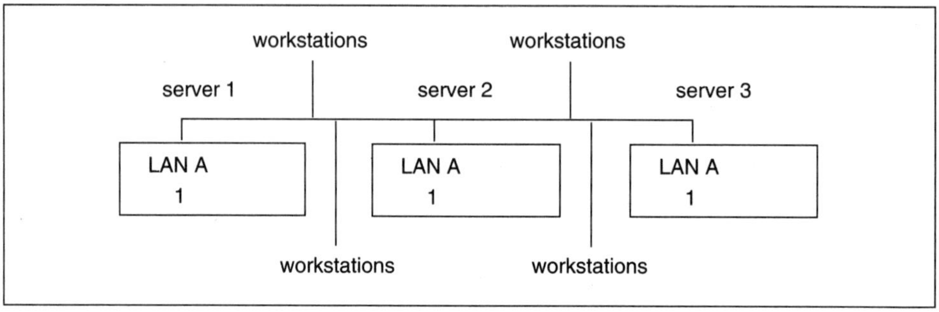

Figure 2-11. Common backbone network

The network design shown in Figure 2-11 facilitates workstation-to-file server connection by allowing the workstations to connect to any file server. This design does not require the services of a particular server to gain access to the network. At the same time, this configuration could be more confusing to the user because it is difficult to determine where each workstation will connect. To clarify, when the network shell (NET3, NET4, etc.) is loaded, it broadcasts a Get Nearest Server message on the LAN to which it is connected. The first file server to respond becomes that workstation's "default" file server. In our example, all workstations and file servers are on the same LAN, thereby giving all file servers an equal chance to hear and respond to a workstation's Get Nearest Server request. The file server that a user logs into becomes that workstation's default server. Each workstation can have only one default server, and connections to other servers are made via the ATTACH command or a utility such as SESSION. The LOGIN utility allows the default file server to be specified.

With NetWare 3.11, Get Nearest Server can be turned off by using:

```
Set Reply To Get Nearest Server = off.
```

at the file server console or in the AUTOEXEC.NCF file.

With NETx version 3.0 and higher, a Preferred Server option can be specified in SHELL.CFG or NET.CFG. (See Chapter 6 for more details.)

The terms *connect* and *connection* should not be confused with node, because it is possible for a single physical address (node) to have several logical file server connections. For instance, Novell's NetWare Access Server does this via DESQview.

IPX Internal Net

With NetWare/386 there is a new IPX address to consider, the IPX Internal Net address, and it is used to uniquely (network-wide) identify all service/clients (NLM applications) that reside in that server.

The IPX Internal Net number is used to uniquely identify a NetWare/386 server throughout the entire internetwork. One of the major reasons for the creation of this address was to eliminate "double routing" (described in a following section of this chapter).

Because each NetWare/386 server is uniquely identified by its IPX Internal Net, the network routers can theoretically send directly to it. Remember a server is "normally" (i.e., NetWare/286) found via its internetwork address plus its NIC's address. If a non-NetWare/386 server has multiple NICs it will be known under the address of its first NIC. However, with the IPX Internal Net number, all NetWare/386 servers are known as one address. That address is the IPX Internal Net plus a node address of 1. One way to see this address is through the use of the command line utility SLIST.

You may wonder why all servers on the same "cable" need to have the same network address for their NICs. Well, the IPX Internal Net address uniquely identifies the server to the internetwork, but for actual routing of each cable segment, a unique network address is still required. For example, if your NetWare/386 server has only one NIC, the server will be known by its IPX Internal Net address. Packets will be sent to that server's workstations via the network address of its network adapter (which "connects" to that workstation) plus the node address of the particular workstation

In short, the IPX Internal Net address uniquely identifies a NetWare/386 server. Each NIC in the NetWare/386 server has its own network address which is used to identify workstations on that cable segment.

Lost Server Syndrome

There is a bug in NetWare version 2.15 that causes external bridges to drop every eighth file server from its routing table. This anomaly, known as "stealth-server," includes any server that accesses the backbone by an external bridge or through another server that is internally bridged to the backbone. The stealth server problem was corrected in version 2.15c. (The upgrade to 2.15c from 2.15a was at one time a no charge upgrade.)

Star File Server Mystery Network

With the release of NetWare/68 2.01, Novell began providing support for an ARCNET adapter in its Star line of file servers (S-net servers). This technology was called RXnet by Novell to avoid infringing on Datapoint's proprietary ARCNET trademark. Regardless of whether that board exists, NetWare will broadcast a message for that board using address 00000002 on the internetwork. This is because Novell ships 2.01 and subsequent releases of NetWare/68 with the RXnet board LAN driver preconfigured to address 00000002.

To understand why this may be a problem, consider the following scenario. Two S-net file servers on an existing internetwork are upgraded to 2.01 or later. Without reconfiguring the RXnet LAN address, chances are the S-net servers will crash soon after they are booted. By changing the RXnet internetwork address of one of the operating systems (NET$OS.SYS) at one of the S-net servers, the problem is corrected. This simply follows the rules for internetwork address assignment, wherein each of the nonexistent (or existent) RXnet boards must have a unique internetwork address.

Double Routing

It is possible to create multiple paths between file servers. This isn't necessarily harmful to network operations, but it can result in extra packets, and consequently complicate management of network traffic. Figure 2-12 shows how such a network might be configured.

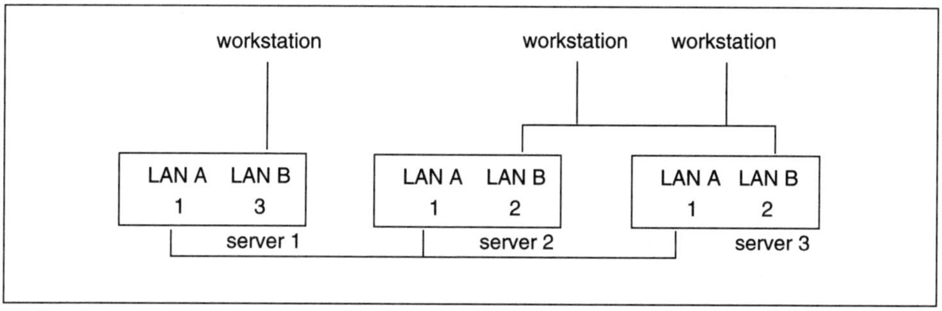

Figure 2-12. A mix of common and file server only network backbones

As shown in Figure 2-12, with NetWare 2.x "double routing" is possible. To demonstrate this, a packet from server 1 would be routed to server 3 via server 2 rather than directly to server 3. Figure 2-13 shows the packet in transit from the workstation to server 3.

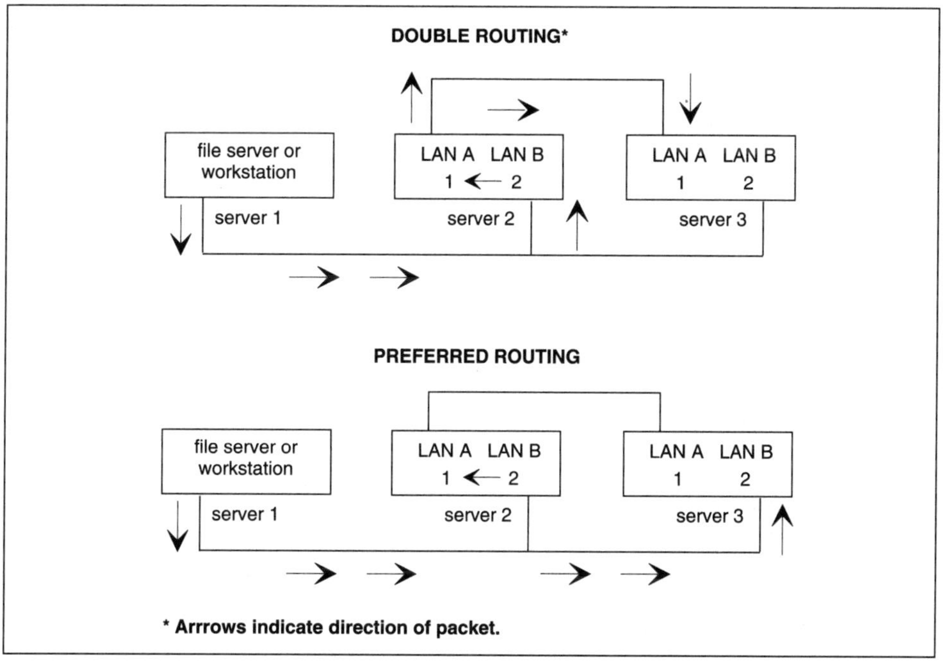

Figure 2-13. Double routing a packet

This anomaly does not occur in NetWare/386, and there is no way to resolve it in NetWare 2.x, other than to avoid multiple paths between file servers. It may not be obvious that a network has a double-routing anomaly but, considering its negative impact on performance, it is wise to check for it. If a double-routing situation is encountered, run performance benchmarks on the network before and after correcting the problem to determine the effect of double routing.

When connecting file servers, make sure that no more than 16 unique internetworks come between any two nodes. Otherwise, these nodes will not be able to communicate with each other, nor with other file servers more than 16 unique internetworks distant. The NetWare router mechanism abandons a packet after 16 different routings.

Defining Users

There are three utilities provided with NetWare to create new user accounts. These are USERDEF (2.1x/2.2x through 3.x), SYSCON (2.0x, 2.1x, and 3.x) and MAKEUSER (2.1x and 3.x). USERDEF is little-known and rarely used by most NetWare supervisors. The other utilities are treated in detail in the NetWare manuals, but the following section covers some important points regarding the definition of users.

Defining a user begins with a login name. It is best that each individual who will be using the LAN have a login name, even persons who make infrequent use of the LAN. Through the login name, a user is tied directly to disk usage and access privileges. Beginning with NetWare version 2.1x, several enhancements were made to the system accounting and security. These enhancements include:

- Simple tracking of user activity while logged into the network
- Prohibiting simultaneous logins of the same login name
- Reporting unsuccessful login attempts and temporarily locking out a login name that repeatedly provides an invalid password
- Requiring users to change their password periodically
- Allowing the supervisor to change passwords, but not to view them

- Encrypting and storing passwords—with ELS, Advanced, and SFT versions of NetWare, passwords are not encrypted as they travel on the network media between the workstations and file servers. However, with NetWare/386, passwords are optionally encrypted as they travel on network media.

In addition to individual users, groups can be defined. Groups can greatly simplify the task of granting privileges to individual users. By making a user a member of a group, that user is granted all of the privileges associated with that group. Likewise, when a new application or disk directory is added, granting access rights to the group gives all members of that group those new rights. This is much more convenient than granting rights to each user individually. One more caution, when granting rights, whether to a group or a single user: only the first 32 rights are used in determining the user's security privilege profile. Thus, if you assign more than 32 rights, they will not all be in effect.

CAUTION: Do not use a backslash or forwardslash following the volume name when typing in the path to a directory. If you do so, and then choose the Trustee Assignments option and answer YES to the prompt about creating a new directory, you will have just deleted that entire directory and its files. Leave the slash out and there is no problem. This problem occurs only with SYSCON 3.62. Version 3.66 fixes the problem.

Groups work best when the members share LAN resources. However, individual rights are still needed for private directories and other private resources. Keep in mind that any changes in user logins and associated rights do not become active and thus are not realized until the next login time for each user. When a change is made, users on the LAN will not realize there has been a change until they logout and login again. If using NetWare/386, changes to rights are immediate, i.e., not requiring a new login to activate the rights changes.

MAKEUSER Error

On a newly-created file server the MAKEUSER utility may produce the following error:

```
ERROR READING THE DEFAULT PROPERTY OF THE SUPERVISOR
```

This error can be fixed by running the SYSCON or NETCON utility and creating a single user (the user may be deleted in the same session). By creating a user, you create the necessary default property. This property can only be created by using SYSCON or NETCON to create the user.

User Names With a Dot (.)

If you define a user name with a dot (.) in it, e.g., USER.NAME, some of the Novell utilities will not operate properly. The "." acts as a separator to most of the NetWare command line utilities (for instance, SEND). And due to the way the Novell utilities parse names with a "." in them, they will likely not work. Thus, you should avoid defining user names with a "." in them. Also, the "." is used as a separator for Novell's upcoming Directory Services.

Login Scripts

The login script is used to define a user's environment during subsequent sessions on the LAN. This environment includes enhanced security, providing access to applications and performing other miscellaneous functions. NetWare uses two levels of login script—the system login script and the user login script. The 2.0x *Menu Utilities* manual and the 2.1x *Supervisor Reference* explain how to create and use login scripts. This section provides additional information to help you better manage login scripts

When a user logs in, the LOGIN program verifies the password entered and then gets the user rights information from the file server. If one exists, the system login script is then executed. This is true for all users logging into the LAN. The system login script is created by the LAN supervisor with the SYSCON utility and is stored in a file named NET$LOG.DAT in the SYS:PUBLIC directory. The system login script is used to define global resources, such as the mapping of shared directories. The language used in the login script processor is very powerful and can serve to greatly simplify administration and use of the LAN. Every LAN supervisor should become intimately familiar with login script capabilities.

Once the system login script has been executed, the LOGIN program checks to see if there is a user login script for the login name being used. It is possible to end the execution of all login scripts from within the system login script, i.e., no user login scripts are executed even if they exist. This can be done using the EXIT login script command in the system login script. Starting with LOGIN version 3.70 the "NO_DEFAULT" command can be inserted into the system login script, which will prevent the default user login script from running. Assuming the system login script does not end the login process, the user login script is executed next. This script is stored in each user's NetWare mailbox directory. A holdover from the days of the Novell Mail program, this directory is set up within the system for each user defined by the LAN supervisor.

NetWare assigns each user or group a unique number when it is created. The SUPERVISOR user number is always 1. All other users and groups are assigned hexadecimal numbers. Since all mail directories are created in the directory SYS:MAIL, the LAN SUPERVISOR's mail directory is SYS:MAIL\1. If, for example, a valid ID number 1C0047 was assigned, the user's mail directory would be SYS:MAIL\1C0047, and that is where that user's private login script would be stored. Note that the file containing the SUPERVISOR's login script (SYS:MAIL\1\LOGIN) should be flagged Read Only to prevent unintentional altering.

An interesting tip concerning the use of EXIT statements in a login script concerns password synchronization. Password synchronization is the process of establishing a common password for every file server to which an individual user has rights. In a network that has multiple servers and that uses NetWare's accounting facilities, password synchronization will not likely occur if the EXIT statement is in the login script —even though it appears to have occurred. A user who EXITs the LAN but then immediately reenters it may be denied access to the other file servers unless a SETPASS is run on each file server where a synchronized password is needed.

The user login script is contained in a file named LOGIN (no extension). For example, the full path name of the SUPERVISOR's user login script is SYS:MAIL\1\LOGIN. The user login script is used to define user-specific resources and environment settings. If a user login script file exists—even if it contains no instructions and has a file length of 0—it will be executed. If it does not exist, then the LOGIN program invokes a default user login script. This can be a source of trouble, as the default user login script might interfere with drive mappings in the system login script. Figure 2-14 displays the default user login script. Starting with LOGIN version 3.70 the NO_DEFAULT command can be inserted into the system login script,*f* which will prevent the default user login script from running.

```
WRITE "Good %GREETING_TIME, %LOGIN_NAME."
MAP DISPLAY OFF
MAP ERRORS OFF
Remark: Set 1st drive to most appropriate directory.
MAP *1:=SYS:; *1:=%LOGIN_NAME
IF "%1"="SUPERVISOR" MAP *1:=SYS:SYSTEM
Remark:  Set search drives (S2 machine-OS dependent).
MAP S1:=SYS:PUBLIC;  S2:=S1:%MACHINE/%OS/%OS_VERSION
Remark:  Now display all the current drive settings.
MAP DISPLAY ON
MAP
```

Figure 2-14. Default user login script

Good login scripts are similar in character to good programs in that many creative, useful, elegant login scripts can be developed to guide the user around the LAN. Conversely, a poor login script can degrade the LAN's performance. The following discussion offers a few tricks that can improve login scripts.

A very specific tip concerns using DAY_OF_WEEK or other "day" functions in the login script. If NetWare 2.1 is installed, it is possible for the calendar to be off by one day. This error is due to an incorrect function in the Lattice C library used to create NetWare version 2.1. Novell has provided a fix for this problem called LEAP.ARC (short for LEAP YEAR FIX) that was previously available from Novell.

The following is a tricky syntax faux pas:

```
IF HOUR24 <= "9" THEN BEGIN
```

can you spot the mistake? Here is how it should read:

```
IF HOUR24 <= "09" THEN BEGIN
```

The insertion of "0" is required for this comparison to operate correctly.

Note: This is also true for the following:

MONTH 01-12
DAY 01-31
MINUTE 01-59
SECOND 01-59

Logging In without Login

Optionally, a user may login to a server without the LOGIN command. The ATTACH command, typically used to attach to additional servers after an initial LOGIN to a primary server, may be used instead of LOGIN for an initial server attachment. Using ATTACH instead of LOGIN does not initiate any login script. Mapping of drives and other tasks usually done in the login script must be done using NetWare utilities or through a batch file. Also, newer versions of the LOGIN utility allow a script override which allows a user to bypass your login script.

A user may also "login" using the MAP command as well as any Novell MENU utility (for example, SYSCON, SESSION, FILER). Currently, it is not possible to prevent user logins without the use of the LOGIN utility. Technically, that way of logging in is ATTACHing to a file server. It will work if the user has access to the ATTACH command (ATTACH.EXE). That means the user must already be logged into a file server or ATTACH.EXE must be in the login directory or on a local drive.

Loading TSRs from Login Scripts

A common mistake is to use the login script # or "execute" option to load TSR (terminate-and-stay-resident) applications. The result is a loss of approximately 75K of RAM at the workstation. This loss is attributed to the fact that the LOGIN program is still in memory when the TSR is loaded. It gets trapped between whatever was in memory prior to login (most likely the network shell) and the newly loaded TSR. For this reason, if any TSRs need to be loaded at login time, use the EXIT statement in a login script to call a DOS batch file. The batch file can load the TSRs without this memory penalty. The other option is to run the login process from a batch file that continues after network login and loads the necessary TSRs.

Installing NetWare Applications

The most important issues influencing applications installation on the LAN are the assignment of rights and the actual configuration requirements for each specific application to be used. The following section provides background information and discusses each of these issues.

NetWare 2.15c (and prior) Trustee Rights

Many options exist to control access to resources in the NetWare environment. The part of NetWare security used most often is trustee rights. A trustee assignment is created by giving certain rights to a user in a file server directory. It is through these trustee assignments that users are granted access to programs and data on the file server.

Various combinations of the basic NetWare 2.15c (and prior) rights—Read, Write, Open, Create, Delete, Parental, Search, and Modify, shown as [RWOCDPSM]—provide a flexible means of defining the security of a LAN. It is very important for the LAN supervisor to have a thorough knowledge of how directory rights work and interact.

Assignment of rights can take two approaches. Taking the trustee approach, rights are granted to users at the user or group level using the SYSCON, MAKEUSER, FILER, or GRANT utilities. With the directory approach, trustees are assigned on a directory-by-directory basis, using the FILER utility.

All of the rights are self explanatory except Parental. Having Parental rights to a directory gives a user the ability to create or delete subdirectories under the subject directory. It also allows a user to grant or revoke trustee assignments to that directory.

Trustee rights consist of both rights assigned to individuals at the user level and rights assigned to groups as a whole. For instance, Read, Open, and Search rights may be assigned at the group level for a certain directory. However, it may be appropriate to grant only one individual in the group Write privileges, which can be assigned at the user level. The only rights that need to be assigned at the user level are those rights that are granted in addition to the rights assigned at the group level.

Once a trustee assignment is granted, it includes all subdirectories beneath the subject directory. For instance, if the Read privilege is granted in the SYS:PUBLIC directory, that Read privilege is automatically allowed in the SYS:PUBLIC\UTILS directory.

The trustee privileges are stored in a hidden system file called DIRSTAMP.SYS, present on all volumes prior to NetWare/386. Users and groups are referenced in the DIRSTAMP.SYS file by a NetWare-assigned ID number. NetWare searches DIRSTAMP.SYS files sequentially up the hierarchical directory structure towards the root. For the user name and each group that the user is a member of and each member that he is an "equivalent" to, NetWare will either fail to find any or all of the applicable IDs, or, at whatever point an applicable ID is found, NetWare will stop looking for that particular ID while continuing to search for the other applicable IDs.

If no applicable IDs are found, the user has no trustee privileges in the directory in question (the point where the operation is attempted on a file and where the first DIRSTAMP.SYS file is inspected).

If only one of the user/group IDs is found in the search, the associated privileges found for that user/group ID are that user's trustee privileges in the target directory.

If two or more IDs are found, i.e., if the user has been granted privileges in the immediate directory or one of its parents and a group to which the user belongs has an applicable trustee assignment, the user's trustee assignments are determined by the summation of all applicable trustee assignments. For instance, assume that:

1. USER1 is a member of the groups EVERYONE and ACCOUNTING.
2. All users are members of EVERYONE.
3. Group EVERYONE has Read, Open, and Search rights in SYS:APPS.
4. Group ACCOUNTING has Write, Create, and Delete rights in SYS: APPS\DATA.
5. USER1 has Parental and Modify rights in SYS:APPS\DATA\USER1.

In SYS:APPS, USER1's trustee rights are equivalent to those assigned to the group EVERYONE. No privileges are assigned to either USER1 or ACCOUNTING at SYS:APPS or above

In SYS:APPS\DATA, USER1's trustee rights are calculated by combining the rights assigned to EVERYONE in SYS:APS and to ACCOUNTING in SYS:APPS\DATA. Figure 2-15 illustrates this calculation.

Directory	Group	Rights
SYS:APPS	EVERYONE	[R O S]
SYS:APPS\DATA	ACCOUNTING	[W CD]
Trustee privileges (in SYS:APPS\DATA		[RWOCD S]

Figure 2-15. Calculation of trustee privileges (from two directories)

The trustee privileges calculated above are still contingent on the rights mask in SYS:APPS\DATA. Effective rights are discussed below.

In SYS:APPS\DATA\USER1, USER1's trustee rights are the combination of rights granted to EVERYONE and ACCOUNTING in parental directories and rights explicitly assigned to USER1 in SYS:APPS\DATA\USER1. This calculation is shown in Figure 2-16.

Directory	Group	Rights
SYS:APPS	EVERYONE	[R O S]
SYS:APPS\DATA	ACCOUNTING	[W CD]
SYS:APPS\DATA\USER1	USER1	[P M]
Trustee privileges (in SYS:APPS\DATA\USER1)		[RWOCDPSM]

Figure 2-16. Calculation of trustee privileges (from three directories)

The above example is unnecessarily complex, but it should clarify the process of determining trustee privileges. USER1 probably would have [RWOCDPSM] rights granted to SYS:APPS\DATA\USER1 by the supervisor to avoid dependence on rights "inherited" from parental directories by group membership.

Effective Rights

To determine a user's effective rights, both the directory's maximum rights mask and the user's trustee rights must be combined. Both the directory's maximum rights mask and user's trustee rights must include a particular right before it is granted. In other words, the resulting right must be the product of a logical AND operation, as shown in Figure 2-17.

```
Directory   &      Trustee=  Effective Rights

[RWOCDPSM]  &      [RWOCDPSM]    =  [RWOCDPSM]
[RWOCD   ]  &      [RWOCDPSM]    =  [RWOCD   ]
[RWOCDPSM]  &      [RWOCD   ]    =  [RWOCD   ]
[RWOCD   ]  &      [     PSM]    =  [        ]
```

Figure 2-17. Determining effective rights

NetWare 2.2 and 3.x Trustee Rights

Previous to NetWare/386, the only rights possible were those that regulated access to directories. Starting with NetWare/386, however, rights can also be assigned to files. In addition, directory right assignments have changed. Many of the new rights correspond to the rights supported under NetWare/286 and earlier versions. The new rights are Supervisory, Read, Write, Create, Erase, Modify, File Scan, and Access Control, with the following new rights "mask":

```
[SRWCEMFA]
```

Supervisory. This assignment grants all rights to the directory, its files, and subdirectories. The Supervisory right overrides any restrictions placed on subdirectories or files with an Inherited Rights Mask. Users who have this right in a directory can grant other users Supervisory rights to that directory, its files, and subdirectories. Once the Supervisory right has been granted, it can only be revoked from the directory to which it was granted. It cannot be revoked from a file or a subdirectory. If disk space restrictions have been assigned and more than one user is assigned to the subdirectories, the user with the Supervisory right to the directory can modify the restrictions in the subdirectories.

Read. This assignment grants the right to open files in a directory, to read their contents, or to execute them if they are programs.

Write. This assignment grants the right to open and write to (i.e., modify the contents of) files.

Create. This assignment grants the right to create files and subdirectories in the directory. If Create is the only right granted at the directory level and no rights are granted below the directory, this right creates a "deposit only" directory. In a deposit only directory, users can create a file and then open and write to it. Once the file is closed, however, they cannot see or modify the file. They can also copy files or subdirectories into a deposit only directory. When they copy, they assume ownership of the files and subdirectories. However, any trustee assignments assigned earlier to the files or the subdirectories are revoked for the copies.

Erase. This assignment grants the right to delete a directory, its files, its subdirectories, and subdirectory files.

Modify. This assignment grants the right to change directory and file attributes. It also grants the right to rename the directory, its files, and subdirectories. This right does not grant the right to modify the contents of a file.

File Scan. This assignment grants the right to see subdirectories and files when viewing a directory.

Access Control. This grants the right to modify a directory's or a file's assignments and Inherited Rights Mask. Users who have this right can grant all rights (except Supervisory) to other users, including rights that they themselves have not been granted.

NetWare /286 and /386 Trustee Rights Compared

These "new" rights can be mapped to the "old" NetWare/286 rights. For instance, with NetWare/286, when users are first added as trustees of a directory, they are granted Read, Open, and Search rights. With NetWare/386, they are granted Read and File Scan rights. The main difference in this case is that, under NetWare/386, the Read and Write rights imply the privilege of opening a file. Figure 2-18 further defines the relationship between directory rights in NetWare/286, Netware 2.2, and /386.

NetWare/286	NetWare 2.2	NetWare/386
Read	Read	Read
Write	Write	Write
Open	Read, Write	Read, Write
Create	Create	Create
Delete	Erase	Erase
Parental	Access Control	Supervisory, Access Control
Search	File Scan	File Scan
Modify	Modify	Modify

Figure 2-18. Relationship of NetWare/286 and /386 directory rights

In a strict comparison of the new rights to the old, only the Supervisory right adds a unique feature. As defined earlier, Supervisory grants a user all rights in a directory, its files, and subdirectories, just as if the user were a LAN supervisor.

Beginning with NetWare/386, trustees can be assigned to files. File rights control access to specific files in a directory. File rights are used to redefine the rights that users can inherit from directory rights. The following describes how these rights control access to specific files.

Supervisory. This assignment grants all rights to the file. Users who have this right can grant any right to another user and can modify all rights in the file's Inherited Rights Mask.

Read. This assignment grants the right to open and read the file.

Create. This assignment grants the right to salvage the file after it has been deleted.

Write. This assignment grants the right to open and write to the file.

Erase. This assignment grants the right to delete the file.

Modify. This assignment grants the right to change the file's attributes and rename the file but not the right to modify the contents of the file.

File Scan. This assignment grants the right to see the filename when viewing the directory. It also grants the right to see the directory structure from the file to the root of the directory.

Access. This assignment grants the right to modify the file's trustee assignments and Inherited Rights Mask. Users who have this right can grant all file rights, except Supervisory, to other users.

Inherited Rights and the Inherited Rights Mask are the NetWare/386 equivalent for the concept of cascading directory rights found in NetWare/286. Although the terminology is different, the manner in which rights are cascaded down directories really has not changed much from NetWare/286.

Just as in NetWare/286, when a directory is created in NetWare/386 it is given a default rights mask containing all rights. The actual rights allowed depend on the individual user's trustee assignments. Other than the Supervisory right which allows full access to all subdirectories, the real difference in assignment shows up on rights allowed with files in subdirectories.

For example, if a user has NetWare/386 trustee assignments of:

```
SYS:1          [RWCEMFA]
SYS:1/2        [R    F ]
SYS:1/2/3      [RWCEMFA]
```

In NetWare/286, the same assignments are:

```
SYS:1          [RWOCDPSM]
SYS:1/2        [R O   S ]
SYS:1/2/3      [RWOCDPSM]
```

Now, if this user was given the NetWare/386 Supervisory right in SYS:1, then that user would have full non-revocable rights in SYS:1/2 and SYS:1/2/3 as well. This is the key difference between NetWare/386 and NetWare/286 directory rights.

An important new feature of trustee directory and file assignments with NetWare/386 is the immediate update of rights for a user. This is very different from

NetWare/286. When users' rights are revoked in a NetWare/286 directory while the user is logged in, they can still access the directory. Users don't learn that their rights have been revoked until the next time they are logged in. Under NetWare/386, rights are effective when they are changed. In the situation just described, that same user would immediately be unable to access that directory, even if that directory is the current directory. These rights updates are performed regardless of whether the trustee assignment is assigned directly to the user or to a group where the user is a member.

Another new feature in NetWare/386 is "unseen" root directories. In NetWare/286, the command

```
F:\>DIR SYS:
```

will list every root directory for that volume, whether or not the user has rights to them. When the same user tries this command on a NetWare/386 file server they will only see the directories to where they have rights. Those rights may be in that root directory or they may be in a subdirectory beneath it. In any event, when users have any directory right, they are able to see the root of that directory. It is important to note that this check is done only when DIR is executed from the root. Once users are in a subdirectory under the root, they can see that subdirectory's entire tree structure.

Tips on Assigning Rights

If users will share rights to a particular directory, trustee assignments should be granted through group membership. When the rights for a group are changed, only the group's trustee assignments need to be modified. Every five trustees assigned to a directory uses one directory entry on the file server. Every file and directory on the network uses a directory entry. In a group membership, only one trustee "slot" is used, regardless of the number of members in the group. All members of the group will automatically have their rights adjusted upon the next login except for NetWare/386, where changes are immediate. Since a group can have several trustee assignments, assigning a member to a group can reduce setup time and simplify trustee rights changes. It can also decrease the number of directory entries used by trustee assignments.

When there is a temporary need for a user to access another user's directory(ies), the security equivalence of the first user can be set to that of the other user. This approach is useful when someone needs to delegate responsibility for work to another person, such as when a manager goes on vacation and has a secretary temporarily handle matters.

Every group to which a user belongs constitutes a security equivalence. Additionally, every time one user is made equivalent to another counts as a security equivalence. When determining effective rights, only the first 32 security equivalences are used. This limitation could result in rights being granted or denied incorrectly because the number of the total security equivalences is exceeded. While this is a rare occurrence, it is an issue worth noting because of the confusion it could create.

There is a special twist to NetWare 2.15 rights. Due mainly to this version's ability to accept Macintoshes on the LAN, the Parental right has slightly changed. Because of this change, the Create rather than the Parental right is necessary to create subdirectories. This change made version 2.15 different from any previous version of NetWare.

Installing User Interfaces

The user interface is one of the most important components of a LAN because it is the way in which most users will interact with the network. The user interface primarily concerns the visual image of the LAN to which users respond, typically a menuing system. However, it also includes behind-the-scenes activities performed on the LAN that shield users from the complexities of NetWare.

One example of a simple, behind-the-scenes interface is a consistent logout process. When a user runs LOGOUT, it is possible for one of a variety of different drive letters to become the new login drive. This variability is due to the state of the user's drive mappings at the time of logout. This can result in a confusing situation. For example, drive M: can suddenly become the login drive, even though drive I: is usually the login drive. Rather than attempting to resolve this predicament through NetWare themselves, users often unnecessarily reboot their workstations in order to login again.

By creating and using two simple files, a consistent logout can smooth the user interface. The first of these files is called LOGOUT.BAT and would normally be located in the SYS:PUBLIC subdirectory. The listing for LOGOUT.BAT follows:

```
MAP F:=FSNAME/SYS:LOGIN
F:
OUT
```

The second is called by LOGOUT.BAT. It is named OUT.BAT and is located in the SYS:LOGIN subdirectory. The sole command in OUT.BAT is

```
LOGOFF
```

In order for these two files to work, NetWare's usual LOGOUT program must be renamed to LOGOFF.

It is important that this particular piece of the user interface be composed of two files. When a file server LOGOUT occurs, all drive attachments are removed. If a batch file were being accessed from one of these now defunct drives, the user would see a message indicating that a batch file is missing. The second batch file prevents this running by executing from a drive/directory that does not disappear when the LOGOUT occurs. When LOGOUT.BAT runs, it will map the current drive to the current file server's SYS:LOGIN directory. Because OUT.BAT is run from that directory and because that directory still exists after LOGOFF (i.e., the renamed LOGOUT), no "batch file missing" messages occur.

DOS DIR Changes Volumes

If you ever type "DIR VOL1:\SOMEDIR" you will notice that your drive suddenly becomes mapped to the volume/directory you just entered, if the volume is different from the one where your drive was mapped when you typed the command.

DIR is a DOS internal command. Consequently, it still uses FCBs to do its stuff. This means that the request sequence is as follows:

- Get current directory
- Change current directory

This uses the path you typed in, for instance, SYS:PUBLIC. If the current drive is a MAP ROOT drive, the MAP ROOT (also known as a fake root) will be removed.

- Get first matching file
- Get next matching file, until all files are retrieved
- Change current directory

This uses the original path without the volume name. However, since the current volume has already been changed, the net result is to remap the current drive to the specified volume/path.

Note that this anomaly does not occur if the current drive is a different server from the one being accessed. But this irregularity does occur even if the current drive is a local drive, through remapping it to the network! You can use the MAP DEL command to remap a local drive back to its local device.

In short, doing a DIR command with a volume label in the path is illegal in DOS. This is a NetWare extension to DOS' capabilities. This problem would be solved if Novell made it illegal in NetWare to do a change directory using a path that includes a volume, or if DOS evolved and started to use the handle based find-first and find-next calls, which do not require the current directory to be changed. In the meantime, you can get around this problem by not using volume labels on fake rooted (or non-fake rooted) drives.

Novell's MENU

Because menuing systems help to define the "look and feel" of the LAN, each one tends to have unique features and shortcomings. Novell's own MENU utility, included with all versions of NetWare 2.x, is a good example of the mix of positive and negative attributes found in a menuing system. On the positive side, MENU comes "in the box" with NetWare and uses the same visual interface as many other NetWare utilities developed using the C-Worthy programming library by Solution Systems.

On the negative side, MENU requires nearly all rights in any directory to which it is assigned. In addition, the larger the menu script file, the slower that MENU will run. Since the script file is held open while the menuing system is active, it is not possible to update the menu script while it is in use.

Fortunately, there are a variety of menuing systems available, both commercially and in the public domain. When looking at alternatives for a menuing system, consider selecting a menuing system that is at least network-aware, if not NetWare-aware.

Beginning with the release of NetWare 4.0, Saber Software's SaberMenu will be included as THE NetWare Menu system. This does away with the C-Worthy based NetWare MENU utility that has been "in the box" since NetWare 2.0's release in April 1986.

Network-Aware Applications

As LANs grow in popularity, more and more applications are being developed with the LAN in mind. Some even go so far as to recognize specific LAN types, e.g., NetWare. Installation of these types of applications is generally straightforward and predictable. The vendors of these applications have put a substantial amount of time into adding LAN support to their products by testing them and providing LAN-specific installation guidelines. As a result, there is little to offer in the way of additional installation tips for these network-aware applications.

However, care needs to be taken in defining where user data and any program configuration files will be stored when installing non-network-aware applications. By doing so, the most apparent problem with a non-network application—the lack of built-in mechanisms for handling any sort of file contention—can be avoided. The classic example is Lotus 1-2-3. If two users on a LAN have separate copies of the same spreadsheet on their PCs and they both save both copies to the same directory and filename on the same file server, the last user to save the file is the one whose file will remain. The user who saved the file first will have his or her copy of the spreadsheet overwritten by the second user's copy. This problem is caused by the way that 1-2-3 opens and closes files. When 1-2-3 reads or saves a worksheet, the worksheet file is only held open for the duration of the read or write. Other applications hold files open that have been read into memory.

Older versions of the word processor WordStar, on the other hand, behave completely differently. If a user running WordStar opens a document, that file is held open while the user works on it. However, WordStar never closes the file properly, even after it is saved and another document is opened by the same user. Therefore files opened by WordStar are not closed, thereby denying access by other users until the original user who opened those files exits WordStar.

These kinds of problems are most prevalent for spreadsheet and word processing applications. About the only way to handle this problem is by giving each user a unique data directory.

Some non-network-aware applications also have configuration files. These files are often tailored to the hardware defined at a particular workstation, which requires multiple configuration files. In order to associate the correct configuration file with the correct workstation, a workstation-specific directory should be created and then mapped during the login process. For example, the following commands could be used to map a workstation-specific search drive to the subdirectory where the hardware-dependent configuration files are stored:

```
IF P_STATION = "0000000000A2" THEN MAP S3:=SYS:CONFIGS\A2
LAST DRIVE = F (unless using the NetWare 4.0 DOS Requester where
  LASTDRIVE=Z is required for proper operation).
```

The directory SYS:CONFIGS\A2 is where the configuration files for workstation A2 are stored. The number inside quotes is the physical node address of the specific workstation in hexadecimal. To determine this address, the NetWare command USERLIST/A is run at that workstation as shown in Figure 2-19.

```
F:\> userlist/a

User Information for Server NS1
Connection    User Name    Network        Node Address     Login Time
------------ ----------   ------------ ------------    -------------


    1          JOHN       [ BOOBABE]  [           1A] 7-03-1990  8:24 am
    5          JACK       [      BAD]  [           A2] 7-11-1990  2:18 pm
    6     *SUPERVISOR     [      BAD]  [           29] 7-10-1990 10:21 am
    7      SUPERVISOR     [      BAD]  [           F4] 7-11-1990  2:55 am
    8          GUEST      [      ACE]  [           55] 7-12-1990  3:49 pm
```

Figure 2-19. Using USERLIST/A to determine physical node addresses

The asterisk next to the user name indicates the connection for the workstation running the USERLIST/A command. For connection 4, the node address is "A2."

The P_STATION variable shown in the example requires a 12-digit hexadecimal number. Therefore, the number "0000000000A2" goes between quotes.

Some non-network-aware applications will not work properly if they are run from a drive that is not within the range of allowable local drives. To remedy this problem, use a combination of DOS and NetWare trickery. First, set the LASTDRIVE command used in CONFIG.SYS to LASTDRIVE=F. This setting makes drives A through F the legal local drive letters and allows the DOS SUBST utility to function with these drive letters. Then, install a non-network-aware application—one that will not run on a network drive. Next, use the NetWare MAP command to remap one of the legal local drive letters to the network directory in which the application is installed. The application should now run, as it thinks it is installed on a valid DOS drive. This approach will allow many non-network-aware applications to operate on the LAN.

Protecting LAN Applications

There are many ways to protect LAN applications. The first option in the NetWare environment is to use the EXECUTE-ONLY flag. This flag, which can be set by the FILER utility, can only be attached to .COM and .EXE files. Once a file is flagged EXECUTE-ONLY it can only be run, and cannot be copied. Nor can protected applications be modified by such things as a computer virus.

Some applications, such as WordPerfect, cannot have their main executable file protected with the EXECUTE-ONLY flag because they either need to write back to the executable file, or need read access to that file. Once a file is flagged EXECUTE-ONLY, that attribute can never be removed. To update the file, it must first be deleted. Be sure to make backup copies of applications before flagging them EXECUTE-ONLY. Applications with built-in virus/integrity checking will fail if flagged EXECUTE ONLY. Remember, once a file is flagged EXECUTE-ONLY it can never be directly opened. Therefore, backups are not possible. (The only backup type—and it is not widely used—that can "backup" files flagged EXECUTE-ONLY is the core-image backup. This type backs up a disk in its entirety, which, in this case, is while the disk is dismounted or when the server is down.)

The EXECUTE-ONLY attribute must NOT be used with any Windows applications because EXECUTE-ONLY allows only "DOS type execution attempts" to utilize the flagged file. Windows applications are NOT DOS applications. And it is important to note that Windows does not actually *execute* applications written for it. Rather, Windows *opens* the application's files and reads them into memory, then acts on their instructions.

A second option for protecting applications is "write protection." This is achieved by flagging the appropriate files as READ-ONLY and ensuring that Modify rights are not granted in the directory (or parent directory) in which the protected files are located. Without Modify rights, users cannot alter the READ-ONLY attribute. This guarantees that a non-supervisor will not be able to alter the application files.

When an application is used on a LAN, it is likely that it will be in use by more than one person at a time. And the number of copies of an application purchased should correspond with the maximum number of simultaneous users. Yet unless the application has built-in software metering, it is difficult to be reasonably sure that the application is not being used by more people than there are authorized copies of the application. (Of course, this licensing issue is avoided altogether in the case where copies are purchased for every workstation on the LAN.) In this respect, software metering products are a third option to consider to protect your investment in LAN applications. These products help to control the maximum number of concurrent users of an application. One such product, SiteLock, offered by Brightwork Development, was written by the author of this book and includes virus protection as well as software metering abilities.

Applications Printing

While LANs are increasingly useful for their electronic messaging and shared processing capabilities, one of the chief benefits is still shared printed output. Printing can be a complex issue for applications on a NetWare LAN. The following section describes some printing highlights.

Serial Port-only Applications

Some applications require all printing to be done via a serial port. This situation is most commonly found with computer aided design (CAD) programs that send data to serial plotters or serial laser printers. Since it is not possible to capture all types of serial port activity to a network printer without specially designed hardware, there would seem to be no choice but to connect an output device to the local workstation's serial port. However, if the application supports printing to a file, there are a couple of alternatives.

The first alternative is to use the CAPTURE command to redirect the PC's parallel port (LPT1:) to the network. (The SPOOL command is CAPTURE's equivalent for NetWare 2.0x and older.) From within the application, specify a "print to file" option and specify the device name LPT1, LPT1:, or PRN as the file name. One or all of these device names should allow the output to actually print to the LAN. This is possible because DOS and NetWare intercept these device names and send the data out through the designated channel.

If the application does not correctly send the data out when the names LPT1, LPT1:, or PRN are used, a second alternative is to save the data to a real file name and then use the NPRINT command to print the file on the LAN.

PRTSC on a Nondedicated File Server

On a nondedicated file server, the combination of the SHIFT and PRTSC keys that normally allows a screenful of data to be printed has been disabled. This one function is disabled because the BIOS routines responsible for the screen print are CPU intensive and slow. If this function were not disabled, workstations on the LAN might lose their connection to the file server while they are busy performing screen prints. Older versions of NetWare which did not disable SHIFT-PRTSC would usually hang the server when these keys were pressed together.

There are several public domain utilities that overcome this limitation. Several of these printer utilities also are available on the CompuServe NetWire forum. There are also several commercially available graphics and word processing packages that include print screen or screen capture utilities.

Mixing 2.0x and 2.1x/2.2x Versions of NetWare

While it is possible to interconnect file servers running NetWare 2.0x and 2.1x/2.2x, there are inherent problems with such a design, mainly due to network printing differences. Below, 2.1x also refers to 2.2x

The main difference between 2.0x's and 2.1x's print process is that they use different LAN printing utilities. In version 2.0x, the SPOOL and ENDSPOOL commands are used, whereas in 2.1x, CAPTURE and ENDCAP are used. Another key difference in printing between 2.0x and 2.1x is the way in which the LAN shell, the ANETx and NETx files, respectively, handle network printing. The biggest difference is that 2.0x's ANETx shell can only "spool" one parallel printer port at a time to a network printer. Version 2.1x's NETx shell can concurrently "capture" data for up to three parallel printer ports. In order for 2.1x to simultaneously capture printer ports, new network printing features were introduced in the CAPTURE command and in the shell.

There are several ways to handle network printing when interconnecting file servers using NetWare 2.0x and 2.1x, none of which are ideal. Two of the three principal approaches discussed here come from the "all-or-nothing" school of thought—either the same version of the network shell is used at all workstations, regardless of the file server NetWare version, or a different shell is used for each workstation, depending on the file server NetWare version.

The first approach is to use the version 2.0x ANETx series of shells at all workstations. This ensures that all workstations are able to "spool" to both 2.0x and 2.1x file servers and, consequently, achieve output through their connected printers. If this approach is taken, it is important to use the S parameter when defining print queues on 2.1x file servers. An example of the 2.1x console command would be "S 0 to PRINTQ_0." The S parameter indicates that a print queue will be compatible with 2.0x's network printing commands. The drawback to this approach is that the LAN will be unable to use 2.1x's rich set of printing features. Among the features not supported by the 2.0x shell are PRINTCON/PRINTDEF-defined printers and the ability to simultaneously "capture" from up to three parallel ports.

The second approach is to use the version 2.1x shells (IPX and NETx) at all workstations. This option offers the advantage of supporting 2.1x's richer network printing conventions. The disadvantage is that this option prevents all 2.0x file servers from being able to share their printers. Neither CAPTURE nor SPOOL, except in one special case discussed below, will work with the 2.1x shell with the destination file server running version 2.0x of NetWare. CAPTURE displays an error message indicating that it will not work, and SPOOL will appear to work, but a message indicating "Not ready error writing device [device name]" will appear when trying to print to the "spooled" printer port. The reported device names include PRN, LPT1, LPT2, and LPT3.

There is one exception that provides for printing to 2.0x file servers from workstations with the 2.1x shell. If the SPOOL command is used and a CREATE file

(SPOOL CR=) is specified, output can be sent to that file and can later be printed to a 2.0x or a 2.1x file server by using the NPRINT command. The version of NPRINT used must be based on the destination file server's version of NetWare.

A third approach involves setting up each workstation with the appropriate shell for a particular file server. This option can be more complicated than the other two approaches simply because all users are not using the same shell. Defining printing specifications for multiple users can become complicated. There is no easy way to build enough intelligence into LAN applications to determine which shell is loaded, or to prevent someone from trying to use a printer on a different file server version. Therefore, this approach is not recommended for printing on more than one file server.

In summary, network printing is the single biggest source of incompatibility between versions 2.0x and 2.1x of NetWare. In the rare case that some other network utility will not support one environment or the other, it usually indicates its limitations as soon as it is executed.

Upgrades

Sooner or later, every LAN Administrator is tempted to upgrade his or her network operating system. An upgrade, though, is something that should not be taken lightly. While an upgrade may relieve some of your current troubles, it can also lead to several new problems. You should never rush into an upgrade without carefully considering your present system configuration and the impact that an upgrade would have.

When evaluating an upgrade, you should ask yourself several important questions. For instance, why do you need to upgrade? Is there something wrong in the system now that an upgrade promises to remedy? Or are you considering an upgrade just to have the "latest and greatest" version of the operating system? This particular motive for performing an upgrade is certainly discouraged. You should never perform an upgrade just because you can. In other words, if it ain't broke, don't fix it.

However, consider that the upgrade may fix or improve features you'll need in the future. In other words, you may wish to fix it before it breaks.

Ask Around

If you do think that an upgrade would be beneficial for your system, you should ask around to see what others in situations similar to yours decided, and also to determine beforehand what potential conflicts, incompatibilities, or other problems you may encounter during the upgrade process.

One good source for input and feedback on your upgrade plans are local user groups. Perhaps the best source of feedback on matters like these, however, are the NetWire forums on CompuServe. Be prepared to answer other configuration-related questions that these experienced users on NetWire may ask in order to offer you advice and guidance. Message section 2 of the NOVC forum is designated for upgrade-related questions and discussions. For instance, you might find that VAP X does not work well with NetWare version Y, and if the two are used together you might lose data, or you might not be able to do something else. You might find out that you should only upgrade the server operating system and not any of the PUBLIC utilities since the new utilities may have some unresolved bugs. Or you might find that you need to load the LOGIN utility from the upgrade to all file servers on your network to ensure compatibility with the new version. For example, many administrators who have upgraded to NetWare 386 3.1 (from either NetWare 286 or NetWare 386 3.0) have found it necessary to load the version 3.1 LOGIN utility on all file servers. Or you could also discover that another upgrade version is on the way and you should wait for it instead of using the current upgrade.

Tips for Upgrades

Assuming that you will be upgrading a system that you are currently using, the first and foremost prerequisite to the upgrade is to have at least two full, coherent backups of your system. You should be prepared to restore your system to what it was before you attempted the upgrade. You could try a practice restore on a directory before trusting the upgrade process alone. Also remember about the console command reset router, which can help restore file server routing tables. The *reset router* command is available with NetWare 286 as well as NetWare 386.

Next, if you have more than one file server to upgrade, you should, at first, only upgrade one. Select the least used of the file servers for the first upgrade. This process will give you a taste for what the upgrade will entail and how much time it will take you to accomplish it. After that server has been upgraded, watch it for a couple of days. Note how it interacts with the rest of the network and what changes, if any, you needed to make to the other file servers or workstations to get the upgraded server to function as expected.

If your upgrade is between NetWare 286 and 386 (or NetWare 386 3.0 and 3.1x), be sure that you have the necessary drivers to allow your current network interface cards (NICs), disk controllers, and disk drives to work correctly. You may be surprised to find that some of these drivers are not available. So you might need to find a comparable card and driver combination that will work with NetWare 386. For instance, say you have an XYZ Ethernet NIC installed in your NetWare 286 file server, but there is no XYZ Ethernet driver for NetWare 386. So before you perform the upgrade, you need to install an ABC Ethernet NIC in place of the XYZ, since ABC has a driver for Netware 386 for its card. As it is an Ethernet card, it is likely compatible at the hardware level (i.e., cable connections) with the other NICs on the network.

You may be wondering why you don't need to change all the NICs on the LAN, if you have to change the file server NIC. The workstation NICs and drivers, though, are not much of a concern, however, since the workstation XYZ drivers from NetWare 286 will work fine with NetWare 386. This consistency is possible because NetWare 386 uses the same IPX/NETx setup as does NetWare 286. Tremendous differences, however, exist between the NetWare 286 and NetWare 386 file server operating systems, which bar the use of NetWare 286 file server drivers on NetWare 386 file servers.

When performing a major upgrade, such as between NetWare 286 and 386, you may also wonder whether or not to run COMPSURF, or another similar utility. The primary reason for running COMPSURF is if the disk drive needs a new low-level format. If the drive has been low-level formatted within the past year, it probably would not benefit from another one now. However, if it has been more than a year or if the drive has experienced read or write errors, you might consider a new low-level format. See Chapter 5 for some additional pointers regarding the low-level format of your file server disk drives.

A new low-level format might be particularly attractive when upgrading between NetWare 286 and 386 because the disk drive's structures (i.e., file allocation table (FAT), directory tables, etc.) will be significantly altered.

While on the subject, note that between NetWare 386 3.0 and 3.1 there is an irreversible alteration of the FAT and directory tables. This modification takes place the first time that NetWare 386 3.1 mounts a NetWare 386 3.0 volume. The change is silent, but is evidenced by two events.

The first is the fact that NetWare 386 3.0 will no longer be able to mount the volume. The second is that the volume will mount significantly faster than it did with NetWare 386 3.0, especially if the volume is sized over 100MB. Faster mounting is possible because of the changes that NetWare 386 3.1 makes to the volume directory structures. Note that your data, however, is unaffected.

For upgrades of NetWare 2.1x/2.2x to NetWare 3.x/4.x, Novell now offers an upgrade utility called the "in place" upgrade. Essentially this method of upgrade allows you to upgrade your file server "in place" without having to upgrade from one server to a new one or to completely destroy an existing server to upgrade it to the new NetWare version. Your purchase of NetWare will probably include this utility; if not, you can find it in Novell's NOVLIB forum on CompuServe.

As you can see, upgrading is a complicated process. And the process is not perfect, either. Before performing the upgrade, you must be certain that the upgrade is really needed. Ask around. See what others are experiencing. Remember that the NetWire forums on CompuServe are perfect for this interaction. Once you have decided to do the upgrade, be sure to have a couple of competent and coherent backups of your system. With some thoughtful planning, your upgrade (should you need it) will go a little smoother.

CHAPTER 3

File Servers

The average size of LANs continues to increase every year. The larger the LAN, the more important file server performance becomes. Although there are other areas to consider when isolating bottlenecks in the network, file server performance will always have a major impact on overall performance. Some of the other areas include workstation performance, network bandwidth, and disk channel bandwidth. Each of these is treated separately in the following chapters.

When purchasing a file server, there are several issues to consider, including manufacturer, speed (CPU), and compatibility.

Choosing a Manufacturer

The file server is one of the most critical parts of the entire network, and as such, should be chosen carefully. Saving a few thousand dollars on the initial investment could end up costing more later if the file server proves unreliable. Any machine purchased as a file server must be of high quality, and should be manufactured by a widely recognized and well-regarded company.

Choosing a CPU Type

Part of choosing a file server is the selection of an 80286-, 80386-, 80486-, or Pentium (sometimes referred to as 80586)-based machine. An 80286-based machine should NOT be considered in any case. Not only can it not run as a NetWare/386 server, it is unable to take advantage of many enhancements of the 80386 and newer processors. All current 80286-based variations of NetWare have been released in their final versions. A few maintenance releases are scheduled that will take care of bug fixes and a few moderate refinements, but the real innovations and enhancements are in NetWare/386.

This narrows the field to 80386 and newer processors. As NetWare/386 implies, it requires at least a 386-based machine. All 386 and newer machines are capable of running current and forthcoming releases of NetWare.

If you are using any version of NetWare/68, there is essentially no choice other than to use one of Novell's S-net file servers. Novell discontinued this server line in March of 1988, but Federal Technologies will handle service for any S-net servers still in use.

BIOS Selection

The BIOS of a microcomputer represents its brains and/or nervous system and, as such, its performance is critical. Under NetWare, older Phoenix BIOSs, older American Megatrends, Inc. BIOSs, and other "no-name" BIOSs can lead to problems with nondedicated file servers. Common failures include the inability to boot the server and a general failure of the server, indicated by random abend messages. Using a different BIOS can eliminate problems associated with running nondedicated file servers as well as some workstation problems. In PCs other than IBM-brand units, a BIOS from Award Software, Inc. usually solves file server problems caused by the BIOS.

Nondedicated Operation

When choosing a file server to run Nondedicated NetWare, it is extremely important to choose a machine that is proven to run it. Good sources for this type of information are Novell, user references, and public forums such as CompuServe's NetWire. The following explains why some machines have problems with Nondedicated NetWare.

The acronym "ND286" stands for Nondedicated NetWare/286 for any version of NetWare from 2.0a through 2.2. ND286 runs DOS applications in the 80286's real mode, while file server processes execute in protected mode. In order to use both real and protected modes, ND286 must switch the 80286 back and forth between the two modes. Switching from real to protected mode is accomplished by executing a special 80286 machine instruction. There is, however, no companion instruction to use when switching from protected to real mode. This missing instruction is one reason why the 80286 is often called a "brain damaged" chip. Performing the switch to real mode requires special hardware and utilization of the IBM ROM

BIOS to reset the 80286. The reset is done through (of all things) the keyboard controller. For many old clones, the ROM BIOS and keyboard controller must be updated to run ND286 (including the original Novell 286A servers). The technique used to accomplish the switch relies on true conformity with the IBM AT standard.

Resetting the hardware is messy and involves a special keyboard processor and some ROM BIOS functions. The keyboard processor is given a command to reset the 80286. A special "shutdown byte" enables the ROM BIOS to recognize at reset time that it is not performing a Power On Self Test (POST). This byte contains different values, depending upon which protected-to-real mode switch has occurred.

The ROM BIOS does not provide any support while the processor is in protected mode, so switching back to real mode is entirely up to the operating system software. Any implementation differences from the IBM AT can cause ND286 to malfunction. Specifically, in doing the reset, NetWare uses shutdown request type 0Ah, which should cause the ROM BIOS to do a JMP DWORD PTR 40h:67h. (For more background on the AT's ROM BIOS refer to IBM's *Technical Reference for the AT.*)

The ROM should not reset any hardware (in particular the interrupt controller) before doing the JMP. The ROM may enable interrupts during processing, but this is of no significance, as NetWare will have masked off all interrupts at the interrupt control chip prior to requesting the reset. NetWare restores the interrupt mask when it receives control back in real mode.

Another critical function in the protected-to-real mode switch involves the keyboard processor contained within the keyboard unit. It is used primarily to pass keyboard scan codes to the resident processor. The keyboard processor also makes the request to enable/disable address line 20 or to reset the 80286. The address line 20 logic controls whether or not the address line 20 bit coming from the 80286 is actually asserted onto the bus. Disabling address line 20 makes the 80286 wrap segments that exist beyond 1MB back into low memory (as in 808x emulation). This wrapping is necessary for the real-to-protected mode switch and takes 1 millisecond (ms) on the IBM AT. On some AT clones, however, it can take up to 50ms or more. This is because the keyboard processor microcode of these clones can only handle passing along the next character once it has a character; it cannot handle the auxiliary request to enable/disable address line 20. This problem manifests itself if the nondedicated file server hangs when a keyboard key becomes stuck.

So, there are two areas that prevent ND286 from operating on clone machines. First, and easier to correct, is the problem of a sluggish keyboard processor. To correct this, replace the existing keyboard with a true IBM keyboard. The second problem occurs when the BIOS in the machine is not entirely emulating an IBM AT BIOS. The culprit is usually an older Phoenix Technologies, Ltd. BIOS. Phoenix seems to have the problem with its AT BIOS and ND286 resolved, but only in the latest revisions of its BIOS. A proven performer is the BIOS available from Award Software Inc. When a machine fails to run ND286 and the keyboard change doesn't cure it, replacing the machine's BIOS with an Award BIOS (or a newer Phoenix BIOS) usually solves the problem. However, be aware that there are some machines that are such poor clones that they will never be able to utilize ND286.

There is yet another problem that may stem from the use of incomplete clones. The 80286 must be properly isolated from the main memory bus or a Direct Memory Access (DMA) being done to or from a network board may become corrupted during an 80286 reset sequence. The result will cause the file server to become unstable and it will usually crash or abend.

When operating a nondedicated file server there are some unusual caveats. The file server's CPU percentage may increase dramatically, perhaps by 80–100 percent whenever the file server is in "DOS" mode. This significant rise in CPU percent (which is likely to be under 30 percent whenever in "CONSOLE" mode) is due to the overhead associated with switching back and forth between real and protected mode. Some clones may push the CPU percentage figure even higher.

File server printing on nondedicated file servers, particularly in "DOS" mode, will appear to be slow and sometimes staggered due to the amount of processing required just to keep the server running. If faster printing speed is needed, a dedicated file server, a nondedicated server kept in "CONSOLE" mode, or a separate print server should be considered. The printing speed may be even slower if a utility or application running at the nondedicated server is loading the CPU with heavy amounts of processing.

33-MH CPUs

In NetWare/286, many timing routines were thrown off by 386/33 and faster CPUs. The CPU is capable of completing tasks before the timing routine expects it to finish, thus destroying the timer's integrity. For instance, file server machines that are 386/33-based can report CPU percentage figures above 100 percent.

This is not a problem but rather a case where hardware performs more efficiently than the software expects. The problem of CPU percentage utilizations greater than 100% has been corrected in NetWare 2.2. Since this problem was innate to the NetWare/286 product line there was never a similar problem in NetWare/386 versions. The ATDISK driver included with 2.15 and earlier versions can corrupt the disk if run on systems faster than 386-25Mhz. Novell has a newer ISADISK that can be used with older 2.15 servers.

Current Server Utilization

The Current Server Utilization statistic of FCONSOLE usually reflects how busy your file server is. If this figure is routinely above 80 percent, it is likely that your file server is overtaxed. Remember, though, that Netware/286 products may have the problem mentioned with inaccurate reporting of file server utilization.

Also, when using NetWare/386 and NetWare Loadable Modules (NLMs), you may observe Current Server Utilization figures that are less than the actual. This inaccuracy is due to the routine that calculates Current Server Utilization, as it does not count all CPU-consuming processes. For instance, if an NLM performs extensive work in loops that take a long time to execute, the file server CPU Utilization figure is not adjusted to reflect this consumption. For instance, when I executed an NLM specially designed to run lengthy loops, the Current Server Utilization statistic read 5 to 10%, but performance from the file server was off 100%, that is, it was twice as slow. This problem may not be limited to NLMs, but they were the only component that could easily be isolated to test for this anomaly.

An additional point regarding Current Server Utilization concerns file servers operating in nondedicated mode. When in "DOS" mode, idle nondedicated file servers should have Current Server Utilization figures under 60 percent, and when in "CONSOLE" mode, the figure should be less than 10 percent. If not, the machine you have chosen as your file server may not be totally appropriate for use with nondedicated NetWare. Be certain the file server you choose has been approved by Novell specifically for use as a nondedicated file server. Your dealer should be able to provide this information.

CPU and RAM Speed

In order to understand how CPU and RAM speed affect file server performance, it is important to first review what a file server is designed to do. The file server's main function is to process requests from the network. All requests processed exist in the form of data in the file server's RAM. Most high-performance machines have a bus dedicated to moving data between the CPU and main memory. One noteworthy exception is IBM's Micro Channel Architecture (formerly referred to by IBM as MCA, but as the result of legal action by the Music Corporation of America, IBM can no longer use this abbreviation). If the machine is based on the Micro Channel Architecture design, then a special bus is not necessarily required. The file server also services the option cards it contains, but the bus servicing these cards is usually running at a considerably slower speed than that of the CPU. Therefore, the main advantage of using a high-speed CPU coupled with a dedicated high-speed memory bus is that processing occurs more quickly.

Depending on the network's topology, the time it takes for a request packet from a workstation to reach the server and the time it takes for a reply packet to return to the workstation are more or less fixed. Improved overall performance is realized only when the time it takes for the file server to process the request is minimized.

The same is also true of the turnaround time between the CPU and internal devices, such as disk controllers. The time for the controller to retrieve the data from the disk and get it back to the CPU is essentially fixed and is not easily reduced beyond a certain point. Thus, given the same network hardware and the same disk controllers, overall performance can be increased by merely replacing an existing CPU and RAM with higher performance ones.

In addition to the speed of the CPU and RAM, the amount of RAM stored in the server is also critical. If there is not enough RAM, the file server will spend much of its time reading and writing from the disk drive(s), as there will be insufficient RAM for cache blocks to store data being transferred to and from the disk. (Fine-tuning RAM performance is discussed in more depth later in this chapter.)

RAM Types

The type of RAM in a PC falls into one of three general classifications: conventional, expanded, or extended. Conventional random-access memory is used by DOS, and is usually limited to 640K, DOS's inherent conventional memory limit.

The 640K limit is related to the 1MB limit of the 8088 or 8086 CPU used in first generation IBM PC computers. There are "DOS extenders" that offer ways to gain additional conventional memory for running large applications.

On an 80286 or higher type of PC, the 1MB of RAM is also known as real-mode memory. When operating in real mode, the 80286 CPU emulates the 8088 or 8086 CPU and is subject to many of the same limitations, such as the 640K limit for conventional memory.

The second type of RAM is expanded memory. Intel Corporation and Lotus Development Corporation initially joined forces to create the Expanded Memory Specification (EMS) version 3.0. Soon thereafter, Microsoft Corporation joined Intel and Lotus and EMS 3.2 was created. It is commonly referred to as the Lotus/Intel/Microsoft (LIM) standard. Later, an enhanced version of the LIM standard was released as LIM 4.0.

Expanded memory operates in a unique manner. It performs "paging" of memory—up to 8MB in the LIM 3.2 standard and 32MB in the LIM 4.0 standard. To accomplish this, EMS uses a 64K segment of RAM, such as D0000h, to hold the current page. An analogy could be drawn to the way you view the night sky through a telescope—you can only view a portion of the sky at a time. EMS memory paging works in a similar fashion in that, even though the PC may have several megabytes of RAM set up as expanded memory, it can only "see" 64K at a time.

EMS memory is controlled through the Expanded Memory Manager (EMM). Only applications that are "EMM-aware" can make direct use of EMS memory. There are also some utilities that allow TSR applications to be stored in EMS memory. EMS memory can be used with any 8086 or higher numbered Intel CPU, i.e., any IBM PC compatible. Note that EMS memory can only be used in 64K windows and does not work with applications requiring contiguous RAM, such as NetWare/286 or NetWare/386.

Extended memory works in a manner similar to conventional memory in that it is available as a continuous block of memory, in which paging does not occur. However, extended memory is memory above 1MB and is only supported on 80286 or higher numbered CPUs. (The conventional memory limit on the 808x CPU line is 640K; the 808x address space is limited to 1MB.) Extended memory is usable only in protected mode operation.

Both NetWare/286 and NetWare/386 utilize protected mode and extended memory. In fact, NetWare uses all of the extended memory it can find—for NetWare/286, up to the first 16MB (although Novell states that only 12MB will be efficiently used); for NetWare/386, up to 4GB. Because NetWare monopolizes extended memory, other applications that normally reside there, such as Windows/386 and DESQview/386, cannot exist in extended memory when NetWare/286 or NetWare/386 is operating. Thus, you should remove all memory managers from the CONFIG.SYS file on the file server. Otherwise, NetWare 3.x will not be able to load if a manager has control of the system memory.

In certain instances, NetWare/286 is unable to use all available memory. This seems to be because of the use of a Transaction Tracking System (TTS) when more than 8MB of extended memory are present. In any case involving NetWare 2.lx and higher, the FCONSOLE utility will reveal the amount of memory the file server recognizes and is using.

Expanded memory for DOS and extended memory for NetWare can be used at the same time by using a nondedicated file server. For instance, a spreadsheet that uses expanded memory can be run on a combination file server/workstation machine. This is possible because the definitions for expanded and extended memory do not conflict. However, it is important to note that the expanded memory must not be extended memory that has been remapped. Often, a separate expanded memory-only board is used.

RAM Requirements

Any machine that will act as a NetWare file server for NetWare versions /68 or /286 should have a minimum of 2MB of extended RAM. This base memory requirement increases to 2.5MB for NetWare/386 versions, with 4MB as a recommended minimum. Obviously, NetWare/86 versions (such as ELS II 2.12 operating in dedicated mode) do not need 2MB of RAM as they are limited to real-mode operations.

It is interesting to note that NetWare/286 versions will crash with General Protection Interrupt (GPI) abend messages or insufficient memory messages when running with insufficient amounts of RAM. For instance, 1MB of RAM is insufficient for NetWare/286 2.lx and a GPI error message often appears. This can leave the installer confused as GPIs usually reflect a physical hardware problem. All in all, as a rule of thumb you should have at least 4MB of extended RAM in a server before it is brought into service. However, with NetWare/386 (3.x, 4.x), the more extended RAM, the better.

Unlike its predecessor, NetWare/386 appropriates all the RAM in the system in a manner that benefits system performance. There is, of course, a point of diminishing returns. But it is important to note that there is not a point where you will incur slower performance because of "too much RAM."

With NetWare/386 the following mini-calculation will produce the minimum RAM your server should have:

- Add together the sizes, in megabytes, of all volumes on the server
- Multiply that number by .023
- Add 2(MB) for the server operating system
- Add x(MB) for any additional NLM products you will use (AppleTalk, 3rd party NLMs, etc.)

For instance, you have:

Volume SYS: with 120MB
Volume SYS1: with 300MB

and you are using the Btrieve NLM, which you guess takes 4MB for your environment.

This would result in:

```
  420 (total volume size)
 x.023
 -----
  = 9.66, round up to 10
```

Next, add everything:

```
 + 10  (from calculation above)
 +  2  (operating system)
 +  4  (Btrieve NLM)
 -----
   16
```

That means you should have, minimally, 16MB of RAM in your server.

If you will have more than 16MB in your server, you will need to implement the AUTO REGISTER MEMORY ABOVE 16 MEGABYTES "SET" command or, if it does not work, the REGISTER MEMORY server console command.

For instance, place the following in your STARTUP.NCF file:

```
SET AUTO REGISTER MEMORY ABOVE 16 MEGABYTES = ON
```

The default for the parameter is already ON and only applies to EISA bus computers anyway. You would want to turn it OFF for an EISA machine if it has 24 bit DMA addressing controllers installed. These will cause a conflict with any memory installed above 16MB. It will have no effect on ISA or Micro Channel machines.

If, once you have booted your server, MONITOR.NLM does not report memory above 16MB, you will need to hard register your server using the command:

```
REGISTER MEMORY <start address(hex)> <length(hex)>
```

To "hard" register 32MB (with the 1st 16MB being recognized by the system):

```
REGISTER MEMORY 1000000 1000000
```

Note that 1000000 in hex is 16MB; also remember that a megabyte is 2 to the 20th power or 1,048,576.

Caching Requirements

Disk caching is one of the principle factors contributing to NetWare's high level of performance. When data is read from or written to a disk in the server, it passes through a section of server RAM set aside as the disk cache. Read access is improved because the cache may contain the requested information left there by a previous read or write request. A workstation performing a write benefits because it does not have to wait for the physical write operation to occur before continuing its own processing.

Cache memory is best described as a high-speed buffer that resides between the CPU and the disk subsystem. NetWare uses disk caching (not to be confused with directory caching) to increase perceived performance of the disk channel. With NetWare 2.lx you can actually see how many cache buffers exist via FCONSOLE, and it is best not to have more than 800 cache buffers. Any more than 800 can cause the cache search time to extend beyond the actual disk access. Each cache buffer is 4K, so 800 buffers consume approximately 3.3MB of RAM.The 800 cache buffer limit is the suggested maximum for file servers running their CPUs at 20 Mhz or lower. For those servers using 25Mhz CPUs (386, not 486), up to 1000 cache buffers can be considered. And for those 33Mhz CPUs (386), up to 1100 cache buffers can be used with a minimum performance degradation due to too many cache buffers. For those using 25 or 33Mhz 486 CPUs, 1200-1400 cache buffers can be used.

Provided there is sufficient memory for all other parts of the operating system, only a small amount of cache memory is needed for the file server to operate. However, the amount of memory available for cache can make the difference between a sluggish network and one that performs efficiently.

NetWare/286 loads all required operating system programs into memory first; whatever memory is left will be used for cache memory. Under NetWare/386 the amount of RAM available for caching may fluctuate as utilities such as NetWare Loadable Modules (NLMs) and Name Spaces are loaded and unloaded, or as these utilities vary, the amount of memory they are using may also vary. Many NetWare/286 VAPs, such as the Macintosh VAPS, require one or more megabytes of memory, which can leave an insufficient amount of RAM for cache memory.

In NetWare/286, cache RAM is broken up into 4K segments called blocks. This segment size matches the minimum storage space used on a NetWare disk, known as a disk block. Every cache block allows for a piece of the disk to be held in RAM. This makes access to the data much faster than if the actual disk were accessed. With NetWare 2.lx and newer, the FCONSOLE utility can be used to monitor the current cache block performance. This is known as the cache block hit ratio or, as seen on the FCONSOLE screen, "Disk Requests Serviced From Cache." A 100 percent cache hit ratio is ideal but generally not possible. Cache hit ratios of 96 percent to 99 percent are usually attainable. If the ratio is less than 96 percent, check the number of cache blocks and try to add at least 100 cache blocks by adding more RAM to the file server.

NetWare /386, however, has no real file server RAM cache limitations. In both NetWare /286 and NetWare /386, hash tables are used to locate items in the cache.

NetWare /386's hash table, however, is much larger than NetWare /286's, which allows for faster cache access times regardless of the amount of cache RAM in use. Also, don't forget, when in doubt, it is okay to add more RAM to a NetWare/386 server. One staple is that the amount of Cache Buffers NOT fall below 60 percent as seen at the top of MONITOR.NLM's Resource Utilization screen.

NetWare and Its Hash Tables Hashing

The following section on hashing originally appeared in BSG's *NetWare Advisor Technical Newsletter,* November, 1990, and was written by Matt Hagen, a consultant with Novell's Systems Research Group in Provo, UT.

Hashing is an indexing technique that enables the NetWare operating system to rapidly find a file (or subdirectory) name in a NetWare volume. Hashing requires that each volume include the following four elements: a Directory Table, a Hashing Index Table, a Duplicate Hashing Index Table, and a Hashing Algorithm.

The Directory Table consists of a number of 4KB blocks. The number of blocks depends on the size of the volume. Each block is divided into 32 128-byte directory entries. Each directory entry accommodates the name of a file or subdirectory and other entry-related information like creation date, attributes, etc. Each directory entry is identified by a zero-based index number called the directory entry number.

The Hashing Index Table is composed of a number of 4-byte slots. The number of slots is dictated by the Hashing Algorithm, but the number is usually much less than the number of slots in the Directory Table and the Duplicate Hashing Index Table. Each slot in the Hashing Table Index accommodates a directory entry number, and each slot is identified by a zero-based index number called a hash index.

The Duplicate Hashing Index Table has one 4-byte slot for each directory entry in the Directory Table. Typically, most of the slots remain empty. When used (as explained later), a slot accommodates a directory number.

Finally, the Hashing Algorithm is code that converts a file or subdirectory name into a hash index.

To better understand the operation of hashing, pretend that you are the NetWare OS and that a client workstation has just asked you to create a file called RED on volume SYS. These are the four steps you would follow to do so (you may want to follow along with a pencil on the diagram in Figure 3.1):

1. Find an empty directory entry in the Directory Table. In this case, you find directory entry 2.
2. Copy the file name and the other file information into the directory entry.
3. Put the ASCII string "RED" into the Hashing Algorithm. Let's say that the Hasher produces the hash index 6.
4. Index into the Hashing Index Table to the zero-based sixth slot and put the directory entry number 2 in the slot.

Now pretend that another workstation client asks you to open the file red. These are the four steps that you would then follow:

1. Hash the string "RED" which produces the hashing index 6.
2. Index into the Hashing Index Table to the sixth slot and find the directory entry number 2.
3. Index into the Directory Table to the second slot and find a file name.
4. Compare the file name in the directory entry with the requested file name red. In this case, the names match and the search is over.

One problem, however, remains. What happens when two or more completely different file names hash to the same hashing index? Pretend again that you are the NetWare OS and a client workstation asks you to create a file called blue on volume sys. Here are the seven steps that you would then follow:

1. Find an empty directory entry in the Directory Table. In this case, you find directory entry 34.
2. Copy the file name and other file information into the directory entry.
3. Put the ASCII string "BLUE" into the Hashing Algorithm. Let's say the Hasher produces the hash index 6.
4. Index into the Hashing Index Table to the sixth slot. This time you find that the slot is already used.
5. Index into the Duplicate Hashing Table to the 34th slot.
6. Copy the directory entry number 2 from the sixth slot in the Hashing Index Table to the 34th slot in the Duplicate Hashing Index Table.
7. Write the directory entry number 34 in the sixth slot in the Hashing Index Table.

Now pretend that a client workstation asks you to open the file red again. Here are the seven steps you would follow:

1. Hash the string "RED" which produces the hashing index 6.
2. Index into the Hashing Index Table to the 6th slot and find the directory entry number 34.
3. Index into the Directory Table to the 34th slot and find the file name blue.
4. Compare the file name blue to the file name red. They don't match.
5. Access the corresponding 34th slot in the Duplicate Hashing Index Table and find the directory entry number 2.
6. Index into the Directory Table to the second slot and find the file name red.
7. Compare the file name red to the requested file named red. In this case, they match and the search is over.

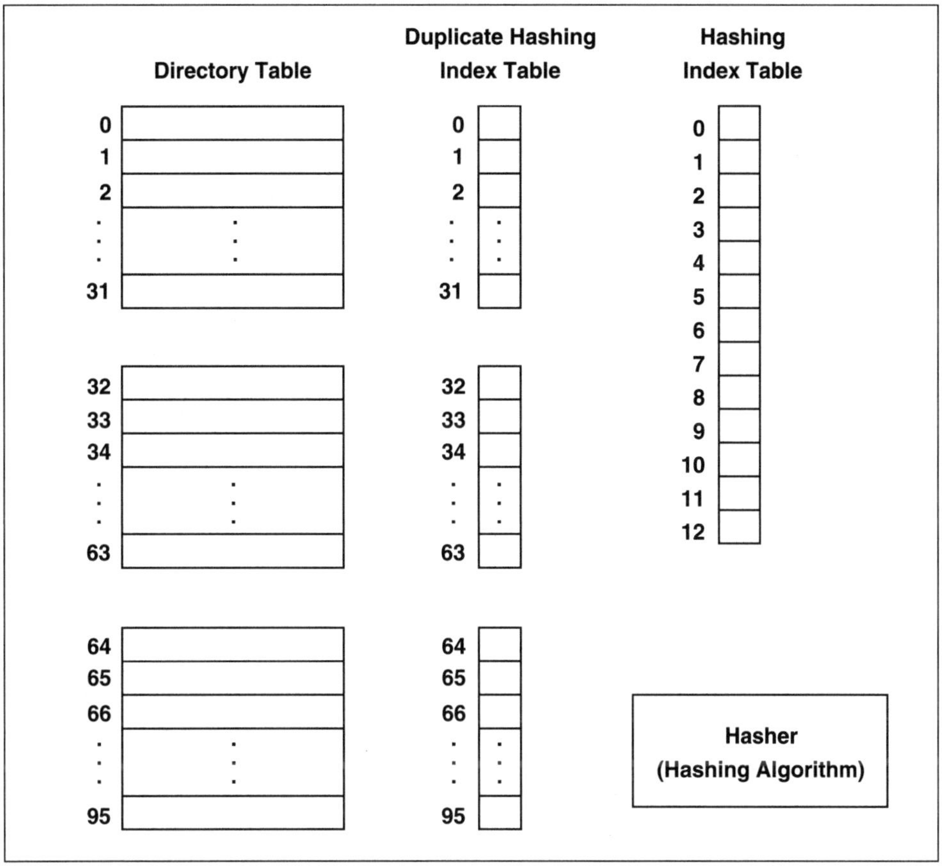

Figure 3-1. Directory Hashing Table

Caching Controllers

Another way to improve file server performance is to install caching disk controllers. Distributed Processing Technology (DPT) and CompuAdd Corporation are examples of two computer and peripherals distributors that are also sources for generic caching disk controllers. Another type is the dedicated caching controller, such as the one available from Racet Computers, Ltd. for use with its line of high-speed drives. This type of hardware-based caching mechanism can improve NetWare's already superior Last Recently Used (LRU)–based file caching. NetWare caches both read and write operations, whereas these caching controllers only fully cache read operations. Because the two caching schemes operate differently, it is possible for the cache on the disk controller to complement the one used by NetWare, thereby improving network performance.

Since it is not possible to disable NetWare/386's file caching, without reducing the amount of RAM, a caching controller is largely a waste of dedicated memory. The memory on the caching controller cannot be used for anything else and, unless its allocation strategy is significantly different from that of NetWare (LRU), it will have no apparent benefit unless your server is short on RAM in the first place. It is recommended that you install more RAM in your server rather than wasting your efforts with a caching controller.

Memory Allocation

Figures 3-2 and 3-3 show the memory usage in a file server running Advanced NetWare/286 and NetWare 2.15, respectively. This information can be used to gauge the base amount of memory needed to achieve a satisfactory level of performance for NetWare 2.x.

Following are descriptions of options 1 through 10 in Figures 3-2 and 3-3.

1. This is the actual size of the operating system program file. Displaying the directory entry for NET$OS.* in SYS:SYSTEM will reveal the file size.
2. The amount of memory for File Allocation Tables (FATs) is based on the total disk space of all of the disks connected to the server. For example, two 47MB Rodime 204Es would use 2 x 47 = 94K of RAM to store the FAT table information in the server RAM.

1) Operating System Program	400K (do an NDIR of NET$OS.*for actual size)
2) File Allocation Table(s)	1K per MB of disk storage space
3) Directory Table(s)–Hashing	4 bytes allocated per entry
4) Directory Table(s)–Caching	32 bytes allocated per entry
5) Dynamic Memory	70-90K
6) Routing Buffers	640 bytes allotted per buffer (average size)
7) VAPs	any size
8) TTS (optional)	22K
9) Indexed files (optional)	1K allocated per file index
10) File Caching	whatever is free after all of the above has been allocated

Figure 3-2. Memory usage in file server (Advanced NetWare/286)

The FAT is a road map to the physical location of a file on a disk. Each disk has its own FAT that describes the path to use when reading or writing a particular file. As the FAT is stored in RAM, whether or not the file is in use, this information is gained much more readily than it would be if it came from the disk itself. Since it is stored, used, and updated in RAM, the FAT is periodically written back to the disk to ensure that the FAT on the disk matches the current status of files on the disk. The operating system further ensures the FAT information by maintaining two copies of it on each disk. (NetWare/386 only stores the most recently used parts of the FAT in RAM because it is impractical to cache all of the FAT when the upper limit on disk capacity is 32 terabytes.)

3. The amount of directory hashing memory used is calculated by multiplying the total number of directory entries (including those defined at installation as well as those in use) x 4 bytes. For example: 5,120 directory entries x 4 bytes = 20,480 bytes or 20K. Directory hashing is the

process performed by the operating system to find a particular file. When the FAT is loaded into memory, each entry, used or not, is given a specific code. This hash code allows for quick access to the exact location of the FAT entry in memory. This is then used to locate the file on the disk. Directory hashing is most beneficial in using search paths, as when searching for a file to load. Older versions of NetWare allowed the installer to activate or deactivate directory hashing per volume to save RAM, often to accommodate large disks without upgrading RAM. But performance suffered significantly, so this option was eliminated. Now, all volume directories are hashed.

1) O/S size	410K	= 410K
2) 183 MB disk FAT table	183MB x 1K per MB	= 183K
3) 7,680 directory entries	7680 x 4 bytes	= 30K
4) 7,680 directory entries	7680 x 32 bytes	= 240K
5) Dynamic memory	92K	= 92K
6) 20 users, 2 buffers/user	20 users x 2 buffers (640 bytes/buffer)	= 26K
7) Btrieve VAP	500K	= 500K
8) TTS	22K	= 22K
9) Indexed files	10 x 1K	= 10K
10) Minimum amount of RAM in server before file caching	1513K	= 1513K

The amount of RAM in excess of the 1513K figure is used for file caching.

Figure 3-3. Memory usage in file server (NetWare 2.15)

4. Directory caching is calculated by multiplying the total number of directory entries (used or not) x 32 bytes. For example: 5,120 directory entries x 32 bytes = 163,840 bytes, or 160K. The actual directory entries are

stored in RAM. Directory caching, in combination with hashing, allows the quickest access to file information on network disks. Although this is an option at installation time, it should be considered a requirement if maximum performance is to be obtained. Also, when a file server boots up and indicates that it has insufficient memory to cache a volume, it is referring to directory caching, not file caching. Furthermore, directory caching is volume-specific, whereas file caching is not. Hence, the volume identification in the boot-time message:

```
not enough memory to cache volume 1.
```

When sufficient RAM is not available to provide directory caching and still leave enough room for file caching, directory caching may be selectively disabled by volume. If in a multivolume system, volume SYS: might be designated to store mostly programs and other non-user data files. Volume VOL1: could be reserved for user data. Depending on the nature of the applications, performance may be maintained with directory caching disabled on one volume type or the other. While it is preferable to add sufficient RAM to avoid having to make these choices, it is not always possible to accomplish this in a timely manner. A good system manager should understand these issues in order to meet the realistic challenges of keeping a LAN "on its feet."

5. Dynamic memory is split into three functional groups (four with NetWare 2.2). The first group, Dynamic Memory Pool 1, is used to store drive mappings and temporary file service request buffers. The amount of RAM used by Pool 1 is not user-definable. The second group, Pool 2, is used to store data regarding open files, file locks, record locks, and semaphores. The amount of RAM used by Pool 2 is configured by adjusting the maximum number of simultaneous file handles. The third group, Dynamic Memory Pool 3, is used to track server and routing information. Its size is fixed. The fourth Dynamic Memory Pool, DMP4, is used for mapping directories. The size of DMP4 cannot be configured.

The first printer assigned to service a queue uses 56 bytes from Dynamic Memory Pool 1. Each additional printer assigned to a queue (already serviced by at least one printer) uses another 8 bytes. Every network drive mapped uses 16 bytes from Dynamic Memory Pool 1. Most VAPs (Btrieve, for instance) use file handles via actual mapped drives or printer queues. Semaphores use different amounts of memory from Dynamic Memory Pool 2, usually in chunks of 100 to 150 bytes each. Finally, each open file handle on the network consumes 62 bytes from Dynamic Memory Pool 2.

6. Routing buffers (also known as communications buffers in version 2.0x) are temporary buffers used to transmit packets of information between devices on the network. Typically, the packets are transmitted between the stations and the server, but they could also be sent between the network printers, other servers, and station to station. Each line used to connect servers requires at least 10 buffers, but it is recommended to increase this number by the total number of stations on each server. For example, suppose Server 1 has 12 stations and Server 2 has 22 stations. The routing buffers would be 12 + 22 +10 = 44 buffers. For each network printer add 2 buffers. If any products use the IPX/SPX protocol or NetBIOS protocol, then add 10 buffers per station used by these products. The server generally requires a base minimum of 10 buffers; all other calculated figures are added to the base 10 buffers.
7. Value Added Processes (VAPs) consume memory after everything but file cache memory has been loaded. VAPs require various amounts of RAM. For instance, the Macintosh VAP can require in excess of 1MB, whereas the keyboard lock VAP requires far less than a 100K. With NetWare/386, NLMs take the place of VAPs in Novell nomenclature. Note that NLMs provide services not supported by VAPs but operate in the same manner as VAPs—that is, they require file server memory to work.
8. The Transaction Tracking System (TTS) requires about 22K of RAM. Approximately 5K is used for data and about 17K is for the TTS program code.

9. File indexing requires 1K per allocation, whether or not a file exists to be indexed. For instance, if a maximum of 10 files can be indexed, then 10K will be reserved. Discussion of file indexing is continued in the next section.
10. File caching uses the amount of memory left after the initial previous nine items are loaded. RAM dedicated to file caching is not directly definable by the user or installer. All the RAM consumed by user-definable parameters eats into the RAM that would otherwise be used for file caching. File caching is the act of loading data into the server's RAM as requested by workstations. These data items are loaded into an organized arrangement of 4K cache blocks. Subsequently, all reads and writes to the network disks will take place through these cache blocks. When data is spooled to network printers, the file cache is accessed, as spooling redirects the user print stream to a temporary file on the server. NetWare/386 differs in the way it uses file server memory. It dynamically assigns memory and fine-tunes memory usage where it can.

The table in Figure 3-4 defines memory usage in a NetWare/386 server.

```
BASE O/S 2MB
CACHING VOLUME SPACE IN MEGABYTES *0.023  (ex:1,000MB,  23MB)  23MB
ALL NLMs (DISK, LAN, NAME SPACES, ETC., just an example)  5MB
TOTAL SERVER MEMORY30MB
```

Figure 3-4. Memory usage in a NetWare/386 server

When a NetWare/386 server boots up, all recognized memory is first set up as cache buffers. From there the NetWare Loader loads the NetWare O/S (both the Loader and the OS are contained in the SERVER.EXE file). What happens next is up to the individual installation. If nothing is defined, prompts for the server's name and internal IPX number are required. From there, the loading of disk drivers, LAN drivers, name spaces, and other NLMs takes place. They all allocate memory from the Cache Buffer pool to one or more of the other memory pools (Permanent Memory, Short Term Memory(Alloc), Cache Movable Memory, and Cache Non-Movable Memory). See Appendix K's CONSOLE SET PARAMETERS for more information on tweaking internal NetWare parameters.

File Service Processes

When NetWare/286 2.1x is used, File Service Processes (FSPs) are extremely important to the system. Each FSP indicates the ability to handle a different, concurrent task. Therefore, having the use of as many FSPs as possible, up to a maximum of 10 for NetWare 2.x, is beneficial.

For example, suppose there is only one FSP. This means that the file server can only perform one task at a time. If someone does an NCOPY of a large file, while that one FSP is busy performing the NCOPY no other users on the network receive service. Even the workstation requesting the NCOPY could miss a "watch dog" pulse from the file server. This would result in an "Error reading or writing" message.

It is also possible for the block of memory used to allocate memory for FSPs to become so overwhelmed by other memory options that no FSPs exist. If there are no FSPs, the file server cannot be utilized.

Note that this problem is not prevalent on 2.0x networks, as they usually have sufficient FSPs. The higher the NetWare/286 version, the less likely you will have many FSPs.

Generally three FSPs are enough for LANs devoted to word processing. For LANs doing database operations, six should be enough. There are two methods of determining how many FSPs exist. The first method is to type CONFIG at the file server. The number of FSPs is indicated by the line:

```
Number of Service Processes: xx
```

For version 2.0x of NetWare, this is the only way to view the number of FSPs. For NetWare 2.1x and later, the Statistics/Summary screen of the FCONSOLE utility also displays this information. The line is labeled:

```
Number of File Service Processes: xx
```

If this number is 2 or less (the maximum is 10 for NetWare/286), your installation would potentially benefit from an increased number of FSPs.

FSPs are allocated from what remains of DGroup memory after a number of other items have been allocated. These items are listed in Figure 3-5 in order of most significant impact to least significant impact. Novell has produced a white paper available on NetWire on this subject.

1. Network Interface Card (NIC) driver packet size
2. Disk space mounted
3. Directory entries defined
4. LAN and disk driver global variables
5. NICs using DMA (Direct Memory Access)
6. Spooled printers (attached to server)
7. Transaction Tracking System (TTS)

Figure 3-5. Factors affecting DGroup memory

Since these items have the biggest impact on DGroup memory, it follows that they are the biggest detractors from your system's ability to allocate FSPs from the DGroup memory pool. Some options for decreasing these items' usage of DGroup memory are fairly clear, such as decreasing your largest defined NIC driver packet size, using non-DMA NICs, and where feasible, disabling TTS.

There are several ways to counter the problem of a FSP deficiency. The most obvious is to use a version of NetWare other than 2.15. As stated above, version 2.15 is the most difficult version with which to acquire a sufficient number of FSPs. Another possible remedy is the removal of all printers (not printer queues) from the file server. These printers can be connected to the workstations. Sharing workstation printers is facilitated by third-party applications and by an add-on product sold by Novell. More details concerning these add-ons are covered in Chapter 10.

NetWare/386 does not suffer from any of these FSP and Dynamic Memory problems. Since up to 16MB of Dynamic Memory can be configured. This roughly equates to 256 times more memory available for FSPs than in NetWare/286. With NetWare/386 you are more likely to overburden the file server than run out of FSPs.

Another problem stemming from the implementation of Dynamic Memory Pool 1 is the holding of workstation drive mappings. Since they are held in Dynamic

Memory Pool 1, which is a preallocated region of memory, this problem cannot readily be solved. However, NetWare 2.2 moves the drive mappings from DMP1 to DMP4, therefore increasing the amount of memory available for FSPs.

If you cannot upgrade to NetWare 2.2, there is a patch program on the Standard Microsystems Corporation forum on CompuServe (GO SMC) that decreases memory available for drive mappings from Dynamic Memory Pool 1. This patch allows more FSPs to exist, but not without the loss of memory from Pool 1. Problems can arise from the use of this patch. Make sure there are at least 6K below the maximum size of Pool 1 before implementing the patch. Otherwise, the result will be fewer drive mappings than were available before the patch. This is because drive mappings are stored in the allocatable portion of Pool 1. In any case, the patch is available and may prove beneficial, especially if you are currently down to only one FSP.

Because of the 80286 processor design (with memory segments of 64K) and the compiler used for NetWare/286, one 64K block of RAM keeps track of many operating parameters. This 64K segment of RAM is what's called DGroup memory. Many items, some optional, share this particular DGroup memory. One block of this DGroup memory contains two important components: Dynamic Memory Pool 1 and FSPs. Contained within this one segment of memory are:

Dynamic Memory Pool 1 (DMP1). Initially, 16K of RAM is allocated for this memory pool. With versions previous to Netware 2.2, workstation drive mappings and print queues will be appropriated from DMP1. DMP1 houses both search and direct drive mappings. With NetWare 2.2, these drive mappings are in DMP4. The rest of the information in this section refers to versions previous to NetWare 2.2. Each directory mapped (whether regular or search) uses 16 bytes of RAM. Each new print queue attached to a printer uses 56 bytes. Each subsequent queue attached to the same printer uses another 8 bytes. DMP1 also houses open semaphores, open Macintosh files, connections in use, mounted volumes, stacks for VAPs, temporary file service requests, open queue capture jobs, queue servers, and Queue Management System queues.

Because DMP1 is of a fixed size in NetWare 286, it can sometimes become completely filled. The most common "hog" of DMP1 is all of the mapped drive information that must be stored there. When DMP1 is filled, additional drive mappings may not be stored there; thus, additional users cannot be supported on that file server. This usually happens when the number of users approaches within 15 to 30 active users of NetWare's proclaimed 100-user limit.

So what can you do to avoid this DMP1 crunch? Limit the number of mapped drives users have by altering your network so that fewer search paths and fewer "direct" path mappings are needed. For example, do not map drives to each application. Rather, it is generally a good practice to map one drive directly to your applications directory and one to your data directory. Then, map search drives to your public and DOS directories.

NIC Drivers. Each Network Interface Card (NIC) driver has a specified maximum buffer size, and for each NIC in the server, one of these buffers is stored here. The buffer size used is that of the largest NIC buffer defined in the system. For instance, if a server has an IBM PC Network card with a buffer size of 2,048 bytes and an IBM Token-Ring card with a buffer size of 1,024 bytes, then two buffers of 2,048 bytes will be allocated from this DGroup memory. A list of known buffer sizes for various NICs is found in appendix A.

Disk Drivers and/or VADDs. Just as with the NIC drivers, a representative buffer is allocated from DGroup for each drive controller in the system. Note that 2.12 has a reduced amount of RAM allocated for these disk processes. Because of this change, Stack Overflow errors are more likely to occur. If you receive a Stack Overflow error with NetWare 2.12 and you are using VADDs or some of the other types of disk controllers, try reducing the number of disk drives and/or VADDS. Chapter 12 contains a patch that increases the disk stack space allocation.

Common Disk Area Memory Table. This memory contains pointers to the segments where the FAT is found. There is a pointer attached to the system for each disk, and a volume map of up to 3K is stored per disk. The larger the disk, the larger the FAT can be, which will require more RAM from this DGroup.

VAPs. For each VAP loaded, a stack size of 128 bytes is used.

Other. Other internal operating system options (like TTS) require various amounts of DGroup memory.

Once all of the above memory requirements have been allocated from the DGroup memory, the remaining memory is divided into FSPs. A maximum of 10 FSPs are possible, each requiring the amount of RAM that is consumed by the largest NIC buffer.

The basic problem with Dynamic Memory Pool 1 is that it resides in DGroup memory, so it interacts with the number of service processes available. Unfortunately, it is not easy to move items out of DGroup memory. There are too many assumptions made in the operating system program (NET$OS) about access to certain types of data from multiple modules. This problem is most likely a result of adding support for the Macintosh. This caused DGroup usage to increase. Novell is planning further maintenance upgrades to the 2.15 product line that may include a reallocation of DGroup memory as it relates to Dynamic Memory Pool 1 and FSPs.

NetWare/286 2.1x File Server Internal Operations

When a file server boots NetWare/286 2.1x, many processes begin operating in order to handle internal file server operations as well as service users and handle other processes.

The first of these processes is initialization of the file server's operating system. It allocates as much memory as the environment has to offer. If insufficient memory exists, NetWare attempts to report an error that explicitly defines the situation. However, when memory is severely limited, a General Protection Interrupt (GPI) error may result instead.

NetWare defines its various internal processes after available memory has been allocated. Two of these processes are Initiating LAN Drivers and Initiating Disk Drivers. Since NetWare/286 is a multitasking operating system, it uses a scheduler process to control which processes receive CPU execution time. While no processes are being scheduled, the scheduler process waits in an idle loop.

One of the first processes NetWare starts after booting is its Server Advertising Protocol (SAP). Through the SAP, the newly booted file server broadcasts its existence to each LAN adapter that it has initiated. This broadcast occurs once a minute.

The next process is the Asynchronous Event Scheduler (AES). It is a background timer process that is part of the IPX driver routines internal to the operating system kernel. The AES is used to coordinate processes that are scheduled to operate in real time, i.e., processes that need to run at certain intervals that are independent of the file server's speed. The AES is similar to a process found in the IPX/SPX interface loaded at each workstation. It is the AES routine that activates the SAP processes every minute to make sure the file server constantly "advertises" its existence.

Next, a set of fundamental processes are started to handle file server disk activity. Among these is a process used to mediate access to the file server's disk drives. This routine is in charge of reading and writing disk data. This read/write routine has all Write operations verified by a subsequent Read operation. And upon the failure of the read-after-write verification, another tightly coupled disk routine is called that governs HOTFIX's operations.

As described earlier, HOTFIX provides resolution for disk write errors, and, when combined with the disk mirroring process, HOTFIX also corrects disk read errors (detailed further in Chapter 5). When in operation, the disk mirroring process continually works to ensure that all mirrored disks attached to the file server are synchronized.

Finally, one of the more involved routines that is inextricably tied to Reading and Writing is elevator seeking. As described later in this chapter, elevator seeking is a NetWare mechanism that provides higher performance when accessing its disk drives.

Another process that is always engaged is one in charge of updating the physical disk drives' FAT and Directory Tables. As described earlier, NetWare provides for directory hashing and caching. Hashing and caching use file server RAM as the basis of operations. Operating out of RAM, hashing and caching are two mechanisms NetWare employs to gain performance. However, since RAM is temporary at best, the data on the disk that the RAM is reflecting (specifically FAT and Directory Tables) must be updated as often as there are changes to these tables. As described in Chapter 5, not one but both sets of FAT and Directory Tables of each disk are kept in concurrence with those in RAM.

NetWare's file caching process operates at a slightly higher logical level. All reads and writes pass through the caching process. The results of Read operations are stored only in a 4K cache block. At some point they are flushed or overwritten. While the result of a Read operation is still current and is stored in the cache, it is available to fulfill ensuing Read requests.

Unlike Read requests, Write operations are intended to eventually make their way to an actual disk drive. Whenever NetWare receives a Write request, it is first stored in the file cache. This step enhances performance because the connection requesting the Write is immediately satisfied. The data is written to RAM and then acknowledged, instead of waiting for the Write operation to actually be completed on the disk drive.

Once a Write request is in RAM, a background cache monitor process ages the Write request and initiates the disk write after three seconds. This delay serves to prevent accessing the disk more often than is necessary, since it is possible for the disk block to be updated several times (remember the cache block is 4K in size) in less than the three second delay. While this cache block is waiting in memory to be written, it is available for new Read requests. Thus, it is possible that a Read request for a particular disk block may arrive and be serviced directly from RAM without ever accessing the disk drive. A Least Recently Used (LRU) replacement algorithm is used to determine the cache block to use when a new one is needed for a Read or Write request.

Working up higher in the file system, there is a process in charge of maintaining the transaction tracking system (TTS) when TTS is implemented. Its sole duty is to guarantee transactions are captured and used to update the actual transaction-tracked file(s).

Handling the actual communication traffic between the file server and external entities are file service processes (FSPs). These processes act independently to perform incoming requests and return appropriate replies. Often the file server is busy with one of these FSPs when an abend condition occurs.

Introduced with NetWare 2.0, a "watchdog" process begins that monitors the viability of workstation connections. This periodically contacts each workstation to get its status. If, after 15 minutes, a workstation's status cannot be ascertained, the watchdog process terminates service to that workstation from the file server where the watchdog process exists.

If the file server has assigned network printers, one or more printer processes monitor the availability of print jobs. When a print job is found, one of these processes handles the submission of the print job to the designated printer. There is a related process that is used to activate these printer processes. Normally this process only "wakes up" printer processes every 15 seconds. Thus, the printer processes may not begin printing immediately upon receipt of a print job.

The NetWare kernel also maintains a process for UPS monitoring, if this feature is installed. This process takes care of predefined UPS monitoring statuses. Otherwise it exists in standby mode.

Always present are the processes that receive and act on keyboard input. For instance, when MONITOR is typed at the file server console, a process brings up the MONITOR screen and initiates another process. This process is in charge of updating the "CPU % Utilization" and "I/O Pending" fields found at the top of the MONITOR screen. The I/O Pending field indicates the number of file cache buffers that have been queued for action.

There are several other processes used at the file server, including an error logging process that updates the SYS:SYSTEM\SYS$LOG.ERR file when certain error conditions occur. Another is an accounting process that periodically updates user account charges. Another is a DOS process on nondedicated file servers to allow the coexistence of DOS and the NetWare operating system. Finally, there is a router table process that maintains a list of current servers (not necessarily file servers) using the SAP.

Setting Adapter Configurations

In order for a file server or workstation to function properly, its various internal hardware must be carefully configured. As a general rule of thumb, two or more different devices cannot share the same memory addresses, I/O ports, Interrupt Request Lines (IRQs), or Direct Memory Access (DMA) channels. In a simple configuration where there are few add-on hardware peripherals, it is easy to avoid conflicts because default settings normally work. However, in a fully loaded file server with several LPT and COM ports and multiple NICs, the configuration is slightly more complicated.

Fortunately, NetWare's NETGEN program (version 2.1x) automates much of the traditional guesswork for configuring a file server. In addition, the IBM PS/2's software-based Reference Disk hardware installation is very helpful in avoiding conflicts. Add-on hardware vendors are usually good about providing technical information on their products, but they typically do not include detailed information about the computers in which their products are installed.

The following scenario illustrates the process of determining the proper configuration of devices using NetWare's NETGEN installation program. While this particular example is for a workstation, the same process applies to the configuration of file servers.

The hypothetical PC in this case is a Compaq Deskpro 386 with 4MB of RAM. It has a Compaq monochrome video board, a standard COM1 serial port, and an LPT1 parallel port. Also in the computer is an IBM Token-Ring adapter that occupies a 64KB page frame address that begins at 0D0000h and (since it is 64KB in size) ends at 0DFFFFH.

The task at hand is to successfully install a NIC into this workstation. A check of the NIC documentation reveals that a minimum of three options are available, as outlined in Figure 3-6.

	IRQ	I/O port	Memory Address	DMA
1)	3	2E0h	0D0000h - 0D3FFFh	not used
2)	7	2E0h	0E0000h - 0E3FFFh	not used
3)	5	2E0h	0CC000h - 0CFFFFh	not used

Figure 3-6. Options for installing an ARCNET NIC

The information in the following figures is necessary to determine which of these options is the most appropriate. Figure 3-7 is a table of IRQs, I/O ports, DMA channels, and memory addresses that correspond to many industry-standard devices. Figure 3-8 is a sample memory map for an 80286- or 80386-based PC. Different models of computers may cause the memory map to vary slightly. The map is divided into major components with an emphasis on portions that are reserved for special use and those that are available for general use.

By using the information in Figures 3-7 and 3-8, the three options outlined in Figure 3-6 can be evaluated.

Device	Int	I/O DECODE (h)	MEM DECODE	DMA
Com1	4	3F8-3FF	-	-
Com2	3	2F8-2FF	-	-
LPT1	7	378-37F	-	-
LPT2 (LPT2 cannot be used with the XT controller due to IRQ5 conflict.)	5	278-27F	-	-
If LPT3 exists then				
LPT1	7	3BC-3BE	-	-
LPT2	5	378-37A	-	-
LPT3	-	278-27A	-	-
XT Disk Controller	5	320-32F	C8000-CBFFF	3
AT Disk Controller	14	1F0-1F8	-	-
Floppy Controller	6	3F0-3F7	-	-
Novell Disk Co-Processor	11 12 10 15	#1 340-347 #2 348-34F #3 320-327 #4 328-32F	- - - -	- - - -
Novell SCSI Adapter	2,3, or 5	340-343	D0000-D7FFF (enhanced only)	1,3, or none
Video Graphics Adapter (VGA)	2 or 9	3C0h-3DAh (color) 3C0h-3BAh (mono)	A000-BFFF C000-C7FFF (VGA ROM)	0
Enhanced Graphics Adapter (EGA)	2 or none	3C0-3CF	A0000-AFFFF B0000-BFFFF C0000-C3FFF (EGA ROM)	0
Monochrome Adapter	-	3B0-3BF	B0000-B3FFF	0
Color Graphics Adapter	-	3D0-3DF	B8000-BBFFF	0

Figure 3-7a. Common hardware devices and their configurations

Device	Int	I/O DECODE (h)	MEM DECODE	DMA
Hercules Monochrome/ Graphics	-	3B4-3BF	B0000-B7FFF	-
IBM SDLC	4 or 3	BiSync 1, 3A0-3AF BiSync 2, 380-38F	-	-
AST clock/ calendar	-	2C0-2C7	-	-
Corvus Omninet				
#0	-	248-24F	-	-
#1	-	258-25F	-	-
#2	-	240-247	-	-
#3	-	250-257	-	-
3COM 3C505 Etherlink Plus				
#0	2	300-307	-	5
#1	3	310-317	-	6
#2	4	320-327	-	7
#3	3	300-307	-	1
#4	4	310-317	-	3
IBM PC Cluster				
#0	3	790-793	D000:0000-7FFF	-
#1	7	B90-B93	-	-
#2	7	1390-1393	-	-
#3	7	2390-2393	-	-
IBM ASYNC Remote Dial In Line				
#0	4	3F8-3FF	-	-
#1	3	2F8-2FF	-	-
IBM Token Ring				
#0	2	A20-A23	CC00:0000-1FFF D800:0000-3FFF	-
#1	3	A24-A27	CE00:0000-1FFF D400:0000-3FFF	-
#2	6	A20-A23	A400:0000-1FFF A000:0000-3FFF	-
#3	7	A24-A27	C400:0000-1FFF C000:0000-3FFF	-

Figure 3-7b. Common hardware devices and their configurations (continued)

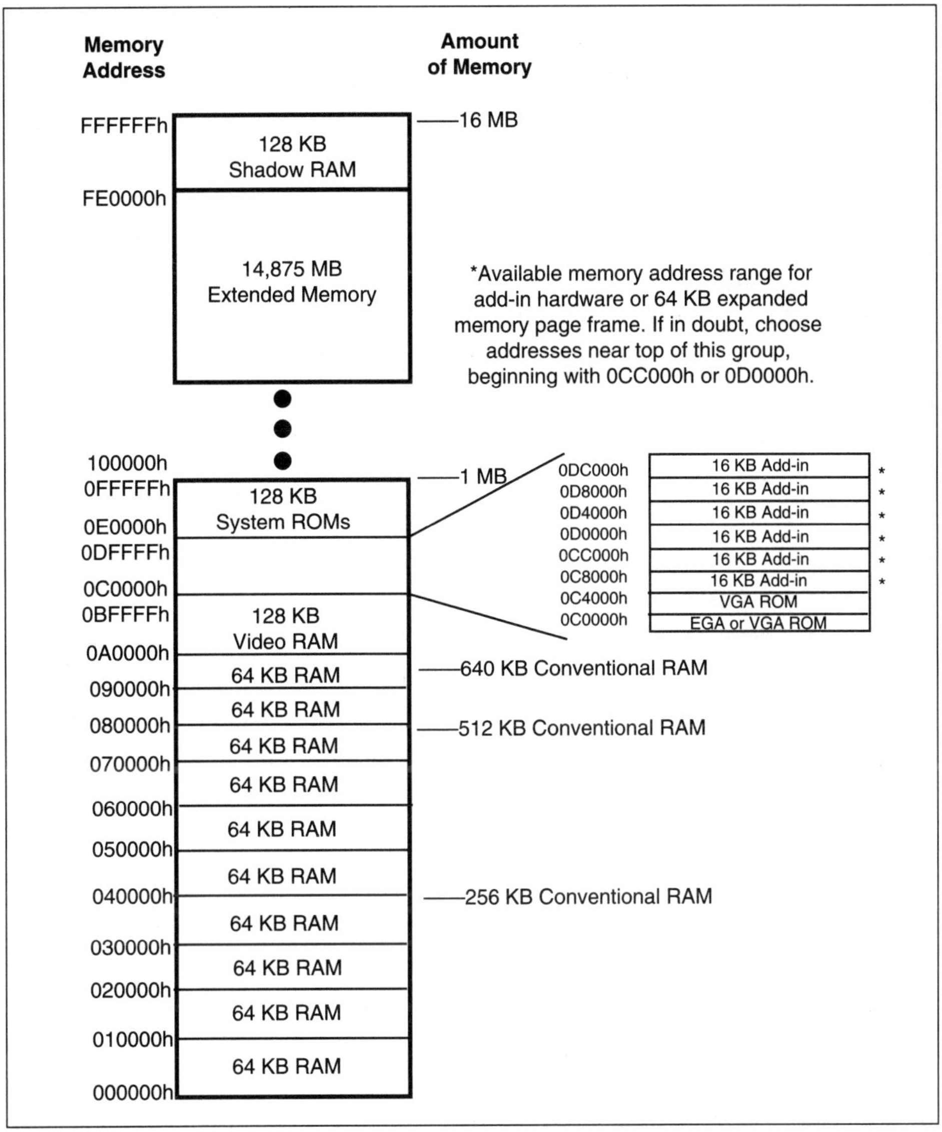

Figure 3-8. Sample memory map for an 80286 or 80386 computer

Option 1 will not work because the NIC's memory address range of 0D0000h - 0D3FFFh conflicts with the beginning of the IBM Token-Ring NIC's page frame memory address range, 0D0000h - 0DFFFFH.

Option 2 will not work because, as shown in Figure 3-7, the range 0E0000h - 0EFFFFH is reserved in most 80286- and 80386-based PCs for system ROMs and should not be used by other devices. This range is only available safely in PC and XT 8088-based computers.

Option 3 is the correct choice. Its IRQ, I/O port, and memory address range are open and unused by the other devices. Confirm this choice by reviewing Figures 3-7 and 3-8.

With NetWare/386 servers, all adapters are configured dynamically when the specific driver is loaded. Thus, there is no concern over setting an adapter in a "permanent" way such as with NetWare/286's NETGEN.

File Access Time and File Fragmentation

The performance of the file server hinges largely upon the amount of time needed to access files. As this time decreases, the efficiency and speed of the entire system increases. NetWare provides several mechanisms to aid in accessing files, including elevator-seeking, disk caching, File Allocation Table (FAT) indexing, and split seeks. Split seeks are discussed in Chapter 5.

Elevator-Seeking

A file is considered fragmented when it does not exist as a contiguous series of blocks on a disk. Accessing a fragmented file usually means much time is wasted waiting for the drive to position the disk's heads to the next portion of the file.

Improved disk performance can be realized when the drives spend less time positioning their heads. The result is better overall system performance. On a standalone PC, hard disk performance improves if the files are contiguously allocated, to minimize activity of the disk's heads when such files are processed. A disk that spends more time positioning its heads than accessing data is said to be *thrashing*.

NetWare minimizes thrashing by using an elevator-seeking mechanism that logically organizes disk requests as they arrive at the server for processing. Several requests received at about the same time are acted upon based on where the data is stored on the disk. As a result of elevator-seeking, the drive heads operate in a sweeping fashion, from one edge of the disk to the other, as opposed to thrashing about. This intervention by NetWare ensures high throughput from the disk, regardless of the amount of activity requested or the actual fragmentation of the files being accessed.

Disk Caching

In addition to elevator-seeking, NetWare also uses a disk caching mechanism. Caching stores the most recently read disk blocks (each cache block is 4K with NetWare/286 and may be 4K, 8K or 16K with NetWare/386) in the server's memory. Caching is also used to temporarily hold blocks that are to be written to disk.

If a requested block of data exists in cache memory, no physical disk activity will occur to retrieve the data. Handling write requests via the cache minimizes wait time for the user. Instead of waiting for the data to be written to the disk, the data is written to cache and the user can continue operations. Write requests stored in cache are written to disk as soon as possible or when the entire cache buffer is updated.

For example, if a file is being updated, NetWare stores the data in the cache. Once the data is in the cache, the application program continues processing because it "thinks" the data has been written to disk. If data in the cache is needed for a read operation before it is actually written to disk, it will be read from the cache.

NetWare performance is greatly improved through elevator-seeking and disk caching. The goal of elevator-seeking is to reduce the amount of time spent positioning a disk's heads, while caching eliminates unnecessary disk accesses. Together, elevator-seeking and caching diminish the effects of file fragmentation in the NetWare environment.

File Allocation Table (FAT) Indexing

Elevator-seeking and caching are built in to all versions of Advanced NetWare. Beginning with SFT NetWare 2.1, Novell added a new feature to further decrease file access time. This new feature, discussed briefly earlier in this chapter, is File Allocation Table (FAT) indexing. The FAT contains the pointers to those disk blocks that contain the data for all files. FAT entries are linked in a daisy-chain fashion to point to all of the blocks for a given file. It is the FAT that resolves the relationship between the logical and physical addresses needed to access files. FAT indexing decreases the time spent finding a specific FAT entry.

To get to a certain FAT entry, the system must start by scanning all of the entries, beginning with the first one. A file flagged for FAT indexing, which is much like a file flagged to be Shareable, has a dynamically constructed index table containing pointers to that file.

Using the index table, NetWare jumps directly to the needed FAT entry, rather than scanning all previous entries. This process is used on files that contain no more than 512 4KB blocks, or that total no more than 2MB in size.

When a file is larger than 2MB, only every other FAT entry (and sometimes every third, or more infrequently, depending on the file's size) is indexed. Even though the file's size is greater than 2MB and the number of FAT entries pointed to by each index entry is increased, performance is better than with sequential FAT access because sequential searches are reduced to a very small number.

SFT 2.1 allows up to 1,000 FAT index tables per server. Each table requires 1K of memory at the server. FAT indexing is best implemented on files that are accessed for specific segments, such as database files, rather than on files accessed for their entire content.

NetWare/386, unlike NetWare/286, automatically creates a FAT index, or in this case "Turbo FAT," for any file larger than 64 FAT entries that is randomly accessed. FAT entries have a one to one relationship with the disk block size; thus a FAT entry may indicate a 4K, 8K, 16K, 32K or 64K portion of a file. Therefore, 64 FAT entries may represent a file that is 256K in size (4K disk block size) up to 4MB (64K disk block size). Note that NetWare/386 does NOT create a Turbo FAT when files are sequentially accessed, only when they are randomly accessed and of minimal size.

Unlike NetWare/286, NetWare/386 has no preset limit on the possible number of Turbo FAT indexes. All it takes is a randomly accessed file (as opposed to sequentially accessed) of the minimum size as described in the previous paragraph. For each Turbo FAT, the server sets aside 8K in the Permanent Memory Pool for the Turbo Fat index table.

Finally, when a Turbo FAT-indexed file is closed, NetWare/386 does not immediately release the Turbo FAT it has built. Remember, under NetWare/286 Turbo FATs are static, so when a file is closed, they are never released. To prevent the server from rebuilding a Turbo FAT index every time the affected file is opened, the SET command:

```
SET TURBO FAT RE-USE WAIT TIME = xx
```

can be used. The default is 5 minutes and 29.6 seconds, and it can range up to one hour, 5 minutes, and 54.6 seconds.

File Defragmentation

If file fragmentation on a NetWare or other network-shared hard disk is still of concern, here are some proven ways to increase network performance:

For any type of network environment:

- Decrease the average access time of shared disks by installing faster hard disks.
- Increase the processing speed of network workstations.

NetWare-specific recommendations:

- Add memory in the file server for file caching, or, if you have more than 800 cache buffers, reduce memory in the file server (For Netware/286).
- Adjust the cache block size. (With NetWare/386 and NetWare 2.0a and below, cache block size can be changed; a 4K block size is optimal with NetWare/286 and below.)
- Increase the speed of the disk channel in the server (e.g., add a DCB or ESDI controller for NetWare/286 or /386, or use faster access disk drives).
- Increase the number of network cards in the file server and split up the network cabling to decrease communication congestion between file server and workstations.

Performance can be increased by as much as ten times by utilizing one or more of the above recommendations. If none of these options seems appropriate, there is a method to defragment any disk. By reformatting the disk and restoring the data file by file, files are written back in contiguous blocks rather than fragmenting. Below are step-by-step instructions.

1. For before-and-after comparison, time such activities as loading a program, spreadsheet, or other applications when no other users are logged on the system.
2. Back up the system completely, at least twice.
3. Reinitialize the disk volumes in question with:
   a. SYSGEN for NetWare/68 versions 2.0 through 2.0la
   b. INSTALL for NetWare/68 2.02x or NetWare/86 and NetWare/286 2.0x or NetWare/386 3.x
   c. NETGEN for NetWare 2.lx/2.2x
   d. ELSGEN for NetWare ELS II 2.lx

If working in a non-NetWare environment, reformat the disk.

1. Reinstall that disk into the system.
2. Restore the system from the backup previously made.
3. Perform the timed activities again, exactly as in step 1, for comparative evaluation.

As a point of reference, experience has shown that after these steps were performed on several NetWare hard disks, they produced no noticeable improvement in performance. The disks were all larger than 100MB and had been in service at least a year before the test.

The premise that fragmented files limit performance is based on a single-user system, or a shared system that practices single-user disk access techniques (such as FIFO). NetWare's elevator-seeking and disk caching features virtually eliminate the need for contiguous files. NetWare is designed to support concurrent disk access by many users. The file caching, elevator-seeking, and multitasking kernel together compensate for any potential loss of performance due to file fragmentation.

NetWare/386 Name Spaces

NetWare/386 includes native support for Macintosh, OS/2, FTAM, and NFS filenames. This is accomplished via Name Spaces. These name spaces are added per volume. To add a name space:

1. Load the name space (for example, LOAD MAC.NAM).
2. Type ADD NAME SPACE MACINTOSH TO VOLUME SYS (supply the correct name space name and appropriate volume name).

From that point forward, each time that volume is mounted, that name space (MAC.NAM) must be loaded. If it is not already loaded, the operating system will attempt to load it; if it is not loadable, then the volume will not fully mount.

Each Name Space entry has at least two directory entries—one for the DOS component, which all non-DOS Name Space entries absolutely map back to, and one for the Native Name Space entry. And, whenever a Name Space is accessed by a "native," both the Name Space and DOS directory entries are accessed. The DOS directory entry is always accessed as it is the only entry that contains information required to find the file on disk and subsequently in cache.

When Name Spaces are needed, there are two basic recommendations. First, consider appropriating separate volumes for Name Space support. This will increase performance because other "DOS-only" volumes will not have the additional disk "bookkeeping" of Name Space support. Also, if the need for volume repair should arise, different volumes for Name Space support will decrease the amount of potential file loss (and recovery time) when a Name Space must be removed to complete volume repair.

Second, whenever using Name Spaces, always try to add them prior to the volume's need for them, in other words, at volume creation time. If the Name Space(s) are added prior to volume usage, then each directory entry maintained (one is maintained for each Name Space, such as DOS or Macintosh) will likely be "together" in the same directory entry block. Thus, directory searches for native Name Space entries (that is, other than DOS) will occur as quickly as possible. Otherwise, if the Name Space is added after the volume has been used, there is almost no chance for the DOS directory entry and the native Name Space directory entry to be located in the same directory block. Thus not one, but two disk reads will be required to access the file natively.

Power Backup Systems

To guard against unscheduled file server down time, follow this simple rule: avoid turning off the file server. Computer components expand and contract with the application of heat or energy. When the file server is in operation, its components expand; when turned off, they contract. The typical file server receives much more activity than "normal" workstations, so its components endure more stress. The additional stress of heating and cooling due to turning the file server on and off often leads to critical hardware faults.

The power surge that occurs when the file server is first turned on adds even more stress. The effect of this initial surge is illustrated by the example of a light bulb which, when turned on, immediately burns out. So, if it is at all possible, always leave the file server on.

One exception to this recommendation, however, occurs when temperatures are likely to exceed 90°F and no one is using the server. When the server is in use, air temperature of no more than 80°F is preferred. The humidity level can also affect the file server. Lack of humidity breeds static electricity, which has the potential to destroy memory chips, keyboard controllers, or many other parts of the file server. A humidity level of 45 percent or higher is preferable to reduce the likelihood of damage due to static electricity.

UPSs and SPSs

There are two basic types of power backup systems to consider—the Uninterruptable Power System (UPS) and the Standby Power System (SPS). Whichever you choose, a good rule of thumb is to have a power backup system that will provide power to the file server for 15 minutes after a power loss. This is enough time for the file server's watchdog processes to automatically close files and connections. When a connection is closed, all resources owned by that connection are released, including such things as memory used for drive mappings. These watchdog processes work under the assumption that the workstations are no longer operating due to the lack of power and will have broken their connections. Other than providing cleaner power, using a full-featured UPS offers little advantage over using a less expensive SPS.

When power is lost, an SPS will supply power from its batteries, just as a UPS would. An SPS sits in-line between the wall socket (or power conditioner, if used) and the file server, along with any disk subsystems. The file server is not aware of the SPS's presence and does not monitor its actions. The SPS is not utilized until a power outage occurs, at which time the SPS supplies power from its batteries until they are exhausted, or until normal power is restored, whichever occurs first. When normal power is available, it flows from the wall socket, through the SPS, and then to the attached devices. This enables the SPS to recharge itself without having to be disconnected from the file server. An SPS does not necessarily provide any protection against surges and spikes coming from the power source, although some units may incorporate such protection. If an SPS without power conditioning is used, it should be plugged into a separate power conditioning device to isolate itself and the file server from surges (over-voltage), brown outs (under-voltage), and spikes (very rapid over- and/or under-voltages).

The UPS works on a slightly different principle. Power comes in to the UPS and is used to recharge the batteries. Power from the batteries is then used to supply any devices attached to the UPS, at all times. As a result, power is automatically conditioned at the file server and other connected devices. Because wall socket power is used solely to refresh the battery power, all chances of line surges and spikes reaching the file server and other attached devices are minimized. Of course, extreme conditions, such as lightning, can still penetrate even this level of protection.

It is very important not to connect any printers to either an SPS or a UPS. This is because all printers have motors that create spurious spikes and surges that can have negative effects on either type of power backup system, as well as on the other devices connected to it. In addition, some printers, particularly laser printers, have large power demands that can overwhelm some SPS or UPS units.

UPS Monitoring

All versions of NetWare since 2.0x are capable of UPS monitoring. UPS monitoring allows the file server to shut down during a loss of power in less than 15 minutes, the time required by the watchdog process. This means that all files and connections are closed before the file server is brought down, thereby protecting the integrity of files on the file server. This level of sophistication in backup power is most critical when individual workstations on a network do not necessarily lose power when the file server does.

If a network includes workstations at other sites, workstations on different power systems, or workstations with their own power backups, a UPS monitoring system will provide the necessary added protection. The main advantage of UPS monitoring is that of advance warning. If workstations are connected to a file server that is experiencing a power outage and it is running on UPS-supplied power, the users need to know if and when the file server is going to go down. This notification is automatically performed by the system when UPS monitoring is in effect. In addition, if a user is not present at a workstation when the notification is given, the system will automatically perform the disconnection from the file server.

Most UPSs will continue to supply power to the file server, even after it has taken itself down. This can result in draining of the UPS's batteries, which must be recharged before the UPS can be used again to protect the file server. Once power is restored, the UPS will continue to report a low battery condition to the server. It is then necessary to disconnect the UPS from the file server while the batteries recharge.

Contrary to statements made in Novell's literature, ELS II 2.12 can participate in UPS monitoring. However, given the nature of ELS II as a less expensive product and its lack of full NetWare functionality, implementation of UPS monitoring could be considered overkill. Information is available on NetWire or directly from Novell. Also, ELS II 2.15, which features UPS monitoring, does not down the file server—a problem that has been corrected with version 2.15c, which was a free upgrade.

Installation of UPS Monitoring

Installing UPS monitoring involves two basic steps. They are:

1. Installing a UPS monitoring board or equivalent in the file server.
2. Creating a CONFIG.UPS (pre-2.15, including 2.0a) or SERVER.CFG (2.15) file in the SYS:SYSTEM directory.

This procedure assumes that the UPS system is capable of providing signals to a Novell file server. These signals are: conventional power "on," low battery, and signal ground.

In order for a file server to use UPS monitoring, the appropriate settings must be made on the UPS monitor board and installed in the file server. You can use any one of the following items as the UPS monitor board:

- Stand-alone UPS monitor board (Novell or other)
- Novell Disk Coprocessor Board (DCB) (37-pin version)
- Novell SS Keycard
- Mouse port (IBM PS/2 only)

Normally, a keycard is not used, as all versions of NetWare 2.12 and higher do not use the keycard for serialization. However, if there is access to a keycard and a 37-pin version DCB is not already being used, the keycard will work fine. Specific board parameter settings are detailed in their respective manuals.

Once the board is installed, either a CONFIG.UPS or SERVER.CFG file must be created in SYS:SYSTEM. Depending on the version of NetWare, either a text file CONFIG.UPS or SERVER.CFG provides the operating system with the following information:

- The type of UPS monitoring hardware being used in the file server
- The UPS monitoring hardware's I/O address (if applicable)
- How long the UPS should run before the file server shuts itself down
- How long the commercial power can be off before workstations are notified that the UPS is supplying temporary power to the server. More information regarding the specific options are covered by the aforementioned installation manuals.

Cabling guidelines for Novell's UPS monitoring boards (37-pin DCB and SS Keycard) and PS/2 Mouse port must also be considered and are described below.

On the 3.5mm RCA jack used on DCB and keycard:

- TIP = UPS-ON-AC-Commercial-Power Signal
- RING = UPS-Low-Battery-Warning Signal
- SLEEVE = Common return for both signals, i.e. Ground

(For 2.1 NetWare, note that the I/O address in the 286 Installation Manual should read "346" not "340.")

Pinout for the PS/2 Model 50, 50Z, 55SX, 60, 70, or 80 Mouse port:

Pin # 1—On-AC Commercial Power Signal
2—Reserved/Not Used
3—Ground
4—Reserved/Not used
5—Low-Battery-Warning Signal (open)
6—Reserved/Not Used

Figure 3-9 shows the file server mouse port.

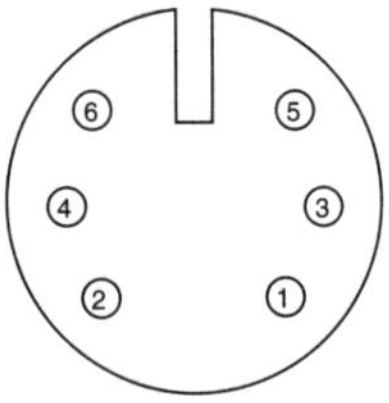

Figure 3-9. Mouse port connector

The NetWare/286 (2.1x) *Installation Manual* contains a more detailed description and explanation of UPS installation. If you have SFT Level II 2.0a, the *UPS Installation Supplement* provides the documentation for UPS monitoring.

Accessing the File Server Floppy Across the Network

For one reason or another, you may need to access the file server floppy from a workstation. This is usually impossible, especially with a dedicated server. If the server is nondedicated, MAP ASSIST from Fresh Technology Group allows the file server floppy drive to be used from a workstation on the network. Other products, like Brightwork Development Inc.'s NETRemote+ provide similar resource sharing across the LAN. MAP ASSIST is primarily intended to allow users to share local floppy and hard disk drives with other NetWare users. Lastly, NLMs under NetWare/386 could be designed to allow access to the file server's local floppy drive. In fact, some NLMs from Novell have been designed to handle these tasks, including EDIT and RCONSOLE.

Performance and Control at the File Server

Performance sets NetWare apart from other network operating systems. A large measure of performance is dictated by control mechanisms. Something must control the order of processing. If there were infinite resources, e.g., unlimited CPU cycles, unlimited RAM, etc., then the notion of control would be less important. However, in our finite world of electronics, the various computer processes, or threads, which are the building blocks of programs, do vie for the use of limited resources. Thus, in an operating system that is multithreaded, that is, running many threads in a concurrent manner, there is the need for some scheduling control so that no one thread dominates a single CPU's time or multiple CPUs' time.

Whether the control is centralized or decentralized is determined by the process scheduler engine. This scheduler determines when processes will be allowed to execute, since they are competing for limited resources.

The processing that occurs in multitasking operating systems is based on one of two scheduling control models—a preemptive model or a nonpreemptive model. Most multi-tasking operating systems, such as OS/2 and UNIX, are preemptive operating systems. NetWare/386, however, is a nonpreemptive operating system. To better understand why the Novell architects chose this scheduling environment for NetWare/386, it is necessary to first understand the logic behind both environments.

Preemption

Within the domain of preemptive control, the operating system itself provides each thread with access to the CPU. However, preemptive scheduling dictates that the operating system may "kick" any process off the CPU at any time in order to allow another thread to run. This process is known as context switching. In general, each thread is given a certain amount of time to execute, but this amount of time is rarely indicated to the thread.

The purpose of stopping and restarting threads is to give all currently operating threads more or less equal CPU time. (Note, however, that different schedule privilege levels may be defined for individual threads.) By fulfilling this purpose, all of the threads are given a chance to run in a timely manner.

However, ensuring that all processes have a certain amount of time in which to execute produces much system overhead. This requirement for additional CPU cycles can slow the execution of the actual operating system code as well as any external code, such as (in the case of NetWare /386) LAN drivers, disk drivers, name space drivers, and NLMs.

Additionally, when different threads interact with each other, there is the need to synchronize their data areas. That is, when threads communicate with one another, they must do so in a synchronized fashion or risk defeating their communications. A lack of synchronization could yield data that is invalid when accessed by different threads.

In a preemptive environment, each different shared data area or structure is synchronized. That is, there is a different lock for each data structure. Thus, when threads in a preemptive setting are preempted, their shared data areas may be locked. This lock would be in place to ensure that the memory is not changed while the lock-owning thread is "asleep." Indeed, each access to shared data regions needs to be synchronized with locks.

But, why synchronize memory at all? The major reason why a preemptive operating system has the need for memory locking is that each thread is not in control of its own destiny. In most cases, the thread has no idea at what point in its processing it was stopped and subsequently restarted. And, because a thread does not actually know when it will be put to sleep, it must protect the shared areas of memory it is dealing with to ensure their integrity. Without the synchronization of memory, their shared data areas could become corrupted. This synchronization is the most important difference between preemptive and nonpreemptive operating systems.

Deadlocks

Most multiuser, or preemptive, operating systems provide semaphores as the lock control method. Semaphores are flags used to limit how many tasks can use or change a resource at the same time. These locks are necessary since the threads, not knowing when they will be preempted, need to access shared data and receive coherent data. However, the basic preemptive model allows for the possibility of a deadlock. The term deadlock refers to the situation where two processes are stuck in a tight loop while waiting for the other to free up resources needed to continue processing; a deadlock implies a lack of synchronization. The methods that the operating system allows to control or synchronize data areas may ensure that a deadlock will not occur, but, in most multiuser operating systems, deadlock is a possibility.

As an example of a deadlock scenario, consider two threads, A and B. They both need to lock data areas 1 and 2 to perform their tasks. When they attempt to lock either data area and cannot, they fall asleep in order to wait for a previously asserted lock to be released.

There are many other examples of deadlock situations, but this one is simple enough to point out the potential problem that any operating system may encounter. In a preemptive operating system, however, where locks on shared data regions are practically required, it is more likely to occur. Not only that, but the enforcement of these locks and their subsequent unlocks only eats up CPU time, thus degrading performance.

Nonpreemption and NetWare /386

By choosing nonpreemption as the scheduling model, the NetWare /386 architects removed a costly barrier to performance. Namely, the need for all threads to perform locks on shared memory. This prerequisite is removed because nonpreemption means that threads are not unknowingly put to sleep at any time. Only in the rare instance when a thread makes a call to another thread that may possibly fall asleep (e.g., when accessing from disk, which can be slow) would a thread be put to sleep. But, because the thread is making a call to another thread that may possibly fall asleep, that calling thread is presumed to know it has a possibility of sleeping. For instance, if a thread makes a disk read request of another thread, as opposed to a faster cache read request, the calling thread should presume it may fall asleep while the read request is fulfilled and make proper preparations for its shared data areas. The proper preparations might include locking the memory (with NetWare /386, threads perform their locking via semaphores), or ordering the disk read request so that it occurs after the thread has completed its use of the shared memory.

However, in NetWare /386's nonpreemptive environment, threads are allowed to run to completion. That is, a thread is active as long as it needs to be to complete an operation. This way a thread can, knowingly, access shared data regions in a continuous manner. Guaranteed access is possible because the thread will only be put to sleep when it explicitly desires to or when it makes a call to another thread which may be put asleep. Once a thread makes a call to another, that calling thread will wait there until the called thread returns. If the called thread goes to sleep, so does the calling thread—sort of an inherited nap.

Because threads are allowed to run to completion and access to shared memory can be trusted (i.e., a thread will not unknowingly be put to sleep), a nonpreemptive operating system is almost entirely freed from the requirement of memory synchronization; almost all data accesses can be performed without synchronization of any kind.

Remember that NetWare /386 currently supports only a single CPU at a time; there is no multiprocessor support. Therefore, when one thread is running, that is it; there are no other threads running until that thread falls asleep or is terminated.

How would multiprocessor support work in a nonpreemptive environment? Certainly, there would be a need for some sort of shared memory locking. While one option in the multiple CPU scenario is for locks on shared memory to be in the operating system software, an arguably better option is locating locking responsibility in the hardware itself. That is, when one CPU is accessing a region of memory, no other CPUs would be allowed to access to that same area. The answer to this problem is still sometime in the future for NetWare.

Nonpreemption Bottlenecks

Because the NetWare /386 operating system is not forcing preemption on its threads, there exists the possibility for a thread to "run away" with CPU time. When creating NLMs, developers must build safeguards into their code, e.g, to allow for the sleeping of threads. However, if their threads are short or they call routines which may put the threads to sleep, there may be no need to insert their own preemption. Likewise, if they have sizable loops where the thread may dominate the CPU for more than 380 milliseconds (ms), then the insertion of a thread sleep period (which can be accomplished through many procedures) would be imperative. NetWare /386 3.1 has the ability to notify a user at the file server console when a thread occupies more than 380ms of continuous CPU time.

The preemptive environment places execution threads in a defensive position, one where they must constantly be on guard against changes to their shared memory. These changes may occur while a thread has been unknowingly put to sleep by the operating system. Therefore, all processes using shared memory must synchronize, or lock, that memory in case they are put asleep — the primary drawback of preemption. Also, with individual locks on different shared data areas, there exists the possibility of deadlocks. The payoff of preemption, however, is that all threads get an equal amount of time to execute (depending on scheduling privilege levels) and no one thread can monopolize the CPU.

With access to shared memory common in NetWare/386 file servers, nonpreemption puts execution threads in the offensive position of being able to ensure, without mandatory locking, that their shared data remains coherent. This assurance is the result of a thread being able to run until it knowingly sleeps. The major downfall of nonpreemption is the possibility that a thread may monopolize CPU time. When this occurs, developers can make simple changes to their code to lower the amount of continuous CPU time that their threads use. The payoff of nonpreemption is that all threads run more quickly, and there is less overhead when switching operations between threads.

Display Relinquish Control Alerts

New to NetWare/386 3.1 is a SET-able parameter called "Display Relinquish Control Alerts." This parameter will, at the file server console, display a message (as shown below) whenever there exists a thread using more than 380 milliseconds (ms) of CPU time:

```
08/10/90 4:36pm: NetWare 31 TesO Process did not relinquish control
  frequently
    Module: NetWare Server Operating System
    Code Offset in module: 73BF0h
```

The only clue you have as to which NLM is executing the offending thread is the name immediately following the date and time stamp. In this case, the name is

"NetWare 3.1 Tes0," which is derived from the module name. If you type MODULES at the file server console prompt, you will see the names of all the modules installed. Look for one whose name matches or starts out the same as the name you see next to the time stamp, less the number, in this case 0. This number indicates the thread number within that module that is using more than 380ms of CPU time.

Interestingly, when a thread is using quite a bit of CPU time, it may not be reflected by the MONITOR.NLM's Utilization field. However, the file server will still be sluggish. This anomaly has been noted when testing certain procedures that were developed explicitly to use more than 380ms of CPU time.

To assist NetWare 386 LAN administrators and developers, Nu-Mega Technologies (Nashua, NH) has produced PROFILE.NLM. PROFILE.NLM works with NetWare/386 3.1x, and "profiles" each NLM or other system module it can find running on that file server. Displayed items include: Module filename, maximum CPU time in milliseconds, total CPU time in hh:mm:ss, average CPU time in ms, and percentage of CPU time used. In fact, it was this PROFILE.NLM that provided the information necessary to determine that NetWare will issue its relinquish control message at the 380ms mark. Also available from Nu-Mega is the NETCHECK NLM. This NLM will display and track any attempts by NLMs to access or write to areas of memory out of their ownership.

SFT III

Initially SFT III NetWare was available only with NetWare 3.11, the 250 user version. Also, only the most minimal support was present. For instance, the only communication protocol supported was IPX/SPX. And the only name space supported was DOS (thus DOS, Windows and OS/2 were supported, however not OS/2's HPFS).

The true, full release of SFT III is not expected until well into 1994. At present, the minimum configuration for SFT III servers is as follows:

- 386/33 or 486/25
- 12MB of RAM (equal amount on each server)
- same monitor hardware
- same or similar LAN adapters
- same server link adapter (Mirrored Server Link or MSL)

In that initial state, SFT III was more of a high-end beta than a broadly applicable commercial product. Just the same, it is quite an advanced "beta," after years of development work, and is proving to be a very viable solution for many companies that use NetWare.

CHAPTER 4

VAPs, VADDs, and NLMs

Novell wants to be sure that everybody and everything can work with NetWare. Of course, the kernel of NetWare, i.e., the NetWare Core Protocol (NCP) is "proprietary"—which means you shouldn't anticipate the code to become public domain any time soon. However, Novell has gone to great lengths to open up NetWare to third-party developers by providing a multitude of "hooks" (i.e., APIs) into its operating system.

From the introduction of version 2.1 of NetWare in late 1987 to the present (including NetWare/386), Novell has provided a specialized set of these "hooks" via two new sets of application program interfaces (APIs). These APIs provide applications programmatic access to the services of the network operating system and the file server.

These two new sets of APIs delivered with version 2.1 of NetWare were Value-Added Processes (VAPs) and Value-Added Disk Drivers (VADDs). VAPs are file server-based applications, and VADDs are specialized file server disk drivers.

In NetWare/386, VAPs and VADDs were replaced by NetWare Loadable Modules (NLMs). NLMs provide a more direct access to a larger number of server functions than can be achieved with VAPs and VADDs. Practically all of the additional applications and other server-based utilities in NetWare/386 are NLMs. There is no conversion utility for instantly making an NLM out of a VAP or vice versa.

VAPs (Value Added Processes)

VAPs are applications that fulfill specific needs at the NetWare file server. These can include locking the file server console keyboard, performing database functions, or assisting in network printing. Other possible functions include archive servers, batch job services, gateways, and other communications services—the only limitation is the software developer's imagination. VAPs offer many potential benefits, such as offloading processing at workstations, providing a single entry point to additional network services, increasing the usefulness of a server by giving it more processing, offering services to the network that would be difficult to implement otherwise, and bettering performance of workstation applications by streamlining their processing.

However, VAPs can also bring about some negative results. For instance, they can crash file servers or dramatically impede server performance. If they do not work correctly, VAPs can make the server unstable. VAPs sometimes require multiple user connections, and under ELS NetWare 2.12 (Level II) this can be a problem since there are only eight user connections available. VAPs can also consume large amounts of server memory, thus requiring more RAM for the server. Optimally, a VAP should only be used to extend a service to network users when no other means is feasible.

VAPs are loaded as separate components that are dynamically linked to the operating system when the file server is booted. VAPs are not integral parts of the operating system.

Examples of VAPs provided by Novell include Btrieve, NetWare for Macintosh VAPs, and Pserver VAP in version 2.2. The Btrieve VAP expedites database program requests by doing all requests at the file server, rather than at an independent workstation. The NetWare for Macintosh VAP provides NetWare file and print services for Macintosh computers.

At the time of this printing, there is no official certification mechanism to ensure the viability of the VAPs not offered by Novell. (Novell has a certification process for NLMs; however, it is costly.) For this reason, caution should be used when loading VAPs and NLMs for the first time. Because they are integrated into the operation of the file server, it is possible for a defective VAP, VADD, or NLM to bring the file server down.

Another potential problem is that two separate VAPs may work when they are used individually, but they then fail when they are loaded at the same time. Using both VAPs simultaneously could bring about their mutual corruption and an eventual lock-up of the file server. This is most common with beta versions of VAP products; production versions do not seem to have this problem.

Some VAPs require separate connections in order to communicate with the file server. These VAPs use the connection(s) to perform tasks requiring file server response, just as a workstation does. An exception is the approach designed into NetWare ELS II 2.15, which does not use up valuable workstation connections. Instead it uses special "VAP connections" that only VAPs may use. This approach leaves regular connections free for actual workstation use. A skilled programmer could theoretically write a VAP that simultaneously handles many user accounts and allows multiple logins through a "VAP connection"—potentially adding several workstation connections.

If too many VAPs are used in the same file server, there is the definite possibility of substantially decreasing file server performance. This drain on performance is the reason Novell advises against using the NetWare for Macintosh VAP in a file server that is near or at capacity. The preferred option is to off-load the Macintosh VAPs to a bridge server.

Another issue influencing the decision to use a VAP is its RAM requirements. If a VAP requires a large amount of RAM (e.g., the Macintosh VAP can require in excess of 1MB of RAM), it is possible that an insufficient amount will remain for file caching. File caching is one of the chief functions used by NetWare to speed network response times.

The file size of the VAP is not a very reliable gauge of how much RAM the VAP will require. A better way to determine VAP memory usage is to use NetWare's FCONSOLE utility. To use FCONSOLE, first boot the file server without loading any VAPs. Use FCONSOLE to see how many cache buffers are available by reviewing the "Statistics/Summary" screen. Next, reboot the file server, this time loading the VAPs. Use FCONSOLE again to check the number of cache buffers. Finally, calculate the difference in the number of cache buffers with and without VAPs loaded and multiply by 4,096 (the size of each cache buffer). The result should provide a good indication of how much RAM the VAP requires. The most reliable method of determining the RAM space that will be used is to contact the VAP manufacturer.

VAPs also use 128 bytes from Dynamic Memory Pool 1, the same area of memory where FSPs are stored. Thus, it is possible that VAP use can decrease the number of FSPs.

VAP Load Order Setup

It is possible to select the load order of your VAPs. To do this, change your VAP's extension from .VAP to .VPx. Replace the x with 0 through 9. Your VAPs will be loaded in ascending numerical order. Remember, you can only load ten VAPs at one time. VAPs that keep the .VAP extensions will be loaded after numerically specified VAPs.

VADDs (Value Added Disk Drivers)

Beginning with NetWare version 2.1, Novell made it possible for OEMs to produce device-specific drivers for disk drives. The drivers are embedded in the operating system. These drivers are needed for many of the high capacity storage devices available today, including SCSI, ESDI, and even WORM drives.

A VADD is merely a special driver type used to interact with a disk subsystem, usually one with a special disk controller. Because they provide a means for outside vendors to sell disk drive subsystems for use on a NetWare file server, VADDs are usually developed by third parties.

One drive type that is not supported by VADDs is the CD-ROM; the data format utilized by CD-ROMs prevents VADD support. Almost every CD-ROM produced uses what is known as the "High-Sierra" format, which is not compatible with the file system used in the /286 versions of NetWare. NetWare/386 (version 3.1) remedies this problem by enabling loadable file systems to support non-NetWare disk formats. However, drivers still must be written to fulfill this need.

Due to the complexities involved in writing such drivers, many OEMs have been forced to revise their VADDs. Be sure to check with your vendor if problems are detected on a VADD-supported disk. A newer release of the VADD, eliminating most of the bugs may be available.

The NetWare version being used may also contribute to the problems you have with a VADD. NetWare version 2.12 has a limited amount of stack space allocated for handling drivers for disk drives. This means that version 2.12 networks are more susceptible to errors that report stack overflow. If moving to another disk drive subsystem is not an option, the answer may be to move to a different version of NetWare, such as versions 2.1, 2.11, or 2.15.

NLMs (NetWare Loadable Modules)

When Novell developed NetWare/386, the designers took the opportunity to dramatically extend the VAP/VADD concept, creating a new breed of file server-based applications called the NetWare Loadable Module. NLMs can be written to service a variety of needs and provide a means of customizing the network to suit a particular environment or situation.

Like VAPs, NLMs link with NetWare when the operating system is loaded and become part of it as if they were hard-coded. However, unlike VAPs, when NLMs are unloaded from the NetWare operating system, they return to the file server all of the memory and resources that had previously been allocated to them. VAPs and VADDs cannot be unloaded. This dynamic loading and unloading is an improvement in overall use of the file server.

NLM design is more flexible and refined than those of VAPs and VADDs. For instance, NLMs can be loaded and unloaded on the fly. An NLM does not need to be loaded all the time, nor does it have to be loaded when the file server is booted. When they are loaded, NLMs attempt to allocate the memory they need. This memory is always taken from the memory in use by cache buffers. When an NLM is unloaded it releases its memory back to the cache memory pool.

There are four basic types of NLMs: utilities and application modules (.NLM filename extension); LAN drivers (.LAN extension); disk drivers (.DSK extension); and modules pertaining to file system name spaces, such as in Macintosh naming conventions (.NAM extension).

The flexibility and range of capabilities these various NLMs bring to NetWare is evident at installation. For example, to install a disk driver, the following steps would be performed:

1. The /386 file server is booted with the appropriate DOS diskette.
2. The DOS diskette is replaced with the NetWare diskette that includes the SERVER.EXE program, and the following command is typed at the DOS prompt:

```
A> server <enter>
```

3. Next, a disk driver is loaded, e.g., ISADISK.DSK (an Industry Standard Architecture disk driver), and the following command is typed at the CONSOLE prompt:

```
: load a:isadisk <enter>
```

The ISADISK.DSK disk driver is now loaded.

Similarly, by executing the NLMs needed to create and edit the NetWare partitions and volumes (INSTALL.NLM) and to load the appropriate LAN driver (NE1000.LAN), a NetWare file server can be literally ready to go in minutes. (Typically, the statements described in this sequence are placed in the STARTUP.NCF or AUTOEXEC.NCF file for loading each time that the file server boots.)

The key advantage of using NLMs is their interface with the NetWare operating system. For example, when the LAN driver NE1000.LAN is loaded, it has access to approximately 30 NetWare routines. Most of these routines are in a section of the NetWare OS called the Link Support Layer (LSL). The remainder of the routines, scattered throughout the NetWare OS, are miscellaneous. Incidentally, the LSL is actually a subset of Novell's Open Data-link Interface (ODI) specification which is being promoted to develop industry standard LAN drivers.

NLM development is fairly straightforward for skilled programmers, and generally regarded as easier than VAP development. There are a few highlights of NLM development worth mentioning.

First, NLM development requires the use of Novell's /386 C Compiler kit. This includes a compiler, linker, a set of standard and NetWare/386-specific libraries and a specialized file called CLIB.IMP. This latter file contains all of the routine functions that an NLM would commonly import during execution, hence the IMP (for Import) extension. The entire kit is also known as the NetWare/386 Software Development Kit (SDK) for version 3.1.

Second, there are three global variables that must be declared for every NLM. NetWare/386 uses these variables when it runs the NLM. These variables could be defined in the linker file, or in the main code, but they must be defined somewhere. They are commonly defined in the .DEF file used by NLMLINK (replaced by WATCOM's WLINK with NetWare/386 3.1's SDK) to product the NLM. They include:

1. Unsigned char NLMDescription[]="Mini command.com emulator." This string is used when the file server lists the NLMs that are currently being run. The example contains a value specific to a sample called NLMCOM produced for the 1989 Novell Developers' Conference.
2. Unsigned long NLMStackSize=8192. This 8K stack size is the default, and so declaring it is somewhat redundant. However, programs requiring a larger stack can be adjusted accordingly.
3. Unsigned char NLMName[]="Minicom." This is a small string that names the NLM, and is again specific to the Developers' Conference example.

Third, programmers must understand the concept of dynamic link libraries and how it is applied in NLM development. The normal job of a linker is to resolve all code components into a single executable. However, in a multi-tasking environment, such as NetWare/386, many programs can be simultaneously loaded into memory. If each of these programs uses the same functions, there can be a serious waste of memory. The solution is to use dynamic link libraries (DLLs), which allow single in-memory functions to be shared by several programs. DLLs are declared in a program's Definition (.DEF extension) file and are set aside in additional Import (.IMP extension) files.

By including the NLM construct in NetWare/386, Novell not only introduced a network operating system developed for the /386 microprocessor, but it provided one that allows relatively easy development of applications.

VAPs and NLMs Compared

When a VAP is loaded (on a NetWare/286 server), it must be loaded when the server is booted up. VAPs were conceived as utilities that would require few special accommodations. In general, to load a VAP, it must be located in the SYS:SYSTEM directory area. NetWare/286 does afford one load time option, either to load all VAPs or to load none of them. NetWare/286 2.15x can load VAPs automatically (using the VAP WAIT command SYS:SYSTEM\ SERVER.CFG), but they cannot be automatically "not" loaded. Practically, this means if you don't want to load a particular VAP, you'll have to answer "No" at the file server console when NetWare asks "Load VAPs?" at boot time.

Additionally, once a VAP is loaded, it cannot be unloaded. The only way to unload a VAP is to reboot the server without that VAP present in the SYS:SYSTEM directory (note that the file's extension, .VAP, could be changed to effectively eliminate it from being loaded).

In contrast, NLMs are loaded only when needed, on demand. The demand may be requested by the server's AUTOEXEC.NCF (NCF=NetWare Command File), which is read when the server is booted. But unlike VAPs, NLMs may be loaded and unloaded at any time while the server is up. Also, NLMs do not have to be located in the SYS:SYSTEM directory. They may exist on the local floppy disk of the file server or on some directory on any server disk volume. In fact, NetWare/386 allows search paths to exist, so the NLM could be loaded off a server-based search path.

VAP vs. NLM Design Differences

VAP and NLM designs differ in five basic areas:

1. Initializing
2. Obtaining Connections
3. Loading/Unloading
4. Availability of APIs
5. Communicating between processes

Initializing. Producing a VAP incurs the creation of its initialization code. This code is in two distinct parts, the VAP header and the actual initialization code. The VAP header is a strictly defined structure that indicates such things as the VAP's name, its keywords (to be used at the server console), whether or not it will use a service connection. The initialization code sets up a VAP's memory allocation needs and spawns a VAP's necessary processes. Once a VAP has been initialized it can no longer allocate new memory. Thus, a VAP needs to statically allocate as much memory as it thinks it will need when it is loaded. In fact, when a VAP is through with its initialization it must actually call a routine InitializationComplete.

With NLMs, Novell provides developers a single prelude module which prepares much of the NLM's, initialization needs. Other items such as dynamic memory allocation, the spawning of processes (called threads in NLMs) can occur at any time provided there is sufficient server memory.

Obtaining Connections. For a VAP to communicate with its server as a user would, it must obtain a connection. To use this connection the VAP must login, just like a workstation-based user. And just like any other user connection, the VAP's connection(s) take away those available to users (except with ELS II NetWare 2.1x). Additionally, if a VAP's login account does not exist or has insufficient rights for the needs of the VAP, a VAP can be rendered useless until the situation is remedied.

An NLM could login as a VAP does to gain server access, but in doing so it would consume a user connection, just like a VAP. However, NLMs can take advantage of a special connection called connection 0. This connection is a direct link to the file server operating system. No official login is necessary and full Supervisor-type rights are always available. The added benefit is that no user connections are forfeited.

One more difference between obtaining connections with an NLM versus a VAP is that if the NLM does login, it does so via one of the 100 "NLM-only" connections supplied on each NetWare/386 server. These connections apply only when an NLM is logging into its local server. If an NLM logs into a server other than the one it is running on, then it does not occupy one of the 100 NLM-only connections at the remote server because the remote server has no way to discern that it is an NLM on another server requesting the login.

Loading/Unloading. As mentioned at the beginning of this section, VAPs can only be loaded at boot time, and once loaded cannot be unloaded. NLMs, however, can be loaded and unloaded at any time.

API Availability. When a VAP communicates with the operating system, it must use some sort of API. This API may be a direct one where each call is made directly by the VAP, or it may be a call made from a predefined library. In either case, the code to process these file server requests must be linked into the VAP's code, artificially inflating the size of the VAP. Because there are at least two different methods for making file server requests, VAPs may make inefficient calls to a file server, wasting precious processing time. Additionally, because each VAP contains the code necessary to make file server requests, there is additional server memory consumed.

NLMs are much more efficient in their use of memory. In the NetWare/386 environment there is a common library definition for NLMs. This library, generally referred to as CLIB or CLIB.NLM, is loaded once. After it is loaded, all NLMs can make calls to it. Thus the NLM creator does not need to be concerned with the actual mechanics of file server requests. And NLMs do not waste server memory by implementing the same file server requests (code wise) over and over again for each NLM. Also, if new versions of NetWare come out, the same NLMs can potentially operate with them; a new CLIB would be the only requirement to accommodate the NLMs.

Communicating between processes. To open a communications path between each other, VAPs must perform a search of all VAPs in memory, to find the one they want. Usually the search scans for a particular VAP name. Once the desired VAP's header is found, the requesting VAP must ascertain the address to call in order to make contact with that VAP. Because the VAP must do all the work of resolving communications references itself, communication between VAPs is unusually complex.

When an NLM needs to communicate with a fellow NLM it calls the needed procedure by name. The only downfall of this method is that an NLM cannot call another NLM unless the calling NLM is loaded after the NLM it is trying to call. Otherwise the calling NLM's procedure call will be unresolvable since the called procedure name is not in memory. Note that not every procedure in an NLM can be called, only those which include NLM exports.

Ring 0 and NetWare/386

There has been some controversy over Novell's choice to use ring 0 (zero) memory protection, also known as Privilege Level 0. Basically, the concern is that applications will cause the file server to "crash." It is possible to create an application which will crash any file server, NetWare or not. But the term "crash" is loosely defined. Most of the concerned voices, however, presume that NetWare/386 is the first NetWare version designed to run all applications at ring 0. Rather, the first version to use ring 0 was NetWare/286 2.1, first delivered in 1987. With NetWare/286, server applications were called VAPs; with NetWare 386 such applications are termed NLMs.

What does ring 0 protection actually provide? Honestly, not much. For instance, DOS applications all run at ring 0. And, it is extremely rare for DOS applications to violate the memory of other applications. Other applications that run at ring 0 include DOS itself, device drivers, TSRs, and other DOS programs. Recognizing that developing a NetWare/386 NLM is similar to creating a DOS application (minus the ability to multithread the code), one would then understand that avoiding the coding of an ill-behaved application (i.e. a program that writes over areas of memory which do not belong to it) is not that difficult.

The worst that an ill-behaved NLM could do is erase your network volumes. This worry can be minimized by a consistent backup strategy.

Once server-based applications begin to show up en masse, another concern that is likely to become an issue is that of CPU scheduling. OS/2 operates with the default that an application does not schedule itself and thus does not have control over when it will execute. This can create programming problems for the application developer. Since the developer has no control of when their application will be running, it is impossible to make simple assumptions such as timeliness of execution, and current state of memory and its values. However, with OS/2's preemptive scheduling (i.e., applications do not schedule themselves), all applications are guaranteed CPU time and thus an equal chance to execute.

With NetWare/386 (as well as /286), scheduling is non-preemptive, i.e. each application is free to run till completion or it may schedule its own preemption. Because of this, it is possible for a NetWare/386 server-based application to run through long sections without giving up the CPU. The application might give up control of the CPU in order to allow execute-time for other applications, including the server operating system itself. By following a few fundamental rules, NLMs can be designed and coded to allow for appropriate preemptive breaks without disturbing its own execution or delaying that of others. In fact, Novell may implement such preemptive breaks each time a library routine is called. Under NetWare/386 (unlike NetWare/286), NLMs all call the same set of Novell-supplied library routines (CLIB). It is these routines where Novell may decide to implement breaks so that performance of a current application is not adversely affected while other applications are given CPU time. Consequently, NetWare 286's VAPs would not benefit from such changes, primarily due to the lack of a common set of library routines.

In the non-preemptive OS found in NetWare/386, there exists the possibility for an NLM to run "till completion" without giving up the CPU for other applications to execute. But, with the implementation of a few basic rules governing program execution, any undue performance penalty an NLM could introduce can be circumvented. If NLM developers wanted to get the most performance from their NLM, they could resort to CPU dominance rather than following guidelines for preemptive programming. However, there are three defenses against this aggressive development. First, users themselves may note a marked decrease in system performance upon the use of such an NLM. And, noting such a decrease, will likely call the vendor to find out what is going on, if indeed this is a concern, and request appropriate changes be made. Second, as noted earlier, Novell may decide to code preemptive breaks in their library routines. Note that an NLM will not have much work to perform if it is not, somehow, using these library routines. (However, it is possible for an NLM to "sit and wait," thus consuming CPU time without doing any library calls, so the insertion of preemption routines in the library can not be 100 percent effective.) Third, a situation where an NLM controls CPU time for an extended amount of time can be detected and Novell may opt to include routines to detect such occurrences. Processes that incur a large amount of contiguous CPU time would be brought to the attention of the network supervisor and then removed from the system. For NetWare/386 3.1, NuMega Technologies has produced PROFILE. PROFILE is an NLM that allows the monitoring of third party NLMs and how much CPU time they are consuming.

NLMs That Use Too Much CPU Time

In NetWare/386 3.1x there exists a settable parameter called "Display Relinquish Control Alerts." For version 3.0 there is no such parameter. This parameter will display a file server console message such as:

```
08/10/90 4:36pm: NetWare 3.1 TesO Process did not relinquish control
  frequently
    Module: NetWare Server Operating System
    Code Offset in module: 73BF0h
```

Whenever there exists a thread using more than 380 milliseconds of CPU time, the only clue you have as to which NLM it is, is the name immediately following the date and time stamp. In this case the name is "NetWare 3.1 Tes0." This name is derived from the module name. If you type MODULES at the file server console prompt you will see the names of all the modules installed. Look for one whose name matches or starts out the same as the name you see next to the time stamp less the number 0. This number 0 indicates the thread number, number 0, within that module that is using more than 380ms of CPU time.

When a thread is using excessive CPU time, it may not be reflected in the MONITOR.NLM's Utilization field. However the file server will still be sluggish. This anomaly has been noted when testing certain procedures. These procedures were developed directly for the purpose of using more than 380ms of CPU time.

To assist NetWare/386 LAN administrators and developers, Nu-Mega Technologies produces the utility PROFILE.NLM, discussed in an earlier section.

CHAPTER 5

Disk Drives and Disk Drive Controllers

Disk drives and controllers are complicated instruments, composed of many parts, created for the specialized purpose of servicing read/write requests by other hardware. It is the intelligent coordination of these components, i.e., the controller, the drive itself, the coprocessor boards, the drive software, etc., that allows disk drives to store and retrieve data.

Disk Drives

Most disk drives are made up of the same basic parts. The disk itself is called a *platter*, and a disk drive can have several. Data is stored on the platter, which spins at speeds from 3,600 up to near 7,200 revolutions per minute (RPM) on magnetic and some optical drives, but usually 1,800 RPM on most optical drives. The actual media, a magnetic coating on the platter, can be one of three types: oxide media, plated media, or sputtered media. Of these, oxide is the oldest (in the PC technological world) and is the least reliable. The newer forms of media, plated and sputtered, offer a higher degree of reliability and a greater frequency range or capacity to hold data. Plated media is the most common type found on drives used in PCs. Plated and sputtered media are usually composed of nickel and cobalt on a substrate, with aluminum serving as the base material.

All platters have two recording sides but, in some cases, only one side is used for recording data. All PC hard disk drives contain two or more platters. Data is stored on each platter on discrete tracks that appear as concentric circles and are often less than 1/1000th of an inch apart. The tracks are further divided into sectors. The most common sector found on PCs is 512 bytes. The number of sectors per track is determined by the encoding method used. These methods (Modified Frequency Modulation (MFM) and Run Length Limited (RLL) are discussed in detail below. Each platter used in a drive has the same number of tracks. Corresponding tracks from each platter are collectively referred to as a *cylinder*. The "physical" appearance is that of a geometric cylinder. A disk drive is sometimes referred to as a *spindle*, although this term technically describes the central axis of the drive.

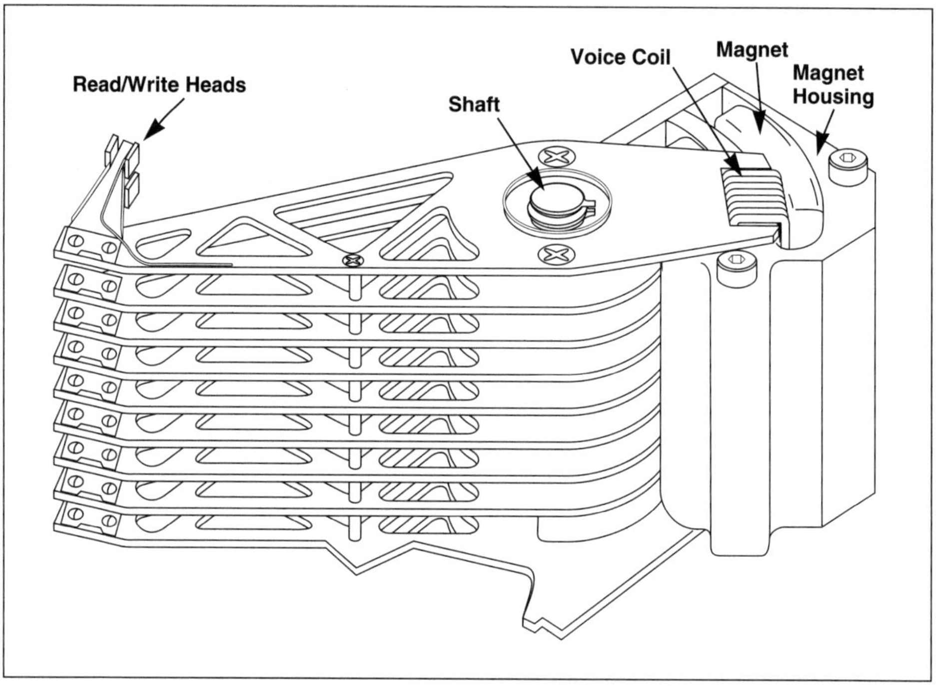

Figure 5-1. Disk drive head positioning system

Data on the platters is written and read by a head, a cross-section of which is shown in Figure 5-1. For each platter side there is a read/write head. For magnetic-based disk drives, this head electromagnetically reads and writes data from and to the disk. The head practically "flies" above the surface of the platter. And, like anything that flies, read/write heads occasionally "crash". When this happens, the read/write head actually has uncontrolled contact with the surface of the platter and damages part of the disk. At the very least, this usually results in total loss of the data stored on that part of the disk. At the worst, it can render the entire disk drive useless when the heads become out of alignment and destroy other areas of the disk platters. However, before considering the drive a total loss, it is worth checking with disk drive refurbishment or repair shops to see if they can cost-effectively fix the unit. To get the name of a reputable refurbishment group, call any large distributor to see who they use in the region.

The heads are positioned by head *actuators*. All of the heads move in unison to a specified location on the disk. With magnetic-based disk drives there are essentially two types of head actuators. The first is a stepper-motor actuator, which is the result of an older technology. The stepper-motor positions the disk heads in a very mechanical way, by stepping the heads across the platters one track (or if you prefer, cylinder) at a time. If the desired track is 10 tracks from where the heads are, 10 individual steps are needed to arrive at the requested location. Normally, stepper-motors do not achieve average access times faster than 55ms. Drives using stepper-motors often employ oxide-coated media for the platters, primarily because there is no need for high-density media or their high tolerances.

The second type of head positioning technology, often used in drives produced today, is the rotary voice-coil (see Figure 5-2). The voice-coil moves the heads in a sweeping manner, placing them directly at a requested location without having to step from track to track. This alone accounts for the improvement in average access times on voice-coil actuated drives over stepper-motor systems. It is not uncommon for voice-coil actuated drives to have average access times below 30ms. There is, however, a penalty when using voice-coil actuation. One entire platter side, usually located on one of the outside platters, must be dedicated to what is called a *servo platter*. Positioning information stored on this server platter is used to properly position the disk heads. The servo information is used as a control signal for the actuator to provide track-crossing signals during seek operations, next track information, and timing information.

Optical-based disk drives (WORMs, Magneto-Optical, and CD-ROM) handle head reads and writes using optical technology. Write Once, Read Many (WORM) drives can write data to the media once and then read it as many times as necessary. During a disk write, the write head essentially "punches out" or "burns" a perforated bit with a laser. Once it has been punched, the direction of the punch, representing either 0 or 1 (binary data), is permanent. The write head cannot return and alter the data.

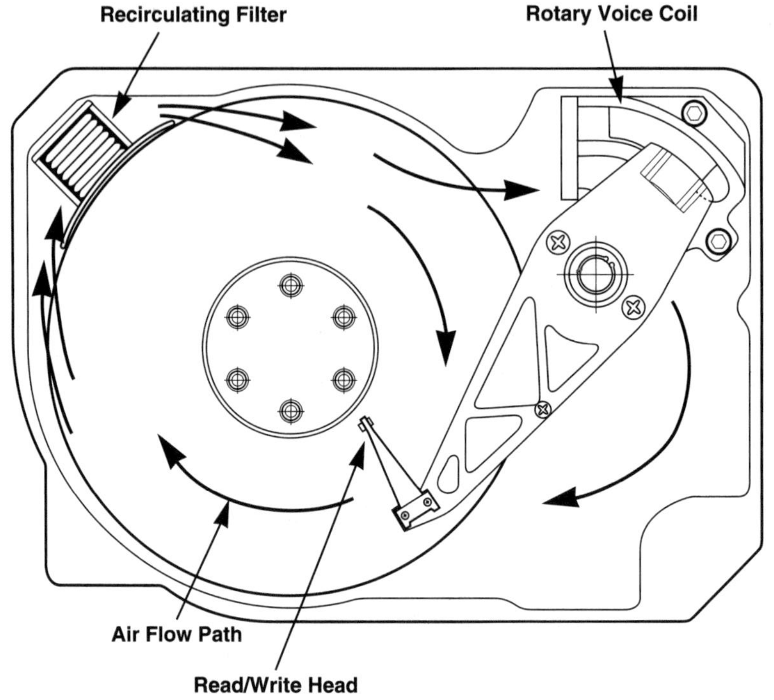

Figure 5-2. Rotary voice-coil

With Magneto-Optical or Erasable Optical disks the write head incorporates a laser that heats the surface of the disk media to 200-300 degrees Celsius above the Curie point of the disk media. This heating is used in conjunction with a magnet to alter the state of the media to indicate a binary 0 or 1. Hence the name, Magneto-Optical disk, or MOdisk.

For all multiple read/write optical disks, there are two sets of optics, each including a laser—one for reading, and one for writing. These heads are positioned high above the disk media, in comparison to magnetic media, thereby making head crashes practically impossible. It is more likely that the drive encasement will be physically destroyed than it is that the head will crash on an optical drive.

On Compact Disk, Read-Only Memory (CD-ROM) disks there is only a read head. CD-ROM disks are purchased with data already written to them. CD-ROMs are production copies created from a master called a *ready disk*. Unique to the CD-

ROM is an industry standard format called the High-Sierra format, which was mentioned earlier in this text. This name was chosen because the meetings that led to its acceptance were held in the Sierra Mountains. Most CD-ROMs adhere to this standard. Note that the media used for CD-ROMs and WORMs are completely different.

Neither conventional magnetic, Erasable Optical, nor WORM media come preformatted. This allows the user to select the most appropriate format. This flexibility is an inherent feature of any media that can be written to.

In the context of file server use, conventional magnetic, WORM, and Magneto-Optical drives can all be used in NetWare file servers running NetWare 2.1x. CD-ROMs are also supportable with version 3.1 and above.

Interleave

All of the aforementioned magnetic-based drive types interleave their disk sectors. Interleave is a measure indicating the number of revolutions a disk must make to read one full track and is most often shown as a ratio (e.g., 1:1, 3:1, etc.). Specified at the time a low-level format is performed, these interleave ratios are best set to the manufacturer's specifications. This is especially important for drives that are translated. Translation is often used for drives that have more sectors per track and/or cylinders available than the ST-506 specification accommodates (discussed later in this chapter). This is true of drives using RLL encoding with ST-506/412 interfaces, both of which are described later in this chapter. Simply stated, the translation allows the most efficient use of all of the disk's sectors and/or cylinders.

Data Encoding Techniques

All disk drives write data in a specified format, often referred to as a data encoding scheme. The encoding method used determines the drive's capacity. There are two dominant encoding schemes used in the PC world: Modified Frequency Modulation (MFM) and Run Length Limited (RLL).

Modified Frequency Modulation

Based on Frequency Modulation (FM), MFM is used on all floppy drives that are rated "double density," and is the predominant data encoding method for hard disk drives found in XT-class and early AT-class machines.

In its most basic form, MFM describes the sequencing of binary 0s and 1s on the surface of a disk's platters. The following definitions describe how these 0s and 1s are represented on the platter: a silence is represented by the absence of a pulse; a silence or pulse represents a "half-bit" of information; a clock extraction is used to coordinate the controller and disk, primarily so that the controller can properly interpret the disk's incoming data. It is the controller that determines this pulse. This clock is like a heartbeat and occurs regularly. A 0 is represented by one of the following patterns: two silences if a pulse occurred at the end of the previous bit, or a pulse followed by a silence if no pulse occurred at the end of the previous bit (i.e., a silence). A 1 is recognized by only one pattern: a silence followed by a pulse.

Data (bits)	MFM encoding (half-bits)
0	if preceding bit is 1: 0 0 if preceding bit is 0: 1 0
1	always 0 1

Figure 5-3. MFM encoding

The result is that there will always be at least one silence between each pulse. Note that MFM uses four half-bits to represent two binary digits (0s, 1s, or a combination; see Figure 5-3). Following this logic, it can be deduced that for every 4 half-bits (2 data bits) on the disk, there will be at least 1 and no more than 3 silences. Consequently, MFM could also be called 1,3 Run Length Limited (RLL) encoding, as described in the next section. The first number, or minimum run length, indicates how compressed the data can be encoded. The second, or maximum run length, indicates how precise the disk controller must be to accurately interpret the data.

MFM translates into a disk format with 17 sectors per track. In the PC world, each of these sectors is 512 bytes, so a single track holds 8,704 bytes of data.

Run Length Limited

Developed by IBM, with its roots in MFM technology, RLL encoding goes a step further. As noted earlier, MFM is actually 1,3 RLL encoding, although it is never referred to as such. RLL is generally used to refer to a disk that uses 2,7 RLL; 3,9 RLL; or, occasionally, 1,7 RLL encoding.

Under the 2,7 RLL encoding scheme, data is encoded into 2 or 4 bits. As its name implies, there are always 2 silences and no more than 7 per set of 8 half-bits. Figure 5-4 illustrates how data is encoded with 2,7 RLL.

Data (bits)	2,7 RLL encoding (half-bits)
0 0	1 0 0 0
0 1	0 1 0 0
1 0 0	0 0 1 0 0 0
1 0 1	1 0 0 1 0 0
1 1 0 0	0 0 0 0 1 0 0 0
1 1 0 1	0 0 1 0 0 1 0 0
1 1 1	0 0 0 1 0 0

Figure 5-4. 2,7 RLL encoding

If the only difference between 1,3 RLL (MFM) and 2,7 RLL was the way bits were stored, the amount of storage space would not increase. However, because the spacing or number of "data slots" between the range of run length is increased—from a minimum of 1 and a maximum of 3 with 1,3 RLL to a minimum of 2 and a maximum of 7 with 2,7 RLL—more data can be squeezed onto the disk. This compression is possible because the clock extraction heartbeat (described in the MFM section above) essentially remains constant. Because it has not changed its heartbeat requirement and the encoded data has loosened up its spacing requirements (so that a clock can be generated when a pulse is read), more data can be squeezed between heartbeats. To make up for this time caused by a surplus of 2,7 RLL encoded silences between relatively constant heartbeats, more data is compacted onto the disk.

What RLL encoding translates into is 25+1 sectors per track, where sectors are 512 bytes long. The 26th or extra (+1) sector per track is used by some controllers during the low-level format operation. If, during the low-level format, a bad sector is found, the controller will try to remap that bad sector to the 26th sector. This procedure is called sector sparing. Some controllers mark either the entire track or just the affected sector as a bad one. If sector sparing is used, the full 25 sectors are still realized and usable. In a PC, each sector is 512 bytes. This means that under 2,7 RLL encoding, a single track holds 12,800 bytes of data; nearly 50 percent more than MFM.

Not all drives are designed with RLL encoding in mind. If a drive is formatted with 2,7 RLL there is a good possibility that the disk drive's useful life (and with it, your data's) will be shortened. Another potential problem is that the drive may lose data if it is unable to support the higher data density required by 2,7 RLL. The combination of these two problems should discourage anyone from using non-RLL rated drives with an RLL controller.

Other Encoding Technologies

Further enhancements to disk drive encoding techniques include Advanced RLL (ARLL) and Enhanced RLL (ERLL). Both ARLL and ERLL offer a 100 percent increase in capacity and transfer rate to systems using MFM encoding. Both ARLL and ERLL use 3,9 RLL encoding.

Several drives now on the market meet the exacting specifications necessary for 3,9 RLL encoding. All of these drives come with an ESDI interface, discussed later in this chapter.

Low-Level Formatting

In low-level formatting, the disk controller writes a sequence of address and control information at the beginning of each sector of the hard disk. This is performed so that the controller will be able to locate each sector on the disk.

NetWare's COMPSURF utility provides extensive testing of the file server's disk drives, making the system more fault tolerant. COMPSURF accomplishes this by finding bad disk areas and marking them as such. COMPSURF records the bad block's logical address (logical block, rather than the physical address of the head, cylinder, and sector) in sectors 17 and 18 of track 0. An alternative technique is to mark a bad track at the actual track itself, but there is no standard way to do this. NetWare's technique is hardware independent. However, the COMPSURF format option, which is a low-level format option, must be used properly, as it overwrites any previous low-level format. It is this option that serves to confuse and trouble network administrators. For a more in-depth discussion of COMPSURF, see Chapter 2.

WARNING: Some older IDE/ATA drives will be rendered useless if low level formatted. Check with the manufacturer to determine the safe method to COMPSURF the drive.

Disk Controller Technology

The disk controller acts as the mediator between the disk and the operating system. While some drives have embedded controllers, most can utilize various types of controllers, the most noteworthy of which are described below.

ST-506/412

Developed by then Shugart Technologies (now Seagate Technologies), the ST-506 is the controller that was used for their 5MB hard disk drive. The ST-506 design is a result of consolidation of pieces from Shugart's SA-450 floppy disk interface and the SA-1000 8-inch disk interface. The resulting interface was built to transfer data at 5Mb/s. It was also designed to allow up to 1,023 cylinders (10 bits worth) and 63 heads (6 bits worth).

The ST-506 design is simple. There are two cables that go between the controller and drive. A 34-pin ribbon cable is used to signal drives into and out of action. This 34-pin cable is connected to all disk drives on the controller. The ST-506 specification indicates a maximum of two drives per controller. A second cable, a 20-pin ribbon cable, is connected to each drive directly from the controller for the transfer of data.

Some controller configurations employ a twisted 34-pin ribbon cable. Where the cable plugs into the hard disk drive, wires 25 through 29 are twisted. This twist, among other things, makes it necessary to use a terminating resistor on both drives connected to the cable. The terminating resistor is used to indicate the end of the physical bus. For controllers using untwisted 34-pin cables, only the last physical drive, logical drive 0, should have a terminating resistor installed.

Soon after ST-506 was introduced, the ST-412 was defined. The ST-412 is based on the ST-506, with the addition of buffered seeks. This allows the disk drive to move its heads at its own pace, rather than being limited to that of the disk controller hardware, as is the case with the ST-506. The ST-506 name is still used even though buffered seeks are utilized, so the controller is really an ST-506/412.

Most ST-506 disk controllers use MFM encoding. There are a number of disk controllers, sometimes called ST-506/RLLs, that use 2,7 RLL. These controllers usually also support transfer rates up to 7.5Mb/s. Remember to verify that a drive is rated for RLL if it is to be used with an RLL controller. If you're using an MFM controller, there should not be any problems. All PC-compatible drives produced are at least MFM capable.

SCSI

Developed by Adaptec and proposed as an ANSI standard in 1982, the Small Computer Systems Interface (SCSI, pronounced "scuzzy") has enjoyed a tremendous following and acceptance as a standard. The first major PC manufacturer to use SCSI was Apple with its Macintosh Plus. Based on the block-multiplex channel used in IBM's mainframe computers, SCSI is hardware independent. Since the SCSI interface is logical rather than physical, SCSI devices can be anything from tape drives to hard disks. As long as the device is block addressable, it can exist on a SCSI bus. As with the ST-506 standard, SCSI supports a 5Mb/s transfer rate for adapters using MFM. SCSI adapters utilizing RLL encoding will provide a transfer rate of 7.5Mb/s. In fact, the SCSI standard allows for transfer rates of up to 32Mb/s, even though the standard AT-style bus will currently handle 4-8Mb/s. However, as faster bus architectures become available, such as the Extended Industry Standard Architecture (EISA), faster SCSI devices will be developed.

The SCSI bus is the first of the four major benefits of using SCSI technology. Up to eight SCSI devices can be chained together on a common bus by using a 50-pin ribbon cable. The last physical device on the bus, logically device 0, terminates the bus.

A second benefit is that of logical, rather than physical, address resolution. This means that any device may be attached to a SCSI controller. The Macintosh has demonstrated the utility of this concept with its SCSI port. Anything from disk drives to tape drives are "plug-and-playable" on the Mac.

A third benefit allows the device controller to be integrated with the SCSI adapter. This can reduce the cost of the overall solution. One example of this is the now discontinued Adaptec 4070 controller, in which the SCSI adapter is implemented with a disk drive interface. The 4070 uses an ST-506/412/RLL disk drive interface. There are even some disk drives that combine the SCSI adapter and disk controller on the disk drive itself. This results in a three-in-one combination. By combining all of these functions, there is no need for separate power supplies for the SCSI adapter and disk drive. Additionally, reliability is improved by having fewer and shorter cables between the SCSI adapter and the disk drive. The price paid for using these embedded SCSI disk drives is a reduction in the overall number of drives supported on the SCSI bus, such as with the Adaptec 4070, where only two drives are allowed per controller. When the SCSI adapter is embedded within the drive, only one drive per SCSI adapter is allowed.

The fourth advantage of SCSI is that of its widespread acceptance. Connecting SCSI devices is fairly straightforward. The interface is a recognized standard and many manufacturers are committed to its implementation and support.

It is important to understand the nature of SCSI. In and of itself, SCSI is not a disk controller. Rather, SCSI provides a data highway from the disk (or other device) controller to other devices, such as a PC. It is very common for SCSI adapters to be merged with a disk controllers, such as one based on the ST-506/412 standard. SCSI's usage, however, is not limited to any one device interface technology. Adaptec manufactures a line of SCSI/ESDI controllers. SCSI/SMD and SCSI/ESMD controllers are also available and are discussed later in this chapter. A final point about SCSI is that many SCSI controllers use bus mastering in the PC AT Bus to maintain high throughput when moving data from the controller to system memory. This technique can conflict with systems with more than 16 MB of system memory installed.

SCSI-II (or SCSI-2)

The SCSI interface has been revised and has a new offspring, SCSI-II. The SCSI-II specification incorporates all the standards of the SCSI (SCSI-I) interface. Thus, all SCSI-I peripherals are compatible with SCSI-II. The SCSI-II specification allows for 8-, 16- or 32-bit data transfers with speeds up to 10MB/sec for the 8-bit interface and up to 40MB/sec for the 32-bit interface.

SCSI-III (or SCSI-3)

Beyond the SCSI-II interface, there is SCSI-III, which is still in proposal. The following are some of the features being considered: Auto Configuration, more than 8 devices per SCSI bus, longer permitted cable lengths, fiber optic attachment, and scatter write/gather read. Remember, at this point, SCSI-3 is still in the proposal stage, being considered by the X3T9.2 ANSI subcommittee.

ESDI

The Enhanced Small Device Interface (ESDI) improves on the ST-506/412 standard. This technology was introduced in 1983 by Maxtor Corporation and is now recognized as a standard. Allowing 10-24Mb/s transfer rates, ESDI was initially conceived of for use in the minicomputer environment.

With ESDI, the job of selecting the clock pulse (as defined under MFM) is moved from the controller and placed in the disk drive itself. This change in the source of the clock timing results in two main advantages. First, the clock pulse closely matches the abilities of the drive. Second, the clock pulse will not degrade, thus providing better resiliency, since it does not have to "ride the bus" between the controller and the disk.

Under an ESDI scheme, all of the signals are transmitted by digital rather than analog means. As a result, the low end of ESDI's transfer rate is 10Mb/s, twice that of ST-506's MFM rate. Like ST-506/412, ESDI was conceived of from the ground up to be a disk drive interface. Although rarely implemented for more than two disk drives, up to seven may be connected to an ESDI controller. Another interesting feature is that ESDI drives can be put into ST-506 compatibility mode. This ST-506 mode is called *step mode*. Pure ESDI mode is called *serial mode*. An ESDI controller can report its configuration and status upon request.

Due to the more streamlined interface controller and the use of digital-only transmissions, ESDI drives and controllers often utilize 1:1 interleave ratios. Throughput is enhanced because the controller can access an entire track during each rotation.

All ESDI drives contain a bad block or defect mapping area. ESDI controllers can use information from this area when low-level formatting the drive. This makes it unnecessary to manually enter bad blocks on the ESDI disk.

To further increase performance, many ESDI drives use a track buffer. When a single sector is requested, its entire track is read into a track buffer. This is done in anticipation of a subsequent request for another sector on that same track. Every read for a sector on a different track results in flushing the previous track from the track buffer so that it can be replaced by the latest track read.

All ESDI controllers currently use 2,7 or 3,9 RLL encoding. It is predicted that in the future ESDI will support further enhancements of RLL, including versions that allow for 53 or more sectors per track (with sector size being 512 bytes). The ESDI standard is an excellent foundation toward achieving this end.

IDE

The Integrated Drive Electronics (IDE) interface is a counterpart to ESDI in that all the mechanisms and electronics that control the drive's operation are built into the drive. As a result, there is no need for a controller card. This puts more processing "goodies" in an IDE drive than in an ESDI drive, which still requires a "type" of controller card. With IDE, simply an 8-bit parallel interface card will do. Each of these interface cards allows for two drives, a slave and a master. IDE is also called the embedded AT interface or AT attachment (ATA).

Remember the ESDI interface is controlled by the Maxtor Corporation. By comparison, IDE is a more open interface, as it was created by Compaq, Western Digital, and Connor. They created it, specifically, to be low-cost. It is completely possible for the ISA.DSK (NetWare/386) driver to operate an IDE drive. However, the ISA.DSK driver bases its assumptions of the drive's capacity on its BIOS table entry. To cure this, Novell provides an IDE-specific driver for all current versions of NetWare.

Since IDE drives offer performance as good as if not better than their ESDI and SCSI counterparts, they are recommended for use in the file server. As a result, ESDI drives are becoming harder and harder to find in servers (except IBM). Even Maxtor has slowed its production of ESDI drives and is now producing more IDE drives than ESDI drives.

Finally, because IDE drives place all drive intelligence at the disk drive, the manufacturers of these drives can enhance them in many ways, such as, increasing the rotation speed, which decreases the problems with rotational latency.

RAID

The Redundant Array of Inexpensive Disks (RAID) is one of the newest disk drive technologies to come to the PC market. Originally produced for the mainframe-set, RAID allows for increased data fault tolerance. Though the performance can be superior to that of other systems, RAID systems are primarily implemented for their data-safety properties.

Unlike any of the other drive technologies discussed, RAID has 6 levels of implementation (0-5). These levels require different hardware configurations. The following section provides a brief description of each RAID level.

0 This level of RAID is similar to NetWare/386 in its ability to link multiple physical disks together to form a virtual volume. This is exactly-what 0 level of RAID does, but it offers no data-safety features. It allows for improved performance but not increased data-safety.

1 This level compares with NetWare's disk mirroring and disk duplexing features. Essentially, one disk is mirrored onto another; if one of the drives fails, the system can continue to operate on the redundant drive.

2 This level of RAID performs very poorly. Essentially, it writes data out to all drives in the array, one bit at a time, (bit interleaving). There is also a checksum drive, or drives, that help to maintain data accessibility in case of a drive failure.

3 Like Level 2, this level is a poor performer. All data is written out to all drives at the bit level, and a single "parity" drive is maintained that allows for the reconstruction of data lost because of drive failure. This is used instead of multiple checksum drives.

4 This level of RAID combines previous levels to achieve byte-level writes (instead of bit level) with a single parity drive. (Byte level writes are called "block data striping." This technique significantly improves write speeds.)

5 This level achieves block data striping and spreads the parity information among all drives. This way, all drives in the array can hold live data, and if one of the drives fails, its complete dataset can be rebuilt from the parity information on all the other drives. Also this level of RAID allows for independent reads and writes to the array's disk drives, which means increased performance over other RAID levels. However, with RAID Level 5 you cannot easily add a drive to the array running counter to NetWare's ability to link multiple drives into a single virtual volume.

However, you can still get higher levels of RAID through NetWare, without the use of RAID hardware. Considering that a drive can be hot-fixed, mirrored, duplexed, and segmented, RAID can do little that cannot be performed with NetWare. To date, the real benefit RAID seems to offer is data-safety in Levels 1-5, with higher performance realized only with Level 5.

Disk Coprocessor Boards

The following discussion of Disk Coprocessor Boards (DCBs) focuses on Novell's DCB. However, the information presented also provides a basis for understanding other manufacturers' DCBs.

Novell's DCB delegates disk requests in a NetWare file server. Normally, the resident CPU (80286, 80386, etc.) in a file server manages all disk requests on its own. This takes processing time and has the effect of slowing the file server. Performance can be enhanced through the use of the DCB. Up to four DCBs can be installed in a file server.

The DCB is a 16-bit board that has an 8MHz Intel 80188 processor, 16K of RAM, EEPROM, firmware, and a SCSI host interface. The DCB/2 (for PS/2 MCA machines) uses an Intel 80186. The Enhanced DCB (or EDCB) also uses an Intel 80186 CPU, however it supports a new feature called SCSI Disconnect. This feature allows the EDCB to request the service of a disk drive and momentarily disconnect from the drive so it can forward (or receive) a request from another disk drive. In other words, SCSI Disconnect allows the EDCB to perform more efficiently than the DCB or DCB/2.

There are two SCSI interfaces, one 50-pin (two vertical rows of 25 pins) internal and one 37-pin or 50-pin external connector located at the rear of the card. The DCB is the SCSI controllers' controller. That is, the DCB can control up to eight SCSI controllers (the DCB/2 and EDCB only support seven) but is not itself a SCSI controller.

When the host CPU has a disk request, it will send it to the DCB. Once the request is sent to the DCB, the host CPU is able to service other requests, such as those that can be performed from the server's RAM. The DCB performs the disk request independently, using its on-board CPU. If the request is a disk write requiring a read-after-write verification, the DCB also performs that task. Once the disk request is complete, the DCB notifies the host CPU. If a read was processed, the host CPU can proceed to pass the data on to the requestor. Similarly, if a write is processed, the verification of the write is passed on. In either case, an error can also be signaled, requiring further action by the CPU.

Overall performance is enhanced because the host CPU is able to service other requests while the DCB is busy handling disk activity. Novell has quoted a strict 34 percent increase in performance over the standard AT-class controller (Western Digital WAx series) disk access interface.

Use of multiple disk drives and DCBs can provide a means of disk mirroring and, more importantly, disk duplexing. Disk mirroring is the process of using two hard disk drives as one. The second drive is used to duplicate the data on the first drive. Disk mirroring is not the same as exact image, since different drives have different bad blocks or unusable areas of the disk. Both disks receive the same updates at the same time. Should one of the disks fail, the other drive (the mirror drive) takes over with no loss of data. Note that upon failure of a drive, the drive will need to be fixed, repaired, or replaced before the file server can be successfully rebooted. This is because the mirroring process is intended to "keep you running" upon the failure of a drive. Once the server is downed, the failed drive must be attended to before the file server can be brought back up.

Duplexing is an extension of mirroring that adds redundancy in the disk channel. Using two disks, two disk channels, and the mirroring option, a file server has what is referred to as duplexed disk drives. Note that the DCB is not necessary for mirroring or duplexing, but its use in mirroring can facilitate disk duplexing. During a read operation, the disk drive that has its heads closest to the requested data will perform the read operation, thus enhancing performance. Novell calls this "split seeks." Duplexing also provides for resiliency in the event of the failure of a DCB, disk controller, or disk. You may opt to have the duplexed disks and controllers (not DCBs) on different power supplies, thereby increasing the amount of protection afforded by duplexing. (More detail on disk mirroring and disk duplexing is provided in the next section.)

Other Controller Technologies

Control Data Corporation developed both the Storage Module Device (SMD) interface, which provides a throughput of up to 14.4Mb/s, and the Enhanced SMD (ESMD), capable of up to 24Mb/s. SMD is generally used with drives having a form factor larger than 5.25", and it is rarely used on PCs. Initially, SMD was used on mainframes, but then became widely used on minicomputers. For instance, 8" Fujitsu Eagle drives can be used with an SMD interface. Because of the availability of better interfaces and the lack of affordable drives, SMD was never widely used in the PC or other microcomputer arena. The previously mentioned drives from Racet make use of the Toshiba ESMD drives.

Plus Development Corporation, manufacturer of the HardCard, developed the Cluster Device Interface (CDI) specification. This specification is used only by Plus Development at this time. The CDI allows for many drives to all use the same disk controller or disk channel. It is a new controller interface that is on the level of SCSI, in that it is not a specific disk interface, but rather, a controller interface. While CDI is supported primarily by Plus Development, more manufacturers are expected to consider adopting this interface.

Disk Information Specific to NetWare

Setting up a NetWare LAN presents the installer with many decisions. Some of these decisions have to do with the various NetWare fault-tolerant options. These options, HOTFIX, disk mirroring, and disk duplexing are discussed in this section.

HOTFIX

Originally introduced in 1986 as part of NetWare 2.0a SFT Level I, every version of NetWare since 2.1 (December, 1987) has included HOTFIX. This feature is used to bypass bad and "weak" blocks on the NetWare disk(s). HOTFIX is a tool with a future. Before going into the details of how HOTFIX works, it is important to understand why there is a need for it in the first place.

Disk drives have improved a lot in a few years, but disk failure is still a legitimate concern. Whether the surface of the platters is metal oxide or nickel-cobalt, it is still a metal and must be applied to the underlying substrate. This application of magnetic material to the disk requires a high level of accuracy. The operating tolerances are very small at this level, and the slightest deviation will render the affected area of the disk unusable. These unusable disk areas are generally noted as hard errors, or errors that are unrecoverable and thus render the affected disk areas useless. These errors are usually listed on the manufacturer's defect map provided with the drive. Most hard errors are the result of a less-than-perfect application of magnetic film to the disk, although a head crash can also create a hard error at the point of impact.

It would be nice if all disk errors were hard errors. Unfortunately, there are also some soft errors that occur. The difference between the two types is that the disk area where a soft error occurs actually has the magnetic media in place. The error occurs because the magnetic media is somewhat shallow and, although the area is still somewhat capable of receiving the information, this information sometimes cannot be read. There is also the potential for a soft area to become even softer with age and use, making it even less capable of retaining data. In a network file server, disk usage is often greater than a typical workstation, thereby lessening the time in which soft errors can appear. It is these soft errors that HOTFIX was intended to handle. Fortunately, HOTFIX also does an admirable job of handling hard errors, which makes it a practical tool for a limited amount of disk testing with COMPSURF. HOTFIX will find any remaining defects on the disk surface.

Now that there is a clear understanding as to why HOTFIX is important, here is how it works.

NetWare keeps a copy of all information to be written to disk in file server RAM. When a WRITE operation occurs, the information that is written is from the copy in file server RAM, and not directly from a workstation or other resource. Once the data is written to the disk, a Read-After-Write verify operation is performed. If the Read-After-Write operation fails, HOTFIX will be invoked and will proceed to map the bad block. If a block is marked bad, it is not used again. Finally, the write is again attempted, but it is sent to one of the blocks in the special redirection area of the disk. The table for the redirection area mapping for NetWare versions previous to 3.x is found on sector 14 of track 0. This redirection area is a pool of disk blocks specifically set aside to handle data from new bad blocks as they are detected. It should be noted that when the redirection area of the disk is filled, HOTFIX will shut down that particular drive. Versions of NetWare before 3.0 will not give any warning before shutting down. NetWare/386 will give a warning message before it shuts down, at which time the server should be brought down and the bad block area increased, if that is indeed the source of the error. For NetWare/386, the OS will dynamically allocate more redirection blocks.

Contrastingly, if an area of the disk goes bad during a READ operation, a read error will result. Recall that the operation invoked is a READ. There was no immediately previous WRITE operation and therefore NetWare has no way of knowing what the data is supposed to look like. The READ error indicates that a disk area (block) has gone bad since the last time it was written to. Below are a few reasons why a READ error might occur:

- The disk is being used with an RLL format and the drive cannot handle the RLL specification.
- The disk was low-level formatted with COMPSURF in a case where the manufacturer's low-level format should have been used.
- The disk and/or controller are having technical difficulty either communicating with one another or in their internal operations.
- The media has decayed since written to. Marginal blocks might be readable immediately after being written, and therefore may not activate HOTFIX.

If a READ error occurs because an area of the disk has gone bad, the data affected is probably unrecoverable. A READ error will usually manifest itself at the workstation as an I/O error. Sometimes, due to its location, the error is bad enough to cause an error at the file server monitor and a broadcast message is issued to all nodes connected to that file server.

Other possible causes of either a READ or WRITE error include:

- Bad RAM (wrong speed, chips with bent legs, dead chips, etc.) in the file server. (See Chapter 12 under GPI and NMI errors heading.)
- Bad disk controller, either on the disk or in the server.
- Random error, such as a power glitch, that does not recur.

Read After Write Verify

A feature operating with HOTFIX is Read After Write Verify. This is a settable option under NetWare/386. The option SET ENABLE DISK READ AFTER WRITE VERIFY = is, by default, always ON. This setting is for all drives on the server, not just one.

Unless you are certain you do not need it, you should leave this option ON. While it is true that most disk controllers do the verification in hardware, it does not mean that the data makes it across the cable correctly. For instance, IDE has no parity checking and SCSI is usually installed with parity disabled.

If you notice that your dirty cache buffer count never goes to zero you might consider turning Read After Write Verify off. However, before doing so, you might investigate your system further to see if there is not some other, more productive change that could be made. To "test the waters," you can temporarily disable Read After Write Verify.

HOTFIX and VREPAIR

There is one final reason for a READ or WRITE error—a disk or disk controller that takes too long to time out. If you are unlucky enough to have a disk READ (or WRITE) failure too severe for HOTFIX to repair, you can use VREPAIR and have a pretty good shot at correcting it. Often, when you get one of these nasty hard disk failures the server will abend with:

```
Abend: AT Disk Time-out call from non-DiskProc process.
Power off and back on to restart

Running Process: MIRROR
```

Note that the indication of running process MIRROR does not imply you are using disk mirroring. Sometimes this error indicates that the disk drive has not been properly low-level formatted. If the disk has been properly low-level formatted, then it may indicate an obnoxious disk error. In any case, when you first run VREPAIR and answer yes to "test for bad blocks?" it will proceed, but when VREPAIR encounters one of these errors it will suffer an abend, quite likely the same abend. Unlike the server operating system, VREPAIR can be "paused" by pressing the pause key.

When the failing disk becomes noisy (most drives will make an audible sound if having trouble), as if it is having trouble reading or writing from/to the disk, press the pause key to stop VREPAIR from timing out. The disk will take somewhere between 30 seconds and 10 minutes until it stops retrying its operation, indicated by the drive's access light going out. For those 30 second errors VREPAIR works fine on its own, and will not time-out. However, on the errors that do take 10 minutes to clear, VREPAIR will time-out unless the pause key is pressed. VREPAIR will stop until another key (i.e., the space bar) is pressed. When VREPAIR is paused, the disk will eventually stop retrying the operation. Then VREPAIR will mark the disk area as "bad" and set up a redirected block to cover the bad block's data (which was inaccessible anyway). This "babying" allows you to use VREPAIR to perform "HOTFIX." Though tedious, if disk space is crucial, it might be the only solution you have.

Disk Mirroring

The discussion has thus far covered the levels of fault tolerance provided by COMPSURF's initial disk integrity check, the Read-After-Write verification, and HOTFIX. NetWare provides two additional levels of fault tolerance: disk mirroring and disk duplexing. The main difference in the two is in the amount of hardware they require.

Disk mirroring, also called disk shadowing, requires two disk drives. One of the disks is the primary disk, or the one that would have been used if disk mirroring had not been implemented. The second disk, which must be at least the same size as the first, is the disk that performs the mirroring operation. If the mirror disk is larger than the primary disk, the mirror disk's extra space will remain unused. All data on the primary disk, other than the redirection table and defective disk area mapping, is replicated on the mirror disk.

Because all disks have different imperfections, the mirror disk is identical only in that the content of the stored data is the same. The actual track and sector location of each piece of data on the mirror disk will most likely differ from those on the primary disk. When disk mirroring is set up, Read-After-Write verify operations and HOTFIX are active on both disks.

If a failure of the primary disk occurs, the mirror disk takes over and no loss of data occurs. When a READ error occurs while disk mirroring is active (see the section on HOTFIX), the requested data will be read from the mirror drive. The disk block that caused the READ error on the primary drive is also marked as bad. To complete the operation, the data from the good block on the mirror disk is written to the primary disk's redirection area. This redundancy of drives combined with HOTFIX provides a mechanism for full recovery from READ/WRITE errors. HOT-

FIX alone handles the write errors and, when combined with disk mirroring, also addresses READ errors.

It should be noted that disk mirroring is merely intended to "keep you going" and is not a final solution to the problem. When a disk fails and the mirror takes over, the failed drive will need to be replaced, repaired, or removed from the system before the server can successfully reboot. The point of disk mirroring is to keep the system running but, once it has stopped, some work is needed to get it running again.

With NetWare/386 it is possible to dynamically mirror and unmirror drives without downing the server, especially if a failed drive is contained in a separate box with a separate power supply. Then it is possible to replace it, bring it back online, and remirror without ever downing the server.

A final note: you should not use dual IDE/ATA drives for disk mirroring. When configured for master and slave, the controller electronics on the master drive controls all read-write operations. If this drive should fail, the slave drive will become unreadable.

Disk Duplexing

Attaining the highest level of fault tolerance available requires having redundant disk controllers as well as redundant disks. This arrangement is called *disk duplexing*, or *channel mirroring*. When installing NetWare, you will note that disk mirroring is a menu option. Disk duplexing can only be activated by implementing a specific layout of the hardware in the disk system, known as redundant disk channels. A disk channel exists for each disk controller card or host interface (such as Novell's DCB) residing in the different slots in the file server bus.

This means that if two Novell DCBs are in the file server, then two disk channels exist. In addition, if two Future Domain controllers, two Western Digital controllers, or two Core controllers reside in the file server, two disk channels exist. Put simply, the difference between disk mirroring and disk duplexing is that the entire disk channel is replicated, including the disk, the disk's controller, and, if applicable, the controller's controller, also called the host interface (such as the DCB). When using host interface connected drive systems, the duplexed disks and controllers may be connected to different power supplies, which will extend the amount of protection afforded by duplexing.

In addition to the fault tolerance gained through duplexing, there are two performance benefits. These are the result of an additional high performance I/O feature of NetWare called split seeks. First, when a read operation is requested and disk duplexing is in effect, NetWare will determine which disk drive is able to respond quickly to the request. This determination is based upon how busy each disk drive is; the one that is less busy receives the request. If the drives are equally busy, the distance from the heads on each drive to the requested data is compared. The drive with its heads closest to the requested data will receive the request.

The second benefit is realized when multiple READ requests are serviced and a true split seek occurs. Note that with NetWare /286, user data-read requests are always for 4K or 8 x 512-byte blocks. With NetWare/386 user read requests can be in increments of 4K up to 64K. And specifically with NetWare 4.0, user requests can be for increments of 512 bytes. If duplexing is in effect, the disks service a mutually distinct set of the read requests received, that is, the read requests are split between the two disks.

As a result, when either type of split seek occurs, disk duplexing doubles the throughput of the disk drive system. As the majority of disk accesses are READ requests, overall performance is significantly improved.

Drive (Volume) Spanning

Unique to NetWare/386 is the ability to combine multiple disk drives to form a single virtual volume. This feature is called drive spanning. Each new physical drive concatenated is assigned a segment number. The original volume disk drive is segment 0. Up to 32 segments may exist for any one volume. And, because NetWare/386 supports up to 64 volumes, there may be up to 2,048 disk drives in use before mirroring.

A beneficial feature of drive spanning is the ability to add more disk drives to a virtual volume "on the fly." As long as there are no more than 32 drives per volume, new drives can be added whenever a volume requires more space. However, if a drive in the span fails, the entire virtual volume is dismounted. Therefore, it is quite important to mirror each disk involved in drive spanning. For best performance, also arrange for disk duplexing to occur. A particular disk drive may not have more than 8 volumes defined.

Directory and File Allocation Tables

Foremost among the remaining fault tolerance features are the redundant directory and File Allocation Tables. Every version of NetWare, has two copies of the directory and FAT tables on each disk. These tables are invaluable in accessing data.

Every time the server is booted, NetWare automatically completes a full self-check of each directory and FAT table. If there are inconsistencies, they will be displayed. (See Chapter 12 for diagnosis of some of these boot time errors.)

Other Facets of Disk Drive Architectures

Although there are many aspects of disk drives in the NetWare environment to be considered, we will focus on just a few. Each disk block is composed of 8 disk sectors. Each sector is 512 bytes, 8 of which make up a 4K disk block. This means that, under NetWare/286 and NetWare/386 through version 3.1x, the smallest available space on a NetWare disk is 4K. With NetWare 4.0, the smallest "sub-allocation" unit is 512 bytes or the size of one sector. For example, a 50 byte batch file will require full use of a 4K area of the disk. Each of these disk blocks resides on a volume that exists inside a *disk partition*, which is an area of the disk dedicated to a specific type of format, such as DOS or NetWare. Within that partition there will be one or more volumes. A volume is a region within a partition that represents a logically separated area of the disk. This separation may be needed for security reasons, or it may be required for NetWare to use the most disk space possible. For instance, older versions of DOS could not have a volume larger that 32MB, however, DOS could use multiple volumes of 32MB (although they were usually not used at the same time unless special add-on utilities were utilized), thereby allowing most of the disk's space to be used. NetWare operates in much the same way, although NetWare's limit is 255MB (for versions previous to NetWare/386).

Normally, it is not possible to change the size of a NetWare volume without destroying all of the data on the volume and, quite likely, adjacent volumes as well. The only exception is that of drives from Racet Computers, Ltd., that contain utilities to allow nondestructive resizing of NetWare disk volumes.

Disk Drive Specifications

As a final note concerning disk drives, PCS publications offers the *Hard Disk Technical Guide*. This guide provides specifications on over 1,450 hard drive models. Not only is it very useful for serious LAN Administrators, Certified NetWare Engineers (CNEs) and Certified NetWare Instructors (CNIs), but it is constantly being updated. Another great reference is Micro House's *Encyclopedia of Hard Drive and Controller Technology.* The addresses and phone numbers for these publishers are listed in appendix E.

CHAPTER 6

Workstations

Almost any PC that can run MS-DOS or IBM PC-DOS can be used as a workstation on a NetWare LAN. In addition, any PC capable of running Windows or OS/2, any Macintosh with at least 512K of RAM, and most machines capable of using NFS, can be used as NetWare workstations. The focus of this chapter is on compatible (MS-DOS and PC-DOS) workstations.

Setting Adapter Configurations

When setting up workstations, it may be necessary to resolve conflicts between the IRQ, I/O, and Base Memory settings of the NIC adapter, and the same settings on other adapters within the PC. These conflicts can be resolved in a manner similar to the approach used for the same problem in file servers, as discussed in Chapter 3.

Configuring the Workstation Software

All computing applications require memory, that is, RAM, at the workstation. A certain amount of RAM usage, often referred to as overhead, is associated with DOS and the LAN shell/requester software. Overhead decreases the total amount of RAM available to run applications on the workstation. This section covers use of DOS and LAN shell/requester RAM. Also included are some tips on conserving RAM and how to regain RAM previously lost to the LAN shell/requester, DOS, and other utilities.

Loading DOS

Starting an IBM PC or compatible begins with booting up DOS. DOS is loaded in layers and is the sum of several parts, as illustrated in Figure 6-1.

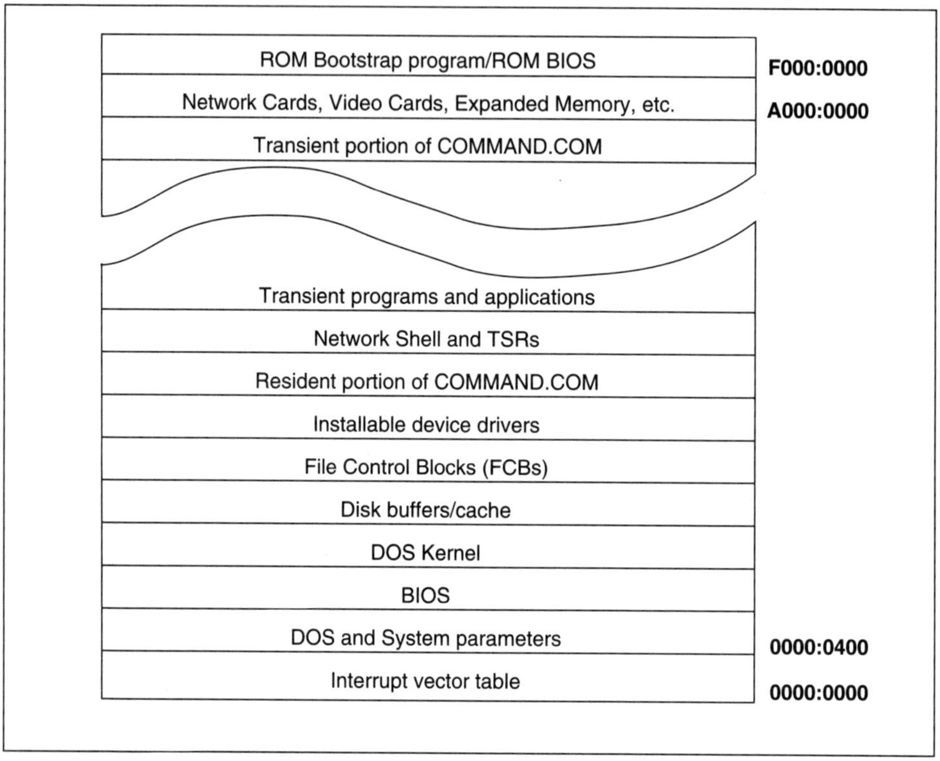

Figure 6-1. Layers of DOS

The BIOS layer (IO.SYS or IBMBIO.COM) is loaded first. The BIOS layer contains software drivers for the display and keyboard (CON), printer (PRN), auxiliary device (AUX), date and time (CLOCK), and the boot disk device.

The next layer to be loaded is the DOS kernel (MSDOS.SYS or IBMDOS.COM). The kernel contains system functions, such as file and record management, memory management, and character device input/output. User-specified device drivers and any other commands stored in CONFIG.SYS are loaded into the system by the kernel. Each of the commands in CONFIG.SYS uses a certain amount of RAM, as described in Figure 6-2.

Command	RAM used (Bytes)
BUFFERS	524-528 per buffer (up to 99 buffers
DEVICE	Varies according to the driver
FILES	68 per file (8-255 file handles)
LASTDRIVE	2112
STACKS	Determined by options

Figure 6-2. CONFIG.SYS command RAM usage

After the kernel is loaded, the command processor (COMMAND.COM) is executed. The command processor provides the interface between the user and DOS, and allows the execution of internal DOS commands such as DIR and COPY.

Loading the NetWare Shell

Prior to running any applications, a user can set other run-time options and otherwise prepare the system for use. This includes such things as setting PATHs, loading Terminate and Stay Resident programs (TSRs), and running a windowing program or menu system. This discussion will focus on loading the NetWare shell, which is comprised of one or more TSRs.

The function of the shell can be divided into two halves. One half deals with the NIC adapter (IPX.COM) and the other half deals with the application/DOS interface (NETx.COM). In NetWare 2.0x, these functions are combined in ANETx.COM.

Starting with version 2.1, the NetWare LAN shell is composed of IPX and NETx (x=2, 3, 4, or 5 depending on the DOS version used). The IPX file contains the NIC adapter's hardware driver and some communication routines. The NETx file contains hardware independent application interface routines. For the same version of NetWare, IPX will vary in the amount of RAM used depending on the NIC adapter used. For instance, under NetWare 2.1, the IPX for a 3Com 3C505 card requires more RAM than the IPX for a Standard Microsystems PC110 card. NETx, on the other hand, remains approximately the same size for all types of NIC adapters. Both IPX and NETx support run-time configuration options, detailed in the following section. (Note that both ANETx and NETx return an ERRORLEVEL 3 if an attempt is made to load them when they are already loaded.)

NetWare Shell Configuration

Just as RAM usage by DOS can be adjusted through entries in CONFIG.SYS, RAM usage by the NetWare shell can be adjusted using entries in SHELL.CFG. All configuration options for IPX and NETx are placed in a file called SHELL.CFG. The SHELL.CFG file needs to be in the same directory from which IPX and NETx are loaded. If a SHELL.CFG is not in that directory, a set of default values will be used.

In the IPX portion of the shell:

Option	Default Value	RAM used by each option(Bytes)	Total RAM consumed with defaults (Bytes)
IPX SOCKETS	20	8	160
SPX CONNECTIONS	15	56	840

In the NETx portion of the shell:

Option	Default Value	RAM used by each option(Bytes)	Total RAM consumed with defaults (Bytes)
CACHE BUFFERS	5	512	2560
FILE HANDLES	40	4	160
PRINT HEADER	64 bytes	user configurable	
PRINT TAIL	16 bytes	user configurable	

Note that CACHE BUFFERS only have an effect on sequential (versus random) reading of non-shared files. Generally, CACHE BUFFERS can be configured with 0 buffers with no loss of performance.

Figure 6-3. SHELL.CFG/NET.CFG option RAM usage

Several SHELL.CFG options are listed in Figure 6-3. Only the ones that affect RAM usage are covered here. See Appendix B of the NetWare *Supervisor Reference* (2.1x) for complete information about SHELL.CFG options.

Search Path Mode Selection

NetWare 2.1x offers two methods for setting search modes. The first method is implemented in the shell; the second method is implemented in the file server. Setting the search modes within the shell involves setting a default workstation search mode that affects all open requests made by that station. Setting the search mode in the file server involves flagging individual programs (files) with their own search modes. This affects each open request made, but does not affect requests from other open programs. The per-program search mode takes precedence over the workstation search mode. The combination of these two modes allows for a great deal of flexibility.

Since the per-program search mode is implemented in the file server, it is not possible to work in this mode without changing the server OS (NET$OS). Consequently, the 2.01-4 (for NetWare 2.0x) shell only works in the workstation search mode.

The workstation search mode for the 2.1x shell is specified in the shell configuration file (SHELL.CFG). This allows the end user to select a workstation search mode. The 2.01-4 shell requires a DEBUG patch to change workstation search modes.

The GENned 2.01-4 shell (ANETx.COM) can be patched at location CS:16A. This byte initially contains a 1, the default mode. Figure 6-4 is a list of the available search modes.

Mode	Description
1	Search if request presents FILENAME (NO PATH). This is the default mode. It is also the mode that has existed in all previous versions.
2	Turn searching off.
3	Search if request presents FILENAME (NO PATH) with READONLY access (in other words, DO NOT search if a WRITE could occur).
5	ALWAYS search, whether PATH is specified or not.
7	ALWAYS search, whether PATH is specified or not IF request prescribes READONLY access.

Note: Modes 4 and 6 do not exist.

Figure 6-4. Available search modes

Figure 6-5 contains the offset, size, and default values of the configurable shell parameters.

Offset	Size	Default	Name
0x158	BYTE	on, 1	Auto Reopen Mode
0x159	BYTE	on, 1	End of Job Mode
0x15A	BYTE	-	Use Internal Error Handler
0x15B	BYTE	on, 1	Broadcast Timer Check Flag
0x15C	WORD	-	Pointer to Header Data
0x15E	WORD	-	Pointer to Current PSP
0x160	BYTE	off, 0	No Question Collapse Flag
0x161	BYTE	off, 0	Hold Files Open Flag
0x162	BYTE	0	Lock Loop Max
0x163	BYTE	1	Lock Delay Count
0x164	WORD	0	Lock Default Delay
0x166	BYTE	on, 1	Share Handles with Child Process
0x167	BYTE	40 decimal	Maximum File Handles
0x168	BYTE	5	Number of Cache Blocks
0x169	BYTE	no, 0	Ignore Printer Defaults

Note: all offsets in hex

Figure 6-5. Configurable shell parameters for all ANETx and NETx

The following section is a description of some of the parameters noted in Figure 6-5.

End of Job Mode. This byte determines whether the EOJ will also close all files, locks, semaphores, etc., used by that program. When a program terminates, an EOJ is generated which, by default, causes these cleanup actions to take place. This mode can be manipulated with the EOJON and EOJOFF utilities.

Hold Files Open Flag. This can be used to force the shell to hold open any files that a program has opened and later tried to close. By default, the shell allows a program to close its files. The files will be closed on program exit. This parameter can be manipulated with the HOLDON and HOLDOFF utilities.

Lock Loop Max, Lock Delay Count, and Lock Default Delay. These bytes correspond to the parameters passed to a DOS IOCTL 0x44 0x0B call to control lock retries and delays.

Share Handles with Child Processes. This option sets whether child processes inherit the same file handle that the parent process had or a copy of the file handle. If this option is on, the child process will inherit the same file handle that the parent process had. If it is off, a new file handle will be created for the child process. The default is to allow the child process to inherit the parent's handles.

Cache Blocks. This byte determines (at load time of ANETx or NETx) the number of 512 byte buffers that the shell will use for local caching of files opened nonshareable with the deny write option. Note that the manner in which the file is flagged does not matter with local caching, how the file is opened determines if the caching will be on or off.

Figure 6-6 provides printer defaults for versions of NetWare using the ANETx shell, prior to version 2.01.

Figure 6-7 provides printer defaults for versions of NetWare using the ANETx shell from version 2.01 and later.

Offset	Size	Default	Name
0x16A	BYTE	0xA0	Print Flags = Print banner, delete file after printing
0x16B	BYTE	8	Tab Expansion
0x16C	BYTE	0	Network Printer Number
0x16D	BYTE	1	Number of Copies
0x16E	BYTE	0	Form Type
0x16F	BYTE	-	unused
0x170	BYTE[14]	none,0	Banner Name
0x17E	BYTE	LPT1:, 0	Local Printer Number
0x17F	WORD	disabled, 0	Printer Time Out Value
0x181	WORD	no, 0	No Auto Endspool on Close
0x183	BYTE[65]		Printer Setup String

Note: all offsets in hex

Figure 6-6. Printer defaults for ANETx (previous to v2.01 of the shell)

Offset	Size	Default	Name
0x16A	BYTE	1	Search Mode
0x16C	BYTE	0xA0	Print Flags = print banner, delete file after printing
0x16D	BYTE	8	Tab Expansion
0x16E	BYTE	0	Network Printer Number
0x16F	BYTE	1	Number of Copies
0x170	BYTE	0	Form Type
0x171	BYTE	-	unused
0x172	BYTE[14]	none,0	Banner Name
0x180	BYTE	LPT1:,0	Local Printer Number
0x181	WORD	disabled,0	Printer Time Out Value
0x183	WORD	no, 0	No Auto Endspool on Close
0x185	BYTE[65]		Printer Setup String

Note: all offsets in hex

Figure 6-7. Printer defaults for ANETx (v2.01 and later of the shell)

Figure 6-8 provides the printer defaults for versions of NetWare using the NETx shell.

Figure 6-9 shows the printer structure defaults for versions of NetWare using the NETx shell.

Tips on Conserving Memory

Each successive version of DOS provides more functionality and consumes more RAM than its predecessor. In order to support these new features, the NetWare shell also requires more RAM. As all versions of DOS are limited to supporting 640K of base RAM, each new version of DOS compounds the problems associated with insufficient memory. This necessitates the search for ways to conserve RAM. Memory can be saved in a number of different ways.

- Use an older version of DOS. In many cases, version 3.1 of DOS will suffice.
- Use entries in the CONFIG.SYS file that minimize the amount of RAM used by DOS. For instance, The BUFFERS= command is practically useless in the NetWare environment unless applications are being run from a local hard disk. Use of LASTDRIVE= can also be avoided in many circumstances. DEVICE=ANSI.SYS may be unnecessary, in which case it can be removed.

- Alter entries in SHELL.CFG. For instance, CACHE BUFFERS= is rarely beneficial, yet the default uses 2.5K of RAM. Fewer buffers can be specified using SHELL.CFG.
- Use specialized memory managers such as Quarterdeck Office Systems' QEMM 386 and Qualitas' 386-To-The-Max to utilize normally empty RAM areas that exist between the addresses of 640K to 960K, sometimes called high RAM. TSR programs, such as the NetWare shell's IPX and NETx, fit quite nicely into high RAM with no reduction in performance. Note, however, that these memory managers work only with PCs running the Intel 80386 processor, owing to the 386's unique ability to dynamically map blocks of memory.

Offset	Size	Default	Name
0x16A	BYTE	1	Search Mode
0x16F	WORD	-	OFFSET of LPT1 printer structure
		-	OFFSET of LPT2 printer structure
0x173	WORD	-	OFFSET of LPT3 printer structure

Note: all offsets in hex

Figure 6-8. Printer defaults for NETx

Offset	Size	Default	Name
0x00	BYTE	0	Status
0x01	BYTE	-	Flags
0x02	BYTE	8	Tab Size (0-18)
0x03	BYTE	0	Server Printer (0-4)
0x04	BYTE	1	Number of Copies
0x05	BYTE	0	Form Type
0x06	BYTE	-	RESERVED
0x07	BYTE[13]	0	Banner Name (ASCIIZ)
0x14	BYTE	0	RESERVED
0x15	BYTE	0	LPT number (0-2 for LPT1 - LPT3)
0x16	WORD	0	Flush Capture Timeout Count
0x18	BYTE	0	Flush Capture on Device Close
0x19	WORD	-	Maximum characters per line
0x1B	WORD	-	Maximum lines per page
0x1D	BYTE[13]	0	Form Name (ASCIIZ)
0x2A	BYTE	0	LPT Capture Flag; 0=clr, 0xFF=set 0x2B
BYTE	0		File Capture Flag; 0=clr, 0xFF=set
0x2C	BYTE	0	Time Out Flag; 0=clr, 0xFF=set
0x2D	DWORD	-	OFFSET:SEGMENT pointer to Printer Setup Buffer
0x31	DWORD	-	OFFSET:SEGMENT pointer to Printer Reset Buffer
0x35	BYTE	-	Connection number of queueing server
0x36	BYTE	0	Capture in process; 0=clr, 0xFF=set
0x37	BYTE	0	Print Queue Flag; 0=clr, 0xFF=set
0x38	BYTE	0	Print Job Valid; 0=clr, 0xFF=set
0x39	DWORD	-	Print Queue ID
0x3D	WORD	-	Print Job Number (1-999)
0x3F through 0x64			RESERVED

Table Size = 101 (0x65) bytes

Note: all offsets in hex

Figure 6-9. Printer structures for NETx

If there is a need to load the NetWare shell (or other TSR) into high RAM on non-80386 workstations, three options exist. For 808x and 80286 PCs, the RYBS Electronics Inc.'s HiCard will work, as will DESQview's QRAM. For 286 PCs only, the All Charge Card from All Computers does the trick. Both of these solutions involve a card that is placed in the PC's bus. The third solution, which can be used with both 80286 and 80386 machines, is LANspace from LAN Systems, Inc. On machines with at least 1MB of RAM, 56K of high RAM can be used to load the NetWare shell.

Generally speaking, the 2.0x ANETx shell is larger than either the 2.1x IPX or NETx files. Whether the ANETx can be moved to high RAM will depend on the actual size of the shell and the amount of available high RAM space. Shell version 3.01 can have its NETx placed into expanded or extended memory.

Removing the Shell

Normally, once the NetWare shell is loaded, the only way to remove it from RAM is to reboot the PC. However, it is possible to remove the NetWare shell from RAM without rebooting the PC by using a special third-party utility. TurboPower Software has altered its public domain utilities, MARK and RELEASE, to allow them to delete difficult-to-remove TSRs. The NetWare shell, as well as DOS's SHARE, MODE, and PRINT all fall into this category. The new utilities, MARKNET and RELNET, were developed solely to remove the NetWare shell. MARKNET stores its information in a file and uses only 144 bytes of RAM as a memory marker. Both MARKNET and RELNET are available on the NetWire forum on CompuServe in the file TSRCOM.ZIP. Also, LANspace has the ability to load and unload the shells. And version 3.01 of the shell can be unloaded from memory via the –u command line switch. See the 3.01 header in the forthcoming Shell Usage section for more information on version 3.01 of the shell.

DOS/NetWare Search Paths

The DOS environment variable PATH can be defined with DOS commands by using one of two different techniques. The correct way to set the PATH variable is to use the PATH= command. Although SET PATH= can also be used to define the PATH, this usage is incorrect. DOS recognizes PATH as an environment variable and will do a little clean-up work on the specified PATH. One thing DOS does is to convert the PATH to all uppercase characters. If SET PATH= is used, DOS does not convert the indicated string. The major reason to use PATH= rather than the SET PATH= command is that some NetWare commands (e.g., MAP) do not accept lowercase letters in the PATH string. If lowercase letters are found for drive letter designations, MAP will remove them from the PATH. It is simple to prevent this by using PATH= when initially defining the PATH. Once on the network, use the MAP command (NPATH for older NetWare versions).

Inserting a Path

The PATH command is most commonly used to create a search path that includes local drives/directories. If local drives are specified in the PATH (usually done at boot time) then it is likely that the user will want them to remain in the PATH after login. This is accomplished by using the MAP INSERT command for each search path defined in a login script, .BAT file, or DOS command line when directly running MAP. By using the MAP INSERT command when mapping search drives, NetWare will *not* destroy the existing path to local drives. Rather, the new search paths will be inserted into the current path. The MAP INSERT command makes it possible to login and logout of the network multiple times without ever losing the local path definitions. NetWare does remove all network drive mappings and the PATH references when the user logs out. However, the MAP INSERT command is available only on version 2.x and later networks. Check the LOGIN and MAP program file dates for version 2.0a. If they are dated 5/86 or later they will support MAP INSERT. If the date shown is earlier, both of these files are available on Novell's NetWire forum on CompuServe. These files are LOGINA.ARC and MAP20A.ARC.

Shell Usage

Because changes occur in NIC adapter hardware and in DOS, Novell has consistently updated its shells to reflect these changes. If working with NetWare version 2.0x, use the version 2.01-4 of the ANET3 shell (unless you are using DOS/2.x, in which case use ANET2). There are many reasons for using 2.01-4, including the fact that it is the last and most stable 2.0x shell released by Novell.

Version 2.0x Shell Revisions

NetWare 2.0x provides support for DOS versions up to 3.3. The shell is linked into a single file, either ANET2.COM or ANET3.COM, depending on the DOS version in use.

To determine the version of the NetWare shell in use, type the file name (ANET2 or ANET3) followed by a space and the letter "I," which stands for inquire shell version and type. Note, however, that the NetBIOS shell does not respond to the "I" command line option.

The following is a list of shell revisions for version 2.0x of NetWare.

2.0b, also known as 2.0a. This shell resolved problems caused by the Microsoft "C" Compiler hanging from spawning a process—under DOS 2.x, printing always sent to printer 0 regardless of the printer that was selected—and ARCNET workstations intermittently hanging when large packets are received.

2.0a++, also known as 2.0c. This revision includes support for function A000h—"Get Installed State of SHARE." NetWare does not need SHARE to share network files since this shell can perform local caching of non-shareable files. Only files opened with the FCB method with sequential reads will take advantage of the local caching feature. This feature is essentially a waste of memory, at 512 bytes a buffer, but it can improve performance for applications that do interspersed sequential reads (such as compilers and sort routines).

2.01. This shell adds support for IBM PC-DOS 3.3. There is also a new driver to support the IBM PC Network II and II/A cards (the existing NetWare Token Ring drivers work with the new IBM Token-Ring Adapter/A).

2.01-2, also known as the 33 Shell. This revision adds additional support for DOS 3.3. It is included in the PS/2 version of NetWare. The following new DOS calls are supported with the 2.01-2 shell:

> Handle Generic IOCTL (Code page switching)–44h(0Dh)
> Get Extended Country Information–65h
> Get/Set Global Code Page–66h
> Set Handle Count–67h

The above calls are all local and are directly passed by the Shell to DOS for processing. There is also a non-local new DOS 3.3 call—Commit File–68h. Commit File flushes any local buffering of data and has the same effect as closing a file and then reopening it. The data is flushed from the local workstation to the file server. When the data has been flushed to the server, it is not automatically flushed to the file server's disks, but is queued for flushing according to NetWare's caching and elevator-seeking schemes. Note that, in general, data written from the workstation to the file server is in the server's memory for no longer than three seconds before it is written to disk.

IPX communication is now accomplished via a FAR CALL. IPX previously used interrupt 7Ah, but this conflicted with some applications, such as the IBM 3270 emulation program. To determine the call address to IPX, perform an interrupt 2Fh with AX=7A00h. The address is returned in ES:DI. In order to support current IPX applications, interrupt 7Ah is still supported by IPX. IPX applications using interrupt 7Ah instead of the FAR CALL will cease to function only when other applications that take over interrupt 7Ah are run in the same workstation.

2.01-4. This shell supports Windows/386 2.x and adds new search modes. Microsoft Corporation and Compaq Computer Corporation worked very closely with NetWare engineers to ensure that Windows/386 would be compatible with NetWare. Windows/386 is very tightly integrated with DOS, to the point that it affects and manipulates some of DOS's internal data structures. Since the NetWare Workstation Shell does much of the same work as DOS, including emulating it in many areas, it was critical that Windows/386 also be able to find and manipulate the NetWare shell's internal data structures. Novell added a new function call to specifically allow Windows/386 to locate some internal structures. Windows/386 actually makes this call when it is installed on top of the shell. This enables it to present a consistent environment, whether the user is in a stand-alone DOS environment or in a network environment. Note that the aforementioned call will only have meaning to Windows-specific applications. It will not be of any benefit to other types of applications.

This shell also provides new search path modes. Originally, these search path modes were intended for introduction in version 2.1. Since Novell was bringing a new shell to market for Windows/386, and because the search modes solved some problems such as overlays with Microsoft C, Novell decided to include them in this shell.

Version 3.x Shell Revisions

3.01. In 1990, Novell released a version of their network shell, and marked the beginning of two new types of shell—shells that will load into expanded and extended memory. The regular shell that loads into DOS memory is also included. The new shells are NET3 and NET4 (note that the IPX (IPX.COM) file does not need to change to use these new shells). These shells work with NetWare 2.1 through NetWare/386, and offer many new features.

3.02. In the spring of 1991, NetWare released a new version of the shell. It offers incremental updates over earlier versions..

New options are placed in the SHELL.CFG file. They include:

- ALL SERVERS
- MAX CUR DIR LENGTH
- MAX PATH LENGTH
- SET STATION TIME
- SPECIAL UPPERCASE
- PREFERRED SERVER
- SHOW DOTS
- ENTRY STACK SIZE (Expanded Memory Shell version only)

With the 3.02 release of the NETx shells:

- DOS NAME
- ENVIRONMENT PAD

ALL SERVERS. Settings for this option include ON and OFF. When ON (which has been the default for all previous versions of the shell), all currently attached (i.e. logged into) servers are sent an End Of Task indicator whenever a task completes. A task completing might be signalled when an application is exited. When turned OFF, only the file servers that have been interacted with will have an End Of Task sent to them. The purpose of turning this option OFF is to reduce the amount of network traffic incurred by the completion of a task. The default is OFF.

MAX CUR DIR LENGTH. Short for Maximum Current Directory Length, this option is configurable from 64 to 255 bytes. This option has been made available so that absolute DOS compliance is possible. Specifically, the DOS call "Get Current Directory" (where AH=0x47) returns a maximum of 64 bytes. Up to 128 bytes were returned with previous versions of the NetWare shell. The default is 64 bytes.

MAX PATH LENGTH. Short for Maximum Path Length, this option allows valid path names to be from 64 to 255 bytes. This option differs from the Max Cur Dir Length in that this option can be used to block the creation of a directory path that is too long. The path name length is the sum of the volume name and directory name lengths. Notice that the file server name and filename are not calculated as part of the Maximum Path Length. The default is 255 bytes.

SET STATION TIME. Settings for this option include ON and OFF. When ON the shell loads the attached file server's current time into the local workstation's clock. This action acts to synchronize the local workstation's time with that of the attached file server. However this is not always desirable. Hence, setting this option OFF turns off the synchronization and the local workstation retains its current time. The default is ON.

SPECIAL UPPERCASE. Settings here include ON and OFF. When ON the shell will translate path name ASCII characters above 127. When ON, this option acts as every other shell version would. When OFF, the shell passes ASCII characters above 127 to the local version of DOS and allows it to determine how to handle the characters. The default is OFF.

PREFERRED SERVER. Use of this option will allow attachment, if possible, to a specified file server. When a file server name is passed to this option, the shell will attempt (up to five times) to connect to that file server first. If no connection can be made, whether the server is out of connections or is nonexistent, an attempt to attach to another server will be made.

SHOW DOTS. SHOW DOTS is not truly unique to shell version 3.01, but it is worth a mention. When set to ON the directory entries "." and ".." will appear when a DIR is performed on a network drive. With versions previous to version 3.0, this was not an option—the dot and dot-dot entries were never shown. The default is OFF.

Note that SHOW DOTS turns on the "." and ".." entries for those applications and utilities using the DOS FILE HANDLE method of directory scanning. For instance, if you type the command DIR (yes, the ubiquitous DOS command) at a DOS prompt you will NOT see the "." and ".." entries on network drives. At first this can be confusing, until you realize that the DIR command operates as it did with DOS 1.0. Under that release of DOS, the DIR command used File Control Blocks (FCBs) rather than file handles to scan the directory. In short, the SHOW DOTS command works only with file handle calls, not FCB calls.

IMPORTANT NOTE: If you use the utility BINDFIX.EXE make sure that it is dated at least 2-12-91 or is at least version 3.52. If you use a lesser version and you have SHOW DOTS=ON you run the EXTREME RISK of COMPLETELY erasing your network disk drives' data. This is especially true if you are logged in with SUPERVISOR equivalent rights.

ENTRY STACK SIZE. Unique to the EMS (expanded memory) shell, this option can be set from 5 to 40 stacks. These stacks are used to store expanded memory page mappings. Whenever the shell is busy and it receives additional requests it must save these mappings. Depending on the applications used, more stacks may be necessary, only "playing" with the number of stacks will provide knowledge of how many stacks will be needed. The default number of stacks is 10.

DOS NAME. This parameter (five characters or fewer) allows a user to set the OS name used in the shell to something other than the default of MSDOS. The %OS variable in the login script uses this variable. For instance, you could use %OS when mapping a search drive to the network DOS directory. Default is MSDOS.

ENVIRONMENT PAD. This parameter defines the number of bytes which will be added to a program's environment space before beginning execution of the program. Increasing this parameter will allow NetWare utilities to update the path environment variable of the current environment when adding search drives. Previously, NetWare utilities did not attempt to update the current environment because of the lack of adequate space for the update.

In addition to new options for SHELL.CFG, there are also new command line parameters. These parameters include: I, U, and PS.

- I Short for Information, this option will show the shell's version, type, and copyright information. This option is available in all versions of the shell subsequent to and including version 2.0. This option does not load the shell.
- U Short for Unload, this option allows the shell to be unloaded from memory. To be removed from memory, the shell must be the last in memory, otherwise an error message will be issued.
- PS Short for Preferred Server, this option requires a server name (PS=FSName). This option acts just as the PREFERRED SERVER option in SHELL.CFG. Note that use of this option overrides the server selected by the PREFERRED SERVER option in SHELL.CFG.

These new shells have different memory requirements than previous versions. The "normal" version requires approximately 41-42K. The expanded memory version requires 7K in "normal" memory and one 64K EMS 4.0 Page Frame. The extended memory version requires 6K in "normal" memory and 64K in extended memory. Also these shells offer the ability to work with Microsoft's Windows 3.0. The file UPILDA.386 is necessary when using IRQ2. VPICDA.386 is included with the v3.01 shell kit and is installed with the INSTALL program, also part of the kit.

3.10. A month after the release of the 3.02 shell, the 3.10 shell was released. This version of the shell was the first to work with DOS 5.0.

3.21. Immediately thereafter, the 3.21 shell release was introduced in July, 1991. This shell marked the end of the shell suffixes of 3, 4, and 5 which referred to the version of DOS for which they were intended. The new "X" suffix replaced them and was used to indicate that the shell could be loaded on any DOS version 3 through 5.

However, the 3.21 shell release brought more than the introduction of the generic X suffix. It also fixed many previous problems and added a few new features.

Some of these new features included the /C=NET.CFG option which allows for the name of the configuration file to be determined at load time. Also the /F option was introduced to allow the shell to be unloaded once loaded high. And finally, support for international date and time formats was introduced.

3.22. Close on the heels of version 3.11, the 3.22 shell was released at the end of July 1991. Its major contribution was to correct a bug that prevented remote booting with DOS 5.0.

3.26. After much preparation, the 3.26 shell was released in February 1992. Its most significant addition was Burst Mode technology, which allows the transfer of multiple packets without reply. More on Burst Mode or Packet Burst later in this chapter.

Version 3.26 fixed several problems. It got rid of trash that appeared on the screen when running CAPTURE, and it allowed queue names to be directly identified. In earlier versions, COMSPEC would point at a network, rather than local drive when unloading the shell. Version 3.26 fixed this problem so that COMSPEC once again pointed at a local drive.

The version 3.26 shell also fixed a critical problem that had caused "Network Errors" to occur when Preferred Server was used when loading the shell and that server had a maximum packet size smaller than the workstation and any intervening servers.

Finally, the 3.26 shell added a couple of new options for SHELL.CFG, or more correctly, NET.CFG:

- SEARCH DIR FIRST
- NCP TIMEOUT

SEARCH DIR FIRST. This option, which can be =ON or =OFF, determines whether files or directories are identified first in a directory search that uses file handles. The default is OFF, which indicates that files are to be returned first. If the option is set to ON, directories are returned first, then files. Once again, this option is only reflected by directory handle searches, not FCB searches. Remember that the DOS command DIR uses FCBs. Thus, the results of this option will only be apparent in most file manager utilities, particularly Windows' File Managers.

NCP TIMEOUT. This option, which has many suboptions, allows for the customization of the shell's time-out period. Note that when a time-out occurs, a "Network Error..." typically results.

The first suboption is FLAG, as in NCP TIMEOUT FLAG=, and can be ON or OFF(default). Specifying the OFF option is the same as not specifying it at all. Also, specifying the ON option and not the following two suboptions is the same as not specifying it at all. However, in order for the two following suboptions to function, the NCP TIMEOUT FLAG=ON must be set.

The second suboption is BASE, as in NCP TIMEOUT BASE=, and can be 1 to 255. The default is 10. Increasing BASE by 1 increases the time-out by 1 timer tick (~18.2 ticks per second).

BASE is then multiplied against the next suboption, MULTIPLIER, as in NCP TIMEOUT MULTIPLIER. This third option can have a value between 1 and 255 and has a default of 4. The BASE * MULTIPLIER equals the shell's NCP TIMEOUT value and the result of that calculation should not exceed 255.

The maximum time-out that can be defined is 255 timer ticks, which is about 14 seconds. The default of 40 timer ticks is just over 2 seconds. By setting the value too low, a large number of "Network Errors" will probably occur. By setting the value too high, the workstation's overall performance will not be affected until there is a real "Network Error." When this occurs, it will take longer for this message to be communicated to the user while the shell waits to "time-out."

Most users will probably not need to use the NCP TIMEOUT option.

3.30. In October 1992, the version 3.30 shell was produced. It was never officially released, but many people received copies through indirect channels, for instance, the Novell developer program. It included multiple fixes and enhancements and even the removal of an enhancement. Overall this was the first shell to offer support for SFT III and NetWare 4.0, but not Directory Services (a NetWare 4.0 option).

Version 3.30 fixed the ability to unload the shell when it was loaded into a DOS Upper Memory Block (UMB). It also fixed a memory allocation error that occurred whenever the ENVIRONMENT PAD option was set to 10 or less, and a "hang" after receiving a broadcast message (i.e., SEND message) when also using IPX-ODI. And, finally, it fixed a "hang" that randomly occurred because of internal shell stack handling.

Note that the SPECIAL UPPERCASE option of SHELL.CFG/NET.CFG introduced by the 3.02 shell was removed. This is largely due to the addition of the ability to handle double-byte and upper ASCII characters in directory and filenames.

Continuing on the internationalization track, the 3.30 shell became "language enabled" and the use of the NETX.MSG file became an option. If loaded in the same directory as NETX (during its initialization), the NETX.MSG file is loaded. The NETX.MSG file is loaded whenever the user desires to send NETX's messages in a language other than English.

Another international feature is employed when the shell receives a broadcast message in a double-byte form. It will show the first half and then, when the user presses CTRL-ENTER, the second half will be shown. This is true only for double-byte messages, not regular (English) messages.

When the shell displays a broadcast message, it will place it at the "true" bottom of the screen rather than line 25. That is, if your screen is in 43 or 50 line mode, the broadcast message will be displayed on the 43rd or 50th line.

The files NETX and BNETX are now EXE files in 3.30. If they are loaded into a directory containing these files with the COM extension, those with the COM extension must be renamed or they will conflict with the loading of the new shells with the EXE extension.

At the packet level, support for Large Internet Packet (LIP) was introduced. For more on the specifics of LIP, refer to the product's documentation. Additionally, support for IPX checksumming on IEEE 802.2 frames was introduced.

A new order of configuration file searching was defined by the 3.30 shell release:

1. The current working directory is searched first looking for NET.CFG.
2. The directory where the LSL was loaded is searched.
3. The current working directory at the time the LSL was loaded is searched.
4. If NET.CFG is still not locatable, the search continues by scanning for a SHELL.CFG file in the current working directory.

3.31. Released in November 1992, the 3.31 shell is the first to offer the NCP Packet Signature option. This shell release also fixes a few problems and has many new features.

The 3.31 shell will now load properly with DR DOS 6.0. Also, a "group" fix for Burst Mode operations was applied. Improving on the last version, it fixes a memory allocation error, an incomplete write problem, and a timing problem which usually manifested itself as a hang under Windows.

Enhancements include the following new NET.CFG options:

- SIGNATURE LEVEL
- LI FRAME MAX
- PB FRAME MAX

SIGNATURE LEVEL. This option, which can be set to 0 through 3, can be used to enhance request security by authenticating the requester. The values 0 through 3 have the following meanings:

0. Packets are not signed (authenticated).
1. Packets are signed only if the server requests it (DEFAULT).
2. Packets are signed if the server is capable of signing.
3. Packets are always signed. If the server is not capable of signing, then the workstation will not be able to interact with the server.

LI FRAME MAX. This option, which can be set from 512 to 16384, is used to determine the maximum frame size when using Large Internet Packet (LIP). The default is 8192 or 8 KB. This value is in bytes. Ordinarily you do not use this option unless you are directed to do so by documentation.

PB FRAME MAX. This option, which can be set from 576 to 8256, is used to determine the maximum frame size possible when using Burst Mode (Packet Burst). The default is 2112. This value is in bytes. As with the LI FRAME MAX option, you do not normally use this option unless you are directed to do so.

Version 1.0 DOS REQUESTER

NetWare 4.0 delivers the new DOS requester, which replaces the concept of the DOS shell. Note that the DOS requester will work with non-4.0 NetWare servers. Also note that the the DOS shell will work with NetWare 4.0, except Directory Services. As with the shell, the requester offers many NET.CFG options, as shown in Figure 6.10.

Parameter	Default	Min	Max	VLM Module affected
USE DEFAULTS	ON	—	—	VLM.EXE
VLM =<path><vlm>	—	—	50VLMs	VLM.EXE
VLM STACK SWITCH	OFF	—		VLM.EXE
CONNECTIONS	8	2	50	CONN.VLM and FIO.VLM
AVERAGE NAME LENGTH	48	2	48	CONN.VLM
MAX TASKS	31	5	254	CONN.VLM
LOAD LOW CONN	ON	—	—	CONN.VLM
LOAD LOW IPXNCP	ON	—	—	IPXNCP.VLM
CHECKSUM	1	0	3	IPXNCP.VLM and NWP.VLM
0=disabled				
1=enable but not preferred				
2=enabled and preferred				
3=enabled and required				
LARGE INTERNET PACKETS	ON	—	—	IPXNCP.VLM
HANDLE NET ERRORS	ON	—	—	IPXNCP.VLM
PREFERRED TREE = <tree name>		—	—	NDS.VLM
NAME CONTEXT = "<name context>" quotes are required)		—		NDS.VLM
PREFERRED SERVER = <server name>		—	—	BIND.VLM
MESSAGE LEVEL	1	0	4	NWP.VLM
0=always display all errors				
1=display warning type messages				
2=display the program load message				
3=display configuration information				
4=display diagnostic information				

Figure 6-10. NET.CFG options for NetWare DOS requester

The single significant difference between the shell and the requester is how each "fits" into the workstation's chain of command. As shown in Figure 6-11, the shell "sits ahead" of DOS and receives all commands, parsing out and sending the DOS requests to it and keeping the NetWare-specific commands to itself so that DOS never sees NetWare's commands. The requester "sits behind" DOS and only receives commands which DOS has filtered down to it.

SIGNATURE LEVEL	1	0	3	NWP.VLM
(Same as the shell's NCP Packet Signature option)				
CACHE BUFFERS	0	0	64	FIO.VLM
BUFFER SIZE	512	64	4096	FIO.VLM
CACHE WRITES	ON	OFF	ON	FIO.VLM
TRUE COMMIT	OFF	OFF	ON	FIO.VLM
PB BUFFERS	3	0	3	FIO.VLM
PRINTER HEADER	64	0	1024	PRINT.VLM
PRINT TAIL	16	0	1024	PRINT.VLM
LOCAL PRINTERS	0	0	4	PRINT.VLM
PRINT BUFFER SIZE	64	0	256	PRINT.VLM
NETWORK PRINTERS	3	0	9	PRINT.VLM
(if 0, PRINT.VLM will not load)				
FIRST NETWORK DRIVE <none>		A	Z	GENERAL.VLM
SEARCH MODE	1	0	2	GENERAL.VLM
READ ONLY COMPATIBILITY	OFF			REDIR.VLM
SHOW DOTS	OFF	OFF	ON	REDIR.VLM
DOS NAME <MSDOS>	1	(char)	5	NETX.VLM and GENERAL.VLM
LONG MACHINE TYPE <IBM_PC>	1	(char)	6	NETX.VLM and GENERAL.VLM
SHORT MACHINE TYPE <IBM>	1	(char)	4	NETX.VLM and GENERAL.VLM
TEMP DRIVE DETECTION	ON	OFF	ON	NETX.VLM
AUTO RECONNECT	ON	OFF	ON	AUTO.VLM and NDS.VLM

Figure 6-10. (continued)

Use of the DOS CONFIG.SYS LASTDRIVE command shows how the Shell and Requester differ in opperation.

With the Shell, LASTDRIVE is used to "reserve or preserve" drive letters for the local workstation. Typically, with the Shell, LASTDRIVE=F is used. This is necessary because the Shell "sits ahead" of DOS, and as such, drive letters needed to be reserved with the LASTDRIVE command.

With the requester, LASTDRIVE is used to "reserve all drives" for DOS at the local workstation. The subsequent use of LASTDRIVE=Z is required to allow the requester to use drive letters A through Z. Note that the drives (drive numbers 27 through 32) are not allowed with the requester.

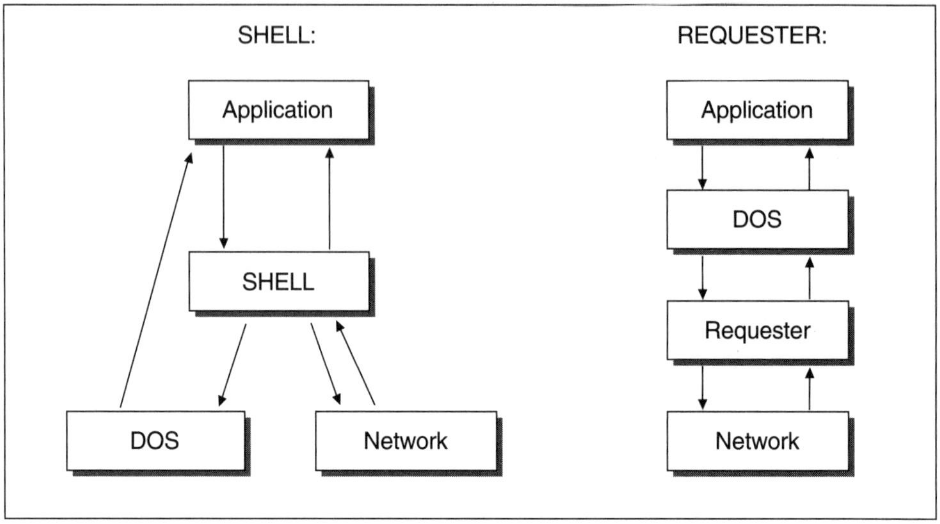

Figure 6-11. Logical difference between operation of NetWare shell and requester

Also, another illustration of how the requester differs from the shell is in the way a simple login process looks. With the shell, it is loaded and then the current drive is generally changed to the first network drive (say it is F:) and when that is done, the prompt appears as "F:\LOGIN." With the requester, this is no longer always true. With NetWare/386, users who are not yet logged in do not have any rights to the root directory of the volume SYS:. When they use the requester they see only a prompt "F:\". Rest assured that this is still the SYS:LOGIN directory, it just won't be completely visible.

A final illustration of how the shell and requester differ is in the number of concurrent server attachments allowed. The shell allows no more than 8 concurrent server attachments. The requester allows up to 50!

The requester introduces a new paradigm for its loading: the Virtual Loadable Module, or VLM. Rather than ganging up all the necessary code for the Requester into one stand-alone module, VLMs allow the selection of just the components that are needed. This way, only the modules needed are loaded. If Bindery Emulation is required, BIND.VLM will be loaded, if Directory Services is needed, NDS.NLM will be loaded, etc. Also, Novell has indicated it will open up the VLM interface to developers so that they may create their own VLMs. Benefits include reduction of concerns writing a "TSR," and resolution of multiple design concerns. For instance, the VLM.EXE load manager takes care of the type of memory the into which the VLM is placed, whether conventional, expanded, or even extended. Also, the VLM Load Manager can ensure that the VLM is loaded, govern the order of loading, and take care of its unloading. Figure 6-12 has a short list of the known VLMs for NetWare 4.0.

VLM Name	Description
AUTO.VLM	Auto-reconnection/auto-retry agent
BIND.VLM	NetWare bindery services agent
CONN.VLM	Connection table manager
FIO.VLM	File Input/output agent
GENERAL.VLM	Miscellaneous function agent for NETX and REDIR VLMs
IPXNCP.VLM	IPX Transport manager
NDS.VLM	Directory services agent
NETX.VLM	NetWare shell compatibility agent
NWP.VLM	NetWare protocol multiplexor manager
PRINT.VLM	Printer redirector agent
REDIR.VLM	DOS Redirector agent
RSA.VLM	RSA Directory services reauthentication encryption agent
SECURITY.VLM	Enhanced NetWare security agent
TRAN.VLM	Transport protocol multiplexor manager
VLM.EXE VLM	Load manager

Figure 6-12. Listing of known VLMs for NetWare 4.0

With the release of these new shells and their new options, Novell has shown that they do listen to users' concerns and are willing to provide solutions. Once you obtain these shells, you will learn how to configure them and how they operate. They can be obtained directly from Novell for $30.00 (call 800 NETWARE or 512-346-8380) or from Novell's NetWire forum on CompuServe.

NET3 2.15b/c Shell Problem

This version of the shell hangs up whenever a filename beginning with the letters "NE" and where the filename is at least four characters long and is copied or "typed out." If the filename is a program, such as NET3.COM, then the program will run normally, that is, without hanging. However, if the same file were copied (to any other filename) then a hang will result. Use of NET3 2.15a (revision A) corrects this anomaly.

IPX Software Interrupts

The IPX portion of the shell provides support for the network communications hardware. Although the filename is IPX.COM, IPX is really a combined IPX/SPX interface. Both IPX and SPX interfaces are contained within IPX.COM. In its original form, IPX.OBJ, this file is linked together with a network driver. Typically, IPX (and the IPX part of ANETx for version 2.0x) will hook into the software interrupts listed in Figure 6-13.

08h	The CLOCK interrupt; IPX gets timing information from this interrupt; IPX also provides timing imformation, via its interface, based on its use of this interrupt
xxh	An interrupt, such as 9h for hardware interrupt 2 or 9. Hardware interrupts are used to talk to the network card (not all network cards use interrupts).
2Fh	The DOS multiplexor interrupt, which, when called, checks to see if the requested interrupt is 7 Ah. If it is, the segment:offset address of the 7Ah interrupt is returned. This information allows an application to use a FAR CALL to call the IPX interrupt, rather than using an interrupt call.
64h	An internal IPX interrupt (actually points to same location as the 7Ah interrupt).
7Ah	The commonly used IPX interrupt, provided for backward compatibility for applications that call it directly. New utilities should perform a FAR CALL to this interrupt's location instead of using an interrupt call.
F4h	An internal IPX interrupt
F6h	An internal IPX interrups
Fxh	May be others in the Fxh range

Figure 6-13. Software interrupts used by IPX

NETx Software Interrupts

Under version 2.1x, the NETx portion of the shell represents the DOS interface. It is complete on its own and is not linked to any hardware drivers. The software interrupts that NETx (and the DOS interface part of ANETx) will hook into are detailed in Figure 6-14.

10th	The BIOS VEDEO interrupt
17h	The BIOS PRINTER interrupt (for parallel printers, i.e., LPT1/PRN,LPT2, and LPT3)
1Bh	The CONTROL-BREAK or CONTROL-C interrupt
20h	The program terminate interrupt (there are equivalent DOS calls; this is an old style of interrupt)
21h	The DOS interrupt, all DOS calls are handled here
24h	The CRITICAL ERROR HANDLER interrupt (i.e. Abort/Retry, etc.)
27h	The terminate-and-stay resident (TSR) interrupt (there are equivalent DOS calls, this is an old style interrupt)
F5h	An internal NETx interrupt

Figure 6-14. Software interrupts used by NETx

Shell Patches Using DEBUG

Common locations in the shell to debug are listed in Figure 6-15.

Released in the fall of 1989, the MAP ROOT command from NetWare 3.x allows workstations using NetWare 2.1x to make a false root. This false root relegates the top of the directory tree to a subordinate subdirectory. This has the appearance and feel of DOS's SUBST utility.

DEBUG ANETx.COM <CR> (also **NETx.COM**)	
-E167 <CR>	Patch the shell for number of file handles.
XXXX:0167 28.xx <CR>	See below for detailed information concerning file handles.
-E168 <CR>	Patch the shell for number of buffers.
XXXX:0168 00.04 <CR>	If you wish to use these buffers, this will set the buffers at 4, the suggested starting point. With most standard configurations the buffers should be kept between 3 and 8. In some extreme circumstances with some stand-alone databases you can increase the buffers even more. These buffers are used only for sequential read operations on files opened by the FCB method (not the file handle method).
E16A <CR>	Patch the shell for search mode.
XXXX:016A 01.xx <CR>	See above listing for search modes and meaning.
When done with DEBUG: **-w <CR>** (write changes) **-q <CR>** (quit debug)	

Figure 6-15. Shell patches using DEBUG

Unfortunately, the 3.x shells, which all allow MAP ROOT, can cause problems with at least two Novell utilities. The problem stems from the use of the SHOW DOTS parameter. When this option is set on—that is, when you see the "." and ".." directory entries when doing a DIR on network drives, there exists the potential of complete single drive data loss. The problem programs are MAKEUSER, versions lower than 3.0, and BINDFIX for NetWare/286. Both these utilities can be used to delete user mailbox directories. With BINDFIX you are actually prompted if you wish to remove mailbox directories of non-existent users. The deletion routine used is the same for both utilities. When these utitities try to delete the mailbox directories and SHOW DOTS=ON, the DeleteAll routine (the actual name of the routine) will not only delete the mailbox directories, but it also finds the ".." entry and proceeds to delete the entire subdirectory tree. That is, the entire SYS: volume (where the mailbox directories are kept) will be erased.

NetWare and Windows 3.0 Setup

When using NetWare and Microsoft Windows 3.0, there are several pieces of information that are useful. Although Windows 3.0 should run on LANs, there are imperfections. For instance, in the SYSTEM.INI file you should have the following at the end of the file:

```
[NETWARE]
RestoreDrives=false
NWSHAREHANDLES=TRUE
```

Without the above lines it is possible for Windows 3.0 to "crash" a NetWare file server (NetWare/286 or /386). It is important to type in those lines as you see them to make sure they are properly recognized. One note, by setting NWSHAREHANDLES = TRUE, each "window" to DOS that you open will have the same drive mappings as any other window. If this value is FALSE then each "window" opened will have its own unique set of drive mappings. One important note is that to run Windows 3.0 on a NetWare LAN you will need to use the NETx (this includes the EMSNETx and XMSNETx shells) shell version 3.0 or higher. There have been many anomalies with the different 3.x versions of NETx. You should try to use version 3.01 revision E or higher. Note that revision 3.01d should be avoided because it does not properly handle some internal DOS calls, especially those used by Emerald Backup Systems under DOS 4.x.

When using NETx 3.x you might want to turn on the feature of SHOW DOTS (as explained earlier in this chapter). By enabling this option you will be able to more freely move about with the Windows 3.0 utilities. Movement will be especially easier with utilities that allow you to manage/scan directories because you will have the . and .. entries. Without these entries your task of scanning directories can become a nuisance.

IMPORTANT NOTE: If you use the utility BINDFIX.EXE make sure that it is dated at least 2-12-91 or is at least version 3.52. If you use a lesser version and you have SHOW DOTS=ON you run the EXTREME RISK of COMPLETELY erasing your network disk drives' data. This is especially true if you are logged in with SUPERVISOR equivalent rights.

NetBIOS

Beginning with version 2.0, all subsequent NetWare packages have included a NetBIOS interface. NetBIOS is used in various network-aware applications to communicate in a peer-to-peer fashion. The NetBIOS part of the shell is optional and should only be loaded when it is needed. The NetBIOS supplied with the version 2.0x works with just one network at a time. Nodes on other physical networks are not reachable.

The final revision of NetBIOS for NetWare 2.0x is 2.0a Revision 3. The NETBIOS.OBJ file is dated 12/86. NetWare versions 2.0a and earlier have a NetBIOS problem when it is used on a nondedicated file server. Since the workstation-to-server connection on the server itself is treated as a separate physical network (observed via the command USERLIST/A), the workstation session at the server cannot participate in NetBIOS activities with other workstations.

NetWare 2.1 includes enhanced support for NetBIOS to handle internetwork routing. Through a combination of workstation NetBIOS and file server routing, NetBIOS packets are distributed across any and all internetworks of which the receiving file server is aware. This all takes place without the need to alter NetBIOS applications. This NetBIOS support is not perfect in version 2.1. Although many of the initial NetBIOS difficulties were worked out in version 2.11 and subsequent versions, a few problems still persist.

Although NetWare can route NetBIOS packets onto an internetwork, this is a NetWare-only extension of NetBIOS.

The message displayed after the header when NetBIOS is initially loaded is shown in Figure 6-16.

```
NetBIOS alternate interface (interrupt 2Ah) loaded.
NetBIOS interface (interrupt 5Ch) loaded.
```

Figure 6-16. NetBIOS loading messages

Alternatively, messages may be displayed which indicate that these inter-faces already exist in this machine. Novell's NetBIOS hooks only into interrupts 2Ah and 5Ch. Interrupt 2Ah is ordinarily one of the DOS Critical Section interrupt handlers and 5Ch is not usually used.

Timeout problems may occur when using a slow link (slower than 150 Kb/s) with NetBIOS communication. Because of this, Novell's Asynchronous Bridge (version 2.1x) does not route NetBIOS traffic. The decision to block NetBIOS routing on these slow links was mostly due to the increased chance of communication faults.

NetBIOS Bugs and Fixes

There are a couple of 2.1x-specific NetBIOS problems and fixes worth mentioning. First, the NetWare manuals state that the use of INT2F is required when using NetBIOS (NetBIOS loads first, then INT2F). This is not totally correct. INT2F is loaded if a specific NetBIOS-aware application is going to use it. The only way to determine if INT2F is needed is to try running the NetBIOS application without INT2F loaded. If the application works, INT2F is not needed. It is safe to say that 99 percent of the time INT2F will not be needed.

Second, a bug exists that prevents the use of NETBIOS SESSIONS in the SHELL.CFG. This bug affects all versions (up to version 2.15) of NETBIOS.EXE. A patch to correct this bug is as follows:

1. Rename NETBIOS.EXE to NETBIOS.DBG
2. DEBUG NETBIOS.DBG <enter>
3. r <enter>
4. Register values are displayed. Make a note of the number to which CX= points. Add, in hexadecimal, 100h to this value. For instance, if the number is 35C2h the result of adding 100h would be 36C2h. (The lowercase "h" is shown to indicate hexadecimal notation. It will not be displayed anywhere in DEBUG.)
5. scs:100 <nnnn> bc 80 00 <enter> where nnnn is the value from step 4 (in assembly, BC 80 00 equates to MOV SP,0080).

A single address is presented, such as: xxxx:2922

6. a2922 <enter>(or whatever the number is)
7. An address prompt is displayed, such as:
   xxxx:2922 _

(the _ is the prompt)
type: MOV SP,C080 <enter>
8. hit <enter> one more time, then
-w <enter>
DEBUG will respond:
Writing xxxx bytes
9. -q <enter>

At the DOS prompt, rename NETBIOS.DBG back to NETBIOS.EXE. The NETBIOS SESSIONS command in SHELL.CFG can now be successfully used.

Note that this type of patch can be dangerous, as it may overwrite a DOS memory control block, causing DOS to crash when the application exits. In the case of NETBIOS.EXE, the patch is fairly safe. As the program never issues a DOS 4Ah call to shrink its memory block, there are no memory control blocks above the program unless a TSR has reserved some high memory.

Because NetBIOS broadcasts go across internetworks, there is a greater probability that a timeout will occur. To minimize this likelihood, use the NETBIOS ABORT TIMEOUT = 2559 (in SHELL.CFG), which is the current maximum value.

Use of File Handles

The various uses of file handles on a network can be confusing. File handles are used in at least three places. The NetWare operating system (NET$OS for NetWare/286, SERVER in NetWare/386) opens file handles at the server. At each workstation the NetWare shell opens file handles on the network, and DOS opens file handles on the local workstation's disks.

Server File Handles

At the file server, there are at least four files that are opened by NET$OS when the server is booted: NET$MSG.SYS, NET$BVAL.SYS, NET$BIND.SYS, and DIRSTAMP.SYS. NET$MSG.SYS (prior to NetWare 3.x only) is a transient file that NET$OS uses for passing kernel messages.

Frequently referred to as the binderies, NET$BIND.SYS and NET$BVAL.SYS are the next two files opened. With NetWare/386 there are three bindery files: NET$OBJ.SYS, NET$PROP.SYS, and NET$VAL.SYS. The bindery files contain data regarding users, groups and file servers such as names, passwords, security equivalences, etc. Together, the bindery files represent the definition of the file server's users and their specific data. Note that the bindery files do not contain directory trustee information. This data is stored in the DIRSTAMP.SYS file on each volume (pre-NetWare/386 only). With NetWare/386, the directory trustee information is stored within each directory.

Finally, DIRSTAMP.SYS (pre-NetWare/386 only) is opened. For every volume defined, a corresponding DIRSTAMP.SYS will be opened, adding to the total number of file handles NET$OS will open. NetWare/286 and NetWare/386 each use a file called BACKOUT.TTS, but it is not defined for every volume.

There are several other files NET$OS opens from time to time. They include NET$ACCT.DAT, NET$REC.DAT, SYS$LOG.ERR, and NET$LOG.DAT. The first two are used for NetWare's accounting services. SYS$LOG.ERR tracks errors that NET$OS detects. NET$LOG.DAT provides an easy way for user applications to log data to the network.

Print Queue File Handles

NET$OS also opens files for the print queues. For every print queue, two files are opened, Q$xxxxxx.SYS and Q$xxxxxx.SRV. These files are only opened at boot time if a printer is servicing a particular queue. Otherwise, the files are not opened until a printer is added to service the queue.

In version 2.1x, an inconsistency exists in the way that print queue file handles are released, depending on how the files were opened. If the print queues are being serviced at boot time and the printer is later removed, only one file handle is freed. This is only true for print queues that are serviced at boot time. A queue that is serviced by a printer added to the server after booting up will take two file handles. When that printer is removed from the queue, both file handles are released.

Workstation File Handles

The workstation uses two types of file handles: network (owned by the file server) and local (owned by DOS). The NetWare shell detects where a file being opened resides. When the shell determines that a file is being opened on the file server, the file handle is stored in both the shell's handle area and in the file server's file handle table. In the case of a file that resides on the local disk, the shell passes the open call to DOS and lets DOS provide space for the resulting file handle.

This leads us to the difference in NetWare FILE HANDLES= (used in SHELL.CFG, detailed in the Supervisor Reference, Appendix B) and DOS's FILES= (used in CONFIG.SYS) parameters. These parameters are completely separate. For example, if a user has FILES=20 in their CONFIG.SYS, then 20 DOS or local files can be opened. If the FILE HANDLES=80 parameter is defined in the SHELL.CFG, then the total number of network files a user may have open at one time is 80 (the default is 40).

Setting Up Diskless Workstations

In addition to the usual PC workstation, there is what is known as a diskless workstation. There are many variations on the diskless workstation but, in essence, it is a PC with a network card and no disk drives. The main difference between diskless workstations and regular PCs is the manner in which they boot. PCs with disk drives boot DOS from the boot disk and then the shell is loaded to connect the PC to the network. Diskless workstations, because they have no boot disk, use a BOOT ROM and boot off the network. One problem posed by this approach is that if the file server is unavailable, the workstation is unusable. (See Chapter 1 for some other points concerning diskless workstations.)

Prior to the release of NetWare 1.0, all stations were required to use BOOT ROMs to load the same DOS image file (the same version of DOS). Beginning with Advanced NetWare version 1.0, it became possible to use BOOT ROMs to load different versions of DOS from the file server.

Multiple DOS Versions

The following procedure explains how to set up a network using ARCNET boards. Assume that two IBM ATs will run IBM DOS 4.01 and three Compaq 386s will use Compaq DOS 3.31. Each ARCNET board on the network is set to a unique physical node address. As the cards are installed on the IBM ATs, their physical node address settings are noted as being 20h and 30h. The Compaq 386s are set to three other unique addresses.

Per the old NetWare DOSGEN procedure, a special disk is formatted to be single-sided, eight sectors per track, and bootable under IBM DOS 4.01. DOSGEN then copies an image of the disk to the SYS:LOGIN directory as IBM$DOS.SYS. With DOSGEN from 1988 or later, no special format is needed—it creates a file called NET$DOS.SYS. This file must be renamed to a unique name with an extension of .SYS, such as IBM401.SYS. A separate single-sided disk is made for Compaq DOS 3.31, and DOSGEN is run. With the old DOSGEN, an image of this disk is also created in the login directory and is named IBM$DOS.SYS.

To allow the IBM ATs with ARCNET boards and node addresses 20h and 30h to boot with the IBM401.SYS file, a BOOTCONF.SYS file is created. This ASCII text file goes in SYS:LOGIN and contains the two entries shown in Figure 6-17.

```
0x20=IBM401.SYS
0x30=IBM401.SYS
```

Figure 6-17. BOOTCONF.SYS file

Note that with other network types, such as IBM Token-Ring, the address will be longer. For instance, a typical BOOTCONF.SYS entry for a typical IBM TRN address would appear similar to Figure 6-18.

```
0x10005A389B10=IBM401.SYS
```

Figure 6-18. BOOTCONF.SYS file

The address specified in a BOOTCONF.SYS entry is the hexadecimal representation. This address is visible if a USERLIST/A is performed while that node is logged into the network.

When the BOOT ROM becomes active, it sends a packet to all file servers on its local network. The responding file server checks the node address of the machine sending the request and checks it against those in its BOOTCONF.SYS file. If there is a match, the server will download the file listed by the node address. If there is no match, or if the "BOOTCONF.SYS" file is not present, IBM$DOS.SYS will be sent. Thus, the Compaqs can be made to boot from an IBM$DOS.SYS file given that there is no match for their ARCNET node addresses in the BOOTCONF.SYS file. If there is more than one file server on the same physical network, it is usually necessary to have the boot files present on all of them to ensure the ability of the diskless workstations to boot onto the network.

Also, when a BOOT ROM finds a file server with which to communicate, it usually first obtains a "load" connection. This connection is used to load the boot image file. A new connection is then obtained, which is used to perform the actual login and to carry on with the session. Unfortunately, the original "load" connection is still open and is tied up for 15 minutes after the boot image file is loaded, regardless of whether or not the user logged in. After this 15 minute (watchdog) period, the connection is freed up. It is freed because there has been no activity from that connection for the past 15 minutes. This double connecting is a particular disadvantage with ELS Level I or ELS Level II version 2.12, where there are few connections available. Not all BOOT ROMs use two connections for loading; however, all of Novell's do.

Limitations

An inherent limitation exists in this method of booting remote stations. If the file server has, for instance, two ARCNET boards (and thus two independent networks), it is possible to have duplicate addresses between the two networks. This could lead to a problem in creating the BOOTCONF.SYS entries in SYS:LOGIN for an address that exists on both ARCNET networks. This problem stems from ARCNET's (e.g., G/NET's, Corvus Omninet's, and others') ability to have node addresses defined at the time of installation. Other network types, such as IBM's Token-Ring and Ethernet, have unique addresses burned into a node address chip located on the board which cannot be changed by the installer or the user. IBM Token-Ring can be an exception if it is using locally administered addresses (LAAs). (See Chapter 7 for more information about Ethernet and Token Ring networks.)

Miscellaneous BOOT ROM Notes

There are a few other things to note regarding the use of BOOT ROMs:

- For any Advanced NetWare/68 system, the procedure described in the previous section will not work with the small older style of NIC boards that use the 2K BOOT ROM.
- When using NetWare/68 Star NICs, the physical node address is determined by the port to which each workstation is connected.
- The RXnet/68 board is set in the same way that all ARCNET board addresses are set during installation.
- The server that responds first to a workstation that is booting up must have the boot file and boot configuration file in its SYS:LOGIN directory.
- It is not possible to boot across servers on NetWare/68 systems when using star ports for workstations.
- Most BOOT ROMs will not work through external bridges.

Sharing Workstation Resources

NetWare supports peer-to-peer communications via IPX, SPX, NetBIOS, and named pipes (OS/2 Requestor version 1.1c and later). This makes it possible to share workstation resources. Of these peer-to-peer communication protocols, IPX and SPX are the most widely used.

Devices that can be shared include, but are not limited to, hard disk drives, CD-ROM drives, WORM drives, printers, modems, and screen/keyboard combinations. Most resource sharing is performed with third party utilities.

Disk Sharing

An example of a product that supports the sharing of disk drives, whether they are hard disks, CD-ROM, or WORM drives, is MAP ASSIST from Fresh Technology Group. With this utility it is possible to "map" from one workstation to another workstation's local disk drive. Only one workstation can map to a drive at a given time. MAP ASSIST uses Novell's IPX for its communications. Performance is not impressive, but is adequate.

Another use of MAP ASSIST is to access local drives via the LAN for the purpose of backup. Maynard Electronics, a manufacturer of tape backup systems, bundles MAP ASSIST with some of their backup systems to facilitate the backup of workstations' local disk drives.

Another disk sharing utility is ManyLink from NetLine, Inc. ManyLink allows file transfer but not the mapping of drives. The Lambda Group and CBIS both offer disk sharing utilities as well.

Print Servers

The need for printers to be located an extended distance from the file server and/or the need for numerous printers may indicate the need for a print server. Available in both dedicated and nondedicated forms, print server software allows a printer attached to a workstation to serve as a network printer. There are several products available to address this type of printer problem for the NetWare environment.

Brightwork Development's PS-Print includes a print server program and a pop-up TSR for the user workstation. This product requires that a user with the appropriate QUEUE_SERVER authority to be logged on at the workstation providing the print server function.

Intel's LANspool uses a VAP to provide print server capabilities. Using a VAP allows the workstation to be used as a print server without having to be logged into the network. This enhances security by eliminating the possibility of unscrupulous users accessing the network via this PC. However, because it is a VAP, LANspool may not be the best choice for those users with minimal RAM at the file server.

Three other print servers are LANport, Netport, and Pserver. LANport and Netport are currently for Ethernet networks. Both are manufactured by MicroTest, but Netport is sold by Intel. PServer, for any LAN topology, is free, and available from Novell's NetWire forum.

Other Server Software

There are additional server software products that can take advantage of workstation resources. The workstation resources manipulated range from modems to the workstation's keyboard and screen. These packages are described in Chapter 9.

Stop Messages with CASTOFF

If you have critical processes—for instance, a backup workstation or a communications server—that run without user intervention, it is quite likely that they should not be interrupted. Regardless of the use of the workstation, a SEND message, from the server or a user, can halt operations on that machine. By using the CASTOFF ALL command, all messages will be blocked so that a machine will not be able to receive messages and, consequently, will not become locked, waiting for someone to press CTRL-ENTER to clear the message.

Macintosh Volume Selection

With the first two releases of NetWare for Macintosh (NetWare/286) came a potential minor problem. This problem stems from the fact that only the SYS: volume has its file server's name preceding it (e.g., a Macintosh user for file server FS1 would see volume SYS: as FS1_SYS). However, if that same server also had a volume VOL1, that volume would appear as VOL1. Note that the file server name is not prepended to volume names other than SYS:. If the Macintosh user is connected to more than one server with the same volume names (beyond the omnipresent SYS volume), it can be extremely difficult to determine which volume is attached to which server.

However, you can avoid this laborious task on Macintoshes with color monitors by color coordinating volumes with servers to allow for easier server/volume correlation. For monochrome Macintosh displays, there is no easy means to match server/volumes. You could insert a directory on each nonSYS: volume that names the controlling server, but this would only be apparent upon opening the volume. Or, the actual volume names can be adjusted so that the file server name is actually embedded in the volume name. NetWare/386's Macintosh release avoids this problem, as it allows you to name the volumes. Macintosh users see the volume name you pick, DOS-based users see the "normal" name.

Packet Burst Mode and Packet Signing

In the second half of 1992, Novell introduced Packet Burst Mode (or Burst Mode, for short). With NetWare 3.1x servers this requires the use of the PBURST.NLM, whereas it is integrated into the operating system with NetWare 4.0. Essentially, Burst Mode allows for the transfer of multiple data (file reads and file writes) packets without requiring that each packet be acknowledged. Previously, the infamous "ping pong" NCP protocol (not IPX, but NCP) required that each read or write packet be acknowledged. Over wide area links that operate at speeds less than the typical LAN segment, this results in a significant performance loss due to the large volume of acknowledgments required by NCP. Burst Mode was designed to minimize this performance loss and make the most of slower speed links, even if only LAN segments are involved.

An added feature that came with Burst Mode was Novell's first volly into packet signing. Included in the PBURST.NLM is the ability to do NCP packet signing. This has many levels (see Console SET Parameters in Chapter 11) and is designed to further ensure that requests from clients are not being duped. Previously NCP had no strict authentication of client requests; thus, a clever programmer could infiltrate a NetWare LAN by pretending to be a user with high security (such as Supervisor) so long as that user was logged in at the same time as the miscreant.

It is important to note that neither Burst Mode nor Packet Signing is available for NetWare/286 servers. However, if there are NetWare/286 and NetWare/386 servers intermingled on the same network, both Burst Mode and Packet Signing can be used. Neither interferes with NetWare/286 servers. Also note that clients of NetWare/286 servers can use Burst Mode options in their shells or requesters and they will not interfere with their operations regarding the NetWare/286 server.

CHAPTER 7

Topologies and Cabling

Building on previous chapters, this chapter addresses the technology behind connecting file servers to workstations and other network resources. The sum of this technology is made up of several concepts, including protocol, topology, and bandwidth, that will ultimately affect your choice of NetWare version, NIC adapters and, perhaps most visibly, cabling. These concepts are explained in the following section to help you better understand the advantages and disadvantages of protocol/topology combinations. Choices for the type of cable used, based on the protocol and topology selected, are also discussed.

Protocols and Topologies

NetWare supports the networking of many topologies and associated protocols that, in turn, dictate the communication medium for a LAN. The factors to consider when choosing a LAN topology are often heavily influenced by their perceived performance. However, the quest for high performance may be overshadowed by economic factors, such as the price of NICs, network cable, and other equipment, and labor necessary to complete the LAN. Other factors complicating the selection process include corporate standards and proprietary technologies that are part of turnkey applications, such as a hospital pharmaceuticals or lab system.

The ability to support a wide variety of network hardware protocols gives NetWare a significant advantage over other network operating systems. NetWare runs on hundreds of manufacturers' NICs, representing many different LAN protocols/topologies. This diversity prevents users from being forced to implement a specific protocol/topology, as is the case with other, more limited network operating systems. In the case of NetWare, Novell has defined a fairly generic NIC interface, through its driver development kit so that other manufacturers can provide the necessary drivers to support Novell's networking hardware.

LAN topologies are divided into three main types: bus, ring, and star. The differences between bus and ring topologies are sometimes only visible when the data link layer is analyzed. In addition to their commercial development, bus and ring topologies have been further refined by the IEEE 802 Standards Committee. Star topology has seen little in the way of this standardization. There are also other non-IEEE 802 standards, each of which will be detailed in the following sections.

In general, each of these topologies has been associated over the years with a network communications protocol, i.e., a standard way for devices to transmit data on the LAN. For the bus, ring, and star topologies, these protocols used to mean carrier sense/multiple access, token passing, and polling, respectively. It is because of the tight coupling of these protocols and topologies that the following sections sometimes refer to them synonymously. Lately, however, associations have become cluttered. For instance, ARCNET is a token-passing bus cabled in a star topology.

Carrier Sense/Multiple Access Networks

The network media access scheme known as Carrier Sense/Multiple Access (CSMA) is utilized by both the IEEE 802.3 and Ethernet standards. Ethernet, developed jointly by Digital Equipment Corporation, Intel Corporation, and Xerox Corporation, is not the same as the IEEE 802.3 standard. Ethernet is based on the experimental ALOHA Network designed in the early 1970s at Xerox's Palo Alto Research Center (PARC). The CSMA mechanism has been further refined by the development of Collision Detection (CSMA/CD), Collision Avoidance (CSMA/CA), and Collision Elimination (CSMA/CE) technologies.

Ethernet

Ethernet was created in 1973 at Xerox PARC during the development of a personal computer called the Alto. Derived from the University of Hawaii's ALOHA Packet Radio Network, Ethernet was originally called Alto ALOHA Network. ALOHA broadcasted packets with randomized retransmissions. Ethernet was publicly introduced in 1976 with the publication of the paper "Ethernet: Distributed Packet Switching for Local Computer Networks" by Robert Metcalfe and David Boggs.

In 1980, Digital Equipment, Intel, and Xerox Corporations jointly developed a standard Ethernet. The result was a 10Mb/s Ethernet called DIX (DEC, Intel, and Xerox) Ethernet.

Ethernet allows all stations to share a network communications cable. This standard indicates only how the communications take place, not the media used. Ethernet can operate on several types of cable media, including:

- Thin Coaxial Cable (RG58 A/U or RG58 C/U), 50 ohm
- Thick Coaxial Cable (no RG equivalent), 50 ohm
- Twisted Wire Pair Cable (22/24 gauge), 150 ohm
- Fiber Optic Cable (100/120/140 micron fiber)

The current Ethernet specification is Version 2.0, which was published in November of 1982. With Ethernet, each station has a controller and a transceiver that attaches it to the network or "ether." The controller is used to build and disseminate packets. The transceiver, which may or may not be a part of the controller, taps into the network to send and receive packets for the controller.

IEEE 802.3

The IEEE 802.3 standard, like Ethernet, uses CSMA/CD as the media access control procedure. The IEEE 802.3 standard differs from Ethernet in the manner in which messages, known as "frames," are formed. The IEEE 802.3 standard has been adopted by the American National Standards Institute (ANSI), the United States Federal Government (FIPS 107), and the International Standards Organization (ISO 8802/3).

Most Ethernet adapters for NetWare actually use 802.3's frame format and not Ethernet's. For current releases of NetWare, there is an ECONFIG utility that allows some Ethernet drivers, which are really standard 802.3, to become viable on Ethernet networks.

The IEEE 802.3 standard was first published in 1985. It incorporates the CSMA/CD access control procedure, based upon Ethernet and 10BASE5. The specification 10BASE5 is shorthand for a 10Mb/s baseband medium with a maximum segment length of 500 meters, using thick Ethernet cable at the physical layer. There have been several adaptations of this initial standard. The first adaptation was based on 10BASE2 (thin RG58 cable) and is commonly known as "Cheapernet." The most evolutionary adaptation is based on the brand new 10BASET standard (T for Telephone twisted pair). Refer to Figure 7-1 for a comparison of 10BASE5 and 10BASE2 standards.

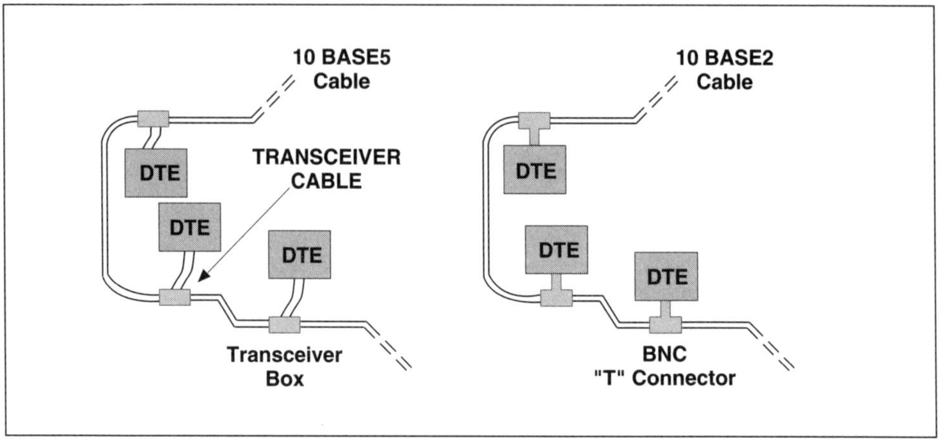

Figure 7-1. Comparison of 10BASE5 and 10BASE2 standards

The IEEE 802.3 standard also has a broadband specification. This specification, 10BROAD36, allows for 10Mb/s broadband media with a maximum segment length of 360 meters, using standard 75ohm CATV coaxial cable. The 10Mb/s rating is maintained to stay compatible with 10BASE5's Attachment Unit Interface (AUI).

The last broadcast medium specified under the 802.3 specification is 1BASE5. This specification was designed to provide for low cost LANs. The only medium used is unshielded twisted pair. 1BASE5 is 1Mb/s baseband and the maximum segment length is 500 meters.

The 10BASET standard provides for 10Mb/s over twisted-pair telephone wire. Instead of using a bus where each station taps directly into the medium, each station taps into a concentrator. The concentrator works as a hub to provide fault isolation and network diagnostics, as well as to propagate network traffic. Some of the objectives for 10BASET Ethernet include coexistence with ISDN, AT&T's StarLan, AT&T's ISN, and 100-meter minimum distance from station to concentrator.

In addition to the richer broadcast medium options (10BROAD36 and 1BASE5) that the 802.3 standard offers, another difference between 802.3 and Ethernet is that the IEEE 802.3 standard divides some of its functions at the data link layer, whereas Ethernet does not. The IEEE 802.3 standard splits the data link layer into the IEEE 802.2 Logical Link Control (LLC) layer and IEEE 802.3 Media Access Control (MAC) layer, as illustrated in Figure 7-2.

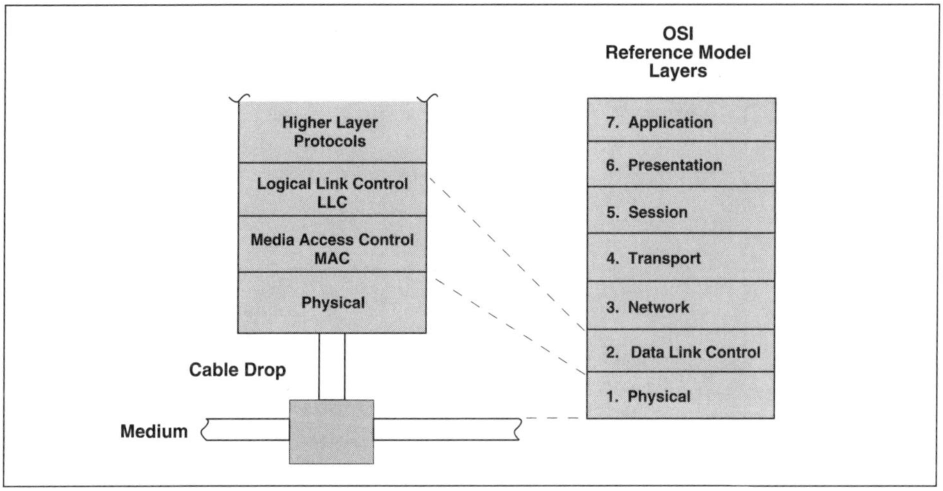

Figure 7-2. Data link layer split by IEEE 802.3

The IEEE 802.2 LLC layer is concerned with establishing, maintaining, and terminating logical links with other devices on the network. The IEEE 802.3 MAC layer is concerned with the actual media access, as in the CSMA/CD algorithm that is at work in the IEEE 802.3 MAC layer.

Comparison of Ethernet and 802.3 Packet Frames

The major difference between the Ethernet and IEEE 802.3 standards is the way the packet frames are built, as shown in Figures 7-3, 7-4a, and 7-4b.

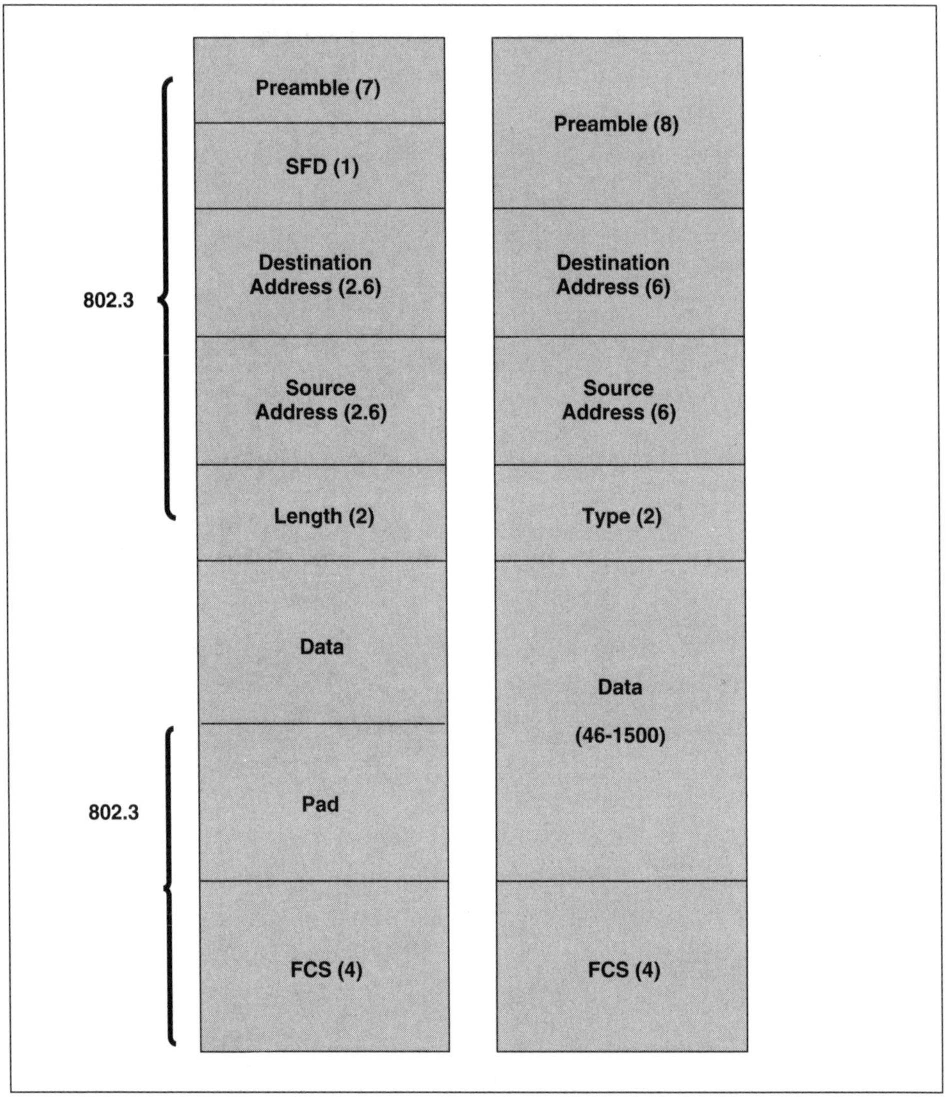

Figure 7-3. Comparison of Ethernet and 802.3 frame formats

THE ETHERNET FRAME FORMAT

72 bytes is the minimum packet size for an Ethernet packet.

THE FRAME FIELDS	Length (Bytes)	DESCRIPTION
PREAMBLE	8 (bytes)	•Provides synchronization and framing •Comprised of the bit pattern 10101010 (repeated 7 times) and the eighth pattern of 10101011
DESTINATION ADDRESS	6	•Represents the address of the receiving station •The most significant bit (MSB) is defined: - 0 indicates the field contains a unique address of the one receiving station, note: all unique address are assigned by the Xerox Corporation, specifically the first 3 bytes are assigned by Xerox and the remaining 3 bytes are specified locally - 1 indicates the field contains a logical group of recipients NOTE: if the field contains all 1's, this indicates this packet (message) is meant for all stations, a broadcast
SOURCE ADDRESS	6	•Always set to the address of the sending station, MSB is 0
TYPE	2	•Specified the higher layer protocol used to disseminate the message data, types are administered by Xerox Corporation
DATA	46-1500	•Represents the content of the message, the data
FRAME CHECK SEQUENCE (FCS)	4	•Computed by the CRC-32 polynomial, note: Data field must be at least 46 bytes in length •Also note that the Ethernet frame must be between 72 and 1526 bytes in length

Figure 7-4a. Detailed frame formats of IEEE 802.3 and Ethernet—The Ethernet frame format

The Frame Fields	Length (Bytes)	Description
PREAMBLE	7	•Provides synchronization •Comprised of the bit pattern 10101010
START FRAME DELIMITER (SFD)	1	•Provides framing, represents the start frame •Bit pattern is 10101011
DESTINATION ADDRESS	2 or 6	•Length depends on implementation, 10Base5 specifies 6 byte addresses) •Represents the address of the receiving station •The MSB is defined: - 0 indicates an individual address, the IEEE assigned all global addresses while local addresses may be defined privately - 1 indicates a group address, may be a multicast group of logically related stations or a full broadcast if all bytes are 1's
SOURCE ADDRESS	2 or 6	•Always set to the address of the sending station, MSB is 0. •If 2 bytes long, the Destination Address must be 2 bytes too •Same is true if this field is 6 bytes long
LENGTH (LEN)	2	•Specifies the length of the data field in bytes
DATA	54-1508 (2 bytes) 46-1500 (6 bytes)	•Represents the content of the message, the data
PAD	n/a	•The minimum frame size minus the Data size plus 2 times the address size plus 6 in length, if the result is non-positive, the Pad value is 0 •Used to Pad the message to ensure its size meets the minimum size requirement, this is necessary when 2 byte destination and source fields are used
FRAME CHECK SEQUENCE (FCS)	4	•Computed by the CRC-32 polynomial, note: frame must be between 72 and 1526 bytes in length •A difference between Ethernet and IEEE 802.3 is that with Ethernet it is the duty of the upper layer protocols to assemble a proper length where such responsibility rests with the IEEE 802.3 MAC layer under IEEE 802.3

Figure 7-4b. Detailed frame formats of IEEE 802.3 and Ethernet—The IEEE 802.3 frame format

Figure 7-5 details the address field formats of an IEEE 802.3 packet.

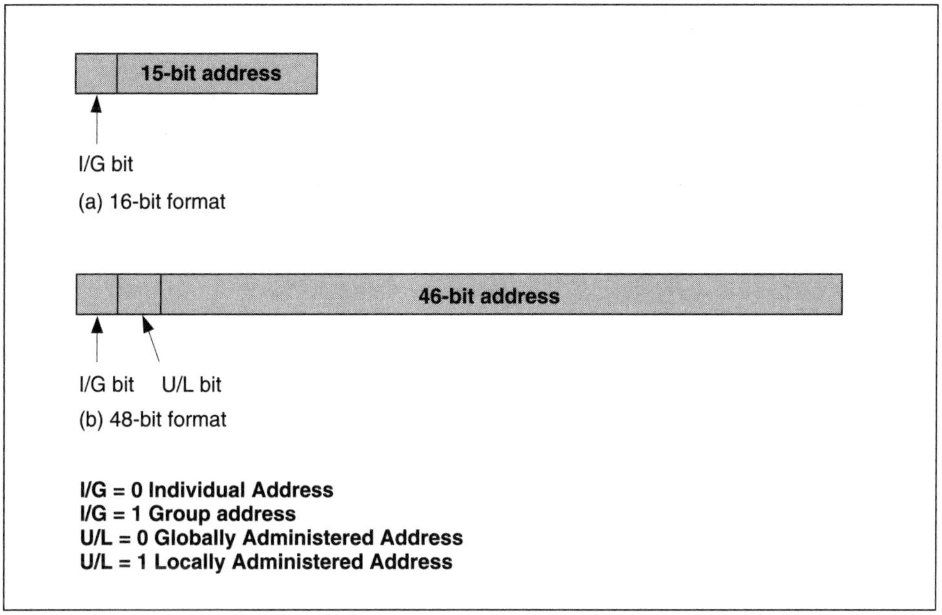

Figure 7-5. Address field formats of an IEEE 802.3 packet

CSMA/CD

The CSMA/CD (collision detection) protocol was originally developed in 1976 by Robert Metcalfe and David Boggs of the Xerox Palo Alto Research Center. Collision Detection means that each station first "listens" to the network, sending a message only if it is quiet—in other words, if no traffic is currently on the network bus. If the bus is not quiet, the station waits a random amount of time before listening again. During and after a message has been transmitted, the device listens to the line to determine whether its message packet has collided with another packet. If a collision is detected, both sending stations wait a random (but different) amount of time before resending their message packets. A collision is illustrated in Figure 7-6.

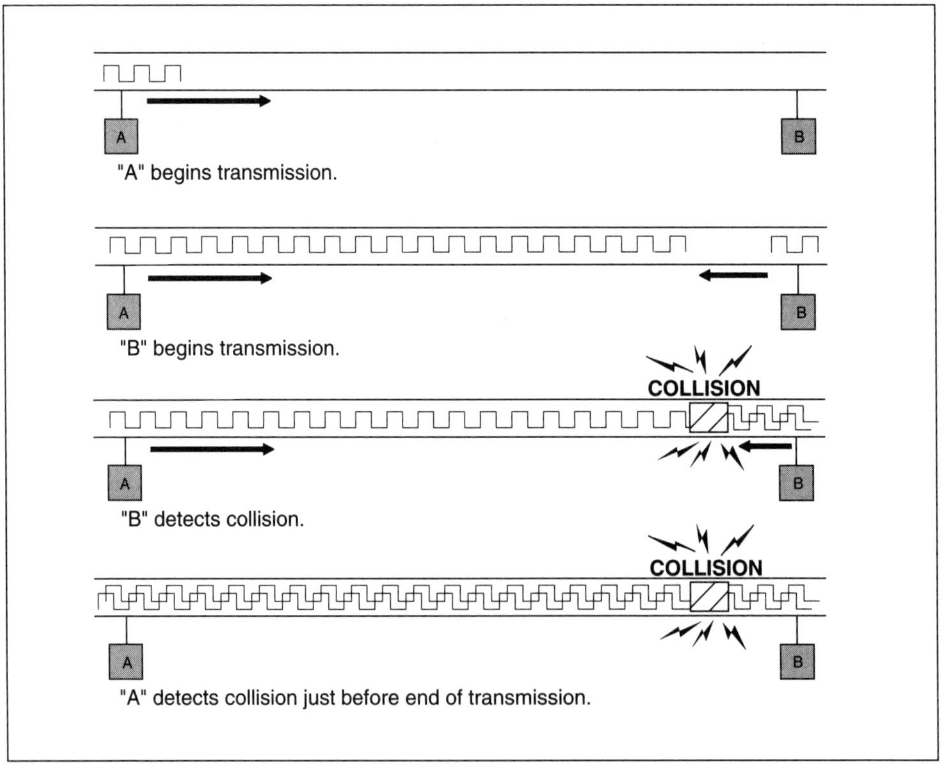

Figure 7-6. A collision

The random wait time used to determine when to retransmit a packet uses a rule known as the *truncated binary exponential backoff*. The wait time is calculated as a random integer x in the range of $0 < x < 2^y$ where $y = \min(z, 10)$; z is the retransmission attempt sequence number (there could be several retransmissions before one is successful). Once the time is calculated, x "slot times" are waited. The slot time is defined so that it will be larger than the sum of the physical round-trip propagation time and the MAC layer jam time. The jam time is the amount of time spent broadcasting a jam signal once a collision is detected. The jam signal lets other nodes on the network know that a collision has occurred. One drawback to the exponential backoff algorithm is that it operates on a LIFO (last in, first out) basis, which means nodes with few collisions may send before a node that has been waiting longer.

CSMA/CA

CSMA/CA (collision avoidance) is very similar to CSMA/CD, in that a particular station listens for a quiet cable before sending. However, a sending station does not continue to monitor the network once a transmission has begun. The CSMA/CA scheme never has knowledge of collisions. Error recovery may be compensated for in the data link or network layer, but there is no strict requirement. The usual method of recovering from lost data, i.e., using time-outs due to collision at the application layer, is rather time-consuming and, as a result, CSMA/CA is rarely implemented.

CSMA/CE

CSMA/CE (collision elimination) is a distributed, contention-based access method that purports to guarantee no data collisions. The CSMA/CE algorithm is proprietary, invented by John McHale of Networth, Inc. Like CSMA/CD and CSMA/CA, CSMA/CE first listens for quiet on the network. Once a quiet state has been detected, an additional wait period is inserted. This additional wait is in the microsecond range. It is termed the Deference Slot Time (DST). The DST is determined by a signal-processing algorithm that is executed locally at the station's controller.

The DST is key to eliminating collisions. If several stations are all waiting when the network becomes idle, the stations do not all try to send their messages at that same moment. Instead, each station waits an additional period of time (DST) before attempting transmission. A unique DST is determined for each station since it is calculated using location-specific information. If the network becomes busy while a station is counting down the DST, then that station will wait until the next idle state and start again. The DST is calculated each time a packet is transmitted, but the DST calculation is embedded in hardware and takes place in a matter of nanoseconds, which does not hamper efficient communication.

CSMA Futures

Ethernet and IEEE 802.3 will, in all likelihood, remain in their current 10Mb/s implementations. The reason for this lies in their simplicity. With Ethernet, the entire protocol is based on the premise of sending a message and then monitoring the network to see if it collides with another message. To sustain speeds higher than 10Mb/s, one of two changes would need to be made. In the first option, the maximum distance allowed between end points on the Ethernet bus could be decreased in order to keep the quiet time required for delivery acknowledgment short, relative to the time to transmit a packet. In the second option, the quiet time and maximum distance need to remain constant, but the packet overhead imposed by the relatively long quiet time becomes a limiting factor in performance. This packet overhead is imposed to keep the packet on the line long enough to detect a collision. Either way, it is reasonable to argue that Ethernet really can't be sped up much beyond its current 10Mb/s implementation.

However, over the horizon lies a new standard for the CSMA/CD protocol, namely, one at 100MB/s. In addition to the methods reviewed, there is another method by which Ethernet's speed could be improved. By guaranteeing no more than 2 nodes on any one cable segment, a collision will always be heard. And, as there are no other nodes competing for access to the wire, no special overhead is required to compensate for the increased speed. Currently there is a feud over how the implementation should occur, with particular contention over the wire type used. In any case, by limiting the maximum number of nodes on any one cable segment to two, Ethernet can have unlimited growth in speed. But, so could practically any protocol. In fact, it is debatable whether or not a protocol as intricate as Ethernet is even required when you have only 2 nodes involved.

CSMA Vendors

While it is important to understand the theory of NetWare operations, it is equally important to understand how some of the various manufacturers have implemented CSMA technology for NetWare. The manufacturers listed do not represent an exhaustive listing, since products such as AT&T's STARLAN are not discussed, but are intended as a sampling of different approaches and characteristics.

G/NET

Gateway Communications, Inc.'s G/NET product uses the CSMA/CA protocol and runs at a transmission speed of 1.43Mb/s. Designed for small networks with fewer than 20 nodes, G/NET can accommodate a maximum of 254 nodes, although it is done quite slowly. In March, 1993, Gateway announced it was discontinuing the G/NET product. It will no longer be commercially available.

Before considering G/NET for a new installation, a careful analysis must be made of your future needs. On the positive side, G/NET NICs, or Network Interface Modules (NIMs), are moderately priced compared to other CSMA implementations. On the negative side, G/NET is available from only one vendor and, as such, lacks widespread support as a standard. Therefore, if the vendor fails, any lifeline to the maintenance and growth of a G/NET network will be imperiled.

G/NET NICs are connected using either RG-58/U (50ohm), RG-59/U (75ohm), or RG-62A/U (93ohm) cable. The /U indicates low loss cable. Although G/NET is a bus topology, it does allow for patch cables up to six feet in length to run from the main bus, as shown in Figure 7-7.

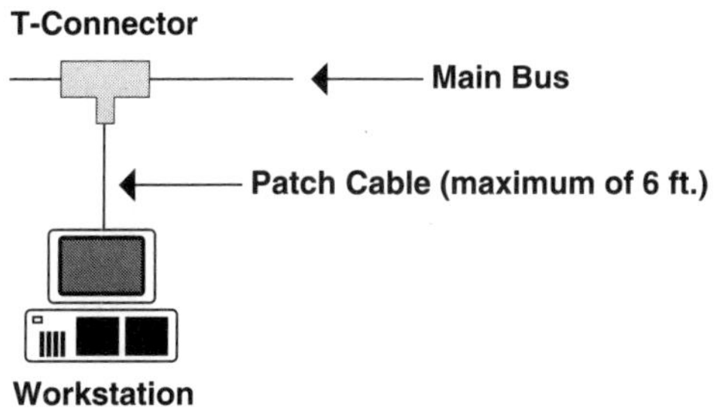

Figure 7-7. Example of G/NET patch cables

Although patch cables are supported, there are good reasons not to use them. Patch cables have the capacity to produce reflections or duplicate signals on the main bus cable. Experience has shown that even one patch cable can cause a drag in network performance or a complete workstation failure, regardless of where the patch cable is located in the network. It is much more advisable to run the main bus up to the back of each PC. If the convenience of a patch cable is required, for instance, when only one cable comes out of the wall instead of two, sources are available that can supply a trustworthy patch, which actually consists of two cables inside of one sheath.

When booting a file server or workstation using G/NET cards, there are other installation issues to consider that are spelled out in the G/NET installation supplement. For example, an error such as "Abend: NIM will not start" or "NIM out of control buffers" may indicate that the NIMLOAD.BIN file does not match the G/NET board's configuration.

OmniNet

Corvus Systems Inc.'s OmniNet is based on CSMA/CD running at 1Mb/s on twisted-pair cable. As with G/NET, OmniNet was not designed with large LANs in mind. In fact, only 63 nodes may exist per physical network. All nodes on an OmniNet network are cabled by patch cables that run from the main bus or trunk cable. Unlike G/NET, OmniNet patch cables can be used without reservation. In OmniNet terminology patch cables are called tap cables and they can be up to 15 feet long. Extenders are available that can be used to cable even greater distances.

The tap cables are attached to tap boxes. Wires from the tap cable are terminated by an RCA jack and run back into the tap box. Inside of the box is a wire guide with wires inserted into the guide from the trunk cable. This combination is free-standing and vulnerable to contamination from oxidation. To provide better operation from the tap box to the trunk cable, it is highly recommended that the installer solder the connections on these wire guides. This alone can remedy some of the network performance problems associated with OmniNet. Note that as with G/NET, OmniNet is available from only one vendor.

Ethernet

Ethernet NICs using CSMA/CD running at 10Mb/s are bountiful, as they are produced by many manufacturers. Under NetWare, these NICs actually run 802.3 but, with an alteration to the NIC's driver file, they can also run Ethernet. Although the IEEE standard defines a maximum trunk length of 600 feet for Thin Ethernet, 3Com's line of NICs, for instance, is capable of supporting maximum trunk lengths up to 1000 feet in length.

As with G/NET, patch cables used on Ethernet introduce reflections onto the network cable and are therefore not supported. However, for relatively small networks, the detrimental effects of using patch cables may not be noticeable.

Token-Passing Networks

The token in a token-passing network is a specialized packet that controls the right of any node to access the LAN. The node in possession of the token has control of the LAN medium. The token is passed from node to node in a manner that creates a ring, which may be logical (ARCNET) or physical (IBM Token-Ring). The ring is fault tolerant, in that it provides maintenance for ring initialization at each node, lost token recovery, and new station addition and deletion from the logical or physical ring (called reconfiguration).

Token-passing networks have been in wide use since 1977 when DataPoint Corporation introduced Attached Resource Computer Network (ARCNET). ARCNET is a token-passing network. The IEEE 802 committee has its own version of the token-passing ring network, described under IEEE 802.5. The IEEE committee has also defined a token-passing bus network in the IEEE 802.4 standard.

Since token-passing networks use a token to control all network traffic, the message packet collisions inherent with CSMA networks are eliminated. As opposed to the statistical nature of a CSMA scheme, token-passing is a deterministic access scheme. There are specific rules by which each node is governed when using the token.

ARCNET

ARCNET, which was originated at DataPoint Corporation by John Murphy, predates the token-passing standards of the IEEE 802 committee. ARCNET originally ran over RG62 coaxial cable, but now also supports twisted-pair, fiber optic, and infrared media. The current implementation of ARCNET offers a 2.5Mb/s transmission speed. To improve upon current performance, however, a 20Mb/s ARCNET standard is under development, with the first NICs based on 20Mb/s ARCNET expected by the end of 1991.

ARCNET is an efficient token-passing network with a distributed star or "unrooted" tree topology. When an ARCNET node sends a message, all of the other nodes receive the message at about the same time. The only limitation is the speed of light in the physical medium. All nodes, except the destination node, ignore the message, as ARCNET passes the token based upon node address. The mechanics of interpreting the token are all taken care of by the MAC level hardware on the ARCNET controller (the COM 9026 in most cases).

The ARCNET protocol uses positive acknowledgments of message receipt and generally has a maximum packet length of 512 bytes. Some vendors provide software drivers that increase the 512 byte message packet size to 4K bytes, thus significantly improving the transmission throughput. The first two bytes are for the source and destination address. The next two bytes indicate the packet data length. The remaining 508 bytes contain the message. Although ARCNET defines up to 256 different node addresses, only 255 are usable because address 0 is reserved for broadcasts to all stations. The remaining 508 bytes contain the message

Each node is offered the token in station number sequence. When a node receives the token, it can transmit a message. The ARCNET protocol specifies a limit of one packet per transmission. Once that transmission is completed and either a positive acknowledgment has been received, or if the node does not need the token, the token is passed on to the next node, as determined by the node's address. If more than one message needs to be transmitted, the sending node must wait until the token has gone around the network again.

In the unlikely event that an extra token is generated, it cannot survive very long because of the manner in which the ARCNET protocol works. Basically, communications from two different nodes will interfere with each other and the end result will be that both tokens would get lost. If a token is lost, the entire LAN assumes an idle state.

Each node continually monitors activity on the LAN. If no activity is detected for 78.2µs (microseconds), a reconfigure timer is started (see Figure 7-8).

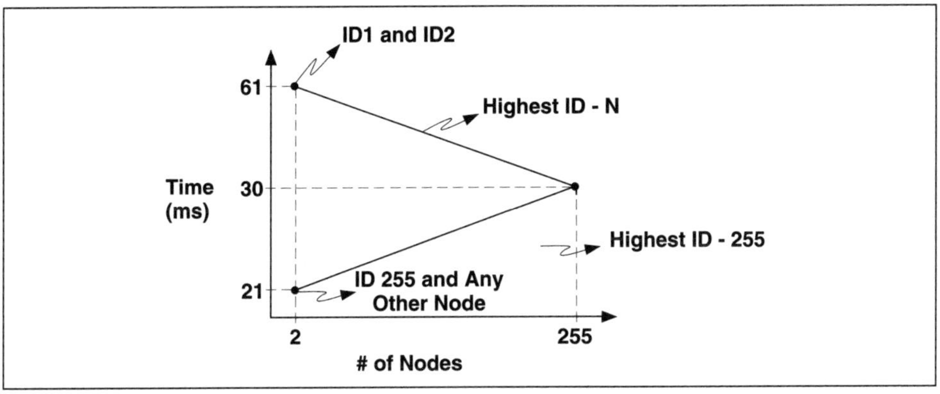

Figure 7-8. Network reconfiguration time

The programmed time is based on each node's address. If node addresses are unique, as they are supposed to be, one node will time-out before all of the others. This node then becomes responsible for initiating a new token. The network reconfigures itself and communication resumes. As this feature illustrates, ARCNET's real elegance is in its simplicity, as compared to the IEEE's 802.4 and 802.5 standards, both of which are detailed in following sections.

The ARCNET protocol can be described as isochronous, because each byte is preceded by a start interval and ended with a stop interval. Unlike asynchronous protocols, there is a constant amount of time separating each data byte. Each byte always consumes eleven clock intervals, with a single clock interval being 400ns (for 2.5Mb/s ARCNET). As a result, one byte is transmitted every 4.4µs.

The ARCNET medium, or line, idles in a logic 0 condition. A logic 0 or "space" is defined as no line activity, and a logic 1 or "mark" is defined as a pulse of 200ns. All transmissions start with an ALERT BURST, consisting of six-unit intervals of mark. Eight-bit data characters are then sent, with each character preceded by two-unit intervals of mark and one unit of space. There are five types of transmissions, each detailed in the list that follows:

1. Invitations to Transmit. An ALERT BURST followed by an EOT (End Of Transmission—ASCII code 04) and two (redundant) DID (Destination IDentification) characters. This message is used to pass the token from one node to another.

2. Free Buffer Enquiries. An ALERT BURST followed by three characters (six bytes): an ENQ (binary 00000101) and two (repeated) Destination Identification (DID) characters, each 2 bytes long. This transmission type is used to "ask" another node if it is able to accept a packet of data.
3. Data Packets. An ALERT BURST after which the following characters appear (each 2 bytes):

    - Start of Header (SOH) binary 00000001
    - Source Identifier (SID), source node address
    - Destination Identifier, repeated (4 bytes), destination address
    - A single COUNT character that is the two's complement of the number of data bytes to follow if a "short packet" is being sent OR two bytes of 0s followed by a COUNT character, which is the two's complement of the number of data bytes to follow if a "long packet" is being sent.
    - N data bytes where COUNT = 256 - N (512-N for a "long packet")
    - Two CRC characters, four bytes, using CRC 16 polynomial

4. Acknowledgments. An ALERT BURST followed by one character, two bytes, the Acknowledgment character (ACK), binary 00000110. This transmission type is used to acknowledge reception of a packet or as an affirmative response to a FREE BUFFER ENQUIRY.
5. Negative Acknowledgments. An ALERT BURST followed by one character, the Negative Acknowledgment character (NAK), binary 00010101. This transmission type is used as a negative response to a FREE BUFFER ENQUIRY.

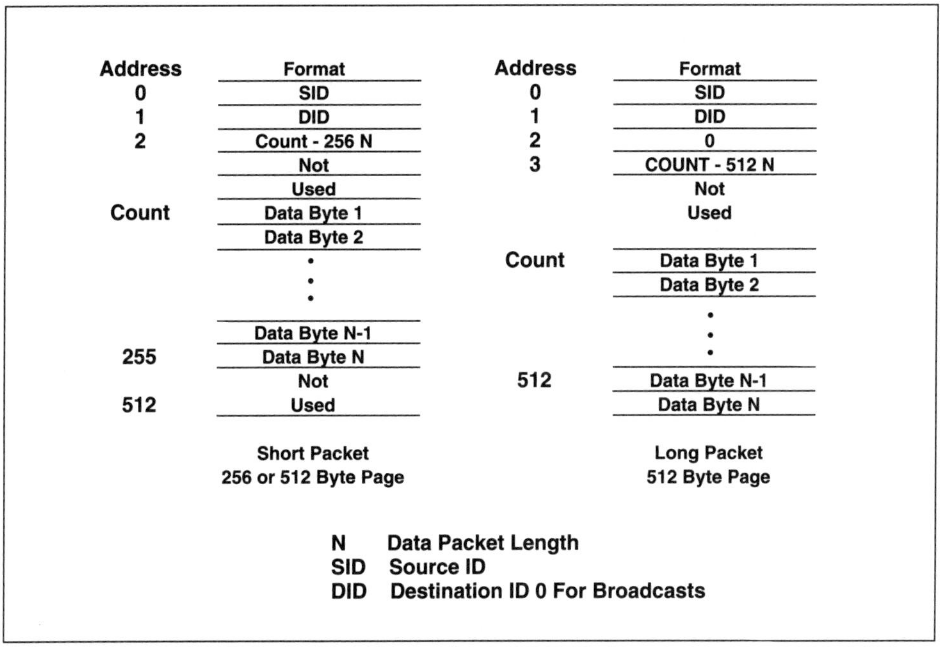

Figure 7-9. RAM buffer packet configurations

ARCNET Vendors

Unlike other topologies, only a few cabling rules apply to ARCNET. Currently all ARCNET products run at 2.5Mb/s and use protocols that are similar in their simple, deterministic nature. Because of its dependable scheme for network access, ARCNET can often outperform non-token passing networks that utilize higher net-work speeds. It is also relatively easy to use ARCNET across different cable types. Hubs are available that allow the combination of twisted-pair, coax, and fiber optic cable to be used on the same network. In contrast, mixing cable types with most other network topologies is not possible without the use of a specialized bridge.

One interesting aspect of ARCNET cabling flexibility is that if IBM 3270 terminals are being replaced by an ARCNET LAN, the 3270 cabling plant may be reused by the network. The reason is that IBM 3270 cable plants use RG62A cable, just like ARCNET. And because the 3270 cable plant is laid out in a star configuration, again like ARCNET, it is immediately ready for ARCNET installation.

Well over 100 manufacturers worldwide produce ARCNET NICs for all types of computers. Some of these manufacturers have formed a trade association called the ARCNET Trade Association (ATA). The ATA, along with Datapoint, SMC, and NCR, has defined a 20Mb/s implementation of ARCNET that can coexist with 2.5Mb/s ARCNET. This product, ARCNET Plus, (from Data Point) is the fastest general purpose LAN topology.

While the ATA was in the process of defining 20Mb/s ARCNET, Thomas-Conrad Corporation had already defined a proprietary derivative of ARCNET. Called the Thomas-Conrad Network System (TCNS), this ARCNET-like network uses a 100Mb/s transmission rate with essentially the same protocol as standard ARCNET, except for some refinements to accommodate the increase in speed. Unlike the ATA's 20Mb/s ARCNET, TCNS will only communicate with other TCNS NICs. Due to the extremely high speed of TCNS, it is very useful as a backbone network between file servers.

Another major ARCNET vendor, Standard Microsystems Corporation (SMC), has also developed a proprietary ARCNET product that defines a nodal priority scheme. Essentially, this scheme allows more active nodes, such as file servers, to participate more frequently in the token-passing protocol, thereby increasing potential network throughput.

The nodal priority scheme works in the following manner. Nodal priority holds the token at the file server long enough to send out several packets of data rather than one, but not long enough to cause a reconfiguration on the LAN. It dynamically configures itself to align with the I/O load on the file server and makes use of the 4K dual-ported RAM of SMC PC500 NICs to queue up multiple packets for distribution.

IEEE 802.4 Token-Passing Bus

In 1985, the first version of the IEEE 802.4 standard for the token-passing bus was finalized. IEEE 802.4 (or token-passing bus) is also recognized by ISO DIS 8802/4, which is a standard supported by the International Standards Organization (ISO).

The 802.4 standard provides definitions for 1Mb/s, 5Mb/s, and 10Mb/s transmissions using both baseband and broadband coaxial cable attachment of nodes to a medium. The token-bus uses a token to control access to the network. The network formed by the token-bus is a logical ring. Each node may transmit its messages, or data frames, when it has received the token. The node may transmit all of the data frames that it contains, but there is generally a time limit that prevents any one node from monopolizing the network. Furthermore, a slot time is defined as the maximum time any node must wait for a response from another node. The slot time is equal to twice the end-to-end propagation delay time of the medium. All nodes assist in error recovery and network management.

All data, token, and general information frames are passed between stations using the frame format illustrated in Figure 7-10.

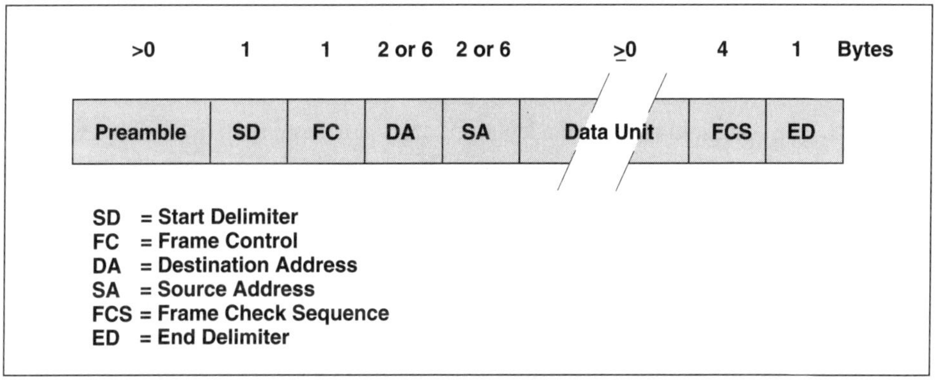

Figure 7-10. General IEEE 802.4 frame format.

The following is a discussion of each element of the frame.

Preamble. The preamble precedes every transmitted frame and has an appropriate length to match the physical medium used. The preamble pattern is chosen in such a way that the receiving nodes will be able to acquire the signal level and phase lock. The preamble also guarantees a minimum ED to SD time period so that all nodes have enough time to process the previously received frame.

Start Delimiter (SD). The start delimiter indicates the beginning of the data frame and is 1 byte in length. There can be up to 8,191 bytes between the SD and ED.

Frame Control (FC). The frame control indicates the class of the frame being sent. FC classes include: claim token, solicit successor, who follows, resolve contention, token, and set successor.

Destination Address (DA). The destination address indicates the destination of the token and may be 2 or 6 bytes in length. Whichever length is chosen is used in all frames. The first bit of the first address byte indicates whether the address is an individual (0) or a group (1) address.

Source Address (SA). The source address indicates the source of the token. Its length is the same as that chosen for the destination address.

Data. The data field may have a length of anywhere from 0 up to 8182 bytes (with 2 byte DA and SA), depending on the frame's class (from the frame control byte).

Frame Check Sequence (FCS). The Frame Check Sequence is used to check the correctness of the data frame being received. The FCS is generated with the standard generator polynomial of degree 32. The FCS is actually the one's complement of two additional computations. See the IEEE 802.4 reference manual for further details.

End Delimiter (ED). The End Delimiter ends the frame and determines the position of the FCS and is 1 byte in length. The seventh bit in the ED indicates if there are more frames to transmit (1), or if this is the end of the transmission (0). The eighth bit is used to indicate if there is an error with the frame (1) or if there is no error with the frame (0). The ED is defined by the transmitting node and is not protected by the FCS that checks the consistency of the rest of the frame.

An aborted frame, abort sequence, or frame abort is defined by a frame that has its SD immediately followed by an ED. A frame that is not a whole number of bytes is also rejected.

The token-passing bus IEEE 802.4 standard is susceptible to several different types of faults. Tokens can be lost, can fail to be passed, or can be duplicated. In addition, nodes can fail or can have duplicate addresses (administrative error). The IEEE 802.4 standard defines methods of trapping and responding to each of these problem conditions.

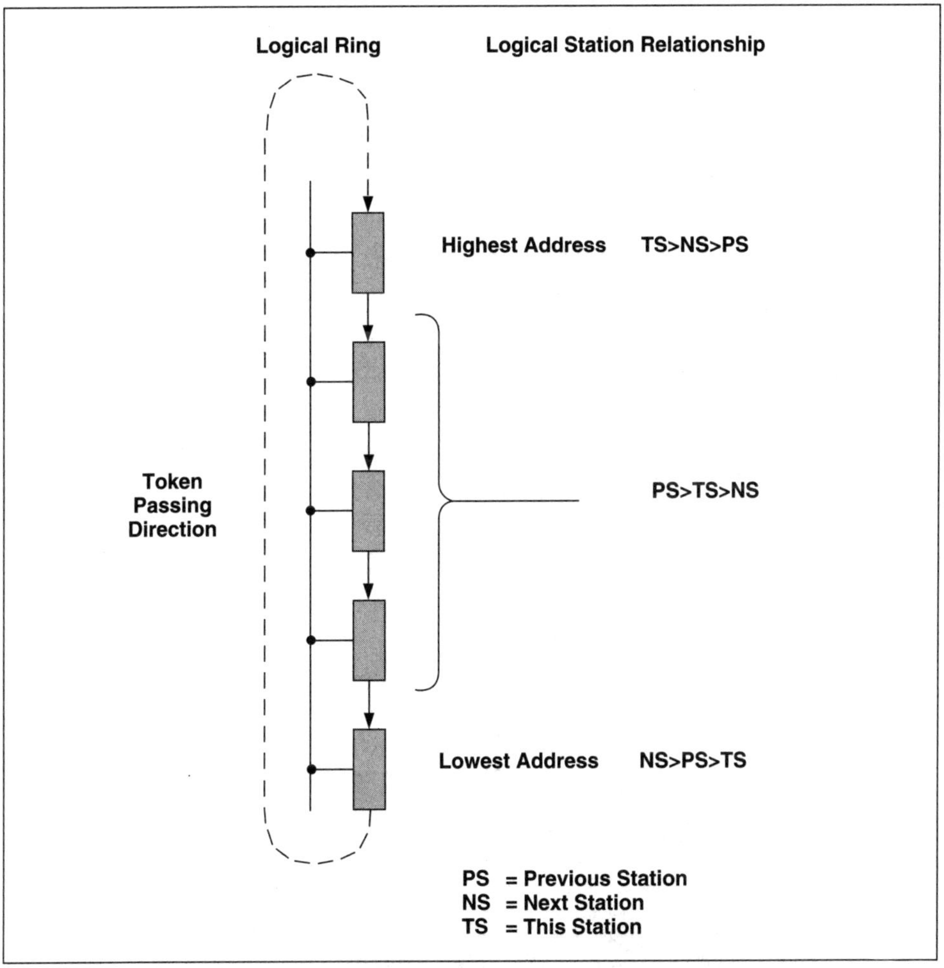

Figure 7-11. Numerical relationship in IEEE 802.4 logical ring

Monitoring for token loss or duplication does not require a special monitoring node. Each node on the network is responsible for handling token loss or duplication. This follows the design of 802.4, which acts as a peer network in which there are no masters.

Once the sending node is done with the token, it passes the token to the next node or "successor." The node passing the token listens for evidence that the successor is active, as illustrated in Figure 7-11.

If a valid frame is heard following the passed token frame, the original sending node "presumes" that the successor has the token and is operating properly. If the original sending node fails to hear a valid token frame, it will try to assess the state of the network.

If the sending node does not find a valid token frame, it will listen to determine what type of tokens are currently active. If the sending node finds only noise or invalid tokens, it will presume the noise or invalid token to be its own token and will retransmit. Once again, the sender listens for a valid frame. If none is heard a second time, the sending node presumes that the successor node has failed. The sender then sends a "who follows" frame in an attempt to ascertain a new successor node address.

All nodes compare the sending node's successor node address, i.e., the failed node's address, with their own previous node address. Each node "remembers" its node address from the last time the token was passed. Whichever node matches the sending node's successor node address with its own previous node address will send a "set successor node address" frame and pass the token to that node. This bridges around the failed node and removes it from the network. If a predefined number of attempts to solicit a successor fail, the sending node will stop soliciting. This will cause the network to either enter an idle state or the sender will attempt to claim the token the next time it has a transmission to send.

If the sending node presumes the successor node has failed when, in fact, the node has not, duplicate tokens result. Duplicate tokens cause chaos and eventually collide, producing noise. The network will either continue on when one of the sending nodes hears a successor or it will reach an idle state. The idle state occurs when all nodes go into a listen state for a predefined multiple of slot times. It is also possible for the sending node to hear a delayed version of its own transmission, and thereby interpret that the successor has taken control of the token. If this happens, the token will be lost. A lost token results in the entire network reaching an idle state.

The token initialization algorithm presumes that more than one node may try to initialize at the same instant. Each node attempting to claim the token issues a "claim token" frame padded by 0, 2, 4, or 6 slot times based on the first two bits of the node's address. After transmitting, a node listens and, if anything is heard, stops trying to claim the token. Otherwise, the node sends out another claim token frame using the next two bits of its address. This process repeats until all of the address bits are used to a point at which the highest numbered node "wins." That is, the node that hears silence after its last claim token frame assumes control of the token. This process is illustrated by the flowchart shown in Figure 7-12.

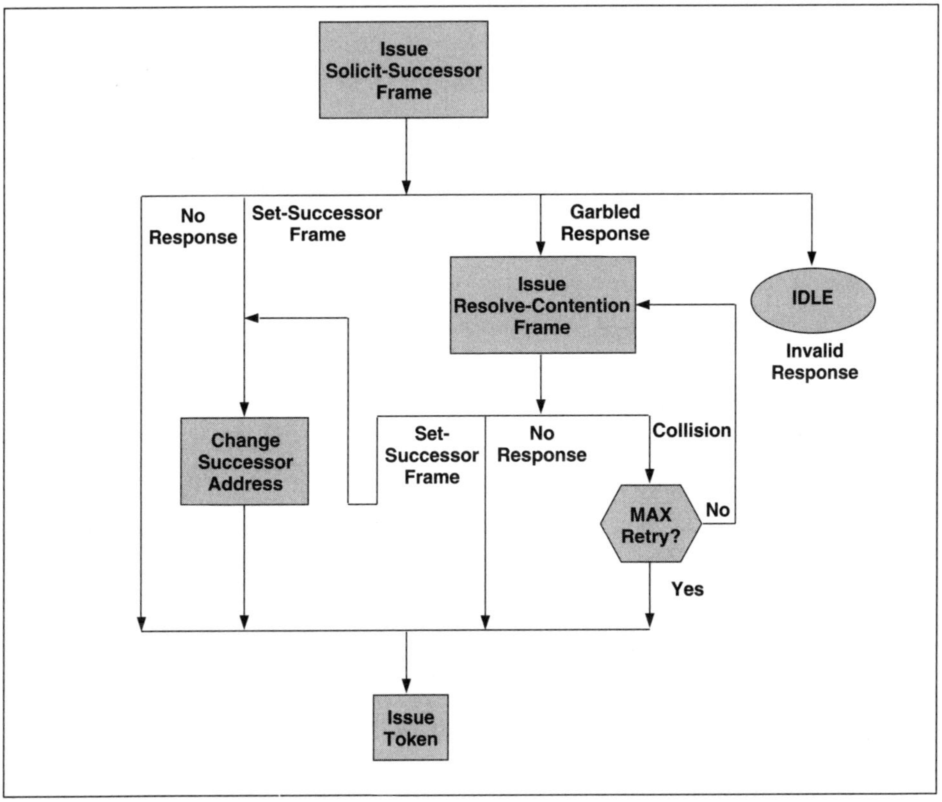

Figure 7-12. Addition of a node

Each active node issues a "solicit successor" frame each time it passes the token. The solicit successor frame is sent for any node with an address between the sending node and the next node in the logical ring. After the frame is sent, the sending station waits one slot time. During this slot time there may be zero, one, or a multiple number of responses. In the case of no response to the solicit successor frame, the token is passed to the successor previously established. If one node responds, a set successor frame is sent and the new node enters the network. If a multiple number of nodes respond, noise will result on the network. The sending node will then issue a "resolve contention" frame and wait for four response windows. Each node attempting to begin participating in the ring issues a set successor frame based on the first two bits of its address. The first node(s) issues the set successor frame in the first response window, and so on. If a contending node hears any frame or noise before its response window is present, it will not transmit. If the original token sender (the one soliciting a successor) receives a valid set successor frame, it will set that node as the next node and pass the token to the successor. If no valid set successor frames are heard during the four response windows, the sending node stops trying to determine a successor and passes the token to the previously established successor.

Nodes are removed or deleted from the network simply by not responding when the token is passed to them. Once the node stops responding, the fault recovery mechanisms previously discussed will remove it from the network.

IEEE 802.5 Token-Passing Ring

The IEEE 802.5 standard is an outgrowth of IBM's research and development. The IEEE 802.5, or token-passing ring, is also recognized by ISO DIS 8802/5. It should be noted that IBM was, and still is, a major influence in the shaping of the IEEE 802.5 standard. The 802.5 standard includes definitions for both 1Mb/s and 4Mb/s token passing schemes using shielded twisted-pair attachment of the node to the medium, including the definition of the medium interface connector.

In 1988, IBM defined a 16Mb/s shielded twisted-pair Token-Ring network in adherence with the IEEE's 802.5 standard. The new 16Mb/s Token-Ring includes an enhancement to the IEEE 802.5 standard called the Early Token Release option. The NIC drivers used with the 4Mb/s mode work with the 16Mb/s mode with no adjustment. However, all nodes on a ring need to run at the same speed—4 or

16Mb/s. Unfortunately, the production of 16Mb/s Token-Ring drivers is still in its infancy, leaving the biggest advantage of using 16Mb/s Token-Ring NICs (or TICs) as that of the larger packet sizes.

Following the IEEE 802.5 standard, IBM offers a 4Mb/s card and a combination 16/4Mb/s card. When using the new 16/4 cards, it is important to use the same speed on all cards in the ring. Note that the 16/4 cards can be run in 16Mb/s mode using the Novell drivers that come with the card, although these drivers are not optimized for the 16Mb/s speed. In mid-1989, Novell released the 16/4 drivers that support the 16Mb/s speed and IBM's source routing protocol addition.

Source routing is another IBM Token-Ring enhancement. With source routing, the originating node provides an explicit route to the destination node through a bridge. The benefit of source routing is intended to provide the ability for multiple virtual paths to exist between sender and receiver, which effectively increases network bandwidth.

The drawback of source routing, which is debatable, is that it unnecessarily complicates Token-Ring hardware. Detractors of source routing claim it should be left out of the hardware, i.e., the data link layer, and placed in each bridge, similar to the approach with which the Xerox Network Standard (XNS) handles internetwork routing. This method is judged by some as superior to that of source routing due to the inherent distribution of network information. If a bridge specified by source routing becomes unavailable, a packet must be unnecessarily returned to its originator for resending. By leaving source routing out of the data link layer, the bridges determine the dynamic route for a packet to take.

Source routing drivers allow IBM bridges to pass NetWare packets, but they do not allow NetWare bridges to pass IBM packets. The file server and all workstations need to be configured in the same manner. Therefore, to bridge between LANs in a source routing environment, the bridge must be changed from NetWare to IBM, and the drivers changed to source routing.

The Token-Ring scheme uses free and busy tokens to control access to the network (see Figure 7-13).

The token is passed around the ring and, when a node needs to transmit data, it first captures a free token and then changes it to a busy token. Once it is done with that token, the node will return a free token to the network. With low network utilization, this technique is quite cumbersome, as a node that is trying to transmit must wait for the token to come back around the network. As network use increases, the token functions in a round-robin manner, thereby providing predictable performance.

The IBM Token-Ring actually passes the token from node to node. While this is an effective way to propagate the signal, it is an extremely burdensome method of transmitting packets. Because of the overhead created, the transmission rate figures quoted with Token-Ring can be misleading. For example, a number of published tests over the years have shown a comparable Token-Ring LAN running at 4Mb/s is easily outperformed by ARCNET running at 2.5Mb/s—albeit this comparison is between a token-passing ring and a token-passing bus.

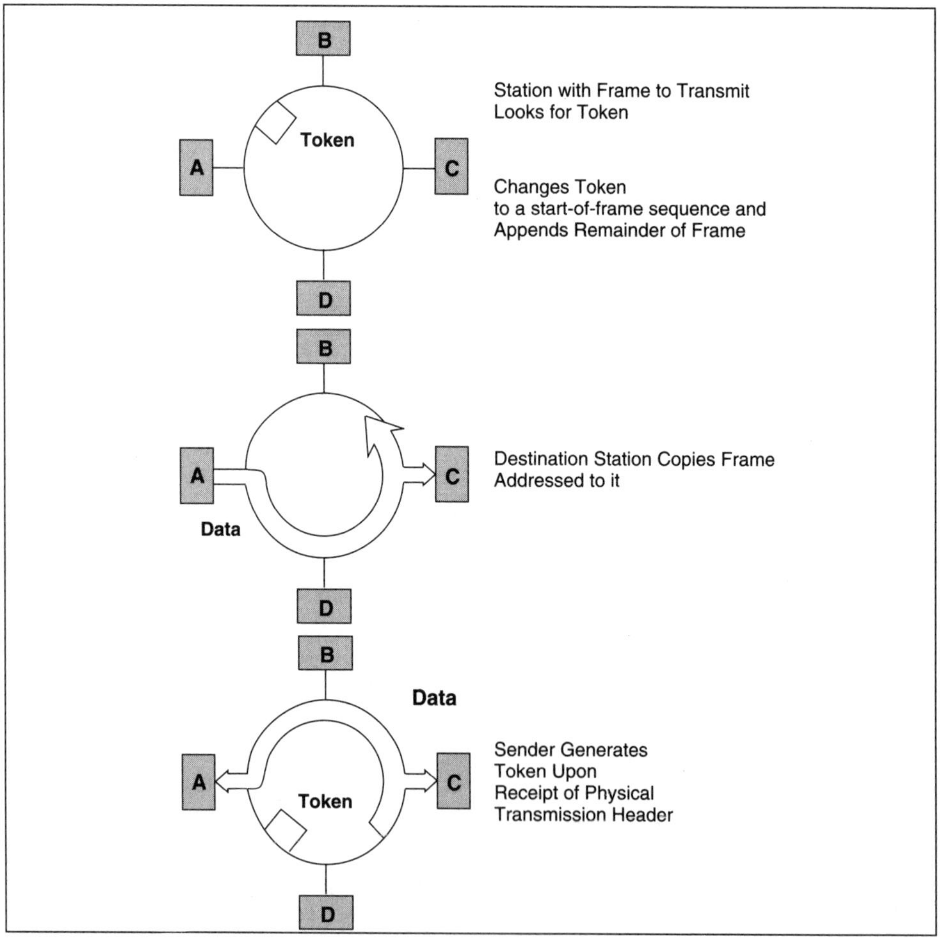

Figure 7-13. Use of tokens in a Token Ring

A new token is released to the network (1) once the sending node has finished its transmission, (2) once the leading edge of its transmitted frame has returned after completing one trip around the ring, and (3) when using the Early Token Release (ETR) option, once the transmitting node completes its transmission, even if it has not yet begun to receive its own transmission. If the bit length of the ring is less than the frame length, the first condition implies the second. If not, a node could release a free token after it has finished transmitting but before it receives its own busy token—the second token is not strictly necessary. If the first, but not the second condition is true, multiple frames may result, requiring fault recovery. In any case, the token guarantees that one, and only one node may transmit at any given time. The next node downstream with data to send will be able to seize the token and transmit once the current node releases a free token.

Figure 7-14 depicts the format of the token and frame generated by the IEEE 802.5 protocol.

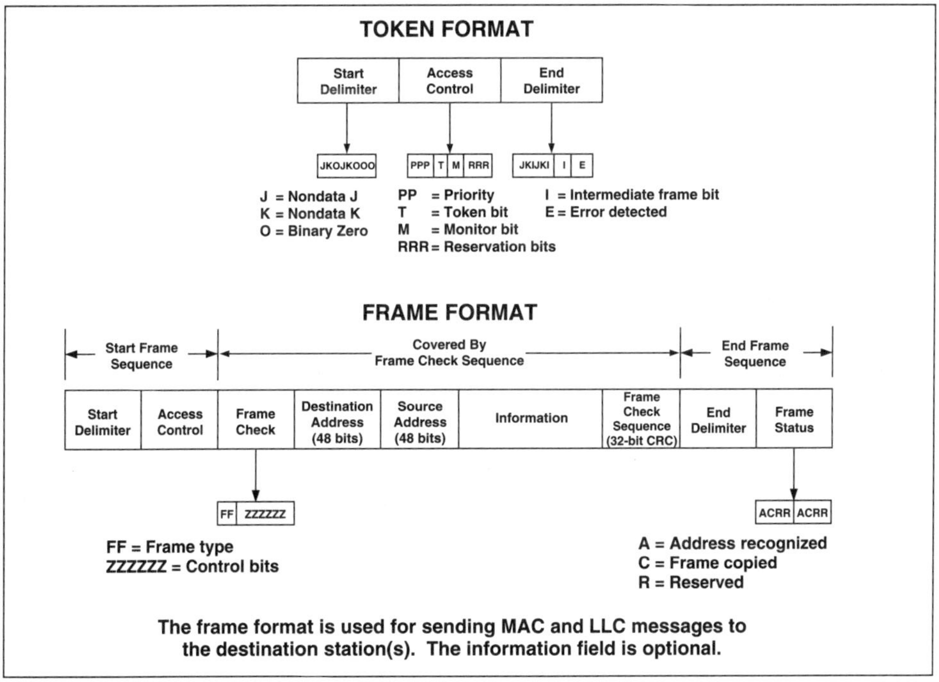

Figure 7-14. Token and frame formats in IEEE 802.5

Start Frame Sequence (SFS)

Start Delimiter (SD). Indicates the start of the token or frame. The SD is made up of signaling patterns, which are always distinguishable from data. It is coded as follows: JK0JK000, where J and K are non-data symbols; 0 is a binary 0; SD is one byte long.

Access Control (AC). Contains the priority and reservation bits, which are used for the priority mechanism and the monitor bit, which is used for ring maintenance. If the message being sent is a token, then the ED is the only other field. AC is one byte long.

Frame Check Sequence (FCS)

The following are covered by the FCS calculation:

Frame Control (FC). Indicates whether this frame contains LLC data or a MAC control frame. If it is MAC, the control bits indicate the type of MAC frame.

Destination Address (DA). This field indicates the intended recipient(s) of this frame. The address may indicate a single node, a group of nodes, or may be global (all addresses/nodes). The address used may be 2 or 6 bytes in length, depending on the implementation. Whichever is used, the address size must be consistent in the SA for all nodes on the same network.

Source Address (SA). Indicates the sending node's address, and uses the same address size as the DA.

Information (INFO). Contains LLC data or control information for the MAC protocol, and may be 0 bytes or more. There is no maximum length, although the size is limited by the amount of time a node may possess the token.

Frame Check Sequence (FCS). This is a CRC-32 polynomial, based on the FC, DA, SA, and INFO fields.

End-of-Frame Sequence (EFS)

Ending Delimiter (ED). Contains non-data symbols to indicate the end of the frame. It also includes indicators to indicate if there are more frames or if an error has been detected in the frame. ED is one byte long.

Frame Status (FS). Frame Status is provided as a redundant check to detect errors. Indicators include the Address recognized and Frame copied, also known as the A and C bits (each is actually 2 bits). Errors include an FCS that appears incorrect and a frame with an incorrect priority.

An aborted frame, abort sequence, or frame abort is defined by a frame that has its SD immediately followed by an ED. Any frame that is not an integral number of bytes is also rejected.

Address fields in 802.5 come with recommended structures to provide for a LAN that is divided into multiple rings. The hierarchical address format provides a convenient method for a bridge to recognize frames that are destined for another ring. For 16-bit and 48-bit address fields, the hierarchical address structure is as follows:

- 16 bit address: |-I/G-|-7 bit ring address-|-8 bit node address-|
- 48 bit address: |-I/G-|-1-|-14 bit ring address-|-32 bit node address-|

I/G indicates whether the frame is for an individual address or for a group/global address. All binary 1s indicate global, otherwise group is indicated. I/G is 1 bit long. The 1 in the 48-bit address indicates a binary 1.

In order for one node to talk to another, the first node must send the message to its nearest neighbor. The neighbor then repeats the message to its neighbor, and so on. Each node introduces approximately a 1-bit time delay, that is, 250ns at 4Mb/s. This delay is the result of the time it takes to examine, copy, or change a bit of the message, as it becomes necessary. Even the destination node repeats the message. Once the destination node receives the token, it sets the frame status byte to indicate that it has copied the frame. When the message is passed back to the originating node, it removes the message from the ring. The sending node can determine from the frame status whether the destination was nonexistent/inactive, if the destination existed but did not copy the frame, or if the frame was copied (received).

Token-Ring maintenance specifies four conditions which can cause the failure of the network. These conditions are:

- the loss of the token
- failure to transmit a free token by the node that last had control of the token
- a physical media interruption
- failure of the monitor node

One node is designated as the active token monitor. In a NetWare environment, this is usually performed by one of the file servers on the ring. The monitor node periodically issues an "active monitor present" control frame so that other nodes are aware that there is an active monitor present on the ring. The monitor is used to detect the loss of the token. To reestablish the token, the monitor purges the ring of any residual data and issues a free token.

The monitor can detect a looping token by inspecting the monitor bit (in the Access Control byte), which it turns on every time it detects a busy token. If a busy token with its monitor bit already set is encountered, the monitor will change the token to a free token. A looping token is caused when the originating node does not issue a free token.

All other nodes participate as passive or standby monitors. If the loss of the active monitor is detected, one of the passive monitors will assume the active monitor duties. If there is contention, the node with the highest address will become the active monitor via a contention resolution algorithm.

Upon entering the network, all nodes transmit a duplicate address test frame. If the frame returns with the "address recognized" bits set to 1 (part of the Frame Status byte), a duplicate address has been detected and the entering node removes itself from the ring and issues an error to the higher level protocols. This error is handled by the IBM Token-Ring drivers if it occurs in a workstation. At the file server, it is handled by the IPX driver, which will cause the server to abort initialization of that LAN driver.

A beacon frame is used to isolate a ring failure, such as a break in the ring or ring medium. When a node is attempting to claim the token, it will time out if it does not achieve a resolution. Once it has timed out, the node issues a beacon to indicate the fault. The monitor purges the beacon frame, clears the ring, and issues a free token.

Token Ring Vendors

Even with IBM's heavy influence on the IEEE 802.5 standards committee and its corporate support of Token-Ring, there are alternatives to IBM's Token-Ring products for NetWare LANs.

For example, Proteon Corporation produces a 10Mb/s token-passing network called ProNET. Although it is regarded as a high performance LAN, two perceived disadvantages of the ProNET product are that it is proprietary and is often more difficult to install and maintain. Once installed correctly, however, ProNET outperforms many other widely used network topologies. Proteon also has 802.5 ProNET 4 (IBM Token-Ring compatible), UTP ProNET 16, and 80Mb/s ProNET 80. Other 802.5 vendors include NCR, Madge Networks, 3Com, Gateway Communications, Racore, and Thomas Conrad.

Another third-party Token-Ring product is Thomas-Conrad Corporation's 16-port Token-Ring MAU. One of the shortcomings of the IBM Token-Ring is its Multistation Access Unit (MAU). It lacks status indicators for nodes and is perceived by some as difficult to use. The Thomas-Conrad MAU has ring activity indicators, push-button reset control, and an "in-ring" indicator. The result is a color-coded, useful display that provides quicker diagnosis of communication faults with Token-Ring.

Star Networks

Star networks usually employ a polling technique much like IBM's SNA. The poll is used to determine which nodes are still active and to maintain the network. However, no special access methods are required on a Star network, since every node is connected directly to a master node. Each node simply sends a request to the master node. If the master node does not respond to the sending node, the sending node resends its message. Star networks are contentionless and the effective bandwidth of the Star network increases every time a new node is added. There are no set standards, such as IEEE, FIPS, or ISO for Star-connected networks.

Star networks are very susceptible to major catastrophe should the master node becomes inoperable, as a backup master node does not usually exist. If there were a backup master node, it would have either a set of connections physically separate from the primary master node or it would share the same connections, perhaps through dual communication controllers at each non-master node. Figure 7-15 illustrates an alternative Star layout.

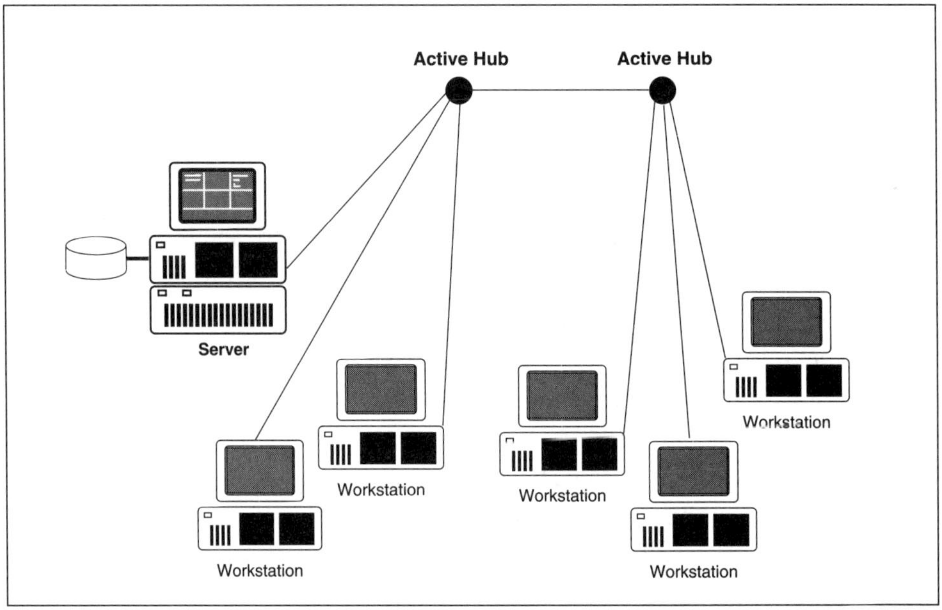

Figure 7-15. Distributed star topology using ARCNET

At one time, the Novell's Star (S-net) server was their premier file server. This time has come and gone. In March of 1988, Novell discontinued the S-net server line, which included the /68, 68A, and 68B. Federal Technologies Corporation has picked up the maintenance of S-net file servers. The last release of NetWare for the S-net file servers was v2.1.

The S-net line of servers allowed up to 24 workstations to be connected via Star ports. If S-nets were interconnected, one or more ports were dedicated to communicating with other file servers.

Beginning with 2.01 and continuing through 2.1 of NetWare /68, the S-net file servers were able to use ARCNET by installing an ARCNET board. Due to a trademark infringement against DataPoint, Novell soon changed the name of its ARCNET products to RXnet. The first release of NetWare to support RXnet, 2.01/68, was defective when used with the RXnet board. Subsequently, Novell has released 2.01a/68 to correct the problem with 2.01.

Cabling

Some of the most common types of local area network mediums include unshielded twisted pair, twisted pair, coaxial, and fiber optic. Wide area transmission mediums for network communication, discussed later, include microwave, infrared, satellite, T1, and, in the future, ISDN.

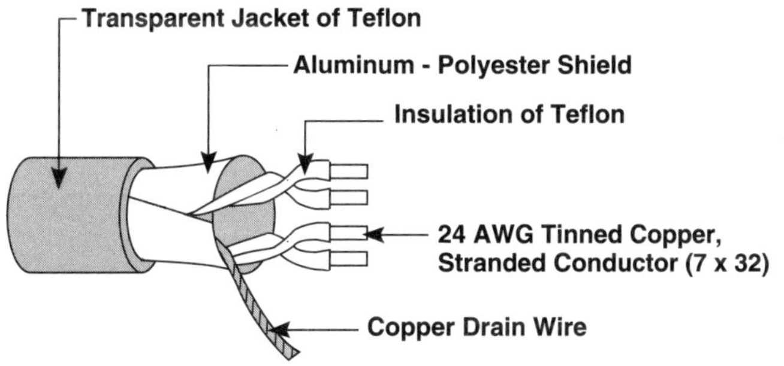

Figure 7-16. Twisted pair cable

Twisted-Pair Cable

Twisted-pair cable, shown in Figure 7-16, is used by many network topologies, including Novell's /68 systems, OmniNet, ARCNET, IBM Token-Ring, and Ethernet. This cable is available in two distinct forms: unshielded twisted pair (UTP) and shielded twisted pair (STP, or TP for short). It is important to realize that twisted pair is susceptible to any kind of electrical interference, from radio frequency (RF) noise to the electromagnetic bursts from a copier machine. Three properties of cabling itself also affect the performance of twisted-pair: attenuation, capacitance, and crosstalk.

Attenuation is the reduction in the amplitude of a transmitted signal (see Figure 7-17). Because the height of a digital communication square wave signal is reduced in attenuation, many listening devices, such as LAN NIC adapters, may confuse incoming signals with noise, if the signals can be detected at all. The waves are used to indicate binary 1s and 0s. If the wave is not tall enough, the desired code, a binary 1, will not be interpreted as such. The listening device can lower its threshold for signals qualifying as 1s. This could lead to errors, since it is easier for noise pulses to register as actual transmission. Therefore, the smaller the amount of attenuation of the signal, the more acceptable it becomes. Since the FCC restricts the strength of the transmitted signal, merely increasing its strength at the transmitter is not a viable solution for mitigating attenuation.

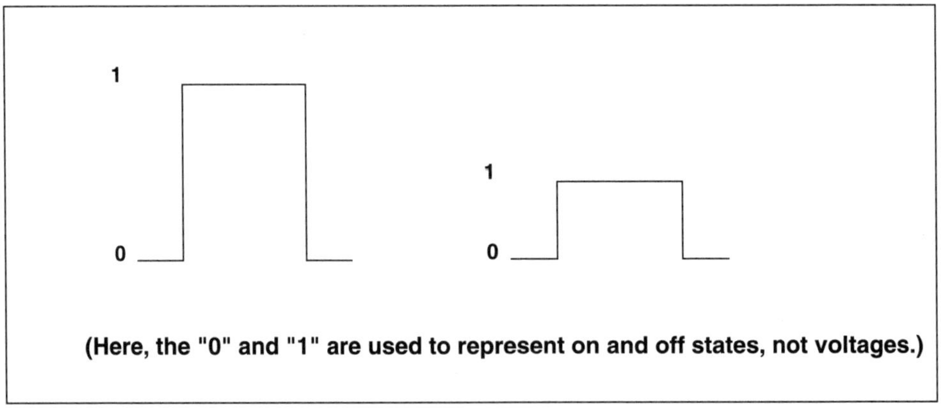

Figure 7-17. Effect of attenuation on digital signals

Capacitance is a measure of a cable's ability to store an electrical charge and to withstand changes in voltage. As with all twisted-pair cable, there is a dielectric constant. The combination of this dielectric constant with the thickness of the insulation provides the capacitance rating. This rating is for a single twisted pair, but it is also influenced by the rating of adjacent twisted pairs. Each pair of wires in a twisted pair has its own capacitance. When twisted pair is used in digital communications, this effect can distort the shape of the digital signal's square wave. This distortion can cause errors and prevent digital communications. PVC-jacketed cable provides the most unacceptable levels of capacitance, while Teflon-jacketed cable has the most acceptable levels.

Crosstalk occurs when the signal is reduced due to interference from other cable. It is rated using a decibel (db) loss index and is always active in twisted pair—especially in telephone wire. Crosstalk is measured by the amount of signal induced by an active or excited pair onto a quiet pair and can affect the suitability of twisted pair for computer use. The lower the db loss index, the stronger the signal becomes. In addition, the smaller the capacitance differences between pairs of cables, the lower the crosstalk effect becomes.

The combined effects of attenuation, capacitance, and crosstalk serve to inhibit network communications over twisted-pair cable. For example, cabling that has both a high attenuation and a high capacitance can be practically useless for digital transmissions (see Figure 7-18).

However, unshielded twisted pair (UTP) is best suited for high-speed computer network communications. This is because the alternative, shielded twisted pair, absorbs or attenuates the signal so that signal loss is greater over shorter distances. Although this makes it easier to comply with FCC regulations, shielded twisted pair can have severe distance limitations when it is used in computer networks.

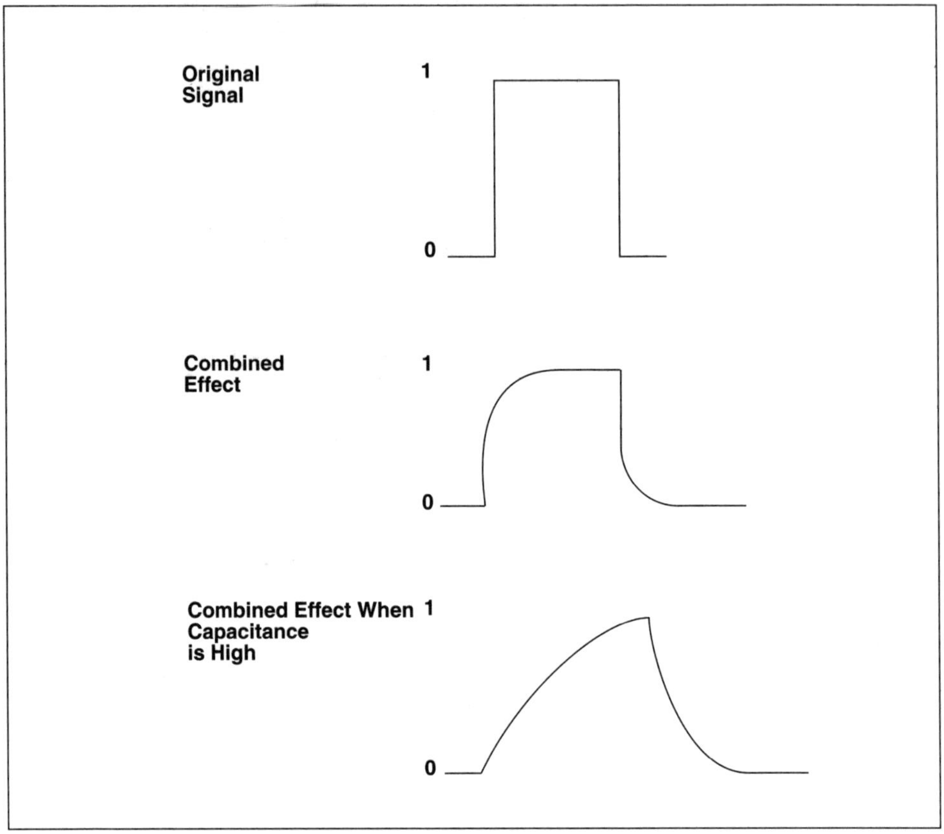

Figure 7-18. Combined effects of capacitance and attenuation on digital signals

Coaxial Cable

Coaxial (coax) cable is often used in Ethernet and ARCNET installations, and as with twisted pair, coax is the product of its physical properties. Among these properties are impedance, attenuation, capacitance, time delay, and velocity of propagation. Using foam core rather than solid core coax cable typically results in a 25 percent increase in cable performance. That is, a length of foam core coax cable transmits signals as quickly and clearly as a somewhat shorter length of solid core coax. Coaxial cable is shown in Figure 7-19.

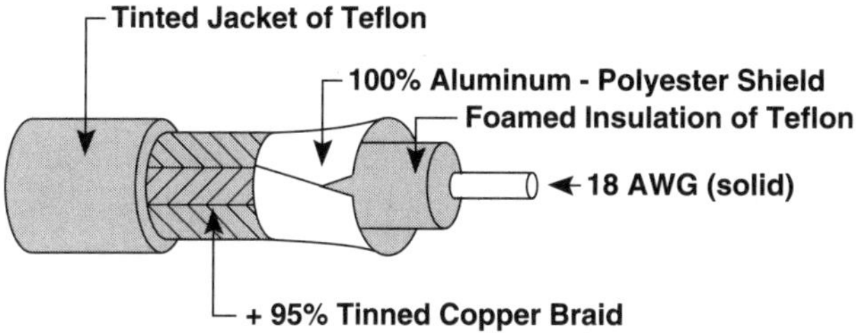

Figure 7-19. Coaxial cable

Coax cable types are differentiated by impedance values. When installing coax cable, take precautions to avoid anything that will produce electronic noise. Coax cable is as susceptible as twisted pair to electrical interference from things such as fluorescent light ballasts and copier machines. The connectors installed on coax are either crimp-on or twist-on. Crimp-on or twist-on connectors can be used with equal success. Crimp-on connectors are more reliable but require the proper tools and experience to install. The easier-to-install twist-on connectors provide a viable solution but have a greater tendency to become loose.

Impedance, measured in ohms, concerns the relationship of current and voltage in a coax cable. The impedance of the cable used must match the impedance expected by the network cards. Use of a cable with a different impedance will greatly shorten the maximum distances across which the network cards will be effective. For instance, most Ethernet installations use 50-ohm cable, while ARCNET installations use 93-ohm cable.

In addition to the connectors and cable, it may be necessary to use terminating resistors at either end of a cable run. This is very common in Ethernet installations using coax cable. The terminating resistors must have resistance values that match the impedance of the selected cable. A mismatch in impedance will result in an environment unfit for network communications. Impedance matching should also be observed in selecting the barrel connectors used in splicing coax, although in most cases the length is usually small enough for impedance to be considered insignificant.

The attenuation in coax cable is a function of the cable's conductor and insulation. Foam-core Teflon has the lowest attenuation, although solid-core Teflon is almost as low.

Capacitance is classified by the dimensions of the inner and outer conductors and the dielectric constant of the core. Most LAN topologies have a maximum capacitance value. Within the operating limits of a particular topology, the lower the capacitance, the longer the cable can be.

The time delay and velocity of propagation properties of a cable are often unknown. Described in nanoseconds per foot (ns/ft), time delay represents the amount of time required for a signal to travel through the cable. It is directly proportional to the square root of the dielectric constant of your cable. Hence, the lower the dielectric constant, the faster the signal can be transmitted through the cable.

Velocity of propagation indicates the speed of transmission in the cable as it relates to transmission in air, and it is inversely proportional to time delay. The closer its value is to 100 percent, the better the velocity of propagation and the lower the time delay.

Baluns

Another aspect of using twisted pair or coax cable concerns baluns. Short for "balance/unbalance," a balun (pronounced "bay lun") allows twisted pair cable to be used with NICs intended for coaxial cable. Baluns provide the heterogeneous link between a coax card and a twisted pair cable on LANs operating at 4Mb/s or slower. For instance, ARCNET LANs can make use of baluns. When using baluns, it is important to choose one manufacturer. Often, a mixture of baluns from a variety of manufacturers can become the Achilles' heel of the LAN, without the installer having any idea that the mixture is the problem.

The function of the balun is also being integrated into some NIC adapters and active hubs. There are a large number of twisted-pair-ready ARCNET cards on the market, as well as coax-to-twisted pair active hubs. This integration allows both twisted-pair and coax cable to be used in the same LAN.

Plenum Cable

Most urban fire and building codes require the use of Teflon-jacketed plenum cable anywhere cable is installed in the air handling system, such as in a suspended ceiling. This requirement is due to plenum's fire-resistant properties and low smoke producing qualities if it is burned.

When non-plenum cable, usually polyvinyl-chloride (PVC), is used, it must be installed in conduit as mandated by local building codes. Since LANs tend to be dynamic in nature, money spent on plenum cable is a good investment, since plenum cable will afford the most flexibility for cable runs, even after the initial installation. In addition, plenum cable generally has better signal propagation properties than non-plenum cable.

Fiber Optic Cable

Fiber optic cable is composed of an inner core of solid glass and a cladding of glass. The cladding is a concentric ring made of a type of glass that has a lower refractive index than that used at the core. Cladding helps to keep the light in the core by bending it back into the core. Both the core and the cladding are housed in an outer jacket, usually made of Teflon. Plastic is sometimes used for the core, but at the expense of higher data loss which, in turn, results in a reduction of maximum allowable cable distances.

Fiber optic cable offers many benefits. It is virtually immune to electromagnetic noise of every type, grounding problems, and differences in ground potential or grounding loops. Because of an almost infinite bandwidth (the capacity to carry data), fiber optic cable will be viable with newer and faster communications technologies as they are developed. These technologies include the ANSI fiber-distributed data interface (FDDI) standard which offers 100Mb/s transmission rates.

There are three types of fiber optic cable. The least expensive and most widely used is step-index multimode. There are also graded-index multimode cable and single-mode fiber optic cable, which is the most expensive. LAN devices that allow use of fiber optic cable are most likely to use step-index multimode fiber optic cable.

One limitation of fiber optic cable is that the signal attenuates or is lost over distance. Repeaters, which refresh the signal, can be used to overcome this limiting factor. However, it is not possible to link long distances of cable together so that it works with a time-bound LAN topology. Many LAN topologies that deal with communications on a contiguous network segment are time-bound.

Another limitation is that today's fiber optic technology can only be used in point-to-point fashion. It is not yet possible to attach multiple nodes to a single fiber optic cable. Although this has been done in research environments, it will quite likely take some time to become commercially available.

Wide Area Transmission Media

Wide area network transmission media—microwave, infrared, satellite, and T1—are all better suited to network applications that require connectivity among multiple geographically distributed sites, or to those that require other special connectivity needs (e.g., as on a factory floor). None of them are inexpensive, nor are they simple to install or maintain.

Microwave must be licensed by the FCC and is very costly to install. It is primarily useful for short point-to-point interconnections. Microwave can be used between two locations that are within line of sight of one another, usually at a distance up to 10 miles. Note that if the signal must pass over different terrestrial formations, such as lakes, concrete, or farm land, the microwave signal can be compromised because of the varying densities of the air through which it will pass.

Infrared can be used when two locations are within a mile of each other, and it does not require an FCC license to use. Infrared can be adversely affected by fog, dense rain, snow, heavy smog, and even birds. As with microwave, infrared is point-to-point. Although it is expensive, infrared is cheaper to install and maintain than microwave. Commercially available infrared LANs are beginning to receive attention in highly mobile office environments and other areas where traditional cabling is impractical. In most cases, their transmission speeds are poor (9600 bits per second [bps]) compared to the speeds of other options. However, there are products being introduced promising full 10Mb/s across infrared links.

Satellite communication borders on being very expensive. Often used for global communications, satellite offers fast throughput, but suffers from comparatively long propagation times due to uplink and downlink delays.

T1 communication connects physically separated sites. It operates via a digital signal level 1 or a DS-1 transmission link at a rate of 1.544Mb/s. T1 is within the reach of many companies and is described in more detail in Chapter 8.

ISDN technology is a specification for a telecommunications network that can conduct data, voice, fax, and graphics. ISDN provides for moderately fast links that are viable for low amounts of network traffic, and is primarily a point-to-point network. When it becomes widely available on a commercial scale, it may be a good connectivity solution; but, for networks requiring moderate-to-high performance, ISDN will probably not provide an adequate solution.

Evaluating Long Cable Run Solutions: An Example

Frequently, it is necessary to connect a group of users to a LAN that are near, yet not close, to the existing LAN; perhaps the new users are located in an office 1,500 feet down the hall. Deciding on the right communications media and protocol can be an involved task. This section will offer useful solutions to these dilemmas. We will present specific environments, relevant to NetWare v2.0 and higher, and useful remedies.

First, let us assume that a new group, located 1,500 feet down a corridor, is to be added to your network. At the moment, you are using unshielded twisted pair (UTP) wiring and your protocol is Ethernet. Now, it is not beneficial to run UTP 1,500 feet when using Ethernet because it will probably refuse to properly operate.

One expensive solution would be to use thick Ethernet cable and trans-ceivers. But thick Ethernet cable is large and heavy, and installing it is not a simple task. So, unless such a cabling plant already exists and is available for use, it would be wise to pass on this first solution.

Next, let's consider a thin Ethernet bridge. First off, you might note that thin Ethernet is designed for cable lengths of no more than, roughly, 600 feet. However, many Ethernet card manufacturers have upped that distance to roughly 1,000 feet. Even with this extended limit, spanning the 1,500 foot distance would involve some sort of repeater or other intermediate connection (such as a NetWare bridge). However, due to the limits of our assumed conduit, only a cable can be run, i.e., we cannot use any repeaters, bridges, or routers.

Fortunately, our simulated condition is not bound to the Ethernet protocol to complete the connection to the new group. Thus, we are free to consider other technologies. Examining the available protocols, we first, serendipitously, find Ethernet—but Ethernet with a twist. This Ethernet has a fiber optic interface. Using this fiber optic interface, we find it possible to use this magical, hair-thin cable to run distances well in excess of 3 miles! And realizing that fiber optic cable is not much more expensive than coaxial cable (per foot), and is also rather easy to run (although installing fiber optic connectors can be difficult), this solution looks promising.

However, we must also consider that the new group has had a network for the past year. They employ ARCNET technology as their specific connectivity protocol. We then realize that we could save a few dollars on hardware by using ARCNET to complete the connection via the aforementioned corridor. In its coaxial form, ARCNET can easily run 2,000 feet. And since there is an available connector on the new group's (ARCNET) active hub, we do not have to incur the additional cost of buying a new hub. In this scenario then, utilizing ARCNET to complete the connection seems to be the most appropriate solution.

"Across-the-Street" Solutions

Sometimes, however, connecting a close but nonlocal distance is not so easily facilitated by running a private cable. For instance, a situation might arise where the two groups to be linked exist across the street from each other. In these instances, it is not always possible (due to the lack of a conduit) to run a private cable. If it were, solving the connectivity needs would not be much different from the above scenario.

Typically, such "across-the-street" connections are made at the expense of performance. Generally, the only feasible solution is to put in an asynchronous bridge. The maximum throughput available with this solution, however, is often a distressingly slow 9600 bits-per-second (bps)—this throughput rate is 260 times slower than ARCNET's 2.5 Mb/s.

By using an Asynchronous Communications Server (ACS), it may be possible to have multiple asynchronous connections. However, because these ACS's are not directly hooked into the network's routing interfaces, these connections can have only one user at a time. Further, the user must run special software to make the necessary connection. And if that weren't bad enough (and it should be!) the side being called must have some sort of PC ready and waiting to process the call. This PC could be a computer-on-a-card (such as Cubix Corporation's QL 1001), it could be a real PC, or it could be the server itself. The last option is rarely used. (See the following section for details.)

Fortunately, there are bridging devices, such as those offered by VitaLink Communications and Advanced Computer Communications, that allow the connection of Ethernet or Token-Ring topologies via telephone circuits and other public data network (PDN) equipment. These bridges do operate at the network's routing layers, and thus require no special software to be run by users. They allow the physically/geographically disparate networks to be united into a usable whole.

There are many other possible solutions, most with hefty costs. Some of these other solutions include infrared, microwave, satellite, T1, and packet radio.

Using the Async Network Driver

When using NetWare, you can usually dedicate a communications (serial) port to receiving incoming "user" calls. A user may call into the network from a remote site and communicate directly with the server. The advantage to this solution is that a dedicated PC is not required to process the remote, call-in user's requests. All such processing takes place at the remote user's PC. The best way to think of the Async option on the file server is to imagine it as nothing more than a very slow LAN connection. Specifically, the server treats the async connection just like any other LAN it services. And, the async option does not function well with modem speeds in excess of 2400K. Beyond these speeds the server will either refuse to communicate, or if it does work, slow the server's performance to a crawl. Even at 2400K, the server's performance will be adversely affected, usually enough to be noted by users on its other LAN connections. Also, since the connection obtained by a remote user is nothing more than a regular (but very slow) LAN connection, all files accessed from the server need to be sent across this slow link to the remote user. Thus, it would be prudent for the remote user to have all programs (and overlay/configuration files) resident at the remote site. For instance, say the LOGIN program had to be retrieved from the network, at 2400K this could take in excess of 15 minutes to download! At a bare minimum, the time required would be 4 minutes. But there is network overhead traffic also. This would be enough to slow down any productive user. Remember, the async option, while available, is not always viable.

CHAPTER 8

Bridges and Routers

Expanding a LAN can involve many different things and can be accomplished in many different ways. When expansion means connecting to other, distant LANs or to dissimilar systems, bridges and gateways can serve to bring them together.

This chapter and Chapter 9 on gateways discuss general technology concepts, as well as many specific products relevant to internetworking. The technology concepts relating to NetWare's communications theory are discussed at length in both chapters. The accompanying product listings are intended to give the reader an idea of the range of possibilities available. The lists provided are neither comprehensive nor complete. Additional product and vendor information can be found in Appendix E.

In a NetWare environment, a router, (which Novell used to refer to as a bridge), is used to connect systems that are either physically separated or that are dissimilar in topology or architecture. The bridge allows nodes on the two systems to communicate with one another via a shared protocol.

All routers (bridges) have a common purpose—to connect two systems for the purpose of data exchange. NetWare supports a variety of means to accomplish this. There are two basic types of bridges, internal and external. This distinction is a physical, rather than a logical distinction, as both types operate in basically the same manner. Examples in each category are discussed in detail in the sections to follow. It is important to note that most of the bridging platforms can also double as support mechanisms for gateways, as discussed in Chapter 9.

Building Internetworks

As systems have grown and evolved, the building blocks of networked systems include not only PCs, but also entire networks. Linking LANs with one another and other, larger computer systems is becoming more and more common, resulting in networked computer systems of all descriptions that support truly distributed information systems.

The means by which LANs are internetworked is often mandated by both the ultimate goals of the internetwork and the existing systems to be linked. For example, if the goal is building E-mail for a business that has multiple operating system platforms, there may be few choices other than some SNA or TCP/IP gateway solutions.

In addition, the number and types of protocols used may limit your internetworking tool options. Using the E-mail example again, if the corporation uses many computers that are non-IBM/non-SNA compliant, SNA may not work.

Novell has traditionally referred to all NetWare products that link LANs over local or wide area networks as bridges. Recently, however, Novell has begun referring to their linking products as routers. In Novell terms, a bridge means router. Devices that link LANs into internetworks include not only bridges in the strictest sense, but also repeaters, routers, gateways, and combinations of these technologies. Each of these devices has unique characteristics in the areas of isolation, protocol support, configurability, filtering, and protocol translation, and it is important to review their respective uses when designing an internetwork.

Repeaters

Repeaters typically extend a physical segment of a LAN beyond the normal maximum distance. They are always specific to topology and sometimes media-specific as well. Ethernet and Token-Ring are two mainstream topology specifications that include repeaters.

The standard repeater is a non-intelligent device—its sole duty is to repeat all traffic it receives. It works as a transparent device at the physical level and, therefore, is transparent to all data link and higher levels of the OSI model.

Twisted-pair Ethernet is one example of the creative use of repeaters. The concentrator (the name for a type of Ethernet repeater) acts as a multiport repeater that treats each unshielded twisted-pair (UTP) attachment as a distinct network segment. All signals are repeated on all segments of the LAN.

A fringe benefit of the concentrator, or "hub," approach is exceptional network management. There are a number of statistical measures that can be taken when centralized equipment, like the concentrator, has unique intelligent connections to each user connection and each backbone attachment. SynOptics Communications, Inc., Cabletron Systems, Inc.,, and other UTP Ethernet vendors have been shipping products that exploit these capabilities for some time.

Novell's Hub Management System is a set a of NetWare Loadable Modules for NetWare 3.11 servers that allows system managers to control hub cards installed in the server. This lets system planners create a low cost intelligent wiring center for NetWare users. The NLMs allow individual port-level monitoring and control of Hub Management Interface (HMI)-compliant cards. Novell has released the HMI specification to allow third party vendors to develop HMI compliant cards so as to offer the user a variety of manufacturers to choose from. HMS is one of the components of the comprehensive NetWare Management System. (See Chapter 11 for more about Novell's NMS.)

Bridges

Bridges, in the strictest sense, are internetworking devices that link LANs at the data link layer (which includes Media Access Control (MAC) and Logical Link Control (LLC)). Primarily, the data link layer is embedded in the firmware on a specific NIC. that is, the software that controls the MAC and LLC is "on the card" and is not in the device driver software loaded at the workstation. They are transparent to IPX/SPX, NetBIOS, and other network layer and higher protocols.

Bridges connect LANs of similar topology and protocol, e.g., Ethernet to Ethernet, or Token-Ring to Token-Ring. They can also be used to link dissimilar cable types, as in the case of UTP Ethernet to coax Ethernet, or Type 1 Token-Ring to Fiber Token-Ring.

There are three major types of bridges: buffered, filtering, and learning. Bridges that include these advanced routing features are often referred to as brouters.

- *Buffered* bridges isolate segments of connected LANs. Collisions are not propagated across segments.

- *Filtering* bridges can be programmed to filter specific packet types. For example, a filtering bridge could filter IPX/SPX packets while propagating TCP/IP packets.
- *Learning* bridges "listen" to all transmissions on all attached segments and build tables of known local addresses. The source addresses of all packets are noted and remembered. On each given segment, the destination address of each packet is compared to the list of addresses known to be on that segment. Only packets whose destination addresses are not known to be on the same local segment are propagated across the bridge.

NetWare internal and external bridges are actually IPX/SPX routers, rather than true bridges. Routers are covered in the next section.

Routers

Routers are internetworking devices that operate at the network layer of the OSI model. Routers support specific protocol suites, such as TCP/IP, IPX/SPX, DECnet, and others.

Routers are normally "blind" to all protocols that they are not explicitly programmed to support. However, some routers, such as those offered by Proteon, Inc. and cisco Systems Inc., can be programmed so that they can concurrently support multiple protocols.

Some routers, such as Proteon's 42xx series and SysKonnect, Inc.'s SK-Net, have the gateway-like capability of encapsulating a packet of one protocol type within another type. This feature is used by several large universities whose TCP/IP campus backbones are used to provide transparent routing of IPX/SPX packets among NetWare LANs scattered across campus.

Before going on, there are a few more points about routers you should know. First, routing tables are kept at each router. The data in each of the routing tables are exchanged via Routing Information Packets (RIP). Finally, routers can route packets between networks of the same or dissimilar media types.

NetWare Routers and Bridges

Routers can be topology- and media-independent. A NetWare bridge is really a router, because it supports the interconnection of both similar and dissimilar LAN topologies and media. Novell now calls their LAN connectivity products routers, hopefully eliminating any confusion.

All NetWare 2.1x/2.2x versions include the ability to generate external bridge software. Under version 2.0a, this external bridge software was included only with 2.0x/68. Other versions of 2.0x (/86 and /286) required that the external bridge software be purchased separately.

Included in the drivers for an external bridge is an Async driver for the serial or COM ports of the external bridge. As a matter of interest, an async bridge is also an option at the file server, although use of this option is not recommended. Due to the interrupt-laden method used for communications to and from the serial ports, file server performance can be severely affected when using the Async driver option.

A close examination of Novell's documentation reveals that the Async driver allows connections to other file servers or to a stand-alone remote workstation. Connecting a single, remote workstation via Novell's Async driver is very tedious. This is because the remote node operates as if it were on the local LAN, which it is not, and it communicates at a relatively slow speed. The fastest speed the Async driver can accommodate at the file server is 2400 baud. Because the node operates as if it were a local node, it downloads files (programs, data, etc.) across the Async link. This connection is not the type that merely sends screens and keystrokes, as would be the case with communications software such as Close-Up, Carbon Copy, or PC Anywhere. It actually downloads everything. Because of these limitations, the Async driver should never be used at a file server. See the end of Chapter 7 for details.

On a more positive note, the Async driver can be used to link remote file servers using an external bridge. In fact, the external NetWare bridge supports the Async driver, a Wide Area Network Interface Module (WNIM), and an X.25 driver, as well as other wide area networking protocols. These are all documented in the NetWare manuals.

There are, however, a few words of warning regarding the use of remote drivers. First of all, the ARCONFIG utility is only for use when configuring the Async driver. If the X.25 driver is being configured, the utility that came with it should be used. Another warning concerns using the Async driver at the file server, in which case the NET$OS file should be modified. On some networks, the NET$OS file is in three parts: NET$OS.EXE, NET$OS.EX1, and NET$OS.EX2—in which case, the NET$OS.EX1 file is the one affected. In this particular instance, the following command syntax should be used from a DOS prompt:

```
util-1\ARCONFIG OSEXE-1:NET$OS.EX1 util-1 S
```

The util-1 reference shows where ARCONFIG is located. This could also be BRUTILS or another disk. The "S" at the end of the line is important, as it indicates the file being configured is part of a "split" file. If "S" is not specified and the file being configured is not an .EXE file, ARCONFIG will abort, indicating it cannot find anything to configure.

Brouters

Another class of bridges includes MAC-layer learning bridges and brouters. These are true bridges operating at the data link layer, but their configuration is more typical of routers operating at the network layer.

Protocol routers make up another class of bridges. Protocol routers are also referred to as routing bridges (or brouters), because they provide the functionality and oneness of bridges with the benefits and control of routers. These devices extend the leg of a network segment. It connects from the LAN to some communications circuit (async, T1, etc.), then to the LAN.

In effect, protocol routers act just like bridges except that they handle the conversion from actual LAN hardware (such as an Ethernet card and cable) to the transmission medium (async, T1, etc.) and back again. All nodes on either side of a protocol router "see" the other nodes as locally attached. This makes for a cohesive WAN that is independent of the upper layer protocols, such as NetWare, TCP/IP, NetBIOS, Named Pipes, etc.

Protocol routers are currently produced only for IBM Token-Ring and Ethernet/802.3-based LANs. VitaLink Communications and Advanced Computer Communications both offer protocol routers.

Gateways

Gateways are internetworking devices that operate at the application layer of the OSI model. The various IBM 3270 Token-Ring and TCP/IP gateways are examples of products that operate between dissimilar LANs or LAN-connected systems to allow interoperation.

As Novell and other vendors continue to migrate towards OSI-compliant networks, they will do so in large part through the use of LAN-based gateways to OSI networks and other LANs. A broader discussion of gateways is presented in Chapter 9.

Remote Internetworks

LANs may be interconnected over wide areas by using remote versions of bridges, routers, and/or gateways. Selection of a remote internetwork device depends on many of the same criteria as selection of a local device. For example, support of multiple protocols requires a remote bridge or multi-protocol router. Dissimilar topologies linked over wide area networks will also require a router.

There is an important distinction between the selection of local and remote internetwork devices. Local internetwork devices attach directly to two or more distinct LAN segments, while remote internetwork devices come only in pairs–each device attaches to one or more local segments, and then connects to its "mate" across a remote link.

Because remote internetworks require additional equipment and communications lines, they should always be architected according to the requirements of the intended applications. For example, the cost of the wide area connection will generally be dominated by the leased line facilities. It pays to architect and build wide area systems to squeeze the most performance from the available communications line bandwidth.

The following scenario demonstrates this point. A hypothetical wide area network connecting a Midwest to a West Coast location using 56Kb/s leased lines costs approximately $3,500 or more per month for using the line, plus $3,000 for installation. Over 12 months, the total telecommunications cost for this system is $45,000.

This type of investment provides ample justification for acquiring two $12,000 devices to make use of the leased lines, even though devices are available at half the price that would still "work," and would certainly give the appearance of being more economically advantageous.

However, spending the $24,000 better leverages the use of the $45,000 per year leased-line facility by providing superior value and reliability. The business mission is more reliably supported because of the additional money spent on superior equipment. The cost of leased communications facility, in most cases, is simply too steep to not ensure and optimize their use.

T1 Communication

Within the past decade, T1 communication has become a well-known and widely implemented service. T1, which provides LAN-like throughput, connects physically separated sites by operating at a rate of 1.544Mb/s via a digital signal level 1 (DS-1) transmission link. This DS-1 signal is often broken into 24 DS-0, or 64Kb/s channels. By splitting the DS-1 signal, it is possible for T1 to be shared by many devices (i.e., Fractional T1). Conversely, it is also possible for the complete DS-1 signal to be used by one device. T1 communicates over various phone company networks. However, it is quite expensive to install and use when compared to slower leased line, dial-up, or packet-switching services. Quite often, troubleshooting T1 problems is a user responsibility. In spite of cost and complexity, both in design and implementation, T1 is often the right choice for networks requiring full-time access by multiple users.

In order to help justify the cost of a T1, companies will often use a T1 to transmit both voice and data, together over the same line. This is accomplished by utilizing T1 multiplexers. T1 multiplexers combine multiple signals, such as voice conversations or LAN data, into one larger signal for transmission over T1 telephone lines by translating any analog signals into digital signals and then sending the voice traffic to another multiplexer at the receiving end of the transmission as a single signal over one of 24 DS-0 channels. A communication device called a channel service unit (CSU), or a combination digital service unit/channel service unit (CSU/DSU) is used to link the T1 multiplexer to the T1 line.

Most T1 multiplexers use time division multiplexing (TDM) to create the one large signal out of several smaller ones. TDM takes pieces of each signal to be sent and combines them into one stream by placing the pieces one after another. The single stream of information the TDM weaves together saves transmission time, because multiple signals do not have to be sent out simultaneously. It also saves resources, because only one channel is being used. Since the whole process happens very quickly, users usually don't notice delays in their phone conversations or have lengthy waits when requesting information from remote LANs.

It is important to note that while the T1 is a link that is primarily external to the physical premises of a corporation, it is imperative to provide fault tolerance for the components that are local. To be prudent, use redundant power supplies on the multiplexers and other communications equipment. Additional fault tolerance can be built into the link by providing a redundant T1 link that will come on-line in the event of the primary line's failure, but the cost/benefits of this option should be considered carefully due to the relatively high cost of this alternative.

NetWare Link/T1 and NetWare Link/64 are two products that permit NetWare LANs to communicate with each other via synchronous communications lines. These products support transmission speeds from 9600 bps to 1.544 Mbps and are designed to route IPX, NetBIOS, and SPX over wide area networks. NetWare routing software dynamically determines the shortest path for each packet based on the current network topology. This means that if one of the aforementioned redundant links were down, one of the operative links would be utilized. To use these products, a Novell Synchronous/+ adapter is required in a dedicated external router.

X.25 Communication

One of the commercially available X.25 solutions used by a number of NetWare LANs is the Eicon X.25 system. Acquired by Novell under an OEM agreement, the Eicon X.25 system is also sold directly by Novell. The software and hardware for X.25 support is packaged in two formats. One product serves as a gateway to a host computer and is described in Chapter 9. The other is a point-to-point, or if you prefer, LAN-to-LAN bridge. Both of these X.25 systems allow for communication speeds of up to 64Kb/s. These systems are designed specifically with NetWare in mind. There are many other packages available for connecting to X.25, but they are not NetWare-aware.

There are several X.25 Public Data Networks (PDNs) in place. The three most prominent are Accunet, Telenet (not to be confused with the TCP/IP Telnet protocol), and Tymnet. These X.25 networks provide a viable communications medium and work well for communicating across international borders and long distances. As with telephone services, these companies charge according to a fee schedule. Charges are usually based on the amount of data sent across the network, so the choice of an X.25 network is influenced by the amount of anticipated traffic. In certain cases, a leased line or dial-up connection may be a more cost-effective solution. Appendix G provides a complete primer on the X.25 standard.

Frame Relay

Frame Relay is an emerging LAN-WAN interconnection method that many consider better suited to a LAN's traffic patterns than the X.25. Additionally, Frame Relay has garnered a great deal of interest because it is priced on a distance- and usage-insensitive basis. T1, for example is priced based on distance—the greater the distance, the more expensive the T1 line. X.25 is price-based on usage—the higher the volume of traffic, the more you pay.

Frame Relay's benefits include low overhead, high capacity with low delay, and reliable data transfer over existing public networks. It is designed to be a public service for interconnecting private local area networks. Frame relay provides service at speeds up to 2 Mbps, and today carriers are rolling out frame relay services in the increments of 56Kbps, fractional T1, and full T1. Frame relay services were just becoming available in the fall of 1991, and services will come from the RBOCs, interexchange carriers, and value-added networks (VANs), including Pacific Bell, CompuServe, Wiltel, and Infonet. (More about frame relay is beyond the scope of this book, but additional information can be found in other books such as BSG's *Enterprise-Wide Networking*, Sams Publishing, 1992.)

Directory Services

Directory services are a feature set of network operating systems that provide a telephone book "White Pages"-like directory of the users and resources that are located on an enterprise-wide network. Well-known examples of directory services include, from a standards body, OSI's X.500, and, from a product vendor, Banyan's StreetTalk.

With NetWare 4.0, Novell provides a new directory services feature set. The service comprises an X.500-compatible hierarchical distributed database that dynamically maps object names to the object's physical location. This allows users to log in once and have access to resources throughout the network. It replaces the flat bindery system in NetWare 2.x and 3.x. A bindery emulation feature will allow those NetWare servers to access 4.0 resources. While little applied information is available from actual usage of Novell's directory services, those services are expected to greatly enhance the ability of Novell to be effective across widely distributed WANs.

CHAPTER 9

Gateways

A gateway provides an interface at all protocol layers that allows the interconnection of the network to other systems. The most common application of a gateway is to allow a workstation on the network to connect to another system as a terminal. Depending on the type of system used (usually referred to as the host), file transfer and printing services may also be made available to the workstation.

Gateways are most often utilized on Wide Area Networks (WANs). These networks, unlike LANs, are not bound by physical size. They provide a timely communication link between geographically separated nodes or networks. Most WANs consist of either a packet-switching network or a direct communication link between two nodes. They are increasingly being used to provide the interchange of E-mail between remote networks.

This chapter describes the operations of several gateway solutions. As is true of the bridging solutions discussed in Chapter 8, the gateway solutions below are offered to give the reader some idea of the range of possibilities available. The list is meant as an overview of what is available and is not comprehensive.

LAN Terminal Servers

Although LAN Terminal Servers are not limited to gateway functions, they do fall into the gateway category by virtue of their ability to connect a network to another system.

A LAN Terminal Server provides one of two basic services. The first permits LAN workstations to call out of the LAN to some other system. The other system can be a communications service, such as MCI Mail, CompuServe, Telenet, or Tynmet; a remote PC; or a minicomputer such as a VAX or an HP3000. The second service a LAN Terminal Server can provide allows a remote device (usually a PC) to call into the LAN and make use of various services available on the LAN. The following are descriptions of several products that accomplish one or both of these goals.

NetWare Access Server

Novell's NetWare Access Server provides a pseudo-gateway function for remote PCs. Access Server is unique in that it is the result of a joint development effort by Novell, QuarterDeck Office Systems, and Symantec-DMA. The resulting product allows up to 15 concurrent remote connections to a single 80386 or compatible system. Access Server allows for remote call-ins to the LAN but does not allow for calls out. This method is by far the simplest hardware approach, in that it requires the least amount of hardware to accomplish the job. Aside from the up to 16 modems that can be connected to it (15 of which can be used concurrently), the system is contained within the one 386 PC/Access Server. Remote PCs calling in send only keystrokes and receive only screens. Access Server does all of the actual processing, so the speed with which the LAN is accessed is equivalent to a locally attached workstation.

To determine which display types are supported, Access Server uses the display type that is installed in the Access Server to define the highest display standard it will support. For instance, if the Access Server has a monochrome video card, only monochrome level screens will be usable. However, if the Access Server has VGA, it will support any level of screens utilized by the remote PC, up to and including VGA.

Single-User Remote Access

When the need to support remote PCs is minimal, the single-user remote access option can be a cost-effective solution. Single-user remote access consists of a workstation with a modem and phone line that is set up to handle incoming calls from remote PCs. This workstation serves as the LAN PC, while the incoming call comes from the remote PC. Support of networks across a wide area can be simplified by this workstation access software and is one of its key benefits.

Several software packages are available that transfer screen and keyboard data between two PCs, including, but not limited to ReachOut, Carbon Copy, PC Anywhere, Co/Session, Close-Up, and Sparkle. This software is used to transfer the keystrokes from a remote PC to a LAN PC, and transfer the screen of a LAN PC to a remote PC. All actual processing occurs on the LAN PC. Since only the screens and keyboard data are transferred, a 2400-baud modem will usually suffice. If the application involves graphics, a higher speed link is helpful. As with Access Server, the lowest common level of graphics between two PCs will be used to decide the level of graphics support. However, some remote software packages may only work with CGA or EGA level graphics, and VGA specific graphics are unsupported.

ReachOut, by Ocean Isle Software is a remote control PC software package that has been optimized for Windows and supports VGA. With ReachOut, mouse movements are completely local, so there is no time delay when using the mouse. The package has been optimized so that only the modified sections of the screen, rather than the entire screen, are sent over the wire when changes are made. This speeds the moving of icons, the opening of software packages, and general use. With V.32bis (14400 baud) modems, Windows performance begins to approach local performance. This package can also be used on a LAN (Novell, Banyan, or LAN Manager) as a support tool. Just as ReachOut works over dial-up lines, it performs a similar function over the LAN, whereby an administrator can take over a user's workstation and help him or her through difficulties.

ReachOut works by taking advantage of Windows' device-independent structure. At the lowest level Windows uses a VGA.DRV, a MOUSE.DRV, and a KEYBOARD.DRV to communicate with the computer's physical devices. ReachOut replaces the generic Windows versions of these drivers with its own versions. The difference is that ReachOut's drivers have asynchronous capability that lets them tell similar drivers on the other end of a dial-up line what they are doing. This keeps the two computers drawing the same objects, and generating the same key-clicks, making the same mouse movements.

Since the VGA driver has the graphics primitives and basic bitmap objects, both machines draw the same objects at roughly the same time without the need for sending any bit-by-bit information (the way Close-Up works). Of course, anything that is a BMP or an ICO—and therefore not defined in the VGA driver—must be sent over the wire. You will, therefore, see performance decrease in proportion to the number of non-stock graphic objects that is used.

Brightwork Development, Inc. has a product called NETRemote that provides the ability for a LAN supervisor to view and control another user's LAN workstation from another workstation. This feature facilitates assisting LAN users. In addition, a package called LAN Support Center aids network administration by supplying a database that logs support activity. By facilitating the diagnosis and cure of user troubles, LAN Support Center can be an indispensable tool to the network manager. Brightwork offers an additional utility for "chatting" that is independent of NETRemote.

Norton-Lambert Corporation's Close-Up LAN product is similar to NETRemote. Among its features are the ability to load the "viewer" as a TSR. The LAN administrator may "hot-key" from a foreground application to view and control other LAN workstations. Up to 16 sessions on 16 remote workstations may be held simultaneously via hot-keying.

In addition to providing the ability to view and access the keyboard of another user's PC, Fresh Technology Group's LAN Assist Plus provides for a chat window, just like Carbon Copy from Microcom, Inc.

The solution offered by each of the products has the obvious drawback of requiring one PC for each incoming call, hence the name single-user remote access. If remote call-ins only occur during non-business hours, then this could be an economical use of LAN PCs—instead of the LAN PCs being used only during business hours, they could be productive during after hours.

In addition to allowing remote access to the LAN, these remote PC-to-PC communication packages also allow file transfer between the remote PC and the LAN PC. In some cases, file transfer can run concurrently with other activities of screen and keystroke transmission. In addition, most of these packages also have a "chat" mode allowing a user at the remote PC to communicate with a user at the LAN PC via a chat window.

LAN Modems

Another alternative connection beginning to develop is the network modem. The RLN (remote LAN node) modem, and the Shiva NetModem are two examples of modem/software combinations that permit remote workstations to act as if they were connected to the LAN via a network interface card. These modems permit the asynchronous transmission of IPX/SPX packets, thereby permitting the connection of LANs over dial-up phone lines. The key point to remember when evaluating this type of alternative is that even V.42/V.42bis modems transmitting at 56Kbps are still a long way from the 10Mbps of Ethernet or 16Mbps of Token Ring in terms of data throughput. As a result, the network modem is not an effective solution for data intensive applications, but it is cost effective for providing standard file retrieval network functionality.

Add-in PCs

Another remote PC architecture uses the equivalent of one or more 8088 or 80286 class PCs on add-in boards that are installed in a NetWare file server or external bridge. The add-in PCs are treated like diskless workstations, as they boot from a boot disk image file stored on the file server. Software is included that allows each add-in PC to boot from a unique boot disk image file. As a result, this architecture supports many creative applications in addition to supporting remote PCs using Close-up, Carbon Copy, or similar software packages.

The Chatterbox Plus by J&L Information Systems Inc. is an example of this kind of product. It can provide the combined functionality of a LAN terminal server, E-mail server, LAN PC, or other functions, depending on the software used. When used to support remote PCs, this architecture can be seen as a hardware implementation of an Access Server or the consolidation of many dedicated LAN PCs in a single chassis.

Novell Asynchronous Communications Server

The Novell Asynchronous Communications Server (NACS) supports both incoming and outgoing calls. A single PC serves as the gateway and can have up to 16 serial connections via Novell Wide Area Network Interface Module (WNIM) cards. Each WNIM handles up to four serial ports that can either be attached to modems or can be directly connected to other machines, such as a DEC VAX minicomputer. The PC acting as the NACS server does not need to be high powered, as the bulk of the processing occurs at the WNIM cards.

Novell's Asynchronous Communication Software is bundled with three major communication packages. The first, and most important one, is the Asynchronous Communication Server (ACS) software. The original product had a number of limitations and in 1987 was revamped as the NetWare Asynchronous Communication Server (NACS). The other two programs are ASCOMIV.EXE and ANYWARE.EXE.

The role of the NACS software is to provide a path to the physical communication hardware, such as a modem or a direct connection. The term path is used because, except for LAN cabling, none of the PCs accessing the hardware are actually physically connected to it. The network cabling, combined with the software being used, emulates the physical connection. The PC executing the ACS software is referred to as the ACS. This PC must be physically configured in the following way:

- No more than 256K of RAM in the machine—this includes memory, whether or not it is configured. For example, if the PC has 512K on the motherboard, the extra 256K RAM chips must be removed or disabled, regardless of whether DOS recognizes the presence of the memory (this limitation is lifted by the newer NACS software).
- At least one WNIM must be installed in the ACS.
- One network card for the appropriate network, as the ACS is a station on the network.
- At least one floppy disk drive.

In addition to the specific physical configuration, the software that will be accessing the ACS must be set up a specific way as well. The following conditions must be present for proper ACS operation:

- The ACS must boot from the floppy disk drive.
- The program called ACS.EXE must be on the boot disk.
- The file CONFIG.SYS should not be present.
- The file AUTOEXEC.BAT should look very similar to Figure 9-1.

```
Echo Off      "hides" the screen output
IPX           For DOS 3.X, use ANET2 for DOS 2.X or IPX for NetWare v2.1x
NET3
ACS           Begins the operation of the ACS
```

Figure 9-1. AUTOEXEC.BAT file

In addition to ACS, ASCOMIV.EXE and ANYWARE.EXE have files that must be initialized in the following manner (this is important only for the ACS):

- Bring the PC that will function as the ACS up on the network as a regular workstation.
- Log in to the network as a user who has rights to the directory that has been set up for these files. (This is discussed in greater detail later.)
- Copy the SETUPACS.EXE file to the directory area that contains the two files to be initialized. (Note that this could be two different directories.)
- Change your current directory to the one containing the two files.
- At the DOS prompt, type: SETUPACS ASCOMIV.EXE and answer "yes" when asked to continue.
- At the DOS prompt, type: SETUPACS ANYWARE.EXE and answer "yes" when asked to continue.
- Delete the SETUPACS.EXE file.

This procedure must be completed before attempting to use any of the three software packages available with the ACS. It must also be performed *immediately* following any change in the way in which the ACS is connected to the network. This includes any change made in the physical station number (port on an S-net server) or in the network number (internetwork address at the server) on which the ACS is located. If the ACS has an Ethernet or Token-Ring adapter, changing out the network card has the same effect as changing the station address.

For S-net servers purchased prior to April 1986, it may be necessary to upgrade the I/O chips on the LAN boards in the server. Revision D of these I/O chips might work, however Revision E will work.

ASCOMIV.EXE

The ASCOMIV communication package allows any workstation on the network to access any hardware device (such as a modem) that is connected to the ACS. An example of this is to connect Smartmodem from Hayes Microcomputer Products, Inc., and external modem, to the first communication port on the first WNIM in the ACS. Once the mode is in place, a user somewhere on the network can then execute the ASCOMIV.EXE, set up a configuration to recognize a Hayes Smartmodem on port 1, and can then place a call.

The way in which ASCOMIV.EXE handles configuration files may not be desirable to many network administrators. When the configuration is saved, the user is prompted to name the file or to use the default name. The problem is that the configuration file is saved in the user's mailbox directory (SYS:MAIL\USERID#) in order to prevent other users from accessing the file. This results in duplicate configurations being saved and wastes disk space. Each duplicate configuration file is approximately 1,159 bytes long and consumes 4K of disk space, as described in Chapter 5. This problem can be resolved by performing a one-time debug on the ASCOMIV.EXE file.

The ASCOMIV.EXE file is hard-coded to use the SYS:MAIL\USERID# user mailbox directory. The following debug sequence will alter the name of the directory to SYS:CNFG. (CNFG is limited only by the following rules: the name must be exactly four characters long; it must be an actual directory name off of the root directory on the SYS volume.)

1. Change the current directory to the directory containing the ASCOMIV.EXE file.
2. Be sure the file is flagged read/write.
3. At the DOS prompt, type: REN ASCOMIV.EXE *.DBG
4. At the DOS prompt, type: DEBUG ASCOMIV.DBG
5. -scs:100 FFFF 'SYS:MAIL'
6. Note the address found. If the address 882h is used, for this example, you will type:

   `-f882 Ld 'SYS:CNFG',0,0,0,0,0` <enter>
7. -w <enter>
8. -q <enter>
9. At the DOS prompt, type: REN ASCOMIV.DBG *.EXE
10. Set the file flags back as they were.

This change will enable multiple users running ASCOMIV from the file server to access the same configuration files from a common dialing directory. Optionally, a disk editor, such as the Norton Utilities from Symantec/Peter Norton, can be used instead of DEBUG.

It may be worthwhile to make both versions of the ASCOMIV program available to users who need or want a private configuration file and dialing directory.

Simply set up two choices on the network menu for ASCOMIV. The first one should be labeled "personal" and the second, "shared." Each menu choice should indicate the way in which the configuration files will be accessed and saved. "Personal" should indicate an unaltered ASCOMIV.EXE file. "Shared" should indicate the debugged file that saves and accesses the configurations in the same directory, regardless of who uses them.

When using the ACS, there is an undocumented feature of the ASCOMIV software that concerns rights within the ASCOMIV directory. The rights mask [RWOCDS] must be assigned in the directory in which the ASCOMIV files reside to any user who will be using the ASCOMIV software. This is a minimum requirement that must be met for proper ACS operation. The system may hang, lock up, or issue a vector error (S-net products only) if the minimum rights mask is absent.

Other NACS Software

So that independent software vendors may take advantage of the NACS's capabilities, Novell provides technical documentation for the NACS called the *NetWare Asynchronous Services Interface* (NASI). Products that make use of the interface described in the NASI include:

- Reflection from Walker Richer & Quinn, Inc.
- Relay Gold from Relay Technology, Inc.
- Procomm Plus from DataStorm Technologies, Inc.
- CrossTalk Mk. 4 from DCA
- Poly-COM/320 from Polygon Inc.
- Smarterm from Persoft, Inc.
- Softerm from Softronics, Inc.
- VSCom from The M/H Group
- ASCOM IV from Symantec-DMA
- NMP2 from Network Products Corporation
  (NMPZ dosen't need the NACS to work; it uses the NASI interface.)

These call-in packages operate with the NACS just as they do for single-user remote access. In fact, the PC Anywhere programs used with Access Server and NACS are simply modified versions of the ones developed for single-user remote access. With NACS, a LAN PC waiting for an incoming call can be anywhere on the LAN. Instead of requiring the waiting PC to be connected to a modem and phone line, the NACS contains the modem, handles the incoming call, and routes data to the LAN PC via the LAN. Other than this difference, the operation of PC Anywhere for NACS and single-user remote access is similar. PC Anywhere for Access Server operates in a similar manner, but only supports incoming calls.

A unique device for capturing serial port activity called the Network Communications Adapter (NCA) is available from J&L Information Systems, whose Chatterbox Plus product is described earlier in this chapter. In the form of a plug-in card, the NCA replaces the standard serial port. With the card installed, all serial port activity can be redirected to another device on the LAN, usually to a Chatterbox. (Note: the NCA is no longer being produced.)

Although it is possible to use software alone to capture all serial port activity, the speed degradation and complexity associated with doing so make it impractical. The hardware in the NCA runs at a much faster speed than any available software, and it offers the additional benefit of utilizing existing communications software without modifications. The penalty is that the NCA requires the use of a slot in the PC to provide this capability and must be installed in each PC that requires such remote communications.

An interesting use of the NCA is that of routing serial port printer activity across the network. This includes sending output to devices, such as certain plotters that require bidirectional communications with the PC.

SNA Gateway Solutions

Gateways are generally most effectively implemented when the mainframe (or minicomputer) host environment is well understood. For this reason, there are many options for IBM gateways—the SNA/SDLC technology has been in the making for 15 years. Refer to Figure 9-2 for an example of many possible connection points for an SNA gateway.

The following text details the connections listed in Figure 9-2.

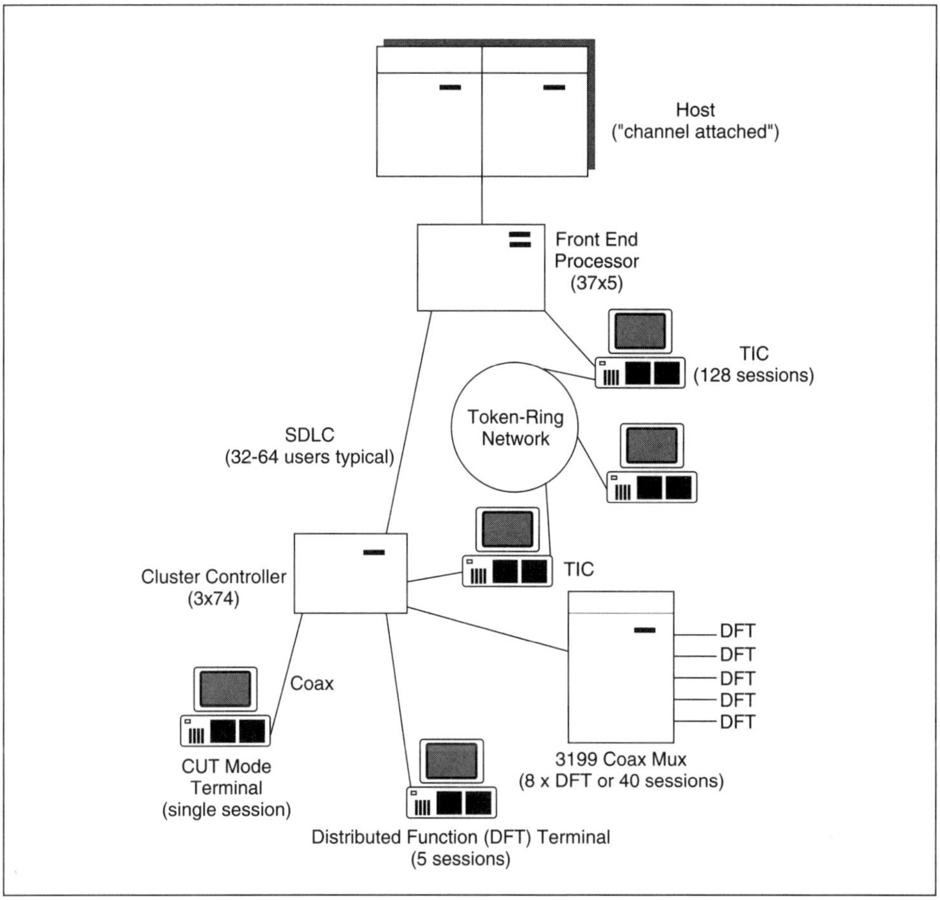

Figure 9-2. Potential SNA gateway connections

SDLC gateway. This is a gateway for synchronous, typically remote connections. It emulates an IBM 3174 (or similar) cluster controller, supporting 32, 64, or more sessions.

CUT-mode terminal gateway. This is a direct connect gateway over coax. It is a poor option because it is a physical connection supporting only one session.

DFT-mode terminal gateway. This is another low-end direct connect gateway over coax. It provides five sessions per physical connection.

Coax Mux gateway. This is a clever configuration using coax. The system "expects" to "see" eight DFT coax channels. The product was originally developed to conserve cables, with the idea of using one cable multiplexed (or muxed) to a cluster of eight terminals, each with a possible five sessions. This enables the gateway to emulate a total of 40 sessions.

Token-Ring gateway. This is the first LAN-specific connection supported by SNA. Most users in an SNA-host environment will probably move to this type of architecture sometime in the future. The Novell Token-Ring gateway supports 97 users and up to 128 sessions.

The Token-Ring gateway configuration may take several distinct variations. For example, PCs on a Token-Ring LAN may communicate directly with the cluster controller. In this instance, the gateway functionality is built into the host and the PC is just a session on the host.

In another example, the PC LAN emulates a cluster controller communicating directly with the host front-end processor. There are other options as well, making connectivity to IBM hosts a much more straightforward and flexible possibility than ever before.

Several products are available today that provide connections to an SNA network. A few of the manufacturers are Novell, Attachmate Corporation, DCA, IBM, and Rabbit Software Corporation. Each of these companies offers a gateway that provides terminal and printer services, and most include an interface that can be programmed as needed.

Connections to IBM mainframes using SNA can be achieved on a station-by-station basis using an emulation card in each workstation. However, in a LAN environment, this process is self-defeating, as it limits the workstations that can access the mainframe and it would unnecessarily tie up valuable ports on the mainframe workstation controller. One exception to this is when graphics-intensive applications are used. In this case, a "direct connection" may perform better than a LAN gateway, although Token-Ring gateways can also yield substantial performance gains.

The best of both worlds is now available through IBM's Token-Ring Interface Card (TIC) facilities for connecting Token-Ring LANs to SNA networks. The TIC is available for IBM FEPs or 3174 controllers. TIC-based gateways offer substantially better performance than regular CUT or DFT controller ports. A TIC appears as a node in a Token-Ring network, even though it still requires a gateway of some sort. The 3174 can act as the gateway for workstations on the same LAN, but Novell's source-routing drivers are needed for the communications to cross Novell bridges.

Novell offers NetWare-aware gateway products that use NetWare's IPX and/or SPX protocols. There are two benefits to using NetWare-aware gateways. First, there is a savings of up to 40K of RAM at the workstation as the NetBIOS emulator is not needed. Second, using the IPX/SPX protocols increases throughput when compared to the NetBIOS interface.

IBM Midrange Gateway Solutions

Systems connected to IBM's System/3x (34, 36, and 38) require a 5250 gateway that is similar, but not identical, to an SNA gateway. There are essentially two ways to connect to a System/3x. One is via the twinax cable that runs out of the local or remote workstation controller. With this method, the gateway acts as a 5251/11 local terminal server and, as such, provides up to seven combined terminal and printer emulations sessions to the LAN via the gateway.

The second means for connecting to a System/3x is via an SNA/SDLC line. Up to eight or nine combined terminal and printer emulations sessions are possible with this remote-type connection, depending on whether the gateway is emulating a 5294 or a 5251/12 cluster controller.

Several manufacturers offer 5250 gateways, including Novell, IDEAssociates, and Eicon Technology Corporation. Most of these gateways require NetBIOS, but a few IPX/SPX versions are available.

One important feature to look for in a 5250 gateway is support for file transfer and virtual printer/disk facilities, such as IBM offers for use with their 5250 terminal emulation products. The software is different for each member of the 3x family. The System/34 uses the File Support Utility for file transfer. The System/36 and System/38 have PC Support/36 and 38, respectively, which include the file transfer, virtual printer, and virtual disk modules. If a workstation accessing the System/3x is using any of the IBM file transfer or virtual printer/disk facilities, it is important to check the gateway product to ensure that it supports IBM's software. As an alternative, some of the 5250 gateway products offer proprietary file transfer software.

The newest member of the System/3x family is the AS/400. Most of the existing 5250 gateway products support terminal emulation to an AS/400. In order to use IBM's file transfer software, the 5250 gateway must emulate the new IBM 5394 cluster controller that supports 16 sessions. Specific vendor support for the AS/400 is constantly changing, so it is advisable to consult a buyer's guide in a current trade publication for available products. The AS/400's native file transfer/virtual printer/shared folders software is called PC Support. The best gateway to choose is one that uses IPX /SPX and works with PC Support for the AS/400. Connectivity to AS/400s will probably best be addressed by a new implementation of portable NetWare. When or if this will be done is uncertain.

Transmission Control Protocol/Internet Protocol

The common denominator of computer communications today is called Transmission Control Protocol/Internet Protocol (TCP/IP). TCP/IP, an entire suite of protocols originated by Vinton Cerf in the early 1970s at Stanford University, offers the most accepted means of inter-LAN connectivity between dissimilar operating systems.

TCP and IP

TCP/IP represents two different levels of communications. IP relates to physical layers, while TCP relates to session layers, which means that TCP specifies the services IP provides.

IP was developed to interconnect heterogeneous networks, thereby allowing nodes on different networks to communicate. IP resides between the Transport and Network layers of the OSI model and is, therefore, hardware independent.

TCP, on the other hand, resides in the Transport layer of the OSI model. It receives data to be delivered from upper layer protocols and provides a *de facto* standard for heterogeneous node communications.

Originally sponsored and then adopted by the Defense Advanced Research Projects Agency (DARPA) and the U.S. Department of Defense (DOD), TCP/IP has been endorsed by a number of companies over recent years, as shown in Figure 9-3.

Year	Companies Accepting TCP/IP
1983	Berkeley, Microdyne, and Sun Microsystems
1984	Wollongong and CMC
1985	Bridge Communications, NRC, and Siemens
1986	Novell, DEC, Ungermann-Bass, and Interlan
1987	IBM and Sytek
1988	Microsoft, Apple, and NCR

Figure 9-3. TCP/IP momentum since 1983

TCP/IP Applied

Microdyne, a division of Novell, offers a workstation-by-workstation solution that involves one of their Ethernet cards. The workstation can concurrently access a TCP/IP network and a Novell network.

Microdyne's TCP/IP solutions run only as a Front End Process (FEP) on EXOS series of adapters. That is, the EXOS board is initialized by running a batch file (TCP.BAT) that downloads the EXOS board operating system and the TCP net module to the card. The batch file then loads a TSR in DOS memory (12K) that allows access to the front-end TCP for DOS applications (FTP, TELNET, etc.). The NetWare drivers require that TCP.BAT has been run and use the TSR driver to gain shared media access with the FEP. Assuming IPX and NETx have been loaded, one example of how this TCP/IP solution is used is as follows. The user is able to copy files on the NetWare volume to a TCP/IP-equipped host with the following command:

```
rcp -r -b f:\filename.ext HOST_NAME=/usr/netware/backup
```

It is interesting to note that, because TCP/IP is run as an FEP, the PC's CPU does not have to construct all of the TCP/IP communications in addition to IPX. With this method, files are moved from the NetWare volume as quickly as with the equivalent DOS command on a local hard disk.

There is no gateway functionality with the Excelan TCP/IP solutions. Only the PC that is equipped with the EXOS series controller has the functionality described above. This obviously limits the viability of the Excelan solution to those workstations equipped with EXOS adapters. Work is currently underway to achieve hardware independence by developing a Host-Resident TCP/IP that can share a common MAC layer interface with IPX.

The Wollongong Group manufactures a unique TCP/IP router, called WIN/TCP for DOS. One workstation operates as the router to the TCP/IP network. The other workstations on the NetWare LAN communicate with this router via IPX. Because of the IPX interface, numerous topologies can be used with this product.

Another product is PC/TCP Network Software for DOS, manufactured by FTP Software, Inc. This TCP/IP Software has the ability to work concurrently with Novell on an assortment of NICs. These NICs need to be Ethernet NICs and, when using NetWare, the IPX.COM shell must be configured using ECONFIG. (Running ECONFIG will make the NICs Ethernet, and not IEEE 802.3 compliant.) ECONFIG is a NetWare 2.1x utility that allows certain Ethernet drivers to be configured for use on an Ethernet, versus an IEEE 802.3, network. Only drivers that include this ability can have ECONFIG used on them.

CompuServe's NetWire forum is a good source of information about the latest developments and product introductions for TCP and related subjects, such as SNMP and SMTP (both of which are discussed in Appendix G, "A TCP/IP Primer").

CHAPTER 10

Printing

In general, the process of determining the exact requirements for network printing is more art than science. For example, while conservative estimates for the maximum length of a parallel printer cable are typically 15 feet, cable lengths up to 50 feet have been used without problems. The same is true for serial printers, which have been used with cables up to 150 feet long, although the conservative recommendation is no more than 50 feet. Because of the variability involved, it is often necessary to "plug-and-play" with a variety of additional items, including line drivers, short-haul modems, low capacitance cables, and printer conversion devices, to arrive at the optimum printer configuration.

Printer Selection

Under current revisions of NetWare, practically any printer can serve as a network printer as long as it has a serial or parallel interface. Printers connected to workstations using third-party printer-sharing software may be shared by LAN users. Check with the manufacturer of the third-party software for more specifics. If a printer is serial or parallel, but not both, and there is not a matching port type available, a conversion device may be used. Conversion devices are available for serial-to-parallel and vice versa.

Parallel printers have a speed advantage—they can accept data two to three times faster than 9600 bps serial printers. Parallel printers work more quickly because of the simultaneous transfer of 8 bits, 1 byte at a time, versus 1 bit-at-a-time transfers for serial printers. The primary advantage of serial printers is that they can utilize printer cable lengths of 50 feet (or longer), while parallel printer cables are generally limited to about 15 feet.

If a parallel printer needs to be installed at a distance of more than 15 feet from the nearest file server, there are three options:

1. Serial cable must be used in tandem with a serial-to-parallel convertor.
2. Another file server must be installed within 15 feet of the new printer in order to provide a close file server connection.
3. A third-party print sharing software package can be installed in a workstation to which the printer is then connected.

PostScript

Use of printers that read PostScript language is becoming increasingly popular. Connecting them to a NetWare file server for shared access is no different than connecting a non-PostScript printer. It is crucial, however, to use the /NT (No Tabs), /NFF (No Form Feed), and /NB (No Banner) flags with the SPOOL or CAPTURE commands. In PRINTCON, specify the following:

```
File contents:     Byte Stream

Suppress form feed: Yes

Print banner:      No
```

Figure 10-1. Using PRINTCON with PostScript language printers

These settings prevent the file server from adding anything to the print stream as it is sent to the printer, except for specified device/mode commands. Note that, regardless of the type of printer being used, whenever graphics are printed, the /NT flag or "File contents: Byte Stream" settings must be used.

Third-party Print Servers

There are a number of situations that could indicate the need for a print server. For example, more printers may be required than there are file servers available to accommodate them. Or the printer may be needed in an area where there are workstations but no nearby file servers. Several products are available to alleviate either of these printer problems.

Brightwork Development Inc. offers a product called PS-Print/QueueIT! that supports both dedicated and nondedicated print server configurations. A pop-up TSR (QueueIt!) that facilitates workstation access to network print functions is included. Another print server that allows up to 15 printers per print server is Fresh Technology Group's Printer Assist.

LANspool (formerly from LAN Systems, now from Intel,) runs as a VAP on a NetWare 2.2 file server or as an NLM on a Netware 3.x server. LANSpool provides an alternate print server capability to replace the NetWare printing services. It also has significantly greater throughput for print jobs, so users demanding extensive graphics capabilities may find LANSpool worth the investment.

Also worth noting, Novell offers its own print server utility called PSERVER for all current shipping versions. PSERVER includes the ability to utilize local workstation printers. Although initial releases of PSERVER had many problems, newer releases have improved. You may find that third party print server products offer more features than PSERVER, though, and may be worth the extra investment.

Print Queues

With NetWare 2.0x, each network printer has an associated print queue. This queue acts merely as an intermediary between the user and the network printer. It is tightly integrated with its assigned network printers and has no other purpose.

NetWare 2.0x print queues allow only 99 entries. If the queue becomes full, additional print jobs are lost by the system. An unsuspecting user has no indication that a job is lost, other than that the print job is not executed. This anomaly does not occur, however, with print jobs created by the NPRINT utility, discussed below.

NetWare 2.1 introduced a new concept for NetWare queues. No longer serving solely as print job repositories, the improved queues allow software developers to specify their use. Two of the most significant characteristics of these new multipurpose queues are that:

- Up to 25 job servers can simultaneously service a single queue.
- Each queue can hold up to 250 jobs, which are identified by any numbers in the range 1-999.

One obvious benefit of these new features is that the same printer queue can be serviced by multiple printers. More importantly, the job servers can act as print servers, archive servers (for doing backups), batch servers (for compiling), mail servers, and more. There is no strict definition of what job server types are allowed.

Because of their flexible and dynamic nature, NetWare 2.1x/2.2x's queues can be arbitrarily attached to one or more job servers. The NetWare manuals contain the actual commands needed to perform these manipulations.

In the event a print queue becomes full, the NPRINT command will notify the user of this condition. If the output is redirected to a network printer via CAPTURE, the following error will be received:

```
Not ready error writing device <device name>
Abort, Retry, Ignore?
```

This is the only warning issued to tell the user the queue is full. Obviously, this message lacks clarity and, to the unknowing user is woefully inadequate. To further complicate matters, if CAPTURE is run with the SHOW option to verify the current print settings, the user will find that output from the indicated <device name> is indeed being captured. Fortunately, queues do not usually become full. If this does appear to have happened, PCONSOLE allows the queue to be directly interrogated.

With NetWare 2.1x/2.2x, queue attachments, such as a definition of which printers will service which queues, are done at boot time. If there is no AUTOEXEC.SYS file in the SYS:SYSTEM directory of the file server, the default queues with names like PRINTQ_0, PRINTQ_1, etc. will be attached to their respective file server printers (PRINTER 0, PRINTER 1, etc.). However, if there is an AUTOEXEC.SYS, this automatic queue attachment is not performed. All printer/queue assignments needed at file server boot time must be specified in the AUTOEXEC.SYS file. An example of the minimum required command in the AUTOEXEC.SYS file is P0 ADD PRINTQ_0. Once the system is up and running, it is possible to define new queues and their attachments and to redefine them.

Printing with Macintosh and AppleTalk

AppleTalk is the overall name given to the Apple networking scheme. LocalTalk is the name of the interface topology built into every Mac, while AppleShare is what Apple calls the networking client software included as part of their operating system.

AppleTalk Filing Protocol (AFP) is a part of the AppleTalk protocols. It is the core transmission protocol used among clients/servers on an AppleTalk LAN, and is conceptually equivalent to Novell's NetWare Core Protocol (NCP). AppleTalk is represented by the presentation layer in the OSI model, controlling file service transactions. The current version of AppleShare file service software which supports Macs, IBMs and IBM clones, and the Apple II family, is AppleShare 2.0.1. AppleShare workstation software began to ship with Apple's System software version 6.0.0. Novell continues to support Macintosh workstations running System 7.

If a network includes Macintoshes, it is likely to have LaserWriter printers. AppleTalk's Printer Access Protocol (PAP) and Name Binding Protocol (NBP) prevent two or more printers from having the same name on the same network. If the first one comes up as "LaserWriter" and the second tries to join the network as "LaserWriter", AppleTalk's NBP will add a character to the end of the name (e.g. "LaserWriter1") without any user intervention. This can cause the printer's name to change from one day to the next, which can cause problems if an AppleShare Print Server or NetWare print queue has captured the printer. For this reason, it is best to name LaserWriters (or networked ImageWriters) using the Namer utility before attaching them to the network.

What happens if you choose the same name for two different queues to the same LaserWriter? AppleShare Print Server won't permit this to happen from the same server. The server used to select the queue will be the one that handles the spooling.

Printing Commands and Utilities

With the advent of NetWare 2.1, Novell introduced new features in their network printing, including two new commands, CAPTURE and ENDCAP, and three new utilities, PRINTCON, PRINTDEF, and PCONSOLE.

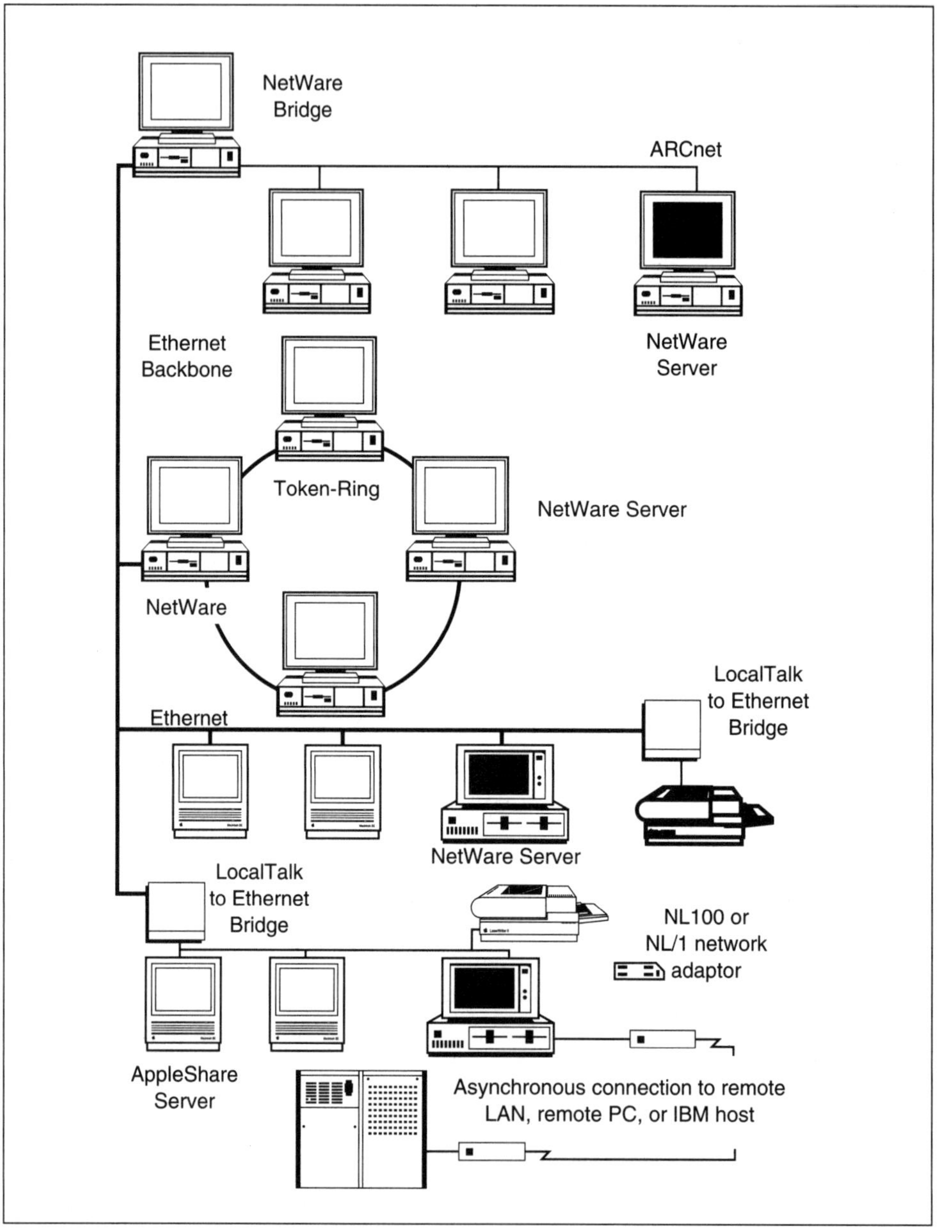

Figure 10-2. Typical networking scheme with Macintoshes

CAPTURE and ENDCAP

With NetWare 2.0x, SPOOL, ENDSPOOL, and NPRINT were the commands most commonly used to send printer output to network printers. Because the printer is not physically attached to the user's workstation, it appears to that workstation as a sort of virtual entity. By eliminating the hardware dependency, output can be redirected, whether or not the workstation has a printer port. In fact, this ability to redirect printer output means that a workstation's parallel port can be spooled to a serial network printer. Note that only workstation parallel ports (LPT1, LPT2, and LPT3) can be redirected to network printers. Under version 2.0x, only one of the parallel ports can be redirected at a time, whereas with version 2.1x/2.2x, it is possible to concurrently redirect all three parallel ports.

New print redirect commands were introduced with NetWare 2.1; CAPTURE and ENDCAP replaced SPOOL and ENDSPOOL, respectively. By and large, CAPTURE and ENDCAP operate just like their counterparts in version 2.0x. The NPRINT utility still exists, with a new array of options made available with CAPTURE. Of these new options, three are particularly significant:

- The ability to redirect output to queues (instead of just to printers)
- The ability to concurrently redirect one, two, or three LPT ports
- The ability to designate predefined configurations

The third option described refers to print jobs defined with the PRINTCON utility which allows print job definitions to be specified and saved in each user's mailbox directory. Whenever CAPTURE or NPRINT is invoked, it searches for the PRINTCON job definitions and uses the default PRINTCON job specifications. The default job is specified in the PRINTCON utility and can be overridden with the /JOB= flag.

It is important to note differences in some default settings used by the new utilities included in 2.1x/2.2x NetWare. The SPOOL utility in NetWare 2.0x defines "no tab expansion" as the default action when invoking SPOOL, thereby sending the redirected printer output to the network printer without alteration. With version 2.1x/2.2x's CAPTURE utility, this default has been reversed so that "tab expansion" is the default. Redirected printer output is altered as it is sent to the network for printing. Also introduced with 2.1x/2.2x are the new terms text mode and byte stream mode, which are used to define a print job with PRINTCON. Text mode is tab expansion mode and byte stream mode is no tab expansion mode. For applications that deal with graphic output, it is necessary to use the /NT flag (No Tab expansion) with the CAPTURE utility or byte stream mode in the PRINTCON job configuration definition.

Another default found in the CAPTURE and SPOOL utilities is the Automatic EndSpool/EndCapture flag. This flag indicates that, if an Interrupt 2Fh subfunction 5 is performed, the network should execute an automatic EndSpool/EndCap to send whatever redirected printer output is not yet released to the network for printing. Interrupt 2Fh occurs every time you arrive at a DOS prompt, such as when an application terminates and returns to DOS. The NetWare shell detects this action and triggers the release of spooled/captured output. The Automatic EndCap flag can be altered with either the CAPTURE utility (/A = enable; /NA = disable) or via a PRINTCON job configuration.

One situation in which disabling the Automatic EndSpool/EndCap would be necessary is when output is being captured to a file using the CREATE option in the CAPTURE utility. With Auto EndSpool/EndCap enabled, it would be inconvenient to spool/capture output to a file, as spooling/capturing is completed after the first item is printed.

Under NetWare 2.0x, the Automatic EndSpool flag is not alterable with the SPOOL utility. For information about a utility called AET.ARC which allows toggling of this flag, contact NetWare SysOps or Novell.

Printing Problems

Several problems may be encountered when printing with NetWare, most of which can be rectified. This section describes some of the most common problems and provides solutions for them.

Slow File Server Printing

A slowdown in file server printing may occur on some clones when nondedicated NetWare is used. This slowdown is attributable to the slowness of the protected-to-real mode switch (detailed in Chapter 3). To restore normal printing speeds, try changing the file server to CONSOLE mode.

Epson DOS

Over the years, every version of Epson DOS has created a hostile environment for NetWare network printing. This has been a long-time problem with Epson DOS and there is only one solution—to replace Epson DOS with that of another company, such as Microsoft or IBM.

Serial Port Redirection

As discussed in Chapter 9, NetWare is unable to redirect serial port activity onto the LAN. This is largely due to the uncompromising nature of serial port activity. While it is true that a BIOS routine exists to handle serial port activity (Interrupt 14h), most programs do not use it for serial port communications. Most applications communicate directly to the serial port via the hardware interrupts and I/O channels (both of which are beyond the scope of this text). Due to this use of serial ports by the majority of applications, serial port redirection is not implemented in software. J&L's NCA hardware allows redirection of serial port activity and can be used to share a serial output device on the network. More information on the NCA can be found in Chapter 9.

Using NetWare on MCA-based PS/2 machines (IBM PS/2 Model 50, 50z, 55, 60, 65, 70, 80, 90, etc.) allows for an expanded range of available printer port designations. A non-MCA PC can have up to five printer ports: LPT1, LPT2, LPT3, COM1, and COM2. The MCA-based PS/2 machines support three additional printer port designations: LPT4, COM3, and COM4. When using the MCA-based PS/2 machine, there is still a limit of five printer ports, three parallel and two serial, but the three new designations can now be used.

The NETGEN (or ELSGEN) utility in NetWare 2.1x/2.2x incorrectly defines some serial port parameters. Please refer to Chapter 12 for information regarding the definition of the file server-stored printer tables. This printer table information makes it possible to correct the parameters.

Nondedicated File Server Printer Aberrations

When defining the network printers at a nondedicated file server, it is possible to set up some or all of the LPT ports as network printers. For each port reassigned as a network printer, NetWare removes its definition from DOS's parallel port definition table. The information stored in this table points to the I/O addresses of the LPT ports.

```
     DEBUG
 -d0040:0008 F <enter>

0040:0008 BC 03 BC 03 BC 03 00 00
          ^LPT1 ^LPT2 ^LPT3 ^LPT4
```

Figure 10-3. Using DEBUG to revive LPT ports

Some application programs actually examine DOS's parallel port definition table to determine the existence of the various LPT ports. Even if the LPT port has been SPOOLed or CAPTUREd to a network printer, such an application will refuse to print to that LPT port, for instance, Lotus 123 objects to printing to an apparently nonexistent LPT port. With these applications, it is necessary to "doctor" the parallel port definition table information to reflect that the LPT port is indeed available for service. This table begins at address 0040:0008h. Figure 10-3 shows how to use the DEBUG command to examine the contents of this table and to revive the LPT ports.

Figure 10-3 illustrates the normal content of the parallel port definition table before any redirection has been invoked. BC 03 is the I/O address of LPT1. It is also the I/O address of LPT2 and LPT3. The fact that BC 03 is repeated three times indicates that only one parallel printer port exists in this machine, so the BIOS automatically assigns the LPT1 definition to the other LPT ports. This ensures that all three LPTs are defined, even though they all point to the same physical I/O address. It is interesting to note that the IBM PS/2 has room for a fourth LPT I/O address that is not otherwise available.

```
0040:0008       00 00 00 00 BC 03 00 00
                ^LPT1 ^LPT2 ^LPT3 ^LPT4
```

Figure 10-4. Parallel printer definition table with LPT1 and LPT2 redirected

Figure 10-4 shows the printer definition table on a nondedicated file server on which LPT1 and LPT2 are redirected to serve network printer duty.

Well-designed DOS applications rely on DOS to send data to the printer port. A few software packages bypass the DOS print mechanism to send output directly to the hardware. Others bypass the DOS print mechanism just to ensure the printer port is defined. In order to determine the I/O address of a particular parallel port, this type of software package directly interrogates the I/O address table. As seen in Figure 10-4, such an interrogation reveals nothing of value, as the printer I/O addresses have been blanked with nulls. To restore use of LPT1 for applications that examine the I/O address table directly, DEBUG can be used to alter the parallel printer definitions, shown in Figure 10-5.

```
-E40:8 <enter>
0040:0008 00._ {the _ is the prompt}
you would enter:
0040:0008 00.BC <space> 00.03 <enter>
-q <enter>
```

Figure 10-5. Using DEBUG to alter parallel printer definitions

At this point, LPT1 has been formally restored. This patch does not revoke the file server printer definition on LPT1—it is purely a cosmetic change for the benefit of certain applications. Restoration can also be achieved with a utility called PRFIX2.ARC, formerly found on CompuServe's NetWire forum, which is simpler to use because it does not involve the DEBUG command. For information about PRFIX2.ARC, contact NetWare SysOps or Novell.

Insufficient Device Command Sequence Buffers

NetWare 2.1x/2.2x uses PRINT HEADERs and PRINT TAILs, as defined in PRINTDEF, to hold the device command strings. These two options can be specified to be up to 255 bytes long. For each LPT there is one PRINT HEAD and one PRINT TAIL. If a situation arises in which 255 bytes is insufficient, a fix is needed to expand the allocated memory space.

To cause the shell to accommodate more than 255 bytes for the PRINT HEAD and PRINT TAIL, begin by looking at offset 16Fh inside the shell. Three two-byte pointers (offset addresses) point to definition structures for the three printers. At an offset inside these structures, there are double word pointers to the PRINT HEAD and TAIL. To expand them, it is necessary to allocate some memory in a separate TSR and to modify the shell so that the PRINT HEAD and TAIL pointers are pointing to the new memory. This fix should be executed only by those who are fairly literate in writing TSR-type applications and in modifying dynamic memory areas. See Chapter 6 for more detailed information on the location and parameters of the shell's printer tables.

Device Strings

From time to time, device strings, which are native to NetWare 2.1x/2.2x, need to be sent to the printer before a banner page. Consider, for example, a PostScript printer that does not correctly print straight ASCII text when certain commands are issued. Unfortunately, it is not possible to directly send a device string before a banner page.

A mediocre solution is to specify different form types for differing print jobs. This can be done either by the submitting user or by content, and form types of 0 to 255 can be used. When the form type change comes to console, all printing stops and the printer can be manually reset for the next job. While resetting it, an option is to have a workstation nearby for downloading fonts.

"Stuck" Files

The phenomenon of "stuck" files is possible under NetWare 2.0x. These existing files somehow errantly become permanently open and are not deletable or renamable. By all appearances, these "stuck" files occur infrequently and, supposedly, only in certain situations. Unfortunately, it is not clear what these situations are. When files do become stuck, they can be "recreated" by using the SPOOL CREATE option. Once an ENDSPOOL is performed, the file can be removed. However, this is not the ultimate solution. Sometimes the CREATE option refuses to work, in which case, it is necessary to use DISKED or VREPAIR. As this phenomena has not been observed with version 2.1x, it appears to be limited to those versions previous to 2.1.

PRINTCON

There is a small design flaw in the PRINTCON utility. Fortunately, the problem is one with which only the network administrator need be aware. This is the inability to globally define the PRINTCON job database, PRINTCON.DAT. This file is used to define a user's commonly used printing parameters so they can be referenced quickly and easily as print job definitions. In its native form, PRINTCON.DAT has to be created and maintained for each user account. These PRINTCON.DATs are stored in each user's personal mailbox directory (SYS:MAIL\xxxxxxxx). It is common for several users to require the same PRINTCON.DAT, but the option to define these files globally, just as the system login script is globally defined, is not provided.

Fortunately, two techniques exist (other than purchasing third-party products) that allow for the sharing of a common PRINTCON.DAT file. The simpler method involves first setting the shell's search mode to 5, which means that a search is always executed during open file requests. (See NetWare manuals referencing SHELL.CFG for an example of this command.) Then use PRINTCON to create the PRINTCON.DAT for the system. This file will be placed in the SYS:MAIL\xxxxxxxx directory for the USERID that is logged in. For instance, the SUPERVISOR user's mailbox directory is always SYS:MAIL\1. Finally, place a copy of the PRINTCON.DAT to be shared in a search directory, such as SYS:PUBLIC. This is the easier of the two methods to implement, but it has the disadvantage of forcing the shell to search on every open file request. This could cause some other applications to unexpectedly read the wrong data.

Although the second method is a bit more technically involved, it offers better control. There are four utilities that read PRINTCON.DAT: PCONSOLE, PRINTCON, CAPTURE, and NPRINT. DEBUG is used to change the file names being

being searched for by these utilities, so it is possible to specify where PRINT-CON.DAT is to be found.

When DEBUG is used to edit a file that has an .EXE extension, it is necessary to first rename the file with a different extension. Once the editing is completed, the original file name is restored. The following procedure outlines the DEBUG steps for CAPTURE.

1. Type: RENAME CAPTURE.EXE CAPTURE.DBG
2. Type: DEBUG CAPTURE.DBG
3. At the - prompt type:

    scs:100 ffff 'sys:mail' <enter>

    or

    scs:100 ffff 'SYS\MAIL' <enter>

    It will bring up an address, something like:

    5E42:8528

Note the number following the colon, in this case, 8528.

4. At the next - prompt type:

    f8528 L1c 'sys:mail\printcon.dat',0,0,0,0,0,0,0<enter>

Notice that the number following the "f" is the same as the number shown after the colon in step 3.

5. At the next - prompt type:

    W <enter>

    Writing xxxx bytes will be displayed.

6. At the next - prompt type:

    Q <enter>

This will quit DEBUG and return you to DOS.

7. Type: RENAME CAPTURE.DBG CAPTURE.EXE
8. Place the global PRINTCON.DAT in the SYS:MAIL directory.

The choice of a directory is arbitrary, as long as you use the same number of characters as shown in the example.

The above patch also works with NPRINT, although the patch address used is different. However, with NPRINT the patch does not work with PCONSOLE.EXE or PRINTCON.EXE. A disk editing utility, such as the Norton Utilities, is used instead of DEBUG to find the 'sys:mail' text in the PCONSOLE.EXE and PRINTCON.EXE files, and to modify the text as demonstrated in Figure 10-6.

```
-d8528
5E42:8520                    73 79 73 3A 6D 61 69 6C     sys:mail
5E42:8530 5C 25 6C 78 5C 25 73 00-70 72 69 6E 74 63 6F 6E  \%lx\%s.printcon
5E42:8540 2E 64 61 74 00 00 53 59-53 3A 50 55 42 4C 49 43  .dat..SYS:PUBLIC
5E42:8550 5C 4E 45 54 24 50 52 4E-2E 44 41 54 00 00 00 00  \NET$PRN.DAT....
5E42:8560 00 B2 0A B2 20 20 00 B0-21 22 23 24 25 26 27 28  .... ..!"#$%&'(
5E42:8570 29 2A 2B 2C 2D 2E 2F 30-31 32 33 34 35 36 37 38  )*+,-./012345678
5E42:8580 39 3A 3B 3C 3D 3E 3F 40-41 42 43 44 45 46 47 48  9:;<=>?@ABCDEFGH
5E42:8590 49 4A 4B 4C 4D 4E 4F 50-51 52 53 54 55 56 57 58  IJKLMNOPQRSTUVWX

5E42:85A0 59 5A 5B 2F 5D 5E 20 60 YZ[/]^
-f8528 l1c 'sys:mail\printcon.dat',0,0,0,0,0,0,0
-d8528
5E42:8520                    73 79 73 3A 6D 61 69 6C     sys:mail
5E42:8530 5C 70 72 69 6E 74 63 6F-6E 2E 64 61 74 00 00 00  \printcon.dat...
5E42:8540 00 00 00 00 00 00 53 59-53 3A 50 55 42 4C 49 43  ......SYS:PUBLIC
5E42:8550 5C 4E 45 54 24 50 52 4E-2E 44 41 54 00 00 00 00  \NET$PRN.DAT....
5E42:8560 00 B2 0A B2 20 20 00 B0-21 22 23 24 25 26 27 28  .... ..!"#$%&'(
5E42:8570 29 2A 2B 2C 2D 2E 2F 30-31 32 33 34 35 36 37 38  )*+,-./012345678
5E42:8580 39 3A 3B 3C 3D 3E 3F 40-41 42 43 44 45 46 47 48  9:;<=>?@ABCDEFGH
5E42:8590 49 4A 4B 4C 4D 4E 4F 50-51 52 53 54 55 56 57 58  IJKLMNOPQRSTUVWX
-w
Writing 8800 bytes
-q
```

Figure 10-6. Modifying SYS:MAIL text in the PCONSOLE.EXE or PRINTCON.EXE file

Queueing System

With NetWare 2.1, Novell introduced their Queue Management System (QMS), an evolutionary step in Novell's queue mechanism scheme. This latest queue system allows for device or server independent queueing of data. This means that data placed in a queue no longer has to go to a printer (or plotter). Rather, due to the truly asynchronous interface of QMS, a server may now be a batch-processing server, an archiving server, or a bulk-data copy server, to name some of the more common options. This is all possible because QMS makes available, for the first time in NetWare's history, a queueing system that allows user applications to attack queueing from the front end (submittal of data) and the backend (processing of that data).

It is the responsibility of the queueing system to reliably gather data from clients (users of the queue system) and place it in the proper queue. The queue is a transitory place (usually residing on disk at a file server) which stores client submissions until they can be processed by a queue server. Once in the queue, the client's data is termed a job. Each job, which has several attributes, is processed, usually in the order it was received. Typically, once a job has been handled, the entry in the queue is deleted, marking its completion.

In the case of NetWare, QMS is handled by the file server, which provides the necessary Application Program Interfaces (APIs) to make NetWare's QMS come alive. For instance, APIs provide the abilities to create queues, for queue servers to attach to queues, and for users to submit jobs to queues. Because QMS is handled by a known agent, namely a file server, QMS can guarantee that the access methods used by the queue clients and queue servers will work consistently. Pre-QMS queue systems were defined individually by third-party developers and therefore did not interoperate.

With NetWare, information regarding queues is stored in the bindery. Each queue is recognized by its name and four other properties:

Q_USERS
: Contains a list of users (or groups) authorized to use this queue

Q_OPERATORS
: Contains a list of all who are authorized to manipulate queue jobs

Q_SERVERS
: Contains a list of servers that are authorized to process jobs from this queue

Q_DIRECTORY
: Contains the directory path of the VOLUME:DIRECTORY on the server (where the queue is defined) where queue jobs are stored

When using NetWare utilities to define queues, the resulting Q_DIRECTORY will always be SYS:SYSTEM\queueID. The directory "queueID" is a hexadecimal number, up to eight characters long, that uniquely identifies that queue. For instance, a queue directory might be: SYS:SYSTEM\20F00EF. (For a trick regarding the alteration of PCONSOLE's use of SYS:SYSTEM, see the following section.)

If a user is not defined as a Q_USER, either directly or by group membership, they will not be allowed to submit jobs to that queue. Likewise, if a user is not defined as a Q_OPERATOR, either directly or by group membership, they will not be allowed to alter jobs in the queue.

Interestingly, Q_SERVERS defines which "servers" are to be allowed to retrieve queue jobs for processing and removes them once processed. These "servers" are not necessarily file servers, as was required under pre-QMS NetWare. The other "servers" are other objects in the bindery; they can be users or they can be other bindery entities (probably created just to be queue servers).

And, unlike pre-NetWare 2.1 queues, each QMS queue can be serviced by as many as 25 simultaneous queue servers. For instance, you could have 25 Hewlett Packard (HP) LaserJets printing jobs from one queue. Also note that a particular job can be routed to a particular job server if the queue submission application is aware of this option.

Because QMS allows for practically any bindery object to be a queue server, applications of QMS are unlimited in respect to previous queue services. Therefore, it is important that the queue submitter and the queue server be as independent as possible. If it were required for a queue server to be active during the submission of a queue job, QMS would not be a true queueing service. However, QMS is a true queueing service—one that defines a rigid structure for job submission (by a queue user or client) and job servicing (by a queue server).

Because of this asynchronous definition, QMS allows any type of job to be submitted for processing by any type of queue server. For instance, NetWare pre-2.1 had a special API call for NPRINTed files. Rather than duplicating the file to be NPRINTed in the queue's directory, NetWare created and placed a small, e.g. 50 byte, file in the queue that directed the server to the location of the file to be NPRINTed. With QMS, NetWare makes no such exceptions—NPRINT jobs are handled just as any other jobs. This is because NetWare now abstracts itself from what is actually going into the queue—it makes no amends for highly NetWare-specific actions (such as NPRINTing) as it did with the pre-QMS system.

With QMS, NetWare has opened up its queueing system to all applications, not just those intrinsic to NetWare. Under this new system, users are given more freedom in the definition and setup of queue servers, and a consistent interface by which access to those queues is made possible.

Changing Q_DIRECTORY's Location

With NetWare, the PCONSOLE utility is often used to create queues. Unfortunately, with current versions, this utility always designates SYS:SYSTEM as the basis for a queue's "job directory." This directory is where queue jobs are stored. The full path of a queue directory might be: SYS:SYSTEM\E30033. However, it is possible to adapt PCONSOLE to use another volume (on the same server) for storage of queue directories and their associated jobs. Just as when modifying PRINTCON, use a utility, such as Norton Utilities, to search for and edit the two SYS:SYSTEM strings within the PCONSOLE.EXE utility. To make it simple to search for the string, you might copy PCONSOLE.EXE to a floppy disk and make your modification(s) there. Afterwards, copy the changed PCONSOLE back to the area where you normally use it.

When modifying the SYS:SYSTEM string, be sure to make the length of the new string match the old one, i.e., do not make the name longer or shorter than 10 characters (which is the length of SYS:SYSTEM). For example, you might use VOL1:QUEUE. The new name that you use will become the basis for the full path of all queues defined using PCONSOLE. You should realize that, if your "other" volume should become unavailable, NetWare's queueing system will be unable to accept queue submissions from users. However, you might just pick another directory on your server, but still on the SYS: volume. Perhaps you would use SYS:QUEUES.

This freedom to locate queue directories is permitted because each queue has a Q_DIRECTORY property that details the directory path of that queue's jobs.

Because of the nature of the files in the queue directories, it is probably not pertinent to back them up. By placing them in their own directory tree, you can easily exclude them from your normal backup routines, instead of typing in the file exclude mask(s) you would use otherwise. To refresh you, those file exclude masks would be: Q$*.SYS and Q$*.SRV or you could use Q$*.* if you have no other files beginning with Q$. With a little experimentation, you should be able to give your queues a home you can both live with.

Serial Handshake Problems with NW286/2.1x

When using the serial (as opposed to parallel) port connected to a file server for network printing, you may experience buffer overflows at your printer. If this is the case, you might try swapping Data Terminal Ready (DTR) or Ready/Busy handshake for the Xon/Xoff handshake at the server. At the printer, set it up for DTR. The reason for using the Xon/Xoff handshake protocol at the server and DTR handshake protocol at the printer is that NetWare's NETGEN (previous to version 2.15c) incorrectly set up the Xon/Xoff protocol. This inconsistency is only in NW286/2.1x (previous to version 2.15c) and results from NETGEN's actions. Another inconsistency with NW286/2.1x versions previous to 2.15c is disabled parity. Only "no parity" works. The odd and even parity selections do not work properly. NetWare/286 2.15 revision C corrects this problem. Otherwise, use no parity where possible. If you do not have access to NW286/2.15c and need to use parity for a serially connected printer/plotter, see Chapter 12 for a discussion of the printer table definition, with the intention you will then be able to modify the printer table directly.

NetWare and Windows 3.0 Printing Problems

In order for Windows 3.0 to properly operate on a NetWare LAN, Novell has provided several driver files and an application file. These Novell files are included on your Windows 3.0 diskettes (as they come from Microsoft). However, in April 1991 Novell provided an update for many of these files. The update was produced to resolve many Windows problems including a major problem of printing anomalies. The printing problem usually resulted in the output being totalled trashed. Also the printing problem usually only manifested itself when operating Windows in Enhanced Mode (/386 mode). Also, these Windows printing problems were made worse by any TSRs loaded (before running Windows) that hooked Interrupt 21h (the DOS interrupt).

The update files are found in the file WINUP7.ZIP in the NOVFILES forum. The files updated include:

README.WIN
NETWARE.DRV
NETWARE.HLP
NETWARE.PIF
NWPOPUP.EXE
VNETWARE.386
INSTALL.EXE
VPICDA.386
BINDFIX.EXE
TBMI.COM
TASKID.COM

The indented filenames are very important for you to update in order to help eliminate your Windows printing problems. If you downloaded a WIN1UP.ZIP before April 10, 1991 you will need to download this (or later) update. This is especially true because the NETWARE.DRV file had some important updates that were not released until the April 10th edition.

CHAPTER 11

Network Management and Maintenance

A supervisor's work does not end when the network is up and running. Keeping the system operational requires continual management and maintenance.

Unfortunately, Novell's documentation includes neither a concise description of the duties of a LAN supervisor nor practical advice on how those duties might be carried out. Novell's *Supervisor's Guide* included with all versions of NetWare since 2.1 is a good primer on LAN concepts, but it does not offer a simple working example for you to follow.

This chapter will fill that void, addressing the set of core responsibilities of a LAN Supervisor. The topics discussed include such basics as:

- Tape backup and archiving
- System programming
- Recordkeeping
- Data integrity and security
- Hardware maintenance
- Software maintenance
- Monitoring file server performance

While some of today's network management issues can be addressed by automation, there is no one product or group of products that addresses all of the issues. With the establishment of the Desktop Management Task Force (DMTF), users may some day have an integrated set of packages to manage their network. However, until then, you will continue to need to interact with a sometimes dizzying array of products. For example, the following few paragraphs highlight basic coverage of the core responsibilities listed in the bullets above.

One must have a strict discipline for backup and restoration of information assets. This includes policies/procedures, a rotation schedule for offsite tapes, security over the tapes, and the backup of nodes on the network.

Most tape backup software is relatively unintelligent and was created around DOS platforms which have typically been small systems. Some users will buy a tape drive that is bigger than the total capacity of the server. As larger disk drives emerge, however, a fundamental change in the way we perform backups is required. With more than 100 gigabytes now available on a server, it is not reasonable to do a full backup every evening. Several products are emerging which support Novell's Storage Management Services (SMS). Legato's Networker is an example of an industrial-strength backup system. Another product worth considering is Palindrome's The Network Archivist (TNA). Remember, the product must support node backup; some nodes now have over 300Mb of data, most of which is unprotected.

Documentation is ignored by most network administrators. It requires a significant amount of time and energy to keep it up to date.

Products like NetWare Management from Frye Computer Systems, Inc., LT Stat from Blue Lance, or Xtree Tools for Networks from Xtree facilitate documentation upkeep. Bindview from the LAN Support Group is a good product to use if you want to filter the information in your final reports based on specific search criteria.

A network inventory includes such information as workstation DOS version, network shell version, CONFIG.SYS file, AUTOEXEC.BAT file, CPU speed, disk drive sizes, and a listing of software on the workstation and server. A network inventory provides essential information for disaster recovery planning. LAN Directory by Frye Computer Systems, Inc., inventories software and permits custom reporting.

The number of network viruses and frequency of attacks are increasing alarmingly. Intel, Corp. and McAffee Associates provide server-based methods of preventing virus infection. They operate as NetWare Loadable Modules (NLM) and monitor the network constantly or, if desired, at specified intervals.

Hardware monitoring ensures that the network server is performing within specific parameters defined in the program. You can be notified when volume space is less than ten percent, if you would like. Early Warning System (EWS) by Frye Computer Systems, Inc. provides a method to notify system administrators of server-based problems before they become critical. In addition, some manufacturers like

Compaq Computer Corporation now offer products such as Insight Manager which monitors over 200 internal statistics. With an additional board (Server Manager/R) you can even monitor temperature and voltage fluctuations. The Server Manager/R also permits secured environment access by the network administrator for troubleshooting and diagnostics. Various methods of notification including e-mail, pager, voice, and fax are available.

Software distribution is becoming a larger issue. Products like Novell's Electronic Software Distribution (ESD), Frye Computer System's Software Update and Distribution System (SUDS) provide an automated way to update nodes on a network. Since keeping nodes current generally is a labor-intensive effort and subject to error, this software can be a substantial time and money saver.

Other products that provide the ability to manage network hardware and software include: Compaq Insight Manager, Frye Utilities for Networks, Frye Early Warning System, Xtree Tools for Networks, Intel's LANDesk. Then there are Novell products, such as Novell's NetWare Management System (NMS), which is discussed in more detail later in this chapter. Because it is modular, it allows third parties to "plug in" to the NMS Console.

This sampling of network management products is just the beginning of what you could find yourself dealing with to manage your network.

The material that follows provides an outline for developing a practical LAN administration strategy and gives some working examples. It assumes that the hardware and NetWare operating system have been selected, installed, and are operational. It further assumes, unless noted otherwise, that the workstations and file servers are IBM compatibles running DOS 3.1 or newer and NetWare/286 version 2.1 or newer. Where additional software or hardware is specified, suggested product names are referenced.

Tape Backup and Archiving

The backup and archiving of network files should be considered the single most important ongoing activity in the administration of a network. With the importance of these backups, it follows that the selection of a backup system is critical.

Performing routine backups of the file server is a critical part of maintaining the integrity of any network. Without proper backups, the smallest problem can turn into a real disaster. In order to assure that backups are available after a catastrophe, such as a flood or fire, a copy of every system backup should be maintained off-site.

A prerequisite to selecting a backup system for a NetWare LAN is that its software must be NetWare-aware. This means that the unit must successfully backup and restore NetWare's bindery files, directory trustees, directory rights, file rights, and with NetWare/386, file transfers.

The choice of which backup system to use depends to some degree on the amount of data it will need to back up. This section examines various backup and archiving methods. Several manufacturers are listed, along with some of their product offerings. The information in this section is meant to be representative of what is available and is not a comprehensive listing of all backup and archiving devices available for LANs. The technology involved in backup and archiving is changing fast. New storage size and technique standards have been introduced since this book was last revised.

Tape Backup Systems for Small LANs

Several appropriate tape backup systems are available for small (150MB of disk space or less) LANs. Manufacturers included in this list are CMS Enhancements, Inc., Emerald Computers, Inc., Everex Systems, Inc., Maynard Electronics, Mountain Computer, Inc., and Sytron.

CMS Enhancements offers 60MB and 150MB 1/4-inch tape cartridge systems.

Emerald offers a 45MB tape cassette system as well as 60MB and 120MB 1/4-inch tape cartridge systems, all of which are quite easy to use, and are well adapted for use in the Novell environment. Emerald's solutions come complete with tape drive, controller, and archiving software.

Everex makes a 60MB tape cartridge system that provides an excellent backup resource for a NetWare LAN.

Maynard offers a 60MB tape cartridge system that is also capable of backing up NetWare files. This system comes with tape drive, controller, and software.

Mountain offers 60MB and 150MB tape units, both of which provide full NetWare compatibility.

Legato systems now has a backup solution for both UNIX and NetWare. They, along with some other manufacturers, now use NLMs to increase backup throughput.

NetWare v3.11 Backup / Restore and Upgrade Subsystem Configuration Matrix

Company / Subsystem	Storage Capacity	SCSI Controllers						QIC02 Controllers		
		Adaptec 1510/152X	Adaptec 154x/164x	174x*	Future Domain	Bus Tech	Prop.	Everex 811	Archive 402/9	Prop
A.D.I.C.										
Data 128	128 MB		M							
Data 256	256 MB		M							
Lambacker 4000	600 MB		M							
Lambacker 8000	1.2 GB		M							
DAT Autochanger	15.6 GB		M							
ARCHIVE										
Archive 2060S	60 MB		X	A	A	A				
Archive 2060L	60 MB		M							A
Archive 2150S	150 MB		X	A	A	A	1			
Archive 2150L	150 MB		M							A
Archive 5250S	250 MB		X	A	A	A				
Archive Python DAT	1.3 GB		X	A	A	A				
CIPHER										
Cipher ST 150	150 MB		X	A		A				
Cipher 540	150 MB		M							A
COMPAQ										
325 COMPAQ	325 MB		X				4			
525 COMPAQ	525 MB		X				4			
COLORADO MEMORY SYSTEMS										
JUMBO 120	120 MB		M							
JUMBO 250	250 MB		M							
QFA 500	500 MB		M							
DATA GENERAL										
150MB SCSI Tape Drive	150 MB		M							
320/525 MB SCSI Tape Drive	525 MB		M							
4mm DAT Tape Drive	1.3 GB		M							
EMERALD										
Rapid Recover	150 MB		X	A	A	A				
LAN-150-2100	150 MB		M						A	
LAN-150-9100	150 MB		M						A	
Rapid Recover 250	250 MB		X	A	A					
Rapid Recover 525	525 MB		X	A	A					
Rapid Recover 1.3GB	1.3 GB		X	A	A	A				
AVAST VAS02G-999	2.2 GB		X	A	A	A				
EXABYTE										
Exabyte 8200	2.2 GB		X	A	A	A	1,2,3			
Exabyte 8500	5.0 GB		X	A	A	A	1,2,3			
GIGATREND										
GigaTrend 101	1.2 GB		X	A						
GigaTrend 103	1.2 GB		M						A	
GigaTrend 107	1.2 GB		X	A	A					
GigaTrend 109	1.2 GB		M						A	
GigaTrend 1236	1.2 GB		M							
ServerDAT 116	1.2 GB		X	A	A					
ServerDAT 117	1.2 GB		X	A	A					
Serve DAT 121	1.2 GB		M			A				

X - Supported in NetWare v3.11 (as TAPEDC00 driver).
M - Contact the device manufacturer for details about which host adapters are supported.
A - Supported in the B/R Driver Kit v.1.0 (as TAPEDC00 driver).
- In "Prorprietary" column, 1 = 3Com, 2 = Netframe 3 =Tricord, 4 = COMPAQ. The Servers contain proprietary SCSI controllers. The drivers for these controllers will be in the B/R Driver Kit v1.0
* - The Apaptec 174x controller board is supported in the NetWare v3.11 Box when configured in 145x mode only.
D - Supported in Server Backup plus (as DIBIDAI2 driver).

Figure 11-1a. SY-TOS tape controller and tape drive compatibility table

NetWare v3.11 Backup / Restore and Upgrade Subsystem Configuration Matrix, *continued*

Company / Subsystem	Storage Capacity	SCSI Controllers						QIC02 Controllers		
		Adaptec 1510/152X	Adaptec 154x/164x	174x*	Future Domain	Bus Tech	Prop.	Everex 811	Archive 402/9	Prop.
HEWLETT-PACKARD										
HP C2224A/DAT	1.3 GB		X	A	A					
HP C1502A/DAT	1.3 GB		X	A	A	A	2			
HP JetStore 2000 DDS			M							
HP Jetstore 5000 DDS			M							
IBM										
Model 3532	2.3 GB		M				A			
Model 6157-002	150 MB		M				A			
Model 6451	2.3 MB		M				A			
Model 7208	2.2 GB		M				A			
IRWIN										
Model 2120	120/240 MB		M							
Model 2320	320/640 MB		X	A						
Model 9131	1.2 GB		X	A						
Model 9231	2.2 GB		X	A						
MOUNTAIN										
Mountain 7150	150 MB		M							
Mountain 7300	300 MB		M							
Mountain 7500	525 MB		M							
Mountain 1200	1.3 GB		X	A	A	A				
Mountain 2100	2.2 GB		X	A						
MAYNARD										
Maynstream150	150 MB		M							
Maynstream 250Q	250 MB		M							
Maynstream 525 Q	525 MB		X							
Maynstream1300 DAT	1.3 GB		X	A	A	A				
Maynstream 2200 HS	2.2 GB		X	A	A	A				
NRC										
6091/2001			M							
6091/2101	2.2 GB		X	A	A	A				
6091/2500	1.0 GB		X	A	A	A				
6091/6100	150 MB		X	A	A	A				
6091/6300	525 GB		X	A	A	A				
NOVASTOR CORPORATION										
NovaDrive			M							
PRESOFT ARCHITECTS										
Media Specialist Driver			M							
SANKYO										
CP150SE	150 MB		X	A	A	A				
CP320SE	525 MB		X	A	A	A				
SAMMUS										
Gigatape 442 (Sony)	1.3 GB		X	A	A	A				

X - Supported in NetWare v3.11 (as TAPEDC00 driver).
M - Contact the device manufacturer for details about which host adapters are supported.
A - Supported in the B/R Driver Kit v.1.0 (as TAPEDC00 driver).
- In "Prorprietary" column, 1 = 3Com, 2 = Netframe 3 =Tricord, 4 = COMPAQ. The Servers contain proprietary SCSI controllers. The drivers for these controllers will be in the B/R Driver Kit v1.0
* - The Apaptec 174x controller board is supported in the NetWare v3.11 Box when configured in 145x mode only.
D - Supported in Server Backup plus (as DIBIDAI2 driver).

Figure 11-1b. SY-TOS tape controller and tape drive compatibility table (continued)

NetWare v3.11 Backup / Restore and Upgrade Subsystem Configuration Matrix, *continued*

Company / Subsystem	Storage Capacity	SCSI Controllers: Adaptec 1510/152X	Adaptec 154x/164x	174x*	Future Domain	Bus Tech	Prop.	QIC02 Controllers: Everex 811	Archive 402/9	Prop.
TANDBERG										
Panther 525 MB	525 MB		X	A						
Panther1000 MB	1.0 GB		X	A						
TDC3660	150 MB		X	A	A	A				
TECMAR										
Proline THS-2000	2.2 GB		X	A	A	A				
Proline 150ES	150 MB		X	A	A	A				
Proline 525ES	525 MB		X	A	A	A				
Proline Data Vault	1.3 GB		X	A	A	A				
TRANSITIONAL TECHNOLOGY										
CTS/4DAT	1.3 GB		X							
CTS/8000/8210/8230	2.2 GB		X							
CTS/8501	5.0 GB		X							
WANGTEK/WANGDAT										
WangDAT 1300	1.3 GB	D	X	A	A	A				
WangDAT 3100	2.0 GB	D	X	A	A	A				
WangDAT 3200	4.0 GB	D	X	A	A	A				
Wangtek 5099ES	60 MB	D	X	A	A	A				
Wangtek 5125ES	125 MB		X	A	A	A				
Wangtek 5150E	250 MB	D	X	A	A	A				
Wangtek 5525ES	525 MB	D	X	A	A	A				
Wangtek 51000ES	1.0 GB	D	X	A	A	A				
Wangtek 6130FS DAT	1.3 GB		X	A	A	A				
Wangtek 6130HS DAT	1.3 GB		X	A	A	A				
Wangtek 6200HS DAT	2.0 GB		X	A	A	A				
Wangtek 9200	2.0 GB	D	X	A	A	A				

X - Supported in NetWare v3.11 (as TAPEDC00 driver).
M - Contact the device manufacturer for details about which host adapters are supported.
A - Supported in the B/R Driver Kit v.1.0 (as TAPEDC00 driver).
- In "Prorprietary" column, 1 = 3Com, 2 = Netframe 3 =Tricord, 4 = COMPAQ. The Servers contain proprietary SCSI controllers. The drivers for these controllers will be in the B/R Driver Kit v1.0
* - The Apaptec 174x controller board is supported in the NetWare v3.11 Box when configured in 145x mode only.
D - Supported in Server Backup plus (as DIBIDAI2 driver).

Storage Devices Compatible with Novadiblnlm or Wangteknlm DIBI-II Driver Software
NetWare v3.11 Backup / Restore and Upgrade Subsystem Configuration Matrix

COMPANY / SUBSYSTEM	STORAGE CAPACITY	SCSI CONTROLLERS: ADAPTEC 1510/152X	ADAPTEC 154X/164X	174X*	FUTURE DOMAIN	BUS TECH	PROP.	QIC02 CONTROLLERS: EVEREX 811	ARCHIVE 402/9	PROP.	WANGTEK
HEWLETT-PACKARD											
HP C 1502AA/OP66			N	N							
WANGTEK/WANGDAT											
Wangtek 5099 EQ	60 MB										W
Wangtek 5125 EQ	125 MB										W
Wangtek 5150 EQ	150 MB										W

W - Supported in NetWare v3.11 (as WANGTEK driver).
N - Supported in NetWare v3.11(as NOVADIBI driver).

Server Backup plus devices support list is based on the following sources: Novell NetWare Version 3.11 Server Backup (SBACKUP) utility, Novell NetWire and third party vendor information. Not all device /host adapter configurations have been tested by Sytron. Sytron assumes no liability for failure of third party hardware to perform as expected. Device support list is subject to change without notice (A)11/12/92).

Figure 11-1c. SY-TOS tape controller and tape drive compatibility table (continued)

Sytron's SY-TOS solution is a bit different in that this product consists of software only. It works with several different tape controllers and tape drive systems. See Figure 11-1 for a listing of valid combinations.

Tape Backup Systems for Large LANs

Several tape backup systems exist for large (more than 150MB of disk space) LANs. Four products, manufactured by Advance Digital Information Corporation (ADIC), Emerald, Maynard, and Palindrome Corporation stand out as preferred solutions.

The ADIC solution, the LANbacker 8000, uses up to ten 120MB tape cartridges to provide a total backup potential of 1.2GB. LANbacker units can be chained together to provide several gigabytes (GB) of data backup.

One solution offered by Emerald allows the chaining together of multiple 60MB or 120MB tape drives to provide a large, unattended backup. The introduction of VAST, Emerald's newest backup system, makes this solution seem impractical and costly but, for a network that already has a single 60MB or 120MB Emerald unit, the drive linking option provides an upgrade path that protects the initial investment.

Although VAST software was initially plagued with problems, the more mature product functions acceptably well. The VAST system offers the ability to store up to 2.2GB on a single 8mm tape cartridge.

Maynard is another source for a 2.2GB tape backup system. The Maynard system was introduced more recently than Emerald's VAST, and has proven to be quite capable.

The new generation 2.2GB tape backup systems employ helical-scan recording, illustrated in Figure 11-2. Exabyte Corporation manufactures most of these helical-scan tape drive units, so the only real difference in them lies in the software they use to operate the drives. Helical-scan recording is a process that uses three rotating heads to write data across the tape in diagonal stripes that are placed quite close together. More conventional technology uses several parallel linear tracks that run the length of the tape. The net effect of using helical-scan recording is that a higher percentage of the tape's surface area is utilized, allowing for a tremendous gain in the amount of data stored on equal amounts of tape. Helical-scan recording is the same technology used in videotape players and recorders.

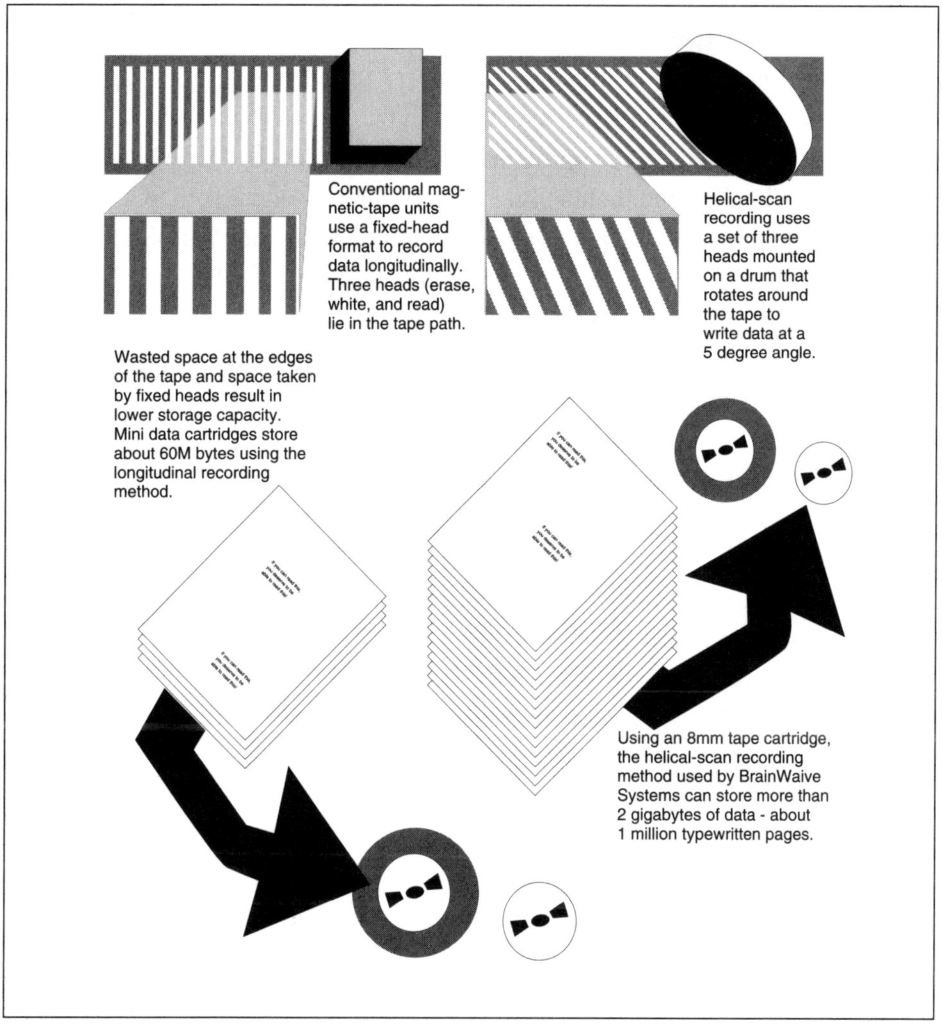

Figure 11-2. Operation of helical-scan

Palindrome offers backup software called Network Archivist that works with any Exabyte 2.2GB helical scan tape drive. The software offers many NetWare-aware features, e.g., using a file's last access date to determine the files that have been least recently used.

Digital Audio Tape

An emerging backup technology is based on 4mm Digital Audio Tape (DAT). DAT is already available in Japan and has been introduced to the U.S. market on a small scale. DAT drives store approximately 1.1GB of data and have bit error rates similar to the 2.2GB, 8mm helical-scan drivers. One advantage of DAT is that the cost of both the drive mechanisms and the media is essentially subsidized by the mass production of DAT for audio applications. One additional reason 4mm DAT will probably prevail in the long run is that the 8mm drive mechanism is made by very few vendors. The 4mm DAT is a wide-open market, and at least two vendors are already shipping DAT to tape drive marketers.

Macintosh Backups

With the advent of NetWare 2.15, file server support has been added for Macintosh file types on NetWare disk drives. These files must be backed up via a "NetWare for Macintosh-aware" backup system, such as those offered by Maynard, Mountain, and Palindrome.

Novell supplies a MACBACK utility, but it suffers from some reliability problems. First, MACBACK "thinks" it has run out of disk space after processing 238 files, and subsequently quits. Second, and more importantly, during a restore it creates resource forks for every file, whether or not the original file had one, which causes gibberish to be tacked on to the end of MAC ASCII files. This problem has been confirmed by Novell. As of this writing, there is no fix from Novell for MACBACK problems.

NBACKUP and SBACKUP ship with all versions of NetWare,and are available on CompuServe's NetWire forum. Even though the documentation states that Macintosh files are backed up, this is not the case with version 1.0 of NBACKUP; all Macintosh application program files are completely ignored.

WORM Backup Systems

Although activity in Write Once/Read Many (WORM) optical technology has been growing recently, there are still only a few products available for the NetWare environment. Optical Storage Solutions (OSS) has come up with an interesting approach that incorporates the use of NetWare.

OSS has a software-only product that is much like Sytron's SY-TOS. The OSS product works with most WORM drives on the market, functioning as an optical disk server. Depending on the drives used, this system can provide a storage capacity of 4GB and up. Software such as Novell's LARCHIVE and LRESTORE can be used for archiving.

Another implementation of WORM technology is to use WORMs as file server drives. Corel Systems, Inc. offers WORM drives that can be used at the file server with NetWare 2.1x.

Backup Speeds

The average tape backup device has a data transfer rate of between 2MB and 4MB per minute. The actual throughput depends almost entirely on the particular network environment. In the case of a low-speed network, such as Corvus Omninet, do not expect a backup unit to achieve its maximum level of performance.

The speed of the network hardware is not the only limiting factor. A heavily loaded network will slow the network backup's throughput. A slow or overtaxed file server will also reduce the backup's performance. Another consideration is the amount of memory available in the PC attached to the backup unit. There should be at least 400K of RAM available before the archiving software is executed, as most of the software products used for tape backup systems use the PC's RAM as a buffer. Lastly, a slow PC will require more time to complete a backup.

DOS's BACKUP Utility

There is an unfortunate problem associated with using DOS's BACKUP utility with files on a NetWare file server. In its current releases, DOS BACKUP and RESTORE do not recognize files that are flagged Shareable. This includes files flagged Shareable Read-Only and Shareable Read-Write. In order to backup Shareable files with the DOS BACKUP utility, it is first necessary to make them non-Shareable. Using DOS to backup NetWare files is archaic, and it is hoped that this problem associated with its use will be enough to persuade users to invest in a more NetWare-aware backup system.

Timed Backups

It is advantageous to run backup sessions during periods of low network activity when most or all of the files will be closed and available for backup. Some backup products provide a means to schedule timed, operator-free backups. However, unattended backups present a certain security risk that must be properly managed.

In order to perform a full system backup, the backup-equipped workstation must be logged in to each file server that has SUPERVISOR equivalence. Specifically, the NetWare bindery files, which make up the database containing user and group definitions, require SUPERVISOR equivalence in order to be archived. Even if the backup does not include the bindery files, access may still be needed to other secured directories. Allowing an unattended workstation to log in with such a high level of security privileges creates a security loophole. Fortunately, there are a number of ways to insure the security of these sessions.

Assuming NetWare 2.1x is being used, start by enabling the SYSCON accounting features that provide restrictions on time, physical station, and concurrent connections. The idea is to create a special user ID for the backup sessions that can log in only once per session, only during certain times (such as 1:00 am to 4:00 am), and only from a specific workstation address.

Next, set up some means by which the workstation can log in with this special user ID at a preset time. A keyboard macro utility can be used for this, but it can also be accomplished via batch files.

There is an obvious need to prevent someone from simply rebooting the backup workstation and using it to log in with the special user ID at 3:00 am. Start by creating a login script for the backup user ID. The script should allow the backup routines to be completed and then should cause the workstation to log out. If the backup device requires several command-line options to operate properly, it may be necessary to use a utility that allows for a batch file from a login script, such as GO-COM.ARC in the libraries of CompuServe's NetWire Forum.

Another potential security risk is the Ctrl-Break (or Ctrl-C) problem. What can be done to keep a user from interrupting the batch job to gain access to the system while the workstation is logged in? A file called CTRLBK.TXT in a library on the CompuServe NetWire Forum contains the instructions necessary to turn the keyboard on and off.

By combining these techniques, it is possible to have a secure, unattended backup session. Once the backup system is set up, simply install the AUTOEXEC.BAT that logs the special user in at the desired time and put a tape in the tape drive (or a disk in the WORM drive).

Last Accessed Date Problems

At least three dates are associated with any file on a NetWare file server: the creation date, the last modified date, and the last accessed date.

The last accessed date is updated every time a file is opened, regardless of whether the file is opened to be run or if it is opened for backup. Knowing the last date a file was accessed can be helpful, as this information can be used to develop a list of unused files. However, performing backups destroys this information, in many cases. Unfortunately, there are precious few backup software products that preserve the file's original last accessed date. Even Novell's own archiving utilities, LARCHIVE and NARCHIVE, do not save the last accessed date.

Brightwork Development offers two utilities, DATESAVE and DATEREST (originally from Integrity Software), that were specifically designed to address this problem. These utilities, which are included in Brightwork's NetReports package, save the last accessed date before the backup is run and restore it immediately after the backup is complete. Palindrome's Network Archivist backup software automatically protects the last backup date.

Novell's internal high-speed tape backup unit also offers a solution to the last accessed date problem. This device requires the file server to be down while backups are run. It bypasses the file server's operating system and makes a virtual image backup of the entire disk drive, thereby preserving the files' last accessed dates.

LARCHIVE and LRESTORE

Novell includes its own backup/restore software with NetWare. Two of these utilities are LARCHIVE and LRESTORE, which allow NetWare disks to be backed up to a local workstation drive. The utility NBACKUP was introduced with 2.15c and 3.x to replace LARCHIVE and LRESTORE.

If a non-NetWare-aware tape backup system is being used, it is necessary to back up NetWare-specific system files, e.g., those files that contain user/group definitions and directory/file trustees. A non-NetWare-aware backup system will backup program and data files, but will not backup the NetWare-specific system files. Backup disks created with LARCHIVE are complete. They can be searched and LRESTOREd in any order, unlike disks created with DOS's BACKUP which requires practically an entire series of disks to be accessed in the correct order. The LARCHIVE and LRESTORE utilities allow the backup of certain NetWare-specific system files that are essential if a complete backup of the system is needed.

Figure 11-3 illustrates how LARCHIVE is used to backup NetWare-specific system files, including the bindery, directory rights, and trustee lists. Use of the LARCHIVE SYSTEM command (instead of the LARCHIVE command) eliminates some of the prompts.

Depending on the target drive, it may be necessary to insert additional disks to complete the backup.

```
E:\> larchive system
Advanced NetWare LARCHIVE V1.13 — Archive to Local Disks
Copyright (C) 1987 Novell, Inc. All Rights Reserved.

You MUST be a supervisor in order to perform a COMPLETE system backup.
If you are not a supervisor, only directories to which you have rights may be backed up.
Back up fixed volume SYS? (Y/N) y

Enter the letter of the LOCAL disk drive on which to archive files:  e
Do you want to print a log report of this session?  (Y/N) n

Select specific directories to be backed up? (Y/N)
(N = Back up all directories) n

Select the backup mode for ALL directories from the following:
        1) Back up ALL qualified files in each directory
        2) Back up ONLY qualified files that have been modified since last backup

Select Option: (1, 2) 1

Do you want to:

        1) Select specific files
        2) Ignore specific files
        3) Backup all files

Select Option: (1-3) 2

Enter list of specifications to be used for ignoring
files or <RETURN> if none. Multiple lines may be entered.
> *.*
>

SYS:SYSTEM
        If you are archiving to a floppy disk drive (or other removable media),
        insert a diskette.
Press the space bar to continue.
        Archiving: +***
SYS:
        Archiving: +*
SYS:SYSTEM
        Archiving: +*
...continues
```

Figure 11-3. Using LARCHIVE to backup system files

Moving User and Group Definitions

With a slight modification of the backup example shown in Figure 11-3, it is possible to back up only the files that define a system's individual and group users, i.e., bindery files. This technique is useful when duplicating the user and group definitions from one server to another.

```
E:\> larchive system
Advanced NetWare LARCHIVE V1.13 — Archive to Local Disks
Copyright (C)1987 Novell, Inc. All Rights Reserved.

You MUST be a supervisor in order to perform a COMPLETE system backup.
If you are not a supervisor, only directories to which you have rights may
be backed up.
Back up fixed volume SYS? (Y/N) y

Enter the letter of the LOCAL disk drive on which to archive files: e
Do you want to print a log report of this session? (Y/N) n

Select specific directories to be backed up? (Y/N)
(N = Back up all directories) y

SYS:SYSTEM
      If you are archiving to a floppy disk drive (or other removable media),
      insert a diskette.
Press the space bar to continue.
      Archiving: +***
SYS:
      Back up? (Y/N)  n
<at this point press CTRL-C>
```

Figure 11-4. Using LARCHIVE to backup bindery files only

Because each user has a specific mailbox directory and specific files (login script, printcon database, etc.), it is also necessary to copy these directories to the other server. This can be accomplished with a second LARCHIVE of just the SYS:MAIL directory, all subdirectories, and corresponding files, as shown in Figure 11-5.

```
Q:\MAIL> larchive
Advanced NetWare LARCHIVE V1.13 — Archive to Local Disks
Copyright (C) 1987 Novell, Inc. All Rights Reserved.

Enter the letter of the LOCAL disk drive on which to archive files: e
Do you want to print a log report of this session? (Y/N) n

Do you want to save directory rights and trustee lists? (Y/N) y
Do you want to archive the system's user and group definitions? (Y/N) y

Select specific directories to be backed up? (Y/N)
(N = Back up all directories) n

Select the backup mode for ALL directories from the following:
1) Back up ALL qualified files in each directory
2) Back up ONLY qualified files that have been modified since last backup

Select Option: (1, 2) 1
Do you want to:

1) Select specific files
2) Ignore specific files
3) Backup up all files

Select Option: (1-3) 3

SYS:SYSTEM
If you are archiving to a floppy disk drive (or other removable media), insert a diskette.
Press the space bar to continue.
Archiving: +***
SYS:MAIL
Archiving: +**
SYS:MAIL/20007
Archiving: +*
SYS:MAIL/1
Archiving: +********
(the process continues...)
```

Figure 11-5. Using LARCHIVE to backup SYS:MAIL

Using LRESTORE, the bindery files and SYS:MAIL directories/files can all be restored at once. This makes it possible to quickly bring up a new server with user definitions from another server.

Note that NetWare/386 uses a different structure for the bindery files. There are three core bindery files and they are not transferable to or from 2.x systems.

For files split across backup disks, they can be recombined with DOS's COPY/B command. For example: COPY/B A:PART1 + B:PART2 C:TOTAL

NBACKUP

In 1989 Novell released NBACKUP as a replacement to the xARCHIVE and xRESTORE utilities (LARCHIVE, NARCHIVE, etc.). Beware, this utility is ineffective at both backing up and restoring. Attempts are currently being made at Novell to correct the following NBACKUP problems:

- Window Based
- File Lumping
- Trail Files
- Other Bugs

Window Based Backup. These utilities perform redundant actions; they largely do the same thing time and time again. By design, a backup utility is boring and routine. While it is pleasant to have a pretty interface, if it is not functional, or if it hinders the routine of backing up, it fails. This is especially true if there is no command line interface and, in the case of NBACKUP, there exists (at this writing) no such interface. Unfortunately, NBACKUP's window interface is hard to use and nonintuitive. Fortunately, Novell listens to its customers and is always improving its utilities.

File Lumping. Unlike the xARCHIVE utilities that NBACKUP replaces, files are not stored on a one-for-one basis. The one-for-one basis indicates that the files are stored, with the possible exception of different filename extensions, in a readily usable state. In fact, the files exist on the backup device as they exist in normal use. NBACKUP, however, lumps files, much in the same manner used in DOS's BACKUP utility. The problem here is two-fold. One, the files are not readily usable nor is it easy to discern which files are on a specific disk. The second part of the problem is that the order in which the disks were stored to is the order which must be used for restoring. In sum, with the older xARCHIVE type utilities, files were stored in a readily usable state and disks could be restored in any order; with the

NBACKUP utility, files are lumped together, not readily usable and disks must be restored in order of backup.

Trail Files. When using NBACKUP for backup there could be a problem with trail files. These trail files are used when restoring the backup session. Unfortunately, NBACKUP leaves these files in the directory where the backup session originated. And, if these files are not copied somewhere and the backup session must be restored, it cannot take place without these exact files. These two files are named BACK$ERR.xxx and BACK$LOG.xxx. The xxx part of the name indicates the sequence number, starting with 000 and continuing with 001, etc. But, the trail file problem does not end here. NBACKUP requires that the same, precise directory path and structure exist for a restore session to succeed. In this case, the directory path is composed of file server name, volume name, and directory name. This makes restore of NBACKUP sessions very difficult, and to the unwitting user, very upsetting.

Other Bugs. There are many other bugs within NBACKUP, not all of which have been uncovered to be sure. However, among those encountered thus far are the inability to completely restore sessions under NetWare/386 3.0. The problem stems from the use of improper directory function calls (where register ah=0xE2) and results in an assortment of error message pertaining to directory errors that do not actually exist. Another bug provides bogus error messages when the trail files do not exist or exist in the wrong directory. Namely, if you have trail files in the wrong directory when a restore session is attempted, those files in the wrong directory will not be shown nor will an error be issued.

All in all, NBACKUP does not provide an adequate replacement for the xARCHIVE and xRESTORE utilities.

System Programming

System programming refers to the installation and maintenance of a front-end user interface for the LAN. The front-end interface allows users to access the most frequently used functions on the LAN without having to learn much, if anything, about DOS or the LAN operating system.

The single largest benefit gained by insulating users from the operating system is not having to train them. The cost of training users is higher than the cost of hardware or software in most computer implementations in business. Reducing or eliminating the need for training in certain areas (such as the operating system) can have a direct impact on the cost of a project.

Efficient use of the system can also have an economic impact. One way to look at this is with a concept called *keystroke economy*. Each time the number of keystrokes required to perform a certain operation is reduced by one, it translates into a savings in time and money. For example, suppose 100 users on a LAN access E-mail at least twice a day. If each user could be saved an average of 10 keystrokes every time they access E-mail, almost 750,000 keystrokes per year would be saved. So, if each keystroke averages a quarter to a half second, this savings works out to between 17 and 35 hours of time. A few such efficiency gains can go a long way toward justifying a LAN supervisor position to management, even though the real benefit of system programming is ease of use.

Workstation Configuration

Let's now move on to what system programming encompasses and how to approach it. The system program begins when a user turns on a PC and it loads the operating system. Many PC users are familiar with the CONFIG.SYS and AUTOEXEC.BAT files, which play important roles in creating their environment. Figures 11-6 and 11-7 show typical CONFIG.SYS and AUTOEXEC.BAT files.

```
files=20
buffers=24
shell=command.com /E:00512 /P
```

Figure 11-6. Typical CONFIG.SYS file

```
REM PURPOSE:        INITIALIZE PC_
REM LOCATION:       ROOT DIRECTORY OF C:
REM AUTHOR:         JOHN Q. PUBLIC
echo off
cls
rem ----------------------------------------------
rem show drive:path in DOS prompt
prompt $P$G
rem ----------------------------------------------
rem set path
path c:\dos;c:\
rem ----------------------------------------------
rem set display type
set DISPLAY=VGA
rem ----------------------------------------------
rem present local menu options
cls
type c:\LCLMENU.TXT
```

Figure 11-7 Typical AUTOEXEC.BAT file with remarks

Note the SHELL command used in the CONFIG.SYS file. This tells DOS to increase the amount of memory allocated for the DOS environment to 512 bytes from the default of 160. The environment space is needed to create environment variables that are used to pass information from one application to another. This saves the user the trouble of reentering this information. Up to 32,768 bytes can be allocated for the environment.

Environment variables are similar to variables used in any programming language. In DOS, variables come in only one type—string variables. These variables are used in DOS batch programming. If you are unfamiliar with the use of environment variables in batch files, refer to a DOS manual for information on the SET and IF...THEN commands.

The first example of an environment variable is shown in the AUTOEXEC.BAT file in Figure 11-7. The statement

```
set DISPLAY=VGA
```

creates a variable called DISPLAY and assigns it a value of VGA. This is a hardware-specific environment variable that refers to the type of display installed. It is used in the login process to help certain applications locate the appropriate drivers for that workstation's display type.

Other statements in the CONFIG.SYS and AUTOEXEC.BAT files are documented with remark statements and should be self-explanatory. Note that there are no user-specific variables in the CONFIG.SYS or AUTOEXEC.BAT files, such as the user's name or ID. It is important to try to separate hardware, software, and user variables as much as possible. Keeping variables of a similar type isolated in separate files reduces the potential for interdependence problems, which might otherwise be caused by mixing the variables together in the same file. For example, although a user will be logging in to the same workstation 95 percent of the time, unnecessary problems can arise if Lotus 123 doesn't work simply because Bill is using Harriet's PC and not his own.

It is important to emphasize that the remark (REM) statements shown in Figure 11-7 do not affect the performance of a batch file. They are shown here to demonstrate that the habit of documenting batch files is good to fall into. These examples contain excessive remarks for the sake of clarity and are not repeated in later figures. Another point worth mentioning pertains to environment variables. Since environment space is limited, it makes sense to use short variables and variable names. The samples are a bit longer than necessary to improve readability.

Local Menu

If the workstation is equipped with a hard disk, a menu program will probably be installed on it. Although there are sophisticated menuing products available, the examples shown in Figures 11-8 and 11-9 represent the simplest form of DOS menu: a text file and supporting batch files. When the PC boots up, the last statement in the AUTOEXEC.BAT displays the LCLMENU.TXT file, which displays available batch files, including CAD.BAT, FMT.BAT, and LAN.BAT.

```
BILL'S PC MENU
CAD Run CAD Program
FMT Format floppy disk
LAN Login to network
```

Figure 11-8. Sample LCLMENU.TXT menu

```
echo off
cls
if X%LOGGED_IN%==XYES goto LANMENU
if X%SHELL%==XLOADED goto LOGIN
ipx
net3
if errorlevel 1 goto ABORT
set SHELL=LOADED
:LOGIN
f:
login %1
goto END
:LANMENU
h:
lanmenu.bat
goto END
ABORT
echo A problem occurred while
echo loading network shell.
echo Contact system supervisor.
:END
```

Figure 11-9. Sample LAN.BAT file

The only batch file of interest is LAN.BAT, as this is the one that initiates a LAN session. In order to optimize execution speed, environment variables are used to determine whether the shell has been loaded and if the user is logged in. If the user is logged in, control is transferred to the LAN menu program. If the shell is loaded but the user is not logged in, the login process is initiated, as described later.

When the PC is turned on and LAN.BAT executes, the two "IF" tests will fail and the shell programs (IPX and NET3) will be loaded. If there is a problem during the loading of the shell programs, the screen will display an error message. The error message is an important aspect of system programming, as it minimizes the user's need to understand how the system works and what might go wrong.

Once the shell has successfully loaded, an environment variable is set accordingly:

```
set SHELL=LOADED
```

Next, the first network drive (assumed here to be F:) is made the current drive and the login program is called. If there is more than one server on the LAN and it is known which server should be the default for a particular workstation, this information could be added so that the batch file would read:

```
login SERVER_1\%1
```

This code would save the user from typing the server name each time they log in. Note that, if there is more than one server and the login does not specify which one to use, the network will select a server at random. The %1 in Figure 11-9 and the variation above permits the user to specify the login name on the command line by typing

```
LAN user-name1
```

(where "user-name1" is the user's login name.)

Login Processing

Once a user has successfully entered a valid login name and password, the system login script is processed. This script is created using the SYSCON utility and resides in a file called NET$LOG.DAT (NET$LOG.OS2 for workstations using OS/2) in the SYS:PUBLIC subdirectory.

In Figure 11-10, a system login script is displayed. Note the WRITE statements are used to personalize the login process. This approach can have a dramatic effect on people who are intimidated by computers. It gives the LAN a personality. IF...THEN logic can also be used to do some creative things during the login process.

```
map display off
write "Good % GREETING_TIME, %FULL_NAME \N"
write "Address # is %P_STATION\N"
set FULL_NAME="%FULL_NAME"
set LOGIN_NAME="%LOGIN_NAME"
set STATION="%STATION"
set PRINTER="0"
set LOGGED_IN="YES"
map f:=SYS:UTILITY
map H:=SYS:HOME\%LOGIN_NAME
drive H:
map insert S1:=SYS:UTILITY
map insert S2:=SYS:DRIVER\%DISPLAY
map insert S3:=SYS:PUBLIC
map insert S4:=SYS:DOS\%OS\%OS_VERSION
```

Figure 11-10. Typical NetWare system login script

The login program has a system of identifier variables of its own, as listed in the *NetWare Supervisor Reference* manual under SYSCON. All identifier variables used in the login script are preceded by a percent sign (%) when used. For clarity, the percent sign will be used to differentiate login script variables from DOS environment variables in this chapter.

- The variable %GREETING_TIME returns either "morning," "afternoon," or "evening," depending on the time of day.
- The variable %FULL_NAME returns whatever was entered when a new user was set up. If SYSCON is used to add users, %FULL_NAME will be found under User Information. If the MAKEUSER utility is used, the %FULL_NAME is specified in the CREATE statement. Note that the MAKEUSER and CREATE commands are features of NetWare versions 2.1 and later.
- The variable %STATION is the logical station number that is dynamically assigned by the server.
- The variable %P_STATION is the 12-character hexadecimal address of the network card in the PC.
- The variable %LOGIN_NAME refers to the name the user enters during the login process.

All of these login script variables can be used in many ways during the login process. The variable %P_STATION notes which workstation is being used. This information may come in handy if any unique hardware combinations exist on the LAN that require special handling in terms of drive mappings. The variable %LOGIN_NAME is the unique identifier that must be used in order to send any messages to a specific user. For instance, a batch file may be needed to send a broadcast message to the user. In the sample login script, these four variables are also set up as DOS environment variables so they may be used by DOS batch programs that will run after the login processing is completed.

In addition to the NetWare login script variables, DOS environment variables can be used to keep track of a user's session on the LAN. Note that two environment variables are set in the system login script that are not login script variables. PRINTER is used at another point in the login sequence to set up the default print job. LOGGED_IN keeps track of whether someone is logged on to the LAN, should the LAN.BAT file be inadvertently run on the user's hard disk while logged in.

The next bit of work accomplished by the system login script involves setting up the drive mappings. The first drive mapping shown in Figure 11-10 sets drive F: to SYS:UTILITY. This will be the directory where all batch files and other miscellaneous commands are located. Think of SYS:UTILITY as being analogous to SYS:PUBLIC. The next mapping sets drive H: to the user's "home" directory. Almost every LAN installation will have some sort of private data area set up for each user. If the login names are kept to eight or fewer characters, a home directory can be created using the login name. It is then possible to map to it automatically using the map statement shown.

Finally, the search mappings are set. Search drives are similar to directories in a DOS PATH, except that the search extends to data files. The drives in the search list are mapped to the SYS:UTILITY, display driver, and public and DOS directories. (Refer to Chapter 6 of this book, and Novell's *NetWare Command Line Utilities* and *Supervisor Reference* manuals for additional information.)

Once the system login script has been processed, LOGIN.EXE will check to see if the user has been assigned a personal login script (see Figure 11-11). The first statement overrides the default value of the PRINTER environment variable set by the system login script. The second statement tells LOGIN.EXE to quit and pass control to LOGUSER.BAT. Note that most of the work was done in the system login script, rather than in the user login script. This approach is superior to other methods that contain lengthy, redundant user login scripts that are harder to maintain. For this reason, it is best to keep user login scripts as short as possible. If there is no user login script, the default login script will execute as shown in Figure 2-12 in Chapter 2.

```
set PRINTER="2"
exit "loguser.bat"
```

Figure 11-11. Sample user login script

Login Batch File

While not altogether necessary, the use of a batch file can be advantageous in completing the login process. If any TSRs are to be loaded at login, it is better to load them using a batch file rather than the login script. This method prevents conflicts between the NetWare login routine and the TSRs. This is also a good place to insert logic that checks for electronic mail and loads any mail programs found.

In this example, the login script for each user exits to LOGUSER.BAT, as shown in Figure 11-12. First, the fact that the user has logged into the network is recorded in the SYS:SYSTEM\NET$LOG.MSG file using the NETLOG program. This program is part of N.E.T. Utilities by Network Enhancement Tools. This utility uses a NetWare-specific routine that writes a record to the NET$LOG.MSG file. This record includes the date, time, user's login name, logical and physical station numbers, and any other text passed to the utility on the command line. This information can be used later to track and analyze usage of various LAN resources.

```
echo off
cls
netlog User_Logged_In
capture P=%PRINTER%
ptr %PRINTER%.PDF
if exist F:NOTICE.TXT list NOTICE.TXT
LANMENU
```

Figure 11-12. Sample LOGUSER.BAT file

The next command sends a print job to the network printer specified in PRINTER. Depending on the arrangement of local and network printers on the LAN, it may be a good idea to start a default print job for all users. This will prevent the workstation from "hanging" should a user inadvertently hit the PRTSC key in the middle of a session.

A default printer assignment is the bare minimum needed for a user to gain full access to all network printing resources. Ideally, printer access can be achieved without bothering to learn the syntax of the CAPTURE command. To this end, the next step in LOGUSER.BAT loads a memory resident utility called PrinTamer (also one of the N.E.T. Utilities) that simplifies access to network printing resources. PrinTamer reads a printer definition file (PDF) as specified in the command line. This PDF contains the setup strings associated with a particular printer. Note the use of the environment variable, PRINTER, to specify which PDF PrinTamer should use.

Once the memory resident utility is loaded, LOGUSER.BAT checks to see if a file called NOTICE.TXT exists in SYS:UTILITY. This system notice is simply an electronic bulletin board that keeps users informed of anything the supervisor desires. The LIST command refers to a public domain utility that permits read-only access to ASCII files and supports scrolling. The DOS TYPE or MORE commands can also be used, although they are less functional. If there aren't any notices to post, simply delete the file from SYS:UTILITY and the instruction is ignored. One nice thing about a system notice is that users can't log in without seeing it. They can ignore it, but at least you tried to tell them that "the system is going down for maintenance at 5:00 PM sharp."

The final step in LOGUSER.BAT is to execute LANMENU.BAT, shown in Figure 11-13. This is a key element in the LAN menu system. Every time a user finishes an application on the LAN, this batch file should execute and redisplay the menu.

```
echo off
cls
cd F:\UTILITY
H:
type LANMENU.TXT
```

Figure 11-13. Sample LANMENU.BAT file

In this example, the same menu technique that was used for the hard disk is used on the LAN. An ASCII file menu, shown in Figure 11-14, contains descriptions of a few batch files used to execute applications on the LAN. This example is not meant to be a recommendation for such a rudimentary approach to menus, but merely a simplification for clarity's sake.

```
WIDGET COMPANY LAN MENU

LOTUS          Lotus 1-2-3
WP             Word Processing
LOGOFF         Log off network
```

Figure 11-14. Sample LANMENU.TXT menu

LANMENU.BAT sets the directory of drive F: back to SYS:UTILITY and changes the drive to H: to make the user's home directory current. The last thing it does is to display the contents of LANMENU.TXT.

Figure 11-15 illustrates how one application might be set up on the LAN. When the user enters the command, LOTUS, first an entry is made to the system log file. Next, drive F: is changed to the SYS:LOTUS directory. Note that, although a network drive is being "remapped" to another directory, it is not necessary to use the

MAP command. This is because the new directory is on the same volume and is using the same drive letter. Since the CD (or CHDIR) command is internal to DOS, it is much faster than the MAP command and can be used whenever a remapping is done to another directory on the same volume.

```
echo off
cls
netlog Lotus_123
f:
cd \LOTUS
OFFNET
```

Figure 11-15. Sample LOTUS.BAT file

SYS:LOTUS, now drive F:, is made the current drive:\directory and the application is loaded. Some activities occur behind the scenes at this point. Lotus looks for a configuration file called 123.SET, which contains the display and printer drivers. Although a different 123.SET file is required for each display type on the LAN, LOTUS will only find the one located in SYS:DEV\VGA, which was mapped as a search drive in the system login script. A different 123.SET needs to be created for each of the various corresponding directories, e.g., SYS:DEV\CGA and SYS:DEV\MONO, for each type of display adapter used by different workstations on the LAN.

Another technique is to use the environment variable to specify the driver set, as follows:

```
lotus %DISPLAY%.SET
```

The SYS:LOTUS directory then needs to contain the required driver sets and name them accordingly, e.g., VGA.SET and CGA.SET. Not all software supports the passing of the driver file as a parameter, so both techniques are shown. Once the user exits the application, in this case LOTUS, the LAN menu is once again displayed. How various menu options are set up on the LAN will depend on how well the software supports NetWare and how you plan to use the application.

Logging Users Off the LAN

Just as the login process is controlled with batch files, so is the logout process. There are two batch files shown here for logging out, and one for reestablishing a connection. The first, LOGOFF.BAT, shown in Figure 11-16, simply passes control to another batch file in the SYS:LOGIN directory. This step is necessary because once the LOGOUT.EXE command is executed, SYS:LOGIN is the only network directory the user can access. The batch file must reside there to complete execution normally.

```
echo off
cls
f:
cd \LOGIN
OFFNET
```

Figure 11-16. Sample LOGOFF.BAT file

The second batch file, OFFNET.BAT, does all of the work. Shown in Figure 11-17, OFFNET.BAT first logs the user's request to exit the LAN. The LOGOUT command actually detaches the user from the LAN, also ensuring that any open print jobs are closed. Then, the presence of the environment variable, SHELL, is tested. If it is not found, it is assumed that the LAN was accessed from a machine that does not have the combination of basic files previously discussed and the logout processing ends there. If SHELL is found, the LOGGED_IN environment variable is changed to "NO." Next, drive C: is made the current drive and the third batch file, found on drive C:, is executed. RESETC.BAT, shown in Figure 11-18, reestablishes the user's local workstation environment and displays the local menu, which brings the user full circle.

```
echo off
cls
netlog User_Logged_Off
logout
if not X%SHELL%==XLOADED goto END
set LOGGED_IN=NO
c:
cd \
resetc
:end
```

Figure 11-17. Sample OFFNET.BAT file

```
set COMSPEC=C:\COMMAND.COM
cls
type c:\LCLMENU.TXT
```

Figure 11-18. Sample RESETC.BAT file

Going back to Figure 11-9, note that LAN.BAT will still work even though the user has already accessed the LAN once. The SHELL environment variable is used to prevent an attempt to load the shell a second time. This was a problem with NetWare prior to version 2.0 when an attempt to load the shell after it was already loaded would "lock up" the PC. In addition, if the user executes LAN.BAT while logged in, it does not repeat the login process but merely executes the LAN menu program.

Recordkeeping

Without proper recordkeeping, the rest of the LAN supervisor's job is made that much more difficult, if not impossible. Careful recordkeeping facilitates efficient support, effective problem determination, and makes it possible to provide an overall high quality of network administration. Proper recordkeeping, or documentation, does not mean an elaborate filing system or on-line database. It simply means that any information that may be needed at some future date should be written down and remain retrievable. A simple paper system should suffice until the need for something more elaborate arises. There is no point in spending a lot of time setting up a complicated recordkeeping system that will never be used.

Log Book

The first thing every LAN supervisor needs is a spiral-bound notebook for keeping a log. Whenever anything is done on the LAN, it should be written down. This should start with the NetWare installation process, even if someone other than the supervisor does it. Every time a new user is added, every time there is a system error, every time anything is changed on the LAN, an entry should be made in the log. The log serves as an audit trail and provides the means to retrace actions. It is also an excellent way for the backup LAN supervisor to see what has been done to the LAN.

Hardware Files

Once the hardware is installed, a file folder should be set up for each piece of equipment. Each folder should contain the purchase order, packing slip, invoice, warranty information, and serial number of the equipment. These records will be needed for warranty repairs and maintenance contracts. As repairs are made to equipment, put a copy of the completed work order in the file. On the inside of the file folder, indicate the location of the equipment's operations guide and how a replacement can be obtained if the original is lost.

Assign each major component a unique number. Use the serial number off of the chassis or use the company's internal asset numbering system. All that matters is that the equipment has a number stuck on it somewhere that won't rub, wash, or fall off. These numbers should be used to organize the files. The next supervisor will be grateful when, years from now, the ordering information for a printer part that needs to be replaced can be tracked down.

There is a multitude of hardware management software packages available, such as PC Tracker by RG Software Systems, Inc., NetManager, by Brightwork Development, Inc., and the Micro Resource Manager from Computer Associates International, Inc. These packages provide a computerized alternative for keeping records.

Another helpful aid is the set of worksheets found in the back of various NetWare manuals, e.g., the *Supervisor's Guide* and the *Installation Guide*. Please note that even if the records are put on-line, the backup paperwork is still necessary. After all, the part you may need is the part that prevents you from accessing your system on-line records.

Cabling

The most difficult piece of hardware to keep track of is cabling. There are no sure-fire methods for tracking cabling. No matter how carefully the records are kept, someone will change something without telling the supervisor and the records will be out-of-sync. At a minimum, cable installers should be required to follow a numbering system specified by the supervisor. The installers should then number each cable using these specifications and provide an "as installed" sketch of any work they do.

The importance of properly numbering the LAN cables cannot be over-emphasized. Use quality materials in labeling cable and avoid handwritten numerals. Remember that Teflon, which is the required material for cable used in some locations, is a nonstick surface by design and will resist even the stickiest adhesive-backed labels. Each end of every segment of cable installed should have a number on it that should be far enough from the end of the cable to allow the connector to be replaced, should that ever be necessary. You should also place this number on the front and back of any wall plates or patch panels where a cable segment terminates.

The file records for the cabling should reflect the start and end point for each cable segment. If a drawing is available, use it to show the actual routing of each segment. Depending on the topology used, it may be important to know the length of the cable in each segment. For example, ARCNET running over RG-62 coaxial cable has a cable segment limitation of 2,000 feet.

When creating a list of cable segments, be sure to include the following pieces of information:

- Cable number
- Starting point
- Ending point
- Cable type
- Cable length
- Installer
- Date installed
- Drawing number

A simple way to record the cable information is to use a spreadsheet. A spreadsheet provides the flexibility of being able to sort on various fields and allows the information to be used in the most advantageous way.

Software

As with each piece of hardware, a file should be maintained for each software package installed on the LAN. Keep copies of the purchase order, packing slip, invoice, and completed registration card, along with any warranty or support contract information. If multiple copies of the same package are purchased, such as a word processor, keep track of who receives the manuals. They are very expensive to replace and have a tendency to disappear within the ranks of the organization because they are so highly valued among users.

When the time comes to upgrade to a new release of a software package, the manufacturer may require the individual serial number for each copy. In some cases, the date purchased will affect the price of the upgrade. For example, Lotus Development Corporation announced a program for purchasers of Lotus 1-2-3, release 2.01. Purchases made after September of 1988 qualified the purchaser for a free upgrade to release 3.0. Keeping accurate records of software purchases can mean direct savings for the organization.

System Configuration

To the supervisor who set up the system, the way in which all the pieces of software on the LAN fit together will be obvious. It may not be so obvious to anyone else and, for that reason, it is important to document the system configuration.

As always, start with something simple. A flowchart showing the chain of events that occur from login to logout, together with a listing of any batch files and login scripts used will explain a large part of the system configuration. To avoid extra effort, always reference the DOS, NetWare, and other software manuals, rather than trying to rewrite them in your own documentation.

Figure 11-19 shows how the system flowchart for our sample system might look. This example assumes a LAN that uses an exit command in each user's private login script to a .BAT file called LOGUSER.BAT. This .BAT file in turn executes MENU.BAT.

Judicious use of comment or remark (REM) statements in the .BAT files and login scripts will eliminate much in the way of separate documentation. The price paid for this self-documenting code is performance, since remark statements in a batch file must be interpreted by DOS when the batch file is executed. Figure 11-13 gives an example of how the file LANMENU.BAT might be commented. The remark statements at the beginning of the file show what it does, where it belongs on the system, and who authored it.

The flowchart in Figure 11-19 illustrates how the pieces fit together. A listing of the individual files describes the role that each plays in controlling the user's environment. This information is essential in isolating problems when a user calls for support.

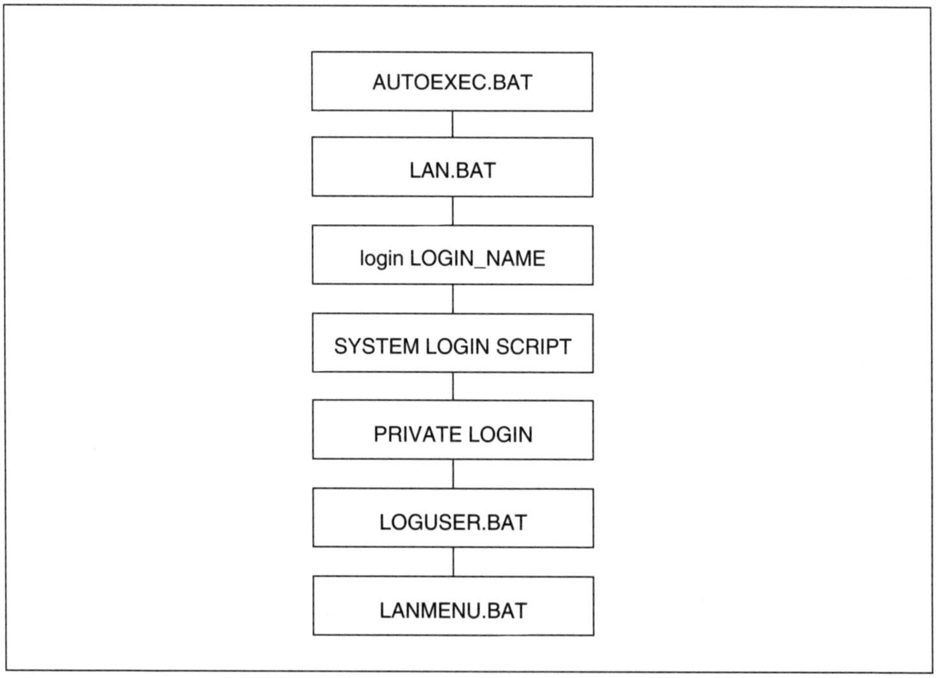

Figure 11-19. Example system flowchart

Software Configuration

The way in which each software package is installed on the LAN is also important. It is especially important with single-user software that has been adapted to work in the LAN environment. Even with network versions of software, there is usually more than one way to install them. Therefore, it is necessary to document the method used.

For each software package or application on the LAN, document the following items:

- Directory(s) where installed
- Trustee rights needed in the directory(s)
- File flags used in the directory(s)
- Default configuration used
- How to modify defaults
- How users access the software or application
- Configuration files needed by user
- Search mappings used, if any
- Any special considerations (hardware or software)
- Other pertinent information

Users, Groups, and Directories

This part of recordkeeping is less complicated, as NetWare stores much of this information in the bindery. The bindery consists of specific files on the server that NetWare uses to control the security of the LAN. However, the only way to get a list of users or groups using NetWare-supplied utilities is through the supervisory program SYSCON. The simple, on-line listings that SYSCON provides are inadequate for documenting the system. In order to keep complete records of the users and groups on the system, an investment in one of the many network management report generators available should be considered.

One way to minimize the rights aspect of recordkeeping is to use groups. Think of a group as a profile for a certain type of user. Anyone who needs access to the files associated with that profile merely needs to be added to the group. Even if only a couple of people share the same profile, it is easier to add another person to the group later to give them all the same rights than it is to grant the necessary trustee rights one by one.

A little planning as to how people are organized functionally will go a long way toward reducing the complexity of LAN administration tasks.

Data Integrity and Security

One of the most important parts of a LAN supervisor's job is to safeguard the centralized data resources from trespass or harm. Before there were LANs, PC users were on their own with regard to data integrity. A single user with a hard disk had full responsibility for the data stored there. Should something happen to that data, the consequences fall entirely on that user.

The LAN changes that, bringing a new set of technological pluses and minuses. On the plus side, one of the savings used to justify LAN technology is the lowered cost of disk sharing. On the minus side, once everyone's data is stored on a shared disk, the LAN supervisor suddenly becomes personally responsible for its safekeeping.

In the traditional mainframe and minicomputer data processing environment, the data is usually protected by multiple levels of passwords, locked rooms, and elaborate backup schemes. LANs are quite often installed in hallways and storage closets. The real security comes from the LAN operating system and the LAN supervisor.

NetWare has a well-earned reputation for being the most secure of the LAN operating systems. There are many options available to the NetWare LAN supervisor when it comes to setting up the security network. NetWare itself has a myriad of built-in features that allow the LAN supervisor to create a security web to control each user's access. In addition, third-party products offer specific enhanced controls and audit trails.

File Attributes

Specific to each file are its attributes or flags. The important ones to know about are the Read, Write, and Shareable attributes. A file can be flagged Read/Write or Read Only. Just as the names imply, the Read Only flag is analogous to having a write-protect tab on a floppy disk, while the Read/Write flag combination does the same thing as removing the write-protect tab.

A file can also be flagged Shareable or Non-Shareable. If a Non-Shareable file is in use by one person, any other attempts to access it will be rejected. These attributes are displayed and changed using the FLAG command, which is discussed in detail in Novell's *Advanced and SFT NetWare Command Line Utilities* reference manual, (for NetWare 2.x) and in *Using the Network* manual (for NetWare 2.2).

Trustee Rights

In addition to file attributes, each directory on a file server has a set of trustee assignments. A directory trustee can either be a group or an individual. Trustee assignments are set up with either SYSCON or FILER, both packaged with NetWare. These utilities are discussed in detail in Novell's SFT and Advanced NetWare Supervisor Reference, or the Using the Network manual.

Trustees assigned to a directory are given rights to actions they can perform within the directory. For an in-depth discussion of NetWare/286 and /386 rights, see Chapter 2.

By combining flags with trustee rights, the LAN supervisor can grant or revoke access to just about everything on the LAN. The trustees associated with a given directory can be listed using the TLIST command.

An example in which flags and trustee rights are combined will better illustrate their use on an everyday basis. Suppose a word processing document is needed for an employee address list. Only one person should be able to modify the document, but everyone needs to be able to view it.

First decide who is going to create and maintain the documentation. Second, grant that user all trustee rights to the directory in which the file is to be located. Third, add the group EVERYONE to the trustee list for that directory using SYSCON or FILER, but only grant Read, Open, and Search trustee rights to the group. This allows EVERYONE to view the document, but only one person to change it. The person creating the document has only to flag it Shareable to permit more than one user to view it at a time.

Audit Trails

An audit trail documents the types of activities that occur on the LAN, who performs them, and when. A good rule of thumb is to always leave an audit trail. Because the data on the system actually belongs to someone other than you as the

LAN supervisor, it is important to get the proper approval before changing access rights. Whenever user or group lists are created, modified, or deleted, the supervisor should get a signed request from the department that owns the data, as the supervisor should not be directly responsible for any security problems caused by the carelessness of others.

Using the signed change request as a source document, be sure to note when the change is made and by whom. Anyone who needs to know (an EDP auditor, for instance) should be able to find out how the LAN's security web was woven and why.

Another form of audit trail involves tracking which applications people use and the files they access. LANtrail by NetWave, Inc. and Blue Lance's LT Auditor are utilities that enhance Novell's security by providing a log of all file accesses according to LAN supervisor definable parameters.

With the release of NetWare 4.0, direct support for audit services exists within NetWare. This includes support for a separate auditor login account that has the ability to receive data being audited. The audit data is stored so that only the auditor user, not the Supervisor, has access. Most client activities can be audited and reported.

Handling User Data

It is essential for a LAN supervisor to be very careful about handling user data, especially in an environment where accountability is a critical issue, such as defense or banking. However, one of the loopholes in NetWare's security scheme is that the network SUPERVISOR and anyone with that security equivalence can look at or change anything on the system. Here are some examples of how to avoid common problems with this issue.

First, if two or more users want to share a file, such as a spreadsheet, give them access to a common subdirectory and show them how to move their own files around.

Second, if it is necessary to restore a file from backup, put the backed up version(s) on a diskette. Then, let the user decide which version of the file to keep and which one to delete.

Third, when a user's name is removed from the system, have someone in that user's department handle the disposition of any files that remain. Once they give the "all clear" to delete any remaining data, be sure to keep an archived copy of it for at least a year.

Granting SUPERVISOR Equivalence

Unless the LAN supervisor performs LAN maintenance on a full-time basis, SUPERVISOR equivalence should not be granted to their personal account. The ID the LAN supervisor uses for personal work should look like that of any other user. This point is often debated, however, the reasons for NOT granting SUPERVISOR equivalence to the LAN supervisor are strong.

First, the LAN supervisor gets a clearer picture of how things work for everyone else by experiencing the LAN from the same rights perspective. If the LAN supervisor has rights to everything, problems that are apparent to other users might not be encountered.

Second, many users do not log out when they are away from their workstations. If the LAN supervisor has SUPERVISOR equivalence and leaves the workstation, the door to the entire system is left wide open.

Third, it is possible to lose track of who has SUPERVISOR equivalence or other broad rights, such as rights over entire volumes. The SECURITY command in NetWare is a utility that will report such loopholes as SUPERVISOR equivalence, volume-level rights, missing or insecure passwords, and missing login scripts. An example of the output given by the SECURITY command is shown in Figure 11-20. This command should be run at least once a month to ensure that there are no serious holes in the security web.

```
File Server Security Evaluation Utility

Checking for network security holes, please wait.

User GUEST
     Has [R O    S ] rights in SYS:SYSTEM (maximum should be[              ])

User SUPERVISOR
     Has [RWOCDPSM] rights in SYS1: (maximum should be [              ])
     Is security equivalent to user SUPERVISOR
     Has unlimited grace logins
     Is not required to change passwords periodically
     Can have passwords that are too short (less than 5)
     Does not require a password

User JPUBLIC

     Is security equivalent to user SUPERVISOR
     Does not have a secure password

Group EVERYONE

Has [RWO      S ] rights in SYS:PUBLIC (maximum should be [R   O      S  ])
```

Figure 11-20. SECURITY command output

Controlling User Access

NetWare versions 2.10 and later include significant improvements in the way a LAN supervisor can manage security on a LAN. The SYSCON utility provides a number of options available from the Default Account Balance/Restrictions menu. These Account Balance/Restrictions features allow the LAN supervisor to specify the following defaults for all users on the system:

- Account expiration date
- Limited number of concurrent sessions
- Required passwords
- Forced password changes
- Maximum disk space allowed

Each option on the menu is explained at length in the NetWare Supervisor Reference and by the help text within SYSCON. In addition to the defaults, each menu option can be tailored to suit a user's needs through use of the User Information menu in SYSCON. The LAN supervisor can also activate an intruder lockout mechanism. This lockout disables a LOGIN ID once an attempt is made to access the system with an incorrect password. Once the intruder lockout option is activated, NetWare will make entries in the system error log (SYS:SYSTEM\SYS$LOG.ERR) indicating the date, time, and nature of the attempted security breach. A supervisor option in SYSCON permits this file to be viewed.

Another option available to the LAN supervisor is to set physical station and time restrictions. The physical station restriction can be useful on a LAN that has mostly diskless workstations. The LAN supervisor may want to restrict all but a select group of users from logging on at the workstations that have diskette drives.

Time restrictions allow the LAN supervisor to determine when users can sign on to the system. This approach can be helpful in scheduling routine system maintenance or backups. As with account restrictions, both of these restrictions can be set as system defaults and/or as individual user defaults.

Maintenance

Machines, especially computers, have to be repaired and otherwise cared for in order to function properly. This requires a skilled technician. Some very large computer installations have specially trained technicians in house, but what about the rest of the world? There are many options available when making arrangements for someone to work on these computers. The primary options available are:

- No arrangement
- Time and materials contract
- Term maintenance contract
- "Hot spares" inventory

Having no arrangement is common in small companies. For standard reasons, including lack of resources or dollars, no attention is given to hardware maintenance until something breaks. When that happens, the *de facto* LAN supervisor makes several frenzied phone calls to the hardware dealer, NetWare dealer, and the installing consultant until someone is found who can fix it. This process can result in an unnecessarily lengthy period of downtime for the LAN.

Time and Materials Contracts

The minimum maintenance arrangement level is a time and materials (T&M) contract. In this arrangement, a service company agrees to provide parts and labor on an "as needed" basis. An agreement of this type will include a schedule that outlines the charges associated with various types of repair work to be performed. Some of the terms to negotiate in a T&M contract are:

1. On-site Technician Billing at a Set Rate Per Hour
   The hourly rate billed for the technician's time should be known in advance for any given situation.
2. Technician Qualifications
   Many service companies use apprentice-level people in the field and keep the experienced people back at the office ready to "walk" them through any tough problems. Know what to expect.
3. Trip Charge
   Is there a trip charge and if so, what is the rate? Anything greater than the cost of one hour of technician time is excessive.
4. Minimum Billed Hour(s) Per Call
   There is usually a minimum number of hours billed per call. If there is more than a two-hour minimum, there should *not* be a trip charge.
5. Equipment Covered
   Just because a service company can fix several brands of PCs does not mean they can work on a laser printer. The preferred approach is to have one T&M contract for all equipment. However, because of specialization, this may be impossible.
6. Response Time Guarantee
   A technician should arrive at the service location within a guaranteed response time after the service call is placed.
7. Warranty Repairs
   Will the service company work on equipment that is still covered under a manufacturer's warranty even though it may have been purchased elsewhere? If so, what charges will be incurred?

Besides these points, there is one more very important issue to remember re-garding a T&M maintenance agreement. Anytime a contractor is working on location, proof of liability insurance and workmen's compensation should be required. This safeguard ensures that the LAN owner is not held financially liable if something should happen and the contractor does not have the proper insurance.

Term Maintenance

A term maintenance contract usually covers a specific piece of equipment, such as a file server, and contains very specific performance requirements for the service company. Unlike the "pay-as-you-go" nature of a T&M contract, term maintenance fixes the cost of all repairs in advance. For a periodic fee, the service company agrees to provide maintenance for that one piece of equipment.

Some of the terms in this type of an agreement include the following:

- Technician qualifications
- Equipment covered
- Spare parts in reserved inventory
- Turnaround time guarantee
- Preventative maintenance performed

Term maintenance can be compared to health insurance: upkeep of the equipment is paid for in advance. Determining whether this option is cost effective will depend on the repair history associated with having the covered equipment down for any length of time. The premium paid for a term maintenance agreement should buy a few things the T&M agreement does not.

First, the service company should guarantee that certain critical spare parts will be kept in inventory specifically for your equipment. If you lose the RAM in a file server, for example, and the chips are on fifteen-week backorder, having an expensive term contract won't do you much good unless the service company has hidden away some RAM.

Second, with a term contract, the turnaround time should be guaranteed. This is the time it takes the service company to get things running from the time they received the call. If they have to supply loaner equipment while they repair something to meet their performance guarantees, it shouldn't cost anything extra.

Third, preventative maintenance of some nature should be included in the contract and periodically performed. This preventative care should include cleaning, visual inspection, and advanced diagnostics, where applicable.

Hot Spares Inventory

The most expensive maintenance arrangement is one in which "hot spares" are available. A hot spare is at least one reliable duplicate of the equipment covered available in stock. Applications that have an inherent high risk associated with equipment failure, such as equipment set up on a factory floor or used for real-time applications, can often justify an inventory of hot spares. Points to keep in mind, in addition to the standard terms for the other types of arrangements, are:

1. Include All Add-ins and Peripherals
   A 386-based file server probably has several megabytes of RAM, large hard disk drives, and any of several kinds of expansion boards. The service company must have the complete configuration available as a hot spare, or the necessary part may not be available when needed.
2. Regularly Test Equipment
   In order to insure that the spares are any better than the defective part they will eventually replace, the spares should be tested at least once per week. Any hot spares purchased should be installed immediately, whether or not the original proves defective. The working "used" parts they replace should then be kept as spares. This approach accomplishes two things. First, the spares are proven good since they have been placed in service. Second, brand new equipment will not go out of warranty while it sits in the box on a shelf as a spare part.

The ultimate preventative care solution to the possibility of hardware failure is fault tolerance. NetWare offers several options to operate redundant hardware on the same LAN through its SFT (System Fault Tolerant) software. With SFT, in the event of certain hardware failures, the LAN continues to operate. For example, one version of SFT NetWare offers the option of redundant hard disk drives, so that if one goes down, the other disk subsystem takes over, keeping the network up and running.

Software Maintenance

In addition to hardware, LAN software maintenance is usually accomplished through maintenance programming. Software maintenance is required to accommodate change, a phenomenon common to all LANs.

Depending on how the LAN is managed, the various duties associated with software (also known as "system") maintenance may or may not be shared among a group of people.

These duties include the following:

- Software revisions (also known as release/version change management)
- Disk space management
- Security profiles maintenance
- Menu system maintenance
- Operating system maintenance

Someone must be responsible for each of these tasks. Since all of these duties interact with one another, it is important that one person act as the coordinator. For example, one LAN supervisor may install a new version of a database package, placing it in a different directory and taking up more hard disk space than the old version of the same package. The disk space management person needs to know how much additional disk space is needed, the menu system person must make the necessary changes so users can access the new version, and the security profiles person needs to grant access privileges to users in the newly created directory. In each case, actions must be taken as a result of some other maintenance activity occurring on the LAN.

Software Revisions

For each software maintenance role, there are specific questions to be asked and duties to be performed. The person in charge of software revisions should keep track of software support agreements and upgrade options. That person should also recognize that installing new versions of applications software can take time in a LAN environment, especially if the software is not written to run on a LAN. Printer drivers may need to be rewritten with new configuration files created for each user.

Most word processing packages use some form of printer driver to describe the settings required to send a document to a specific printer. If the word processing software is centrally located on a file server, it then becomes the LAN supervisor's job to maintain the printer driver. In addition, configuration files may be set up for various users that "customize" the word processing software for their use. Updating the word processing software may require an update on those users' configuration files.

Another software revision issue to be considered is that of differences in installation from one version of an application to another. For example, OfficeWriter 5.0, a word processor application, requires that the directory in which the program's files are located be mapped as a search drive in order to load correctly. OfficeWriter 6.1 eliminates this requirement.

A special case concerning software revisions is custom applications. If modifications are being made to the code of an existing custom-written application, is there a way to lock users out while these modifications are being made? A simple technique to use is to rename the executable file so that menu options and batch files won't work.

Disk Space Management

Disk space management involves more than making sure no one person is "hogging" all of the disk space. It ranges from mundane hard disk "housekeeping" chores, such as deleting old or useless files from the system, to sophisticated analysis of disk usage data using NetWare's FCONSOLE utility and the disk subsystem's advanced diagnostics.

Housekeeping is the least exciting part of disk space management. You should periodically go through a listing of all the files in all of the subdirectories (other than individual users' private directories) to see if any unused files have accumulated there. One easy way to track accumulation is to flag all files in the NetWare and application directories as Shareable/Read-Only. The default for new files is always Non-Shareable/Read/Write.

The toughest aspect of housekeeping is controlling the amount of disk space wasted by users. Some users will be so wary of the LAN that they will store very little data in a private directory and keep anything of value on diskettes. Other users think of the file server as an infinite resource and keep every file (including several generations of revisions) they ever had on it. The common system for dealing with these latter users involves the LAN supervisor begging and pleading with file server "hogs" to archive unneeded data off the LAN.

NetWare 2.1x and 3.x have a feature that allows you to limit the amount of disk space for any one user. Once the limit is reached, the user's only choice is to remove unneeded data or to get the limit increased by the LAN supervisor. Note that under all versions of NetWare, queue (spool) files that users create when sending output to network printers count against their total disk space used. With NetWare 2.1x disk space limitations were server-based. That is, all volumes disk spaces counted towards the user's limit. Under NetWare 386, disk space limitations can be per volume. Therefore, it is important to note that unless specifically changed (see chapter 10, Queue Directory Relocation), all queue files are stored on the SYS: volume and will deduct from users' disk space limitation on volume SYS:.

Another option is to provide a facility that allows users to archive data for long-term storage. This can be as simple as creating a directory that is backed up to tape once a week and then cleared. One method to promote user archiving is as follows:

1. Set up a directory called SYS:ARCHIVE, in which the group EVERYONE has all rights, except DELETE, PARENTAL, and MODIFY.
2. Instruct your users to put anything they don't need anymore but want saved in that directory.
3. Once a week, copy the files users want saved to tape and then delete them from the network.

By maintaining a catalog of the archive tapes, using a product such as EMLIB from Emerald Systems, access to those files can be achieved fairly quickly.

A standard structure for each volume on the file server should be established and should be enforced in order to simplify disk space maintenance. For example, only the NetWare operating system files provided on the release diskettes go in the SYS: root directories created by the INSTALL program. These directories include:

- SYS:SYSTEM
- SYS:MAIL
- SYS:PUBLIC
- SYS:LOGIN

Following this subdirectory approach will simplify operating system upgrades later. One exception to this rule might be in the treatment of the SYS:LOGIN subdirectory, which is the only directory accessible from a workstation prior to logging in. For example, a copy of EDLIN.COM in the SYS:LOGIN directory can be very handy for tasks like editing the AUTOEXEC.BAT or CONFIG.SYS files when servicing workstations that do not have a full copy of DOS. If non-NetWare installed files are put in the SYS:LOGIN directory, they should be carefully documented.

All applications should be organized under a common volume or root directory with no more than one copy of each application in a given directory. This type of organization simplifies the task of upgrading application software as new releases/versions become available.

Reclaiming Disk Space

In rare instances, it is possible to run out of disk space with NetWare 2.x. If TTS is used, the file server will load and then halt with the message: "Abend: Error writing transaction." It will then ask to be powered off and rebooted. This creates an endless cycle. The solution requires reducing the amount of space being used on the SYS volume without actually bringing up the server. To accomplish this, you should first run NETGEN and reload the system files. If using NetWare 2.0a, use INSTALL rather than NETGEN but, instead of using the working NetWare diskettes, make a series of "fake" disks with much smaller files given the same volume and file names. For example, create a set of PUBLIC disks with small text files renamed to represent the real NetWare commands. In place of the actual MAP.EXE, for instance, create a small text file named MAP.EXE.

Once the files are installed, up to 3MB of disk space can be reclaimed. The next step is to perform whatever maintenance is needed to legitimately free space on volume SYS. Boot the file server and start erasing the fake files. When the disk is cleaned up, run INSTALL or NETGEN again and use the real PUBLIC disks to restore the real PUBLIC files.

Security Profiles Maintenance

Security maintenance for the LAN involves overseeing security profiles that include a user's ID, password, list of groups, security equivalences, and trustee assignments. Security profiles are very important to the integrity of the LAN. In order to properly maintain them, strict control must be kept over who can authorize and make any changes.

A common mistake made by many LAN supervisors is to grant one user access to another user's files without permission from someone in authority. Adding security profiles for every new user may seem like overkill, unless you consider that most users assume their private directories are really private. Part of a LAN supervisor's job is to ensure that privacy.

Menu System Maintenance

The duties of the person in charge of menu maintenance are crucial, particularly in light of the fact that the menu system may be the one part of the LAN that is most important to the user. It is essential that the menus a user sees work 100 percent of the time, or the LAN supervisor's credibility may become suspect.

Whenever an application is added or modified, the menu system should be thoroughly tested to verify that everything still works. This includes signing on to several workstations with a non-supervisory login ID and trying the affected menu option. It should also be verified that the application works on a variety of workstation configurations and that it can be accessed with normal user rights. It is also a good idea to sign on with each new user's ID to verify that the trustee assignments that permit the menu (and applications) to function properly are correct.

Operating System Maintenance

Operating system maintenance is the most obvious aspect of software maintenance on a LAN. NetWare has gone through frequent revisions, as Figure 11-21 illustrates. Contact Novell for the latest upgrade information. If you are in the USA, call 1-800-UPDATE1. Upgrading can be a lengthy process and is typically done during off-hours to avoid system down time.

Probably the worst part of a NetWare upgrade is installing new shell files on every workstation. This task may involve accessing every workstation on the LAN to copy the new shell files onto a boot disk or hard disk and modifying the necessary batch file to allow access to the LAN.

Latest Software	Latest Version	Previous Software	Previous Versions
ELS NetWare	2.15c	ELS II	None
Advanced NetWare	2.15c	NetWare	4.6x
		Advanced NetWare/86	2.0a, 2.0, 1.02a, 1.02, 1.01, 1.0a, 1.0
		SFT Level I	2.0a
		Advanced NetWare	2.12, 2.11, 2.0a, 1.02a, 1.02
SFT NetWare	2.2	SFT Level II	2.0a
		SFT	2.15, 2.12, 2.11, 2.1
NetWare /386	3.11	3.10	3.0, 3.10

Figure 11-21. List of previous NetWare assurance upgrades

It is possible to enable the LAN to automatically download the shells to each workstation. The following two key criteria must be met:

- The name(s) of the shell files cannot have changed between versions
- The old shell files must still allow users to log in to the new operating system

For example, assume NetWare version 2.11 is being upgraded to version 2.15. If a homogeneous network is in place, i.e., a network in which all workstations share the same type of network card and all have version 3.x of DOS, the shell files needed are NET3.COM and IPX.COM. Figure 11-22 lists a sample batch file that would automatically update both floppy and hard disk-based workstations.

Some notes of interest about this batch file include:

1. The file is divided into seven components. Any one of the component routines can be enhanced to include more sophisticated logic or messages. These components are:

    - An initial decision point that determines the remaining flow of the procedure
    - A routine for hard disk-based workstations
    - A routine for floppy disk-based workstations
    - A routine for workstations already containing the updated shell
    - A closing routine
    - An error message routine
    - An end statement

2. The file MARKER.215 is a "dummy" file used to indicate the version of shell files installed on that boot disk. Therefore, it does not need to contain any data, although you might want to put a line of text that describes its purpose.
3. This procedure assumes that the shell files for the workstation are in the root directory, but they don't have to be.

This technique is not foolproof, but it will take care of at least 75 percent of the workstations on most LANs. Any problems can be handled as they arise.

```
@echo off
if exist c:\NET3.COM goto hard
if exist a:\NET3.COM goto floppy
goto errmsg

:hard
if exist c:\MARKER.215 goto ok
copy f:\login\NET3.COM c:\
copy f:\login\IPX.COM c:\
del c:\MARKER.*
copy f:\login\MARKER.215 c:\
goto done

:floppy
if exist a:\MARKER.215 goto ok
echo Please remove diskette from
echo drive a: and make sure the
echo write protect notch is NOT
echo covered with a write protect
echo tab.
pause
copy f:\login\NET3.COM a:\
copy f:\login\IPX.COM a:\
del a:\MARKER.*
copy f:\login\MARKER.215 a:\
goto done

:ok
rem marker file found. No update
rem necessary.
goto end

:done
echo Your boot disk has been updated
echo with new network files. If you
echo experience any problems, please
echo call Lanny Ministrator at x555
pause
goto end

:errmsg
echo A problem has been detected
echo with your boot disk. Please
echo call Lanny Ministrator at x555.
pause
:end
```

Figure 11-22. NEWSHELL.BAT sample code listing

Monitoring File Server Performance

File server performance provides a good indication of a network's overall state of well-being. NetWare version 2.0x provides very little in the way of tools to monitor this performance. Advanced NetWare users can keep an eye on the CPU percentage displayed on the console's MONITOR display. SFT users have the additional option of using the console's DISK command.

Console DISK command

The DISK command has three different types of parameters. The first is DISK *. This command displays a screen similar to Figure 11-23.

```
:DISK * <enter>    ...screen clears
 FILE SERVER VOLUMES
 Volume Name    Phy Drv Mir Drv          Volume Name Phy Drv    Mir Drv
 SYS      00
```

Figure 11-23. DISK * Parameter

This screen provides a listing of up to 32 volumes. These are the names of the volumes on this particular file server. Once the volume name is known, more information is available via the DISK <volume name> command, as illustrated in Figure 11-24.

```
:DISK SYS <enter>  ...screen clears

Information For Volume SYS

Physical drive number          :  00
Physical drive type            :  IBM AT Hard Disk "C"  type 045
I/O errors on this drive       :      0
Redirection blocks available   :   473
Redirection blocks used        :    70

Mirror physical drive number   :  no mirror drive

Other volumes sharing these physical drive(s):
none

:
```

Figure 11-24. DISK <volume name> command

The "I/O errors on this drive" error indicates how many I/O errors have occurred on the drive since the server was last rebooted. Each I/O error translates directly into a redirection block created by HOTFIX. If the DISK display indicates five I/O errors, then five HOTFIX redirection blocks are used. If the drive has a mirror, this fact is indicated. If the drive is divided into more than one volume, the other volume names will be indicated.

The third use of DISK does not utilize any parameters. The command DISK provides an overview of disk status on the file server. Figure 11-25 shows the DISK output for an SFT 2.0x NetWare system. For version 2.1x NetWare, refer to the Console Reference manual.

```
:DISK <enter>    ...screen clears

                    PHYSICAL DISKS STATUS AND STATISTICS
   cha con  drv  stat IO  Err Free  Used cha  con  drv  stat IO Err Free Used
 00  0  0  0  OK    0     473 70

  0   0   0   0   0   0   0   0   0   0   0   0   0
  0   0   0   0   0   0   0   0   0   0   0   0   0
  0   0   0   0   0   0   0   0   0   0   0   0   0
  0   0   0   0   0   0   0   0   0   0   0   0   0
  0   0   0   0   0   0   0   0   0   0   0   0   0
```

Figure 11-25. DISK command

The 00 displayed indicates the drive number. This is the number displayed when there is a disk error. The next 0 is the disk drive channel. The 0 that appears under "con" is the controller number on that channel. The column marked "drv" gives the physical drive number of the controller on that disk channel. Beneath "stat" is the current drive status.

The values for stat include:

- OK, which indicates the drive is available and HOTFIX is on.
- NO HOT, which indicates that the drive is operating without HOTFIX being on.
- OFF, which indicates the drive is unavailable; probably turned off.

I/O Err indicates the number of HOTFIX blocks used on that drive since the file server was last rebooted. The "Free" and "Used" columns indicate how many more blocks HOTFIX can redirect and how many have already been used on this drive.

The FCONSOLE utility offers a tremendous amount of information with NetWare 2.1x that you can use to assist you in your network's installation. In this section exploring FCONSOLE, we take a close look at the cache and disk statistics that are reported by the utility. Understanding what these statistics actually mean can assist you greatly in fine-tuning your NetWare installation.

Before going too far, however, note an important tip that will help you learn how to use each FCONSOLE screen. By pressing the F2 key, you will put any screen that displays constantly updated information on hold. When you put these screens on hold, a message indicating "Update Paused" appears in the upper right corner of the FCONSOLE header. By pressing F2 a second time, screens will return to continuous update.

But, first, before starting, note that the following are maximum values for each field: Cache Read Requests, Cache Write Requests, Cache Hits, Cache Misses, Physical Read Requests, Physical Write Requests, Cache Get Requests, Full Write Requests, Partial Write Requests, Background Dirty Writes, Background Aged Writes, Total Cache Writes, and Cache Allocations all have a maximum value of 4,294,967,295; all other fields are 65,535.

Cache Statistics

When data is read from or written to a disk in the file server, it passes through a section of file server RAM set aside as the disk cache. Cache memory is perhaps best described as a high-speed buffer that resides between the CPU and the disk subsystem. Read access is improved because the cache may still contain the requested information left there by a previous Read or Write request. Also, a workstation performing a Write operation benefits from disk caching because it does not have to wait for the physical Write to occur before continuing its own processing.

With NetWare 2.1x, you can actually see how many cache buffers exist by using FCONSOLE. Upon selecting Cache Statistics from the Statistics sub-menu, you are presented with a screen full of information, including the number of cache buffers, the cache buffer size, the numbers of dirty cache buffers, cache Read and Write Requests, cache hits and misses, and other measurements. The meaning behind each of these statistics is explained below, along with hints for using them in the installation process.

Number of Cache Buffers. This number indicates how many file cache buffers exist. (There are also directory cache buffers, discussed later.) This number depends on a couple of factors, the first being the cache buffer size, which is shown on the same screen. With NetWare 2.1x/2.2x, the cache buffer size is typically 4,096 bytes. This figure directly correlates with the sector size used in NetWare 2.1x/2.2x to store information on physical disk drives. Conveniently, this means that for every Read or Write NetWare does to a physical disk, the information is transferred in chunks that fit evenly into one cache block.

The number of cache buffers also depends on the amount of file server RAM. As NetWare is loaded, it first initializes all of its parameters and loads the required operating system programs into memory. Once this operation is complete, any remaining memory is assigned to cache buffers. Note that there must be enough memory for at least a few cache blocks to exist; if not, NetWare will not run.

When there is a shortage of RAM, NetWare may indicate during booting that there is "not enough memory to cache volume xx." However, this message has nothing to do with the file cache buffers we have been discussing so far. Instead, it refers to the directory cache buffers, used for caching directory entries. NetWare does not distinguish between drives when setting up file cache buffers. Instead, it makes this distinction when setting up directory cache buffers, which are set up for each disk volume.

The number of cache buffers designated by the FCONSOLE Cache Statistics screen can greatly affect system performance. Too few and your system becomes bottlenecked by the speed of your physical disk drive(s). Too many and your system, during Read Requests, can spend too much time searching RAM for a cache entry that is not there before retrieving the information from disk. As stated by NetWare engineers, an optimal number of cache buffers for NetWare 2.1x/2.2x is between 800 and 900. You can change the number of cache buffers by adjusting the amount of RAM in your file server.

Cache Buffer Size. With a new NetWare 2.1x/2.2x installation, you cannot choose the cache buffer size—it is always 4,096 bytes. This size provides optimal speed because it matches the unit of transfer NetWare uses for physical disks. However, this size may not reflect an optimal use of file server memory.

For instance, if your network experiences heavy database traffic with records that do not exceed 512 bytes, then a smaller cache buffer size would give you a more optimal use of cache memory. Unfortunately, while NetWare 2.0x offered the option of reducing the cache buffer size, NetWare 2.1x/2.2x does not. With NetWare 2.0x, cache buffers could be 512, 1024, 2048, or 4096 bytes although all cache buffers defined had to be of the same size—there could be no mixture of different size buffers.

Dirty Cache Buffers. Unlike either of the two statistics described so far, the Dirty Cache Buffers statistic represents real-time data. That is, the number reflects how many dirty buffers there are at any one moment—the number is not cumulative. Besides being displayed on the Cache Statistics screen of FCONSOLE, the number of dirty cache buffers is also indicated by the Disk I/O Pending field on the file server's MONITOR screen.

The Dirty Cache Buffers number indicates how many cache buffers are ready to be written to disk. These dirty buffers hold information that is new or that updates data already on the disk drive. Note that the workstation that submits the data to be written has already received an acknowledgment from the file server that its data has been written to disk. Actually, the data has not been written to disk at that moment, but it is queued to be written to disk within three seconds, or when the cache buffer is filled with new information.

The advantage of pre-acknowledging the workstation is mainly for optimizing speed. As long as the file server has the data to be written, it is immediately available for incoming Read Requests, whether or not that data has yet been written to disk. The disadvantage, of course, is if the file server goes down before cleaning up all its dirty cache buffers, those updates are lost. This point alone is a very good reason to incorporate an uninterruptible power supply (UPS) into your LAN.

Cache Read and Write Requests. These two statistics indicate how many Read and Write Requests have been issued. Additionally, the Cache Write Requests field is the sum total of the Full Write Requests and the Partial Write Requests fields, both of which are described in more detail later.

There is, however, an anomaly that occurs in the accumulation of the Cache Read Requests number, owing to the requirement that a Read must be performed before a Partial Write Request. Because Partial Write Requests require a Read of a sector, that Read Request may be satisfied from a cache block in memory. If it can be satisfied from the file cache, that Read Request is not recorded for the number of Cache Read Requests. Instead, it is tallied in the Cache Hits field, discussed next. While this operation seems odd, after personally spending many, many hours figuring out what produces the Cache Hits number, it does seem to be the case. Further proof is offered in the following equation, which should theoretically hold true, but rarely ever does:

```
(Cache Read Requests + Cache Write Requests) = (Cache Hits - Cache
  Misses)
```

Novell is presently unable to confirm this finding, although they agree that it is possible.

Cache Hits. This number indicates the sum of Cache Read Requests, Cache Write Requests, and the "magical" Cache Reads just discussed, less the number of Cache Misses.

Cache Misses. This number is the sum total of the Cache Allocations and LRU Block Was Dirty statistics, both of which are coming up later. In short, these are the requests that could not be serviced directly from an existing cache block.

Physical Read and Write Requests. These numbers are self-de-scribing. However, note that the number of Write Requests is the sum of the Total Cache Writes and Fragmented Writes.

Cache Get Requests. This statistic is the sum total of Cache Read Requests and Partial Write Requests. It indicates how many times a cache block was requested from disk, no matter whether it existed in cache RAM already or not. The only Read Request not counted in this case is the Read Request performed for a Partial Write Request that was satisfied from cache RAM without requiring an actual disk

Read. (This possibility was discussed earlier in the Cache Read and Write Requests section).

Full Write Requests. This number indicates how many times disk sectors were updated without having to pre-read the sector. Because there was no pre-read, the entire sector was overwritten, hence the name Full Write Request.

Partial Write Requests. This field indicates how many times a disk sector was pre-read before it was rewritten. The sector was pre-read before the Write because the sector only partially changed. Had the entire sector changed, the Write Request would have been counted under the Full Write Requests.

Background Dirty Writes. This number is an accumulation of the data reported by the constantly updated Dirty Cache Buffers statistic. The only time a Write Request is counted for this statistic is when it is not immediately processed. Also note that only full cache buffers are counted here.

Background Aged Writes. This is the number of partially-filled dirty cache buffers that were written to disk, after they remained unwritten to disk for more than three seconds.

Total Cache Writes. This is the total number of Write Requests processed that filled one or more than one contiguous 4,096 byte disk units, or clusters (contrast this to the Fragmented Writes field, described below). This number, plus the Fragmented Writes number, produces the Physical Write Requests total.

Cache Allocations. This is the number of cache blocks allocated from a pool of free (i.e., not dirty, where dirty means that the block had data to be written to disk before it could be reallocated) cache blocks.

Thrashing Count. This is the number of times a cache block was needed but no cache block was available for use. This situation requires the file server to issue a standby message to workstations submitting requests that require cache blocks, resulting in an overall slowdown in network performance. Generally, adding RAM to the file server (within the confines described previously in the Number of Cache Buffers section) will help to alleviate this problem.

LRU Block Was Dirty. This is the number of cache blocks that were allocated from a pool of dirty cache blocks. Note that LRU stands for Least Recently Used, which is the principal of the algorithm that NetWare uses to determine which cache block to allocate.

Read Beyond Write. This is the number of times that data was retrievable (for a Read Request) from the cache RAM but the entire Read Request was not retrievable. For instance, the first x bytes were available in the cache RAM, but the next y bytes were read from disk.

Fragmented Writes. This is the number of times a series of noncontiguous 4,096 byte disk units (clusters) was written (as opposed to Total Cache Writes, which records only contiguous Writes). In other words, a number of Physical Disk Writes were necessary because the data was not contiguously formed on the disk.

Hit On Unavailable Block. This is the number of times a requested cache block was in memory but was not available because, at that moment, the cache block was either being read in from the disk or being written to the disk. Because the request was for a cache block "in action," the requesting process has to wait until the disk activity is completed.

Cache Blocks Scrapped. This number provides a definite "for trivia" statistic. Indicated here is the number of times a process was put on hold because the cache block it was trying to allocate for a Read Request was dirty. When the process was put back in action, another process had already read in the data the first process was going to retrieve. Thus, the first process no longer needed the cache block allocated to it, so the cache block was returned to the free pool of cache blocks.

Disk Statistics

When selecting the Disk Statistics option, you will be prompted to choose a physical disk drive. Note that the drives are not identified by their volume names, even if the disk has only one volume, but by their physical disk number. Once you have chosen a drive, you will see a full screen of information regarding that drive. Most of these fields are self-explanatory. However, a few fields that do require a bit more explanation are described in the following sections.

I/O Error Count. This statistic indicates how many I/O (Input/Output, i.e., Read/Write) errors have occurred on the selected disk since the last time the file server was initialized (or, if you prefer, booted). It is not cumulative between file server up periods. That is, every time a file server is downed, this field is set to 0. If you see a count greater than 0, your physical disk may be having trouble either at the disk itself, at the disk's controller, or possibly in the file server RAM.

HOTFIX Enabled. This number indicates the current status of HOTFIX on the selected disk. (See the cover story of the July 1989 issue of the *NetWare Advisor* for more detailed information on what HOTFIX is and how it operates.) One of three different conditions will be displayed in this field—HOTFIX is either Enabled, Disabled, or Not Available.

If Enabled, HOTFIX will be working as it normally does. If Disabled, HOTFIX has had multiple failures (I/O Errors) on the selected disk and has turned itself off for that drive. If this condition occurs, you should down the server as soon as possible (unless use of the drive is not critical to you and your data) and run VREPAIR in an attempt to correct the drive problems. Be sure, as always, to have a good and current backup (preferably two) of your file server's data, just in the off chance that VREPAIR does more harm than good.

Finally, the HOTFIX Not Available message indicates that the selected file server (with this disk drive) does not support HOTFIX. This condition is extremely unlikely, as FCONSOLE will not even run on a file server running a version of NetWare below 2.1. And, starting with NetWare 2.1, every version of NetWare (including ELS) supports HOTFIX.

HOTFIX Table Size. This field indicates the total number of disk blocks that have been allocated for HOTFIX, but does not indicate the number of disk blocks in use. You can increase the HOTFIX Table Size with NETGEN for NetWare 286 or with PREPARE for NetWare 2.0x.

To find out the size of the table with a NetWare 2.0x server, type DISK <disk volume name> at the server's colon prompt. For example, type DISK SYS <enter> and note the field labeled Redirection Blocks Available. The Table Size plus the Table Start field (from FCONSOLE) will indicate the approximate size of your disk drive in blocks. Note that your Table Size should be at least 2 percent of this total size.

HOTFIX Remaining. This is the number of free blocks that are available for HOTFIX to use. The next time there is a disk I/O Error that HOTFIX can remedy, it will use one of these blocks. If your disk should run out of disk blocks, you could expand the HOTFIX table on your disk, or you might consider four other options.

First, perform a new low-level format of the disk. Begin by backing it up first. Then, when running COMPSURF, answer "No" to the "Format disk?" prompt, unless your disk is connected to a DCB (Disk Coprocessor Board). The reasoning here is that your drive may have had a low-level format that was not good, especially if COMPSURF's Format option was used and the drive was not connected to a DCB. (See the July 1989 issue of the NetWare Advisor for more concerning difficulties with COMPSURF).

Second, you could expand your HOTFIX table and note if the table fills up again. Be sure to backup the disk in question when expanding this table.

Third, you could try replacing the drive.

Or fourth, when all else fails, you might widen your search for the culprit and suspect your disk controller or your file server's RAM. You might try testing your file server's RAM and potentially replacing chips that show up as questionable or bad.

LAN I/O Statistics

Upon entering the LAN I/O screen, a large amount of information is displayed. Some of this data is self explanatory, but most of it is not casually understood. Therefore the following explanations are offered. Before starting, note that the following maximum values apply to each field: Total Packets Received, Packets Routed, File Service Packets and NetBIOS Broadcasts have a maximum value of 4,294,967,295; all other fields are 65,535. See the "What is a Packet?" section later in this chapter for more information on packets.

Packets Routed. Found here is the number of IPX packets the file server has received and then forwarded to another network. The recipient on the other network might be a file server, or it might be another workstation. The packets were received by this file server (the one whose FCONSOLE data is being reported) because it found itself between the originating workstation and the destination network. In other words, this file server acted as a router for these packets.

File Service Packets. Indicated here is the number of packets received that turned out to be requests for some file server service. The service might be some actual file activity, but it might also be a request for something else. The service might have been a bindery request, it might have been a login request. Point is, a "file service" is not strictly limited to activity against files, it can be any file server offered service.

NetBIOS Broadcasts. New to NetWare 2.1x was the ability to make NetBIOS operate across an internetwork. By design, NetBIOS did not understand internetworks and as such did not naturally work with them. However, through some modifications at the file server, NetWare allows NetBIOS to operate on an internetwork, specifically a NetWare Internetwork. When NetBIOS initializes it broadcasts out its "name" in search of it. If it finds its name already "out there" it will not complete its initialization.

When this name is broadcast it is sent out to all listening nodes. To make sure all possible listening nodes hear the broadcast, NetWare file servers intercept the broadcast of the local NetBIOS requester. Then the NetBIOS broadcast is issued to all other servers and networks for rebroadcast throughout the internetwork. The number of times a file server does this is the number indicated by this field. Note that because NetBIOS is timing sensitive, you might find it necessary to increase the NetBIOS time-out (using SHELL.CFG at each workstation) to its maximum to ensure NetBIOS does not time-out before all possible answers to its broadcast are received.

Packets With Invalid Slots. When file servers receive requests from workstations, a connection number (slot) is included. If this number is 0 or is greater than the maximum number of connections supported by the file server, then that request is counted here. Normally this does not occur. If it does, it could be a bad packet. And, bad packets can be caused by bad network cards, bad cabling, electrical interference, etc. If it is continuously updated (increasing) then it could likely be a bad network card. It could also be cause by someone goofing around and playing with packets as they go out on the network.

Invalid Connections. This number indicates the number of packets received with valid slot (connection) numbers but the workstation address does not match that of the connection's "owning" workstation. That owning workstation may be none, that is, no workstation logged in on that connection. This counter can be increased for the same reasons as Packets With Invalid Slots. It can also be caused by a workstation trying to communicate with a file server that has gone down and back up since the last time the workstation attempted communications with that file server. This indicates that a workstation that once had a valid connection has lost it (because the file server went down) and it has become invalid when the file server came back up.

Invalid Sequence Numbers. When workstations communicate with the file server the dialogue is ordered by sequence numbers. Each new communication from a workstation needs to have a sequence number one higher than its previous communication. If not, it is counted here. Normally this does not occur, but could be caused by a workstation's communication being lost and the workstation finished retrying the operation and proceeded with a new one. However, this is unlikely, it could also be caused by the same conditions outlined under Packets With Invalid Slots.

Invalid Request Types. If the file server receives a request it does not understand, it will count it here. This situation could be caused by a workstation using a utility that is either very old or very new. In either case, the file server operating system is not old enough (compatible enough) or new enough to know the request and how to respond to it.

Detach With Invalid Slot. This indicates the number of times a detach (logout) command was issued from a workstation with an illegal connection number. This usually does not occur, and conditions under Packets With Invalid Slots might be occurring.

Forged Detach Requests. If this counter increases, it would indicate that a detach (logout) request came from a workstation and the connection number indicated is incorrect. This is quite unlikely to occur, but it could be due to conditions outlined under Packets With Invalid Slots.

New Request During Processing. This is usually only incremented during the following sequence: Workstation sends request to file server; file server processes request; workstation times out while awaiting a reply so it reissues the request; file server finishes request just as workstation reissues the request; workstation receives reply immediately after reissuing request; file server receives re-request just after sending original reply and begins to reprocess the request; workstation, upon receiving reply, issues a new request; file server, who is still working on reissued previous request, receives new request. If this scenario occurs, it is indicated here by an increment of this field. An incrementation here might indicate that the file server is heavily loaded, it might also mean the communications channel between the file server and workstation is very slow.

New Attach During Processing. The same scenario under New Request During Processing applies here. The only difference being that the new request (after the reissued request) from the workstation is one to attach to the file server. This would only occur if the workstation reloaded the network shell (after a possible reboot) before issuing the attach command. This condition is unlikely to actually occur.

Ignored Duplicate Attach. If a file server receives an attach command from a workstation that is already attached, it is counted here. This is unlikely to occur, but if it does, it probably indicates some software package operating without proper regard for a workstation's connection status.

Reply Cancelled By New Attach. If a New Attach During Processing occurred, it is likely that this field will also be incremented. If the file server is processing a file service request when a new attach is issued by a workstation, then the response to that file service request will be cancelled and this counter incremented. This is unlikely to occur.

Detach During Processing Ignored. If a file server receives a detach request from a workstation while the file server is processing a request for that workstation, it will ignore the detach request. This condition is unlikely to occur.

Reexecuted Requests. This counter will be incremented whenever a file server re-executes the same request from a workstation (as indicated by the packet sequence number). This would occur if the workstation timed out while waiting for a file server reply and reissued its request just as the file server issued its reply to the original request.

Duplicate Replies Sent. This counter is incremented to indicate the number of times a file server could send a reply to a reexecuted request directly from its memory. The server could send the result from its memory because it stores the last reply in memory. This would need to occur for some types of requests where a full re-execution would result in a different reply than the original request. However, there are some requests that would require a new execution to get a proper response.

Positive Acknowledgments Sent. This counter indicates the number of times a file server received a duplicate request from a workstation. But unlike the condition under Reexecuted Requests, the file server has not yet finished its processing. In this case, the file server will proceed to send an "I'm busy" reply to the workstation who will wait for another time-out before reissuing the request.

File Service Used Route. This counter indicates the number of times the server was unable to immediately act on a request. That is, no file service process (FSP) was available. Consequently the request was queued into a routing buffer. And as soon as a FSP becomes available the request will be processed.

Packets Discarded Because They Crossed More Than 16 Bridges. In a Novell network it is presumed that a packet that crosses more than 16 internetworks is either lost or travelling in circles and is discarded. The number of such packets discarded is tallied here. This condition is unlikely to occur except in large internetworks.

Packets Discarded Because Destination Network Is Unknown. When a file server receives a packet to be routed, the file server examines the destination network (not node) to find an available route. If one cannot be found, the packet is discarded because the file server is unable to route the packet. Usually this would occur if a file server went down and a workstation issued a request before the workstation found out that the file server went down.

Incoming Packets Lost Because Of No Available Buffers. Indicated here is the number of times a packet was received and no buffer was available to hold its contents. This can occur if insufficient routing buffers exist.

Outgoing Packets Lost Because of No Available Buffers. Indicated here is the number of times a packet could not be sent to its destination due to a lack of buffer space to hold the contents before they are sent. This can occur if there are insufficient routing buffers available.

The most often referred to screen in FCONSOLE is the Summary screen. Here you will find most of the more useful information offered by FCONSOLE on one screen. Some of the information presented here is obvious. However, some are worth a mention, therefore the following explanations are offered. But first, note the following maximum values for each field: Number Of File Service Processes, Current server Utilization and Disk Requests Serviced From Cache have a maximum value of 255; Packets Routed, Total Packets Received, File Service Packets, Total server Memory, Unused server Memory and all the Dynamic Memory fields have a maximum value of 4,294,967,295; all other fields are 65,535.

FCONSOLE Highlights

NetWare version 2.1x includes the FCONSOLE utility, which allows a workstation user to view most of the file server performance data. FCONSOLE does not simultaneously display information pertaining to all file server drives, as does the DISK command at the file server.

Many aspects of file server performance can be monitored by FCONSOLE, which facilitates a quick diagnosis of the file server's condition. In addition, the context-sensitive help screens contain descriptions of the figures displayed. Some of the more important file server and network statistics accessed via FCONSOLE include:

Number of File Service Processes (FSPs). This is the FSP count noted in Chapter 3.

Current Server Utilization. This indicates the current level of CPU use at the file server. If this figure is routinely above 80%, it is likely that your file server is being overtaxed. Sometimes, however, the Current Server Utilization statistic can be inaccurate.

As noted in Chapter 3, when running NetWare/286 on an 80386 33MHz CPU, you may notice that the Current Server Utilization figure is greater than 100%. Due to an unforeseen timing loop problem, versions of NetWare through 2.15c running on an 80386 33MHz CPU cannot properly register the Current Server Utilization. (NetWare/386 does not suffer from this problem).

Also, when using NetWare/386 and NetWare Loadable Modules (NLMs), you may observe Current Server Utilization figures that are less than the actual figure. This inaccuracy is due to the fact that the routine which calculates Current Server Utilization does not count all CPU-consuming processes. For instance, if an NLM performs extensive work in loops that take a long time to execute, the file server CPU Utilization figure is not adjusted to reflect this consumption. For instance, when I executed an NLM specially designed to run lengthy loops, the Current Server Utilization statistic read 5 to 10%, but performance from the file server was off 100%, that is, it was twice as slow. This problem may not be limited to NLMs, but they were the only component that could easily be isolated to test for this anomaly.

An additional point regarding Current Server Utilization concerns file servers operating in nondedicated mode. When in "DOS" mode, idle nondedicated file servers should have Current Server Utilization figures under 60%, and when in "CONSOLE" mode, the figure should be less than 10%. If not, the machine you have chosen as your file server may not be totally appropriate for use with nondedicated NetWare. Be certain the file server you choose has been approved by Novell specifically for use as a nondedicated file server. Note that placing a nondedicated file server into CONSOLE mode substantially decreases CPU usage and results in a corresponding increase in overall performance.

Disk Requests Serviced from Cache. This is also called the disk cache hit ratio or the cache hit percentage. If this figure falls below 96 percent, chances are the file server would perform better with more RAM available for disk caching. The closer the cache hit percentage is to 100 percent, the better the file server's performance will be. While it is not realistic to ever achieve 100 percent, a range of 96-98 percent is a reasonable expectation.

Total Number of Cache Buffers. This indicates the number of cache buffers that the system has allocated after all other file server options have been loaded. This can be used to gauge how much RAM is used by a new option, such as a VAP. The cache block size is 4K. To verify the cache block size, view the Cache Statistics screen available under the Statistics main menu option of FCONSOLE. A cache block size of 4K is optimal for disk activity, as it is equal to the block size used by NetWare (2.x). If the number of cache buffers on your NetWare/286 file server exceeds 1000 (NetWare/386 has no such limitation), reducing RAM so that there are fewer cache buffers will most likely improve your system's performance. (Note that 1MB equals 256 cache buffers.) Having too many cache buffers means that NetWare may spend excessive time searching the cache RAM before accessing the disk channel to fulfill a data request.

A good rule of thumb is to have from 800 to 1000 cache buffers (i.e., 3 to 4MB of cache buffers) available. One situation where less than 800 cache buffers might be acceptable is when you use a disk controller that has its own caching. Note, however, that most disk controllers cache only read operations; all write operations must still be handled by NetWare's cache RAM. NetWare handles write requests by holding them in cache RAM until the operating system gets a chance to perform the writes in the background. If there is no cache buffer available to receive a write, that write must be performed immediately, in the foreground of processing, thereby slowing the overall performance of the file server. So, if you are operating in a write-intensive system, you must be certain that there are sufficient NetWare cache RAM buffers available to handle these write requests. A read-only caching disk controller will help relieve NetWare of some of its read-caching duties, but not of its write-caching duties.

NetWare 386, however, has no real file server RAM cache limitations. In both NetWare 286 and NetWare 386, hash tables are used to locate items in the cache. NetWare 386's hash table, however, is much larger than NetWare 286's, which allows for faster cache access times regardless of the amount of cache RAM in use.

Total Server Memory. As the name indicates, this is the total amount of available RAM that NetWare detects in the server. If you are using nondedicated NetWare, expect the RAM available for NetWare to equal the total RAM less the amount used for DOS, which is usually just over 1MB. (If you are using a Compaq, it is usually just over 1.3MB.) Therefore, if your server/workstation has 3MB of RAM, only 2MB is available for NetWare. (On a Compaq, just under 1.7MB is available.)

Unused Server Memory. This indicates how much memory cannot be allocated. It usually represents fragments of memory that are left over from memory initialization at server boot time. There appears to be a bug in TTS of NetWare 2.1x that disrupts memory allocation for cache blocks which can leave several megabytes of memory unused. This bug has been observed, but it has not been verified.

Routing Buffers. The size of these buffers depends on the LAN drivers installed in the file server. The largest maximum packet size required by the selected LAN drivers determines the routing buffer size. These buffers hold incoming requests until they can be processed. As these buffers are shared by all of the LAN drivers, they all need to be sized according to the largest packet that could be received. One effect to consider is that adding a new LAN driver to an existing file server can result in fewer cache buffers. This happens only if the new driver has a larger maximum packet size than any of the previously installed drivers. (Remember, cache buffers are allocated after everything else has been allocated.)

Dynamic Memory. This is described in Chapter 3.

It is possible to monitor the number of HotFix blocks used on the Disk Statistics screen and at the file server console. It is important to keep track of this information because every time this number increases, it means that NetWare has found a new bad block on the disk. If bad blocks continue to appear, the disk could be failing. It could also mean that the drive was not low-level formatted properly, or that a hardware failure exists elsewhere in the system. For instance, if the disk controller operates inconsistently, HotFix blocks might also be used. So there may not be anything wrong with the disk, but rather with the controller. This particular problem can be difficult to track down.

Optimizing File Server Disk Subsystem Performance

To get the best performance from your file server, you must optimize the performance of your file server's disk subsystem, which is responsible for storing and retrieving files from the file server. A file server with a painfully slow disk subsystem is not much of a file server at all.

This section focuses on several aspects of disk subsystem performance, including external NetWare bridges, disk duplexing, multiple volumes on a single drive, caching controllers, and the amount of NetWare file cache RAM.

Limit External NetWare Bridges. The performance that you realize from your disk subsystem is greatly dependent on the speed of the file server-to-workstation connection. One of the most influential determinants of file server-to-workstation connection speed is the use of external NetWare bridges. Note that the "internal" bridge within a single file server that services the workstations, i.e. the network adapter, is not the type of bridge referred to here. An external NetWare bridge between a file server and a workstation will, however, significantly reduce the speed of the file server-to-workstation connection, thereby reducing the performance potential of your file server's disk subsystem. Third-party bridges and routers do not usually impact performance as severely as NetWare bridges. However, you should work closely with your third-party vendor to determine any potential performance impacts.

Inserting a NetWare bridge between a file server and a workstation degrades performance because NetWare bridges (in their current incarnation) can only pass data in 512-byte packets. This limitation is particularly significant if you are using packet drivers that can pass packets larger than 512-bytes.

For example, a Thomas-Conrad 4KB ARCNET packet driver transfers data between workstations and file servers that are directly connected (i.e., with no intervening external bridge) in 4KB packets. However, passing these packets through a NetWare bridge cuts the packet size to 512-bytes. This reduction results in a packet one-eighth of its potential size, and is accompanied by a similar drop in performance.

Keep in mind that a 4KB packet driver receives 4KB packets from IPX, but then breaks them down so that they may pass through the physical layer, i.e., the media.

For maximum performance, you should limit the number of external NetWare bridges that you use by directly connecting as many workstations as possible to the appropriate file server. Inserting a NetWare bridge may nullify any disk subsystem performance tuning that you may have implemented previously.

Several other factors also affect the speed of file server-to-workstation con-nections. These factors include file server and workstation CPU speed, media throughput, number of users requesting services from the file server, and soundness of the cable plant (i.e., proper cable types, impedances, termination, etc.). The specific recommendations regarding these factors depend greatly on your particular implementation, but in general, you should use the fastest machines you can afford, running on a sound media implementation and cabling plant.

Performance Impacts of Disk Duplexing. Disk duplexing, a System Fault Tolerance (SFT) feature, refers to the mirroring of two disks which are controlled by different disk controllers, such as Novell's Disk Coprocessor Boards (DCBs). Disk duplexing can enhance disk subsystem performance by enabling split seeks. Split seeks are a type of "load balancing" of READ requests between the drives. That is, READ requests are split between the two disks' channels. As a result, disk duplexing increases the throughput of the disk drive system. And since the majority of disk accesses are READ requests, overall file server performance is also improved.

However, there is little that can be done to improve the efficiency of file server WRITE operations. NetWare caches WRITE requests immediately and returns an "OK" to the workstation, even though the WRITE request has not actually been performed yet. NetWare will perform the WRITE request in the background when it has the opportunity. Because of this "lying WRITE," there is little more that you can do to improve WRITE throughput other than ensuring that there is sufficient cache RAM available. If there is insufficient cache RAM available, the file server must perform the WRITE before it returns an "OK" to the workstation.

Defining Multiple Volumes on a Single Drive. A guideline when you have multiple volumes on the same drive is to carefully plan where you place data that is accessed often for READ operations. By evenly spreading the data across the volumes, you can balance how the volumes are accessed. For example, consider three volumes—VOLA, VOLB, and VOLC—on a single drive. If you place the most frequently accessed data on VOLA and VOLC, the disk drive's heads will constantly be jumping back and forth across the drive, skipping VOLB's data area because it is infrequently accessed. To achieve the best performance from NetWare 286 drives with multiple volumes, therefore, you should place the most frequently accessed data on contiguous volumes.

Since NetWare/386 does not impose a maximum volume size limitation, you do not need to split a drive into multiple volumes. Rather, you should create one volume per drive and let NetWare arrange the files on the drive as it sees fit. With NetWare 386, you can define a single volume that spans across many physical disk drives. This capability is referred to as drive spanning. Drive spanning allows quicker access to data because data from one file may be scattered across multiple drives. When a request comes in to READ that file, multiple drives can then service that request.

Drive spanning is particularly beneficial when used in combination with SCSI disk controllers that employ the SCSI disconnect feature. This feature enables the controller to request data from a drive, and then to "disconnect" from it and request data from another drive—the controller does not have to wait for the drive to retrieve the information. The SCSI disconnect feature allows up to eight SCSI disk drives off a single host controller (such as a DCB) to simultaneously service disk requests.

Caching Controllers. Some disk controllers include a built-in caching function, making them caching controllers. These controllers can often increase NetWare's performance, although there are some instances in which they do not. For example, caching controllers that cache WRITE operations are of little benefit to NetWare, since NetWare itself caches all WRITE operations, as previously discussed. However,WRITE-caching controllers can be of some benefit if there is insufficient cache RAM available for the file server to cache its own WRITE requests.

Caching controllers that cache READ requests, on the other hand, can more often improve file server performance. Note, however, that a caching controller that uses a Least Recently Used (LRU) algorithm to flush old data out of cache may only duplicate NetWare's caching efforts. The LRU algorithm is the same algorithm that NetWare uses to cache file server operations. Therefore, unless the LRU caching controller has more cache RAM than the file server, you will realize an only marginal performance increase. The degree of enhanced performance (if any) that will result from using caching controllers on your system is not easily predictable. You will simply need to try out the various options to determine what works best.

File Cache RAM. NetWare/286's internal file caching mechanism has a definite point of diminishing returns in regards to cache size. That point of diminishing returns is somewhere between 800 and 1400 cache buffers. With more than this amount of cache buffers, it becomes just as fast or faster to access the disk directly than to search through such a large cache for the requested data. Unlike NetWare/286, NetWare/386 and later versions have no point at which there can be "too much file cache RAM." In fact, when in doubt, add memory to a NetWare/386 server. See Chapter 3 for more information about cache buffers.

What is a Packet?

When data travels between network nodes, it does so in the form of packets. A packet is the unit of data exchange between, for instance, workstations and file servers. A packet's size is variable and hardware dependent.

With NetWare 2.1x you can monitor the number of packets each file server senses. The "Total Packets Received" field found on the Statistics/Summary and Statistics/LAN I/O Statistics screens indicate how many packets that file server has received.

The packets counted include file server requests, packets routed to other networks and packets received for non-file server request, such as those to VAPs.

However, this number may not reflect a number anywhere near actual totals. When NetWare counts packets received it is counting how many packets have been handed off by the NIC driver. Packets that are actually "on the network cable" may not be the same number reflected by the screens of FCONSOLE. This is because some NIC driver's ship packets in a virtual manner. Because some packets are shipped in a virtual format, there may be 8 or more physical packets received for each packet counted by the FCONSOLE statistics.

For instance, on an ARCnet LAN, at the hardware or physical level, ARCNET sends a maximum of 504 bytes per packet. However, with NetWare, all NIC drivers must be able to send and receive at least 576 bytes. This is the size Novell uses when routing packets across internetworks. This size was chosen because it matches Xerox's Network Standard (XNS), which was the model used when Novell's Internetwork Packet eXchange (IPX) protocol was created. The Internetwork Datagram Protocol (IDP) of XNS expects a maximum packet length of 576 bytes, unlike NetWare, which allows negotiation on maximum packet size.

Packet Negotiations

When, a workstation node and file server node exist on the same network (i.e. both have the same network address) NetWare allows a negotiation to occur concerning the maximum packet size. This negotiation permits workstations and file servers on the same network to send and receive packets larger than 576 bytes. The maximum packet size used is determined by the smallest maximum packet size that is acceptable to both the workstation and file server.This determination occurs when the workstation first connects to a file server. In other words, the workstation must initiate the negotiation, otherwise the file server uses the default size of 576 bytes

For instance, NetWare Requester for OS/2, versions 1.2 and 2.0, does not negotiate packet sizes with file servers, it just uses 576 bytes as its maximum send and receive size. However, the NetWare Requester for OS/2 does negotiate packet sizes with file servers, and is thus capable of sending and receiving NetWare packets larger than 576 bytes.

For network topologies that are physically able to send and receive large packet sizes, the FCONSOLE Packets Received statistic will likely be accurate. However, for topologies such as ARCNET where there is a maximum physical packet size of 504 bytes (data-wise) the NIC driver must use multiple physical packet transfers to equal the movement of one "NetWare packet." This feat is accomplished by the NIC driver, which splits up the NetWare packet into usable chunks. Then the NIC driver sends its multiple physical packets (the chunks) and the receiving NIC driver reassembles the pieces. Thus, for a topology such as ARCNET, a 4KB packet size (NetWare packet) is sent as 9 physical packets.

Note that many types of NetWare requests will fit into a 504 byte packet. Thus, as there is a mixture of NetWare packets, there will a different number of physical packets sent. A file copy will likely use the 4KB size, i.e. 9 physical packets to every one NetWare packet. But a request to get the current file server time will fit into one physical packet.

Routing Packets

When NetWare routes packets, (that is, sends them between LANs,) it mandates a maximum of 576 bytes per NetWare packet. This is true because there is no breakdown and reassembly of packets at the file server when it routes packets. The packet's origin, the workstation must not therefore form a packet larger than 576 bytes when it is determined that the packet will cross an inter-network boundary. A file server will not accept a 4KB packet to route to another network. it will only receive a 576 byte (or smaller) packet to be routed. Insuring the packet is within the size limit is the responsibility of the NetWare shell, not the NIC driver. Remember that the physical hardware may still send multiple physical packets to accommodate the 576 byte packets being routed.

NetWare Management System

In early 1992, Novell announced the NetWare Management System (NMS). NMS provides an open and modular object-oriented environment for management of NetWare networks and the devices that support them. Novell provides several management service modules that can be used separately or, under NMS, become one very highly integrated management system. The modules include:

Network Services Manager—A Microsoft Windows 3.1 and OS/2 graphical application that gives the system manager a single integrated window of all the devices in the network. NSM allows the services manager to build graphics hierarchical maps of their networks, including countries, states, cities, building, floors, network segments. The services manager can then select a device and get performance and error statistics for that object, and, if necessary, can reconfigure the device remotely.

Hub Service Manager—Allows NSM to control HMI compliant hub cards down to the port level.

LANtern Service Manager—This allows the NSM to monitor the traffic, performance, and error statistics of remote networks. The LSM can be configured with various thresholds that, if crossed, will trigger an alarm at the NSM console. The LSM also allows remote packet capture and decode. This can allow SM administrators to do very detailed problem diagnosis without leaving their offices.

Communication Service Manager—Allows for remote monitoring of the Novell NetWare SAA gateway services to the SNA environment. This module provides connection status information to NSM allowing the system administrator to monitor the gateway sessions to the host. Configuration also can be monitored and controlled remotely through the single integrated NSM console.

Third Party Service Managers—Novell has developed an extensive set of APIs for use by developers to add NMS functions to their products, including remote monitoring and control.

Client/Server Applications

Currently receiving much attention in LAN computing circles are client/server (client/server) applications. Most articles on client/server applications discuss database servers, but there is a lot more to client/server computing than the embodiment of database servers.

In its simplest form, client/server computing involves the transferring of services between two nodes. These nodes are usually a client workstation and a server workstation. For instance, when you login to your NetWare file server, you are operating a client application with the goal of receiving service from a file server. Client/server computing is a name for the operations between a node requesting services and one providing such services. Client/server computing does not necessarily mean that server applications need to run at some particular type of network node. You do not have to use a file server for client/server applications.

Indeed, in client/server computing, the clients and servers can literally be any node on the network. For instance, a NetWare file server becomes a client in at least one situation—namely, when the NetWare file server issues an "are you alive" packet (called the "watchdog") to a workstation. The NetWare file server (client) is requesting a response from a workstation (server). If the workstation answers "Yes, I'm alive," then the process is complete. However the workstation may be gone, (for whatever reason,) and upon a specified time-out the NetWare file server will presume the workstation to be no more. Whether or not the "server" (workstation) responds, the "client" (NetWare file server) has requested a service.

The basic premise of client/server computing is that the components of client and server are split to maximize performance. For instance, with the case of a SQL-based database server, the client wishes to perform an SQL operation. The client builds the request and sends it to the database server (say, one based on Sybase's SQL Server product) to be processed. The SQL server contains the mechanisms to process the SQL request, whereas the client has only the ability to build a SQL request. Here, the splitting of processes has determined which node is the client and which is the server.

The details on how communications are established between nodes are not defined by client/server computing. Communicating between the clients and servers can be as simple as a common file or it can be something network-specific like IPX or SPX. Some available communication protocols for client/server computing include IPX/SPX, NetBIOS, Named Pipes, MHS, RPC, and TCP/IP.

Novell has been encouraging and supporting the growth of client/server computing since the introduction of VAPs with NetWare 2.1x. VAPs opened up the world of server applications, that is, applications that run on the file server (providing services to workstations, if the VAP was programmed to do so). Then NetWare 3.x saw the introduction of a better server application engine, namely, NLMs. Now, there are dozens of NLMs that provide a variety of database, network management, and numerous other features for Novell networks. With NetWare 4.0, Novell has completed the client/server loop by introducing the virtual loadable module (VLM) for the workstation (or client) side of the network.

CHAPTER 12

Diagnostics and Troubleshooting

A LAN is typically made up of a mixture of assorted hardware and software from a variety of different vendors. This can present a real challenge when analyzing and diagnosing LAN problems. In the sections that follow, several key areas of fault diagnosis will be examined. Specific products that are useful in LAN troubleshooting are also reviewed, along with examples of how to use them.

There are three classifications of tools for network diagnostics and troubleshooting: monitors, time domain reflectometers (TDRs), and protocol analyzers. Monitors are available for a variety of LAN types and are used to examine diagnostic or statistical data concerning network traffic. The TDR is used to isolate cable faults. The protocol analyzer is usually protocol- and topology-specific and allows the contents of an individual packet to be analyzed.

Monitors

Monitors provide statistical analysis of a network's performance on a continuous basis. They are used both to measure throughput and to monitor errors. Both functions are useful in determining the status of the network. Performance monitoring is especially useful when combined with trend analysis. Performance trend information is used for capacity planning or predicting when the network will fail. The latter would permit preemptive action to avoid a potential catastrophe. Performance monitoring should allow concurrent monitoring of select traffic and aggregate network utilization. Note that analyzers using Token-Ring chip sets may provide erroneous data. If the network interface loses data, the statistics provided in monitoring will be wrong.

Error monitoring involves recording network error conditions and can assist in isolating problems. Error monitoring is distributed among the network stations in

Token Ring. Each station in use records errors and periodically reports the error counts to an error monitor. Token-Ring protocol analyzers should support error monitoring as a diagnostic tool. Network problems and failures are easily identified through the use of error monitoring.

Monitor Products

A monitor should support periodic logging to disk, so that it is not necessary to constantly watch the monitor. Programmable thresholds should be available on the statistics display to alert the network administrator to a potential problem.

Monitoring the activity of a NetWare LAN can be done using any one of several products, including Brightwork Development's ARCmonitor and Emonitor, Thomas-Conrad Corporation's TxD, Cheyenne Software Inc.'s Monitrix, Novell's NetWare Care, and Sarbec's NWRanger, among other products. New network monitoring products are constantly being announced and updated.

ARCmonitor from Brightwork Development, Inc., designed specifically for ARCNET networks, provides a tool to test an individual network interface card and its associated cabling. ARCmonitor can also be used to analyze general network conditions.

Emonitor, also from Brightwork, is designed specifically for Ethernet networks. This product provides a means to test an individual network interface card and its associated cabling and can also be used to analyze general network conditions.

Cheyenne Software Inc.'s Monitrix utility provides analysis of network traffic and can test connections between any two workstations.

NetWare Care from Novell provides a map of the network and displays diagnostic information concerning each node. NetWare Care is only available for NetWare 2.1x/2.2x. NetWare Care is an IPX-level diagnostic as opposed to most of the other diagnostics described here, which are dependent upon a particular physical topology. NetWare Care is recommended in conjunction with any appropriate low-level diagnostic.

A product similar to NetWare Care is Thomas Conrad's TxD diagnostic software which allows for monitoring of network traffic flows. It also allows testing of connections between any two workstations.

NWRanger from Sarbec can be used to create a map of network nodes, to measure network traffic, and to perform point-to-point tests. It also collects information from nodes that appear to be operating outside the realm of normal use. NWRanger requires at least NetWare 2.1, and, similar to NetWare Care, is an IPX/SPX-level diagnostic tool.

Time Domain Reflectometer and Other Hardware Tools

The task of troubleshooting and isolating cabling problems accounts for almost 70 percent of all LAN problems. Selecting the hardware tools to be used for cable troubleshooting will depend on whether the cable is metallic or fiber-optic. The tools most commonly used for metallic cable include a time domain reflectometer (TDR), a spectrum analyzer (which is used to determine the bandwidth of a particular cable), and a continuity checker. An Optical Time Domain Reflectometer (OTDR), a bandwidth test set, and a power set are generally used to test fiber-optic cable.

In terms of the International Standard Organization's (ISO) Open Systems Interconnect (OSI) model, these cable troubleshooting tools work at the lowest protocol layer, the *physical layer*. They provide information that helps determine if the cable will correctly transmit signals. They will not test the content of the transmitted signals on the cable, i.e., anything in the other six layers of the OSI model.

Of the tools mentioned above, the TDR is perhaps the most beneficial in troubleshooting and isolating cabling faults. While the other tools can help to determine if a cabling problem exists, a TDR can save a significant amount of time by pinpointing the location of one of the three most common faults:

- A cable short
- An "open" on any single wire
- A break, where all wires are open

Troubleshooting Cable

As with all other aspects of troubleshooting and maintaining LANs, it makes sense to use a systematic approach when looking for cable problems. Diagnosis should be done by someone familiar with the specific network type being used and its associated characteristics, including topology, protocol, and bandwidth. When troubleshooting, all of the appropriate tools and devices should be available. To isolate a defect, only one component should be changed each time the cable is tested.

New cable should be tested while it is still on the spool. This will ensure cable integrity prior to running it over, under, around, and through ceilings and walls.

When a TDR is used, measurements should be taken from the end of a cable segment, rather than from a tee or tap along the segment. This approach will produce the most accurate measurement by reducing multiple reflections of the signal.

Good documentation is also important. Every segment of cable should be labeled at both ends, indicating where it is connected. This procedure should be followed up with documentation that includes a diagram showing all points of access after cable installation. This diagram will prove invaluable in the event of trouble with a connector or a terminator, as it will make it possible to determine what and where the problem may be.

What is a TDR and How Does it Work?

A TDR is like a radar device attached to the cable. It sends electronic signals down the cable and awaits a return. Cable faults in the form of impedance changes reflect some of the electronic signal back to the TDR. Based upon the signal it receives, the TDR can build a representative wave form of the cable under test. As each fault has a characteristic way of reflecting the signal, the type of fault can be predicted fairly accurately, either by viewing a display of the actual wave forms on a TDR's monitor or by allowing the TDR to interpret the wave form and tell the user in plain English the probable cause of the fault.

TDRs can also be used to display data reflecting the traffic, or packet activity, of a properly operating network. Under normal operating conditions, activity on a network should change frequently. If the network shows no activity, something is probably wrong. On the other hand, constant activity can also indicate problems.

Each particular LAN topology has specific guidelines that include maximum cable lengths. With a TDR, it is possible to determine cable length and to test each cable segment as it is installed. When an installation requires several cable segments, such as in a floor-to-floor and an on-floor installation, each segment should be tested separately before connecting the cable segments.

There are TDRs that will operate on many types of cable. It is advantageous to get a TDR that supports multiple cable types, such as Token-Ring (Type II), twisted-pair, Ethernet (thick and thin), and ARCNET. TDRs can also be used to troubleshoot data terminal problems, for example, on a UNIX system using RS-232 cables.

Why Use a TDR?

TDRs detect changes in cable characteristics over the cable's entire length, allowing the installer/troubleshooter to identify faulty splices, connectors, and severe bends along the cable. TDR success stories probably provide the best argument for using them. The following two examples are from actual LAN installation experiences, and will offer a good illustration of the benefits of having a TDR and the drawbacks of not having one.

The first example involves a network installation consisting of a 10-node Novell Ethernet network and included approximately 1,500 feet of cabling. The cable was first tested while it was still on the spool. Everything checked out okay on the TDR. Next, the cable was pulled and terminated. Again, it was tested, but this time, the TDR displayed the message "OPEN at 59." This message indicated a cable problem 59 feet away, which was traced to a loose BNC connector. Another message, "OPEN at 79," led to a kink in the cable, that was severe enough to break the core conductor of the cable. Since this portion of the cable was in the ceiling, it is quite likely a lot more time would have been spent locating the problem without the use of a TDR.

The second example involves a LAN similar to the first, but which experienced a number of problems with one particular PC after the installation was completed. The PC operated intermittently and was able to log on but periodically came up with one or more network errors. The network interface card was suspected at first. After a visual check of the cables, examining the connections numerous times, changing out the network card and, finally, tracing down each segment, it was determined that a "T" connector was at fault, since it was the only component not already replaced. This not only solved the problem with the individual PC, but also dramatically increased network response time. In this example, using a TDR from the beginning would have immediately pointed to the connector problem, which could have saved a significant amount of time and frustration.

In the past, TDRs have been viewed as special-case-only service and support tools. However, recent developments in technology and pricing have helped to bring TDRs into the mainstream of LAN installation tools. Microtest, Inc. makes the Cable Scanner, a hand-held TDR with an LCD display for messages and a number of useful cable attachment options. Tektronix, Inc. is another manufacturer that has made TDRs for many years.

Protocol Analyzers

Protocol analyzers should be evaluated using the following criteria:

1. The protocol decodes available.
2. The internal architecture of the analyzer.
3. The performance of the analyzer during collection.
4. Data filter and trigger capabilities.
5. Transmit capabilities and performance.
6. Monitoring capabilities and performance.
7. Ease of setup.
8. Ease of use and interpretation of the decode displays.
9. The physical characteristics of the unit.

Protocol Decodes

Protocol Decodes are needed by developers, systems integrators, and network managers for three different purposes. Developers need to test protocols that are under development, using the analyzer as a means of validating their interpretations of the protocol. Systems integrators need to isolate conformance and interoperability problems in multi-vendor networks. This enables them to determine which product is at fault. Systems integrators also need to streamline the protocols, to maximize efficiency by tuning the protocol parameters for the best network performance. Network managers need access to utilization statistics and error conditions on the network to keep it running efficiently. When a network goes down, the network manager must have access to any and all available information.

The number of protocols available for each analyzer does not need to be overwhelming. Product choices should be based on the protocols that are currently in use or are planned for the near future. This will reduce the number of choices to consider in evaluating protocol analyzers.

There are several protocol analyzers available. Two of the best known are Network General's Sniffer and Novell's LANalyzer. Sniffer is an example of a very capable and well-known product. In its various configurations it is able to analyze

ARCNET, Ethernet, StarLAN, and Token-Ring networks. Both of these protocol analyzers can decode of Novell's NetWare Core Protocol (NCP).

In the case of a network running multiple protocols simultaneously, such as Novell NCP and IBM SNA, automatic protocol recognition is a must. This feature allows frames from different protocols to be interleaved on the analyzer display during analysis. This simplifies the job of isolating the problems associated with existing protocols. Network General's Sniffer supports automatic protocol recognition.

Software Protocol Decoders

In addition to hardware protocol decoders there are now several software-only protocol decoders available. Most are only viable on Ethernet LAN hardware, though a few support Token-Ring and ARCNET. These software-only protocol decoders not only support Novell's NCP, but AppleTalk, TCP/IP, and IPX/SPX. Developers include Intel (NetSight Analyst), Novell (LANalyzer for Windows), FTP Software (LANWatch), and Klos Technologies (PacketView).

These software-only decoders cannot, in general, detect faults at the same level as their hardware-based big brothers. They are however, much less expensive, and, in many cases provide what is needed. Their availability makes the dream of having a protocol decoder much more possible for most LAN administrators.

Architecture

The performance of a protocol analyzer is directly related to its internal architecture. The most common architecture consists of a network interface card, processor card, interconnecting backplane, disk drives, display/keyboard, and standard I/O ports. The network interface card is the most important part of the analyzer—it determines the collection capabilities, transmit capabilities, and performance of the analyzer.

Interfacing to and collecting data from an Ethernet network is quite straightforward. This is due to the simplicity of the access control mechanism. As a result, good data collection performance is easy to achieve.

The access mechanism for Token-Ring networks is considerably more com-plex than the one used in Ethernet. Most Token-Ring protocol analyzers use an industry standard Token-Ring adapter card as the network interface. These cards perform quite well for communications purposes, but their performance in the role of protocol analysis is questionable during heavy load conditions. This is true for 4Mb/s Token-Ring networks and the problem is magnified for 16Mb/s operation.

Program execution and data buffering are accomplished by using RAM memory. This RAM must be dedicated to act as the capture buffer, thereby allowing data to be moved from the network to the capture buffer as it arrives. The preferred arrangement includes having the RAM memory located on the network interface card. This will guarantee 100 percent data capture.

Standard microprocessors lack the performance required to process the amount of data transmitted over today's local area networks. Processing of the data must be done by a high-speed dedicated processor. This ensures that unwanted data is ignored and the collection of the desired data is guaranteed. The processing power of a PC/AT is sufficient for display processing, file management, and storage of data to disk. In fact, support for MS-DOS is highly desirable in a protocol analyzer, as most users are familiar with the operating system. In addition, numerous spreadsheet and database programs are available to analyze captured network data and related statistics.

Disk drives are used to store both data and any analyzer setup configurations. Large disk capacities are desirable due to the bulk of data that needs to be managed. Files containing captured data or statistics logs in excess of 5MB are not uncommon.

Collection Performance

The most important specification of any protocol analyzer is its performance in the collection mode of operation, whether it is collecting actual data frames or statistics. If the network interface of the analyzer cannot guarantee capture of 100 percent of the network activity, it must indicate whenever data loss has occurred. Most network problems occur during heavy network loads. If data is lost by the analyzer during these peak loading periods, the data presented will be incorrect and will only complicate the process of locating a problem. The analyzer should not introduce any uncertainty when isolating problems.

Be sure that the performance specifications provided by the vendor are for the model and configuration of the analyzer being evaluated. Vendor data can often be misleading, specifying performance for only one configuration (This is typical of

Ethernet) and by implying that all configurations perform equally well. It is important to keep in mind that collection performance is determined by the network interface and the internal architecture of the analyzer. The network interface will be different for each network type.

An analyzer's performance should be specified for two capture rates. The first is the maximum data rate or "burst rate" at which the analyzer guarantees no data loss, even if the network is operating at maximum capacity. This burst rate specification should be accompanied by a maximum data buffer capacity, as the data is typically stored in the network interface RAM.

The second performance specification is a sustained data rate at which the analyzer can store data directly to disk, bulk memory, or some other mass storage device for long-term collection of very select traffic (e.g. errors, station-to-station data, etc.). This mode of operation should provide ample buffer space. Analyzing initialization scenarios between network devices, for example, requires the storage of large amounts of data. During sustained collection, the burst rate buffering should accommodate bursts of data by acting at a surge capacity, thereby smoothing the peak network conditions.

All collected data should be time-stamped. The time-stamp resolution should be minute enough to distinguish the smallest frames on the network. This means a 1-microsecond resolution for most of today's networks. For example, a 25-byte frame on a 16Mb/s Token-Ring network is 12.5 microseconds long, and a token is 1.5 microseconds long.

Filters and Triggers

Filters and triggers provide a means to isolate data on the network, select the data that you want to see, and ignore the rest. Filters reduce the data rate by ignoring unwanted frames and capturing only those desired. This provides observation of select communications on busy networks. The filters setup menus should be presented to the user in an easy-to-understand format. Pattern-match filters require the user to specify a hexadecimal pattern located within the frame at either a data or frame offset. While this may offer a great deal of flexibility, the process of setting such filters is often too complex.

Triggers are used to start or stop the capture of data when one or more network events occurs. This captures all events relating to a given network condition. The time of day can even serve as an important trigger criteria, since the user is not always next to the analyzer when it should be looking for a problem.

Transmit Capabilities

The analyzer's ability of an analyzer to transmit frames on a network greatly increases it utility. Transmission capabilities allow the analyzer to be used for such functions as capacity planning, benchmarking, interactive diagnostics, and station control. The transmission capability should be able to specify all fields within the frame. Some are limited to a single source address within a frame, the analyzer's station address.

The ability to simultaneously send multiple frames is desirable for testing certain network components, such as bridges and gateways. The limitations of these type of components are often determined by the number of connections or the number of stations a properly equipped analyzer uses to simulate this environment. High data rates are also useful for capacity planning and performance benchmarking.

Set-Up Displays

Protocol analyzers typically make use of easy-to-learn menus. This is especially important to the infrequent user who is often prone to forgetting complex commands or key sequences.

Setup programs should have on-line help text to assist users, thereby eliminating the need for a manual. Setup should include the option to assign recognizable names to represent the physical station addresses. Analysis of network traffic data is made more difficult if the physical station addresses are only depicted by their 48-bit representations.

Decode Displays

Protocol analyzers capture data and present it to the user in easy-to-read formats. An analyzer should be capable of displaying data frames at any of the applicable protocol layers, allowing a user to examine the frame layer-by-layer. A lost or delayed frame at the network layer may be the cause of a problem at the application layer. The ability to analyze each layer is necessary if this type of problem is to be detected.

Time-stamp information should be available in multiple formats to assist in problem isolation. Delta time between frames, time-of-day, and time relative to a reference frame are the predominant formats used. Delta time formats can be used to uncover race conditions; time-of-day is helpful in correlating problems to peak traffic periods; time relative to a reference frame can detect time-out problems.

Automatic protocol identification is mandatory in heterogeneous, multi-protocol networks. Representations for non-frame events (e.g. tokens, noise bursts, frame fragments, carrier detect, etc.) are essential to isolate certain network hardware problems.

Other Features

Another important feature to look for in a protocol analyzer is a remote control capability. The analyzer should be controllable from a remote site through dial-up or similar means. This feature should employ a common device, such as a personal computer or another protocol analyzer.

Application Program Support

Application program support is also a real plus in a protocol analyzer. These application programs provide network-specific support in such areas as station diagnostics, learning about network stations, acting as a Token-Ring parameter server, or measuring Token-Ring utilization and capacity through analysis of token rotation time. Each of these application programs can provide a direct answer to a specific networking problem or question.

Physical Characteristics

The physical characteristics of the protocol analyzer determine how and where it can be used. Most are constructed for portability so the analyzer can be moved to the problem. The analyzer should be rugged enough to withstand the wear and tear of day-to-day use and transport. This can include its being moved to car trunks, air conditioned offices, factory floors, and airplane overhead compartments. Storage of accessory items, such as power cords, network cables, and diskettes, should be accommodated handily. Setup time is also important for the sake of personnel who move the analyzer frequently.

File Server Diagnostics

With every copy of NetWare, Novell has included several utilities on the diskettes, with the sole purpose of directly interacting with the disk drive sub-system. These utilities principally include COMPSURF, VREPAIR, and DISKED.

The procedure for using COMPSURF, a utility used to format and test hard disk drives, is well-documented in the NetWare manuals, especially the */286 Maintenance* manual. VREPAIR, which corrects minor hard disk problems without destroying the data on the disk, is also documented in the */286 Maintenance* manual, although to a lesser degree than COMPSURF. Of the three utilities, DISKED is the only one not documented anywhere in the NetWare manuals.

The following sections help explain what VREPAIR and DISKED are, provide the basics of using them, and propose some situations where they may be put to work. COMPSURF is discussed in detail in Chapters 2 and 3.

Using VREPAIR

The VREPAIR utility is provided for NetWare 1.0x and higher (and in-cluded with version 2.x and later) and is perhaps one of the chief file server diagnostic tools available to network managers. It is used to repair the File Allocation Tables (FAT) and Directory Tables and to remap bad blocks. VREPAIR replaces the VOLFIX utility that came with earlier versions of NetWare.

The following four examples outline what could happen that might result in the need for VREPAIR level disk maintenance.

1. When using SFT NetWare on a disk that has a DOS partition occupying the last cylinders of the disk, there is a risk of data loss. NetWare stores data in redirection blocks at the end of the disk. As DOS is not aware that NetWare is using this area of the disk, DOS may overwrite a redirected block, thereby destroying part of the data in the NetWare partition. One solution is to reduce the high cylinder number DOS occupies by 5 or so. The preferred solution is to remove the DOS partition altogether. Note that NetWare 2.15c corrects the DOS partition problems, as does NetWare/386.
2. When using SFT NetWare, it may still be possible to get data errors on

the DOS partition altogether. Note that NetWare 2.15c corrects the DOS partition problems, as does NetWare/386.

2. When using SFT NetWare, it may still be possible to get data errors on the disk (such as "IO error during random read or write errors at sector xxx"). This most likely indicates that there is a problem with RAM or a power problem manifesting itself as a RAM problem. It can also result from a bad disk controller or a bad network card. In any event, the disk surface probably isn't involved unless the disk wasn't properly low-level formatted before it was installed as a NetWare drive.
3. On non-SFT systems, a bad sector has developed when a disk error persists, is reproducible, and, in some cases, can be overcome by multiple retries.
4. VREPAIR should be used on any NetWare system, SFT or not, when FAT and/or directory errors are displayed during server bootup. The one exception to this is the error message that includes "marked used with no file." This is not a real error but rather an informational message. The circumstance that causes that particular message is resolved as the disk is used. (See the detailed discussion later in this chapter.)

VREPAIR Bug Fix

If you use your file server's ability to "share printers" at the server then you may have encountered the following problem: You run VREPAIR at your file server (after the server has been downed and properly backed up) and you receive the following:

```
Abend: Invalid printer definition table. Run NETGEN to fix it.
```

(If you have NetWare 2.0x, the word NETGEN will be replaced with INSTALL.)

Now, what VREPAIR is doing is looking for the number of defined server-attached printers, defined meaning actually set up by you, not just printer ports. Anyway, if that number exceeds 3, VREPAIR will display this message. Now, this is silly because NetWare normally allows up to five printers to be connected to the server. Why would VREPAIR only allow three? Furthermore, why would VREPAIR really care since, even in its "worst case," it will never use more than one printer itself. Also, since VREPAIR never actually checks the printer table definitions, just *how* does it know they are invalid anyway? All it looks at is offset 100 hex of sector 15 decimal of the disk drive. If that number is greater than three it dies with that Abend message. So, in an effort to remedy this nagging problem, there are two solutions: First, use NETGEN (or INSTALL) to reduce the number of defined server printers to three or less. This method has the side effect of having to be undone so that the printers are usable after VREPAIR has run.

Second, use DOS's DEBUG utility to change one byte in VREPAIR. That byte will be currently be three and we will change it to five, to correspond to NetWare's "normal" capacity for five server-attached printers. The patch is given below.

Copy `VREPAIR.EXE to V.`
Type: `DEBUG V.`
at the - prompt: `-scs:100 ffff 83 F9 03` <enter>
You will receive back one result, perhaps: 2355:0EA0 (if you get more than one, only use the first)

The first number is the segment (2355)—ignore it. The second number is, in this case, 0EA0. Remember your number may be different, so please substitute it for my number in the following text. We need to add the number 2 to this number, to do this:

type at the - prompt: `-h 0EA0 2` <enter>
You will get: `0EA2 0E9E`
Use the first number, then type: `-E 0EA2` <enter>
You get: `03.`
type: `5` <enter>
at the next - prompt, type `W` <enter>,
It will say "Writing xxxx bytes."
type `Q` <enter>.

To complete this process, copy V. to VNEW.EXE (or whatever name you desire, perhaps V286.EXE, etc.). Now you can run VREPAIR (under this new name) without having to modify your printer tables in NETGEN (or INSTALL).

Be sure to have a good backup copy (or two) of your system before using VREPAIR! This is always the case, whether or not you use this patch.

VRepair and NetWare 3.x Name Spaces

If name spaces have been installed on a volume which is to be VRepaired, it is important to have the associate V_*.NLM available for VRepair to load. For instance, V_MAC.NLM for Macintosh and V_OS2.NLM for OS/2, or, more properly, HPFS name spaces. Without these, VRepair will be unable to fully repair a damaged volume.

Understanding DISKED

DISKED is included with all versions of NetWare available today. It has been available since before Advanced NetWare version 1.0. In the most fundamental sense, DISKED is just what its name implies—a disk editor. With DISKED, the disk drive subsystem can be modified on a byte-by-byte level. When it's in use, DISKED most resembles the DEBUG utility available with Microsoft's MS-DOS, or the NU utility available with Symantec/Peter Norton Group's Norton Utilities.

DISKED must be run when the file server is down. The file server is then rebooted with an MS-DOS boot diskette and DISKED is executed from the DOS prompt. Regardless of the version of NetWare, the initial screens for DISKED look similar to the example in the figure from NetWare/86.

```
Novell Advanced NetWare/86 Disk Editor V2.00
(C)Copyright Novell Inc. 1983,1984,1985

1 disk drives are attached to this PC:
   1. IBM XT or compatible

Maximum number of sectors per request = 77
```

Figure 12-1. Initial screen of DISKED

DISKED is a terse utility, somewhat primitive in its functionality, and unforgiving when it comes to recovering from or undoing mistakenly made commands. To put it another way, DISKED has the ability to wipe out all data (system and user) on the file server's disk drive subsystem if it's not used with caution. Therefore, be certain to backup the entire system before using DISKED.

Using the DISKED Commands

Referring back to the figure, note that DISKED's prompt is the ">" (i.e., greater than) symbol. DISKED is not a menu-driven utility, so a list of choices is not provided—the user must learn and know the command set. There is a Help command, which displays one screen of help text. Any one command is invoked by typing its letter at the DISKED prompt, for example, typing:

```
>h
```

displays the help screen. DISKED is not case sensitive, so either upper or lower case letters may be typed. Figure 12-2 displays the DISKED help screen.

```
>h
Available commands are:
R Num Num — Read sector for count
W Num Num — Write sector for count
D Address — Display Buffer from an address
C Address — Change bytes till "."
F Byte Start End — Fill buffer with a byte
M Start End Dest — Move buffer to a destination
N — New drive selection *Note-Not all versions have this option
Q — Exits to MS-DOS
    * All values are Hex except "Num" in R & W
    * If no values are entered on the write command
      then the values of the previous read will be used
    * The buffer will hold a maximum of 64 sectors
    * The default value for the sector counts is 1
      and for the  End values it is the buffer end.
      All other values default to 0
```

Figure 12-2. DISKED help screen

Each sector referred to in the commands is composed of 512 bytes, regardless of the version of NetWare or make/model of the disk drive subsystem. The buffer referred to in the commands describes the area of memory that the disk sector is read into. One of the simpler operations, other than the HELP command, is the READ command. For example, by typing

```
>r0 <enter>
```

DISKED will read sector zero of track zero of the disk into the buffer. The disk "busy" light will flash when the command is issued, after which the DISKED prompt will return. Keep in mind that r0 only reads one sector. Using decimal as opposed to hex notation, however, allows multiple sectors be read. For example, to be read the first 15 sectors of track zero, type:

```
>r0 15 <enter>
```

In a similar manner, other DISKED commands will work simultaneously on multiple sectors. However, for simplicity, all operations discussed in the following examples will be for one sector at a time.

The next DISKED command to review, is the DISPLAY command, which comes in logical sequence after the READ command. Notice the resemblance to DOS's DEBUG when referring to the DISPLAY command illustrated in Figure 12-3.

```
>d <press enter>
0000  FA EB 74 43 6F 70 79 72 69 67 68 74 20 28 63 29
...etc. up to the first 256 bytes
```

Figure 12-3. DISPLAY command

The DISPLAY command will show the first 256 bytes of the current 512-byte sector in hexadecimal format. There will be 16 lines of data, with 16 bytes per line. The hex number at the far left is the address of the data in the buffer. To view the other 256 bytes of the sector, press the <enter> key at the next DISKED prompt.

The CHANGE command, illustrated in Figure 12-4, allows the value(s) of any displayed data to be changed. When using this command, the address of the data to be changed must be entered in hexadecimal. This address is relative to the current sector you Read. For illustrative purposes, assume that the most current Read was of track and sector zero (">r0").

```
>ce
000E 63<- 64  <enter>
000F 29<-  .

>
```

Figure 12-4. DISKED's CHANGE command

Reviewing Figure 12-4, note that the "e" just right of the letter "c" is the byte to change in hex. It represents the fifteenth byte in the sector. After the command is typed, DISKED returns the address and value to be changed. The new value is typed immediately to the right of the "-", where the cursor is waiting for the new information. The change is entered, in this case "64", and the <enter> key is pressed. DISKED then prompts for the next byte to change, in this case the sixteenth byte (or hex "f"), which has a current value of 29.

When all changes are entered, type the period symbol (".") and press the <enter> key. To view the change, type:

```
>d0 <enter>
```

to indicate that you wish to display the top of the first sector just read.

It is important to understand that the CHANGE command only changes the values in RAM. To make the change to the disk sector, the Write command must be utilized. To permanently make the changes to the sector displayed and changed in Figures 12-3 and 12-4, type:

```
>w0 <enter>
```

In this situation, the "0" parameter isn't really necessary, because of the default usage explained on the help screen, "If no values are entered on the write command, then the values of the previous read will be used." However, explicitly typing the sector number is recommended, as there is then no question as to which sector is being written.

Another DISKED command to consider is the FILL command, which allows the value(s) of any data read to be replaced with another designated byte. One of the more common uses of this command is to wipe out certain disk information. For example, the FILL command can be used if the boot track of the file server disk drive becomes corrupted. Often, the only way to remedy this problem is to erase the boot track and reload it (versus totally reinitializing the disk via COMPSURF). Simply reloading the boot track without erasing it may have no effect. If wiping out the boot track is necessary, all of its sectors must be filled with 0s. (The sectors of the boot track are listed, along with other relevant sectors, as seen in Figure 12-5.)

To use the FILL command in the example above, the disk sector filled must first read through a command such as ">r0". Then, at the next DISKED prompt, type:

```
>f0 <enter>
```

which indicates that all bytes in the current sector are to be filled with 0s. Finally, to complete the operation, use the WRITE command, such as ">w0" to rewrite the sector that is now filled with 0s.

The final DISKED command to examine is the MOVE command. MOVE is essentially a copy command that allows a specified range of data that has been read into the buffer to be moved from the disk drive to another area in the buffer. The MOVE command is used less frequently than the other commands because it requires a more advanced understanding of buffer manipulation on the user's part.

When finished with DISKED, press "q" to exit to the MS-DOS prompt.

Putting DISKED to Work

DISKED can be used to handle a number of disk maintenance chores, beyond rebuilding the boot track as discussed earlier.

Figure 12-5 describes the key disk sectors found in the NetWare/286 environment that are available for exploration with DISKED. Note that all of the sector numbers in Figure 12-5 are in decimal, because the READ and WRITE commands use decimal format.

Sector	Use
0-13	Boot Area (regardless of where the disk is in the system, this area is reserved as the boot area). On some systems, fewer sectors are used.
14	HOTFIX redirection table (for SFT versions of NetWare) Mirror Tables
15	Indication of NetWare level, such as "NetWare or "Advanced NetWare" where NetWare is v4.61 or older (pre-1985). Also contained here are the file server name (offset is 06h), the cache block size (prior to 2.1), the maximum number of open file handles, file server printer definitions and number of FAT indexes allowed.
16	Map of all disk volumes on this physical disk drive.
17	Map of all disk volumes in the system (partially on sector 16).
18	Media defect table (bad block list).
19-31	Unused.
32	Beginning of First FAT for first volume.

Figure 12-5. Disk sectors to explore with DISKED

One possible use of DISKED could be editing the File Allocation Table (FAT). For example, it is possible to have a file on the network that cannot be deleted. This situation could occur, albeit infrequently, when using NetWare version 2.0x and older.

Two copies of the FAT exist for each NetWare volume, regardless of the version of NetWare being used. If the file's entry is found in the first FAT, the file's information can be edited or even deleted. If the file cannot be found in the first copy of the FAT, it's possible that the data might have been overlooked, e.g., if the second 256 bytes of data were not viewed via the DISPLAY command.

When the first FAT is edited with DISKED, the second FAT is not automatically updated. If the file server is booted after the first FAT has been changed, a "Mirror Mismatch" error will result. However, if the volume mount is continued, the copy of the first FAT will replace that of the second FAT, thus restoring their equality.

The first of six redirection block pointers begins at offset 0008 (immediately after REDIRECTD). These six blocks (two bytes each) are always the first to be allocated from the total number of specified HOTFIX blocks. Therefore, there will always be six HOTFIX blocks in use. Figure 12-6 provides a sample of a redirection table.

```
>r14
>d
0000 52 45 44 49 52 45 43 54 C4 09 00 00 CC 09 00 00 REDIRECTD...L...
0010 D4 09 00 00 DC 09 00 00 E4 09 00 00 EC 09 00 00 T...\...d...l...
0020 C4 09 00 00 00 08 00 00 00 00 00 00 00 00 00 00 D...............
```

Figure 12-6. View of redirection table (Sector 14)

Figure 12-7 details the layout of Sector 15. The disk format is indicated beginning at offset 0000. AN10 indicates that the disk in Figure 12-7 is in an Advanced NetWare 1.0 format. The next two zeros (00 00) is reserved to indicate other NetWare versions, although they are not used for any version earlier than version 2.15. The 48 bytes beginning at offset 0006 contain the file server name, which is null terminated. In this example, the file server name is L8088.

```
                                                                        >r15
>d
0000 41 4E 31 30 00 00 4C 38 30 38 38 00 00 00 00 00 AN10..L8088.....
0010 00 00 00 00 00 00 00 00 00 00 00 00 00 00 00 00 ................
0020 00 00 00 00 00 00 00 00 00 00 00 00 00 00 00 00 ................
0030 00 00 00 00 00 00 00 00 00 00 00 00 00 00 00 00 ................
0040 00 00 00 00 00 00 00 00 00 00 00 00 00 00 00 00 ................
0050 00 00 31 28 00 00 49 42 4D 2D 58 54 20 64 72 69 ..1(..IBM-XT dri
006076 65 20 43 00 00 00 00 00 00 00 00 00 00 00 00 ve C............
0070 00 00 00 00 00 00 00 00 00 00 00 00 AF ED 00 00 ............/m..
0080 00 00 00 00 00 00 00 00 00 00 00 00 00 00 00 00 ................
0090 00 00 00 00 00 00 00 00 00 00 00 00 00 00 00 00 ................
00A0 00 00 00 00 00 00 00 00 00 00 00 00 00 00 00 00 ..c.............
00B0 00 00 00 00 00 00 00 00 00 00 00 00 00 00 00 00 ................
00C0 00 00 00 00 00 00 00 00 00 00 00 00 00 00 00 00 ................
00D0 00 00 00 00 00 00 00 00 00 00 00 00 00 00 00 00 ................
00E0 00 00 00 00 00 00 00 00 00 00 00 00 00 00 00 00 ................
00F0 00 00 00 00 00 00 00 00 00 00 00 00 00 00 00 00 ................
>
010003 00 F3 00 00 00 00 00 00 00 00 00 00 00 00 00  ..c.............
10 00 80 00 00 00 00 00 00 00 00 00 00 00 00 00      ................
0120 00 81 00 00 00 00 00 00 00 00 00 00 00 00 00 00 ................
0130 00 00 00 00 00 00 00 00 00 00 00 00 00 00 00 00 ................
0140 00 00 00 00 00 00 00 00 00 00 00 00 00 00 00 00 ................
0150 00 00 00 00 00 00 00 00 00 00 00 00 00 00 00 00 ................
0160 00 00 00 00 01 01 00 00 00 01 01 0D 01 00 23 00 ..............#.
0170 00 00 00 00 00 00 00 00 00 00 00 00 00 00 00 00 ................
0180 00 00 00 00 00 00 00 00 00 00 00 00 00 00 00 00 ................
0190 00 00 00 00 00 00 00 00 00 00 00 00 00 00 00 00 ................
01A0 00 00 00 00 00 00 00 00 00 00 00 00 00 00 00 00 ................
01B0 00 00 00 00 00 00 00 00 00 00 00 00 00 00 00 00 ................
01C0 00 00 00 00 00 00 00 00 00 00 00 00 00 00 00 00 ................
01D0 00 00 00 00 00 00 00 00 00 00 00 00 00 00 00 00 ................
01E0 00 00 00 00 00 00 00 00 00 00 00 00 00 00 00 00 ................
01F0 F4 00 00 00 00 00 00 00 00 03 34 12 CD AB 02 00 t.........4.M+..
```

Figure 12-7. Sector 15 layout

At offset 0049 we find the maximum number of FAT indexes allowed. This number is stored in the default Intel low-high format.

Setup information regarding file-server-attached printers is stored starting at offset 0100. Figure 12-8 provides the location of the printer tables for NetWare-spooled printers.

Offset (hex)	Length (decimal)	Description
0100	1	Number of Spooled Printers (Max = 5)
0101	16	Printer Table for Spooled Printer 0
0111	16	Printer Table for Spooled Printer 1
0121	16	Printer Table for Spooled Printer 2
0131	16	Printer Table for Spooled Printer 3
0141	16	Printer Table for Spooled Printer 4

Figure 12-8. Storage of server printer information (Sector 15)

Each 16-byte printer table entry is further sub-divided into a number of meaningful bits of information. This information is detailed in Figure 12-9.

The maximum number of simultaneous open files is found at the end of sector 15. At offset 01F0 is the maximum number of simultaneous open files, in low-high order. In Figure 12-9, it is: F4 00, which is 244 in decimal. For NetWare 2.x/86 and /286, this number can be up to E8 03 (in low-high order), which is 1,000 in decimal. For NetWare 2.0x/68, the number may be up to A0 F0 (in low-high order), which is 4,000 in decimal.

Offset (hex)	Length (decimal)	Description
0	1	Printer number with high-bit set if Parallel Printer further, LPT1 (parallel port 1) would be represented as 80h, LPT2 would be 81h.
1	1	Serial printer configuration byte Bit Pattern = BBBPPSLL BBB = Baud rate 0=110 -bit pattern: 000 1=150-bit pattern: 001 2=300-bit pattern: 010 3=600-bit pattern: 011 4=1200-bit pattern: 100 5=2400-bit pattern: 101 6=4800-bit pattern: 110 7=9600-bit pattern: 111 PP = Parity 0=None-bit pattern: 00 1=Odd-bit pattern: 01 3=Even-bit pattern: 11 S = Stop bits 0=1 Stop b it 1=2 Stopbits LL = Word Length 2=7 bits bit pattern: 10 3=8 bits bit pattern: 11
2	1	Xon/Xoff Flag 0=No 1=Yes
3	13	Reserved

Figure 12-9. Example printer table entry

Non-destructive Recovery of the Supervisor's Account

The following procedure allows recovery of the Supervisor password with the use of DISKED. Note, however, that these instructions are applicable only to versions 1.x and 2.x of NetWare.

1. Boot the file server using MS-DOS.
2. Run the DISKED utility.
3. Starting with sector 32, perform the following commands:

```
>r32
>d
```

4. Begin looking for the files NET$BIND.SYS and NET$BVAL.SYS. Continue viewing each sector in sequence, i.e., 33, 34, etc., alternating the READ and DISPLAY commands until you see one or both of these files.
5. Keep track of the number of the current sector you are displaying. It is possible, although not likely, that these two files are not in the same sector.
6. Assuming that they are in the same sector, once you find the files, identify the starting offset address of the first letter of the NET$BIND.SYS file (the letter "N").
7. Using the CHANGE command, change this address from 4E to 4F. Its character representation is now the letter "O".
8. Repeat steps 6 and 7 for the NET$BVAL.SYS file, if it exists in the same sector as NET$BIND.SYS. Otherwise, continue with Step 9.
9. Next, change the file attribute for each file. For example, say the 4E changed in Step 7 was the third character in the sample display line:

```
00E0      00 02 4E etc.
```

   Directly under it will be a line similar to:

```
00F0      26 00 00 etc.
```

Use the CHANGE command again to change the attribute byte from "26" to "20". Be sure to change this byte for both files. When you are done, be sure to enter a "." to indicate that there are no more changes to be made.

10. When you have finished changing the sector, use the Write command to write the changes to the disk drive, for example:

```
>w36
```

WARNING! Writing to the wrong sector can prevent successful re-entry into the system. Therefore, it is imperative to have the correct sector number when performing this command.

11. If NET$BVAL.SYS is in a different sector, begin looking for it, repeating steps 4 through 10. When finished, type "q" and press <enter> to return to the MS-DOS prompt.
12. Next, reboot the file server. The NET$OS file will then look for the binderies, which it will not find. When it doesn't find them, it will create them, specifically with the SUPERVISOR and GUEST accounts. Once the system is rebooted, you can login as the SUPERVISOR. You will get a mirror mismatch when you boot the server—do not be alarmed, simply continue booting up.
13. To continue getting the old binderies back, perform LARCHIVE SYSTEM (see Figure 11-3 in Chapter 11), e.g., to a floppy diskette. Backup the binderies, excluding all files (i.e., "*.*") and answering "y" to questions about backup rights, as shown in Figure 12-10.
14. When the first "Backup? (Y/N)" appears, press <CTRL-C> to stop it, as shown in Figure 12-11.

```
D:\T>larchive system
Advanced NetWare LARCHIVE V1.01a — Archive to Local Disks
Copyright(C) 1984, 1985 Novell, Inc. All Rights Reserved.
You MUST be a supervisor to perform a COMPLETE system backup. If you are not a
supervisor, only directories to which you have rights may be backed up.

Back up fixed volume SYS? (Y/N) y
Back up fixed volume SYS1? (Y/N) n
Back up fixed volume SYS2? (Y/N) n


Enter the letter of the LOCAL disk drive on which to archive files:  d

Do you want to print a log report of this session? (Y/N) n

Select specific directories to be backed up? (Y/N)
(N = Back up all directories) y
```

Figure 12-10. The LARCHIVE command

```
SYS:SYSTEM

If you are archiving to a floppy disk drive (or other removable media), insert a diskette.

Press the space bar to continue.
     Archiving: +**
SYS:
     Backup? (Y/N)    <press CTRL-C here>

Archive session terminated
```

Figure 12-11. Using CTRL-C to terminate LARCHIVE

15. Two "empty" binderies were backed up. The files OET$BIND.SYS and OET$BVAL.SYS will be in the directory SYS:SYSTEM. Perform the following command, assuming LARCHIVE SYSTEM was saved to the D: drive:

```
F:\SYSTEM> copy   o*.sys   D:n*.*
```

When the copy process is completed, you should have the original bindery files in a directory, similar to Figure 12-12. Then perform LRESTORE SYSTEM. Respond "y" when asked if the binderies should really be overwritten.

```
D:\>dir

Volume in drive D is 386 Stealth
Directory of D:\

.                   <DIR>              1-01-90  10:20p
..                  <DIR>              1-01-90  10:20p
ARCHIVE     LOG         206            1-01-90  10:20p
ARCHIVER    LOG          11            1-01-90  10:21p
NET$BIND    SYS     22784              1-01-90  10:23p
NET$BVAL    SYS       2090             1-01-90  10:23p
            6 File(s)    86720 bytes free
```

Figure 12-12. Recovered password files

16. The final step is to run the SYSCON utility. Check the passwords if you have NetWare version 2.0x or older, or change the passwords if the version of NetWare is more recent than version 2.0x.

Non-Destructive Recovery of the Supervisor's Account for NetWare/386

If the need arises to recover the SUPERVISOR account on a NetWare/386 file server, the methods just described for NetWare/286 servers will not work. While this is unfortunate, you still have options. For example, a simple NLM will allow you to change the supervisor password. Figure 12-13 shows sample NLM code (in C) that will change the supervisor's password.

```
main( )
{

int Result,

SetCurrentConnection(0); /* set to internal KERNEL
  connection for NLMs */

Result=ChangeBinderyObjectPassword("SUPERVISOR", 1, " ", " ");

printf("\nChange Supervisor password to NULL was [%x], should
  be 0",Result);
}
```

Figure 12-13. Sample NLM code to change supervisor's password

If your server is a NetWare 4.0 file server and Directory Services are installed, remember that this NLM will only function if bindery emulation is enabled.

NetWare 2.15c Trouble with 2 MFM Drives

Many users have complained of performance problems when upgrading their networks to version 2.15c. Specifically, the complaints were related to performance of the disk drive subsystem when it had 2 MFM drives attached to an internal disk controller (e.g., the Western Digital MFM internal disk controller). The problem largely stemmed from using the ISADISK disk driver shipped with 2.15c. To fix the problem, use the old ATDISK driver. It can be found on the NetWire forum NOVA on CompuServe in library 3 as ATDISK.ZIP

NetWare Error Messages and Meanings

NetWare users find error messages frustrating enough. But this frustration is doubled when the error is represented symbolically as a numeric code. Figure 12-14 offers translations of the most common numeric-based error codes generated by NetWare command line and Novell's menu-based utilities (SYSCON, FILER, SESSION, etc.) .

Code	Meaning
128	File locked during file open or file create
129	Out of file handles (the file server is out of file handles)
130	No Open privileges (during file open)
131	Hard Disk I/O Error on Read (error reading on network disk)
132	No Create privileges (during file create)
133	No Create/Delete privileges (during file Create or Delete)
134	Create file exists w/Read Only attribute (during file Create)
135	Wild cards In Create filename (during file Create)
136	Invalid file handle, file may be closed or unlocked
137	No Search privileges (in directory specified)
138	No Delete privileges (in directory specified)
139	No Rename privileges (in directory specified)
140	No Modify privileges (in directory specified)
141	Some files affected others in use (during Delete, Rename, Set file attributes on a set of files, i.e. *.*)
142	No files affected others in use (during Delete, Rename, Set file attributes on a set of files, i.e. *.*)
143	Some files affected others Read Only (during Delete, Rename, Set file attributes on a set of files, i.e. *.* and some files are flagged Read Only)
144	No files affected others Read Only (during Delete, Rename, Set file attributes on a set of files, i.e. *.* and some files are flagged Read Only)
145	Some files renamed others name exists already (during Rename)
146	No files renamed others name exists already (during Rename)
147	No Read privileges (in directory specified)
148	No Write privileges or file Read Only (during Write)

Figure 12-14. NetWare error messages

Code	Meaning
149	File detached (during Read or Write) (File may become detached if it was open when a Release File Set (Function 0xCB) was issued. A detached file can be reattached by using Lock File Set (Function 0xCD))
150	No dynamic memory available (file server ran out of dynamic memory)
151	No disk space for Spool File
152	Volume does not exist, an unknown volume was specified
153	Directory full, all free directory slots have been allocated
154	Renaming across volumes, a rename can be used to move a file between directories, however, this convenience is not extended to moving and renaming between volumes
155	Bad directory handle, usually only occurs when the server is rebooted and workstation is not, can also indicate a corrupt shell
156	Invalid path (an invalid path was specified)
157	No more directory handles, the workstation's allocation of file handles (which up to 255 may be specified) is exhausted
158	Invalid filename (during create)
159	Directory active, indicates an attempt to delete directory that is in use by another workstation, i.e. the other workstation has drive letter mapped to this directory or one of its subdirectories
160	Directory not empty, indicates, during a directory delete attempt, that the directory still contains files and or subdirectories
161	Directory I/O error, indicates a fatal, nonrecoverable I/O error has occurred in the directory area of the disk, this also indicates that both copies of the directory table are affected by the I/O error
162	Read file with record lock, occurs during a Read of a locked area of a file (a physical lock)
192	No account privileges
193	Login denied, no account balance
194	Login denied, no credit
195	Account too many holds
197	Intruder detection lock
198	No console operator
208	Queue error
209	No Queue
210	No Queue server

Figure 12-14. NetWare error messages (continued)

Code	Meaning
211	No Queue rights
212	Queue full
213	No Queue job
214	Encrypted login needed or No Queue job rights
215	Password not unique (Queue servicing)
216	Password too short (Queue not active)
217	Login denied, no connection to server (station not server)
218	Unauthorized login time (Queue halted)
219	Unauthorized login station (Queue servicing)
220	Account disabled
222	Password has expired, no grace logins remaining
223	Password has expired
*** Bindery error messages:**	
232	Attempt to Write Property to a group
233	Group add request for member already in group
234	Group request for nonexistent member
235	Group request made for nongroup property
236	No property value to retrieve (in read/write)
237	Property already exists (in create)
238	Object already exists (in create)
239	Object name contains illegal characters
240	Attempt to use wild cards in wrong place
241	Attempt to change security to bindery-only status
242	No Object Read (property scan) privileges
243	No Object Rename privileges
244	No Object Deletion privileges
245	No Object Creation or Change privileges
246	No Property Deletion privileges for object
247	No Property Creation or Change privileges for object
248	No Write privileges for property
249	No Read privileges for property
251	No such Property
252	No such Object
253	Unknown bindery request
254	Bindery temporarily locked, try later
255	Unrecoverable/Unknown error

Figure 12-14. NetWare error messages (continued)

Packed File is Corrupt

This error results when a file cannot be read correctly. Novell uses Microsoft compilers to produce many of its network utilities. When one of these utilities is run, it first "unpacks" itself and performs a checksum to verify that the unpack was successful. If the checksum does not verify, then a Packed File is Corrupt error results.

There are several possible reasons why the checksum would fail. The file may, in fact, be corrupt. It can also result from a bad NIC adapter, because some cards will occasionally reverse bytes, causing this error to occur. Some combinations of IPX, NIC driver, DOS, and other programs can affect the environment in such a way that it will cause this error.

To isolate the cause of this problem, begin by loading a fresh copy of the suspect utility from a workstation drive. If the copy works and other utilities run properly from the server, the file is probably corrupted.

File Server Troubleshooting

From time to time the file server may experience an abnormal ending or "abend." Any version of NetWare can report abends. Two specific abend messages are the most common, yet they are the most difficult to resolve. These two errors are General Protection Interrupt and Non-Maskable Interrupt, or GPI and NMI, respectively. A discussion of reasons for their occurrence and what to do about them follows.

NetWare/386 3.0

If you are using NetWare/386 3.0, it is time to upgrade. This version of NetWare contains several severe bugs and should not be used. If you are experiencing any file server problems with version 3.0, your best option is probably to upgrade to version 3.10 or 3.11. Or, if you need the features of enterprise networking provided by NetWare 4.0, you might consider upgrading to it.

NetWare/386 and Old API Warning

If you load an NLM and receive a message such as:

```
THIS MODULE IS USING 3 NETWARE 3.00 API CALLS.
YOU SHOULD UPGRADE TO A NETWARE 386 3.11 MODULE WHEN IT
  BECOMES AVAILABLE.
```

Note that this message does not indicate that running the NLM will be treacherous to your file server's operations. In the case of certain APIs such as ClearFile, LogFile, and sprintf the message is relatively meaningless.

If you want to see what old APIs are being used, type the following command at the console prompt:

```
set display old api names = on
```

Then load your NLM to see a list of the old API names.

GPIs and NMIs—Maladies of the Network File Server

GPI/NMIs often result from some sort of hardware deficiency. This might be as simple as not having sufficient RAM in the file server. For instance, most versions of 2.1x/2.2x NetWare require at least 1.5MB of RAM before the file server can boot and begin to issue meaningful error messages. A GPI/NMI received after the cold boot loader message is displayed, but before any of NetWare's initialization messages are displayed, may indicate an insufficient amount of RAM in the server.

Most other GPI/NMIs result from memory problems of one sort or another. Some possible causes of memory problems are:

- Power glitch, i.e., over- or under-voltage
- Static electricity, generally an over-voltage
- Phone wires, if there is a modem installed in the server and it is connected to an active phone line
- Bad RAM chips

A RAM chip problem can cover an assortment of RAM problems. As a rule, all of the chips used as extended memory in a file server should have the same speed rating, if they are not of the same type. The speed rating is noted in nanoseconds (ns). It is important that all chips on a given memory board are the same speed and meet the board manufacturer's specification. If there are multiple memory boards in the file server, it is acceptable for each board to use RAM chips of different speeds.

RAM chips can also be defective. In most cases, failure of an electronic component due to a defect will occur during the first 10 days of use, that is, the first 10 days of time during which the device is active with power appropriately applied. A GPI/NMI message within the first few days of operation may indicate that a RAM chip has failed.

Yet another problem is that of improperly installed RAM. When installing RAM, it is important to be extremely careful to make sure all legs of the chips are inserted into their sockets. As a final check, hold the board at eye level and look underneath the chips, visually inspecting for any misaligned chip legs. Another thing to remember when installing RAM chips is that they only work when correctly oriented in the socket. Most RAM chips have a "half moon" on one end of the chip, either drawn on the chip or as part of its shape. The memory chip socket has a corresponding half moon indicator drawn at one end of the memory chip socket. A chip installed backwards will probably be destroyed when power is applied.

If GPI/NMI messages only occur during periods of increased network activity, there may be a RAM problem that exists high up in memory. Simply put, this memory is not accessed unless the cache RAM begins to fill up. On the rare occasion when it is accessed, faulty operation causes the abend to occur. Ways to resolve such memory problems include:

- Physical verification of proper installation including:
  correct RAM chip speeds
  correct installation of chips in their sockets
- Application of a power protection system including:
  line conditioner
  battery backup
  uninterruptible power supply
  testing of power received at socket (your local power company probably has this available as a service)
- Test of RAM using a specific test utility, such as the RAM testing program from Brown Bag Software, Inc.
- Removal of RAM so that only a minimum amount of RAM remains. If the RAM problem still occurs removed memory can be swapped with base memory in an attempt to isolate the cause of the error.

Any other board in the file server has the potential to cause a GPI/NMI error condition. It is more likely that a hardware problem on another card would first manifest itself in some way other than as a GPI/NMI error but, if memory checks out, it is advisable to look at the other boards in the server.

With version 2.1x/2.2x of NetWare, VAPs (Value Added Processes) and VADDs (Value Added Disk Drivers) were both added as options. Both represent a type of application. VAPs are used to add utility to the server. VADDs are added to specifically control disk drives and/or disk controllers. If adding one or the other to a system results in GPI/NMI abends, it could be one of several things. Since a new VAP or VADD will require additional memory, the problem may be the result of using heretofore unused RAM. It could also be more directly related to the VAP or VADD itself, as in the case of a product that contains bugs.

Moving outside of the file server, another piece of hardware that may masquerade as a memory problem is a printer attached to the file server. This can happen in one of two ways. As was mentioned earlier, a power surge at the server can cause GPI/NMI errors to occur. A printer attached to the same power source can cause the power fluctuations. The other problem stemming from a server attached to a printer is that of ungrounded data cables. In the case of a serial printer, check pins 1 and 7 on the 25-pin connector or pin 5 on the 9-pin connector. The parallel cable usually gets its ground through the printer cable's shield. If they're not properly connected, either can serve as the source of a GPI/NMI abend.

If a GPI/NMI error is not reproducible, it is likely the problem can be attributed to a power fluctuation.

One known cause of file server abends in some clones running NetWare 2.0a is worth mentioning. If a 1.2MB floppy disk is inserted at the time the file server begins to initialize itself, an invalid OP code interrupt (another abend message) results. To avoid this problem, use a high performance disk controller, e.g., Western Digital, or, if you can, boot from the hard disk, ensuring there is no floppy in the disk drive when you do so.

This covers the most prevalent reasons for GPI and NMI abend messages. With a little detective work, it is usually possible to remove the source of the GPI/NMI. If you receive unusual error messages or random error messages at the file server the same resolution techniques discussed for GPI/NMI are valid.

BINDFIX WARNING

If you use the utility BINDFIX.EXE make sure that it is dated at least 2-12-91 or is at least version 3.52. If you use an earlier version and you have SHOW DOTS=ON you run the EXTREME RISK of COMPLETELY erasing your network disk drives' data (SYS: volume). This is especially true if you are logged in with SUPERVISOR equivalent rights. The problem stems from the availability of the . and .. entries. Older versions of BINDFIX were NOT expecting to find these entries. When these entries ARE found by an older BINDFIX, it causes BINDFIX to go up and down the ENTIRE directory tree of the SYS volume. If this occurs, all directories and all files will be deleted on volume SYS:. This only occurs if you answer YES to the question:

```
Delete mail directories of users that no longer exist
```

If you are unsure about whether or not your version of BINDFIX has this problem, answer NO to this question.

Marked Used with no File

One of the most frequent and misunderstood FAT boot time messages is:

```
*** WARNING *** FAT Entry <xxxx> Marked Used with no File.
```

This "error" is totally harmless; it is a "for your information" type of error message. When a file is opened on the network for Write activity, an extra disk block is automatically reserved for that file's private use. If it is not closed properly, such as when the server is abruptly downed, the station locks up (which is more likely with versions before 2.0) and thus that extra block remains. Furthermore, the extra block is not physically linked into that file until it is used. So, if a file is not closed properly, the extra block will still be marked "in use," but will not be "attached" to any file.

The NetWare file system "knows" the difference between a current "in use" block, and a block that was in use before the last reboot of the server. The latter a file is not closed properly, the extra block will still be marked "in use," but will not be "attached" to any file.

The NetWare file system "knows" the difference between a current "in use" block, and a block that was in use before the last reboot of the server. The latter blocks, marked "used with no file", are reused as soon as possible but, because Novell does a "best fit" for large block operations such as file copies, they may not be used immediately. The integrity of the system is therefore unaffected by the "marked used with no file" blocks. Only serious errors like data mirror mismatch, multiple allocation, out-of-order, file-out-of-bounds, and the like compromise the integrity of the system.

If these errors do occur (most notably by the "abandon volume mount?" prompt), do not let the server reboot. Run VREPAIR first, making certain a complete backup exists. If the server is allowed to reboot, note that the first copy of the FAT and DIR tables will replace the second, "mirror copy," in an attempt to make everything "match.

Abandon Volume Mount?

This prompt is generated when booting the file server and should be preceded by a message indicating a problem. In other words, the "abandon volume mount" prompt gives users the opportunity to abort booting the file server when it encounters conditions that it interprets as possibly jeopardizing its integrity.

If this question is answered "No," the file server will continue to try and boot and the boot procedure will try to fix the problem reported previous to the Abandon Volume Mount. If the question is answered "Yes," the file server will continue to boot, because of the possibility of other volumes existing on the file server. However, if that volume was the only volume in the file server, i.e., the SYS: volume, you will not be able to log in to the file server. This will seem odd, as the file server is up, but with no active volumes. Without active volumes, the file server is essentially useless, i.e., unable to accept workstation requests.

Network Printing with Plotters

NetWare 2.12 has some sketchy undocumented problems with using serial ports for printing, particularly with more complex devices such as plotters. One problem that will occur is that printers and plotters will work for a time, but then will report framing or data transfer errors. For instance, a printer will report an error 40 ("Error occurred while transferring data from computer"). Even taking down the file server and bringing it back up does not always correct the problem.

There are two approaches to use for this problem that may yield a solution. First, connect the device to a parallel port on the file server. If the printer is serial only, get a parallel-to-serial convertor. Make certain that the convertor converts all 8 bits, since some convert only 7 bits, stripping the high bit. Second, try "reverse" protocols, such as the server using Xon/Xoff and the printer using DTR, or vice versa. While this reversing of hardware protocols seems counter intuitive, it works in many cases.

Increasing the Stack Size in NET$OS

If NetWare repeatedly provides a stack overflow message and all of the normal performance tuning steps have been taken to no avail, there is a way to increase the stack size in the operating system file NET$OS. The following procedure will implement this change in SFT 2.15, but can be tried for any version of NetWare experiencing stack overflows.

1. Make a backup copy of the SFTOBJ diskette.
2. Insert the SFTOBJ disk and type:

   ```
   DEBUG SFT_1.OBJ
   ```

3. Search for 8B E5 81 06 00 00 8C 00 BB 8C 00 53 BB by typing:

   ```
   SCS: 100  FFFF  8B  E5  81  06  00  00  8C  00  BB  8C  00  53
   BB  <enter>
   ```

   XXXX:YYYY will be an address returned. There should be only one address.

4. Take the offset YYYY, add 6 (giving the offset of the first 8C). The result is YYZZ.

5. Edit this address:

```
E  YYZZ <enter>
type:    FE <enter>
```

6. Add 3 to YYZZ. This is the offset of the second 8C. The result is YYAA.

```
E  YYAA <enter>
Type:  FE <enter>
```

7. Type: `W <enter>`
   This writes the changes back to the disk.

8. REGEN the operating system using NETGEN.

Workstation Diagnostics and Troubleshooting

Support of a network can be simplified with the help of workstation-access software. This genre of software allows one workstation on a LAN to share control of the screen and keyboard functions of another workstation on the same LAN. In this manner the support person can view a user's screen and have simultaneous keyboard control of that user's workstation. The most common analogy in a non-LAN context is Microcom's Carbon Copy software which provides remote control of a PC via modems.

One example of a workstation-access product is Brightwork's Net-Remote. LAN Support Center, also from Brightwork, tracks support activity in a database. Keeping track of the diagnosis and resolution of user problems can prove indispensable to the network manager.

In addition to providing workstation access, Fresh Technology's LAN Assist Plus has a chat window, just like Carbon Copy.

Intel's LANSight is another workstation access product that provides: hardware configuration information, IPX/SPX traffic statistics, and a conventional memory mapper utility.

TRACK ON, TRACK OFF

A rarely used, yet useful console command combination for some mediating LAN diagnostics on the NetWare file server is TRACK ON and TRACK OFF. The messages normally displayed by TRACK ON are file server broadcasts. Each file server advertises itself once every minute. The "IN" prefix indicates a message received by the file server and the "OUT" prefix indicates a message sent out by the file server.

The address within the brackets [ ] following the IN or OUT indicates where the message is from or where it is going, and is given in terms of the physical node address. For example, an address of [x:FFFFFFFFFFFF] indicates a broadcast message to all nodes on the internetwork serviced by that network card.

One simple diagnostic aid provided with the use of TRACK ON is monitoring of network shell loading at a workstation. To see how this works, type TRACK ON at the file server prompt. Next, load the shell (ANETx or IPX+NETx) at a workstation. The console display at the file server should display something similar to:

```
IN  [A:0000000000A2] Get Nearest Server
OUT [A:0000000000A2] Give Nearest Server <file server name>
```

If the "A:" is some other letter, e.g. B, C, or D, then the following will also be displayed.

```
IN  [x:10005A385510] Route Request
OUT [x:10005A385510] 0000153 1 / 2
```

where the x: is "B:", "C:", or "D:."

The numbers in the "x/y" format indicate file server "hop" counts, minimum and maximum hops to an address from the address noted on that line. The address noted is eight characters long, representing the internetwork address.

When everything is working properly, the server will acknowledge the workstation in this manner and a connection will be established. On the other hand, if the workstation shell does not load and the IN/OUT lines are repeated several times when attempting to load the shell at the workstation, this most likely indicates that the workstation is unable to receive the information from the file server. A conflict of interrupts or a defective network card at the workstation can cause this.

Another case to consider is when no IN/OUT lines are displayed at all when loading the workstation shell. This can indicate the same problems with the workstation as noted above, but it can also mean there is a problem with the network card in the file server or with the cabling to the file server. To isolate the fault, connect a single workstation to the file server with a cable that is known to work. If there are still no IN/OUT lines, then replacing the file server card may be in order.

Workstation Fault Diagnosis

Every LAN administrator tends to develop their own approach to diagnosing LAN ills, just as physicians do with patients. The following suggestions offer a base-line set of steps to perform for diagnosing workstation problems.

1. At the file server type TRACK ON; at the workstation try to load NETx. Observe tracking messages at the file server. If several Get/Give Nearest Server messages are displayed, then the file server is getting the request and the workstation cannot "hear" the reply. In this case, check the workstation NIC, as its configuration may be in conflict with another device.
2. Type CONFIG at the file server and note the number of Service Processes. If there are less than two Service Processes, then this is the most likely cause of the problem. To correct this, reconfigure the operating system so that there are at least two FSPs. In some cases, one will work. (FSPs are discussed in greater detail in Chapter 3.)
3. The next thing to check is cabling. If a TDR is available, use it to verify the network cabling. If not, then place the workstation close enough to the server so that all of the cabling used can be visually verified. This will eliminate cabling as the fault.
4. Check the NIC's workstation address (not applicable to those that are Ethernet-based or IBM Token-Ring-based and not using LAA) to be sure its con-figured address does not conflict with that of any other NIC on that network segment.

5. Replace the workstation NIC with one that is known to work.
6. Replace the file server NIC (unless it already works with other workstations).
7. Seek help on the CompuServe NetWire forum or with other technical persons.

File Read/Write Errors

Three methods to correct consistent read or write errors on a certain file or a set of certain files are detailed below.

1. Rename the affected files (e.g., to *.BAD) and flag them read-only so they won't be deleted by mistake. Then restore the original files from a backup or create them anew.
2. Bring the file server down and run VREPAIR to find the affected files. Allow VREPAIR to make the changes it suggests. Be sure to have at least two good backups of the system before trying to use VREPAIR.
3. If the first two options fail, this may suggest that the disk was not low-level formatted per the suggestions found in Chapter 2. If this is the case, perform the low-level format of the drive again to make a permanent fix.

Communication Faults

Another common source of errors is communication faults. Error messages such as "Error Reading/Receiving ..." or "Error Writing/Sending ..." can be diagnosed as follows:

1. Did it occur at all stations at once?
   If so, the file server is probably down, its NIC is having trouble, or a portion of the network cable has been cut or disconnected. Any hubs should also be checked for a good connection and power. A bad network card spewing out packets and causing network congestion can also cause this error.

2. Does it occur only at certain workstations?

Check the workstation's NIC, which may have failed. Check the network cable plant. In the case of Ethernet, or nodes may be too closely spaced or there may be a patch cable where one is not allowed. It may also be a bad port on an active hub (ARCNET) or MAU (Token-Ring). On S-net (/68) connections, check the port on the file server where the node is connected, particularly the I/O chip on the LAN board(s). Figure 12-15 represents a portion of a LAN board found in S-net file servers. The three chips shown are replicated on the board six times. The I/O chip should be Revision E or higher. If it is Revision D or lower, upgrade the chips.

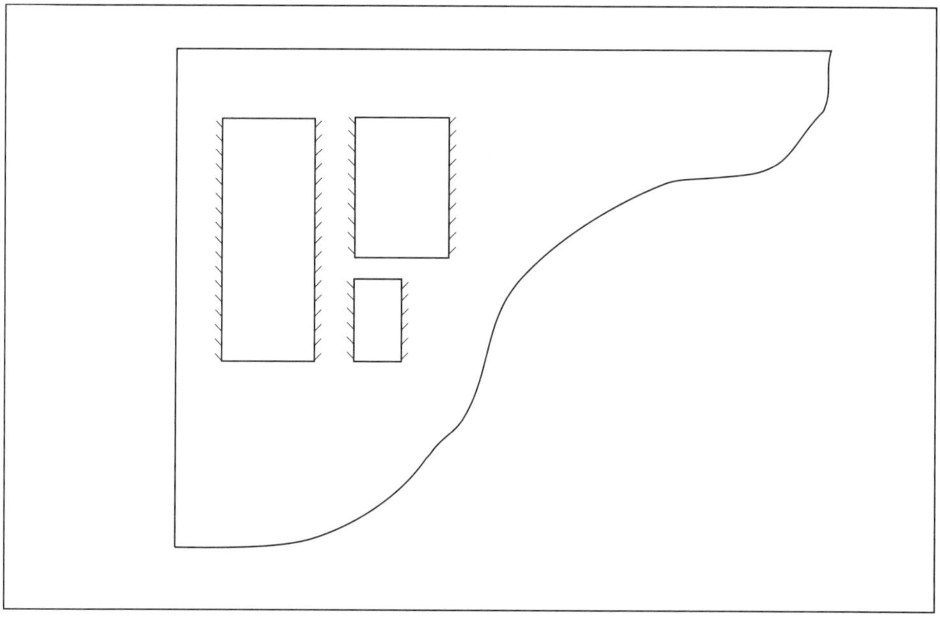

Figure 12-15. The I/O chip of a LAN board (S-net file servers)

3. Does it occur at all workstations or randomly?
   If the file server is NetWare 2.1x or higher, check the number of communications buffers using FCONSOLE. If the peak used is equal to the maximum number, more communications buffers are needed. Use the DCONFIG utility as noted in Chapter 2 to increase the number of communication buffers. Check the number of file service processes (especially true for version 2.1x). If there is only one, this is probably the cause of the problem. One fix is to try removing a NIC from the network operating system configuration. If there is more than 6K available in dynamic memory pool 1, use the FSP patch available on the SMC forum. Also check the file server NIC, it may be at fault.
4. For programmers—Does it occur after a network call?
   Check the size of the reply buffer, which is probably too short. Even if it doesn't appear to be too short, add a couple of bytes to it. More than one network call has been documented incorrectly.
5. Is the network topology Token-Ring?
   If it is Token-Ring with Type 3 cabling, be sure to use media filters to assist with diagnosing the problem.

NetWare Publications

Novell now publishes the NetWare Application Notes. these notes are produced monthly and contain several in-depth articles involving current NetWare issues. The notes are available electronically or hard copy. To retrieve the NetWare Application Notes electronically, access NOVA on CompuServe. The notes are found in Library 11. To receive the notes in hard copy, call (801) 429-7550. Currently, a one year subscription is $95 (US).

Another monthly publication specifically for NetWare administrators is *Inside NetWare*, published by the Cobb Group, a division of Ziff-Comm Publishing. This technical journal has been in publication for nine years and contains numerous tips and techniques. The coauthors of this book are frequent contributors. A one year subscription is currently $89 (US) for the USA and $109 (US) outside the USA. *Inside NetWare* is also available in a Japanese (Kanji) edition. To order the *Inside NetWare,* call 1-800-223-8720.

The Last Resort

When all else fails, and you've even tried the NetWire forums on CompuServe, there is one last, almost foolproof method for diagnosing network problems. Isolate the file server from everything else on the system except for a couple of workstations. From that point, start adding things (hardware and software) back onto the system in an attempt to recreate and pinpoint the problem.

APPENDIX A

Buffer Sizes of Selected LAN NICs

MAX PACKET SIZE	HARDWARE OPTION TEXT
2048	IBM PC Network
2048	IBM PC Network (286 mode)
512	IBM PC Cluster
1024	IBM Token-Ring
512	Orchid / Santa Clara / AST PCNet
512	Allen-Bradley Vista LAN/PC
1024	Proteon ProNET with Checksum
4096	Standard Microsystems ARCnet
512	Nestar PLAN 2000
512	Corvus Omninet
512	Novell Star Intelligent NIC
1024	3Com EtherLink
1024	3Com 3C505 EtherLink Plus
512	Gateway GNet
512	AT&T StarLAN
512	IBM ASYNC Remote Dial-in Line
512	Ungermann-Bass
1024	Novell E-Net
1024	MICOM-InterLAN 5010/NP600
512	Novell RX-Net
4096	Thomas Conrad ARCnet

APPENDIX B

Acronyms/Abbreviations

3270	Generic name for IBM SNA/SDLC protocol
5250	Generic name for IBM 3x minicomputers terminal/controllers

ABM	Asynchronous Balanced Mode
ACS	Asynchronous Communications Server
ADCCP	Advanced Data Communication Control Procedures (ASA's)
AES	Asynchronous Event Schedule
AFP	Apple Filing Protocol
ANSI	American National Standards Institute
ANW	Advanced NetWare
ARCnet	Attached Resouce Computer network
ARM	Asynchronous Response Mode
ARPANET	Advanced Research Projects Agency NETwork, (replaced by Internet)
ASCII	American Standard Code for Information Interchange
ATA	ARCnet Trade Association

BBS	Bulletin Board System
BIOS	Basic Input/Output System
bit	A single unit of information, either 0 (no) or 1 (yes)
byte	8 bits (2 nybbles)

CCITT	Comite' Consultatif International Telephonique et Telegraphique
CDI	Compact Disk Interactive
CDI	Cluster Device Interface
CDROM	Compact Disk-Read Only Memory
CICS	Customer Information Control System (IBM specific)CUT Control Unit Terminal (IBM specific)
CNE	Certified NetWare Engineer
CPU	Central Processing Unit
CSMA	Collision Sense/Multiple Access

DDCMP	Digital Data Communications Management Protocol (DEC)
DLE	Data Link Escape, 000100 in ASCII
DCB	Disk Coprocessor Board
DCE	Data Circuit terminating Equipment
DEC	Digital Equipment Corporation
DFT	Distributed Function Terminal (IBM specific)
DIX	Digital, Intel, Xerox
DMP	Dynamic Memory Pool (as in DMP1, DMP2, DMP3)
DOS	Disk Operating System
DRAM	Dynamic Random Access Memory
DSE	Data Switching Equipment
DTE	Date Terminal Equipment

EBCDIC	Extended Binary Coded Decimal Information Code
ECB	Event Control Block
EEPROM	Electronically Erasable Programmable Read Only Memory
EIA	Electronic Industries Association (created RS-232 standard)
EISA	Extended Industry Standard Architecture
E-mail	Electronic Mail
ESDI	Enhanced Small Device Interface
ESR	Event Service Routine
ETB	End of Transmitted Block, (0000100 1110100 in ASCII)

ETR	Early Token Release
FAT	File Allocation Table
FCB	File Control Block
FEP	Front End Processor
FSP	File Service Processes
GB	Gigabyte
GIGO	Garbage In Garbage Out
GPI	General Protection Interrupt
HDLC	High-level Data-Link Control
IATA	International Air Transport Association
ICAO	International Civil Aviation Organization
IDE	Integrated Drive Electronics
IMS	Information Management System (IBM Specific)
ISAM	Indexed Sequential Access Method (IBM Specific)
IMP	Interface Meassage Processor (node in Internet network)
INT	Interrupt, usually refers to a software interrupt
I/O	Input/Output
IOCTL	Input/Output ConTroL
IPX	Internetwork Packet eXchange, a protocol used by Novell, derived from Xerox's XNS standard
IRQ	Interrupt ReQuest line, usually refers to a hardware interrupt
ISA	Industry Standard Architecture
ISO	International Standards Organization
K	Kilobyte (1024 bytes)
KB	Kilobyte (1024 bytes)
Kb	Kilobit (1024 bits)
Kb/s	Kilobits per second
LAA	Locally Administered Address

LAN	Local Area Network
LAP	Link Access Protocol
LAPB	Link Access Protocol Balanced
LSB	Least Significant Bit
LSL	Link Support Layer
MAN	Metropolitan Area Network
MB	MegaByte, (1,048,576 bytes)
Mb	Megabit (1,048,576 bits)
Mb/s	Megabits per second
MCA	MicroChannel Architecture (IBM specific)
MFM	Modified Frequency Modulation
MHz	Megahertz
MHS	Message Handling Service
MIPS	Millions of Intructions per Second
MLID	Multiple Link Interface Driver
μs	microsecond
ms	Millisecond
MSB	Most Significant Bit
MVS	Memory Virtual System (IBM Specific)
MVS/XA	Memory Virtual System/eXtended Architecture (IBM Specific)
NAP	Network Access Protocol
NAR	NetWare Async Router
NARR	NetWare Async Remote Router
NetBIOS	Network Basic Input/Output System
NFS	Network File System
NLM	NetWare Loadable Module
NIC	Network Interface Card
NOS	Network Operating System
NSF	National Science Foundation
nybble	4 bits (half a byte)
ODI	Open Data-Link Interface

OS	Operating System
OSI	Open Systems Integration
PAD	Packet Assembler/Disassembler
PARC	Palo Alto Research Center
PC	Personal Computer
PDU	Protocol Data Unit
POST	Power On Self Test
PROM	Programmable Read Only Memory
PVC	PolyVinyl Chloride
RAM	Random Access Memory
RFNM	Ready-For-Next-Message, pronounced 'rufnum' (used in ARPANET, which is now Internet)
RJE	Remote Job Entry
RLL	Run Length Limited
ROM	Read-Only Memory
RPL	Remote Procedure Load (IBM specific)
SAP	Server Advertising Protocol
SDLC	Synchronous Data-Link Control (IBM specific)
SFT	System Fault Tolerant
SCSI	Small Computer Systems Interface
SMD	Storage Module Device
SNA	Systems Network Architecture (IBM specific)
SPP	Sequenced Packet Protocol
SPS	Standby Power System
SPX	Sequenced Packet eXchange (Novell's derivation of Xerox's SPP)
SWIFT	Society for Worldwide Interbank Financial Transactions
TCAM	TeleCommunications Access Method (IBM specific)
TCPIP	Transmission Control Protocol/InterNet Protocol
TDR	Time Domain Reflectometer
TIP	Terminal Interface Processor (node w/no host in Internet)

TP	Twisted Pair
TRN	Token-Ring Network
TSR	Terminate and Stay Resident
TTS	Transaction Tracking System
UDLC	Universal Data Link Control (from Sperry)
UPS	Uninterruptable Power Supply
UTP	Unshielded Twisted Pair
VADD	Value-Added Disk Driver
VAP	Value-Added Process
VAR	Value-Added Reseller
VAX	Virtual Address eXtension (DEC)
VLSI	Very-Large-Scale Integration
VMS	Virtual Memory System
VTAM	Virtual Terminal Access Method (IBM specific)
WAN	Wide Area Network
WORM	Write Once, Read Many times (type of optical disk drive)
WSTN	Workstation
X.25	Interface between data terminal equipment and data circuit-terminating equipment for terminal operating in the packet mode on public data networks
XNS	Xerox Network System

APPENDIX C

History of NetWire

The first implementation of a Novell on-line support forum BEGAN in April of 1986. It was available on The SOURCE and it was called NetWire. As it turned out, the SOURCE was not the most effective public access medium (both in terms of cost and ease of use) and Novell did little to promote NetWire usage or to nurture it. After about a year of minimal usage, Novell began reevaluating NetWire and the SOURCE as its host. In November of 1987, after two months of analysis and proposals, NetWire officially moved to CompuServe. The benefits Novell cited in moving NetWire to CompuServe included:

1. Improved on-line response time
2. Lower daytime usage rates
3. On-line sign-up (previously took two to three weeks)
4. Lower sign-up costs
5. Optional elimination of monthly minimums
6. Increased revenues (An $8/hr surcharge, which Novell planned to use to subsidize their LANSWER support team, was added to NetWire when it moved to CompuServe.)

Having moved to CompuServe on November 15, 1987, NetWire also remained on the SOURCE until December 31, 1987 to permit a smooth transition. In perspective, the "forum" on the SOURCE handled about five messages in a good month and so this redundancy was hardly necessary.

During the initial months of the CompuServe NetWire, users scorned Novell for the $8/hr surcharge. The International NetWare Users Advisory Board (now NetWare Users International) took up the cause on behalf of all NetWare users. Things began to progress a bit, and at the 4th Annual Developers' Conference in February of 1987, the INU, with Glenn Fund at the lead, scheduled discussions with Novell to either drop the additional fee or to create a new, unsurcharged forum. The compromise proposal that emerged was to leave the existing forum (and surcharge) in place for "guaranteed 24-hour, official Novell responses." In addition, a new user-to-user forum would be created that would be sanctioned by Novell, but would be administered by users and would not incorporate any surcharge. The INU reasoned that increased usage would make up for any lost revenue. The key Novell contact for NetWire at that time was Jared Blaser, one of the original Novell employees. Graig Taylor, Novell's Senior VP for User and Government Relations, was the internal sponsor for the INU position.

Continued efforts of Graig Taylor and Glenn Fund to establish a new users' forum finally gained the necessary corporate support within Novell. Mr. Fund was given the task of querying NetWire users, asking for new user SysOp volunteers, and making recommendations to Mr. Taylor. As a result of these efforts, five user systems operators (SysOps) were selected: Glenn Fund, Jeff Grammer, Dave Kearns, Bart Mellink and John McCann. All were invited to PC EXPO in New York in June of 1988 for an intensive planning session, where details of the new users' forum would be worked out. Four of the five volunteer SysOps were there to meet with the necessary parties from within Novell and CompuServe. The meeting adjourned with the initial sections and libraries outlined.

A good part of July 1988 was spent preparing the forum using CompuServe's tool kit. With coding complete, an initial pre-production announcement of the new forum, NOVUSER, was made to some of the patrons of the existing NetWire forum, NOVFOR. Initially, forum membership was "by invitation only," meaning users had to request admittance, which would then be granted or denied by one of the SysOps.

Initial announcements of NOVFOR began to appear, and additional comments on NOVFOR led a number of users to request membership in NOVUSER. All who asked were granted access, and the new forum soon became a viable complement to NOVFOR. In September of 1988, Novell had completed all of the contractual obligations necessary for CompuServe to turn on automatic user "join." This is the normal situation with CompuServe forums. At this time, Novell also posted an official notice that NOVUSER was open to the public.

Users were encouraged to try the new NOVUSER forum via personal E-mail (EasyPlex) and NOVFOR messages. By the end of September, the new NOVUSER forum had as much daily traffic (sometimes more) as NOVFOR. At that point, the five designated user SysOps had reduced their ongoing support of NOVFORUM and attended to the growing demand within NOVUSER.

In October and November of 1988, NOVFOR eliminated most of the files in its libraries because NOVUSER had a duplicate set of files in its unsurcharged libraries. Files remaining in the surcharged NOVFOR were drivers and utilities that were only available from Novell at a cost.

Support from Novell on NOVFOR declined during this period. Novell had not augmented the efforts of Doug Baird, who now was the only Novell employee officially assigned to this task. Users again were beginning to take up some of the slack, although many questions began to go unanswered. Many users preferred to get their user-to-user answers in the unsurcharged and much more active NOVUSER forum.

Novell also had not encouraged use of the new NOVUSER forum, other than at largely overlooked events at NetWorld '88 and a very small footnote in PC Week. NOVUSER had not received the publicity that it deserved. The success of NOVUSER was the direct result of the technical efforts of each of the volunteer SysOps.

In early December of 1988, Novell began to see the light. They decided that users were important and that their talents could significantly enhance Novell's limited support resources, products, and bottom line. *LAN Times*, Novell's monthly publication for NetWare users, requested that the SysOps send them the "top questions" posted during the past month to be included in a new user's section of the publication, which first ran in January of 1989. This small amount of publicity for

NOVUSER, with examples of what it could do to support NetWare users, was responsible for a noticeable increase in users.

Because CompuServe only allowed 999 active messages per forum, it became necessary to split NetWire into three forums at the time. (Compuserve has since modified its software to allow several thousand active messages per forum.) In late 1989, the latest version of the NetWire forums debuted. The forums are named NOVA, which contains all library files, NOVB, and NOVC. To see a list of the topics available on any of the three forums, type the command NAMES at the first NetWire prompt.

With these changes in place, the future is bright for the continued growth of NetWire. In addition, increased on-line and SysOp backup support by LANSWER and each of Novell's product groups has also been promised to bolster Novell's presence on NetWire. While some questions still go unanswered, the forum has provided quite a bit in the way of technical support and promises to remain an invaluable source of information for NetWare users and supporters.

NetWire continues to grow. On CompuServe, Novell is finally offering a hotline to answer technical support questions on the forums which now include NETW2X, NETW3X, NOVDEV, NOVVEN, etc. The "original" NOVA/B/C are still there though their specific duties have changed. Note that NOVDEV, which was opened March 31, 1991, is a developer-specific forum and requires specific permission to be allowed to join it. Being a member of Novell's Professional Developer Program (PDP) allows immediate access as long as Novell knows your CompuServe ID. Contact Novell at 76701,171 to submit your request for access to NOVDEV

By the way, you can contact me, John T. McCann, at 70007,3430, and on the Internet: "70007.3430@compuserve.com" (without the quotes). And this revision (the fifth!) of the *NetWare Supervisor's Guide* is dedicated to my son, NLM (that's Nicholas Lee to you uninitiated!). Remember that NetWare computing is constantly changing and that NetWire remains the sole source for the most current information, both from the field and from the source.

APPENDIX D

Hardware Ready Reference Guide

Novell's Hardware Ready Reference Guide is an invaluable addition to the technical library that no LAN supervisor should be without. Currently in Revision 1.01, this manual is a quick reference for Novell hardware. It is not intended to be a complete guide for installing or troubleshooting, but simply a concise, common source for the settings of the wide variety of Novell hardware.

Figure D-1 provides a condensed table of contents for the Guide. It is spiral bound, so new pages can't currently be added, but there is sufficient white space on each page and extra blank pages at the end of each section to leave personal notes.

NetWare File Servers
68A Server
68B Server
286A Server
286B Server
386A and 386AE Servers

Disk Drives and Disk Interface Boards
DIB and DCB
Disk Controllers
Disk Drives
Tape Controllers

Communication Boards
WNIM Settings

NetWare Interface Cards
S-Net
RXNet
Ethernet
G/Net
Token-Ring
ProNet
Node Address Settings

Miscellaneous Information
Common Devices
Port Pinouts
BIOS Tables

Figure D-1. Topics in Novell's Hardware Ready Reference Guide

The Hardware Ready Reference Guide is rich with clean, simple illustrations, providing everything from the PAL and jumper locations on a Disk Co-processor Board (DCB), as shown in Figure D-2, to charts presenting the proper settings for boards, as shown in Figure D-3. It also has one of the most extensive listings of common devices and their configurations (a similar but expanded version of Figure 3-4) that can be found anywhere.

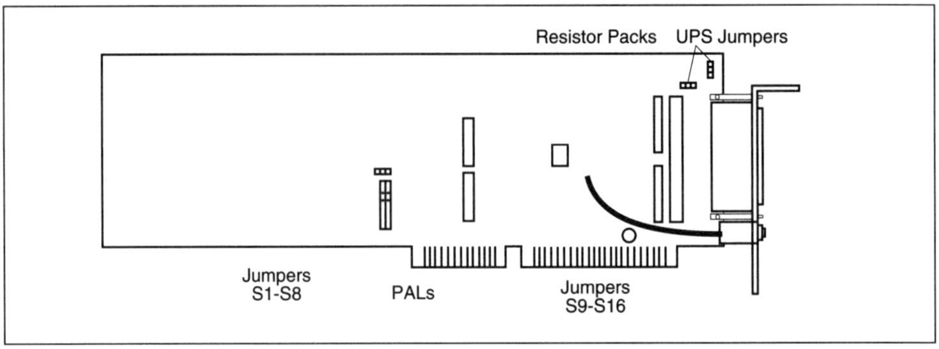

Figure D-2. Disk Co-processor Board

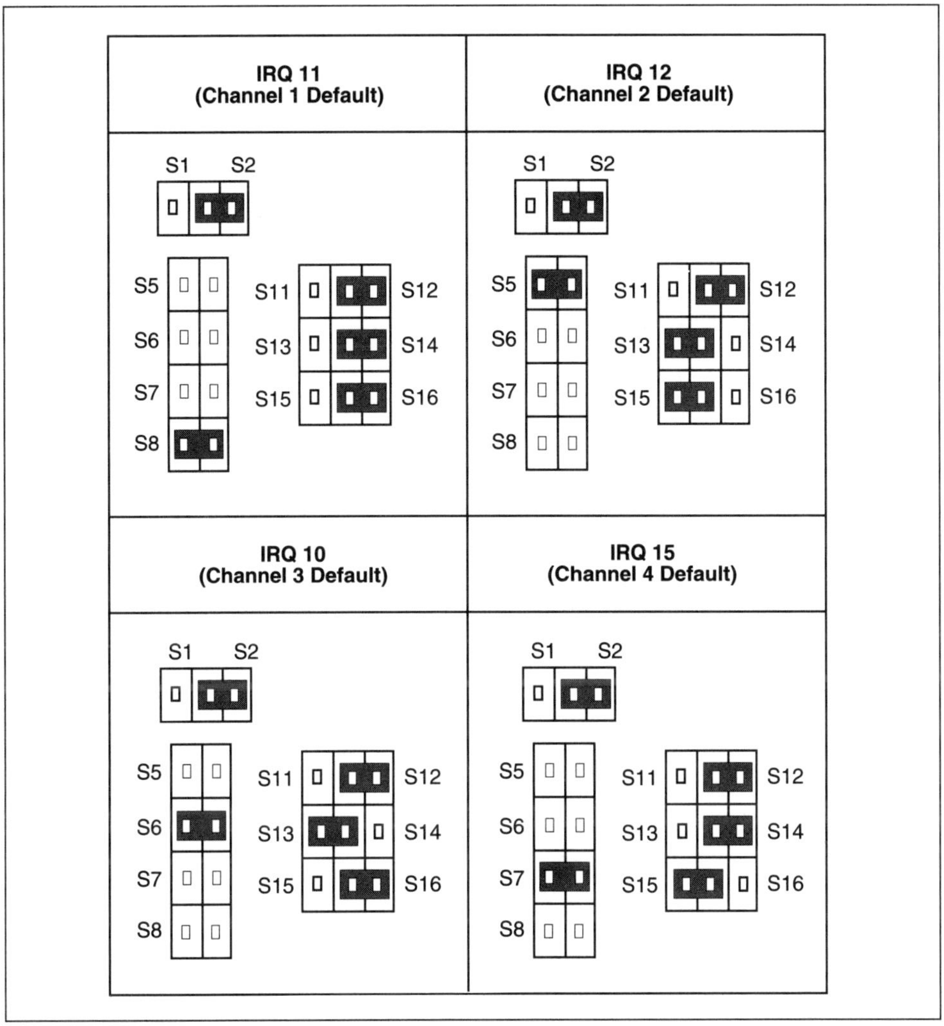

Figure D-3. Disk Co-processor Board IRQ settings

A copy of this guide can be acquired by contacting Novell and requesting document number 100-000385-001. It is also provided with other course materials as part of the Certified NetWare Engineer training courses.

APPENDIX E

Selected Manufacturers of LAN Products

AST Research, Inc.
16215 Alton Parkway
P.O. Box 57005
Irvine, CA 92619-7005
(800) 876-4278

Adaptec
691 S. Milpitas Blvd.
Milpitas, CA 95035
(800) 934-2766

Advanced Computer Communications
10261 Bubb Road
Cupertino, CA 95014
(800) 444-7854

All Computers, Inc.
1220 Yonge St., Second Fl.
Toronto, Ontario
Canada M4T 1W1
(800) 627-4825

Alloy Computer Products, Inc.
25 Porter Road
Littleton, MA 01460-1410
(800) 800-2556

Apple Computer, Inc.
20525 Mariani Ave.
Cupertino, CA 95014
(800) 776-2333

Artisoft, Inc.
691 E. River Road
Tucson, AZ 85704
(800) 846-9726

Attachmate Corporation
3617 131st Ave., SE
Bellevue, WA 98006
(800) 426-6283

Award Software, Inc.
130 Knowles Drive
Los Gatos, CA 95030
(408) 370-7979

Banyan Systems, Inc.
120 Flanders Road
Westboro, MA 01581
(800) 828-2404

Black Box Corporation
P.O. Box 12800
Pittsburg, PA 15241-0800
(800) 552-6816

Blue Lance
1700 West Loop South
Ste. 1100
Houston, TX 77027
(713) 680-1187

Brightwork Development, Inc.
766 Shrewsbury Ave.
Jerral Center West
Tinton Falls, NJ 07724
(800) 552-9876

BSG, Inc.
11 Greenway Plaza, Ste. 900
Houston, TX 77046-1102
(713) 965-9000

CBIS, Inc.
5875 Peachtree Ind. Blvd.
Bldg. 100, Ste. 170
Norcross, GA 30092
404) 446-1332

cc:Mail, Inc.
2141 Landings Drive
Mountain View, CA 94043
(800) 448-2500

CMS Enhancements, Inc.
2722 Michelson Drive
Irvine, CA 92715
(714) 222-6000

Cheyenne Software, Inc.
55 Bryant Ave.
Roslyn, NY 11576
(800) 243-9462

cisco Systems, Inc.
1525 O'Brien Drive
P.O. Box 3075
Menlo Park, CA 94026-1435
(800) 553-6387

Colorado Memory Systems, Inc.
800 S. Taft Ave.
Loveland, CO 80537
(800) 432-5858

COMPAQ Computer Corp.
20555 SH 249
P.O. Box 692000
Houston, TX 77269-2000
(800) 345-1518

CompuAdd Corporation
12303 Technology Blvd.
Austin, TX 78727
(800) 456-3116

Computer Associates International, Inc.
One Computer Associates Plaza
Islandia, NY 11788-7000
(800) 225-5224

Concept Development Systems
P.O. Box 1988
Kennesaw, GA 30144
(404) 424-8995

Core International
7171 N. Federal Highway
Boca Raton, FL 33487
(800) 688-9910

Corel Systems, Inc.
1600 Carling Ave.
Ottawa, Ontario,
Canada K1Z 8R7
(800) 836-7274

Corvus Systems, Inc.
160 Great Oaks Blvd.
San Jose, CA 95119
(408) 281-4100

DCA
1000 Alderman Drive
Alpharetta, GA 30201-4199
(404) 442-4000

Data Interface Systems Corp.
8701 N. Mopac Expressway, Ste. 415
Austin, TX 78759
(800) 351-4244

Datapoint Corporation
8400 Datapoint Drive
San Antonio, TX 78229-8500
(800) 334-9968

Da Vinci Systems Corp.
P.O. Box 17449
Raleigh, NC 27619-7449
(800) 328-4624

Digital Equipment Corporation
146 Main St.
Maynard, MA 01754-2571
(508) 493-5111

Eicon Technology Corporation
14755 Preston Road, Ste. 620
Dallas, TX 75240
(214) 239-3270

Elgar Corporation
9250 Brown Deer Road
San Diego, CA 92121
(800) 733-5427

Enterprise Technology Center
11 Greenway Plaza, Ste. 900
Houston, TX 77046-1102
(713) 965-9000

Everex Sytems, Inc.
901 Page Ave.
Fremont, CA 94538
(800) 821-0806

Exabyte Corporation
1685 38th St.
Boulder, CO 80301-9803
(800) 392-2983

Fresh Technology Group
1478 N. Tech Blvd
Ste. 101
Gilbert, AZ 85234
(800) 793-7374

Fujitsu Computer Products of America, Inc.
3055 Orchard Drive
San Jose, CA 95134-2022
(800) 626-4686

Future Domain Corporation
2801 McGaw Ave.
Irvine, CA 92714
(800) 879-7599

Gateway Comminications, Inc.
2941 Alton Ave.
Irvine, CA 92714
(800) 367-6555

GigaTrend, Incorporated
2234 Rutherford Road
Carlsbad, CA 92008
(619) 931-9122

Hayes Microcomputer Products, Inc.
5923 Peachtree Industrial Blvd.
Norcross, GA 30092
(404) 840-9200

Hercules Computer Technology, Inc.
3839 Spinnaker Court
Fremont, CA 94538
(800) 532-0600

Hyundai Electronics America
166 Baypointe Parkway
San Jose, CA 95134
(800) 727-6972

International Business Machines (IBM)
Old Orchard Road
Armonk, NY 10504
(800) 426-3333

IDEAssociates, Inc.
29 Dunham Road
Billerica, MA 01821
(800) 257-5027

Intel Corporation
P.O. Box 58119
2200 Mission College Blvd.
Santa Clara, CA 95052-8119
(800) 346-3028

J & L Information Systems, Inc.
9238 Deering Ave.
Chatsworth, CA 91311
(818) 709-1778

J.A. Lomax Associates
15 Jackson Court
Novato, CA 94947
(800) 225-6629

Lotus Development Corporation
55 Cambridge Parkway
Cambridge, MA 02142
(800) 343-5414

M/H Group
300 W. Adams St.
Chicago, IL 60606
(312) 443-1222

Maxtor Corporation
211 River Oaks Parkway
San Jose, CA 95008
(800) 262-9867

Maynard Electronics
36 Skyline Drive
Lake Mary, FL 32746
(800) 821-8782

Meridian Data, Inc.
5615 Scotts Valley Drive
Scotts Valley, CA 95066
(800) 767-2537

Meridian Technology Corp.
11 McBride Corporate Center Drive,
Ste. 250
Chesterfield, MO 63005-1406
(314) 532-7708

MICOM Communications Corp.
4100 Los Angeles Ave.
Simi Valley, CA 93063
(800) 642-6687

Micro House
4900 Pearl East Circle, Ste. 101
Boulder, CO 80301
(800) 926-8299

Microsoft Corporation
One Microsoft Way
Redmond, WA 98052-6399
(800) 426-9400

MicroTest, Inc.
4747 N. 22nd St.
Phoenix, AZ 85016-4708
(800) 526-9675

Miramar Systems, Inc.
201 N. Salsipuedes, Ste. 204
Santa Barbara, CA 93103
(800) 862-2526

Mountain Network Solutions, Inc.
240 E. Hacienda Ave.
Campbell, CA 95008-6623
(800) 458-0300

NCR Corporation
1700 S. Patterson Blvd.
Dayton, OH 45479
(800) 225-5627

NetWare Advisor
c/o The Cobb Group
9420 Bunsen Parkway, #300
Louisville, KY 40220
(800) 223-8720

Netwise, Inc.
2477 55th St.
Boulder, CO 80301
(800) 733-7722

Network General Corporation
4200 Bohannon Drive
Menlo Park, CA 94025
(800) 695-8251

Network Products Corp.
1440 W. Colorado Blvd.
Pasadena, CA 91105
(800) 638-7765

NetWorth, Inc.
8404 Esters Road
Irving, TX 75063
(800) 544-5255

Norton-Lambert Corporation
P.O. Box 4085
Santa Barbara, CA 93140
(805) 964-6767

Novell, Inc.
122 E. 1700 S.
Provo, UT 84606-6194
(800) 453-1267

NuMega Technologies
PO Box 7780
Nashua, NH 03060-7780
(603) 889-2386

Ontrack Computer Systems, Inc.
6321 Bury Drive
Stes. 15-19
Eden Prairie, MN 55346
(800) 752-1333

Palindrome Corporation
600 E. Diehl Road
Naperville, IL 60563
(708) 505-3300

Persoft, Inc.
465 Science Drive
P.O. Box 44953
Madison, WI 53744-4953
(800) 368-5283

Phoenix Technologies, Ltd.
846 University Ave.
Norwood, MA 02062-3950
(800) 344-7200

PRIAM Systems Corporation
1140 Ringwood Court
San Jose, CA 95131
(408) 954-8680

Prime Computer, Inc.
100 Crosby Road
Bedford, MA 01730
(800) 349-2540

ProComp USA, Inc.
6777 Engle Road
Cleveland, OH 44130
(216) 234-6387

Proteon, Inc.
9 Technology Drive
Westborough, MA 01581-1799
(800) 545-7464

Pure Data, Inc.
1740 S. I-35
Carrollton, TX 75006
(214) 242-2040

Qualitas
7101 Wisconsin Ave.
Ste. 1386
Bethesda, MD 20814
(800) 733-1377

Quarterdeck Office Systems
150 Pico Blvd.
Santa Monica, CA 90405
(800) 354-3222

RG Software Systems, Inc.
6900 E. Camelback, Ste. 630
Scottsdale, AZ 85251
(602) 423-8000

RYBS Electronics, Inc.
3109 28th St.
P.O. Box 4521
Boulder, CO 80301
(303) 444-6073

Rabbit Software Corporation
7 Great Valley Parkway E.
Malvern, PA 19355
(800) 722-2482

Racore Computer Products, Inc.
170 Knowles Drive, Ste. 204
Los Gatos, CA 95030
(800) 635-1274

Rodime Systems, Inc.
7700 W. Camino Real, Second Fl.
Boca Raton, FL 33433
(800) 277-4144

Saber Software Corp.
5944 Luther Lane, Ste. 1007
Dallas, TX 75225
(800) 338-8743

Samsung Information Systems, Inc.
3655 N. First St.
San Jose, CA 95134-1708
(408) 434-5400

Seagate Technology
920 Disc Drive
Scotts Valley, CA 95066
(800) 468-3472

Soft-Switch, Inc.
640 Lee Road
Wayne, PA 19087
(215) 640-9600

Standard Microsystems Corporation
80 Arkay Drive
Hauppauge, NY 11788
(800) 762-4968

Storage Dimensions, Inc.
1656 McCarthy Blvd.
Milpitas, CA 95035
(800) 765-7895

Sun Microsystems, Inc.
2550 Garcia Ave.
Mountain View, CA 94043
(800) 821-4643

Symantech-DMA
1776 E. Jericho Turnpike
Huntington, NY 11743
(516) 462-0440

Symantech-Peter Norton Group
2500 Broadway
Santa Monica, CA 90404
(310) 453-4600

SynOptics Communications, Inc.
P.O. Box 58185
4401 Great America Parkway
Santa Clara, CA 95052-8185
(800) 776-6895

Sytron Corporation
134 Flanders Road
Westboro, MA 01581
(508) 898-0100

Tektronix, Inc.
P.O. Box 1000, M/S 63-630
26600 SW Parkway
Wilsonville, OR 97070
(800) 835-6100

Thomas-Conrad Corporation
1908-R Kramer Lane
Austin, TX 78758
(800) 332-8683

3Com Corporation
P.O. Box 58145
5400 Bayfront Plaza
Santa Clara, CA 95052-8145
(800) 638-3266

Tiara/10Net
7777 Washington Village Drive
Dayton, OH 45459-3957
(513) 433-2238

TurboPower Software
P.O. Box 49009
Colorado Springs, CO 80949-9009
(800) 333-4160

Ungermann-Bass, Inc.
P.O. Box 58030
3900 Freedom Circle
Santa Clara, CA 95052-8030
(800) 777-4526

Vitalink Communications Corp.
48761 Kato Road
Fremont, CA 94538
(800) 443-5740

Walker Richer and Quinn, Inc.
2815 Eastlake Ave., E
Seattle, WA 98102
(800) 872-2829

Western Digital
8105 Irvine Center Drive
Irvine, CA 92718
(800) 832-4778

Wollongong Group, Inc.
P.O. Box 51860
1129 San Antonio Road
Palo Alto, CA 94303
(800) 872-8649

WordPerfect Corporation
1555 N. Technology Way
Orem, UT 84057
(800) 451-5151

XTree Company
4115 Broad St., Bldg. 1
San Luis Obispo, CA 93401-7993
(800) 876-6368

Xerox Corporation
P.O. Box 24
Rochester, NY 14692
(800) 832-6979

APPENDIX F

The OSI Model

A variety of international standards are defined by the International Standards Organization (ISO). The American National Standards Institute (ANSI) represents the United States to ISO. The most notable contribution of ISO in the data communications world is the Open Systems Interconnection (OSI) Reference Model.

The OSI Reference Model

ISO undertook development of a reference model for computer communication protocols in 1978, and published the OSI Reference Model in 1984. Figure F-1 shows the familiar seven-layer model. Each of the seven layers are described separately in the following sections.

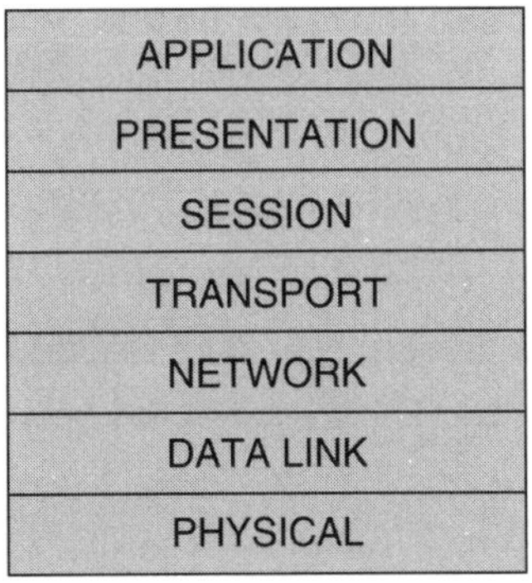

Figure F-1. The seven-layer OSI Reference Model

Physical Layer

The physical layer is the most fundamental layer in the OSI Model. It is the interface to the physical medium and provides standards for electrical, mechanical, and functional transmission parameters.

Data Link Layer

The data link layer deals with procedures and services related to the transfer of data from node to node. Its main purpose is to ensure error-free delivery of data packets from a point-to-point network viewpoint. Hence, it is concerned with such problems as error detection, error correction, and retransmission. However, since the data link layer is highly dependent upon the physical medium, there is not a universal protocol at this level. Individual protocols include HDLC for point-to-point and multipoint connections, as well as IEEE 802.2 with Media Access Control (MAC) and/or Logical Link Control (LCC) for Local Area Networks (LANs).

Network Layer

The network layer ensures that a packet generated at the source arrives at its destination in a reasonable amount of time. Therefore, this layer handles routing procedures as well as flow control functions. It hides the physical implementation of the network from the upper layers that need not know whether fiber optics, LANs, or satellite communications are used. Hence, it creates a media-independent transmission from the point of view of the upper layers.

Transport Layer

The transport layer is the lowest among the layers that only provide services locally for an end user. It ensures that the lower three layers are providing adequate services for application communication, as far as the transmission medium and the information flow are concerned. The transport layer creates a logical transparent "pipe" between end users.

Session Layer

The session layer controls communication between applications. It is responsible for ensuring synchronization so data exchange is performed in an orderly manner. Two-way simultaneous and two-way alternate communication are allowed by the session layer.

Presentation Layer

The presentation layer deals with the differences in data representation between communicating applications. A syntax is provided by this layer so that any application can understand the content of the piece of information received.

Application Layer

The application layer is the only one that does not provide any service to another layer. it deals with the user applications and handles communication at a semantics level. The application layer is concerned with problems such as interprocess communication, file transfer, virtual terminal and manipulation services, and job transfer and broadcast communication.

APPENDIX G

A TCP/IP Primer

Transmission Control Protocol/Internet Protocol (TCP/IP) is an entire suite of protocols originated by Vinton Cerf at Stanford University in the early 1970s. Its development was sponsored by the Advanced Research Projects Agency (ARPA) and the Department of Defense (DOD). TCP/IP represents two different levels of communications. IP relates to physical layers, while TCP relates to session layers, which means that TCP specifies the services IP provides (see Figure G-1).

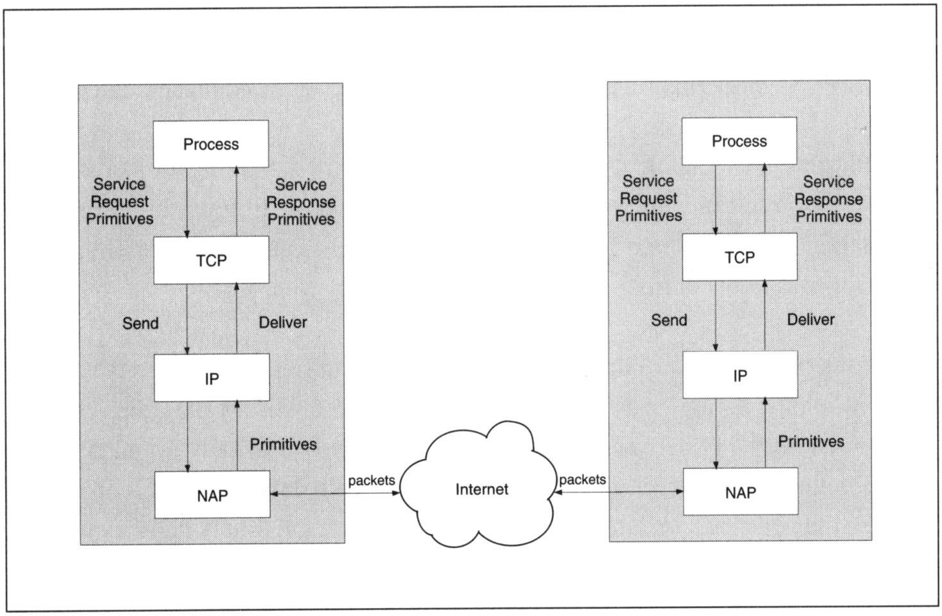

Figure G-1. Use of TCP and IP service primitives

Internet Protocol

IP was developed to interconnect heterogeneous networks, thereby allowing nodes on different networks to communicate. IP, which is also recognized by the nomenclature DOD IP, MIL-STD-1777, resides between the Transport and Network layers of the OSI model and is, therefore, hardware independent.

IP provides for connectionless service between nodes or hosts. IP involves datagrams and so does not develop a logical connection between nodes, nor does it guarantee that the data packet (datagrams) will be delivered. As is also the nature of datagrams, the order in which data packets are received is not necessarily the same as the order in which they are transmitted.

By providing connectionless service, IP does offer a number of benefits:

Robustness. Each datagram (data packet) is routed independently through the network or internetwork by virtual paths. This allows each datagram to be routed individually along the best possible path, including around nodes that are out of service. For this reason, datagrams can arrive at their destination in any order.

Adaptability. IP can be operated across disjointed network services, i.e., networks such as those that offer connection-oriented service and those that do not.

Modular. TCP can be used in conjunction with IP for applications requiring routing, flow control, and connection-oriented protocols. IP provides definitions for datagram life, datagram fragmentation and defragmentation, addressing, routing, error, and flow control.

Datagram life. Every datagram has an upper limit on its lifetime that determines when the datagram is removed from the internetwork. Datagrams that are transported normally between source and destination will usually not be affected by this boundary. However, the possibility exists that a datagram will loop indefinitely in the network, consuming resources, preventing the timely delivery of data, and even halting network operations. The boundary on lifetime eventually eliminates these infinitely looping datagrams.

Timely delivery is achieved through the use of TCP with IP; this is discussed further under the TCP heading.

Datagram Fragmentation. Due to IP's versatile nature, specifically its ability to utilize heterogeneous networks, datagrams may be divided into fragments according to the physical limitations of intervening networks. IP does not define a standard packet (datagram) size. As a datagram can continually be fragmented during its journey, defragmentation occurs at the destination node. Defragmentation is not performed at intervening gateways. This would require buffers to absorb all of the pieces of a datagram and would prevent the use of dynamic routing (as all packets would have to be gathered at some intermediary point to be reassembled).

Each datagram (whole or fragmented) has a header that indicates an ID, data length, offset, and a *more* flag. The ID is used to uniquely identify the originating node, and includes the source and destination addresses of the datagram and a sequence number. The data length is the size of the data field in bytes. The offset is the position of the fragment in the original datagram, as indicated in multiples of 64 bits. The *more* flag is a boolean indicator that indicates if more fragments are to follow. For instance, the original datagram (before it is transmitted) would have a data length equal to the length of the datagram's entire data field and would have an offset of 0 with the *more* flag set to "false."

IP does not guarantee delivery. It is quite possible that a datagram or a fragment of a datagram will not arrive at the destination node. IP requires that the lifetime be indicated in the header of each datagram or fragment. As a fragment is received, a timer based on the datagram's lifetime starts to count down. As each subsequent fragment is received, the timer is incremented by the lifetime of that fragment. If the timer expires before all fragments are received, the entire datagram is rejected.

Addressing. IP uses the hardware addressing scheme of the underlying network. IP does not concern itself with the correct destination address, although it does support the source address. The destination address is handed down from higher level protocols, such as TCP.

Routing. Each IP node and gateway maintains a routing table that indicates the best node or gateway route for each datagram to follow. These routing tables can either be static or dynamic. Static tables generally include alternate routes, in case the primary route is unavailable. Dynamic routing tables work by maintaining current information about the network. If a gateway becomes unavailable, nodes or gateways that were using it will send out messages to other nodes and gateways indicating that the gateway is down.

IP also allows for source routing. In this type of routing, the transmitting node defines a list of gateways in the datagram. This list indicates the route that will provide security or priority for the datagram. IP can also use route recording, in which each node the datagram visits on its journey has its address appended to the end of the datagram. This allows for network analysis and debugging. Note that this type of source routing differs from the type used in IBM's Token-Ring. IP's source routing resides in the network and transport layers of the OSI model, whereas IBM's resides in the data link layer. (This type of routing is further detailed in Chapter 7.)

Error Control. Although the IP does not guarantee delivery, there is an error control facility for rejected datagrams. When a datagram is refused because its lifetime has expired, the receiving node (if the underlying network configuration allows it) will attempt to return information concerning the discarded datagram to the originating node. Datagrams may also be discarded if an error is detected in the datagram. However, due to the bit error, the datagram may not have the recognizable ID to identify the datagram and its source.

Flow Control. IP alone does not specify flow control. The Internet Control Message Protocol (ICMP), which resides in the same layers as IP but is, in fact, a user of IP, provides flow control. Detailed information on ICMP messages is provided later in this appendix. The following illustrates the initiation and transmission of an IP datagram:

1. The sending node constructs the IP datagram based on the SEND PRIMITIVES received.
2. The checksum is calculated and inserted into the IP datagram.
3. The route is determined. The datagram moves toward its destination either directly or via an intervening gateway.
4. The IP datagram is passed to the data link and physical layers for delivery. At each gateway:

5. The datagram performs the checksum calculation. If the calculated checksum does not match the one in the datagram, the datagram is purged from the network.
6. The datagram lifetime counter is decremented. If the time has expired, the datagram is purged from the network.
7. The gateway decides where the datagram will be routed next.
8. The datagram is fragmented if necessary.
9. The IP header is reconstructed to reflect the new datagram lifetime, fragmentation, and new checksums.
10. The IP datagram is passed to the data link and physical layers for delivery.
11. At the destination node, the checksum is calculated. If the calculated checksum does not match the one contained in the datagram, the packet is purged.
12. If the datagram received is a fragment, it is buffered in anticipation of the receipt of the remaining fragments. When all of the fragments have been received, the datagram is reassembled. If the lifetime counter expires during reassembly, the datagram is purged.
13. If the datagram arrives successfully, the data and parameters are passed up to the higher layers (TCP).

ICMP Messages

Each of the nine types of ICMP messages are discussed below. They are:

- Destination unreachable
- Echo
- Echo reply
- Parameter problem
- Redirect
- Source quench
- Time exceeded
- Timestamp
- Timestamp reply

Each of these messages has five fields, as described in Figure G-2.

Field	Size (bytes)	Explanation
Type	1	the type of ICMP message
Code	1	parameters of the message
Checksum	2	checksum of entire ICMP message
Parameters	4	any necessary parameters
Information	n	additional message information

Figure G-2. ICMP message fields

The destination unreachable message can indicate one of several conditions, including:

- A datagram defines a route that is unavailable.
- A node determines that the user protocol or another high-level protocol is unavailable.
- A gateway determines that the destination is unreachable.
- The gateway cannot determine how to route the datagram to its destination.
- A datagram has its don't fragment indicator on and an intervening gateway needs to fragment the datagram.

The first 8 bytes of the IP header are returned in the *data unreachable* message.

The echo and echo reply messages are used to test communication between two nodes. The originating node sends an echo message and the destination node sends back an echo reply message. The first 8 bytes of the IP header are returned in this message.

The parameter problem message indicates a semantic or syntactic error in the header of a datagram. The parameter field includes a pointer to the header location at which the error is suspected. The first 8 bytes of the header are returned.

The redirect message is sent by a gateway to indicate to the sending node that a quicker route can be obtained by sending the data via another gateway. The gateway will then forward the original datagram to its destination. The address of the alternate gateway (contained in the parameter field) and the first 8 bytes of the original datagram header are returned in the redirect message.

The source quench message provides primitive flow control. A gateway or a node may send this message to the sending node. The source quench message is a request to decrease the rate at which datagrams are being sent. The first 8 bytes of the offending datagram are sent to the originating node.

The time exceeded message is sent by a node to indicate that the lifetime of the datagram has expired before its delivery was complete and its first 8 bytes are returned.

The timestamp and timestamp reply messages are used to sample delay characteristics of the intervening network between two nodes. The originating timestamp is included in the information field. The receiving node appends its timestamp and returns the message as a timestamp reply.

Transmission Control Protocol

Transmission Control Protocol (TCP) was originally developed for use in ARPANET and is now used as the transport protocol standard for the U.S. Department of Defense (DOD). TCP has also been combined with IP (TCP/IP) to provide a *de facto* standard protocol for heterogeneous node communications. Acceptance of TCP/IP following DOD acceptance is outlined in Figure G-3.

Year	Companies Accepting TCP/IP
1983	Berkeley, Excelan and Sun Microsystems
1984	Wollongong and CMC
1985	Bridge Communications, NRC and Siemens
1986	Novell, DEC, Ungermann-Bass and Interlan
1987	IBM and Sytek
1988	Microsoft, Apple and NCR

Figure G-3. TCP/IP momentum since 1983

'TCP resides in the transport layer of the OSI model. It receives data to be delivered from upper layer protocols and provides reliable transportation of the data, in segments, to its destination. TCP is a connection-oriented protocol and provides the following services: connection, data transport, multiplexing, flow control, expedited delivery and receipt, and error reporting.

TCP's services are provided by a set of primitives and parameters. Figures G-4, G-5, and G-6 illustrate the use of TCP's Request and Response Primitives and Service Parameters.

PRIMITIVE	PARAMETERS	DESCRIPTION
Unspecified Passive Open	source port, [timeout], [timeout-action], [precedence], [security-range]	Listen for connection attempt at specified security and precedence from any remote destination
Fully Specified Passive Open	source port, destination port, destination address [timeout], [timeout-action], [precedence], [security-range]	Listen for connection attempt at specified security and precedence from specified destination
Active Open	source port, [timeout], [timeout-action], [precedence], [security]	Request connection at a particular security and precedence to a specified destination
Active Open With Data	source port, destination port, destination address [timeout], [timeout-action], [precedence], [security], data, data length, PUSH flag, URGENT flag	Request connection at a particular security and prcedence to s spefied destination and transmit data with the request
Send	local connection name, data, data length, PUSH flag, URGENT flag, [timeout], [timeout-action]	Transfer data across named connection
Allocate	local connection name, data length	Issue incremental allocation for receive data to TCP
Close	local connection name	Close connection gracefully
Abort	local connection name	Close connection abruptly
Status	local connection name	Query connection status

Note: Square brackets indicate optional parameter

Figure G-4. TCP service request primitives

PRIMITIVE	PARAMETERS	DESCRIPTION
Open ID	local connection name, source port, destination port,* destination address*	Informs user of connection name assigned to pending connection requested in an Open primitive
Open Failure	local connection name	Reports failure of an Active Open request
Open Success	local connection name	Reports completion of a pending Open request
Deliver	local connection name, data, data length, URGENT flag	Reports arrival of data
Closing	local connection name	Reports that remote TCP user has issued a Close and that all data sent by remote user has been delivered
Terminate	local connection name, description	Reports that the connection has been terminated and no longer exists: a description of the reason for termination is provided
Status Response	local connection name, source port, source address, destination port, destination address, connection sate, receive window, send window, amount awaiting ACK, amount await-receipt, urgent state, precedence, security, timeout	Reports current status of connection
Error	local connection name, description	Reports service request or internal error

***Not used for Unspecified Passive Open**

Figure G-5. TCP service response primitives

Parameters	Description
Source Port	Identifier of the local TCP user.
Timeout	The longest delay allowed for data delivery before automatic connection termination or error report.
Timeout-action	In the event of a timeout, determines if the connection is terminated or an error is reported to the user.
Precedence	Actual or requested precedence level for a connection. Takes on values zero (lowest) through seven (highest). Same parameter as defined in IP.
Security range	Security structure that specifies the allowed ranges in compartment, handling restrictions, transmission control codes, and security levels.
Destination Port	Identifier of the remote TCP user.
Destination Address	Internet address of the remote host.
Security	Security information (including security level, compartment, handling restrictions, and transmission control code) for a connection. Same parameter as defined in IP.
Data	Block of data sent by a TCP user or delivered to a TCP user.
Data Length	Length of block of data sent or delivered.
PUSH Flag	If set, this indicates that the associated data are to be provided with the data stream push service.
URGENT Flag	If set, this indicates that the associated data are to be provided with the urgent data signaling service.
Local Connection Name	The shorthand identifier of a connection defined by a (local socket, remote socket) pair. Provided by TCP.
Description	Supplementary information in a Terminate or Error primitive.

Figure G-6. TCP service parameters

Parameters	Description
Source Address	Internet address of the local host.
Connection State	State of referenced connection (CLOSED, ACTIVE OPEN, PASSIVE OPEN, ESTABLISHED, CLOSING).
Receive Window	Amount of data in octets the local TCP entity is willing to receive.
Send Window	Amount of data in octets permitted to be sent to remote TCP entity.
Amount Awaiting ACK	Amount of previously transmitted data awaiting acknowledgment.
Amount Awaiting	Amount of data in octets buffered at the local TCP and Receipt pending receipt by local TCP user.
Urgent State	Indicates to the receiving TCP user whether there is urgent dataavailable or whether all urgent data, if any, has been delivered to the user.

Figure G-6. TCP service parameters (continued)

TCP operates as an intermediary between applications and the internetwork. It eliminates the need for higher application layers to become involved in the complex matter of maintaining and communicating with other nodes. The services of IP are used by TCP to provide the actual exchange of data and, as IP is not reliable, TCP makes the following assumptions:

- Segments may be lost or may arrive somewhere with errors
- Segments may not be received in the order in which they were transmitted
- Segments may be delayed at a variable rate that delays communications

TCP sequentially numbers each segment to manage its receipt. The segments can then be properly assembled at their destination by their sequence numbers. Segments, like datagrams, can be lost. TCP sends an acknowledgment (ACK) segment for each segment it receives. If the sending TCP does not receive an ACK within a reasonable amount of time, it presumes the segment is lost and sends it again.

The repeated segment is generally sent with the same sequence number previously assigned to it. TCP is able to resend the missing segment because a segment buffer holds each transmitted segment until an ACK is received.

TCP establishes a dual purpose connection (session) between two sockets (nodes). First, it defines all connection characteristics, including security. Second, the connection allows each TCP socket to maintain information about the state of the connection. This includes such information as the last sequence number used, the last sequence number received, and the last sequence number acknowledged.

TCP is designed to service requests of multiple processes within a single node. For instance, a node that is a Unix host is likely to have several processes that use TCP services running concurrently. Each process using a TCP service is identified by a port. A port and an internet address are combined to form a socket that is unique throughout the entire internet. The socket is the basic communication mechanism and is a communication end-point in each TCP. Interestingly, two processes within the same node could actually use TCP to communicate with each other because of their unique sockets.

The fields of the TCP segment frame are illustrated and described in Figures G-7 and G-8. The scope of TCP's checksum is illustrated in Figure G-9.

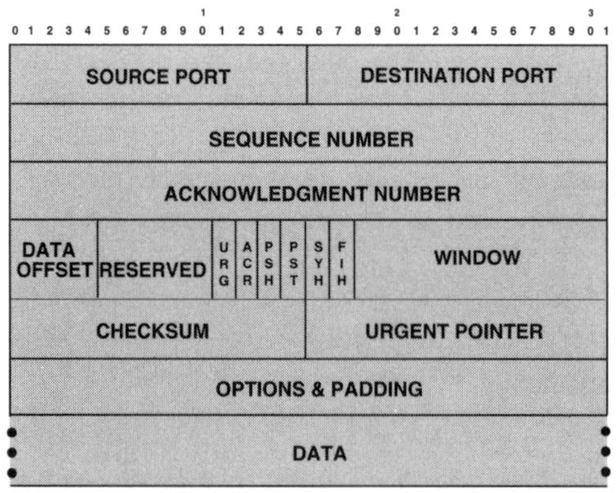

Figure G-7. TCP header format

Field	Size (bytes)	Explanation
Source port	2	indicates source port
Destination port	2	indicates destination port
Sequence No	4	indicates the sequence number of the first data byte in this segment, except when SYN is present. When SYN is present, it is the initial sequence number (ISN) and the first data byte is ISN + 1.
Acknowledgment	4	sequence number of the next byte that the TCP entity expects to receive; used for piggyback acknowledgments
Data offset	1 nybble	number of 32-bit words in the header
Reserved	6 bits	not currently used
Flags	6 bits	URG: Urgent pointer field significant ACK: Acknowledgment field significant PHS: Push Function RST: Reset connection SYN: Synchronize the sequence numbers FIN: End of data from sender
Window	2	number of data bytes beginning with the one indicated in the acknowledgment field that the sender is willing to accept
Checksum	2	One's complement of the sum mod 2^16 - 1 of all the 2-byte words in the segment plus a 96-bit pseudo-header that contains the source internet address, destination internet address,protocol, and TCP segment length.
Urgent Pointer	2	indicates the byte following the urgent data; allows the receiver to know how much urgent data is coming.
Options (variable)	1	maximum accepted segment size

Figure G-8. TCP message fields

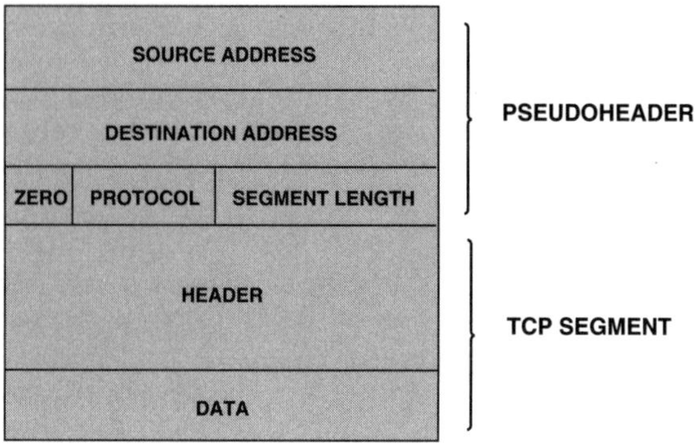

Figure G-9. Scope of TCP checksum

The TCP standard supplies a specific protocol for communication between TCP entities. TCP also supplies several implementation options called policies. These policies are send, deliver, accept, retransmit, and acknowledge. Each is discussed separately.

Send Policy. When the Data Stream Push (expedited delivery) is not exercised, the sending TCP can transmit data whenever it is appropriate. User data is buffered by TCP, which sends each set of user data as its own segment, or accumulates some predetermined amount of user data before assembling a segment. The type of implementation chosen can affect performance by increasing or decreasing the network load.

Deliver Policy. Without the use of the Data Stream Push, a recipient TCP node is free to deliver data to its client at its convenience. Data may be delivered in the order in which it is received, or TCP may buffer several data segments and deliver a lump of segments. The chosen method of delivery affects TCP performance.

Accept Policy. The receiving TCP can choose to accept only segments that arrive in sequential order or to accept segments within the same receive window. If the TCP determines that it will only accept segments arriving in sequential order, extra communication is necessary to reject and retransmit segments. If it accepts any segment arriving in the current receive window, the TCP is responsible for delivery of all segments in the proper order.

Retransmit Policy. A sending TCP maintains a queue of segments that have been transmitted but not acknowledged. The TCP protocol specifies that the sending TCP will retransmit any segment that is not acknowledged within a specified period of time. The sending TCP has three options with regard to the retransmission of unacknowledged segments:

First-only. One timer is maintained for the entire queue. When an acknowledgment is received, that segment is removed and the timer is reset. If the timer expires, the segment at the beginning of the queue is retransmitted. The first-only policy is useful because only unacknowledged segments are retransmitted. Note that an acknowledgment may be lost on its way back to the sending TCP, and its segment therefore remains unacknowledged at the sending TCP. A drawback of this option is considerable delays in segment communication.

Batch. One timer is maintained for the entire queue. When an acknowledgment is received, the segment is removed and the timer is reset. If the timer expires, the entire queue of unacknowledged segments is retransmitted and the timer is reset. The batch policy reduces the chance of delays, but at the price of possible excessive retransmissions. The batch policy can be useful for receiving nodes that must receive segments in sequence.

Individual. A timer is maintained for each segment in the queue. When an acknowledgment is received, the corresponding segment is removed and its timer is cancelled. When a timer expires, that segment is retransmitted and its timer is reset. The individual policy is generally the most useful policy. The cost, however, is extra overhead at the sending TCP, which should be weighed against the communication needs of the network.

Acknowledge Policy. The receiving TCP has two options when acknowledging received segments. Segment acknowledgments are either sent upon the arrival of each segment, or they are delayed. In the latter case, as each segment is received, its arrival is noted internally. Meanwhile, TCP waits for an outbound segment on which to piggyback an acknowledgment. In the event that no outbound segment is realized, a timer is used to force the acknowledgment to be sent after a specified period of time.

The immediate acknowledgment is straightforward and keeps acknowledgments current at both ends of the connection. Extra segment transmissions may be required to achieve this result.

The time acknowledgment policy demands additional overhead at the receiving TCP and may result in extraneous retransmissions from the sending TCP.

APPENDIX H

An X.25 Primer

The International Telephone and Telegraph Consultative Committee (CCITT) has formulated the X.25 packet switching recommendation. This recommendation specifies the protocol to be followed by the user devices (nodes) in accessing public packet-switching networks. Internationally agreed upon, the X.25 protocol specifies the details of the interactions between each user packet-mode device and the network nodes, as shown in Figure H-1.

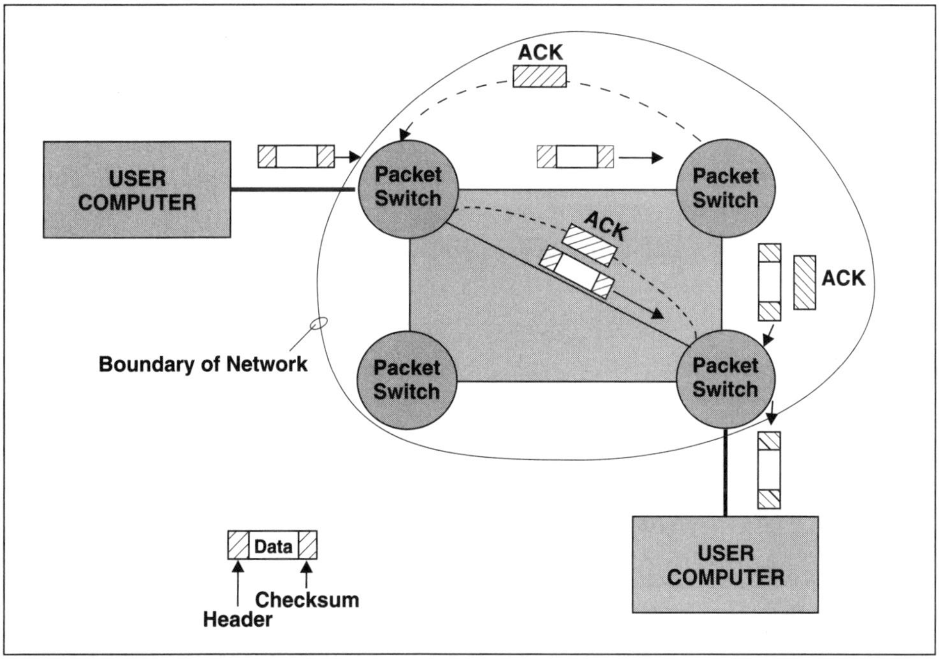

Figure H-1. A simple model of packet switching

The network node and user packet-mode devices are called Data Circuit-Terminating Equipment (DCE) and Data Terminal Equipment (DTE), respectively. The actual equipment used and the design of the packet-switched network is not of concern when implementing the X.25 protocol. In the case where the communication network utilized does not use packet switching, each DTE is connected to a Packet Assembler/Disassembler (PAD) and the DTE is referred to as a character-mode device, as opposed to a packet-mode device (see Figure H-2).

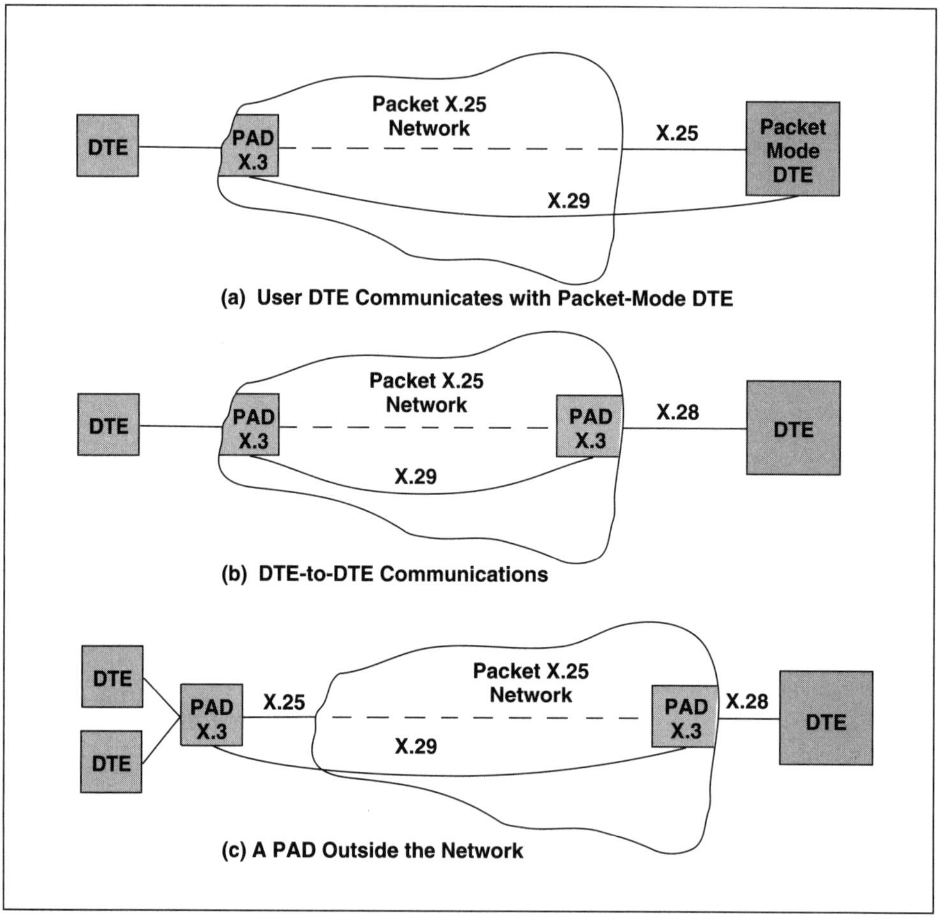

Figure H-2. Network configurations using PADs

Layers of Communication

The actual implementation of the X.25 protocol is primarily through the use of software in an intelligent terminal, host, or network processing node. The CCITT Recommendation X.25 specifies three layers of communications: physical, data-link, and network.

In reference to the OSI model, the physical layer defines the interface between the network and the node. Currently, the bulk of data communications uses telecommunications circuits that were originally designed for voice communications. There are two types of telecommunications circuits available: dial-up and leased-line. Connected by modems, the signals that travel along these circuits are defined by CCITT definitions such as V.24. In most cases, packet-switched systems use leased lines. If the communications circuit is fully digital, the interface used is defined by the CCITT Recommendation X.21. The definition of X.25 also specifies which facilities of X.21 it uses; some of the facilities X.21 offers aren't needed by a simple point-to-point X.25 network. Simply stated, the X.21 interface provides for end-to-end digital transmission between DTEs and DCEs.

With an X.21 circuit-switched network, the DTE (or user) alerts the DCE (or network) that it wishes to "make a call." This is a Call Request, which is similar to lifting the handset on a telephone in the hopes of getting a dial-tone. The "dial tone" that the DTE is expecting is termed Proceed to Select, which is provided by the DCE.

Once the DTE receives a Proceed to Select the DTE "dials" by providing a Selection Signal Sequence. The DCE will respond within 20 seconds of the end of the Selection Signal Sequence with a Call Progress signal. Instead of a busy signal, no answer, or "Hello," the X.21 DTE receives one of the codes listed in Figure H-3.

Code	Meaning	Category
00	Reserved	
01	Terminal called	
02	Redirected call	
03	Connect when free	Successful
20	No connection	
21	Number busy	
22	Selection Signal procedure error	Cleared due to short-term conditions
23	Selection Signal transmission error	
41	Access barred	
42	Changed number	
43	Not obtainable	
44	Out of order	
45	Controlled not ready	
46	Uncontrolled not ready	
47	DCE power off	
48	Invalid facility request	
49	Network fault in local connection	
51	Call information service	Cleared due to long-term conditions
52	Incompatible user class of service	
61	Network congestion	Cleared due to short-term conditions
71	Long-term network congestion	Cleared due to long-term conditions
72	RPOA out of order	
81	Registration/cancellation confirmed	
82	Redirection activated	Cleared by DTE procedure
83	Redirection deactivated	

Figure H-3. Call progress signals (from the CCITT recommendation X.96)

Each "call" established through a packet-switched network creates a virtual circuit. Each DTE node can have up to 15 virtual circuits or logical channel groups, each with up to 255 logical channels. Once both DTEs, the calling and the receiving, have entered the Ready For Data state, data exchange begins. The call can be ended by either the DCE or DTE signalling a Clear.

The Recommendation X.21 is not, however, necessary to provide communication for X.25. Instead, X.21 bis may be used. This was designed for conventional analog connections using the CCITT V.24 or EIA RS 232C modem connections. The ability to connect V.24 DTEs and X.21 DTEs is defined by X.21 bis. Note that the Call Progress signals are not supported in X.21 bis connections. There are procedures for the manual answering of calls with call request time-outs of 2 (normal) to 60 seconds.

The second layer of communication is the data-link layer. The Recommendation X.25 specifies data link procedures that provide for the exchange of data via frames that can be sent and received. Errors in the physical layer can be detected by the data link layer. The data link layer used by X.25 is defined by a subset of High-Level Data Link Control (Balanced-Asynchronous) (HDLC(BA)) called Link Access Procedure Balanced (LAPB).

The third layer, the network layer (also known as the packet layer), is where the real substance of the Recommendation X.25 is found. The network layer is where X.25 provides the virtual circuit interface to packet-switched service.

Each X.25 packet indicates one of 15 available logical channel groups (see Figure H-4).

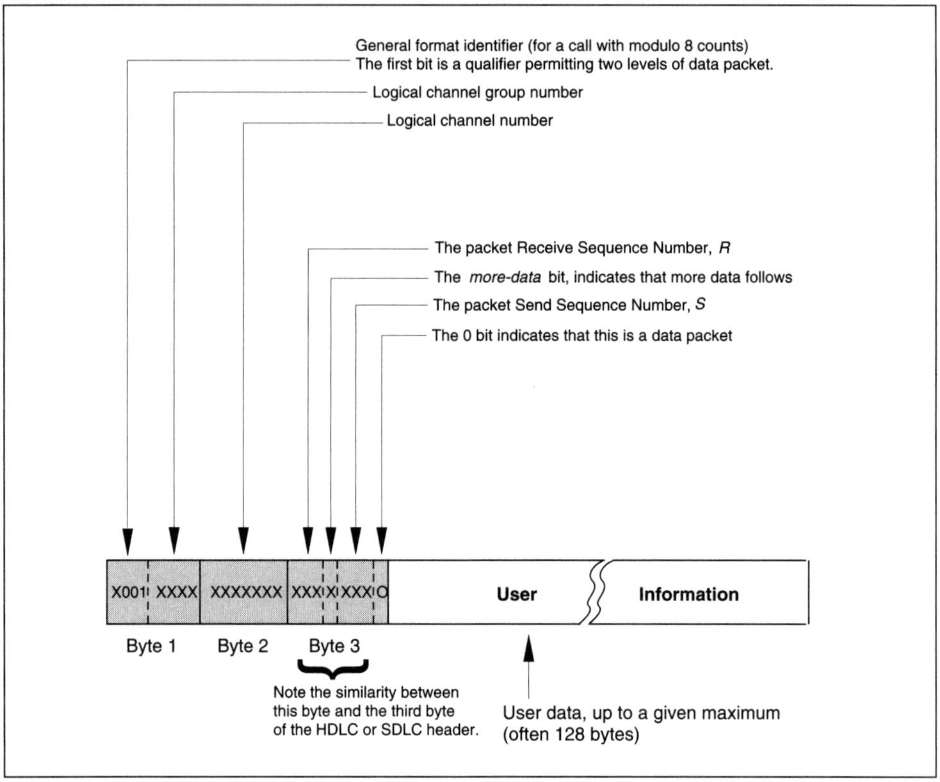

Figure H-4. Format of the X.25 data packet (with 3-bit counts)

This channel identifies the packet as being on a switched or permanent virtual circuit for both directions of communications. The actual range of valid logical channel numbers is defined between the DTE and the network service being used. The logical channel numbers are only significant between the communicating DTE and DCE interface pair, shown in Figure H-5.

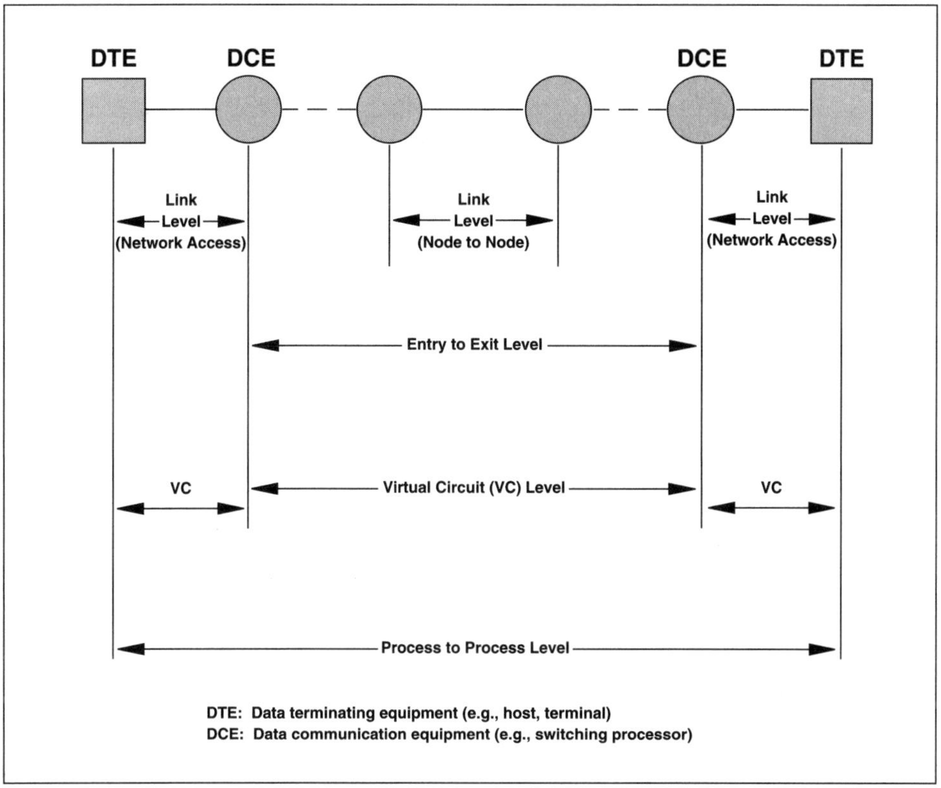

Figure H-5. Network protocol layers

Any one DTE may communicate with many other DTEs, each using a switched and/or permanent virtual circuit. Recommendation X.25 includes the packet types outlined in Figure H-6.

Packet Type		Service	
From DCE to DTE	From DTE to DCE	VC	PVC
Call Set-Up and Clearing			
Incoming call	Call request	X	
Call connected	Call accepted	X	
Clear indication	Clear request	X	
DCE clear confirmation	DTE clear confirmation	X	
Data and Interrupt			
DCE data	DTE data	X	X
DCE interrupt	DTE interrupt	X	X
DCE interrupt confirmation	DTE interrupt confirmation	X	X
Flow Control and Reset			
DCE RR	DTE RR	X	X
DCE RNR	DTE RNR	X	X
	DTE REJ	X	X
Reset indication	Reset Request	X	X
DCE reset confirmation	DTE reset confirmation	X	X
Restart			
Restart indication	Restart request	X	X
DCE restart confirmation	DTE restart confirmation	X	X
Diagnostic			
Diagnostic		X	X
Registration			
Registration confirmation	Registration request	X	X

VC = Virtual Call PVC = Permanent Virtual Circuit

Figure H-6. X.25 packet types

Permanent Virtual Circuits

Just like dial-up lines, X.25 offers the user a virtual circuit or call. And, like leased lines, X.25 offers Permanent Virtual Circuits (PVCs). The biggest difference is that there are no call setup or disconnect operations when PVCs are used.

When a user DTE connects to another user DTE via a virtual circuit, a free logical channel number is selected. If the connection is a permanent virtual circuit, the logical channel number is permanently assigned. Once again, there are as many as 255 logical channels per group, and each node (DTE) may have up to 15 groups (see Figure H-7).

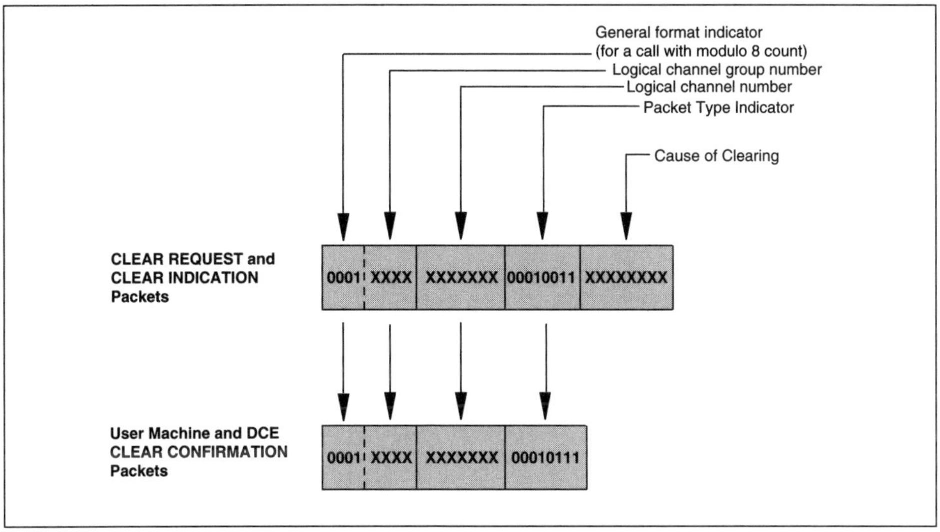

Figure H-7. Packet formula used when disconnecting a virtual call

Initiating a Call

Once the calling DTE selects a free logical channel, it sends a Call Request message to its DCE. The format of the call request is shown in Figure H-8.

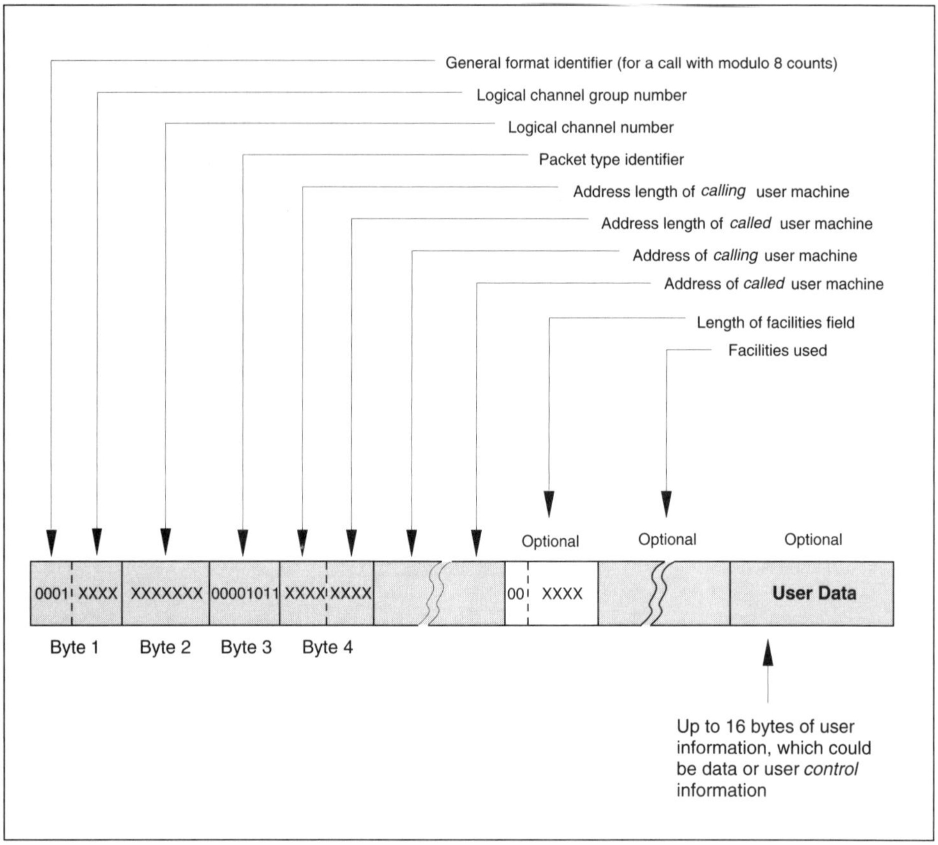

Figure H-8. Format of the Call Request and Incoming Call packets

This message usually has the address of the destination node and may contain the address of the sending node. Both addresses are variable in length and may be followed by facilities fields which are also variable in length. A facilities field is present when the sending node requires a call with some optional characteristics. For example, a maximum data length may be specified to accommodate limited buffer capacity at either node, and a maximum window size may be specified for flow control.

When the DCE receives the Call Request from the DTE, the DCE then sends the information to the network in an attempt to initiate communication. Meanwhile, the DTE changes from the Ready state to the DTE Waiting state.

The receiving DTE receives an Incoming Call message from its DCE. The receiving DTE will then determine if it is able to establish communication. If it can, a Call Accepted message is sent back to the originating DTE/DCE.

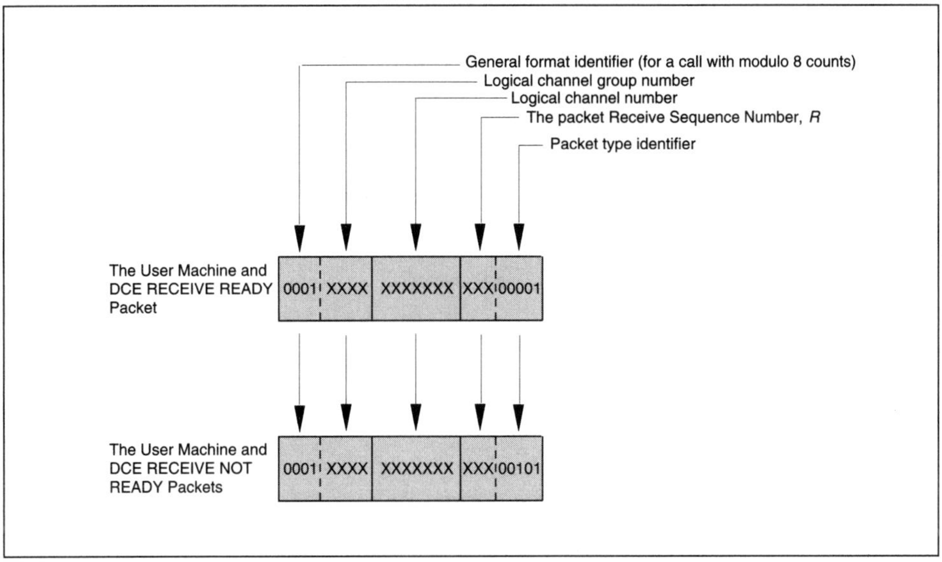

Figure H-9. Format of packets used to acknowledge a Data packet

The DCE receives the message and sends a Call Connected message to its DTE. One fault that may occur is that the waiting DCE (at the originating node) may receive a Call Request from another node with which it is not currently communicating. If this incoming Call Request is for the same logical channel in the same group as the call currently being established, a Call Collision state is entered. The DCE will reject the incoming Call Request and proceed normally with the Call Accepted message that is pending or due. When the Call Request fails, the originating DCE will receive a Clear Indication that specifies the reason why the Call Request was rejected.

To satisfy the need to temporarily stop interactive communication, the Recommendation X.25 incorporates the use of Interrupt packets.

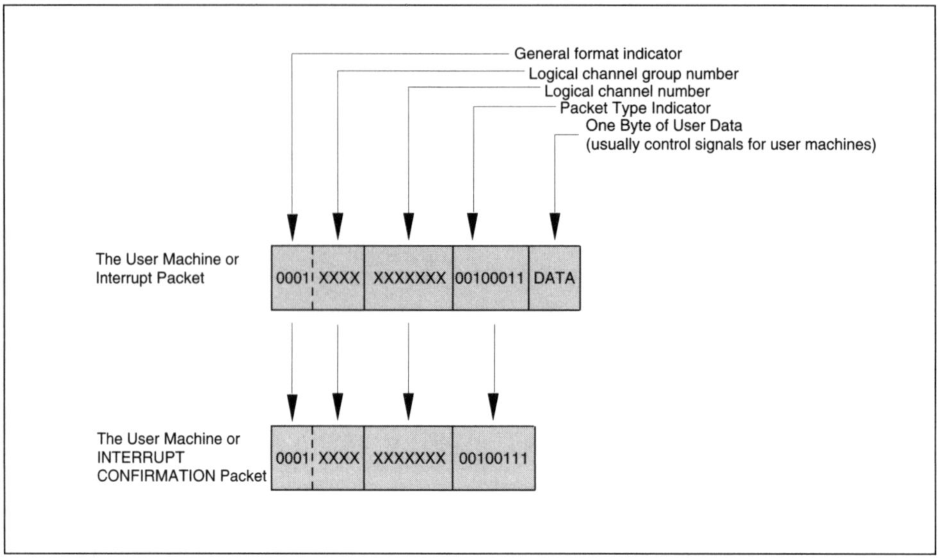

Figure H-10. Formats of the Interrupt and Interrupt Confirmation packets

An Interrupt packet bypasses the normal flow of information, jumping ahead of Data packets in the normal queues. Normally, the Interrupt packet contains only one byte of information, although it can have more. However, any one DTE cannot have more than one outstanding Interrupt packet on any virtual call in each direction. This allows for the dedication of a single one byte buffer space for each logical channel to use to capture any incoming Interrupt packet. Further, the Interrupt packet does not use a sequence number. A receiving DTE will send an Interrupt Confirmation packet to acknowledge the receipt of an Interrupt packet. Once the original sending DTE receives the Interrupt Confirmation packet, it may once again use an Interrupt packet on that logical channel within that logical channel group. The network is capable of detecting protocol errors between DTEs or the need for a DTE to discard a message, whether it be in transit or buffered at one end of the link. When the network detects an error condition or other unknown state, it issues a request.

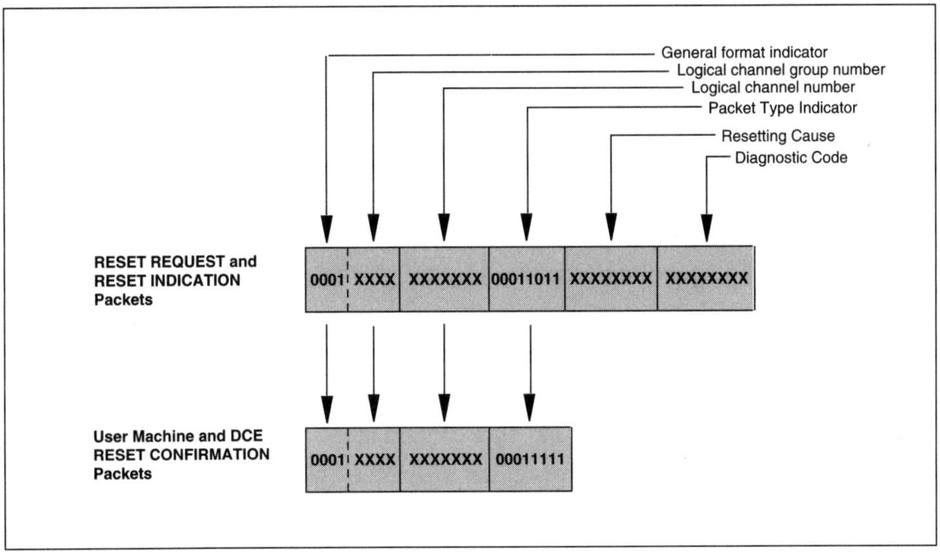

Figure H-11. Format of packets used for Resetting

When the network generates this request, both DTEs on the link receive the packet. The network will be reset when both DTEs have replied with a Reset Confirmation packet. It is also possible for one of the DTEs to generate the Reset Request. The network will intercept the Reset Request and the receiving DTE will get a Reset Indication packet. This DTE will then send a Reset Confirmation packet. Once the reset is complete, both the SSN and RSN counters will have been set to 0. In addition, any Data or Interrupt packets that were in transit will have been discarded.

Once communication is complete, a DTE may disconnect. To accomplish this, the DTE sends a Clear Request packet to its DCE. When it is ready to clear the channel, the DCE responds with a Clear Confirmation packet. The DCE then proceeds to send the Clear Request to the other DCE. The receiving DCE will send a Clear Indication to its DTE. When that DTE sends a Clear Confirmation back to its DCE, the channel is cleared and once again enter the Ready state.

Packet Assembler/Disassembler

The Packet Assembler/Disassembler (PAD) is a device that provides dumb character terminal emulation while using a complex packet-switched network. In other words, the PAD is used to connect character-mode terminals to packet-switched networks utilizing the Recommendation X.25. The PAD is defined by the three CCITT Recommendations X.3, X.28, and X.29. The X.3 protocol defines the service provided to the terminal by the PAD. The X.28 protocol defines how start-stop terminals are connected to the PAD via a telephone or other link, and how they can control the PAD's functions. X.28 also defines the user interface to the X.3 services. The X.29 protocol defines the interaction between the PAD and the host machine using the X.25 protocol.

Packet-switched networks are most efficient when exchanging relatively large blocks of data. This is not the case with a character-mode terminal, which is typically set up to send and receive one byte of data at a time. Included in the PAD is software (or firmware) and hardware that provide a buffering service between the character-mode terminal and the block-mode packet-switched network. In a typical implementation, an end-of-message or terminating character is defined. When this character is received from the terminal, the PAD sends the buffered input from the terminal to its destination.

Different systems do not necessarily use the same end-of-message character. The use of Recommendations X.3, X.28, and X.29 is an attempt to provide a general solution. Unfortunately, these three recommendations are from the CCITT and do not conform with the OSI model. But, the X.25 and PAD recommendations are widely accepted and are used on a global basis. So, usability has won over conformity with the ISO model. In effect, the OSI model is partially ignored by the X.25 and PAD Recommendations.

There are a variety of PADs used to fit different terminal arrangements. PADs generally support more than one terminal, with options ranging from 1 to 32 terminals per PAD. Each terminal using the PAD is assigned a unique logical channel number for its communication.

In addition, each terminal connected to the PAD has 22 separate parameters which control the response of the PAD as it receives data from the terminal. These parameters allow the session between the terminal and PAD to be customized to suit the needs of the terminal. The host, PAD, or terminal user may alter the PAD's parameters. The following details each of these 22 parameters.

Parameter 1: Escape to PAD command state on receipt of DLE. The default of this parameter is 1, which indicates that escape to the PAD command state is possible. Typically, this would be used if a user wanted to initiate the end of a call from the PAD rather than from the host. After the DLE command is sent to the PAD, the PAD then prompts for a command, such as Clear or Reset. If this parameter is set to 0, escape is not possible. This setting is useful, however, if the escape sequence, DLE, might be issued during some other processing, such as with graphics.

Parameter 2: Character echo. This parameter defaults to 1, which indicates that echoing will be performed, meaning that the PAD will echo each character back to the terminal as it is typed. Normally, the terminal is connected to the PAD in full duplex so that each character is not displayed on the terminal until the PAD has echoed it. This parameter is set to 0 if no echoing is desired, such as when a password or other security code is being typed at the terminal.

Parameter 3: Data forwarding characters. The data forwarding characters refer to the same terminating or end-of-message characters discussed earlier. Since the PAD deals with a variety of terminals, this parameter informs the PAD which character codes indicate the end of a message.

If, while entering information, the PAD runs out of buffer space and the terminal flow control (parameter 5) is not enabled, the overflow characters will be discarded and the PAD will issue a BEL (hex code 07) character to the terminal. Once forwarded to the host system by the PAD, data can no longer be edited by the terminal.

Data forwarding may also take place if parameter 4, data forwarding on timeout, is used. The count down timer for parameter 4 is reset each time a character is received from the terminal. Parameter 4 is especially useful when no forwarding character can be defined.

The following encoding is used to select the data forwarding character(s):

0 -	receipt of the 129th character or time-out only
1 -	A-Z, a-z, and 0-9
2 -	CR
4 -	ESC, BEL, ENQ, ACK
8 -	DEL, CAN, DC2
16 -	ETX, EOT
32 -	HT, LF, VT, FF
64 -	All other characters less than hex 20 in value and DEL (hex 08)

Figure H-12. Encoding used to select data forwarding characters

To customize the data forwarding characters, the above values may be summed to indicated the desired characters. For instance, if parameter 3 is set to a value of 6, then CR, ESC, BEL, ENQ, and ACK can all be used to indicate that the data buffered by the PAD needs to be forwarded.

If parameter 3 is set to 0, a high traffic load may result on the network due to the continuous manner in which messages are exchanged.

Parameter 4: Data forwarding on time-out. If parameter 3 is set to 0, the value of this parameter will be used as the method of forwarding buffered data from the PAD to the host. This parameter may be set from 0 to 255, with 0 indicating that no time-out will ever be signalled. If set to some value between 1 and 255, the PAD will wait 0.05 seconds times the value before sending the buffered data to the host. The maximum delay is 12.75 seconds, which corresponds to a parameter 4 value of 255.

Parameter 5: Flow control of the terminal by the PAD. When the PAD is connected to an intelligent terminal, the PAD may be overwhelmed with data to send to the host because an intelligent terminal can send data faster than a user can type it. If parameter 5 is set to 0, the PAD will discard all data that it cannot buffer. The PAD will also echo the BEL character back to the terminal to indicate that the most recently received data has been discarded. If this parameter is set to 1, the PAD will issue an XOFF (DC3) character when its buffer becomes full, thereby inhibiting the terminal from accepting additional input. Once the PAD is again able to buffer data, the XON (DC1) character will be issued.

Parameter 6: Suppression of service signals from the PAD. The PAD issues service signals in response to external events, such as the network being Cleared or Reset. If this parameter is set to 0, these service messages will not be echoed on the terminal. If set to 1, the terminal will be sent the messages as they are received by the PAD.

Parameter 7: Receipt of a break signal from the terminal. The break signal is a predefined sequence that is used to signal the host that a terminal needs attention. On some PADs, the break signal is executed when the connection between the terminal and PAD is held in the space condition for more than 100ms. Figure H-13 indicates the action the PAD will take when the break signal is detected, depending on the value of parameter 7:

0	No action
1	Transmit an X.25 Interrupt packet to the host
2	Transmit an X.25 Reset packet to the host
5	Transmit an X.25 Interrupt packet and an Indication of Break
8	The PAD enters command state awaiting a command from the user, thus leaving the Data Transfer state
21	Same as 5, but parameter 8 (discussed below) is set to 1

Figure H-13. PAD Parameter 7 options

Option 21 is useful for slower terminals since parameter 8 is set to 1, thus discarding any messages that are buffered for display on the terminal. Once the PAD receives an acknowledgment of the Indication of Break, it will set parameter 8 to 0, thus restoring the terminal's ability to receive messages.

Parameter 8: Data delivery to the terminal. When this parameter is set to 0, data will be sent to the terminal as fast as it can receive it. When set to 1, all data destined for the terminal is discarded. Receipt of a Reset indication or confirmation sets this parameter to 0.

Parameter 9: Padding after Carriage Return. This parameter controls the number of pad characters inserted after a Carriage Return (CR). The CR may have originated from the terminal or from the host. In any case, the pad characters are used to allow TTY or simple mechanical terminals sufficient time to return their print head to the margin so that they can begin printing a new line. If this parameter is set to 0, no pad characters are generated. But if the PAD, under control of parameter 10, generated the CR, then 2 or 4 pad characters are generated. The number of pad characters generated depends on the terminal's speed. If parameter 9 is set between 1 and 7, one to seven pad characters will be issued regardless of the origin of the CR.

Parameter 10: Line folding. Parameter 10 is used to prevent the loss of data if the terminal has a narrower print line than the host. The PAD keeps track of how many non-format-effectors it has sent to the terminal. If this count reaches the value of the line folding parameter, the PAD automatically generates a CR. If parameter 9 is non-zero, additional pad characters will also be generated. If parameter 10 is 0, the PAD will not insert any format effectors. Otherwise, if this parameter is set between 1 and 255, the PAD will issue a CR after the set number of non-format-effectors are displayed on the terminal.

Parameter 11: Terminal speed. The CCITT sets the values for possible terminal speeds, though in a seemingly illogical manner:

Value	Speed (bps)
0	110
1	134.5
2	300
3	1200
4	600
5	75
6	150
7	1800
8	200
9	100
10	50
11	75/1200
12	2400
13	4800
14	9600
15	19.2 (Kb/s)
16	4800
17	56 (Kb/s)
18	64 (Kb/s)

Figure H-14. CCITT values for terminal speeds

This parameter is read-only; the host may view it, but cannot change it. The value is also included as an option in the Call Request packet, sent when the virtual circuit is initialized.

Parameter 12: Flow control of the PAD by the terminal. When the terminal has intelligence and some manner of recording its messages, the terminal may instruct the PAD to temporarily stop sending data. The terminal accomplishes this by sending an XOFF signal to the PAD. The PAD resumes data transmission once it receives an XON signal from the terminal. Parameter 12 is only in effect when it is set to 1. If set to 0, this parameter has no effect. If the PAD enters the command state, it will be cleared as if an XON had been issued.

Parameter 13: Line Feed insertion after Carriage Return. To accommodate the variety of terminals and hosts that may be connected to the PAD, the following options are supported with respect to line feed insertion:

0	None
1	Inserted after every CR transmitted
2	Inserted after every CR received from host
4	Line Feed inserted after every CR locally echoed to the terminal
5	values 1 + 4
6	values 2 + 4
7	values 1 + 2 + 4 (data transfer only)

Figure H-15. PAD Parameter 13 options

Parameter 14: Padding characters inserted after Line Feed. This parameter has the same effect as Parameter 9, except that pad characters are sent after a Line Feed to the terminal. If this parameter is set to 0, no padding occurs; if set between 1 and 7, that many pad characters will be inserted. Optionally, from 8 to 255 pad characters may be used.

Parameter 15: Editing. This parameter, if set to 1, allows editing of characters in the send buffer. If set to 0, editing is not allowed. Also, if parameter 15 is set to 1, parameters 16, 17, and 18 have significance.

Parameter 16: Character Delete character. When this parameter is set to 0, deletion of characters in the PAD's buffer is not allowed. When non-zero, the value used indicates the character code that performs backspacing and deleting. Often the value of 08 is used.

Parameter 17: Buffer Delete character. As with parameter 16, this parameter has no effect when set to 0. Otherwise, this value indicates the character code that erases the entire buffer prior to transmission. Typically, the value used (in hex) is 18, which happens to be the Cancel character in the ASCII code table.

Parameter 18: Buffer Display character. This parameter must also be set to a non-zero value to have an effect. When non-zero, the value indicated is the character code that displays the contents of the PAD's buffer on the terminal. Usually DC2, ASCII code 12h is used to display the current buffer contents.

Parameter 19: Editing PAD service signals. This parameter controls the format of the editing PAD service signals.

0 - no editing
1 - editing for printing terminals
2 - editing for display terminals
8 - editing using characters from the character code range 20h-7Eh

Figure H-16. PAD Parameter 19 options

Parameter 20: Echo mask. This parameter controls which characters will and will not be echoed to the terminal when Parameter 2 is enabled.

0 - all characters echoed
1 - no echo of CR
2 - no echo of LF
4 - no echo of VT, HT, or FF
8 - no echo of BEL or BS
16 - no echo of ESC or ENQ
32 - no echo of ACK, NAK, STX, SOH, EOT, ETB, or ETX
64 - no echo of editing characters

Figure H-17. PAD Parameter 20 options

Parameter 21: Parity treatment. This parameter dictates how the checking and generation of parity on characters sent to and from the terminal will be performed.

0 - no parity detection or generation
1 - parity checking
2 - parity generation
3 - values 1 + 2

Figure H-18. PAD Parameter 21 options

Parameter 22: Page wait. This parameter indicates the number of lines to be displayed before waiting for a continuation prompt from the terminal.

0 - no page wait
23- number of line feed characters before waiting; optionally, may be other values.

Figure H-19. PAD Parameter 22 options

CCITT Recommendation X.28

Recommendation X.28 defines how control of the data flow between the non-packet mode user terminal and the PAD is performed. The terminal issues commands to the PAD as outlined above. These commands summarize the procedures for establishing the link, initializing the service, and exchanging the data and control data in an orderly fashion. Recommendation X.28 requires the PAD to respond when a terminal sends a command. The link established may be either simple or transparent. If simple, the terminal has access to the X.3 commands. If transparent, the services of the PAD are transparent to both the terminal and the host (or other terminal).

CCITT Recommendation X.29

Recommendation X.29 defines how the PAD and a remote node exchange control information during an X.25 call. The remote node is either another PAD or an X.25 DTE. As introduced earlier, the Qualifier bit of the General Format Identifier field does not have a specific definition. With the use of X.29, the Qualifier bit is set to 0 to indicate that the packet has user data, or is set to 1 to indicate that the packet contains PAD control information.

Recommendation X.29 has seven control messages, called PAD messages:

0: Parameters Indication	Returned by the PAD in response to the Read, and Set and Read messages
1: Invitation to Clear	Allows X.25 call clear by a remote DTE; PAD clears to local connection
2: Set Parameters:	Changes an X.3 value
3: Indication of Break	PAD indicates that the terminal has transmitted a break
4: Read Parameters	Reads an X.3 value
5: Error	Response to an invalid PAD message
6: Set and Read	Changes an X.3 value and requires the PAD to confirm the change

Figure H-20. X.29 PAD control messages

Other CCITT Recommendations

In addition to X.25, the CCITT has issued other recommendations that help shape the standards for internetworks, especially international Wide Area Networks (WANs). Two of these are explained in the following sections.

CCITT Recommendation X.400

The CCITT proposed a series of recommendations for message-handling systems which are referred to as the X.400 recommendations. The X.400 standard, as it has come to be known, was approved in 1984 by the CCITT, and has since gained widespread acceptance and continues to be implemented.

The X.400 standard specifies the guidelines for message exchange between two different computers. The set of eight recommendations contained in X.400 positions it in the Presentation and Application Layers of the OSI model. It is designed to interface to the Session Layer.

The X.400 standard has two key functional modes, referred to as the CEPT and CEN/CENELEC profiles. The CEPT functional standard provides for message exchange between private companies via a public network. The CEN/CENELEC functional standard provides for the description of interfaces used by message-handling systems within private companies.

As mentioned previously, the X.400 standard is a collection of eight recommendations:

1. X.400 System model-service elements
2. X.401 Basic service elements and optional user facilities
3. X.408 Encoded-information-type conversion rules
4. X.409 Presentation transfer syntax and notation
5. X.410 Remote operations and reliable transfer server
6. X.411 Message transfer layer
7. X.420 Interpersonal messaging user agent layer
8. X.430 Access protocol for Teletex terminals

X.400 describes the basic Message Handling System (MHS) in accordance with the OSI model and is limited to the Application Layer. In essence, X.400 describes how the user interacts with the User Agent (UA) in order to prepare, edit, send, and receive messages. When sending a message, the user is referred to as the originator; when receiving, the recipient. X.400 also specifies how the UA supports and interfaces to the Message Transfer Agent (MTA) (responsible for the delivery and receipt of messages from the network) and other UAs (P2, P3, and P7). Both the UA and MTA describe naming and addressing conventions.

X.401 details services and facilities provided for both the MTA and X.420 (described below).

X.408 specifies recommendations for code and format conversion, e.g., ASCII to Teletex.

X.409 defines presentation transfer conventions. X.409 specifies encoding rules for messages and control information to be used by the subcomponents of the Application Layer. The Application Layer is logically divided into two sublayers, the lower one consisting of two components. X.410, X.411, and X.420 describe services provided by these sublayers.

X.410 provides for remote operations and an entity labeled the Reliable Transfer Server (RTS), which is a separable subcomponent of the MTA. The RTS is the newest defined subcomponent of the Application Layer and makes use of the Basic Activity Subset (BAS) of the OSI Session Layer. The RTS provides for reliable and recoverable transfer of individual messages between communicating MTAs (see Figure H-21).

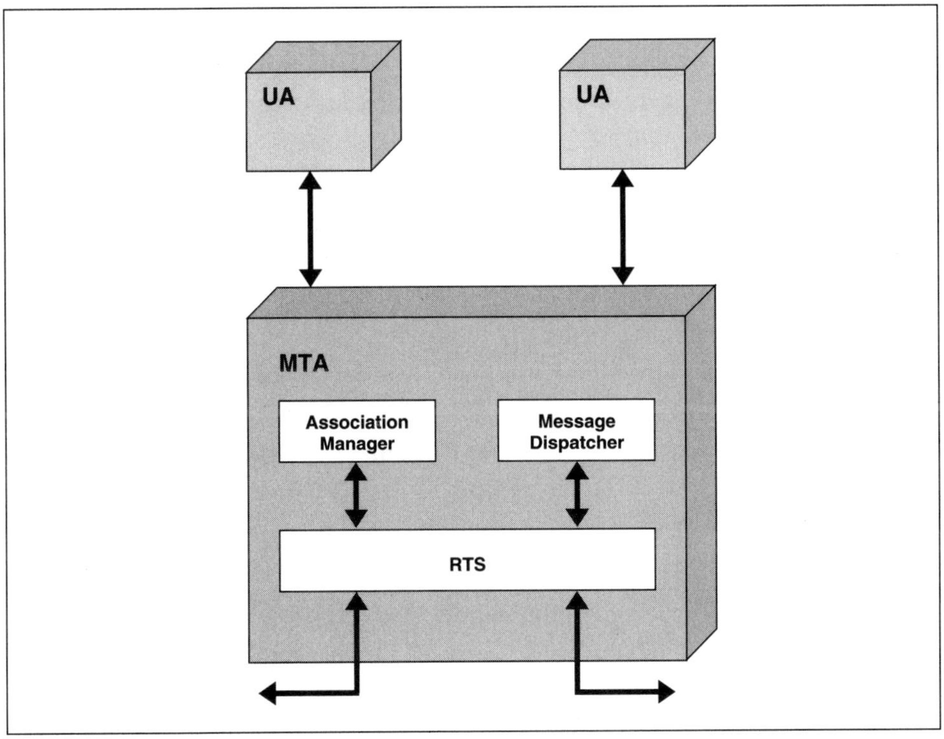

Figure H-21. Associations with MTAs

X.411 describes the Message Transfer Layer (MTL) service. The MTL service dictates how the UA transfers messages and provides delivery of messages within a specific period. Also, MTL provides for type conversion of the message contents. The transfer services include specification of the P1 and P3 protocols, as shown in Figure H-22.

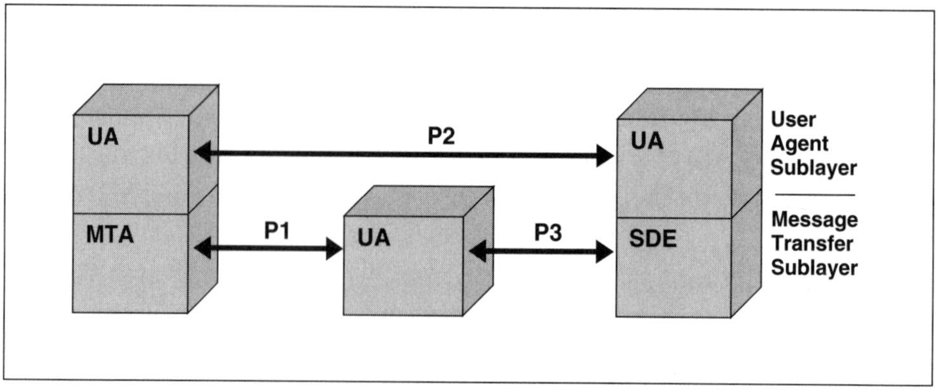

Figure H-22. Sublayers and protocols of an Interpersonal Messaging System

The P1 protocol specifies rules for message transfer between MTAs, and the P3 protocol identifies the protocol used by an MTA and a Submission and Delivery Entity (SDE). The SDE sends and receives messages from an MTA. Whenever the two communicating MTAs are not in the same system, the SDE is used as a remote delivery agent. Since the P3 protocol was developed largely on minicomputers and mainframes, a new protocol, P7, is being developed for microcomputers. The main difference between P3 and P7 is that P7 allows for the MTA to be located in a central MHS server, where microcomputers can occasionally check for or send messages.

X.420 defines the Interpersonal Message Service (IPM) which provides the semantics and syntax involved in the sending and receiving of interpersonal messages. X.420 also specifies how transmission of E-mail protocol data units (PDUs) is achieved through the network. X.420 is a user agent definition, and other user agents can be defined to suit the needs of the community using the X.400 standards. The Recommendation X.420 also specifies the P2 protocol for peer-to-peer communication between UAs and the format of the messages exchanged between UAs, according to the encoding rules specified in X.409.

X.430 describes the interface between the MHS and Teletex devices. X.430, like X.420, also defines a user agent known as a Teletex Access Unit (TTXAU). The TTXAU provides for access to the X.400 standard using Teletex terminals and is intended to ease migration to X.400.

X.500 Worldwide E-mail Directory

In early 1988, the CCITT and ISO drafted the Recommendation X.500. Recommendation X.500 is intended to be a globally distributed database system that contains E-mail addresses of all persons using any E-mail system. The primary goal of X.500 is to provide a workable means by which different E-mail system users can exchange messages with one another. It also serves to supplement the X.400 series of standards. Recommendation X.500 has seen limited implementations.

The X.500 Directory is made up of Directory System Agents (DSAs). The DSAs are individual portions of the Directory that exist in X.500 hosts. The DSAs are accessed by users, either human or data communication entities, through the Directory User Agents (DUAs).

APPENDIX I

The IEEE Project 802 Groups

IEEE 802.0	Executive Committee
IEEE 802.1	High Layer Interface (HILI) Work Group
IEEE 802.2	Logical Link Control (LLC) Work Group
IEEE 802.3	CSMA/CD Work Group
IEEE 802.4	Token Bus (TBUS) Work Group
IEEE 802.5	Token Ring (TRING) Work Group
IEEE 802.6	Metropolitan Area Network (MAN) Work Group
IEEE 802.7	Broadband Technical Advisory Group (BBTAG)
IEEE 802.8	Fiber-Optic Technical Advisory Group (FOTAG)
IEEE 802.9	Integrated Voice and Data (IVD) LAN Work Group
IEEE 802.10	Standard for Interoperable LAN Security (SILS) Work Group

APPENDIX J

ANSI.SYS Commands

This appendix documents many of the commands that can be used to make ANSI.SYS dance and sing. Be sure to load ANSI.SYS in CONFIG.SYS to enable its workings.

The place you are most likely to use these commands is with the PROMPT command. However, if you are writing a program or utility you can use these same commands, just "write" them to the screen. For instance, with the DOS AH=9, DS:DX=BUFFER, INT21H API, i.e.

```
MOV     AH,9
PUSH    CS
POP     DS ;presuming DS and CS are in the same segment
MOV     DX, OFFSET THINGS_TO_DISPLAY
INT     21H
```

Before continuing note that the "$" used in the commands below is for use with PROMPT, if you intend to use these commands in a program replace the "$" with the ESCAPE (hex = 1Bh) character. Now, the commands.

Macro Commands:

$b |
$d current date
$g >
$h backspace
$l <

$n current drive

$q =

$t current time

$_ (underscore) more cursor to next line

Positioning Commands:

$e[yA	move cursor up y rows
$e[yB	move cursor down y rows
$e[xC	move cursor right x columns
$e[xD	move cursor left x columns
$e[y;xf	move cursor to row y column x
$e[y;xH	same as $e[y;xf
$e[H	move cursor to upper left corner
$e[2J	clear screen and move cursor to upper left corner (home position)
$e[K	erase current line from cursor to end of line
$e[s	record cursor's current position
$e[u	move cursor to position saved by $e[s

Coloring Commands:

$e[aa;bb;...m	changes the foreground or background attribute/color, semicolons separate each choice and the "m" ends the command, the following is a list of attributes and colors

Attributes:

0 = no special attributes

1 = high intensity

2* = low intensity

3* = italic

4 = underline

5 = blink

6* = rapid blink

7 = everse video

8* = concealed text (no display)

* entries may have no effect with DOS, but will on true ANSI terminals

Colors:

30 = foreground black
31 = foreground red
32 = foreground green
33 = foreground yellow
34 = foreground blue
35 = foreground magenta
36 = foreground cyan
37 = foreground white

40 = background black
41 = background red
42 = background green
43 = background yellow
44 = background blue
45 = background magenta
46 = background cyan
47 = background white

Screen Mode Commands:

$[=nh Set Screen mode where n is:

0 = 40 x 25, 16 color text (color burst off)
1 = 40 x 25, 16 color text
2 = 80 x 25, 16 color text (color burst off)
3 = 80 x 25, 16 color text
4 = 320 x 200, 4 color graphics
5 = 320 x 200, 4 color graphics (color burst off)
6 = 620 x 200, 2 color graphics
14 = 40 x 200, 16 color graphics (EGA, DOS v4.0)

15 = 640 x 350, 2 color graphics (EGA, DOS v4.0)
16 = 640 x 350, 16 color graphics (EGA, DOS v4.0)
17 = 640 x 480, 2 color graphics (MCGA and VGA, DOS v4.0)
18 = 640 x 480, 16 color graphics (VGA, DOS v4.0)
19 = 320 x 200, 256 color graphics (MCGA and VGA, DOS v4.0)

$[=nl same as $[=nh

$[=7h Enable line wrap
$[=7l Disable line wrap

Keyboard Redefinition Commands:

$[keyCode;newValue;keyCode;newValue....p

keyCode is the code for the key to change, the list of keycodes follows, newValue is a string that contains the new value for that key, the string needs to be in ""; alternatively for a single character you may use that character's ASCII representation, for instance,

"Z" and 90 have the same effect

Key	Alone	Shifted	Ctrl	Alt
F1	0;59	0;84	0;94	0;104
F2	0;60	0;85	0;95	0;105
F3	0;61	0;86	0;96	0;106
F4	0;62	0;87	0;97	0;107
F5	0;63	0;88	0;98	0;108
F6	0;64	0;89	0;99	0;109
F7	0;65	0;90	0;100	0;110
F8	0;66	0;91	0;101	0;111
F9	0;67	0;92	0;102	0;112
F10	0;68	0;93	0;103	0;113
Home	0;71	55	0;119	

Key	Alone	Shifted	Ctrl	Alt
Up Arrow	0;72	56		
Page Up	0;73	57	0;132	
Left Arrow	0;75	52	0;115	
Right Arrow	0;77	54	0;116	
End	0;79	49	0;117	
Down Arrow	0;80	50		
Page Down	0;81	51	0;118	
Insert	0;82	48		
Delete	0;83	46		
PrtSc				0;114
A	97	65	1	0;30
B	98	66	2	0;48
C	99	67	3	0;46
D	100	68	4	0;32
E	101	69	5	0;18
F	102	70	6	0;33
G	103	71	7	0;34
H	104	72	8	0;35
I	105	73	9	0;23
J	106	74	10	0;36
K	107	75	11	0;37
L	108	76	12	0;38
M	109	77	13	0;50
N	110	78	14	0;49
O	111	79	15	0;24
P	112	80	16	0;25
Q	113	81	17	0;16
R	114	82	18	0;19
S	115	83	19	0;31
T	116	84	20	0;20
U	117	85	21	0;22
V	118	86	22	0;47
V	118	86	22	0;47

Key	Alone	Shifted	Ctrl	Alt
W	119	87	23	0;17
X	120	88	24	0;45
Y	121	89	25	0;21
Z	122	90	26	0;44
1	49	33		0;120
2	50	64		0;121
3	51	35		0;122
4	52	36		0;123
5	53	37		0;124
6	54	94		0;125
7	55	38		0;126
8	56	42		0;127
9	57	40		0;128
0	48	41		0;129
	45	95		0;130
=	61	43		0;131
Tab	9			0;15
Null				0;3

NetWare 3.1x and NetWare 4.0 Console SET Parameters

Alloc Memory Check Flag (NW4.0 ONLY)
Category: Memory
Default is OFF. This parameter can be set in STARTUP.NCF.
When ON, it enables corruption checking in Alloc memory (Alloc Short Term Memory Pool) nodes.

Allow Change To Client Rights
Category: Communications (NW3.1x) NCP (NW4.0)
Default is ON. This parameter may be set in STARTUP.NCF. When ON, a print or job server is allowed to assume the rights of a queue job's submitter as it services that queue job. This parameter's effect is always ON in versions of NetWare previous to 3.1. NetWare 3.1x requires PBURST.NLM for this parameter to exist.

Allow Deletion Of Active Directories (NW4.0 ONLY)
Category: File System
Default is ON. This parameter, when ON, allows the removal of directories that other connections have mapped. In previous versions of NetWare, an active directory could never be removed, thus causing a hunt for the connections that had the directory mapped, or the abandonment of the directory removal attempt.

Allow Invalid Pointers (NW4.0 ONLY)
Category: Memory
Default is OFF. This parameter can be set in STARTUP.NCF. When ON, it will allow an invalid pointer to cause a non-existent page to be mapped in and will notify the console only once. This setting should be left OFF, except during debugging.

Allow LIP
Category: Communications (NW3.1x) NCP (NW4.0)
Default is ON. This parameter may be set in STARTUP.NCF. When ON, it allows Large Internet Packet (LIP) support to operate. NetWare 3.1x requires PBURST.NLM for parameter to exist.

Allow Unencrypted Passwords
Category: Miscellaneous
Default is OFF. If set to ON, it allows older login utilities to function.

Automatically Repair Bad Volumes (NW4.0 ONLY)
Category: Miscellaneous
Default is ON. This parameter can be set in STARTUP.NCF. If ON when a volume fails to mount, VRepair will automatically attempt to correct the volume so that it will mount.

Auto Register Memory Above 16 Megabytes
Category: Memory
Default is ON, and this parameter can be set only in STARTUP.NCF. Works mainly on EISA bus machines. Use the "Register Memory" command if this Auto Register command does not appear to work. For instance, "Register Memory 1000000 1000000" would indicate to register16MB, starting at the address of 16MB, that all numbers are in hex.

Auto TTS Backout Flag

Category: Transaction Tracking

Default is OFF, and this parameter can be set only in STARTUP.NCF. If ON, it will skip the prompts when the server is brought up, and TTS backouts will be required due to incomplete file updates.

Bindery Context (NW4.0 ONLY)

Category: Miscellaneous

Default is nothing. It may be set up to 256 bytes in length and represents the bindery context used by Directory Services when performing bindery emulation. Typically this paramenter is set when Directory Services is installed, and it need not be changed later.

Cache Buffer Size (NW3.1X ONLY)

Category: Memory

Default is 4096 bytes in a range of 4096 to 16384 bytes and can only be set in STARTUP.NCF. This parameter sets the size of each cache buffer in memory. For maximum memory efficiency it should remain at its default. (This parameter is not part of NetWare 4.0.)

Compression Daily Check Start Hour (NW4.0 ONLY)

Category: File System

Default is 0. It may be set from 0 to 23: 0=midnight, 23=11 p.m. This parameter defines the hour when the file compressor will begin its scan for compressible files on enabled volumes.

Compression Daily Check Stop Hour (NW4.0 ONLY)

Category: File System

Default is 6. It may be set from 0 to 23: 0=midnight, 23=11 p.m. This parameter defines the hour when the file compressor stops scanning enabled volumes for files that need to be compressed. If this parameter is equal to the Compression Daily Check Starting Hour, then compression checking will start every day at the starting hour and continue for as long as necessary to complete compression of all affected files.

Concurrent Remirror Requests (NW4.0 ONLY)
Category: Disk
Default is 4. It may be set from 2 to 32. This parameter defines the number of remirror requests per logical partition. There may be no more than one remirror request per logical partition, of which there may be up to 32.

Console Display Watchdog Logouts
Category: Communications
Default is OFF. If ON it will display an alert message at the server console whenever a user is logged out because of a watchdog time-out.

Convert Compressed To Uncompressed Option (NW4.0 ONLY)
Category: File System
Default is 1. It may be set from 0 to 2. This parameter defines the action to take place when a compressed file is accessed. Note that the file is accessed, it is first uncompressed in its entirety. The value of 0 means always leave the compressed version in place. One (1) means to leave the file compressed if there is only one read request after it is uncompressed within the time frame defined by the Days Untouched Before Compression parameter. Upon the second read access, remove the compressed version; 2 means always remove the compressed version after uncompressing. In any case, if an uncompressed file is written to, then its compressed version will be rendered stale and will be removed.

Days Untouched Before Compression (NW4.0 ONLY)
Category: File System
Default is 7. It may be set from 0 to 100000. This parameter defines the number of days since a file's last access before queueing the file for compression. In many systems the default of 7 days may cause the system to go "compression happy" and compress too many files. Chances are this option is best set higher, perhaps to 30 or 60 days, while requesting specific files to be immediately compressed when the need arises. Remember that compression must be enabled per volume, so not all volumes may be affected, and the default may then be justified.

Decompress Free Space Warning Interval (NW4.0 ONLY)

Category: File System

Default is 31 minutes and 18.5 seconds. It may be set from 0 seconds to 29 days, 15 hours, 50 minutes, and 3.8 seconds. If not 0, this parameter defines the interval between alerts that indicate when the file system is not permanently changing compressed files to uncompressed files due to insufficient free disk space.

Decompress Percent Disk Space Free To Allow Commit (NW4.0 ONLY)

Category: File System

Default is 10. Its value may be set from 0 to 75. This parameter defines how much free disk volume space is required for file decompression to change the compressed file to its uncompressed version permanently. This prevents newly uncompressed files from entirely filling up volume disk space. Remember that compressed files, as a group, may easily exceed available volume space when uncompressed. Also remember that when an uncompressed file is written to its compressed version, it will be rendered stale and will be removed.

Delay Before First Watchdog Packet

Category: Communications

Default is 4 minutes and 56.6 seconds. It may be set from 15.7 seconds to 20 minutes and 52.3 seconds. This determines how long the server will wait to "hear" from a workstation. If, after the delay elapses, the workstation has not been "heard" from, the server will send an "are you there" request to the workstation. If the server cannot make contact with the workstation, it will logout the workstation after the specified number of watchdog packets has been reached.

Delay Between Watchdog Packets

Category: Communications

Default is 59.3 seconds. It may be set from 9.9 seconds to 10 minutes and 26.2 seconds. This delay indicates the amount of time the server will wait for a reply to its "are you there" watchdog packet before sending another. If the specified number of watchdog packets have been sent to the workstation, each without reply, the server will logout the connection.

Deleted Files Compression Option (NW4.0 ONLY)
Category: File System
Default is 1. It may be set from 0 to 2. This parameter defines deleted files' compression action. 0 means do not compress deleted files; 1 means compress deleted files the next day, and 2 means compress deleted files immediately. Remember that immediate compression requests are queued until the next Compress Daily Check Start Hour.

Developer Option (NW4.0 ONLY)
Category: Miscellaneous
Default is ON. This parameter, which can be set in STARTUP.NCF, enables options associated with the developer environment. As Figure K-1 shows, the Developer Option can be used to troubleshoot an application when a page fault is detected. Through a series of SET commands that include Read and Write Fault Emulation and Notification, and Allow Invalid Pointers, a person developing applications in the NetWare server environment is given a great degree of flexibility for reacting to such page faults.

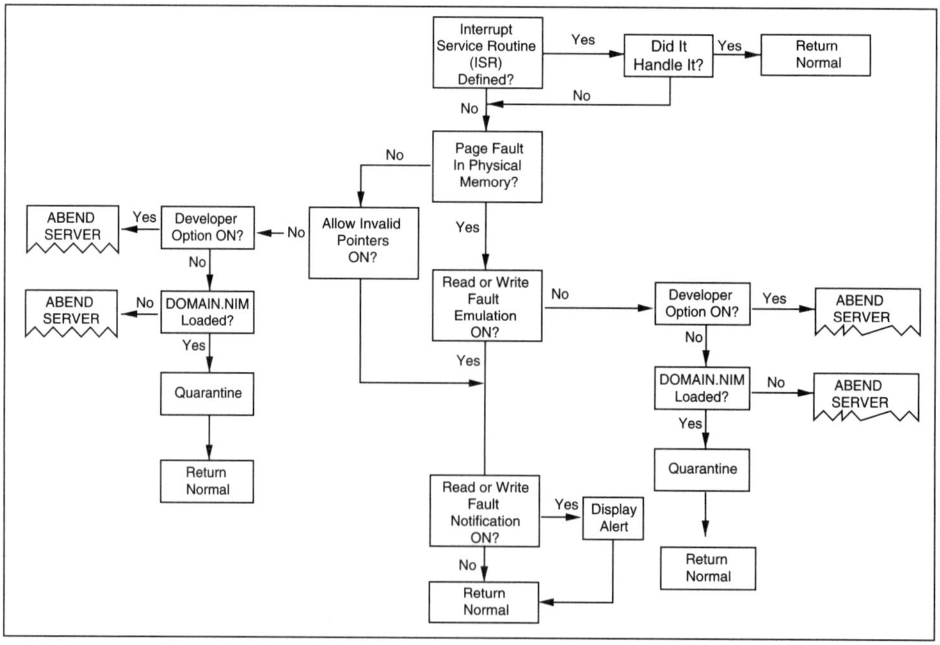

Figure K-1 Example of Parameters for NetWare 4.0

Directory Cache Allocation Wait Time

Category: Directory Caching

Default is 2.2 seconds. It may be set from .5 second to 2 minutes. This delay represents how much time the server will wait before creating a new directory cache buffer. If this parameter is set too high, the server will be forced to flush directory cache buffers that may still be in use, resulting in a thrashing problem where the server is constantly going back to disk to retrieve the directory block because it is unable to allocate a new one "in time." It is best to keep this option at its default, though tweaking it up should not hurt performance.

Directory Cache Buffer Nonreferenced Delay

Category: Directory Caching

Default is 5.5 seconds. It may be set from 1 second to 5 minutes to determine how long a directory cache buffer will be "left alone" before it is reused. If you set this option too high, the server will most likely waste memory by creating new directory cache buffers when it could have reused them more quickly.

Dirty Directory Cache Delay Time

Category: Directory Caching

Default is .5 seconds. It may be set from 0 to 10 seconds to determine how long the server will wait before updating the disk with a "dirty" (read: modified) directory cache buffer. Suppose the size of a file changes or its owner changes. With the time delay increased, there is more of a chance for the directory cache buffer to be further modified; however, it will be further modified without being flushed to disk, which is a precarious predicament.

Dirty Disk Cache Delay Time

Category: File Caching

Default is 3.3 seconds in a range from .1 to 10 seconds. This is the length of delay before flushing a file cache buffer to a disk that is only partly modified. The delay allows for the submission of further modifications to the buffer before it is flushed to disk. Increasing the time will allow for more modifications to occur, but at the expense of not recording them to disk for a longer period of time. For instance, if the server is in an environment that experiences many small write operations, setting this parameter to its maximum will result in better overall performance because more modifications to the cache buffers will be allowed before forcing a flush to disk.

Display Disk Device Alerts

Category: Miscellaneous

Default is OFF. It can be set in STARTUP.NCF. When ON, it will display alert messages whenever a disk device is added, deleted, mounted, dismounted, activated, deactivated, and so on.

Display Incomplete IPX Packet Alerts

Category: Miscellaneous

Default is ON. It can be set in STARTUP.NCF. When ON, it will display alert messages on the console whenever an incomplete IPX packet is received by the server. This can be caused by someone trying to fake an IPX packet or by a hardware error. It can also be caused by a bug in a workstation shell or requester.

Display Lost Interrupt Alerts

Category: Miscellaneous

Default is ON. It can be set in STARTUP.NCF. When ON, it will display alert messages on the console whenever a lost interrupt is detected by the interrupt controller. Typically this is provoked by a hardware incompatibility or malfunction.

Display NCP Bad Component Warnings (NW4.0 ONLY)

Category: NCP

Default is ON. This parameter can be set in STARTUP.NCF and, when ON, will display an alert whenever an NCP packet is received with bad components (wrong parameters). These packets can be rejected by setting the Reject NCP Packets With Bad Components parameter to ON.

Display NCP Bad Length Warnings (NW4.0 ONLY)

Category: NCP

Default is ON. This parameter can be set in STARTUP.NCF and, when ON, will display an alert whenever an NCP packet is received with a wrong length. These packets can be rejected if the Reject NCP Packets with Bad Lengths parameter has been set to ON.

Display Old API Names

Category: Miscellaneous

Default is OFF. It can be set in STARTUP.NCF. When ON, it will display the names of "old APIs" that an NLM uses when it is loaded. The "old APIs" are translated to their new counterparts so that the NLM may still function, but it should be updated.

Display Relinquish Control Alerts

Category: Miscellaneous

Default is OFF. It can be set in STARTUP.NCF. If ON, it will display alert messages when a process fails to yield the CPU, which occurs after approximately 380 ms of continuous CPU use by the process.

Display Spurious Interrupt Alerts

Category: Miscellaneous

Default is ON. It can be set in STARTUP.NCF. When ON, it will display alert messages whenever a spurious interrupt is detected by the interrupt controller. As with Lost Interrupts, this alert is often the result of a hardware incompatibility or malfunction.

Enable Disk Read After Write Verify
Category: Disk
Default is ON. This option, when ON, rereads data from disk to insure its correctness. (see Chapter 5)

Enable File Compression (NW4.0 ONLY)
Category: File System
Default is ON. This parameter, when ON, will allow compression to occur on so-enabled volumes. Compression will begin at the starting hour (Compression Daily Check Starting Hour), and all immediate compress requests will be queued until compression is scheduled.

Enable IPX Checksums (NW4.0 ONLY)
Category: NCP
Default is 1. It may be set from 0 to 2 in STARTUP.NCF. If set to 0, then no IPX packet checksumming is performed; at 1, checksumming is performed if the client is capable; 2 requires that all IPX packets be checksummed.

File Delete Wait Time
Category: File System
Default is 5 minutes and 29.6 seconds. Wait time may be set from 0 seconds to 7 days. This option is the normal wait time after a file is deleted before it is purged from disk. This value should be greater than that of the Minimum File Delete Wait Time parameter. If the Immediate Purge Of Deleted Files parameter is ON, this parameter is not relevant.

Garbage Collection Interval (NW4.0 ONLY)
Category: Memory
Default is 15 minutes. It may be set from 1 minute to 1 hour. This parameter, which can be set in STARTUP.NCF, sets the maximum time between memory cleanup (Garbage Collection) events.

Global Pseudo Preemption (NW4.0 ONLY)

Category: Miscellaneous

Default is OFF. If ON, it will require all threads to be monitored for Pseudo Preemption needs.

Halt System On Invalid Parameters (NW4.0 ONLY)

Category: Miscellaneous

Default is OFF. This parameter may be set in STARTUP.NCF. If ON when an invalid parameter or condition is detected, it will halt the system, rather than displaying a system alert and continuing. In all but test situations, it is highly recommended that this parameter remain at its default.

Immediate Purge Of Deleted Files

Category: File System

Default is OFF. If ON, this parameter will purge files from disk immediately after they are deleted, which eliminates the ability of the SALVAGE command to perform any meaningful duties. Also, the server's performance will be slightly higher because it does not need to keep up with the list of salvageable files.

Maximum Alloc Short Term Memory

Category: Memory

Default is 2097152 bytes. It may be set from 50000 to 16777216 bytes. This parameter defines the maximum amount of memory that can be used for the work dynamic memory pool. (This parameter is not part of NetWare 4.0.)

Maximum Concurrent Compressions (NW4.0 ONLY)

Category: File System

Default is 2. It may be set from 1 to 8 to determine how many concurrent compression processes will be allowed. In any case, only one compression process per enabled volume will be allowed. Setting this option beyond one has an effect only when more than one volume is compression enabled.

Maximum Concurrent Directory Cache Writes
Category: Directory Caching
Default is 10. It may be set from 5 to 50 buffers. This parameter defines the maximum number of concurrent directory cache writes that will be placed in the disk's elevator queue. Typically the number defined is how many directory cache buffers will be set up to be written to disk at once. The more of these buffers there are to write (in the disk's elevator queue), the less space is left for actual disk read and write requests. In a write-intensive environment, it is important to keep the modified directory cache buffers updated on disk since the disk files are constantly being modified.

Maximum Concurrent Disk Cache Writes
Category: Directory Caching
Default is 50. It may be set from 10 to 100 buffers. This parameter defines how many concurrent disk cache writes will be allowed. In a write-intensive environment, increasing this value will improve performance. In a read-intensive environment, a lower value will benefit performance.

Maximum Directory Cache Buffers
Category: Directory Caching
Default is 500. It may be set from 20 to 4000. It simply indicates the maximum number of directory cache buffers the server will be able to allocate. In environments with large numbers of files (not necessarily large files) this default may need to be increased. If not, performance can lag as the directory cache buffers are reused too often.

Maximum Extended Attributes Per File Or Path
Category: File System
Default is 16. It may be set from 4 to 512. This controls the number of extended attributes for files and paths. Typically this is not altered unless a specific product requires it to be.

Maximum File Locks

Category: Locks

Default is 10000. It may be set from 100 to 100000. This controls the maximum number of files that can be locked at once on the server, including both explicit and implicit file locks (open files).

Maximum File Locks Per Connection

Category: Locks

Default is 250. It may be set from 10 to 1000 to control the maximum number of locked files a workstation can have at once, including both explicit and implicit file locks (open files).

Maximum Interrupt Events (NW4.0 ONLY)

Category: Communications

Default is 10. It may be set from 1 to 1000000. This parameter defines the maximum number of interrupt time events (for instance, IPX Routing) allowed before guaranteeing that a ThreadSwitch has occurred, thus allowing other processes to run. This parameter ensures that excessive interrupt events will not delay server processing of user requests.

Maximum Outstanding NCP Searches

Category: Miscellaneous (NCP under NW4.0)

Default is 51. It may be set from 10 to 1000. This is the maximum number of concurrent NCP directory searches a connection may have. If an alert occurs indicating this number has been exceeded, the user should increase it to 100.

Maximum Packet Receive Buffers

Category: Communications

Default is 100. It may be set from 50 to 2000. This parameter represents the maximum number of packet receive buffers the server will be allowed to allocate. The buffer size is determined by the Maximum Physical Receive Packet Size. The memory used for this parameter comes from the permanent memory pool. This value should be greater than the Minimum Packet Receive Buffers parameter.

Maximum Percent Of Volume Space Allowed For Extended Attributes

Category: File System

Default is 10. It may be set from 5 to 50 percent of volume space. This parameter sets the maximum amount of volume space that will be used to store extended attributes. Typically, this setting will not need to be changed.

Maximum Percent Of Volume Used By Directory

Category: File System

Default is 13. It may be set from 5 to 50 percent of volume space. This parameter controls how much volume space the directory may allocate, which implicitly controls the number of files that the volume will be able to accommodate. In any case, 2,097,152 files is the maximum number that can be created on any one volume. The way you derive this is by starting with the 16,777,216 directory entries per volume and dividing that by 8 name spaces, to get 2 million files.

Maximum Physical Receive Packet Size

Category: Communications

Default is 1514. It may be set anywhere from 618 to 4202. This parameter can be set only in STARTUP.NCF. It should be set to accommodate the largest packet size at the file server. If it is set too high, it will result in wasted memory. The LAN Adapter manufacturers should indicate the maximum size necessary for their products. Simply use the largest size. The Receive Packets are allocated into a general pool and are assigned as required to incoming packets regardless of their originating LAN Adapter. Thus, it is important to use the largest packet size among the LAN Adapters installed in the server.

Maximum Record Locks

Category: Locks

Default is 20000. It may be set from 100 to 200000. This parameter defines how many locks—based physically, logically, or semaphorically—may exist at this server at any one time. If set too low, operations requiring these locks will fail, and applications will report their inability to obtain a required lock.

Maximum Record Locks Per Connection

Category: Locks

Default is 500. It may be set from 10 to 10000. This parameter identifies how many record locks—based physically, logically, or semaphorically—a single connection may have in use at once from this server. Note that a connection may represent a workstation that is logged into several servers. This maximum reflects only upon locks acquired from this server.

Maximum Service Processes

Category: Miscellaneous

Default is 40. It may be set from 5 to 40 (NW3.1x) or 5 to 100 (NW4.0). This parameter defines the maximum number of service processes the server will be allowed to create. Each SP is capable of handling a concurrent user request. Thus, if there were 10 SPs, then 10 concurrent user requests could be handled. The default should be changed in a busy environment where the number of service processes has been reached or is within 5 of the maximum. The current number of SPs can be checked on MONITOR.NLM's main screen.

Maximum Subdirectory Tree Depth

Category: File System

Default is 25. It may be from 10 to 100 and can be set only in STARTUP.NCF. This parameter defines how may levels of subdirectories may be on any volume at this server. For instance, DOS allows up to 32 levels. This setting is rarely changed, except perhaps to a lower value.

Maximum Transactions

Category: Transaction Tracking

Default is 10000. It may be set from 100 to 10000. This parameter defines how many concurrent transactions TTS will be allowed to handle at this server.

Minimum Compression Percentage Gain (NW4.0 ONLY)
Category: File System
Default is 2. It may be set from 0 to 50. This parameter defines the minimum amount a file must be compressed for it to remain compressed. The default—as of this writing, 2—is impractical. The minimum should be higher. Perhaps a minimum of 20 would yield more effective use of NetWare 4.0's compression.

Minimum Directory Cache Buffers
Category: Directory Caching
Default is 20. It may be set from 10 to 2000. This parameter defines how many directory cache buffers the server will allocate before delaying. If the number is too low, initial system performance will be sluggish as new directory cache buffers will be delayed allocation because of the time-out value assigned to the parameter Directory Cache Allocation Wait Time. After the system has been in use (time since last boot up) for a while, this minimum parameter will not have as much impact on system performance.

Minimum File Cache Buffers
Category: File Caching
Default is 20. It may be set from 20 to 1000. This parameter is important because it reserves the indicated number of cache buffers for the exclusive use of the file cache. This means, for instance, that an errant NLM could not allocate memory away from the pool of file cache buffers. Also, the parameter can be used as a high water mark to further ensure that there is at least enough memory for file caching. Thus, if NLMs are loaded without proper checking, they will not be allowed to decrease this reserve pool but will either fail to load or stop functioning due to the lack of memory they can allocate.

Minimum File Cache Report Threshold

Category: File Caching

Default is 20. It may be set from 0 to 1000. This parameter should be set equal to or higher than the Minimum File Cache Buffer parameter. When the indicated number or fewer file cache buffers remain, the server will issue an alert indicating it is getting low on memory. If the value is set below the Minimum File Cache Buffers count, then the server will be operating on reserved memory and will probably already be in trouble.

Minimum File Delete Wait Time

Category: File System

Default is 1 minute and 5.9 seconds. It may be set from 0 seconds to 7 days. This parameter defines the minimum time the server will wait after a file is deleted before purging it from disk. This value should be less than or equal to the File Delete Wait Time parameter. In a situation where disk space is needed, this minimum wait time will dictate which files can be purged to gain needed space. If no space can be gained because the delete time has not yet expired, the disk space allocation will fail (probably at a user workstation). If the Immediate Purge Of Deleted Files parameter is ON, then this parameter is not relevant.

Minimum Free Memory For Garbage Collection (NW4.0 ONLY)

Category: Memory

Default is 8000. It may be set from 1000 to 1000000. This parameter, which can be set in STARTUP.NCF, sets the minimum number of freed allocated memory bytes needed for garbage collection to occur.

Minimum Packet Receive Buffers

Category: Communications

Default is 100 (NW3.x) 10 (NW4.0). It may be set from 10 to 1000. This parameter can be set only in STARTUP.NCF. It is used to initially allocate packet receive buffers. This value should be below the Maximum Packet Receive Buffer count. To gauge an appropriate minimum, watch the server's MONITOR.NLM (main screen) after the server has been in use for a while (at least one week). Note the number of Packet Receive Buffers. This number should identify the proper minimum number for that particular server. If the minimum is too low for the load at the server, initial performance after bringing up the server will be sluggish as packet receive buffers are allocated.

NCP File Commit

Category: File System (NW3.1x) NCP (NW4.0)

Default is ON. If ON, this parameter allows applications to flush all pending file writes to disk. Typically there is no reason to have this option OFF.

NCP Packet Signature Option

Category: Communications (NW3.1x) NCP (NW4.0)

Default is 1. It may be set from 0 to 3. This parameter may be set in STARTUP.NCF. Zero (0) means do not do packet signatures; 1 means do packet signatures only if the client requires them; 2 means do packet signatures if the client is capable; 3 means require packet signing. If clients are not capable, they will not be allowed access to the server. After the server is brought up, this parameter's value can only be increased. To decrease it, the server must be downed. NetWare 3.1x requires PBURST.NLM for this parameter to exist.

New Packet Receive Buffer Wait Time

Category: Communications

Default is .1 second. This parameter may range from .1 second to 20 seconds. If a packet is received into the server by the LAN Adapter hardware when no packet receive buffer is available, the server will return the error message NO ECB AVAILABLE, and the sender (probably a user workstation) will eventually time-out and resubmit its request. In the meantime, if this wait time has expired, the server will have created a new packet receive buffer, and/or a packet receive buffer that was in use will have been freed. In either case, the sender will have his or her request received by the server. For maximum system performance this value should always be left at the default of .1 second and the number of packet receive buffers controlled by the Maximum Packet Receive Buffer parameter.

New Service Process Wait Time

Category: Miscellaneous

Default is 2.2 seconds. It may be from .3 second to 20 seconds. This parameter controls how long the server will wait before creating a new Service Process. Each SP is capable of handling a concurrent user request. Typically, most user requests can be handled in less than 2.2 seconds, so the default is a good indicator of when a new SP should be acquired. Setting below the default can result in more SPs being created than will actually be used efficiently. The current number of Service Processes is found on MONITOR.NLM's main screen.

Number Of Frees For Garbage Collection (NW4.0 ONLY)

Category: Memory

Default is 5000. It may be set from 100 to 100000. This parameter, which can be set in STARTUP.NCF, sets the minimum number of "frees" needed for garbage collection to occur. A free is an operation that returns allocated memory to the memory scheduler.

Number Of Watchdog Packets

Category: Communications

Default is 10. It may be set from 5 to 100. This parameter, when combined with the Delay Before First Watchdog Packet and Delay Between Watchdog Packets, identifies how many watchdog packets will be sent to a workstation before it is forcibly logged out due to nonresponsiveness.

Pseudo Preemption Time (NW3.1X)

Category: Miscellaneous

Default is 2000. It may be set from 1000 to 10000. This parameter, for NetWare 3.1x, identifies the amount of time in .84 microsecond (millionths of a second) increments to allow an NLM to run before forcing it to relinquish control (ThreadSwitch) on the next system read or write call, even if the call can be satisfied from cache. Pseudo Preemption is enabled with each NLM. There is nothing to set. Whenever an NLM (any of its threads/processes) occupies the CPU continuously enough to trigger the Pseudo Preemption Time, the preemption will be forced as previously described. In any case, if a thread does not relinquish control often enough (about every 380 ms), then an alert can be displayed if Display Relinquish Control Alerts is ON.

Pseudo Preemption Time (NW4.0)

Category: Miscellaneous

Default is 10. It may be set from 1 to 4294967295. This parameter, for NetWare 4.0, identifies the number of times to allow threads to make system read or write calls without relinquishing CPU control before a relinquish control is forced (ThreadSwitch). This parameter is set either with each NLM thread or globally for all threads. The Global Pseudo Preemption parameter indicates whether all threads are affected. In any case, if a thread does not relinquish control often enough (about every 380 ms), then an alert can be displayed if Display Relinquish Control Alerts is ON.

Read Ahead Enabled (NW4.0 ONLY)

Category: File Caching

Default is ON. This parameter, when ON, will do background reads whenever sequential file access occurs on a file. When the read ahead occurs, files that are accessed sequentially—the loading of an application for instance—will be accessed more quickly because they are already cached.

Read Ahead LRU Sitting Time Threshold (NW4.0 ONLY)

Category: File Caching

Default is 10 seconds. It may be set from 0 seconds to 1 hour. This threshold defines how long a read ahead buffer is "kept" without actually being accessed, before it is marked for purging. Remember, not all read ahead buffers may be accessed. Read ahead can occur on data files as well as executables. If set to 0, Read Ahead will not occur.

Read Fault Emulation (NW4.0 ONLY)

Category: Memory

Default is OFF. This parameter, which can be set in STARTUP.NCF, when ON, will emulate a read after a read fault is caused by access to a nonpresent memory page. This parameter is used mainly for debugging purposes.

Read Fault Notification (NW4.0 ONLY)

Category: Memory

Default is ON. When ON, this parameter, which can be set in STARTUP.NCF, will produce a message on the server console and record in the error log any emulated read page faults. This parameter is used mainly for debugging purposes.

Reject NCP Packets With Bad Components (NW4.0 ONLY)

Category: NCP

Default is OFF. This parameter can be set in STARTUP.NCF. When ON, it will refuse NCP packets that have incorrect parameters.

Reject NCP Packets With Bad Lengths (NW4.0 ONLY)
Category: NCP
Default is OFF. This parameter, which can be set in STARTUP.NCF, when ON, will refuse NCP packets of incorrect lengths (that is, they fail boundary checking).

Remirror Block Size (NW4.0 ONLY)
Category: Disk
Default is 1. It may be set from 1 to 8. This parameter defines the remirror block size in 4K increments with 1 being 4K, 2=8K, 3=12K, 4=16K, 5=20K, 6=24K, 7=28K, and 8=32K. This parameter is best left at its default.

Replace Console Prompt With Server Name (NW4.0 ONLY)
Category: Miscellaneous
Default is ON. When ON, the familiar server console prompt, ":", is replaced with "server_name:" as in "FS1:".

Reply To Get Nearest Server
Category: Communications
Default is ON. This parameter identifies whether or not this server will respond to the IPX inquiry "GET NEAREST SERVER" (as seen on the TRACK ON screen). If there are numerous servers on a backbone and only a few are actually required for initial login, this parameter can help limit the amount of network traffic created when workstation shells or requesters load.

Reserved Buffers Below 16 Meg
Category: File Caching
Default is 16. It may be set from 8 to 200. This option can be set only in STARTUP.NCF. This number identifies how many file cache buffers will be kept for device drivers unable to access memory above 16 megabytes. Examples are 16-bit adapters and some DMA-enabled cards. Most affected manufacturers indicate when to use this parameter.

Sound Bell For Alerts (NW4.0 ONLY)
Category: Miscellaneous
Default is ON. When ON, a beep will sound whenever an alert is displayed on the server console.

TTS Abort Dump Flag
Category: Transaction Tracking
Default is OFF. If ON, data from aborted transactions will be written to a log file.

TTS Backout File Truncation Wait Time
Category: Transaction Tracking
Default is 59 minutes and 19.2 seconds. It may be set from 1 minute and 5.9 seconds to 1 day, 2 hours, 21 minutes, and 51.3 seconds. This parameter defines the amount of time to wait before truncating the TTS backout file. In most cases the default is viable.

TTS UnWritten Cache Wait Time
Category: Transaction Tracking
Default is 1 minute and 5.9 seconds. It may be set from 11 seconds to 10 minutes and 59.1 seconds. This represents the amount of time TTS can block a cache buffer write from being written to disk.

Turbo FAT Re-Use Wait Time
Category: File System
Default is 5 minutes and 29.6 seconds. It may be set from .3 second to 1 hour 5 minutes and 54.6 seconds. As described in Chapter 3, this parameter defines how long the server will wait after an affected file is closed before reusing its Turbo FAT Index for another purpose. Typically files that are FAT Indexed are always in use, so this parameter may not need to be changed from its default. If a Turbo FAT must be rebuilt regularly, system performance will be affected, so be sure this parameter is set accordingly.

Upgrade Low Priority Threads (NW4.0 ONLY)
Category: Miscellaneous
Default is OFF. When ON, it causes low priority threads to be scheduled at regular priority. This would be turned on when an NLM is running in the system that shut out processing of lower than regular priority threads, thus disabling system processes such as file compression.

Volume Low Warn All Users
Category: File System
Default is ON. When the Volume Low Warning Threshold is met while this parameter is ON, a message will be sent to all current connections to indicate which server/volume is running low on space.

Volume Low Warning Reset Threshold
Category: File System
Default is 256. It may be set from 0 to 100000. This indicates the number of disk blocks (disk block size is defined per volume—see Chapter 5) above the Volume Low Warning Threshold where the warning trigger is reset. For instance, if the volume block size is the default of 4K, 256 blocks is 1MB.

Volume Low Warning Threshold
Category: File System
Default is 256. It may be set from 0 to 1000000. This indicates the threshold where a warning is issued that the volume is getting low on disk space. This value is in volume blocks, set per volume. See Volume Low Warning Reset Threshold for more information.

Worker Thread Execute In A Row Count (NW4.0 ONLY)
Category: Miscellaneous
Default is 10. It may be set from 1 to 20. This parameter defines the number of consecutive times the process scheduler will dispatch new worker threads before allowing other threads to run. For maximum performance, this value should be lowered. Worker threads are reduced priority threads designed to perform their duties when the system has no other immediate demands.

Write Fault Emulation (NW4.0 ONLY)

Category: Memory

Default is OFF. This parameter, which can be set in STARTUP.NCF, when ON, will emulate a write when a write fault is caused by access to a nonpresent memory page. This parameter is used mainly for debugging purposes.

Write Fault Notification (NW4.0 ONLY)

Category: Memory

Default is ON. This parameter, which can be set in STARTUP.NCF, when ON, will produce a message on the server console and record in the error log any emulated write page faults. This parameter is used mainly for debugging purposes.

About the Writers

John T. McCann is an independent systems developer and President of Integrity Software. He has developed software for Novell and other leading third-party applications and utilities vendors, including Brightwork Development, Inc. He has served as the lead system operator (SYSOP) for the popular Novell user's forum, NetWire, and is a frequent contributor to various technical magazines, including *LAN Magazine*. John has an M.S. degree in computer science from Texas A&M University. He is also the author of Brightwork's SiteLock utility.

Adam T. Ruef is a senior supervisor in the Applications Development and Office Automation group of Mobil Chemicals Company. He is a founding member and former Chairman of the International NetWare User's Group. Adam has been a guest speaker and moderator for many industry shows such as COMDEX and NetWorld.

Steven L. Guengerich is Chief Infrastructure Officer and Editor-in-Chief of Publications for BSG, a nationally recognized systems integration company headquartered in Houston, Texas. With a background in systems consulting for Business Systems Group and other Big Eight consulting divisions, he has been involved in the management of strategic planning, design, installation, and support of several Novell and non-Novell networks. Steve is coauthor of the book *Microcomputers in Government* and a regular columnist for various technical publications.

Index

B

C

D

E

G

H

M

N

Q

R

T

U

V

W

X

Z